PENGUIN BOOKS

# THE PENGUIN BOOK OF HISTORIC SPEECHES

Brian MacArthur was founder editor of *Today* and *The Times Higher Education Supplement*, and editor of the *Western Morning News*. He was deputy editor of the *Sunday Times* and executive editor of *The Times*. He has written *Surviving the Sword: Prisoners of the Japanese 1942–1945*. He has been interested in the power of oratory since first hearing Aneurin Bevan on the hustings in 1956 and has edited *The Penguin Book of Modern Speeches* and *The Penguin Book of Twentieth-Century Protest*.

Brian MacArthur lives in Norfolk and London and has two daughters.

THE PENGUIN BOOK OF

•

# HISTORIC SPEECHES

•

EDITED BY BRIAN MacARTHUR

PENGUIN BOOKS

PENGUIN BOOKS

Published by the Penguin Group
Penguin Books Ltd, 80 Strand, London WC2R ORL, England
Penguin Group (USA) Inc., 375 Hudson Street, New York, New York 10014, USA
Penguin Group (Canada), 90 Eglinton Avenue East, Suite 700, Toronto, Ontario, Canada M4P 2Y3
(a division of Pearson Penguin Canada Inc.)
Penguin Ireland, 25 St Stephen's Green, Dublin 2, Ireland (a division of Penguin Books Ltd)
Penguin Group (Australia), 250 Camberwell Road, Camberwell, Victoria 3124, Australia
(a division of Pearson Australia Group Pty Ltd)
Penguin Books India Pvt Ltd, 11 Community Centre, Panchsheel Park, New Delhi – 110 017, India
Penguin Group (NZ), 67 Apollo Drive, Rosedale, Auckland 0632, New Zealand
(a division of Pearson New Zealand Ltd)
Penguin Books (South Africa) (Pty) Ltd, Block D, Rosebank Office Park,
181 Jan Smuts Avenue, Parktown North, Gauteng 2193, South Africa

Penguin Books Ltd, Registered Offices: 80 Strand, London WC2R ORL, England

www.penguin.com

First published by Viking 1995
Published in Penguin Books 1996
Reissued in this edition 2012
002

The selection copyright © Brian MacArthur, 1995
All rights reserved

The moral right of the editor has been asserted

The acknowledgements on pp. xxii–xxiii constitute an extension of this copyright page

Printed in England by Clays Ltd, St Ives plc

ISBN: 978-0-241-95326-6

www.greenpenguin.co.uk

MIX
Paper from
responsible sources
FSC® C018179

Penguin Books is committed to a sustainable
future for our business, our readers and our planet.
This book is made from Forest Stewardship
Council™ certified paper.

ALWAYS LEARNING                    PEARSON

For Tessa MacArthur

# CONTENTS

## TOWARDS CIVIL WAR 203

## THE AGE OF IMPROVEMENT 265

THE AGE OF LINCOLN 335

There are two arts which raise men to the highest places of preferment: one is that of the great soldier, the other that of the accomplished orator; for by the former the glories of peace are preserved, by the latter the perils of war are driven away.

Cicero

The business of the orator is not to convince, but persuade; not to inform, but to rouse the mind; to build upon the habitual prejudices of mankind (for reason of itself will do nothing) and to add feeling to prejudice, and action to feeling.

William Hazlitt on William Pitt the Elder

A speech is a soliloquy, one man on a bare stage with a big spotlight. He will tell us who he is and what he wants and how he will get it and what it means that he wants it and what it will mean when he does or does not get it . . . He looks up at us on the balconies and clears his throat. 'Ladies and Gentlemen . . .' We lean forward hungry to hear. Now it will be said, now we will hear the thing we long for. A speech is part theatre and part political declaration; it is personal communication between a leader and his people; it is art, and all art is paradox, being at once a thing of great power and great delicacy. A speech is poetry: cadence, rhythm, imagery, sweep! A speech reminds us that words, like children, have the power to make dance the dullest beanbag of a heart . . . Speeches are important because they are one of the great constants of our political history. They have been not only the way we measure public men, they have been how we tell each other who we are . . . They count. They more than count, they shape what happens.

Peggy Noonan

# INTRODUCTION

The speeches of Moses, Jesus of Nazareth and Muhammad to their followers are still inspiring men and women to lead lives based on a moral code and still, today, changing the course of history. Two thousand years on it is all too easy to wonder whether the speeches of any of our contemporary leaders – Clinton, Major, Kohl or Mitterrand, Pope John Paul, Archbishop George Carey or the mullahs of Iran – will still be read in the year 4,000, let alone with any inspirational effect. Even as global television magnifies the power of oratory and propels contemporary speakers to audiences undreamt of in the days of Chatham and Fox, Webster and Lincoln, Disraeli and Gladstone – audiences counted in hundreds of millions – contemporary wisdom mourns the decline of oratory. Yet, as this anthology demonstrates, the twentieth century has produced speakers – Gandhi, Roosevelt, Hitler, Churchill – who stand comparison with the greatest orators of the past; and even in the 1990s the speeches of Vaclav Havel and Nelson Mandela transcend national boundaries and inspire mankind.

The aim of this anthology is to collect together some of the greatest speeches made during our (mainly Western) history and to show their power to move hearts or inspire great deeds, to uplift spirits or cast down enemies. Studying oratory, moreover, offers powerful insights into the motives and ideals of the men and women who made history. There is a bias towards speeches that still read well, which were spoken nobly and with eloquence, and which contained phrases – or soundbites – that were immortal. Most of the speeches changed votes or changed minds and swayed the course of history whether within their nations or across the world. Many have the poetry and the beauty of great literature. Above all, they were genuinely historic.

When Demosthenes spoke, he roused the Athenians to march on Philip of Macedonia. When Cicero spoke, even Caesar trembled – and only when Demosthenes and Cicero were silenced did despotism triumph in Greece and Rome. When Queen Elizabeth I spoke, men bowed at her knees. Yet when John Pym raised the 'cry of England', a king lost his head. When James Otis and Andrew Hamilton and John

Hancock defied the British colonialists they raised the flag of American independence.

'Who can doubt,' said the great American orator Daniel Webster, 'that in our struggle for independence, the majestic eloquence of Chatham, the profound reasoning of Burke . . . had influence on our fortunes in America? They tended to diminish the confidence of the British ministry in their hopes to subject us. There was not a reading man who did not struggle more boldly for his rights when those exhilarating sounds, uttered in the two Houses of Parliament, reached him across the seas.' Mirabeau, by the power of his oratory, directed the storm of the French Revolution. When he told the King's emissary: 'Slave, go tell your master that we are led by the will of the people and will depart only at the point of the bayonet,' his words sounded the trumpet throughout Europe and sealed the fate of Louis XVI.

When the nullifiers of South Carolina threatened the federal Constitution, it was Webster himself who raised the banner. 'As the champion of New England closed the memorable peroration of his reply to Hayne,' according to one contemporary account, 'the silence of death rested upon the crowded Senate chamber . . . The sharp rap of the President's hammer could hardly awaken the audience from the trance into which the orator had thrown them.'

The speeches of Lord Chatham (William Pitt the Elder) feature strongly in any discussion of oratory. Their power, the power detected across the sea by Webster and the power which throbs throughout this anthology, was never better captured than by William Hazlitt: 'His genius . . . burnt brightest at the last. The spark of liberty which had lain concealed and dormant, buried under the dirt and rubbish of state intrigue and vulgar faction, now met with congenial matter and kindled up "a flame of sacred vehemence" in his breast. It burst forth with a fury and a splendour that might have awed the world and made kings tremble. He spoke as a man should speak, because he felt as a man should feel in such circumstances. He came forward as the advocate of liberty, as the defender of the rights of his fellow citizens, as the enemy of tyranny, as the friend of his country and of mankind . . . He did not try to prove those truths which did not require any proof but to make others feel them with the same force that he did and to tear off the flimsy disguises with which the sycophants of power attempted to cover them. The business of the orator is not to convince, but persuade; not to inform, but to rouse the mind; to build upon the habitual prejudices of mankind (for reason of itself will do nothing) and to add feeling to prejudice, and action to feeling.'

It is that power which this anthology celebrates, but oratorical power does not arise only from passionate declamation. Abraham Lincoln, the greatest American orator, demonstrated the equal power of passionate conviction allied to simple but eloquent words, quietly spoken, unheard, indeed, by many who thronged the cemetery when the Gettysburg address was delivered. The main address at Gettysburg that day was delivered by Edward Everett, president of Harvard and considered then the best American orator of his day. Everett spoke in his ornate, florid and mannered style for two hours and nobody now remembers a word of what he said. When Lincoln delivered a few dedicatory 'remarks', he spoke 270 words. Yet in those ten sentences he delivered the best short speech since the Sermon on the Mount.

Apart from the Sermon on the Mount, no speech has been so heavily analysed by scholars. A study of the Gettysburg address nevertheless teases out several of the issues that so preoccupy scholars and critics of modern oratory and its alleged decline. Lincoln himself considered his speech a failure. Yet as Garry Wills, the latest scholar, argues, Lincoln used words as weapons of peace which called up a new nation out of the blood and trauma of war. So the Civil War is to most Americans what Lincoln wanted it to mean, a war against slavery for the equality of man. According to Wills, all modern political prose descends from the Gettysburg address. Those 272 words rendered obsolete the style of Everett and forged a new, lean language to redeem the first modern war.

As has happened with each generational change in the style of oratory, it was that 'new' language, used as Lincoln adapted to the development of telegraphy, that undoubtedly baffled his contemporary critics, just as the generation that followed the era of Chatham and Burke and Fox was critical of the pedestrian speech of the age of Peel. Chatham and Fox addressed an aristocratic society in an aristocratic age. The great speakers were drawn from a few families, often connected by intermarriage, educated at the same few schools and the ancient universities of Oxford and Cambridge, where they were schooled in public speech. When William Pitt the Younger went up to Cambridge, his father insisted that he made a special study of Thucydides. Pitt responded gladly and read and translated the celebrated orators of the ancient world. He was as familiar with Virgil, Horace, Cicero and Juvenal as with Shakespeare.

When Pitt and his contemporaries went to the House of Commons, they quoted their favourite authors, surpassed each other's efforts, understood their rivals' quotations – and dissected, criticized and applauded each other's speeches. They addressed a small, self-admiring social caste. After the Reform Bill of 1832, Parliament changed – and so did the style of speaking, as Members of Parliament adapted to a concern with legislation rather than administration and with a House that was often empty. With the rise in power of the whips and the rival party machines, moreover, there were fewer independently minded MPs and speeches became more standardized. Yet this era of 'decline' was the age of Peel, Brougham, Disraeli, Bright and Gladstone.

As Lloyd George, Churchill and Roosevelt adapted subsequently to the age of the wireless, critics again mourned the state of oratory, as they do today in the age of global television, even though it is this age that has brought us John F. Kennedy, Martin Luther King and Nelson Mandela and given more powerful worldwide power and effect to their speeches than Chatham or Webster or Lincoln could have dreamed of. Oratory, therefore, is always in decline, yet somehow is always surviving as the supreme art of politicians, the principal criterion by which they are judged and by which they seize and maintain power and address their parties and followers.

What has changed – which is where the Gettysburg address crops up again, albeit incidentally – is that most great speeches are now prepared by a team of speechwriters instead of by the orators themselves, a tradition that survived into the early twentieth century. President Roosevelt, for instance, wrote the first draft of his 1933 inaugural in four hours and only then submitted it to scrutiny, and Churchill wrote and rehearsed his own speeches.

It was President Kennedy in 1961 who made liberal use of speechwriters, notably Theodore Sorensen, and who offers us the most detailed insight into the making of a modern speech. Sorensen's first instruction from the incoming president was to study the Gettysburg address. His conclusion, which applied to the drafting of Kennedy's inaugural (see the use of biblical quotation and the use of 'Let' to start eight sentences), was that Lincoln never used a two- or three-syllable word where a one-syllable word would do and never used two or three words where one would do. Kennedy also instructed Sorensen that he wanted the shortest inaugural of the century, focusing on foreign policy, neither partisan, pessimistic nor critical of his predecessor. Above all it should set the tone for the Kennedy era that was about to begin.

Serious drafting began a week before the address was due. Pages, paragraphs and complete drafts had poured in, solicited from J.K. Galbraith, Arthur Schlesinger, Adlai Stevenson and others, unsolicited from newsmen and strangers. Biblical quotations were obtained from Billy Graham and Isaac Franck, director of Washington's Jewish Community Council. Sorensen describes Kennedy's dissatisfaction with each attempt to outline domestic goals, ending with a decision to drop the 'domestic stuff' and eliminate all 'I's from the address. Sorensen also shows the evolution of a great speech. When he accepted nomination, Kennedy said:

> Man . . . has taken into his mortal hands the power to exterminate the entire species some seven times over.

By the inaugural, that sentence had been polished by the speechwriters into something simpler and more eloquent:

> For man holds in his mortal hands the power to abolish all forms of human poverty and all forms of human life.

The opening sentence had three drafts:

> We celebrate today not a victory of party but the sacrament of democracy,

> We celebrate today not a victory of party but a convention of freedom,

and finally . . .

> We observe today not a victory of party but a celebration of freedom.

Meanwhile the phrase that is most often quoted was transformed between September campaigning and the January inaugural from:

> We do not campaign stressing what our country is going to do for us as people. We stress what we can do for our country, all of us,

to a sentence that is still quoted more than thirty years later:

> And so, my fellow Americans, ask not what your country can do for you; ask what you can do for your country.

The question that lingers after this exegesis of the 1961 inaugural – as it also does of the speeches crafted for Ronald Reagan by his speechwriter Peggy Noonan – is whether the address was by Kennedy or by Sorensen.

The answer has to be that it was Kennedy's speech. It was he who knew what he wanted, he who insisted on draft after draft until he got what he wanted, and he who both delivered the address and accepted the responsibility for the ideals he set forth. So, too, it was Reagan's sincere and schmaltzy delivery of Noonan's words that worked the alchemy on her speeches and made people weep.

One criticism that may be made of this anthology, certainly in the 1990s, is that it features so few women. There are three reasons. One is that until the emancipation of Western women in the mid twentieth century few featured on the great stages of world politics. Another, given by some feminists, is that women have wanted no part in the macho game of domination by speech. The third is physical – women's voices are not made by nature for oratory. They are not deep enough (as Margaret Thatcher discovered until she trained herself to acquire more depth to her voice and was no longer described as shrill).

Voice, moreover, is the most important asset of the orator. According to Lloyd George, speeches succeeded by a combination of word, voice and gesture in moving their audiences to the action the orator desired. As we read the speeches in this anthology, we go back to the days when orators addressed their audiences directly, without the restraining intervention of radio and television, and attracted thousands to walk miles to hear them – and when word, voice and gesture were crucial, whether in attracting the crowds or dominating Parliament or Senate.

Chatham, with his flashing eye and forbidding manner, owed his supremacy as much to his voice as to his other gifts. He could roar so loud in the Lords that he could almost be heard in the Commons, yet whisper so as to be heard on the furthest bench. At the age of twenty-one, William Pitt the Younger ruled Britain by the sonorous depths of his voice, a voice that filled the House of Commons with its sound. Although he had a shrill, penetrating voice, Charles James Fox learned to use it well, at times pitching his tone low to good effect, and his rapid rate of speaking had a compelling quality that swept his listeners along with him. Webster's voice, described as deep, rich, musical and of prodigious volume and force, was compared to an organ, as were the voices of Daniel O'Connell and William Gladstone. Robert Peel had a strong flexible voice that could range effortlessly from soft persuasiveness to sonorous defiance, from sly banter to a grave solemnity that hushed the Commons to silence.

Although it is not always obvious from the page, there is still a thrill to be gained from setting the speakers who feature in this anthology on to the stages from which they spoke and to try to sense the excitement they generated. How, for instance, did the vast multitudes that Daniel O'Connell drew to Mullaghmast manage to hear his speech when there were no microphones? 'It was this way,' said one of the old men, who was there. 'The people said there was half a million of men, not counting women. It was a mighty gathering. Everybody heard Dan. For Dan raised his hand and told all about the platform to repeat his words. He said "Silence", and silence came to us as the wind upon the barley. Then each man spoke after Dan, and every other man said the words, and out to us all on the edge of the crowd came the speech of Dan O'Connell.'

With his melodious voice, Gladstone could also attract the crowds. 'The outstanding feature of Gladstone's oratory,' says his biographer Philip Magnus, 'was the way in which it was adapted to its audience. He combined in an unusual degree the arts of exposition and debate. He had an unerring instinct for any weak points in an opponent's argument and he would swoop on them like a hawk . . . Beneath that smooth expression an unseen volcano blazed. It erupted at intervals and shot forth pillars of flame and clouds of smoke. The controls were colossal but Gladstone's mind was seismic . . . He used the masses to provide himself with the response which his nature craved but which he had ceased to find in the social world in which he moved. He rewarded the masses . . . by appealing not to their self-interest but to their self-respect. He invested them with the quality of a supreme tribunal before which the greatest causes could be tried. And by that means he completed, in the political field, the work of spiritual emancipation which Wesley had begun . . . The mood which Gladstone kindled was one which priests, orators, poets and artists have sought to kindle throughout the ages. It is the mood in which mortal men are made to feel that they are somehow "greater than they know".'

Orators, in that tribute to Gladstone, are placed alongside artists, poets and priests. It is the aim of this anthology to show that that is where they belong – that the great historic speeches of the past and the present can still be read with the pleasure that comes with reading the greatest poetry and literature and the profit that comes from understanding the historical forces that have shaped our world.

# ACKNOWLEDGEMENTS

No anthology can be compiled without substantial help from friends, historians and libraries. So I acknowledge with sincere gratitude the help I have received from Bridget, Tessa and Georgie MacArthur, Sandra Bourne, Barry Turner, Mary Fulton, Maureen Waller, David Glencross, Michael James, Roy Greenslade, Edward Pearce, George Darby, David Evans, John Morrill, Melvyn Matthews, Richard Bourne, Edward Wild, David Mutton, Peter Stothard, Hilary Mantel, Douglas Johnson, Antonia Fraser, Erica Wagner, Hilary Rubinstein, Tony Lacey, Ruth Salazar, Lynne Truss, Jill Fenner, Suzan Richmond, Brenda Maddox and Peter Riddell.

I owe a special debt to the London Library and its staff, but also to the Highgate Library and Scientific Institution, the reference library of the United States Embassy in London, the Gladstone Library at Bristol University and the librarian of the National Liberal Club.

Several books have been particularly helpful – all the Penguin history dictionaries and Penguin histories of England, *Chambers Biographical Dictionary* and the *Cambridge Dictionary of Biography*. A special debt is owed to the work of Robert Blake, Hugh Brogan, Roy Foster, J.H. Plumb, Philip Magnus and J.P. Kenyon.

The publishers would like to thank the following for permission to reprint copyright material:

Betty Friedan: to Curtis Brown Ltd for 'A woman's civil right' (1969) from *It Changed My Life* (1991). Copyright © 1963, 1964, 1966, 1970, 1971, 1972, 1973, 1974, 1975, 1976, 1985, 1991 by Betty Friedan.

David Lloyd George: to Express Newspapers plc and Macmillan Publishing Company, New York, for 'The great pinnacle of sacrifice' (1914) from *Slings and Arrows* (London, Cassell, 1929).

Martin Luther King: to the Heirs to the Estate of Martin Luther King, Jr, c/o Joan Daves Literary Agency for 'I have a dream' (1963). Copyright 1963 by Martin Luther King, Jr, copyright renewed 1991 by Coretta Scott King.

Nelson Mandela: to Fatima Meer and Penguin Books Ltd for 'An ideal for which I am prepared to die' (1964) from *Higher Than Hope: The Authorized Biography*.

Emmeline Pankhurst: to Richard Pankhurst and Fawcett Library, London Guildhall University, for 'The laws that men have made' (1908).

'La Pasionaria': to Lawrence & Wishart Ltd for 'Fascism shall not pass' (1936) from *Speeches and Articles 1936–1938* by Dolores Ibarruri (Lawrence & Wishart, 1938).

Every effort has been made to identify and contact copyright holders. The publishers will be glad to rectify, in future editions, any omissions or corrections brought to their notice.

# ANCIENT TIMES

# MOSES
## *c.* 1250 BC

### 'Thou shalt not . . .'

*As a child in Egypt, Moses was saved from the slaughter of all male Jewish children by being hidden in bulrushes in the Nile. He was found and brought up by one of Pharaoh's daughters in the Egyptian court. He became a prophet and lawgiver and led the people of Israel out of Egypt. After forty years' wandering in the desert wilderness, they drew within sight of the promised land of Canaan. Moses called his people together on Mount Sinai, where he delivered the Ten Commandments, one of the two most influential speeches in Western civilization.*

Hear, O Israel, the statutes and judgements which I speak in your ears this day, that ye may learn them, and keep and do them.

The Lord our God made a covenant with us in Horeb.

The Lord made not this covenant with our fathers, but with us, even us, who are all of us here alive this day.

The Lord talked with you face to face in the mount out of the midst of the fire (I stood between the Lord and you at that time, to shew you the word of the Lord: for ye were afraid by reason of the fire, and went not up into the mount), saying,

I am the Lord thy God, which brought thee out of the land of Egypt, from the house of bondage.

Thou shalt have none other gods before me.

Thou shalt not make thee any graven image, or any likeness of anything that is in heaven above, or that is in the earth beneath, or that is in the waters beneath the earth:

Thou shalt not bow down thyself unto them, nor serve them: for I the Lord thy God am a jealous God, visiting the iniquity of the fathers upon the children unto the third and fourth generation of them that hate me,

And shewing mercy unto thousands of them that love me and keep my commandments.

Thou shalt not take the name of the Lord thy God in vain: for the Lord will not hold him guiltless that taketh his name in vain.

Keep the sabbath day to sanctify it, as the Lord thy God hath commanded thee.

Six days thou shalt labour, and do all thy work:

But the seventh day is the sabbath of the Lord thy God: in it thou shalt not do any work thou, nor thy son, nor thy daughter, nor thy manservant, nor thy maidservant, nor thine ox, nor thine ass, nor any of thy cattle, nor thy stranger that is within thy gates; that thy manservant and thy maidservant may rest as well as thou.

And remember that thou wast a servant in the land of Egypt, and that the Lord thy God brought thee out thence through a mighty hand and by a stretched out arm: therefore the Lord thy God commanded thee to keep the sabbath day.

Honour thy father and thy mother, as the Lord thy God hath commanded thee: that thy days may be prolonged, and that it may go well with thee, in the land which the Lord thy God giveth thee.

Thou shalt not kill.

Neither shalt thou commit adultery.

Neither shalt thou steal.

Neither shalt thou bear false witness against thy neighbour.

Neither shalt thou desire thy neighbour's wife, neither shalt thou covet thy neighbour's house, his field, or his manservant, or his maidservant, his ox, or his ass, or anything that is thy neighbour's.

These words the Lord spake unto all your assembly in the mount out of the midst of the fire, of the cloud, and of the thick darkness, with a great voice: and he added no more. And he wrote them in two tables of stone, and delivered them unto me.

And it came to pass, when ye heard the voice out of the midst of the darkness (for the mountain did burn with fire), that ye came near unto me, even all the heads of your scribes, and your elders;

And ye said, Behold, the Lord our God hath shewed us his glory and his greatness, and we have heard his voice out of the midst of the fire: we have seen this day that God doth talk with man, and he liveth.

Now therefore why should we die? for this great fire will consume us: if we hear the voice of the Lord our God any more, then we shall die.

For who is there of all flesh, that hath heard the voice of the living God speaking out of the midst of the fire, as we have, and lived?

Go thou near, and hear all that the Lord our God shall say: and speak thou unto us all that the Lord our God shall speak unto thee; and we will hear it, and do it.

And the Lord heard the voice of your words, when ye spake unto me; and the Lord said unto me, I have heard the voice of the words of this

people, which they have spoken unto thee: they have well said all that
they have spoken.

O that there were such an heart in them, that they would fear me, and
keep all my commandments always, that it might be well with them, and
with their children for ever!

Go say to them, Get you into your tents again.

But as for thee, stand thou here by me, and I will speak unto thee all
the commandments, and the statutes, and the judgements, which thou
shalt teach them, that they may do them in the land which I give them
to possess it.

Ye shall observe to do therefore as the Lord your God hath commanded you: ye shall not turn aside to the right hand or to the left.

Ye shall walk in all the ways which the Lord your God hath
commanded you, that ye may live, and that it may be well with you, and
that ye may prolong your days in the land which ye shall possess.

Deuteronomy 5
Authorized Version

●

## PERICLES
### 431 BC

### *'Athens crowns her sons'*

*The funeral oration which Thucydides puts in the mouth of Pericles, the Athenian
statesman, is one of the great statements of human achievement, an apologia for the
democratic principles and system of government of Athens. It was delivered during
the winter of 431–430 BC at the funeral of the dead in battle of the Peloponnesian
War.*

*Modern translations of the speeches of Pericles, Demosthenes and Socrates can
leave the reader with only a tantalizing insight into their greatness. This extract is
from a translation by Benjamin Jowett, Regius Professor of Greek at Oxford
University from 1855 to 1893.*

In the hour of trial Athens alone among her contemporaries is superior
to the report of her. No enemy who comes against her is indignant at
the reverses which he sustains at the hands of such a city; no subject
complains that his masters are unworthy of him. And we shall assuredly

not be without witnesses; there are mighty monuments of our power
which will make us the wonder of this and of succeeding ages; we shall
not need the praises of Homer or of any other panegyrist whose poetry
may please for the moment, although his representation of the facts will
not bear the light of day. For we have compelled every land and every
sea to open a path for our valour, and have everywhere planted eternal
memorials of our friendship and of our enmity. Such is the city for
whose sake these men nobly fought and died; they could not bear the
thought that she might be taken from them; and every one of us who
survive should gladly toil on her behalf.

I have dwelt upon the greatness of Athens because I want to show
you that we are contending for a higher prize than those who enjoy
none of these privileges, and to establish by manifest proof the merit of
these men whom I am now commemorating. Their loftiest praise has
been already spoken. For in magnifying the city I have magnified them,
and men like them whose virtues made her glorious. And of how few
Hellenes can it be said as of them, that their deeds when weighed in the
balance have been found equal to their fame! Methinks that a death such
as theirs has been gives the true measure of a man's worth; it may be the
first revelation of his virtues, but is at any rate their final seal. For even
those who come short in other ways may justly plead the valour with
which they have fought for their country; they have blotted out the evil
with the good, and have benefited the state more by their public services
than they have injured her by their private actions. None of these men
were enervated by wealth or hesitated to resign the pleasures of life;
none of them put off the evil day in the hope, natural to poverty, that a
man, though poor, may one day become rich. But, deeming that the
punishment of their enemies was sweeter than any of these things, and
that they could fall in no nobler cause, they determined at the hazard of
their lives to be honourably avenged, and to leave the rest. They resigned to hope their unknown chance of happiness; but in the face of death
they resolved to rely upon themselves alone. And when the moment
came they were minded to resist and suffer, rather than to fly and save
their lives; they ran away from the word of dishonour, but on the battlefield their feet stood fast, and in an instant, at the height of their fortune,
they passed away from the scene, not of their fear, but of their glory.

Such was the end of these men; they were worthy of Athens, and the
living need not desire to have a more heroic spirit, although they may
pray for a less fatal issue. The value of such a spirit is not to be
expressed in words. Any one can discourse to you for ever about the

advantages of a brave defence. But instead of listening to him I would have you day by day fix your eyes upon the greatness of Athens, until you become filled with the love of her; and when you are impressed by the spectacle of her glory, reflect that this empire has been acquired by men who knew their duty and had the courage to do it, who in the hour of conflict had the fear of dishonour always present to them, and who, if ever they failed in an enterprise, would not allow their virtues to be lost to their country, but freely gave their lives to her as the fairest offering which they could present at her feast. The sacrifice which they collectively made was individually repaid to them; for they received again each one for himself a praise which grows not old, and the noblest of all sepulchres – I speak not of that in which their remains are laid, but of that in which their glory survives, and is proclaimed always and on every fitting occasion both in word and deed. For the whole earth is the sepulchre of famous men; not only are they commemorated by columns and inscriptions in their own country, but in foreign lands there dwells also an unwritten memorial of them, graven not on stone but in the hearts of men. Make them your examples, and, esteeming courage to be freedom and freedom to be happiness, do not weigh too nicely the perils of war. The unfortunate who has no hope of a change for the better has less reason to throw away his life than the prosperous who, if he survive, is always liable to a change for the worse, and to whom any accidental fall makes the most serious difference. To a man of spirit, cowardice and disaster coming together are far more bitter than death striking him unperceived at a time when he is full of courage and animated by the general hope.

Wherefore I do not now commiserate the parents of the dead who stand here; I would rather comfort them. You know that your life has been passed amid manifold vicissitudes; and that they may be deemed fortunate who have gained most honour, whether an honourable death like theirs, or an honourable sorrow like yours, and whose days have been so ordered that the term of their happiness is likewise the term of their life. I know how hard it is to make you feel this, when the good fortune of others will too often remind you of the gladness which once lightened your hearts. And sorrow is felt at the want of those blessings, not which a man never knew, but which were a part of his life before they were taken from him. Some of you are of an age at which they may hope to have other children, and they ought to bear their sorrow better; not only will the children who may hereafter be born make them forget their own lost ones, but the city will be doubly a gainer. She will not be left desolate, and she will be safer. For a man's counsel cannot have equal weight or worth, when he alone has no children to risk in the general danger. To those of you who have passed their prime, I say: 'Congratulate yourselves that you have been happy during the greater part of your days; remember that your life of sorrow will not last long, and be comforted by the glory of those who are gone. For the love of honour alone is ever young, and not riches, as some say, but honour is the delight of men when they are old and useless.'

To you who are the sons and brothers of the departed, I see that the struggle to emulate them will be an arduous one. For all men praise the dead, and, however pre-eminent your virtue may be, hardly will you be thought, I do not say to equal, but even to approach them. The living have their rivals and detractors, but when a man is out of the way, the honour and goodwill which he receives is unalloyed. And, if I am to speak of womanly virtues to those of you who will henceforth be widows, let me sum them up in one short admonition: To a woman not to show more weakness than is natural to her sex is a great glory, and not to be talked about for good or for evil among men.

I have paid the required tribute, in obedience to the law, making use of such fitting words as I had. The tribute of deeds has been paid in part; for the dead have been honourably interred, and it remains only that their children should be maintained at the public charge until they are grown up: this is the solid prize with which, as with a garland, Athens crowns her sons living and dead, after a struggle like theirs. For where the rewards of virtue are greatest, there the noblest citizens are enlisted in the service of the state. And now, when you have duly lamented, every one his own dead, you may depart.

•

# SOCRATES
## 399 BC

### 'No evil can happen to a good man'

*The Greek philosopher Socrates (469–399 BC) was born in Athens, where he spent his life and died. With Plato and Aristotle, he is one of the three great figures in ancient philosophy. The 'Socratic method' was to ask for definitions of concepts like justice and courage, to elicit by cross-examination contradictions in the responses of his interlocutors, and by demonstrating their inconsistencies to*

*prompt them to profounder thought. It was this unpopular activity which contrib-*
*uted to demands for his conviction for impiety and 'corrupting youth'. At the age*
*of seventy he was tried, found guilty, and sentenced to die by drinking hemlock.*
    *At his trial, Socrates spoke eloquently in his defence.*

Thou doest wrong to think that a man of any use at all is to weigh the
risk of life or death, and not to consider one thing only, whether when
he acts he does the right thing or the wrong, performs the deeds of a
good man or a bad ...

If I should be found to be wiser than the multitude, it would be in this,
that having no adequate knowledge of the Beyond, I do not presume that
I have it. But one thing I do know, and that is that to do injustice or turn
my back on the better is alike an evil and a disgrace. And never shall I fear
a possible good, rather than avoid a certain evil ... If you say to me,
'Socrates, Anytus fails to convince us, we let you go on condition that
you no longer spend your life in this search, and that you give up
philosophy, but if you are caught at it again you must die' – my reply is
'Men of Athens, I honour and love you, but I shall obey God rather than
you, and while I breathe, and have the strength, I shall never turn from
philosophy, nor from warning and admonishing any of you I come across
not to disgrace your citizenship of a great city renowned for its wisdom
and strength, by giving your thought to reaping the largest possible
harvest of wealth and honour and glory, and giving neither thought nor
care that you may reach the best in judgement, truth, and the soul' ...

So God bids, and I consider that never has a greater good been done
you, than through my ministry in the city. For it is my one business to
go about to persuade young and old alike not to make their bodies and
their riches their first and their engrossing care, but rather to give it to
the perfecting of their soul. Virtue springs not from possessions, but
from virtue springs possessions and all other human blessings, whether
for the individual or for society. If that is to corrupt the youth, then it is
mischievous. But that and nothing else is my offending, and he lies who
says else. Further I would say, O Athenians, you can believe Anytus or
not, you may acquit or not, but I shall not alter my conduct, no, not if I
have to die a score of deaths.

*Uproar ensued on these words in court, but Socrates appealed for a hearing, and went on.*

You can assure yourselves of this that, being what I say, if you put me
to death, you will not be doing greater injury to me than to yourselves.

To do me wrong is beyond the power of a Meletus or an Anytus. Heaven permits not the better man to be wronged by the worse. Death, exile, disgrace – Anytus and the average man may count these great evils, not I. A far greater evil is to do as he is now doing, trying to do away with a fellow-being unjustly.

O Athenians, I am far from pleading, as one might expect, for myself; it is for you I plead lest you should err as concerning the gift of God given unto you, by condemning me. If you put me to death you will not easily find another of my sort, who, to use a metaphor that may cause some laughter, am attached by God to the state, as a kind of gadfly to a big generous horse, rather slow because of its very bigness and in need of being waked up. As such and to that end God has attached me to the city, and all day long and everywhere I fasten on you, rousing and persuading and admonishing you . . .

Be not angry with me speaking the truth, for no man will escape alive who honourably and sincerely opposes you or any other mob, and puts his foot down before the many unjust and unrighteous things that would otherwise happen in the city. The man who really fights for justice and right, even if he expects but a short career, untouched, must occupy a private not a public station . . .

Clearly, if I tried to persuade you and overcame you by entreaty, when you have taken the oath of judge, I should be teaching you not to believe that there are gods, and my very defence would be a conviction that I do not pay them regard. But that is far from being so. I believe in them as no one of my accusers believes. And to you I commit my cause and to God, to judge me as seemeth best for me and for you.

*Then the result is declared amid a strained hush – 'Guilty.' Socrates again stands forth to speak.*

Men of Athens, many things keep me from being grieved that you have convicted me. What has happened was not unexpected by me. I am rather surprised at the number of votes on either side. I did not think the majority would be so little. As it is the transference of thirty votes would have acquitted me . . .

A fine life it would be for one at my age always being driven out from one city and changing to another. For I know that whithersoever I go the young men will listen to my words, just as here. If I drive them away, they themselves will have me cast out, and if I don't drive them away their fathers and relatives will cast me out for their sakes.

*Again there is an anxious interval while the jurors decide between the penalties. When the decision is announced, the word is 'Death.'*

O men, hard it is not to avoid death, it is far harder to avoid wrongdoing. It runs faster than death. I being slow and stricken in years am caught by the slower, but my accusers, sharp and clever as they are, by the swifter wickedness. And now I go to pay the debt of death at your hands, but they to pay the debt of crime and unrighteousness at the hand of Truth. I for my part shall abide by the award; let them see to it also. Perhaps somehow these things were to be, and I think it is well . . .

Wherefore, O Judges, be of good cheer about death, and know of a certainty that no evil can happen to a good man, either in life or after death. He and his are not neglected by the gods, nor has my own approaching end happened by mere chance. But I see clearly that to die and be released was better for me; and therefore the oracle gave no sign. For which reason, also, I am not angry with my condemners, or with my accusers; they have done me no harm, although they did not mean to do me any good; and for this I may gently blame them.

Still I have a favour to ask of them. When my sons are grown up, I would ask you, O my friends, to punish them, and I would have you trouble them, as I have troubled you, if they seem to care about riches, or anything, more than about virtue; or if they pretend to be something when they are really nothing, then reprove them, as I have reproved you, for not caring about that for which they ought to care, and thinking that they are something when they are really nothing. And if you do this, I and my sons will have received justice at your hands.

The hour of departure has arrived, and we go our ways – I to die, and you to live. Which is better God only knows.

•

## DEMOSTHENES
### 330 BC

*'I have always made common cause with the people'*

*The speech delivered by the Athenian statesman Demosthenes (384–322 BC) at his trial is considered the greatest speech of the ancient world's greatest orator. By modern standards it is long and often obscure; its greatness, moreover, is difficult to capture in translation, even in this early nineteenth century version by Henry Lord Brougham, the eminent British politician and social reformer.*

*From 351 BC, Demosthenes led the desperate struggle of the Athenians to maintain the freedom of the city states against the imperialist ambitions of Philip of Macedon. His speeches denouncing Philip – the Philippics – incited the Athenians to war, but resulted in the defeat of Chaeronia in 338 and the establishment of Macedonian supremacy.*

*A proposal to award Demosthenes a loser's crown was opposed by Aeschines, who had negotiated the peace with Philip. At his trial Aeschines set out to destroy Demosthenes, whose courage is demonstrated in his speech. He turns the attack on Aeschines, assesses his career, dares to state unpopular truths, and demolishes his opponent.*

It was my lot, Aeschines, when a boy, to frequent the schools suited to my station, and to have wherewithal to avoid doing anything mean through want. When I emerged from boyhood, I did as was consistent with my origin; filled the office of Choregus, furnished galleys, contributed to the revenue, and was wanting in no acts of munificence, public or private, but ready to aid both my country and my friends. When I entered into public life, I deemed it proper to choose the course which led to my being repeatedly crowned both by this country and the other Greek states, so that not even you, my enemies, will now venture to pronounce the part I took other than honourable. Such then were my fortunes . . .

But you, venerable man, who look down upon others, see what kind of fortunes were yours compared with mine! Brought up from your boyhood in abject poverty, you both were helper in your father's school, and you ground the ink, sponged the forms, and swept the room, doing the work of a household slave, not of a freeborn youth. When grown up, you recited your mother's books as she performed her mysteries, and you helped in her other trickeries. At night, dressed like a bacchanal, and draining the goblet, and purifying the initiated, and rubbing them with clay and with bran, rising from the lustration, you ordered them to cry, 'I've fled the evil; I've found the good'; bragging that none ever roared so loud before; and truly I believe it; for do not doubt that he who now speaks out so lustily, did not then howl most splendidly . . .

I come to the charges that apply to your life and conversation. You chose that line of policy (ever since the plan struck your mind) by which, as long as the country flourished, you led the life of the hare, frightened, and trembling, and perpetually expecting the scourge for the offences of which you were conscious; but when all others were suffering, you were seen in high spirits by all. But he who was so cheerful after the death of thousands of his fellow-citizens, what does he deserve to suffer at the hands of the survivors? . . .

Draw then the parallel between your life and mine, Aeschines, quietly and not acrimoniously; and demand of this audience which of the two each of them had rather choose for his own. You were an usher – I a scholar; you were an initiator – I was initiated; you danced at the games – I presided over them; you were a clerk of the Assembly, I a member; you, a third-rate actor, I a spectator; you were constantly breaking down – I always hissing you; your measures were all in the enemy's favour – mine always in the country's; and, in a word, now on this day the question as to me is whether or not I shall be crowned, while nothing whatever is alleged against my integrity; while it is your lot to appear already as a calumniator, and the choice of evils before you is that of still continuing your trade, or being put to silence by failing to obtain a fifth of the votes . . .

Among all other men I observe these principles and these distinctions to prevail. Does any one wilfully do wrong? He is the object of indignation and of punishment. Does any one commit an error unintentionally? He is pardoned, not punished. Has one who neither does any wrong nor commits any error devoted himself to a course which to all appeared expedient, and has he been in common with all disappointed of success? It is not fair to reprobate or to attack him, but to condole with him. All this is established not only in all our jurisprudence, but by Nature herself in her unwritten laws, and in the very constitution of the human mind. Thus has Aeschines so far surpassed all other men in cruelty and calumny, that those same things which he enumerates as misfortunes he also imputes to me as crimes . . .

In what circumstances then ought a statesman and an orator to be vehement? When the State is in jeopardy upon the ruin of affairs – when the people are in conflict with the enemy – then it is that the strenuous and patriotic citizen appears. But when Aeschines cannot pretend to have any ground whatever for even charging me with any offence in public life, or, I will add, in private, either in the name of the country or his own – for him to come forward with a vamped up attack on my crowning and my honours, and to waste so many words upon this subject, is the working of personal spite and envy, and a little mind, and shows no good man.

To me, indeed, Aeschines, it appears from these speeches of yours, as if you had instituted this impeachment through a desire of making a display of vociferation, not of punishing any one's misconduct. For it is not the speech of the orator, Aeschines, that avails, nor yet the compass of his voice, but his feeling in unison with the community and bearing enmity or affection towards them whom his country loves or hates. He that thus possesses his soul speaks ever with right feeling. But he that bows to those from whom the country has danger to apprehend, does not anchor in the same roadstead with the people; accordingly he does not look for safety from the same quarter. But mark me, I do: for I have always made common cause with the people, nor have I ever taken any course for my peculiar and individual interest. Can you say as much? Then how? – You, who, instantly after the battle, went on the embassy to Philip, the cause of all that in these times befell your country; and that after refusing the office at all former periods, as every one knows? – But who deceives the country? Is it not he that says one thing and thinks another? And who is he upon whom at every assembly solemn execration is proclaimed? Is it not such a man as this? What worse charge can any one bring against an orator than that his words and his sentiments do not tally? Yet you have been discovered to be such a man; and you still lift your voice and dare to look this assembly in the face! . . .

What alliance ever accrued to the country of your making? Or what succours, or goodwill, or glory of your gaining? Or what embassy, or what other public functions, whereby the state acquired honour? What domestic affair, or concern of the Greek states, or of strangers, over which you presided, was ever set right through you? What galleys, what armaments, what arsenals, what repairs of the walls, what cavalry? In what one of all these particulars have you ever proved useful? What benefit has ever accrued to either rich or poor from your fortunes? None. – 'But, hark!' says some one, 'if nothing of all this was done, at least there existed good dispositions and public spirit.' Where? When? you most wicked of men? – Your contributing nothing was not owing to your poverty but to your taking special care nothing you did should ever counteract the schemes of those to whom all your policy was subservient. In what, then, are you bold, and when are you munificent? When any thing is to be urged against your countrymen, then are you most copious of speech – most profuse of money – most rich in memory – a first-rate actor – the Theocrines of the stage! . . .

Two qualities, men of Athens, every citizen of ordinary worth ought to possess (I shall be able in general terms to speak of myself in the least invidious manner): he should both maintain in office the purpose of a firm mind and the course suited to his country's pre-eminence, and on all occasions and in all his actions the spirit of patriotism. This belongs to our nature; victory and might are under the dominion of another power. These dispositions you will find to have been absolutely inherent in me. For observe; neither when my head was demanded, nor when they dragged me before the Amphyctions, nor when they threatened, nor when they promised, nor when they let loose on me these wretches like wild beasts, did I ever abate in any particular my affection for you. This straightforward and honest path of policy, from the very first, I chose; the honour, the power, the glory of my country to promote – these to augment – in these to have my being. Never was I seen going about the streets elated and exulting when the enemy was victorious, stretching out my hand, and congratulating such as I thought would tell it elsewhere, but hearing with alarm any success of our own armies, moaning and bent to the earth like these impious men, who rail at this country as if they could do so without also stigmatizing themselves; and who, turning their eyes abroad, and seeing the prosperity of the enemy in the calamities of Greece, rejoice in them, and maintain that we should labour to make them last for ever!

Let not, oh gracious God, let not such conduct receive any manner of sanction from thee! Rather plant even in these men a better spirit and better feelings! But if they are wholly incurable, then pursue themselves, yea, themselves by themselves, to utter and untimely perdition by land and by sea; and to us who are spared vouchsafe to grant the speediest rescue from our impending alarms, and an unshaken security!

•

## MARCUS TULLIUS CICERO
### 63 BC

### 'Among us you can dwell no longer'

*Marcus Tullius Cicero (106–43 BC) had confirmed his reputation as an orator in 70 BC when he impeached the corrupt governor Gaius Verres. Seven years later, as consul of Rome, he foiled a conspiracy led by Lucius Catiline to raise an insurrection, set Rome on fire and massacre the Senate. Cicero was kept informed of Catiline's plot by Fulvia, the mistress of one of the conspirators. Two days later Cicero summoned the Senate to the temple of Jupiter in the Capitol – which Catiline had the audacity to attend. Cicero was so provoked that he addressed*

*Catiline in the first of four thundering and vituperative indictments of his enemy.
It is his most famous speech and was used as a school exercise in the instruction of
rhetoric, even by kings, for centuries.*

*The speech, given here in the translation by C.D. Yonge, was a triumph and
Cicero played a principal part in saving Rome from a* coup d'état. *He convinced
an incredulous Senate that the danger was real. Catiline was sentenced to
execution. He refused to surrender and was killed on the battlefield the following
year.*

When, O Catiline, do you mean to cease abusing our patience? How
long is that madness of yours still to mock us? When is there to be an
end of that unbridled audacity of yours, swaggering about as it does
now? Do not the nightly guards placed on the Palatine hill – do not the
watches posted throughout the city – does not the alarm of the people,
and the union of all good men – does not the precaution taken of
assembling the Senate in this most defensible place – do not the looks
and countenances of this venerable body here present, have any effect
upon you? Do you not feel that your plans are detected? Do you not see
that your conspiracy is already arrested and rendered powerless by the
knowledge which every one here possesses of it? What is there that you
did last night, what the night before – where is it that you were – who
was there that you summoned to meet you – what design was there
which was adopted by you, with which you think that any one of us is
unacquainted?

Shame on the age and on its principles! The Senate is aware of these
things; the consul sees them; and yet this man lives. Lives! aye, he comes
even into the Senate. He takes a part in the public deliberations; he is
watching and marking down and checking off for slaughter every
individual among us. And we, gallant men that we are, think that we are
doing our duty to the republic if we keep out of the way of his frenzied
attacks.

You ought, O Catiline, long ago to have been led to execution by
command of the consul. That destruction which you have been long
plotting against us ought to have already fallen on your own head . . .

I wish, O conscript fathers, to be merciful; I wish not to appear
negligent amid such danger to the State; but I do now accuse myself of
remissness and culpable inactivity. A camp is pitched in Italy, at the
entrance of Etruria, in hostility to the republic; the number of the enemy
increases every day; and yet the general of that camp, the leader of those
enemies, we see within the walls – ay, and even in the Senate – planning

every day some internal injury to the republic. If, O Catiline, I should now order you to be arrested, to be put to death, I should, I suppose, have to fear lest all good men should say that I had acted tardily, rather than that any one should affirm that I acted cruelly. But yet this, which ought to have been done long since, I have good reason for not doing as yet; I will put you to death, then, when there shall be not one person possible to be found so wicked, so abandoned, so like yourself, as not to allow that it has been rightly done. As long as one person exists who can dare to defend you, you shall live; but you shall live as you do now, surrounded by my many and trusty guards, so that you shall not be able to stir one finger against the republic: many eyes and ears shall still observe and watch you, as they have hitherto done, though you shall not perceive them.

For what is there, O Catiline, that you can still expect, if night is not able to veil your nefarious meetings in darkness, and if private houses cannot conceal the voice of your conspiracy within their walls – if everything is seen and displayed? Change your mind: trust me: forget the slaughter and conflagration you are meditating. You are hemmed in on all sides; all your plans are clearer than the day to us; let me remind you of them. Do you recollect that on the 21st of October I said in the senate, that on a certain day, which was to be the 27th of October, C. Manlius, the satellite and servant of your audacity, would be in arms? Was I mistaken, Catiline, not only in so important, so atrocious, so incredible a fact, but, what is much more remarkable, in the very day? I said also in the Senate that you had fixed the massacre of the nobles for the 28th of October, when many chief men of the Senate had left Rome, not so much for the sake of saving themselves as of checking your designs. Can you deny that on that very day you were so hemmed in by my guards and my vigilance, that you were unable to stir one finger against the republic; when you said that you would be content with the flight of the rest, and the slaughter of us who remained? What? when you made sure that you would be able to seize Praeneste on the first of November by a nocturnal attack, did you not find that that colony was fortified by my order, by my garrison, by my watchfulness and care? You do nothing, you plan nothing, you think of nothing which I not only do not hear, but which I do not see and know every particular of.

Listen while I speak of the night before. You shall now see that I watch far more actively for the safety than you do for the destruction of the republic. I say that you came the night before (I will say nothing obscurely) into the Scythedealers' street, to the house of Marcus Lecca;

that many of your accomplices in the same insanity and wickedness came there too. Do you dare to deny it? Why are you silent? I will prove it if you do deny it; for I see here in the Senate some men who were there with you.

O ye immortal Gods, where on earth are we? in what city are we living? what constitution is ours? There are here – here in our body, O conscript fathers, in this the most holy and dignified assembly of the whole world, men who meditate my death, and the death of all of us, and the destruction of this city, and of the whole world. I, the consul, see them; I ask them their opinion about the republic, and I do not yet attack, even by words, those who ought to be put to death by the sword. You were, then, O Catiline, at Lecca's that night; you divided Italy into sections; you settled where every one was to go; you fixed whom you were to leave at Rome, whom you were to take with you; you portioned out the divisions of the city for conflagration; you undertook that you yourself would at once leave the city, and said that there was then only this to delay you, that I was still alive. Two Roman knights were found to deliver you from this anxiety, and to promise that very night, before daybreak, to slay me in my bed. All this I knew almost before your meeting had broken up. I strengthened and fortified my house with a stronger guard; I refused admittance, when they came, to those whom you sent in the morning to salute me, and of whom I had foretold to many eminent men that they would come to me at that time.

As, then, this is the case, O Catiline, continue as you have begun. Leave the city at last: the gates are open; depart. That Manlian camp of yours has been waiting too long for you as its general. And lead forth with you all your friends, or at least as many as you can; purge the city of your presence; you will deliver me from a great fear, when there is a wall between me and you. Among us you can dwell no longer – I will not bear it, I will not permit it, I will not tolerate it . . .

You are summoning to destruction and devastation the temples of the immortal gods, the houses of the city, the lives of all the citizens; in short, all Italy. Wherefore, since I do not yet venture to do that which is the best thing, and which belongs to my office and to the discipline of our ancestors, I will do that which is more merciful if we regard its rigour, and more expedient for the state. For if I order you to be put to death, the rest of the conspirators will still remain in the republic; if, as I have long been exhorting you, you depart, your companions, those worthless dregs of the republic, will be drawn off from the city too.

What is the matter, Catiline? Do you hesitate to do that when I order you which you were already doing of your own accord? The consul orders an enemy to depart from the city. Do you ask me, Are you to go into banishment? I do not order it; but, if you consult me, I advise it.

For what is there, O Catiline, that can now afford you any pleasure in this city? for there is no one in it, except that band of profligate conspirators of yours, who does not fear you – no one who does not hate you. What brand of domestic baseness is not stamped upon your life? What disgraceful circumstance is wanting to your infamy in your private affairs? From what licentiousness have your eyes, from what atrocity have your hands, from what iniquity has your whole body ever abstained? Is there one youth, when you have once entangled him in the temptations of your corruption, to whom you have not held out a sword for audacious crime, or a torch for licentious wickedness?

What? when lately by the death of your former wife you had made your house empty and ready for a new bridal, did you not even add another incredible wickedness to this wickedness? But I pass that over, and willingly allow it to be buried in silence, that so horrible a crime may not be seen to have existed in this city, and not to have been chastised. I pass over the ruin of your fortune, which you know is hanging over you against the ides of the very next month; I come to those things which relate not to the infamy of your private vices, not to your domestic difficulties and baseness, but to the welfare of the republic and to the lives and safety of us all.

If your parents feared and hated you, and if you could by no means pacify them, you would, I think, depart somewhere out of their sight. Now, your country, which is the common parent of all of us, hates and fears you, and has no other opinion of you, than that you are meditating parricide in her case; and will you neither feel awe of her authority, nor deference for her judgement, nor fear of her power?

And she, O Catiline, thus pleads with you, and after a manner silently speaks to you: – There has now for many years been no crime committed but by you; no atrocity has taken place without you; you alone unpunished and unquestioned have murdered the citizens, have harassed and plundered the allies; you alone have had power not only to neglect all laws and investigations, but to overthrow and break through them. Your former actions, though they ought not to have been borne, yet I did bear as well as I could; but now that I should be wholly occupied with fear of you alone, that at every sound I should dread Catiline, that no design should seem possible to be entertained against me which does not proceed from your wickedness, this is no longer endurable. Depart, then, and deliver me from this fear; that, if it be a just one, I may not be destroyed; if an imaginary one, that at least I may at last cease to fear.

If, as I have said, your country were thus to address you, ought she not to obtain her request, even if she were not able to enforce it? What shall I say of your having given yourself into custody? what of your having said, for the sake of avoiding suspicion, that you were willing to dwell in the house of Marcus Lepidus? And when you were not received by him, you dared even to come to me, and begged me to keep you in my house; and when you had received answer from me that I could not possibly be safe in the same house with you, when I considered myself in great danger as long as we were in the same city, you came to Quintus Metellus, the praetor, and being rejected by him, you passed on to your associate, that most excellent man, Marcus Marcellus, who would be, I suppose you thought, most diligent in guarding you, most sagacious in suspecting you, and most bold in punishing you; but how far can we think that man ought to be from bonds and imprisonment who has already judged himself deserving of being given into custody?

Since, then, this is the case, do you hesitate, O Catiline, if you cannot remain here with tranquillity, to depart to some distant land, and to trust your life, saved from just and deserved punishment, to flight and solitude? Make a motion, say you, to the Senate (for that is what you demand), and if this body votes that you ought to go into banishment, you say that you will obey. I will not make such a motion, it is contrary to my principles, and yet I will let you see what these men think of you. Be gone from the city, O Catiline, deliver the republic from fear; depart into banishment, if that is the word you are waiting for. What now, O Catiline? Do you not perceive, do you not see the silence of these men; they permit it, they say nothing; why wait you for the authority of their words when you see their wishes in their silence? . . .

And yet, why am I speaking? that anything may change your purpose? that you may ever amend your life? that you may meditate flight or think of voluntary banishment? I wish the gods may give you such a mind; though I see, if alarmed at my words you bring your mind to go into banishment, what a storm of unpopularity hangs over me, if not at present, while the memory of your wickedness is fresh, at all events hereafter. But it is worth while to incur that, as long as that is but a private misfortune of my own, and is unconnected with the dangers of the republic. But we cannot expect that you should be concerned at your own vices, that you should fear the penalties of the laws or that you should yield to the necessities of the republic, for you are not, O Catiline, one whom either shame can recall from infamy, or fear from danger, or reason from madness.

Wherefore, as I have said before, go forth, and if you wish to make me, your enemy as you call me, unpopular, go straight into banishment. I shall scarcely be able to endure all that will be said if you do so; I shall scarcely be able to support my load of unpopularity if you do go into banishment at the command of the consul; but if you wish to serve my credit and reputation, go forth with your ill-omened band of profligates; betake yourself to Manlius, rouse up the abandoned citizens, separate yourself from the good ones, wage war against your country, exult in your impious banditti, so that you may not seem to have been driven out by me and gone to strangers, but to have gone invited to your own friends . . .

Now that I may remove and avert, O conscript fathers, any in the least reasonable complaint from myself, listen, I beseech you, carefully to what I say, and lay it up in your inmost hearts and minds. In truth, if my country, which is far dearer to me than my life – if all Italy – if the whole republic were to address me, Marcus Tullius, what are you doing? will you permit that man to depart whom you have ascertained to be an enemy? whom you see ready to become the general of the war? whom you know to be expected in the camp of the enemy as their chief, the author of all this wickedness, the head of the conspiracy, the instigator of the slaves and abandoned citizens, so that he shall seem not driven out of the city by you, but let loose by you against the city? Will you not order him to be thrown into prison, to be hurried off to execution, to be put to death with the most prompt severity? What hinders you? is it the customs of our ancestors? But even private men have often in this republic slain mischievous citizens. – Is it the laws which have been passed about the punishment of Roman citizens? But in this city those who have rebelled against the republic have never had the rights of citizens. – Do you fear odium with posterity? You are showing fine gratitude to the Roman people which has raised you, a man known only by your own actions, of no ancestral renown, through all the degrees of honour at so early an age to the very highest office, if from fear of unpopularity or of any danger you neglect the safety of your fellow-citizens. But if you have a fear of unpopularity, is that arising from the imputation of vigour and boldness, or that arising from that of inactivity and indecision most to be feared? When Italy is laid waste by war, when cities are attacked and houses in flames, do you not think that you will be then consumed by a perfect conflagration of hatred? . . .

Though there are some men in this body who either do not see what threatens, or dissemble what they do see; who have fed the hope of Catiline by mild sentiments, and have strengthened the rising conspiracy by not believing it; influenced by whose authority many, and they not wicked, but only ignorant, if I punished him would say that I had acted cruelly and tyranically. But I know that if he arrives at the camp of Manlius to which he is going, there will be no one so stupid as not to see that there has been a conspiracy, no one so hardened as not to confess it. But if this man alone were put to death, I know that this disease of the republic would be only checked for awhile, not eradicated for ever. But if he banishes himself, and takes with him all his friends, and collects at one point all the ruined men from every quarter, then not only will this full-grown plague of the republic be extinguished and eradicated, but also the root and seed of all future evils.

We have now for a long time, O conscript fathers, lived among these dangers and machinations of conspiracy; but somehow or other, the ripeness of all wickedness, and of this long-standing madness and audacity, has come to a head at the time of my consulship. But if this man alone is removed from this piratical crew, we may appear, perhaps, for a short time relieved from fear and anxiety, but the danger will settle down and lie hid in the veins and bowels of the republic. As it often happens that men afflicted with a severe disease, when they are tortured with heat and fever, if they drink cold water, seem at first to be relieved, but afterwards suffer more and more severely; so this disease which is in the republic, if relieved by the punishment of this man, will only get worse and worse, as the rest will be still alive.

Wherefore, O conscript fathers, let the worthless begone – let them separate themselves from the good – let them collect in one place – let them, as I have often said before, be separated from us by a wall; let them cease to plot against the consul in his own house – to surround the tribunal of the city praetor – to besiege the Senate-house with swords – to prepare brands and torches to burn the city; let it, in short, be written on the brow of every citizen, what are his sentiments about the republic. I promise you this, O conscript fathers, that there shall be so much diligence in us the consuls, so much authority in you, so much virtue in the Roman knights, so much unanimity in all good men, that you shall see everything made plain and manifest by the departure of Catiline – everything checked and punished.

With these omens, O Catiline, begone to your impious and nefarious war, to the great safety of the republic, to your own misfortune and injury, and to the destruction of those who have joined themselves to you in every wickedness and atrocity. Then do you, O Jupiter, who were consecrated by Romulus with the same auspices as this city, whom we rightly call the stay of this city and empire, repel this man and his companions from your altars and from the other temples – from the houses and walls of the city – from the lives and fortunes of all the citizens; and overwhelm all the enemies of good men, the foes of the republic, the robbers of Italy, men bound together by a treaty and infamous alliance of crimes, dead and alive, with eternal punishments.

•

# JESUS OF NAZARETH
## *c.* 33

### *'Blessed are the poor in spirit'*

*When his disciples came to him on the mountain, Jesus of Nazareth delivered the most famous and enduring speech in Christendom. Nearly 2,000 years later, the moral code contained in the Sermon on the Mount remains the foundation of Western morality.*

Blessed are the poor in spirit:
For theirs is the kingdom of heaven.

Blessed are they that mourn:
For they shall be comforted.

Blessed are the meek:
For they shall inherit the earth.

Blessed are they which do hunger and thirst after righteousness:
For they shall be filled.

Blessed are the merciful:
For they shall obtain mercy.

Blessed are the pure in heart:
For they shall see God.

Blessed are the peacemakers:
For they shall be called the children of God.

Blessed are they which are persecuted for righteousness' sake:
For theirs is the kingdom ofheaven.

Blessed are ye, when men shall revile you, and persecute you, and shall
    say all manner of evil against you falsely, for my sake.
Rejoice, and be exceeding glad: for great is your reward in heaven: for so
    persecuted they the prophets which were before you.

Ye are the salt of the earth: but if the salt have lost his savour, wherewith shall it be salted? it is thenceforth good for nothing, but to be cast
out, and to be trodden under foot of men.

Ye are the light of the world. A city that is set on a hill cannot be hid.
Neither do men light a candle, and put it under a bushel, but on a candle-
stick; and it giveth light unto all that are in the house. Let your light so
shine before men, that they may see your good works, and glorify your
Father which is in heaven.

Think not that I am come to destroy the law, or the prophets: I am
not come to destroy, but to fulfil. For verily I say unto you, 'Till heaven
and earth pass, one jot or one tittle shall in no wise pass from the law,
till all be fulfilled.' Whosoever therefore shall break one of these least
commandments, and shall teach men so, he shall be called the least in the
kingdom of heaven: but whosoever shall do and teach them, the same
shall be called great in the kingdom of heaven. For I say unto you,
'Except your righteousness shall exceed the righteousness of the scribes
and Pharisees, ye shall in no case enter into the kingdom of heaven.'

Ye have heard that it was said by them of old time, 'Thou shalt not
kill'; and whosoever shall kill shall be in danger of the judgement. But I
say unto you, 'Whosoever is angry with his brother without a cause shall
be in danger of the judgement: and whosoever shall say to his brother,
"Raca," shall be in danger of the council: but whosoever shall say,
"Thou fool," shall be in danger of hell fire.' Therefore if thou bring thy
gift to the altar, and there rememberest that thy brother hath ought
against thee; leave there thy gift before the altar, and go thy way; first be
reconciled to thy brother, and then come and offer thy gift. Agree with
thine adversary quickly, while thou art in the way with him; lest at any time
the adversary deliver thee to the judge, and the judge deliver thee to the
officer, and thou be cast into prison. Verily I say unto thee, 'Thou shalt by
no means come out thence, till thou has paid the uttermost farthing.'

Ye have heard that it was said by them of old time, 'Thou shalt not commit adultery.' But I say unto you, 'Whosoever looketh on a woman to lust after her hath committed adultery with her already in his heart. And if thy right eye offend thee, pluck it out, and cast it from thee: for it is profitable for thee that one of thy members should perish, and not that thy whole body should be cast into hell. And if thy right hand offend thee, cut it off, and cast it from thee: for it is profitable for thee that one of thy members should perish, and not that thy whole body should be cast into hell.' It hath been said, 'Whosoever shall put away his wife, let him give her a writing of divorcement.' But I say unto you, 'Whosoever shall put away his wife, saving for the cause of fornication, causeth her to commit adultery: and whosoever shall marry her that is divorced committeth adultery.'

Again, ye have heard that it hath been said by them of old time, 'Thou shalt not forswear thyself, but shalt perform unto the Lord thine oaths.' But I say unto you, 'Swear not at all; neither by heaven; for it is God's throne: nor by the earth; for it is his footstool: neither by Jerusalem; for it is the city of the great King. Neither shalt thou swear by thy head, because thou canst not make one hair white or black. But let your communication be, "Yea, yea"; "Nay, nay": for whatsoever is more than these cometh of evil.'

Ye have heard that it hath been said, 'An eye for an eye, and a tooth for a tooth.' But I say unto you, 'Resist not evil: but whosoever shall smite thee on thy right cheek, turn to him the other also. And if any man will sue thee at the law, and take away thy coat, let him have thy cloak also. And whosoever shall compel thee to go a mile, go with him twain. Give to him that asketh thee, and from him that would borrow of thee turn not thou away.'

Ye have heard that it hath been said, 'Thou shalt love thy neighbour, and hate thine enemy.' But I say unto you, 'Love your enemies, bless them that curse you, do good to them that hate you, and pray for them which despitefully use you, and persecute you; that ye may be the children of your Father which is in heaven: for he maketh his sun to rise on the evil and on the good, and sendeth rain on the just and on the unjust.' For if ye love them which love you, what reward have ye? do not even the publicans the same? And if ye salute your brethren only, what do ye more than others? do not even the publicans so? Be ye therefore perfect, even as your Father which is in heaven is perfect.

Take heed that ye do not your alms before men, to be seen of them: otherwise ye have no reward of your Father which is in heaven.

Therefore when thou doest thine alms, do not sound a trumpet before thee, as the hypocrites do in the synagogues and in the streets, that they may have glory of men. Verily I say unto you, 'They have their reward.' But when thou doest alms, let not thy left hand know what thy right hand doeth: that thine alms may be in secret: and thy Father which seeth in secret himself shall reward thee openly.

And when thou prayest, thou shalt not be as the hypocrites are: for they love to pray standing in the synagogues and in the corners of the streets, that they may be seen of men. Verily I say unto you, 'They have their reward.' But thou, when thou prayest, enter into thy closet, and when thou has shut thy door, pray to thy Father which is in secret; and thy Father which seeth in secret shall reward thee openly. But when ye pray, use not vain repetitions, as the heathen do: for they think that they shall be heard for their much speaking. Be not ye therefore like unto them: for your Father knoweth what things ye have need of, before ye ask him. After this manner therefore pray ye:

> Our Father which art in heaven,
> Hallowed be thy name.
> Thy kingdom come.
> Thy will be done
> In earth, as it is in heaven.
>
> Give us this day
> Our daily bread.
> And forgive us our debts,
> As we forgive our debtors.
> And lead us not into temptation,
> But deliver us from evil:
>
> For thine is the kingdom,
> And the power,
> And the glory,
> For ever. Amen.

For if ye forgive men their trespasses, your heavenly Father will also forgive you: but if ye forgive not men their trespasses, neither will your Father forgive your trespasses.

Moreover when ye fast, be not, as the hypocrites, of a sad countenance: for they disfigure their faces, that they may appear unto men to fast. Verily I say unto you, 'They have their reward.' But thou, when thou fastest, anoint thine head, and wash thy face; that thou appear not unto men to fast, but unto thy Father which is in secret: and thy Father, which seeth in secret shall reward thee openly.

> Lay not up for yourselves treasures upon earth,
> Where moth and rust doth corrupt,
> And where thieves break through and steal:

> But lay up for yourselves treasures in heaven,
> Where neither moth nor rust doth corrupt,
> And where thieves do not break through nor steal.

For where your treasure is, there will your heart be also.

The light of the body is the eye: if therefore thine eye be single, thy whole body shall be full of light. But if thine eye be evil, thy whole body shall be full of darkness. If therefore the light that is in thee be darkness, how great is that darkness!

No man can serve two masters: for either he will hate the one, and love the other; or else he will hold to the one, and despise the other. Ye cannot serve God and Mammon.

Therefore I say unto you, 'Take no thought for your life, what ye shall eat, or what ye shall drink; nor yet for your body, what ye shall put on.' Is not the life more than meat, and the body than raiment? Behold the fowls of the air: for they sow not, neither do they reap, nor gather into barns; yet your heavenly Father feedeth them. Are ye not much better than they? Which of you by taking thought can add one cubit unto his stature? And why take ye thought for raiment? Consider the lilies of the field, how they grow; they toil not, neither do they spin: and yet I say unto you that even Solomon in all his glory was not arrayed like one of these.

Wherefore, if God so clothe the grass of the field, which today is, and tomorrow is cast into the oven, shall he not much more clothe you, O ye of little faith? Therefore take no thought, saying, 'What shall we eat?' or, 'What shall we drink?' or, 'Wherewithal shall we be clothed?' (for after all these things do the Gentiles seek): for your heavenly Father knoweth that ye have need of all these things. But seek ye first the kingdom of God, and his righteousness; and all these things shall be added unto you. Take therefore no thought for the morrow: for the morrow shall take thought for the things of itself. Sufficient unto the day is the evil thereof.

Judge not, that ye be not judged. For with what judgement ye judge, ye shall be judged: and with what measure ye mete, it shall be measured to you again. And why beholdest thou the mote that is in thy brother's eye, but considerest not the beam that is in thine own eye? Or how wilt thou say to thy brother, 'Let me pull out the mote out of thine eye'; and, behold, a beam is in thine own eye? Thou hypocrite, first cast out the beam out of thine own eye; and then shalt thou see clearly to cast out the mote out of thy brother's eye.

> Give not that which is holy unto the dogs,
> Neither cast ye your pearls before swine,
> Lest they trample them under their feet,
> And turn again and rend you.
>
> Ask, and it shall be given you;
> Seek, and ye shall find;
> Knock, and it shall be opened unto you:
> For every one that asketh receiveth;
> And he that seeketh findeth;
> And to him that knocketh it shall be opened.

Or what man is there of you, whom if his son ask bread, will he give him a stone? Or if he ask a fish, will he give him a serpent? If ye then, being evil, know how to give good gifts unto your children, how much more shall your Father which is in heaven give good things to them that ask him? Therefore all things whatsoever ye would that men should do to you, do ye even so to them: for this is the law and the prophets.

Enter ye in at the strait gate: for wide is the gate, and broad is the way, that leadeth to destruction, and many there be which go in thereat: because strait is the gate, and narrow is the way, which leadeth unto life, and few there be that find it.

Beware of false prophets, which come to you in sheep's clothing, but inwardly they are ravening wolves. Ye shall know them by their fruits. Do men gather grapes of thorns, or figs of thistles? Even so every good tree bringeth forth good fruit; but a corrupt tree bringeth forth evil fruit. A good tree cannot bring forth evil fruit, neither can a corrupt tree bring forth good fruit. Every tree that bringeth not forth good fruit is hewn down, and cast into the fire. Wherefore by their fruits ye shall know them.

Not every one that saith unto me, 'Lord, Lord,' shall enter into the kingdom of heaven; but he that doeth the will of my Father which is in heaven. Many will say to me in that day, 'Lord, Lord, have we not prophesied in thy name? and in thy name have cast out devils? and in thy name done many wonderful works?' And then will I profess unto them, 'I never knew you: depart from me, ye that work iniquity.'

Therefore whosoever heareth these sayings of mine, and doeth them, I will liken him unto a wise man, which built his house upon a rock; and the rain descended, and the floods came and the winds blew, and beat upon that house; and it fell not: for it was founded upon a rock. And every one that heareth these sayings of mine, and doeth them not, shall be likened unto a foolish man, which built his house upon the sand: and the rain descended, and the floods came, and the winds blew, and beat upon that house; and it fell: and great was the fall of it.

Matthew 5–7
Authorized Version

•

## MUHAMMAD
### 7th century

### *'Turn thy face towards the Sacred Mosque'*

*The angel Gabriel appeared to Muhammad on Mount Hira, near Mecca, in 610, when he was about forty, and told him he was the messenger of God. About four years later Muhammad became a preacher, and he preached for the next twenty-two years. The result is one of the great books of mankind, the Koran, containing the words of Muhammad delivered in a series of revelations taken down by his entourage. Muslims believe that through Muhammad, the Founder of Islam, God delivered his last message to mankind. He founded a religion which today has 700 million adherents. This is a central part of his preaching.*

It is not righteousness that ye turn your face towards the east or the west, but righteousness is [in] him who believeth in God and the Last Day, and the angels and the Scripture, and the Prophets, and who giveth wealth for the love of God to his kinsfolk and to orphans and the needy and the son of the road and them that ask and for the freeing of slaves, and who is instant in prayer, and giveth the alms; and those who fulfil their covenant when they covenant, and the patient in adversity and affliction and in time of violence, these are they who are true, and these are they who fear God.

Say: We believe in God, and what hath been sent down to thee, and what was sent down to Abraham, and Ishmael, and Isaac, and Jacob, and the tribes, and what was given to Moses, and to Jesus, and the prophets from their Lord – we make no distinction between any of them – and to Him are we resigned: and whoso desireth other than Resignation [Islam] for a religion, it shall certainly not be accepted from him, and in the life to come he shall be among the losers.

Observe the prayers, and the middle prayer, and stand instant before God. And if ye fear, then afoot or mounted; but when ye are safe remember God, how he taught you what ye did not know.

When the call to prayer soundeth on the Day of Congregation (Friday), then hasten to remember God, and abandon business; that is better for you if ye only knew: and when prayer is done, disperse in the land and seek of the bounty of God.

Turn thy face towards the Sacred Mosque; wherever ye be, turn your faces thitherwards.

Give alms on the path of God, and let not your hands cast you into destruction; but do good, for God loveth those who do good; and accomplish the pilgrimage and the visit to God: but if ye be besieged, then send what is easiest as an offering.

They will ask thee what it is they must give in alms. Say: Let what good ye give be for parents, and kinsfolk, and the orphan, and the needy, and the son of the road; and what good ye do, verily God knoweth it.

They will ask thee what they shall expend in alms; say, The surplus.

If ye give alms openly, it is well; but if ye conceal it, and give it to the poor, it is better for you, and will take away from you some of your sins: and God knoweth what ye do.

O ye who believe, make not your alms of no effects by taunt and vexation, like him who spendeth what he hath to be seen of men, and believeth not in God and the Last Day: for his likeness is as the likeness of a stone with earth upon it, and a heavy rain falleth upon it and leaveth it bare; they accomplish nothing with what they earn, for God guideth not the people that disbelieve. And the likeness of those who expend their wealth for the sake of pleasing God and for the certainty of their souls is as the likeness of a garden on a hill: a heavy rain falleth on it and it bringeth forth its fruit twofold; and if no heavy rain falleth on it, then the dew falleth; and God seeth what ye do.

Kind speech and forgiveness is better than alms which vexation followeth; and God is rich and ruthful.

The hearts of men are at the disposal of God like unto one heart, and He turneth them about in any way that He pleaseth. O Director of hearts, turn our hearts to obey Thee.

The first thing which God created was a pen, and He said to it, 'Write.' It said, 'What shall I write?' And God said, 'Write down the quantity of every separate thing to be created.' And it wrote all that was and all that will be to eternity.

There is not one among you whose sitting-place is not written by God whether in the fire or in Paradise. The Companions said, 'O Prophet! since God hath appointed our place, may we confide in this and abandon our religious and moral duty?' He said, 'No, because the happy will do good works, and those who are of the miserable will do bad works.'

The Prophet of God said that Adam and Moses (in the world of spirits) maintained a debate before God, and Adam got the better of Moses; who said, 'Thou art that Adam whom God created by the power of his hands, and breathed into thee from His own spirit, and made the angels bow before thee, and gave thee an habitation in His own Paradise: after that thou threwest man upon the earth, from the fault which thou committedst.' Adam said, 'Thou art that Moses whom God elected for His prophecy, and to converse with, and He gave to thee twelve tables, in which are explained everything, and God made thee His confidant, and the bearer of His secrets: then how long was the Bible written before I was created?' Moses said, 'Forty years.' Then Adam said, 'Didst thou see in the Bible that Adam disobeyed God?' He said, 'Yes.' Adam said, 'Dost thou then reproach me on a matter which God wrote in the Bible forty years before creating me?'

•

# OF COMMONERS AND KINGS

## 'We do not wish to molest you'

*Ethelbert (c. 552–616) was the Saxon King of Kent who met Augustine and his followers on their mission to convert England. It was a remarkable meeting – Ethelbert seated on the bare ground as Augustine and his forty companions advanced from the shore chanting a solemn litany, with a huge silver cross borne before them and beside it a large picture of Christ, painted and gilded on an upright board. Neither could understand the other's language, but the priests accompanying Augustine stepped forward as interpreters. The King listened and then gave his answer.*

Your words are fair, and your promises – but because they are new and doubtful, I cannot give my assent to them, and leave the customs which I have so long observed, with the whole Anglo-Saxon race. But because you have come hither as strangers from a long distance, and as I seem to myself to have seen clearly, that what you yourselves believed to be true and good, you wish to impart to us, we do not wish to molest you; nay, rather we are anxious to receive you hospitably, and to give you all that is needed for your support, nor do we hinder you from joining all whom you can to the faith of your religion.

*Augustine later became the first Archbishop of Canterbury.*

•

## WILLIAM THE CONQUEROR
1066

## 'Be ye the avengers of noble blood'

*William the Conqueror (c. 1027–87) invaded England with 7,000 men in 1066, claiming that he had been bequeathed the throne by his kinsman, Edward the Confessor. At the Battle of Hastings he defeated and killed Harold II and was crowned king.*
*On the morning of battle, still as Duke William of Normandy, he addressed his troops and summoned them to war.*

Normans! bravest of nations! I have no doubt of your courage, and none of your victory, which never by any chance or obstacle escaped your efforts. If indeed you had, once only, failed to conquer, there might be a need now to inflame your courage by exhortation; but your native spirit does not require to be roused. Bravest of men, what could the power of the Frankish King effect with all his people, from Lorraine to Spain, against Hastings my predecessor? What he wanted of France he took, and gave to the King only what he pleased. What he had, he held as long as it suited him, and relinquished it only for something better. Did not Rollo my ancestor, founder of our nation, with our fathers conquer at Paris the King of the Franks in the heart of his kingdom, nor had the King of the Franks any hope of safety until he humbly offered his daughter and possession of the country, which, after you, is called Normandy.

Did not your fathers capture the King of the Franks at Rouen, and keep him there until he restored Normandy to Duke Richard, then a boy; with this condition, that, in every conference between the King of France and the Duke of Normandy, the duke should wear his sword, while the King should not be permitted to carry a sword nor even a dagger. This concession your fathers compelled the great King to submit to, as binding for ever. Did not the same duke lead your fathers to Mirmande, at the foot of the Alpes, and enforce submission from the lord of the town, his son-in-law, to his own wife, the duke's daughter? Nor was it enough for you to conquer men, he conquered the devil himself, with whom he wrestled, cast down and bound him with his hands behind his back, and left him a shameful spectacle to angels. But why do I talk of former times? Did not you, in our own time, engage the Franks at Mortemer? Did not the Franks prefer flight to battle, and use their spurs? While you – Ralph, the commander of the Franks having been slain – reaped the honour and the spoil as the natural result of your usual success. Ah! let any one of the English whom, a hundred times, our predecessors, both Danes and Normans, have defeated in battle, come forth and show that the race of Rollo ever suffered a defeat from his time until now, and I will withdraw conquered. Is it not, therefore, shameful that a people accustomed to be conquered, a people ignorant of war, a people even without arrows, should proceed in order of battle against you, my brave men? Is it not a shame that King Harold, perjured as he was in your presence, should dare to show his face to you? It is amazing to me that you have been allowed to see those who, by a horrible crime, beheaded your relations and Alfred my kinsman, and that their own heads are still on their shoulders. Raise your standards, my brave men, and set neither measure nor limit to your merited rage. May the lightning of your glory be seen and the thunders of your onset heard from east to west, and be ye the avengers of noble blood.

•

## JOHN BALL
### June 1381

### 'Cast off the yoke of bondage'

*The Peasants' Revolt of 1381 was the first great popular protest in English history. Led by Wat Tyler and John Ball, rebel forces marched on London from Essex and Kent in protest at the capping of wages after the Black Death and the imposition by Richard II of a poll tax of one shilling a head. John Ball made this address to the rebels at Blackheath, to the south of London.*

> *When Adam delved and Eve span,*
> *Who was then the gentleman?*

From the beginning all men by nature were created alike, and our bondage or servitude came in by the unjust oppression of naughty men. For if God would have had any bondmen from the beginning, he would have appointed who should be bond, and who free. And therefore I exhort you to consider that now the time is come, appointed to us by God, in which ye may (if ye will) cast off the yoke of bondage, and recover liberty. I counsel you therefore well to bethink yourselves, and to take good hearts unto you, that after the manner of a good husband that tilleth his ground, and riddeth out thereof such evil weeds as choke and destroy the good corn, you may destroy first the great lords of the realm, and after, the judges and lawyers, and questmongers, and all other who have undertaken to be against the commons. For so shall you procure peace and surety to yourselves in time to come; and by dispatching out of the way the great men, there shall be an equality in liberty, and no difference in degrees of nobility; but a like dignity and equal authority in all things brought in among you.

*Both Ball and Tyler were subsequently executed.*

•

# THOMAS CRANMER
## 21 March 1556

### '*I shall declare unto you my very faith*'

*Thomas Cranmer (1489–1556), who composed the 39 Articles and rephrased the English Book of Common Prayer, one of the noblest examples of English prose, won the favour of Henry VIII when he enabled the King to divorce Catharine of Aragon, and was appointed Archbishop of Canterbury in 1533. He used his position against the rights of Queen Catharine. Under Edward VI, in 1553, he signed a patent excluding Mary and Elizabeth from the succession in favour of Lady Jane Grey. On the accession of Mary, daughter of Catharine of Aragon, he was sent to the Tower of London for treason. He was tried a year later in 1554 before the papal commissioner and formally degraded in 1556. He signed the last of seven recantations on 21 March and was told that he was to be burnt. He went to his death nobly, retracting his recantations and naming the Pope as Christ's enemy. At the stake, he knelt down and said the Lord's Prayer. Then he made his final speech.*

All men desire, good people, at the time of their deaths, to give some good exhortation that others may remember after their deaths, and be the better thereby. So I beseech God grant me grace that I may speak something, at this my departing, whereby God may be glorified and you edified.

First, it is an heavy case to see that many folks be so much doted upon the love of this false world, and so careful for it, that for the love of God, or the love of the world to come, they seem to care very little or nothing therefor. This shall be my first exhortation. That you set not overmuch by this false glozing world, but upon God and the world to come; and learn to know what this lesson meaneth, which St John teacheth, that the love of this world is hatred against God.

The second exhortation is that next unto God you obey your King and Queen willingly and gladly, without murmur and grudging, and not for fear of them only, but much more for the fear of God, knowing that they be God's ministers, appointed by God to rule and govern you. And therefore whoso resisteth them, resisteth God's ordinance.

The third exhortation is, That you love altogether like brethren and sisters. For, alas! pity it is to see what contention and hatred one Christian man hath toward another; not taking each other as sisters and brothers, but rather as strangers and mortal enemies. But I pray you learn and bear well away this one lesson, To do good to all men as much as in you lieth, and to hurt no man, no more than you would hurt your own natural and loving brother or sister. For this you may be sure of, that whosoever hateth any person, and goeth about maliciously to hinder or hurt him, surely, and without all doubt, God is not with that man, although he think himself never so much in God's favour.

The fourth exhortation shall be to them that have great substance and riches of this world, that they will well consider and weigh those sayings of the Scripture. One is of our Saviour Christ himself, who sayeth, It is hard for a rich man to enter into heaven; a sore saying, and yet spoken by him that knew the truth. The second is of St John, whose saying is this, He that hath the substance of this world and seeth his brother in necessity, and shutteth up his mercy from him, how can he say he loveth God? Much more might I speak of every part; but time sufficeth not. I do but put you in remembrance of these things. Let all them that be rich ponder well those sentences; for if ever they had any occasion to show their charity they have now at this present, the poor people being so many, and victuals so dear. For though I have been long in prison, yet I have heard of the great penury of the poor. Consider that which is given to the poor is given to God; whom we have not otherwise present corporally with us, but in the poor.

And now, for so much as I am come to the last end of my life, whereupon hangeth all my life passed and my life to come, either to live with my Saviour Christ in heaven in joy, or else to be in pain ever with wicked devils in hell; and I see before mine eyes presently either heaven ready to receive me, or hell ready to swallow me up; I shall therefore declare unto you my very faith, how I believe, without colour or dissimulation; for now is no time to dissemble, whatsoever I have written in times past.

First, I believe in God the Father Almighty, Maker of heaven and earth, and every article of the catholic faith, every word and sentence taught by our Saviour Christ, His Apostles and Prophets, in the Old and New Testaments.

And now I come to the great thing that troubleth my conscience, more than any other thing that ever I said or did in my life; and that is, the setting abroad of writings contrary to the truth. Which here now I renounce and refuse, as things written with my hand, contrary to the truth which I thought in my heart, and writ for fear of death, and to save my life, if it might be; and that is, all such bills, which I have written or signed with mine own hand since my degradation, wherein I have written many things untrue. And forasmuch as my hand offended in writing contrary to my heart, therefore my hand shall be punished; for if I may come to the fire it shall be first burned. And as for the Pope, I refuse him as Christ's enemy and Anti-christ with all his false doctrine.

*As the fire was put to him, Cranmer stretched out his right hand and thrust it into the flame, crying with a loud voice, 'This hand hath offended.'*

•

## QUEEN ELIZABETH I
### 9 August 1588

### *'I have the heart and stomach of a king'*

*When the Spanish Armada of 130 ships with nearly 17,000 soldiers sailed for England in May 1588, Queen Elizabeth I (1533–1603) rose to heights of true greatness and saved England by her personal supervision of the high command set up to resist invasion.*

*As the Armada approached England, she went to Tilbury by barge to review the troops and stiffen morale. On 8 August, 'full of princely resolution and more than feminine courage, she passed like some Amazonian Empress through all her army'. The next day she rode out to address the troops, mounted on a fine white horse and carrying a small silver staff. She watched a mimic battle, reviewed the army, and then addressed her soldiers, with the words read out to the companies by their officers.*

My loving people, we have been persuaded by some that are careful of our safety, to take heed how we commit ourselves to armed multitudes, for fear of treachery. But I assure you, I do not desire to live to distrust my faithful and loving people. Let tyrants fear ... I have always so behaved myself that, under God, I have placed my chiefest strength and safeguard in the loyal hearts and good will of my subjects, and therefore I am come amongst you as you see at this time, not for my recreation and disport, but being resolved, in the midst and heat of the battle, to live or die amongst you all, to lay down for my God, and for my kingdom, and for my people, my honour and my blood, even in the dust. I know I have the body of a weak and feeble woman, but I have the heart and stomach of a king, and of a king of England too, and think foul scorn that Parma or Spain or any Prince of Europe should dare to invade the borders of my realm, to which, rather than any dishonour shall grow by me, I myself will take up arms, I myself will be your general, judge and rewarder of every one of your virtues in the field. I know already for your forwardness you have deserved rewards and crowns, and we do assure you, in the word of a Prince, they shall be duly paid you ... By your valour in the field, we shall shortly have a famous victory over these enemies of my God, of my kingdom and of my people.

*The Queen was still at Tilbury when reports arrived that the Armada had been overwhelmed and dispersed by Francis Drake.*

*The historian Carole Levin, in* The Heart and Stomach of a King, *says that this speech contains the key sentiment of Elizabeth's reign: the only way a woman could assume leadership without contradiction was by combining in herself the attributes of King and Queen.*

•

## QUEEN ELIZABETH I
### 30 November 1601

### 'To be a king'

*Elizabeth I was sixty-nine and in the forty-fourth year of her reign as Queen of England and Ireland in November 1601 when 140 members went to Whitehall to hear the Queen's last wooing (as the historian J. E. Neale puts it) of her 'faithful, troublesome Commons'. The speech she made was known for generations as the 'Golden Speech' – worthy to be written in gold.*

*She spoke with the majesty that stoops to conquer. 'The inimitable perfection of her art was heightened by the thought, which must have been in every mind, that she was practising it for the last time,' says Neale. 'In effect, if not in strict fact, these were her last words to the realm she had loved and served with her whole being.' At first, the members of the Commons knelt to hear her speak.*

Mr Speaker, we perceive your coming is to present thanks unto us. Know I accept them with no less joy than your loves can have desire to offer such a present, and do more esteem it than any treasure, or riches;

for those we know how to prize, but loyalty, love, and thanks, I account them invaluable; and though God hath raised me high, yet this I account the glory of my crown, that I have reigned with your loves. This makes that I do not so much rejoice that God hath made me to be a queen, as to be a queen over so thankful a people, and to be the means under God to conserve you in safety, and preserve you from danger, yea to be the instrument to deliver you from dishonour, from shame, and from infamy, to keep you from out of servitude, and from slavery under our enemies, and cruel tyranny, and vile oppression intended against us; for the better withstanding whereof, we take very acceptable their intended helps, and chiefly in that it manifesteth your loves and largeness of hearts to your sovereign. Of myself I must say this, I never was any greedy scraping grasper, nor a strict fast-holding prince, nor yet a waster, my heart was never set upon any worldly goods, but only for my subjects' good. What you do bestow on me I will not hoard up, but receive it to bestow on you again; yea mine own properties I account yours to be expended for your good, and your eyes shall see the bestowing of it for your welfare.

Mr Speaker, I would wish you and the rest to stand up, for I fear I shall yet trouble you with longer speech.

Mr Speaker, you give me thanks, but I am more to thank you, and I charge you thank them of the Lower House from me; for had I not received knowledge from you, I might a' fallen into the lapse of an error, only for want of true information.

Since I was Queen, yet did I never put my pen to any grant but upon pretext and semblance made me, that it was for the good and avail of my subjects generally, though a private profit to some of my ancient servants, who have deserved well; but that my grants shall be made grievances to my people, and oppressions, to be privileged under colour of our patents, our princely dignity shall not suffer it.

When I heard it, I could give no rest unto my thoughts until I had reformed it, and those varlets, lewd persons, abusers of my bounty, shall know I will not suffer it. And, Mr Speaker, tell the House from me, I take it exceeding grateful, that the knowledge of these things are come unto me from them. And tho' amongst them the principal members are such as are not touched in private, and therefore need not speak from any feeling of the grief, yet we have heard that other gentlemen also of the House, who stand as free, have spoken as freely in it; which gives us to know, that no respect or interests have moved them other than the minds they bear to suffer no diminution of our honour and our subjects love unto us. The zeal of which affection tending to ease my people, and knit their hearts unto us, I embrace with a princely care far above all earthly treasures. I esteem my people's love, more than which I desire not to merit: and God, that gave me here to sit, and placed me over you, knows, that I never respected myself, but as your good was conserved in me; yet what dangers, what practices, and what perils I have passed, some if not all of you know; but none of these things do move me, or ever made me fear, but it's God that hath delivered me.

And in my governing this land, I have ever set the last judgement day before mine eyes, and so to rule as I shall be judged and answer before a higher Judge, to whose judgement seat I do appeal: in that never thought was cherished in my heart that tended not to my people's good.

And if my princely bounty have been abused; and my grants turned to the hurt of my people contrary to my will and meaning, or if any in authority under me have neglected, or converted what I have committed unto them, I hope God will not lay their culps to my charge.

To be a king, and wear a crown, is a thing more glorious to them that see it than it's pleasant to them that bear it: for myself, I never was so much enticed with the glorious name of a king, or the royal authority of a queen, as delighted that God hath made me his instrument to maintain his truth and glory, and to defend this kingdom from dishonour, damage, tyranny, and oppression. But should I ascribe any of these things to myself or my sexly weakness, I were not worthy to live, and of all most unworthy of the mercies I have received at God's hands, but to God only and wholly all is given and ascribed.

The cares and troubles of a crown I cannot more fitly resemble than to the drugs of a learned physician, perfumed with some aromatical savour, or to bitter pills gilded over, by which they are made more acceptable or less offensive, which indeed are bitter and unpleasant to take; and for my own part, were it not for conscience sake to discharge the duty that God hath lay'd upon me, and to maintain his glory, and keep you in safety, in mine own disposition I should be willing to resign the place I hold to any other, and glad to be freed of the glory with the labours, for it is not my desire to live nor to reign, longer than my life and reign shall be for your good. And though you have had and may have many mightier and wiser princes sitting in this seat, yet you never had nor shall have any that will love you better.

Thus, Mr Speaker, I commend me to your loyal loves, and yours to my best care and your further councils; and I pray you, Mr Controuler and Mr Secretary, and you of my council, that before these gentlemen depart into their countries, you bring them all to kiss my hand.

•

KING JAMES I
21 March 1609

*'Kings are justly called Gods'*

*James VI, King of Scots (1566–1625) and son of Mary, Queen of Scots, became King James I of England, Scotland and Ireland on the death of Elizabeth I in 1603. His concept of monarchy was based on the doctrine of the divine right of kings (subsequently challenged and defied with dramatic results during the reign of his son, Charles I).*

*MPs became increasingly restless as James, who spoke with a stutter, insisted on frequent reiteration of his divine rights. As this speech demonstrates, he was, however, willing to make substantial concessions. James admits that in any advanced society the absolute power of kings is regulated by laws and by an implied contract with the people.*

The state of monarchy is the supremest thing upon earth; for kings are not only God's lieutenants upon earth, and sit upon God's throne, but even by God himself they are called Gods . . .

Kings are justly called Gods, for that they exercise a manner or resemblance of divine power upon earth. For if you will consider the attributes to God, you shall see how they agree in the person of a king. God hath power to create, or destroy, make or unmake at his pleasure, to give life or send death, to judge all, and to be judged nor accountable to none. To raise low things, and to make high things low at his pleasure, and to God are both soul and body due. And the like power have Kings: they make and unmake their subjects: they have power of raising, and casting down: of life and of death: judges over all their subjects, and in all causes, and yet accountable to none but God only. They have power to exalt low things, and abase high things, and make of their subjects like men at the chess. A pawn to take a bishop or a knight, and to cry up or down any of their subjects, as they do their money. And to the king is due both the affection of the soul, and the service of the body of his subjects . . .

A king governing in a settled kingdom, leaves to be a king, and degenerates into a tyrant as soon as he leaves off to rule according to his laws. In which case the king's conscience may speak unto him, as the poor widow said to Philip of Macedon; either govern according to your law, *Aut ne Rex sis*. And though no Christian man ought to allow rebellion of people against their prince, yet doth God never leave kings unpunished when they transgress these limits; for in that same psalm where God saith to kings, *Vos dii estis*, he immediately thereafter concludes, *But ye shall die like men*.

The higher we are placed, the greater shall our fall be. *Ut casus sic dolor*: the taller the trees be, the more in danger of the wind; and the tempest beats forest upon the highest mountains. Therefore all kings that are not tyrants, or perjured, will be glad to bound themselves within the limits of their laws; and they that persuade them the contrary, are vipers, and pests, both against them and the commonwealth. For it is a great difference between a king's government in a settled state, and what kings in their original power might do in *Individuo vago*. As for my part, I thank God, I have ever given good proof, that I never had intention to the contrary. And I am sure to go to my grave with that reputation and comfort, that never king was in all his time more careful to have his laws duly observed, and himself to govern thereafter, than I.

I conclude then this point touching the power of kings with this axiom of divinity, that as to dispute what God may do, is blasphemy, but *quid vult Deus*, that divines may lawfully, and do ordinarily dispute and discuss; for to dispute *A posse ad esse* is both against logic and divinity: so is it sedition in subjects to dispute what a king may do in the height of his power. But just kings will ever be willing to declare what they will do, if they will not incur the curse of God. I will not be content that my power be disputed upon, but I shall ever be willing to make the reason appear of all my doings, and rule my actions according to my laws.

•

## SIR JOHN ELIOT
### 3 June 1628

### *'The exchequer . . . is empty . . . the jewels pawned'*

*Sir John Eliot (1592–1632) was one of the main agitators in the House of Commons against King Charles I. He denounced arbitrary taxation and imprisonment. As a leading defender of the rights of the Commons, he made this speech during a debate on the Petition of Right, which proposed that no loan or tax could be levied by the King without the consent of Parliament.*

The ignorance and corruption of our ministers, where can you miss of instances? If you survey the court, if you survey the country; if the church, if the city be examined; if you observe the bar, if the bench, if the ports, if the shipping, if the land, if the seas – all these will render you variety of proofs; and that in such measure and proportion as shows the greatness of our disease to be such that, if there be not some speedy application for remedy, our case is almost desperate.

The exchequer, you know, is empty, and the reputation thereof gone; the ancient lands are sold; the jewels pawned; the plate engaged; the debts still great; almost all charges, both ordinary and extraordinary, borne up by projects! What poverty can be greater? What necessity so great? What perfect English heart is not almost dissolved into sorrow for this truth? . . .

The oppression of the subject . . . needs no demonstration. The whole kingdom is a proof; and for the exhausting of our treasures, that very oppression speaks it. What waste of our provisions, what consumption of our ships, what destruction of our men there hath been. Witness that expedition to Algiers – witness that with Mansfeldt – witness that to Cadiz – witness the next – witness that to Rhé – witness the last (I pray God we may never have more such witnesses) – witness, likewise, the Palatinate – witness Denmark – witness the Turks – witness the Dunkirkers – witness all! What losses we have sustained! How we are impaired in munitions, in ships, in men!

It is beyond contradiction that we were never so much weakened, nor ever had less hope how to be restored.

These, Mr Speaker, are our dangers; these are they who do threaten us, and these are, like the Trojan horse, brought in cunningly to surprise us. In these do lurk the strongest of our enemies, ready to issue on us; and if we do not speedily expel them, these are the signs, these are the invitations to others! These will so prepare their entrance that we shall have no means left of refuge or defence. If we have these enemies at home, how can we strive with those that are abroad? If we be free from these no other can impeach us. Our ancient English virtue (like the old Spartan valour), cleared from these disorders – our being in sincerity of religion and once made friends with Heaven; having maturity of councils, sufficiency of generals, incorruption of officers, opulency in the King, liberty in the people, repletion in treasure, plenty of provisions, reparation of ships, preservation of men – our ancient English virtue, I say, thus rectified, will secure us; and unless there be a speedy reformation in these, I know now not what hopes or expectations we can have.

*The King consented reluctantly to the petition four days later – but only after MPs forcibly held down the Speaker of the House while resolutions were passed condemning the raising of taxes without parliamentary approval. A year later Charles I imprisoned Eliot in the Tower of London after he refused to agree that his speeches had offended the monarchy. He died in the Tower in 1632.*

•

## THOMAS WENTWORTH, EARL OF STRAFFORD
### 13 April 1641

*'You, your estates, your posterity, lie at the stake!'*

*Thomas Wentworth (1593–1641) became the chief adviser to King Charles I in 1639 and was made Earl of Strafford and Lord Lieutenant of Ireland.*

*When Scotland rebelled against Charles, Strafford failed to keep the Scots out of the north of England and negotiated with Spain for support. He called the Long Parliament of 1640 in an attempt to outbid John Pym and impeach him for treason for negotiating with the Scots. He was outmanoeuvred and himself impeached by Pym for treason.*

*Pym led his trial before the Lords, when Strafford defended himself with the moving eloquence of this speech.*

My lords, I stand before you, charged with high treason. The burden of the charge is heavy, yet far the more so because it hath borrowed the authority of the House of Commons. If they were not interested, I might expect a no less easy, than I do a safe issue. But let neither my weakness plead my innocence, nor their power my guilt. If your lordships will conceive of my defences as they are in themselves, without reference to either party – and I shall endeavour so to present them – I hope to go hence as clearly justified by you, as I now am in the testimony of a good conscience by myself.

My lords, I have all along, during this charge, watched to see that poisoned arrow of treason, which some men would fain have feathered in my heart; but, in truth, it hath not been in my quickness to discover any such evil yet within my breast, though now, perhaps, by sinister information, sticking to my clothes . . .

It is hard, my lords, to be questioned upon a law which cannot be shown! Where hath this fire lain hid for so many hundred years, without smoke to discover it, till it thus bursts forth to consume me and my children? My lords, do we not live under laws? and must we be punished by laws before they are made? Far better were it to live by no laws at all, but to be governed by those characters of virtue and discretion which Nature hath stamped upon us, than to put this necessity of divination upon a man, and to accuse him of a breach of law before it is a law at all! If a waterman upon the Thames split his boat by grating upon an anchor, and the same have no buoy appended to it, the owner of the anchor is to pay the loss; but if a buoy be set there, every man passeth upon his own peril. Now, where is the mark, where is the token set upon the crime to declare it to be high treason?

My lords, be pleased to give that regard to the peerage of England as never to expose yourselves to such moot points, such constructive interpretations of law. If there must be a trial of wits, let the subject matter be something else than the lives and honour of peers! It will be wisdom for yourselves and your posterity to cast into the fire those bloody and mysterious volumes of constructive and arbitrary treason, as the primitive Christians did their books of curious arts, and betake yourselves to the plain letter of the law and statute, which telleth what is, and what is not, treason, without being ambitious to be more learned in the art of killing than our forefathers. These gentlemen tell us that they speak in defence of the Commonwealth against my arbitrary laws. Give me leave to say I speak in defence of the Commonwealth against their arbitrary treason!

It is now full two hundred and forty years since any man was touched for this alleged crime to this height before myself. Let us not awaken those sleeping lions to our destruction, by taking up a few musty records that have lain by the walls for so many ages, forgotten or neglected.

My lords, what is my present misfortune may be for ever yours! It is not the smallest part of my grief that not the crime of treason, but my other sins, which are exceeding many, have brought me to this bar; and, except your lordships' wisdom provide against it, the shedding of my blood may make way for the tracing out of yours. You, your estates, your posterity, lie at the stake!

•

## JOHN PYM
### 13 April 1641

*'He should perish by the justice of that law
which he would have subverted'*

*Sensing that the great occasion of his life had come, Pym rose as Strafford finished his defence. 'With him,' says John Forster (in The Statesman of the Commonwealth of England), 'it now finally rested whether or not the privileges so long contested, and the rights so long misunderstood, of the great body of the people should win at last their assured consummation and acknowledgement.'*

*Pym was convinced Strafford was morally guilty whether or not the laws declared him technically innocent. He immediately answered Strafford's opening barb about the 'poisoned arrow of treason'.*

My lords, many days have been spent in maintenance of the impeachment of the Earl of Strafford by the House of Commons, whereby he stands charged with high treason; and your lordships have heard his defence with patience, and with as much favour as justice will allow. We have passed through our evidence; and the result is, that it remains clearly proved that the Earl of Strafford hath endeavoured by his words, actions, and counsels, to subvert the fundamental laws of England and Ireland, and to introduce an arbitrary and tyrannical government.

This is the envenomed arrow for which he inquired in the beginning of his replication this day, which hath infected all his blood; this is that intoxicating cup (to use his own metaphor) which hath tainted his judgement, and poisoned his heart! From hence was infused that specifical difference which turned his speeches, his actions, his counsels into treason – not cumulative, as he expressed it, as if many misdemeanours could make one treason; but formally and essentially. It is the end that doth inform actions, and doth specificate the nature of them, making not only criminal, but even indifferent, words and actions, to be treason, when done and spoken with a treasonable intention.

That which is given to me in charge is to shew the quality of the offence, how heinous it is in the nature, how mischievous in the effect of it; which will best appear, if it be examined by that law to which he himself appealed, that universal, that supreme law, Salus Populi. This the element of all laws, out of which they are derived; the end of all laws, to which they are designed, and in which are they perfected. How far it stands in opposition to this law, I shall endeavour to show; in some considerations, which I shall present to your lordships, arising out of the evidence which hath been opened.

The first is this – it is an offence comprehending all other offences. Here you shall find several treasons, murthers, rapines, oppressions, perjuries. The earth hath a seminary virtue, whereby it doth produce all herbs and plants, and other vegetables: there is in this crime a seminary of all evils hurtful to a state; and if you consider the reasons of it, it must needs be so.

The law is that which puts a difference betwixt good and evil, betwixt just and unjust. If you take away the law, all things will fall into a confusion. Every man will become a law to himself, which, in the depraved condition of human nature, must needs produce many great enormities. Lust will become a law, and envy will become a law, covetousness and ambition will become laws; and what dictates, what decisions such laws will produce, may easily be discerned in the late government of Ireland!

The law hath a power to prevent, to restrain, to repair evils. Without this, all kinds of mischief and distempers will break in upon a state. It is the law that doth entitle the King to the allegiance and service of his people; it entitles the people to the protection and justice of the King. It is God alone who subsists by himself; all other things subsist in a mutual dependence and relation. He was a wise man that said that the King subsisted by the field that is tilled: it is the labour of the people that supports the crown. If you take away the protection of the King, the vigour and cheerfulness of allegiance will be taken away, though the obligation remain.

The law is the boundary, the measure, betwixt the King's prerogative and the people's liberty. Whilst these move in their own orbs, they are a support and a security to one another – the prerogative a cover and defence to the liberty of the people, and the people by their liberty enabled to be a foundation to the prerogative; but if these bounds be so removed that they enter into contestation and conflict, one of these mischiefs must ensue – if the prerogative of the King overwhelm the liberty of the people, it will be turned into tyranny; if liberty undermine the prerogative, it will grow into anarchy . . .

It is the end of government, that virtue should be cherished, vice suppressed; but where this arbitrary and unlimited power is set up, a way is open not only for the security, but for the advancement and encouragement of evil. Such men as are apt for the execution and maintenance of this power are only capable of preferment; and others who will not be instruments of any unjust commands, who make a conscience to do nothing against the laws of the kingdom and liberties of the subjects, are not only not passable for employment, but subject to much jealousy and danger. It is the end of government, that all accidents and events, all counsels and designs, should be improved to the public good; but this arbitrary power is apt to dispose all to the maintenance of itself. The wisdom of the council-table, the authority of the courts of justice, the industry of all the officers of the crown, have been most carefully exercised in this; the learning of our divines, the jurisdiction of our bishops, have been moulded and disposed to the same effect; which, though it were begun before the Earl of Strafford's employment, yet hath been exceedingly furthered and advanced by him. Under this colour and pretence of maintaining the King's power and prerogative, many dangerous practices against the peace and safety of the kingdom have been undertaken and promoted. The increase of popery, and the favours and encouragement of papists, have been, and still are, a great grievance and danger to the kingdom.

The invocation, in matters of religion, upon usurpations of the clergy, the manifold burthens and taxations upon the people, have been a great cause of our present distempers and disorders; and yet those who have been chief furtherers and actors of such mischiefs have had their credit and authority from this, that they were forward to maintain this power. The Earl of Strafford had the first rise of his greatness from this; and in his apology and defence, as your lordships have heard, this hath had a main part.

The royal power and majesty of kings is only glorious in the prosperity and happiness of the people. The perfection of all things consists in the end for which they were ordained. God only is his own end. All other things have a further end beyond themselves, in attaining whereof their own happiness consists. If the means and the end be set in opposition to one another, it must needs cause an impotency and defect of both . . .

This treason, if it had taken effect, was to be a standing, perpetual treason, which would have been in continual act; not determined within one time or age, but transmitted to posterity, even from one generation to another.

The last consideration is this – that as it is a crime odious in the nature of it, so it is odious in the judgement and estimation of the law.

To alter the settled frame and constitution of government, is treason in any state. The laws whereby all other parts of a kingdom are preserved would be very vain and defective, if they had not a power to secure and preserve themselves . . .

The forfeitures inflicted for treason, by our law, are of life, honour, and estate, even all that can be forfeited; and this prisoner having committed so many treasons, although he should pay all these forfeitures, will be still a debtor to the commonwealth. Nothing can be more equal than that he should perish by the justice of that law which he would have subverted. Neither will this be a new way of blood. There are marks enough to trace this law to the very original of this kingdom; and if it hath not been put in execution, as he allegeth, these 240 years, it was not for want of law, but that all that time hath not bred a man bold enough to commit such crimes as these!

*Strafford was abandoned by the King and beheaded before a crowd of 200,000 on 12 May.*

•

## JOHN PYM
### 11 January 1642

### 'The cry of all England'

*After Pym published the Grand Remonstrance, a statement of the King's misgovernment and the grievances of the people, he was one of five Members of Parliament whom the King named for high treason on 3 January.*

*The five accused members withdrew from the Commons to the city. When the King arrived with an armed force to seize them, he made his famous remark: 'I see all the birds are flown.' As the humiliated King left London for Hampton Court, the securely guarded Commons welcomed back the five members, led by Pym, who had become director of the State.*

*Next day he expounded to a joint conference of the Lords and Commons on the dangers in which the country stood. The speech – the 'cry of all England' – was a masterpiece – and revolutionary in its declaration that the Commons were prepared to act independently of the Lords and that the Commons constituted Parliament.*

*The Civil War was now imminent. Pym became leader of the parliamentary party.*

My lords, in these four petitions you may hear the voice, or rather the cry, of all England; and you cannot wonder if the urgency, the extremity of the condition wherein we are, do produce some earnestness and vehemency of expression more than ordinary. The agony, terror, and perplexity in which the kingdom labours, are universal; all parts are affected with them; and therefore in these you may observe the groans and miserable complaints of all.

Divers reasons may be given why those diseases which are epidemical are more dangerous than others. First, the cause of such diseases is universal and supernal, and not from an evil constitution, or evil diet, or any other accident; such causes, therefore, work with more vigour and efficacy than those which are particular and inferior. Secondly, in such diseases there is a communicative quality, whereby the malignity of them is multiplied and enforced. Thirdly, they have a converting, transforming power, that turns other diseases and ill affections of men's bodies into their own nature . . .

We have often suffered under the misinterpretation of good actions, and false imputation of evil ones which we never intended; so that we may justly purge ourselves from all guilt of being authors of this jealousy and misunderstanding. We have been, and are still, ready to serve His Majesty with our lives and fortunes, with as much cheerfulness and earnestness of affection as ever any subjects were; and we doubt not but our proceedings will so manifest this, that we shall be as clear in the apprehension of the world, as we are in the testimony of our own consciences.

I am now come to a conclusion. I have nothing to propound to your lordships by way of request or desire from the House of Commons. I doubt not but your judgements will tell you what is to be done. Your consciences, your honours, your interests, will call upon you for the doing of it. The commons will be glad to have your concurrence and help in saving of the kingdom; but, if they fail of it, it shall not discourage them in doing their duty. And whether the kingdom be lost or saved (I hope, through God's blessing, it will be saved!), they shall be sorry that the story of this present Parliament should tell posterity that, in so great a danger and extremity, the House of Commons should be enforced to save the kingdom alone, and that the peers should have no part in the honour of the preservation of it, having so great an interest in the good success of those endeavours in respect of their great estates and high degrees of nobility.

My lords, consider what the present necessities and dangers of the commonwealth require, what the commons have reason to expect, to what endeavours and counsels the concurrent desires of all the people do invite you! So that, applying yourselves to the preservation of the king and kingdom, I may be bold to assure you, in the name of all the commons of England, that you shall be bravely seconded!

•

## THOMAS RAINBOROWE
### 29 October 1647

### 'The poorest he'

*The Levellers wanted all free-born Englishmen to sign a social contract, an Agreement of the People, and to enjoy full rights of participation in a decentralized, democratic state. It was their commitment to religious freedom, however, that attracted Oliver Cromwell and his army, officers and men. At the Putney debates, held near Putney church to the south of London in 1647, Cromwell's officers and army agitators debated the Leveller proposals. The Leveller, Colonel Rainborowe, argued the soldiers' case – that since it was they who had won the victory, they should now be allowed to vote.*

The poorest he that is in England hath a life to live, as the greatest he; and therefore truly, sir, I think it's clear, that every man that is to live under a government ought first by his own consent to put himself under that government; and I do think that the poorest man in England is not at all bound in a strict sense to that government that he hath not had a voice to put himself under; and I am confident that, when I have heard the reasons against it, something will be said to answer those reasons, insomuch that I should doubt whether he was an Englishman or no, that should doubt of these things . . .

I do very much care whether [there be] a king or no king, lords or no lords, property or no property; and I think, if we do not all take care, we shall all have none of these very shortly. I do hear nothing at all that can convince me, why any man that is born in England ought not to have his voice in election of burgesses. It is said that if a man have not a permanent interest, he can have no claim; and [that] we must be no freer than the laws will let us be, and that there is no [law in any] chronicle will let us be freer than that we [now] enjoy. Something was said to this yesterday. I do think that the main cause why Almighty God gave men reason, it was that they should make use of that reason, and that they should improve it for that end and purpose that God gave it them. And truly, I think that half a loaf is better than none if a man be anhungry: [this gift of reason without other property may seem a small thing], yet I think there is nothing that God hath given a man that any [one] else can take from him. And therefore I say, that either it must be the Law of God or the law of man that must prohibit the meanest man in the kingdom to have this benefit as well as the greatest. I do not find anything in the Law of God, that a lord shall choose twenty burgesses, and a gentleman but two, or a poor man shall choose none: I find no such thing in the Law of Nature, nor in the Law of Nations. But I do find that all Englishmen must be subject to English laws, and I do verily believe that there is no man but will say that the foundation of all law lies in the people, and if [it lie] in the people, I am to seek for this exemption.

•

## KING CHARLES I
### 30 January 1649

### *'I go from a corruptible to an incorruptible crown'*

*The trial and execution of Charles I was something new and terrible. It shocked all Europe. The Stuart court – whose favourite entertainment was the masque eulogizing the divine right of kings – was a carefully staged affair, isolated from the King's subjects. So it seemed that his trial and execution were only the last acts in a drama, with the King playing a central, magnificent role.*

*It was bitterly cold on the day of the execution; the King walked between rows of armed guards from St James to Whitehall. At the Banqueting House he passed under the Rubens ceiling he had commissioned in honour of his father, James I, the great proponent of the King's supremacy on earth. He stepped out of a window of the palace on to the black-draped scaffold; fearing reprisals, the executioner and his assistant were masked and disguised beyond recognition. The block was built low purposely and the crowd was kept far back to hear the King's last words; he addressed only the group around him. Charles Stuart, 'that man of blood', accused of waging war against his people, now propagated his own myth: to this day he is commemorated as 'Charles the Martyr', a most potent description of his own making. As the executioner held up the severed head, a great groan escaped from the crowd, and women fainted. A few intrepid souvenir hunters rushed forward to dip handkerchiefs in the blood.*

I shall be very little heard of anybody here; I shall therefore speak a word unto you here; indeed I could hold my peace very well, if I did not think that holding my peace would make some men think that I did submit to the guilt, as well as to the punishment; but I think it is my duty to God first and then to my country for to clear myself both as an honest man and a good king and a good Christian. I shall begin first with my innocency. In troth I think it not very needful for me to insist long upon this, for all the world knows that I never did begin a war with the two Houses of Parliament, and I call God to witness, to whom I must shortly make my account, that I never did intend for to encroach upon their privileges; they began upon me, it is the militia, they began upon, they contest that the militia was mine, but they thought it fit for to have it from me; and to be short, if anybody will look to the dates of the commissions, of their commissions and mine, and likewise to the declarations, will see clearly that they began these unhappy troubles, not I; so that as the guilt of these enormous crimes that are laid against me, I hope in God that God will clear me of it, I will not, I am in charity; God forbid that I should lay it upon the two Houses of Parliament; there is no necessity of either, I hope they are free of this guilt, for I do believe that ill instruments between them and me has been the chief cause of all this bloodshed; so that by way of speaking as I find myself clear of this, I hope (and pray God) that they may too: yet for all this, God forbid that I should be so ill a Christian as not to say that God's judgements are just upon me: many times he does pay justice by an unjust sentence, that is ordinary; I will only say this, that an unjust sentence that I suffered for to take effect is punished now, by an unjust sentence upon me; that is, so far I have said, to show you that I am an innocent man.

Now for to show you that I am a good Christian: I hope there is a good man that will bear me witness, that I have forgiven all the world; even those in particular that have been the chief causes of my death; who they are, God knows, I do not desire to know, I pray God forgive them. But this is not all; my charity must go farther, I wish that they may repent, for indeed they have committed a great sin in that particular; I pray God with Saint Stephen that they may take the right way to the peace of the kingdom, for my charity commands me not only to forgive particular men, but my charity commands me to endeavour to the last gasp the peace of the kingdom: so, sirs, I do with all my soul, and I do hope (there is some here will carry it further) that they may endeavour the peace of the kingdom. Now, sirs, I must show you both how you are out of the way and will put you in a way; first, you are out of the way, for certainly all the way you ever had yet as I could find by anything is in the way of conquest; certainly this is an ill way, for conquest, sir, in my opinion is never just, except there be a good just cause, either for the matter of wrong or just title, and then if you go beyond it, the first quarrel that you have to it, that makes it unjust at the end, that was just as first: But if it be only matter of conquest, then it is a great robbery; as a pirate said to Alexander, that he was the great robber, he was but a petty robber; and so, sir, I do think the way that you are in, is much out of the way.

Now, sir, for to put you in the way, believe it you will never do right, nor God will never prosper you, until you give God his due, the King his due (that is, my successor), and the people their due; I am as much for them as any of you; you must give God his due by regulating rightly his church according to his Scripture which is now out of order: for to set you in a way particularly now I cannot, but only this, a national synod freely called, freely debating among themselves, must settle this, when that every opinion is freely and clearly heard.

For the king, indeed I will not . . . [*At this point a gentleman touched the axe and the King said, 'Hurt not the axe that may hurt me.'*] For the King: the laws of the land will clearly instruct you for that; therefore, because it concerns my own particular, I only give you a touch of it.

For the people. And truly I desire their liberty and freedom, as much as anybody whomsoever; but I must tell you that their liberty and their freedom consists in having of government those laws by which their life and their goods may be most their own. It is not for having share in government, sir, that is nothing pertaining to them. A subject and a sovereign are clean different things; and therefore, until they do that, I mean, that you do put the people in that liberty as I say, certainly they will never enjoy themselves.

Sirs, it was for this that now I am come here: if I would have given way to an arbitrary way, for to have all laws changed according to the power of the sword, I needed not to have come here; and therefore, I tell you (and I pray God it be not laid to your charge) that I am the martyr of the people.

In troth, sirs, I shall not hold you much longer; for I will only say this to you, that in truth I could have desired some little time longer, because that I would have put this I have said in a little more order, and a little better digested, than I have done; and therefore I hope you will excuse me.

I have delivered my conscience, I pray God, that you do take those courses that are best for the kingdom, and your own salvation.

[Dr Juxon: Will Your Majesty (though it may be very well known Your Majesty's affections to religion, yet it may be expected that you should) say somewhat to the world's satisfaction.]

I thank you very heartily, my lord, for that; I had almost forgotten it. In troth, sirs, my conscience in religion, I think, is very well known to the world; and therefore I declare before you all that I die a Christian according to the profession of the church of England, as I found it left me by my father; and this honest man [pointing to Dr Juxon] will witness it. Sirs, excuse me for this same. I have a good cause, and I have a gracious God; I will say no more. I go from a corruptible to an incorruptible crown, where no disturbance can be, no disturbance in the world.

•

## OLIVER CROMWELL
### 20 April 1653

#### 'In the name of God, go!'

*By 1653, Oliver Cromwell (1599–1658) was becoming increasingly impatient with the Rump Parliament. It had sat since the execution of Charles I in 1649 and was reluctant to dissolve itself. Cromwell wanted an interim council of MPs and officers to work out a new constitution. On 19 April, the Rumpers had agreed to discuss dissolution. So Cromwell was infuriated the following day when he heard they were pushing through an act to prolong their sitting.*

*He hastened to the House but left a file of musketeers at the door and in the lobby. At first he sat slumped in his seat. Then he began to speak. He put on his hat and walked up and down in the middle of the House and as his anger increased started kicking the ground and shouting. He was finally provoked beyond endurance when Sir Peter Wentworth accused him of using strange language, 'unusual within the walls of Parliament'.*

It is high time for me to put an end to your sitting in this place, which you have dishonoured by your contempt of all virtue, and defiled by your practice of every vice; ye are a factious crew, and enemies to all good government; ye are a pack of mercenary wretches, and would like Esau sell your country for a mess of pottage, and like Judas betray your God for a few pieces of money; is there a single virtue now remaining amongst you? is there one vice you do not possess? ye have no more religion than my horse; gold is your God; which of you have not barter'd your conscience for bribes? is there a man amongst you that has the least care for the good of the Commonwealth? ye sordid prostitutes have you not defil'd this sacred place, and turn'd the Lord's temple into a den of thieves, by your immoral principles and wicked practices? Ye are grown intolerably odious to the whole nation; you were deputed here by the people to get grievances redress'd, are yourselves become the greatest grievance. Your country therefore calls upon me to cleanse this Augean stable, by putting a final period to your iniquitous proceedings in this House; and which by God's help, and the strength he has given me, I am now come to do; I command ye therefore, upon the peril of your lives, to depart immediately out of this place; go, get you out! Make haste! Ye venal slaves be gone! So! Take away that shining bauble there, and lock up the doors. In the name of God, go!

*The 'bauble' was the parliamentary mace, which Cromwell gave to a musketeer before removing the Speaker of the House. After the speech the House was locked and the key and the mace carried away. On the same afternoon Cromwell dissolved the Council of State. As Commander in Chief of the army, he remained as sole ruler.*

*The speech was quoted by the British Conservative MP Leo Amery on 7 May 1940, when he demanded the resignation of Neville Chamberlain, the Prime Minister. Winston Churchill succeeded Chamberlain three days later.*

•

## OLIVER CROMWELL
### 4 February 1658

### *'Let God be judge between me and you'*

*Oliver Cromwell's first Protectorate Parliament insisted on trying to amend the 1653 Constitution to bring the executive under parliamentary control and was dissolved in January 1655. 'It is not for the profit of these nations, nor for common and public good, for you to continue here any longer,' Cromwell told them, adding in familiar words, 'And therefore I do declare unto you, that I do dissolve this Parliament.'*

*A year later Cromwell, needing to raise money to wage war on the Dutch and to obtain a legal basis for his power, was forced to call another Parliament. About 100 radical MPs were excluded from the second Protectorate Parliament, which amended the Constitution so that Cromwell could name his successor and added a second chamber. Yet after he accepted the new Constitution, the excluded radicals were allowed to sit and about thirty of his supporters were promoted to the second chamber. When the radicals started to attack the second chamber and to air the soldiers' grievances, Cromwell once again lost his temper. He ordered a coach to Westminster, strengthened himself with a cup of ale and delivered a violent speech defending the concept of a second chamber and dissolving a Parliament by personal fiat for the third time.*

My Lords, and gentlemen of the House of Commons, I had very comfortable expectations that God would make the meeting of this Parliament a blessing; and, the Lord be my witness, I desired the carrying on the affairs of the nation to these ends. The blessing which I mean, and which we ever climbed at, was mercy, truth, righteousness, and peace, which I desired might be improved.

That which brought me into the capacity I now stand in was the petition and advice given me by you, who, in reference to the ancient constitution, did draw me to accept the place of Protector. There is not a man living can say I sought it; no, not a man or woman treading upon English ground. But contemplating the sad condition of these nations, relieved from an intestine war into a six or seven years' peace, I did think the nation happy therein. But to be petitioned thereunto, and advised by you to undertake such a government, a burden too heavy for any creature; and this to be done by the House that then had the legislative capacity – certainly I did look that the same men who made the frame should make it good unto me. I can say in the presence of God, in comparison with whom we are but like poor creeping ants upon the earth, I would have been glad to have lived under my woodside, to have kept a flock of sheep, rather than undertaken such a government as this. But undertaking it by the advice and petition of you, I did look that you who had offered it unto me should make it good.

I did tell you, at a conference concerning it, that I would not undertake it, unless there might be some other persons to interpose between me and the House of Commons, who then had the power, and prevent tumultuary and popular spirits; and it was granted I should name another house. I named it of men that shall meet you wheresoever you go, and shake hands with you, and tell you it is not titles, nor lords, nor party that they value, but a Christian and an English interest – men of your own rank and quality, who will not only be a balance unto you, but to themselves, while you love England and religion.

Having proceeded upon these terms, and finding such a spirit as is too much dominant, everything being too high or too low, when virtue, honesty, piety, and justice are omitted, I thought I had been doing that which was my duty, and thought it would have satisfied you; but, if everything must be too high or too low, you are not to be satisfied.

Again, I would not have accepted of the government, unless I knew there would be a just accord between the governor and the governed, unless they would take an oath to make good what the Parliament's petition and advice advise me unto. Upon that I took an oath, and they took another oath upon their part, answerable to mine; and did not every one know upon what condition he swore? God knows I took it upon the conditions expressed in the act of government, and I did think we had been upon a foundation and upon a bottom, and thereupon I thought myself bound to take it, and to be advised by the two Houses of Parliament; and we standing unsettled till we were arrived at that, the consequences would necessarily have been confusion, if that had not been settled. Yet there are not constituted hereditary lords, nor hereditary kings, the power consisting in the two Houses and myself. I do not say that was the meaning of the oath to yourselves; that were to go against my own principles, to enter upon another man's conscience. God will judge between me and you. If there had been in you any intention of settlement, you would have settled upon this basis, and have offered your judgement and opinion.

God is my witness, I speak it; it is evident to all the world, and all people living, that a new business hath been seeking in the army against this actual settlement made by your own consent. I do not speak to these gentlemen or lords (*pointing to his right hand*), or whatsoever you will call them. I speak not this to them, but to you; you advised me to run into this place, to be in capacity by your advice, yet, instead of owning a thing taken for granted, some must have I know not what; and you have not only disjointed yourselves, but the whole nation, which is in likelihood of running into more confusion in these fifteen or sixteen days that you have sat, than it hath been from the rising of the last session to this day, through the intention of devising a commonwealth again, that some of the people might be the men that might rule all; and they are endeavouring to engage the army to carry that thing. And hath that man been true to this nation, whosoever he be, especially that hath taken an oath, thus to prevaricate? These designs have been made among the army to break and divide us. I speak this in the presence of some of the army, that these things have not been according to God, nor according to truth, pretend what you will. These things tend to nothing else but the playing the King of Scots game, if I may so call him, and I think myself bound to do what I can to prevent it.

That which I told you in the banqueting-house was true, that there were preparations of force to invade us. God is my witness, it has been confirmed to me since, not a day ago, that the King of Scots hath an army at the waterside, ready to be shipped for England. I have it from those who have been eye-witnesses of it; and while it is doing there are endeavours from some, who are not far from this place, to stir up the people of this town into a tumulting. What if I had said into a rebellion? It hath been not only your endeavour to pervert the army, while you have been sitting, and to draw them to state the question about the commonwealth, but some of you have been listing of persons, by commission of Charles Stuart, to join with any insurrection that may be made. And what is like to come upon this, the enemy being ready to invade us, but ever present blood and confusion? And if this be so, I do assign it to this cause – your not assenting to what you did invite me to by your petition and advice, as that which might be the settlement of the nation. And if this be the end of your sitting, and this be your carriage, I think it high time that an end be put to your sitting, and I do dissolve this Parliament; and let God be judge between me and you.

# THE BIRTH OF
# THE UNITED STATES

# JOHN WINTHROP
## 1630

### 'We shall be as a city upon a hill'

*The Massachusetts Bay Company was founded in 1629 after inheriting a struggling plantation at Naumkeag (now Salem) in New England. In 1630 it put to sea a fleet of eleven ships, carrying 700 passengers, 240 cows, 60 horses, the royal charter of the company (so that self-government was legally possible) and a leader, John Winthrop (1588–1650), the governor of the company and the colony.*

*Winthrop, a Suffolk gentleman who came from the same generation as Pym and Cromwell, was the first great American. It was his decision to establish the seat of government on the Shawmat peninsula (which became Boston); his faith sustained the settlers through the starving winter after their arrival, and he led the Puritans in stamping their character on American society.*

*Winthrop set out his vision of government in the New World in this famous sermon made on board the* Arbella *as it sailed the Atlantic to New England. After an elaborate discussion of Christian love and charity, he concluded by speaking of the great work on which they had embarked and the means by which it was to be accomplished.*

Thus stands the case between God and us. We are entered into a covenant with him for this work. We have taken out a commission. The Lord hath given us leave to draw our own articles. We have professed to enterprise these and those ends, upon these and those accounts. We have hereupon besought of him favor and blessing. Now if the Lord shall please to hear us, and bring us in peace to the place we desire, then hath he ratified this covenant and sealed our commission, and will expect a strict performance of the articles contained in it; but if we shall neglect the observation of these articles which are the ends we have propounded, and, dissembling with our God, shall fall to embrace this present world and prosecute our carnal intentions, seeking great things for ourselves and our posterity, the Lord will surely break out in wrath against us; be revenged of such a (sinful) people, and make us know the price of the breach of such a covenant.

Now the only way to avoid this shipwreck, and to provide for our posterity, is to follow the counsel of Micah, to do justly, to love mercy, to walk humbly with our God. For this end, we must be knit together, in this work, as one man. We must entertain each other in brotherly affection. We must be willing to abridge ourselves of our super-fluities, for the supply of other's necessities. We must uphold a familiar commerce together in all meekness, gentleness, patience, and liberality. We must delight in each other; make other's condition our own; rejoice together, mourn together, labor and suffer together, always having before our eyes our commission and community in the work, as members of the same body. So shall we keep the unity of the spirit in the bond of peace. The Lord will be our God, and delight to dwell among us, as his own people, and will command a blessing upon us in all our ways. So that we shall see much more of his wisdom, power, goodness and truth, than formerly we have been acquainted with. We shall find that the God of Israel is among us, when ten of us shall be able to resist a thousand of our enemies; when he shall make us a praise and a glory, that men shall say of succeeding plantations, 'The Lord make it likely that of New England.' For we must consider that we shall be as a city upon a hill. The eyes of all people are upon us.

So that if we shall deal falsely with our God in this work we have undertaken, and so cause him to withdraw his present help from us, we shall be made a story and a by-word throughout the world. We shall open the mouths of enemies to speak evil of the ways of God, and all professors for God's sake. We shall shame the faces of many of God's worthy servants, and cause their prayers to be turned into curses upon us till we be consumed out of the good land whither we are a-going.

I shall shut up this discourse with that exhortation of Moses, that faithful servant of the Lord, in his last farewell to Israel (Deuteronomy 30). Beloved, there is now set before us life and good, death and evil, in that we are commanded this day to love the Lord our God, and to love one another, to walk in his ways and to keep his commandments and his ordinance and his laws, and the articles of our Covenant with him, that we may live and be multiplied, and that the Lord our God may bless us in the land whither we go to possess it. But if our hearts shall turn away, so that we will not obey, but shall be seduced, and worship and serve other Gods, our pleasure and profits, and serve them; it is propounded unto us this day, we shall surely perish out of the good land whither we pass over this vast sea to possess it; therefore let us choose life that we, and our seed may live, by obeying his voice and cleaving to him, for he is our life and our prosperity.

*The 'city upon a hill' section of the sermon is chiselled in stone on Boston Common. The words were used by both President Kennedy and, frequently, President Reagan.*

•

## ANDREW HAMILTON
### 4 August 1735

### 'The cause of liberty'

*Andrew Hamilton (1656–1741), the most eloquent advocate in Pennsylvania, was eighty when a New York printer, John Zenger, was imprisoned on a charge of seditious libel after his paper, the* New York Weekly Journal, *attacked the government. Hamilton went from Philadelphia to New York to plead for Zenger, arguing that juries were judges of the law and that if a statement was true it was not a libel.*

*As he reached his conclusion, Hamilton declared that what was at stake was not the cause of a poor printer – but of America and liberty.*

The loss of liberty to a generous mind is worse than death; and yet we know there have been those in all ages who, for the sake of preferment or some imaginary honor, have freely lent a helping hand to oppress, nay, to destroy, their country. This brings to my mind that saying of the immortal Brutus, when he looked upon the creatures of Caesar, who were very great men, but by no means good men: 'You Romans,' said Brutus, 'if yet I may call you so, consider what you are doing; remember that you are assisting Caesar to forge those very chains which one day he will make yourselves wear.' This is what every man that values freedom ought to consider; he should act by judgement and not by affection or self-interest; for where those prevail, no ties of either country or kindred are regarded; as, upon the other hand, the man who loves his country prefers its liberty to all other considerations, well knowing that without liberty life is a misery . . .

Power may justly be compared to a great river; while kept within its bounds, it is both beautiful and useful, but when it overflows its banks, it is then too impetuous to be stemmed; it bears down all before it, and brings destruction and desolation wherever it comes. If, then, this be the nature of power, let us at least do our duty, and, like wise men who value freedom, use our utmost care to support liberty, the only bulwark against lawless power, which, in all ages, has sacrificed to its wild lust and boundless ambition the blood of the best men that ever lived.

I hope to be pardoned, sir, for my zeal upon this occasion. It is an old and wise caution that 'when our neighbor's house is on fire, we ought to take care of our own'. For though, blessed be God, I live in a government where liberty is well understood and freely enjoyed, yet experience has shown us all (I am sure it has to me) that a bad precedent in one government is soon set up for an authority in another; and therefore I cannot but think it mine and every honest man's duty that, while we pay all due obedience to men in authority, we ought, at the same time, to be upon our guard against power wherever we apprehend that it may affect ourselves or our fellow subjects.

I am truly very unequal to such an undertaking, on many accounts. And you see I labor under the weight of many years and am borne down with great infirmities of body; yet old and weak as I am, I should think it my duty, if required, to go to the utmost part of the land, where my service could be of any use in assisting to quench the flame of prosecutions upon informations, set on foot by the government to deprive a people of the right of remonstrating, and complaining too, of the arbitrary attempts of men in power. Men who injure and oppress the people under their administration provoke them to cry out and complain, and then make that very complaint the foundation for new oppressions and prosecutions. I wish I could say there were no instances of this kind. But, to conclude, the question before the court, and you, gentlemen of the jury, is not of small nor private concern; it is not the cause of a poor printer, nor of New York alone, which you are now trying. No! It may, in its consequence, affect every free man that lives under a British government on the main continent of America. It is the best cause; it is the cause of liberty; and I make no doubt but your upright conduct, this day, will not only entitle you to the love and esteem of your fellow citizen, but every man who prefers freedom to a life of slavery will bless and honor you as men who have baffled the attempt of tyranny, and, by an impartial and uncorrupt verdict, have laid a noble foundation for securing to ourselves, our posterity, and our neighbors that to which nature and the laws of our country have given us a right – the liberty of both exposing and opposing arbitrary power (in these parts of the world at least) by speaking and writing truth.

•

# JAMES OTIS
24 February 1761

### 'A man's house is his castle'

*James Otis (1725–83) was the King's advocate-general in Boston in 1760 when the revenue officers demanded his help in obtaining search warrants allowing them to enter any man's house in search of smuggled goods. Otis refused. He appeared as counsel for the merchants of Massachusetts and passionately denounced the writs of assistance issued to the royal customs collectors, arguing that they were against natural law, therefore against the English Constitution and illegal whatever Acts of Parliament said. Otis made the simple appeal to natural law, right and justice which the Declaration of Independence used in 1776 as the justification for the colonies' rebellion.*

*Otis spoke for five hours but only the beginning of the speech was preserved.*

I will to my dying day oppose with all the powers and faculties God has given me all such instruments of slavery, on the one hand, and villainy, on the other, as this writ of assistance is.

It appears to me the worst instrument of arbitrary power, the most destructive of English liberty and the fundamental principles of law, that ever was found in an English lawbook . . .

I was solicited to argue this cause as Advocate General; and because I would not, I have been charged with desertion from my office. To this charge I can give a very sufficient answer. I renounced that office, and I argue this cause from the same principle; and I argue it with the greater pleasure, as it is in favor of British liberty, at a time when we hear the greatest monarch upon earth declaring from his throne that he glories in the name of Briton, and that the privileges of his people are dearer to him than the most valuable prerogatives of his crown; and as it is in opposition to a kind of power the exercise of which, in former periods of history, cost one king of England his head and another his throne. I have taken more pains in this cause than I ever will take again, although my engaging in this and another popular cause has raised much resentment. But I think I can sincerely declare that I cheerfully submit myself to every odious name for conscience' sake; and from my soul I despise all those whose guilt, malice, or folly has made them my foes. Let the consequences be what they will, I am determined to proceed. The only principles of public conduct that are worthy of a gentleman or a man are to sacrifice estate, ease, health, and applause, and even life, to the sacred calls of his country.

These manly sentiments, in private life, make the good citizen; in public life, the patriot and the hero. I do not say that when brought to the test I shall be invincible. I pray God I may never be brought to the melancholy trial; but if ever I should, it will be then known how far I can reduce to practice principles which I know to be founded in truth. In the meantime I will proceed to the subject of this writ.

Your honors will find in the old books concerning the office of a justice of the peace precedents of general warrants to search suspected houses. But in more modern books you will find only special warrants to search such and such houses, specially named, in which the complainant has before sworn that he suspects his goods are concealed; and will find it adjudged that special warrants only are legal. In the same manner I rely on it that the writ prayed for in this petition, being general, is illegal. It is a power that places the liberty of every man in the hands of every petty officer. I say I admit that special writs of assistance, to search special places, may be granted to certain persons on oath; but I deny that the writ now prayed for can be granted, for I beg leave to make some observations on the writ itself, before I proceed to other acts of Parliament. In the first place, the writ is universal, being directed 'to all and singular justices, sheriffs, constables, and all other officers and subjects'; so that, in short, it is directed to every subject in the king's dominions. Everyone with this writ may be a tyrant; if this commission be legal, a tyrant in a legal manner, also, may control, imprison, or murder anyone within the realm. In the next place, it is perpetual; there is no return. A man is accountable to no person for his doings. Every man may reign secure in his petty tyranny, and spread terror and desolation around him, until the trump of the archangel shall excite different emotions in his soul. In the third place, a person with this writ, in the daytime, may enter all houses, shops, etc., at will, and command all to assist him. Fourthly, by this writ, not only deputies, etc., but even their menial servants, are allowed to lord it over us. What is this but to have the curse of Canaan with a witness on us; to be the servant of servants, the most despicable of God's creation? Now, one of the most essential branches of English liberty is the freedom of one's house. A man's house is his castle; and whilst he is quiet, he is as well guarded as a prince in his castle. This writ, if it should be declared legal, would totally annihilate this privilege. Customhouse officers may enter our houses when they please; we are commanded to permit their entry. Their menial servants may enter, may break locks, bars, and everything in their way; and whether they break through malice or revenge, no man, no court, can inquire. Bare suspicion without oath is sufficient.

*Another radical Boston lawyer, John Adams, who was to become President, dated the revolution from this speech. 'Otis' oration . . . breathed into this nation the breath of life,' he said. 'Otis was a flame of fire . . . American independence was there and then born, the seeds of patriots and heroes were there and then sworn . . . There and then was the first scene of the first act of opposition to the arbitrary claims of Great Britain.'*

•

## WILLIAM PITT, 1st EARL OF CHATHAM
### 14 January 1766

### *'I rejoice that America has resisted'*

*When William Pitt (1708–78), a cornet in the Blues, made his maiden speech, it was compared favourably with Cicero and Demosthenes. 'We must muzzle this terrible cornet of horse,' said Walpole, and dismissed him from the army.*

*But the cornet was never muzzled. 'The spark of liberty . . . burst forth with a fury and a splendour that might have awed the world and made kings tremble,' William Hazlitt said of Pitt, subsequently the 1st Earl of Chatham. 'He came forward as the advocate of liberty, the defender of the rights of his fellow-citizens, as the enemy of tyranny, the friend of his country and mankind.'*

*After a long period of mental illness, Chatham returned to London in 1766 at the height of the debate over the Stamp Act, which imposed taxes on British citizens in America who were not represented in Parliament. It was clear that the years had ravaged him when he rose to speak. He was gaunt, pale, physically the wreckage of a man – but that only increased the power of his words.*

I hope a day may soon be appointed to consider the state of the nation with respect to America. I hope gentlemen will come to this debate with all the temper and impartiality that His Majesty recommends and the importance of the subject requires; a subject of greater importance than ever engaged the attention of this House, that subject only excepted when, near a century ago, it was the question whether you yourselves were to be bond or free. In the meantime, as I cannot depend upon my health for any future day (such is the nature of my infirmities), I will beg to say a few words at present, leaving the justice, the equity, the policy, the expediency of the act to another time.

I will only speak to one point – a point which seems not to have been generally understood, I mean to the *right*. Some gentlemen seem to have considered it as a point of honour. If gentlemen consider it in that light, they leave all measures of right and wrong, to follow a delusion that may lead to destruction. It is my opinion that this kingdom has no right to lay a tax upon the colonies. At the same time, I assert the authority of this kingdom over the colonies to be sovereign and supreme, in every circumstance of government and legislation whatsoever. They are the subjects of this kingdom, equally entitled with yourselves to all the natural rights of mankind and the peculiar privileges of Englishmen; equally bound by its laws and equally participating in the Constitution of this free country. The Americans are the sons, not the bastards, of England! Taxation is no part of the governing or legislative power. The taxes are a voluntary *gift* and *grant* of the Commons alone. In legislation the three estates of the realm are alike concerned; but the concurrence of the peers and the Crown to a tax is only necessary to clothe it with the form of a law. The gift and grant is of the Commons alone.

In ancient days, the Crown, the barons, and the clergy possessed the lands. In those days, the barons and the clergy gave and granted to the Crown. They gave and granted what was their own! At present, since the discovery of America, and other circumstances permitting, the Commons are become the proprietors of the land. The Church (God bless it!) has but a pittance. The property of the Lords, compared with that of the Commons, is as a drop of water in the ocean; and this House represents those Commons, the proprietors of the lands; and those proprietors virtually represent the rest of the inhabitants. When, therefore, in this House we give and grant, we give and grant what is our own. But in an American tax, what do we do? 'We, your Majesty's Commons for Great Britain, give and grant to Your Majesty' – what? Our own property! No! 'We give and grant to Your Majesty' the property of your Majesty's Commons of America! It is an absurdity in terms.

The distinction between legislation and taxation is essentially necessary to liberty. The Crown and the peers are equally legislative powers with the Commons. If taxation be a part of simple legislation, the Crown and the peers have rights in taxation as well as yourselves; rights which they will claim, which they will exercise, whenever the principle can be supported by power.

There is an idea in some that the colonies are *virtually* represented in the House. I would fain know by whom an American is represented here. Is he represented by any knight of the shire, in any county in this kingdom? Would to God that respectable representation was augmented to a greater number! Or will you tell him that he is represented by any representative of a borough? – a borough which, perhaps, its own representatives never saw! This is what is called the rotten part of the Constitution. It cannot continue a century. If it does not drop, it must be amputated. The idea of a virtual representation of America in this House is the most contemptible idea that ever entered into the head of a man. It does not deserve a serious refutation.

The Commons of America, represented in their several assemblies, have ever been in possession of the exercise of this their constitutional right of giving and granting their own money. They would have been slaves if they had not enjoyed it! At the same time, this kingdom, as the supreme governing and legislative power, has always bound the colonies by her laws, by her regulations, and restrictions in trade, in navigation, in manufactures, in everything, except that of taking their money out of their pockets without their consent . . .

Gentlemen, sir, have been charged with giving birth to *sedition* in America. They have spoken their sentiments with freedom against this unhappy act, and that freedom has become their crime. Sorry I am to hear the liberty of speech in this House imputed as a crime. But the imputation shall not discourage me. It is a liberty I mean to exercise. No gentleman ought to be afraid to exercise it. It is a liberty by which the gentleman who calumniates it might have profited. He ought to have desisted from his project. The gentleman tells us America is obstinate; America is almost in open rebellion. I rejoice that America has resisted. Three millions of people, so dead to all the feelings of liberty as voluntarily to submit to be slaves, would have been fit instruments to make slaves of the rest . . .

Since the accession of King William, many ministers, some of great, others of more moderate abilities, have taken the lead of government. None of these thought, or even dreamed, of robbing the colonies of their constitutional rights. That was reserved to mark the era of the late administration. Not that there were wanting some, when I had the honour to serve His Majesty, to propose to me to burn my fingers with an American stamp act. With the enemy at their back, with our bayonets at their breasts, in the day of their distress, perhaps the Americans would have submitted to the imposition; but it would have been taking an ungenerous, an unjust advantage. The gentleman boasts of his bounties to America! Are not these bounties intended finally for the benefit of this kingdom? If not, he has misapplied the national treasures!

I am no courtier of America. I stand up for this kingdom. I maintain that the Parliament has a right to bind, to restrain America. Our legislative power over the colonies is sovereign and supreme. When it ceases to be sovereign and supreme, I would advise every gentleman to sell his lands, if he can, and embark for that country. When two countries are connected together like England and her colonies, without being incorporated, the one must necessarily govern. The greater must rule the less. But she must so rule it as not to contradict the fundamental principles that are common to both.

If the gentleman does not understand the difference between external and internal taxes, I cannot help it. There is a plain distinction between taxes levied for the purposes of raising a revenue and duties imposed for the regulation of trade, for the accommodation of the subject; although, in the consequences, some revenue may incidentally arise from the latter.

The gentleman asks, when were the colonies emancipated? I desire to know, when were they made slaves? . . .

A great deal has been said without doors of the power, of the strength, of America. It is a topic that ought to be cautiously meddled with. In a good cause, on a sound bottom, the force of this country can crush America to atoms. I know the valour of your troops. I know the skill of your officers. There is not a company of foot that has served in America out of which you may not pick a man of sufficient knowledge and experience to make a governor of a colony there. But on this ground, on the Stamp Act, which so many here will think a crying injustice, I am one who will lift up my hands against it.

In such a cause, your success would be hazardous. America, if she fell, would fall like the strong man; she would embrace the pillars of the state, and pull down the Constitution along with her. Is this your boasted peace – not to sheathe the sword in its scabbard, but to sheathe it in the bowels of your countrymen? Will you quarrel with yourselves, now the whole house of Bourbon is united against you; while France disturbs your fisheries in Newfoundland, embarrasses your slave trade to Africa, and withholds from your subjects in Canada their property stipulated by treaty; while the ransom for the Manilas is denied by Spain, and its gallant conqueror basely traduced into a mean plunderer – a gentleman whose noble and generous spirit would do honour to the proudest grandee of the country?

The Americans have not acted in all things with prudence and temper: they have been wronged: they have been driven to madness by injustice. Will you punish them for the madness you have occasioned? Rather let prudence and temper come first from this side. I will undertake for America that she will follow the example. There are two lines in a ballad of Prior's, of a man's behaviour to his wife, so applicable to you and your colonies, that I cannot help repeating them:

> Be to her faults a little blind;
> Be to her virtues very kind.

Upon the whole, I will beg leave to tell the House what is my opinion. It is that the Stamp Act be repealed absolutely, totally, and immediately. That the reason for the repeal be assigned – viz., because it was founded on an erroneous principle. At the same time, let the sovereign authority of this country over the colonies be asserted in as strong terms as can be devised, and be made to extend to every point of legislation whatsoever; that we may bind their trade, confine their manufactures, and exercise every power whatsoever, except that of taking money from their pockets without consent.

*The Stamp Act was repealed, but a year later the Townshend Acts imposed new taxes on American ports and lit the flame of revolution.*

•

## JOHN HANCOCK
### 5 March 1774

### 'The tremendous bar of God!'

*With James Otis and John Adams, John Hancock (1737–93), Boston's richest merchant, was another of the patriot leaders of Massachusetts and a fearless champion of the colonists against British oppression. He was president of the Continental Congress and the first to sign the Declaration of Independence. He made this speech in memory of the 1770 Boston Massacre.*

The troops, upon their first arrival, took possession of our Senate house, and pointed their cannon against the judgement hall, and even continued them there whilst the supreme court of judicature for this province was actually sitting to decide upon the lives and fortunes of the King's subjects. Our streets nightly resounded with the noise of riot and debauchery; our peaceful citizens were hourly exposed to shameful insults, and often felt the effects of their violence and outrage. But this was not all: as though they thought it not enough to violate our civil rights, they endeavored to deprive us of the enjoyment of our religious privileges, to vitiate our morals, and thereby render us deserving of destruction. Did not a reverence for religion sensibly decay? Did not our infants almost learn to lisp out curses before they knew their horrid import? Did not our youth forget they were Americans, and regardless of the admonitions of the wise and aged, servilely copy from their tyrants those vices which finally must overthrow the empire of Great Britain? And must I be compelled to acknowledge that even the noblest, fairest part of all the lower creation did not entirely escape the cursed snare? When virtue has once erected her throne within the female breast, it is upon so solid a basis that nothing is able to expel the heavenly inhabitant. But have there not been some, few, indeed, I hope, whose youth and inexperience have rendered them a prey to wretches, whom, upon the least reflection, they would have despised and hated as foes to God and their country? I fear there have been some such unhappy instances, or why have I seen an honest father clothed with shame? or why a virtuous mother drowned in tears? . . .

Ye dark designing knaves, ye murderers, parricides! how dare you tread upon the earth, which has drunk in the blood of slaughtered innocents, shed by your wicked hands? How dare you breathe that air which wafted to the ear of Heaven the groans of those who fell a sacrifice to your accursed ambition? But if the laboring earth doth not expand her jaws; if the air you breathe is not commissioned to be the minister of death; yet, hear it and tremble! The eye of Heaven penetrates the darkest chambers of the soul, traces the leading clue through all the labyrinths which your industrious folly has devised; and you, however you may have screened yourselves from human eyes, must be arraigned, must lift your hands, red with the blood of those whose death you have procured, at the tremendous bar of God!

Surely you never will tamely suffer this country to be a den of thieves. Remember, my friends, from whom you sprang. Let not a meanness of spirit, unknown to those whom you boast of as your fathers, excite a thought to the dishonor of your mothers. I conjure you, by all that is dear, by all that is honorable, by all that is sacred, not only that ye pray, but that ye act; that, if necessary, ye fight, and even die, for the prosperity of our Jerusalem. Break in sunder, with noble disdain, the bonds with which the Philistines have bound you.

•

## WILLIAM PITT, 1st EARL OF CHATHAM
### 20 January 1775

### 'The kingdom is undone'

*As the situation in America deteriorated and British troops under General Gage became an impotent army stuck in Boston, Chatham saw his last chance to save his country. He tabled a motion to withdraw the troops from Boston. His speech, says his biographer J.H. Plumb, was of his best – eloquent, dramatic and full of the invective of which he was such a master.*

When I urge this measure of recalling the troops from Boston, I urge it on this pressing principle – that it is necessarily preparatory to the restoration of your peace and the establishment of your prosperity. It will then appear that you are disposed to treat amicably and equitably; and to consider, revise, and repeal, if it should be found necessary, as I affirm it will, those violent acts and declarations which have disseminated confusion throughout your empire.

Resistance to your acts was necessary, as it was just; and your vain declarations of the omnipotence of Parliament, and your imperious doctrines of the necessity of submission, will be found equally impotent to convince, or to enslave, your fellow-subjects in America, who feel that that tyranny, whether ambitioned by an individual part of the legislature, or the bodies who comprise it, is equally intolerable to British subjects.

The means of enforcing this thraldom are found to be as ridiculous and weak in practice as they are unjust in principle . . .

I therefore urge and conjure your lordships immediately to adopt this conciliating measure. I will pledge myself for its immediately producing conciliatory effects by its being thus well timed; but if you delay till your vain hope shall be accomplished of triumphantly dictating reconciliation, you delay for ever. But admitting that this hope, which in truth is desperate, should be accomplished, what do you gain by the imposition of your victorious amnity? You will be untrusted and unthanked.

Adopt, then, the grace while you have the opportunity of reconcilement, or at least prepare the way. Allay the ferment prevailing in America, by removing the obnoxious hostile cause – obnoxious and unserviceable, for their merit can be only inaction. *Non dimicare et vincere* – their victory can never be by exertions. Their force would be most disproportionately exerted against a brave, generous, and united people, with arms in their hands, and courage in their hearts – three millions of people, the genuine descendants of a valiant and pious ancestry, driven to those deserts by the narrow maxims of a superstitious tyranny. And is the spirit of persecution never to be appeased? Are the brave sons of those brave forefathers to inherit their sufferings, as they have inherited their virtues? Are they to sustain the infliction of the most impressive and unexampled severity, beyond the accounts of history or description of poetry. '*Rhadamanthus habet durissima regna, castigatque, auditique.*' So says the wisest poet and perhaps the wisest statesman and politician. But our ministers say, the Americans must not be heard. They have been condemned unheard. The indiscriminate hand of vengeance has lumped together innocent and guilty, with all the formalities of hostility has blocked up the town [*Boston*], and reduced to beggary and famine thirty thousand inhabitants.

But His Majesty is advised that the union in America cannot last. Ministers have more eyes than I, and should have more ears; but with all the information I have been able to procure, I can pronounce it a union, solid, permanent, and effectual. Ministers may satisfy themselves and delude the public with the report of what they call commercial bodies in America. They are not commercial; they are your packers and factors; they live upon nothing – for I call commission nothing. I mean the ministerial authority for this American intelligence; the runners for government, who are paid for their intelligence. But these are not the men, nor this the influence, to be considered in America when we estimate the firmness of their union. Even to extend the question, and to take in the really mercantile circle, will be totally inadequate to the consideration. Trade indeed increases the wealth and glory of a country; but its real strength and stamina are to be looked for amongst the cultivators of the land; in their simplicity of life is found the simpleness of virtue; – the integrity and courage of freedom. These true, genuine sons of the earth are invincible; and they surround and hem in the mercantile bodies; even if these bodies, which supposition I totally disclaim, could be supposed disaffected to the cause of liberty. Of this general spirit existing in the British nation (for so I wish to distinguish the real and genuine Americans from the pseudo-traders I have described), of this spirit of independence animating the nation of America, I have the most authentic information. It is not new among them; it is, and has ever been, their established principle, their confirmed persuasion; it is their nature and their doctrine.

I remember some years ago, when the repeal of the Stamp Act was in agitation, conversing in a friendly confidence with a person of undoubted respect and authenticity on that subject; and he assured me with a certainty which his judgement and opportunity gave him, that these were the prevalent and steady principles of America – that you might destroy their towns, and cut them off from the superfluities, perhaps the conveniences of life; but that they were prepared to despise your power, and would not lament their loss, whilst they have – what, my lords? – their woods and their liberty. The name of my authority, if I am called upon, will authenticate the opinion irrefragably. (*It was Dr Franklin.*)

If illegal violences have been, as it is said, committed in America, prepare the way, open the door of possibility, for acknowledgement and satisfaction; but proceed not to such coercion, such prescription; cease your indiscriminate inflictions; amerce not thirty thousand; oppress not three millions, for the fault of forty or fifty individuals. Such severity of injustice must for ever render incurable the wounds you have already given your colonies; you irritate them to unappeasable rancour. What though you march from town to town, and from province to province; though you should be able to secure the obedience of the country you leave behind you in your progress, to grasp the dominion of eighteen hundred miles of continent, populous in numbers possessing valour, liberty and resistance?

This resistance to your arbitrary system of taxation might have been foreseen; it was obvious from the nature of things, and of mankind; and above all, from the Whiggish spirit flourishing in that country. The spirit which now resists your taxation in America is the same which formerly opposed loans, benevolences, and ship-money in England; the same spirit which called all England on its legs, and by the Bill of Rights vindicated the English Constitution; the same spirit which established the great fundamental, essential maxim of your liberties – that no subject of England shall be taxed but by his own consent.

This glorious spirit of Whiggism animates three millions in America, who prefer poverty with liberty to gilded chains and sordid affluence; and who will die in defence of their rights as men, as freemen. What shall oppose this spirit, aided by the congenial flame growing in the breasts of every Whig in England, to the amount, I hope, of double the American numbers? Ireland they have to a man. In that country, joined as it is with the cause of colonies, and placed at their head, the distinction I contend for is and must be observed. This country superintends and controls their trade and navigation; but they tax themselves. And this distinction between external and internal control is sacred and insurmountable; it is involved in the abstract nature of things. Property is private, individual, absolute. Trade is an extended and complicated consideration; it reaches as far as ships can sail or winds can blow; it is a great and various machine. To regulate the numberless movements of its several parts, and combine them with effect, for the good of the whole, requires the superintending wisdom and energy of the supreme power in the empire. But this supreme power has no effect towards internal taxation, for it does not exist in that relation; there is no such thing, no such idea in this constitution, as a supreme power operating upon property. Let this distinction remain for ever ascertained; taxation is theirs, commercial regulation is ours. As an American, I would recognize to England her supreme right of regulating commerce and navigation; as an Englishman by birth and principle, I recognize to the Americans their supreme unalienable right to their property – a right which they are justified in the defence of to the last extremity. To maintain this principle is the common cause of the Whigs on the other side of the Atlantic, and on this. ''Tis liberty to liberty engaged', that they will defend themselves, their families, and their country. In this great cause they are immovably allied; it is the alliance of God and nature – immutable, eternal, fixed as the firmament of heaven.

To such united force, what force shall be opposed? What, my lords? A few regiments in America, and seventeen or eighteen thousand men at home! The idea is too ridiculous to take up a moment of your lordships' time. Nor can such a rational and principled union be resisted by the tricks of office or ministerial manoeuvre. Laying of papers on your table, or counting numbers on a division, will not avert or postpone the hour of danger; it must arrive, my lords, unless these fatal Acts are done away; it must arrive in all its horrors, and then these boastful ministers, spite of all their confidence, and all their manoeuvres, shall be forced to hide their heads. They shall be forced to a disgraceful abandonment of their present measures and principles, which they avow but cannot defend – measures which they presume to attempt, but cannot hope to effectuate. They cannot, my lords, they cannot stir a step; they have not a move left; they are checkmated.

But it is not repealing this Act of Parliament, it is not repealing a piece of parchment, that can restore America to our bosom; you must repeal her fears and her resentments; and you may then hope for her love and gratitude. But now, insulted with an armed force posted at Boston, irritated with an hostile array before her eyes, her concessions, if you could force them, would be suspicious and insecure; they will be *irato animo*; they will not be the sound, honourable passions of freemen, they will be dictates of fear, and extortions of force . . .

When your lordships look at the papers transmitted us from America, when you consider their decency, firmness, and wisdom, you cannot but respect their cause, and wish to make it your own. For myself, I must declare and avow that in all my reading and observation – and it has been my favourite study: I have read Thucydides, and have studied and admired the master-states of the world – that for solidity of reasoning, force of sagacity, and wisdom of conclusion, under such a complication of difficult circumstances, no nation or body of men can stand in preference to the General Congress at Philadelphia. I trust it is obvious to your lordships, that all attempts to impose servitude upon such men, to establish despotism over such a mighty continental nation, must be vain, must be fatal. We shall be forced ultimately to retract; let us restrain while we can, not when we must. I say we must necessarily undo these violent oppressive Acts; they must be repealed – you will repeal them; I pledge myself for it, that you will in the end repeal them; I stake my reputation on it: – I will consent to be taken for an idiot, if they are not finally repealed. Avoid, then, this humiliating, disgraceful necessity. With a dignity becoming your exalted situation, make the first advances to concord, to peace, and happiness; for that is your true dignity, to act with prudence and justice. That you should first concede is obvious, from sound and rational policy. Concession comes with better grace and more salutary effect from superior power; it reconciles superiority of power with the feelings of men, and establishes solid confidence on the foundations of affection and gratitude . . .

If the ministers thus persevere in misadvising and misleading the King, I will not say that they can alienate the affections of his subjects from his crown; but I will affirm that they will make the crown not worth his wearing. I will not say that the King is betrayed; but I will pronounce that the kingdom is undone.

•

# EDMUND BURKE
## 22 March 1775

### 'This spirit of American liberty'

*Edmund Burke (1729–97), an Irish Protestant, made his career in London and dominated the British Parliament for a generation by the power of his oratory and his timeless battle against oppression, whether in India, France or America.*

*Chatham's eloquence on 20 January had failed to secure the removal of General Gage's troops from Boston. Now it was time for Burke to play his part. Speaking for more than three hours in defence of the rights of the American colonists, he proposed thirteen resolutions for conciliation.*

America, gentlemen say, is a noble object. It is an object well worth fighting for. Certainly it is, if fighting a people be the best way of gaining them. Gentlemen in this respect will be led to their choice of means by their complexions and their habits. Those who understand the military art will, of course, have some predilection for it. Those who wield the thunder of the State may have more confidence in the efficacy of arms. But I confess, possibly for want of this knowledge, my opinion is much more in favour of prudent management than of force; considering force not as an odious, but a feeble instrument for preserving a people so numerous, so active, so growing, so spirited as this, in a profitable and subordinate connection with us.

First, sir, permit me to observe, that the use of force alone is but temporary. It may subdue for a moment, but it does not remove the necessity of subduing again; and a nation is not governed which is perpetually to be conquered.

My next objection is its uncertainty. Terror is not always the effect of force; and an armament is not a victory. If you do not succeed, you are without resource; for, conciliation failing, force remains; but, force failing, no further hope of reconciliation is left. Power and authority are sometimes bought by kindness, but they can never be begged as alms by an impoverished and defeated violence.

A further objection to force is that you impair the object by your very endeavours to preserve it. The thing you fought for is not the thing which you recover; but depreciated, sunk, wasted, and consumed in the contest. Nothing less will content me than *whole* America. I do not choose to consume its strength along with our own, because in all parts it is the British strength that I consume. I do not choose to be caught by a foreign enemy at the end of this exhausting conflict, and still less in the midst of it. I may escape; but I can make no insurance against such an event. Let me add, that I do not choose wholly to break the American spirit, because it is the spirit that has made the country.

Lastly, we have no sort of experience in favour of force as an instrument in the rule of our colonies. Their growth and their utility have been owing to methods altogether different. Our ancient indulgence has been said to be pursued to a fault. It may be so; but we know, if feeling is evidence, that our fault was more tolerable than our attempt to mend it; and our sin far more salutary than our penitence.

These, sir, are my reasons for not entertaining that high opinion of untried force, by which many gentlemen, for whose sentiments in other particulars I have great respect, seem to be so greatly captivated.

But there is still behind a third consideration concerning this object, which serves to determine my opinion on the sort of policy which ought to be pursued in the management of America, even more than its population and its commerce – I mean its temper and character. In this character of the Americans a love of freedom is the predominating feature which marks and distinguishes the whole; and, as an ardent is always a jealous affection, your colonies become suspicious, restive, and untractable, whenever they see the least attempt to wrest from them by force, or shuffle from them by chicane, what they think the only advantage worth living for. This fierce spirit of liberty is stronger in the English colonies, probably, than in any other people of the earth, and this from a variety of powerful causes, which, to understand the true temper of their minds, and the direction which this spirit takes, it will not be amiss to lay open somewhat more largely.

The people of the colonies are descendants of Englishmen. England, sir, is a nation which still, I hope, respects, and formerly adored, her freedom. The colonists emigrated from you when this part of your character was most predominant; and they took this bias and direction the moment they parted from your hands. They are, therefore, not only devoted to liberty, but to liberty according to English ideas and on English principles. Abstract liberty, like other mere abstractions, is not to be found. Liberty inheres in some sensible object; and every nation has formed to itself some favourite point which, by way of eminence, becomes the criterion of their happiness.

Permit me, sir, to add another circumstance in our colonies, which contributes no mean part toward the growth and effect of this untractable spirit – I mean their education. In no other country, perhaps, in the world is the law so general a study . . . This study renders men acute, inquisitive, dexterous, prompt in attack, ready in defence, full of resources. In other countries, the people, more simple, and of a less mercurial cast, judge of an ill principle in government only by an actual grievance; here they anticipate the evil, and judge of the pressure of the grievance by the badness of the principle. They augur misgovernment at a distance; and snuff the approach of tyranny in every tainted breeze . . .

Perhaps a more smooth and accommodating spirit of freedom in them would be more acceptable to us. Perhaps ideas of liberty might be desired, more reconcilable with an arbitrary and boundless authority. Perhaps we might wish the colonists to be persuaded that their liberty is more secure when held in trust for them by us, as guardians during a perpetual minority, than with any part of it in their own hands. But the question is not whether their spirit deserves praise or blame. What, in the name of God, shall we do with it? You have before you the object, such as it is, with all its glories, with all its imperfections on its head. You see the magnitude, the importance, the temper, the habits, the disorders. By all these considerations we are strongly urged to determine something concerning it. We are called upon to fix some rule and line for our future conduct which may give a little stability to our politics, and prevent the return of such unhappy deliberations as the present. Every such return will bring the matter before us in a still more untractable form. For, what astonishing and incredible things have we not seen already? What monsters have not been generated from this unnatural contention? . . .

We are indeed, in all disputes with the colonies, by the necessity of things, the judge. It is true, sir; but I confess that the character of judge in my own cause is a thing that frightens me. Instead of filling me with pride, I am exceedingly humbled by it. I cannot proceed with a stern, assured, judical confidence, until I find myself in something more like a judicial character. Sir, these considerations have great weight with me, when I find things so circumstanced that I see the same party at once a civil litigant against me in point of right and a culprit before me; while I sit as criminal judge on acts of his whose moral quality is to be decided on upon the merits of that very litigation. Men are every now and then put, by the complexity of human affairs, into strange situations; but justice is the same, let the judge be in what situation he will.

In this situation, let us seriously and coolly ponder, what is it we have got by all our menaces, which have been many and ferocious. What advantage have we derived from the penal laws we have passed, and which, for the time, have been severe and numerous? What advances have we made toward our object by the sending of a force which, by land and sea, is no contemptible strength? Has the disorder abated? Nothing less. When I see things in this situation, after such confident hopes, bold promises, and active exertions, I cannot, for my life, avoid a suspicion that the plan itself is not correctly right.

If, then, the removal of the causes of this spirit of American liberty be, for the greater part, or rather entirely, impracticable; if the ideas of criminal process be inapplicable, or, if applicable, are in the highest degree inexpedient, what way yet remains? No way is open but the third and last – to comply with the American spirit as necessary, or, if you please, to submit to it as a necessary evil.

If we adopt this mode, if we mean to conciliate and concede, let us see of what nature the concessions ought to be. To ascertain the nature of our concessions, we must look at their complaint. The colonies complain that they have not the characteristic mark and seal of British freedom. They complain that they are taxed in Parliament in which they are not represented. If you mean to satisfy them at all, you must satisfy them with regard to this complaint. If you mean to please any people, you must give them the boon which they ask; not what you may think better for them, but of a kind totally different.

Such is steadfastly my opinion of the absolute necessity of keeping up the concord of this empire by a unity of spirit, though in a diversity of operations, that, if I were sure the colonists had, at their leaving this country, sealed a regular compact of servitude; that they had solemnly abjured all the rights of citizens; that they had made a vow to renounce all ideas of liberty for them and their posterity to all generations, yet I should hold myself obliged to conform to the temper I found universally prevalent in my own day, and to govern two millions of men, impatient of servitude, on the principles of freedom. I am not determining a point of law. I am restoring tranquillity, and the general character and situation of a people must determine what sort of government is fitted for them. That point nothing else can or ought to determine.

My idea, therefore, without considering whether we yield as matter of right, or grant as matter of favour, is to admit the people of our colonies into an interest in the Constitution, and, by recording that admission in the journals of parliament, to give them as strong an assurance as the nature of the thing will admit, that we mean forever to adhere to that solemn declaration of systematic indulgence.

The Americans will have no interest contrary to the grandeur and glory of England, when they are not oppressed by the weight of it; and they will rather be inclined to respect the acts of a superintending legislature, when they see them the acts of that power which is itself the security, not the rival, of their secondary importance. In this assurance my mind most perfectly acquiesces, and I confess I feel not the least alarm from the discontents which are to arise from putting people at their ease; nor do I apprehend the destruction of this empire from giving, by an act of free grace and indulgence, to two millions of my fellow citizens, some share of those rights upon which I have always been taught to value myself.

A revenue from America transmitted hither – do not delude yourselves – you never can receive it – no, not a shilling. We have experienced that from remote countries it is not to be expected. If, when you attempted to extract revenue from Bengal, you were obliged to return in loan what you had taken in imposition, what can you expect from North America? for certainly, if ever there was a country qualified to produce wealth, it is India; or an institution fit for the transmission, it is the East India Company. America has none of these aptitudes. If America gives you taxable objects on which you lay your duties here, and gives you, at the same time, a surplus by a foreign sale of her commodities to pay the duties on these objects which you tax at home, she has performed her part to the British revenue. But with regard to her own internal establishments, she may, I doubt not she will, contribute in moderation; I say in moderation, for she ought not to be permitted to exhaust herself. She ought to be reserved to a war, the weight of which, with the enemies that we are most likely to have, must be considerable in her quarter of the globe. There she may serve you, and serve you essentially.

For that service, for all service, whether of revenue, trade, or empire, my trust is in her interest in the British Constitution. My hold of the colonies is in the close affection which grows from common names, from kindred blood, from similar privileges, and equal protection. These are ties which, though light as air, are as strong as links of iron. Let the colonies always keep the idea of their civil rights associated with your government; they will cling and grapple to you, and no force under heaven will be of power to tear them from their allegiance. But let it be once understood that your government may be one thing, and their privileges another; that these two things may exist without any mutual relation; the cement is gone; the cohesion is loosened; and everything hastens to decay and dissolution. As long as you have the wisdom to keep the sovereign authority of this country as the sanctuary of liberty, the sacred temple consecrated to our common faith, wherever the chosen race and sons of England worship freedom, they will turn their faces toward you. The more they multiply, the more friends you will have. The more ardently they love liberty, the more perfect will be their obedience. Slavery they can have anywhere. It is a weed that grows in every soil. They may have it from Spain; they may have it from Prussia; but, until you become lost to all feeling of your true interest and your natural dignity, freedom they can have from none but you. This is the commodity of price, of which you have the monopoly. This is the true Act of Navigation, which binds to you the commerce of the colonies, and through them secures to you the wealth of the world. Deny them this participation of freedom, and you break that sole bond which originally made, and must still preserve, the unity of the empire. Do not entertain so weak an imagination as that your registers and your bonds, your affidavits and your sufferances, your cockets and your clearances, are what form the great securities of your commerce. Do not dream that your letters of office, and your instructions, and your suspending clauses, are the things that hold together the great contexture of this mysterious whole. These things do not make your government. Dead instruments, passive tools as they are, it is the spirit of the English communion that gives all their life and efficacy to them. It is the spirit of the English Constitution which, infused through the mighty mass, pervades, feeds, unites, invigorates, vivifies every part of the empire, even down to the minutest member.

Is it not the same virtue which does everything for us here in England?

Do you imagine, then, that it is the land tax which raises your revenue, that it is the annual vote in the committee of supply which gives you your army? or that it is the mutiny bill which inspires it with bravery and discipline? No! surely no! It is the love of the people; it is their attachment to their government, from the sense of the deep stake they have in such a glorious institution, which gives you your army and your navy, and infuses into both that liberal obedience, without which your army would be a base rabble, and your navy nothing but rotten timber.

All this, I know well enough, will sound wild and chimerical to the profane herd of those vulgar and mechanical politicians, who have no place among us; a sort of people who think that nothing exists but what is gross and material, and who, therefore, far from being qualified to be directors of the great movement of empire, are not fit to turn a wheel in the machine. But to men truly initiated and rightly taught, these ruling and master principles, which, in the opinion of such men as I have mentioned, have no substantial existence, are in truth everything and all in all. Magnanimity in politics is not seldom the truest wisdom; and a great empire and little minds go ill together. If we are conscious of our situation, and glow with zeal to fill our place as becomes our station and ourselves, we ought to auspicate all our public proceeding on America with the old warning of the church, *sursum corda!* We ought to elevate our minds to the greatness of that trust to which the order of Providence has called us. By advertising to the dignity of this high calling, our ancestors have turned a savage wilderness into a glorious empire, and have made the most extensive and the only honourable conquests, not by destroying, but by promoting, the wealth, the number, the happiness of the human race. Let us get an American revenue as we have got an American empire. English privileges have made it all that it is; English privileges alone will make it all it can be.

In full confidence of this unalterable truth, I now, *quod felix faustumque sit*, lay the first stone in the temple of peace; and I move you, 'That the colonies and plantations of Great Britain in North America, consisting of fourteen separate governments, and containing two millions and upwards of free inhabitants, have not had the liberty and privilege of electing and sending any knights and burgesses, or others, to represent them in the high court of parliament.'

*Burke spoke for so long that he lost most of his audience. His resolution was defeated by 270 votes to 78.*

•

## PATRICK HENRY
### 23 March 1775

### *'Give me liberty, or give me death!'*

*As Edmund Burke made his plea in the British House of Commons for conciliation with the American colonies, the Virginia Convention to the Continental Congress was meeting in St John's Church in Richmond. One delegate was the Virginian patriot and successful lawyer Patrick Henry (1736–99), who had delivered the first speech to the Congress in 1774. Henry rose and handed to the clerk a series of resolutions stating that a militia was the only security of free government, that a militia was necessary to protect American rights and liberties and that Virginia be put immediately into a posture of defence.*

*With the revolutionary fervour of the colonists at fever pitch, Henry defended his resolutions. 'The tendons of his neck stood out white and rigid, like whip cords,' wrote a Baptist clergyman as he described the climax of Henry's speech. 'His voice rose louder and louder, until the walls of the building and all within them seemed to shake and rock in its tremendous vibrations. Finally his pale face and glaring eyes became terrible to look upon.' According to Thomas Jefferson, he was the leader of the revolution. The American revolution in the biggest colony started from this speech.*

Mr President, it is natural to man to indulge in the illusions of hope. We are apt to shut our eyes against a painful truth, and listen to the song of that siren, till she transforms us into beasts. Is this the part of wise men, engaged in a great and arduous struggle for liberty? Are we disposed to be of the number of those who, having eyes, see not, and having ears, hear not, the things which so nearly concern their temporal salvation? For my part, whatever anguish of spirit it may cost, I am willing to know the whole truth; to know the worst and to provide for it.

I have but one lamp by which my feet are guided; and that is the lamp of experience. I know of no way of judging of the future but by the past. And judging by the past, I wish to know what there has been in the conduct of the British ministry for the last ten years, to justify those hopes with which gentlemen have been pleased to solace themselves and the House? Is it that insidious smile with which our petition has been lately received? Trust it not, sir; it will prove a snare to your feet. Suffer not yourselves to be betrayed with a kiss. Ask yourselves how this gracious reception of our petition comports with these war-like prepara- tions which cover our waters and darken our land. Are fleets and armies necessary to a work of love and reconciliation? Have we shown ourselves so unwilling to be reconciled, that force must be called in to win back our love? Let us not deceive ourselves, sir. These are the implements of war and subjugation; the last arguments to which kings resort. I ask gentlemen, sir, what means this martial array, if its purpose be not to force us to submission? Can gentlemen assign any other possible motives for it? Has Great Britain any enemy, in this quarter of the world, to call for all this accumulation of navies and armies? No, sir, she has none. They are meant for us; they can be meant for no other. They are sent over to bind and rivet upon us those chains which the British ministry have been so long forging. And what have we to oppose to them? Shall we try argument? Sir, we have been trying that for the last ten years. Have we anything new to offer on the subject? Nothing. We have held the subject up in every light of which it is capable; but it has been all in vain. Shall we resort to entreaty and humble supplication? What terms shall we find which have not been already exhausted? Let us not, I beseech you, sir, deceive ourselves longer. Sir, we have done everything that could be done, to avert the storm which is now coming on. We have petitioned; we have remonstrated; we have supplicated; we have prostrated ourselves before the throne, and have implored its interposition to arrest the tyrannical hands of the ministry and Parliament. Our petitions have been slighted; our remonstrances have produced additional violence and insult; our supplications have been disregarded; and we have been spurned, with contempt, from the foot of the throne. In vain, after these things, may we indulge the fond hope of peace and reconciliation. There is no longer any room for hope. If we wish to be free – if we mean to preserve inviolate those inestimable privileges for which we have been so long contending – if we mean not basely to abandon the noble struggle in which we have been so long engaged, and which we have pledged ourselves never to abandon until the glorious object of our contest shall be obtained, we must fight! I repeat it, sir, we must fight! An appeal to arms and to the God of Hosts is all that is left us!

They tell us, sir, that we are weak; unable to cope with so formidable an adversary. But when shall we be stronger? Will it be the next week, or the next year? Will it be when we are totally disarmed, and when a British guard shall be stationed in every house? Shall we gather strength by irresolution and inaction? Shall we acquire the means of effectual resistance, by lying supinely on our backs, and hugging the delusive phantom of hope, until our enemies shall have bound us hand and foot? Sir, we are not weak, if we make a proper use of the means which the God of nature hath placed in our power. Three millions of people, armed in the holy cause of liberty, and in such a country as that which we possess, are invincible by any force which our enemy can send against us. Besides, sir, we shall not fight our battles alone. There is a just God who presides over the destinies of nations; and who will raise up friends to fight our battles for us. The battle, sir, is not to the strong alone; it is to the vigilant, the active, the brave. Besides, sir, we have no election. If we were base enough to desire it, it is now too late to retire from the contest. There is no retreat, but in submission and slavery! Our chains are forged! Their clanking may be heard on the plains of Boston! The war is inevitable – and let it come! I repeat it, sir, let it come!

It is in vain, sir, to extenuate the matter. Gentlemen may cry peace, peace – but there is no peace. The war is actually begun! The next gale that sweeps from the north will bring to our ears the clash of resounding arms! Our brethren are already in the field! Why stand we here idle? What is it that gentlemen wish? What would they have? Is life so dear, or peace so sweet, as to be purchased at the price of chains and slavery? Forbid it, Almighty God! I know not what course others may take; but as for me, give me liberty, or give me death!

•

## SAMUEL ADAMS
### 1 August 1776

### 'Be yourselves, O Americans'

*Among the patriot leaders of Massachusetts, Samuel Adams (1722–1803) was the most effective; according to Hugh Brogan, he was the first Democrat, the first professional American politician. It was Adams (second cousin of John, the second American president) who wrote the circular letter from Massachusetts to all the other colonial assemblies affirming Americans' rights and denouncing the Townshend Acts, and who led the protest in Massachusetts. Adams was chief agitator at the Boston Tea Party, a delegate to the first and second Continental Congresses and a signatory of the Declaration of Independence. A month later he delivered an eloquent address at the State House of Philadelphia on American independence.*

We are now on this continent, to the astonishment of the world, three millions of souls united in one cause. We have large armies, well disciplined and appointed, with commanders inferior to none in military skill, and superior in activity and zeal. We are furnished with arsenals and stores beyond our most sanguine expectations, and foreign nations are waiting to crown our success by their alliances. There are instances of, I would say, an almost astonishing Providence in our favor; our success has staggered our enemies, and almost given faith to infidels: so we may truly say it is not our own arm which has saved us.

The hand of Heaven appears to have led us on to be, perhaps, humble instruments and means in the great providential dispensation which is completing. We have fled from the political Sodom; let us not look back, lest we perish and become a monument of infamy and derision to the world. For can we ever expect more unanimity and a better preparation for defense; more infatuation of counsel among our enemies, and more valor and zeal among ourselves? The same force and resistance which are sufficient to procure us our liberties will secure us a glorious independence and support us in the dignity of free, imperial states. We cannot suppose that our opposition has made a corrupt and dissipated nation more friendly to America, or created in them a greater respect for the rights of mankind. We can therefore expect a restoration and establishment of our privileges, and a compensation for the injuries we have received, from their want of power, from their fears, and not from their virtues. The unanimity and valor which will effect an honorable peace can render a future contest for our liberties unnecessary. He who has strength to chain down the wolf is a madman if he let him loose without drawing his teeth and paring his nails.

We have no other alternative than independence, or the most ignominious and galling servitude. The legions of our enemies thicken on our plains; desolation and death mark their bloody career; whilst the mangled corpses of our countrymen seem to cry out to us as a voice from Heaven.

Our union is now complete; our constitution composed, established, and approved. You are now the guardians of your own liberties. We may justly address you, as the *decemviri* did the Romans, and say: 'Nothing that we propose can pass into a law without your consent. Be yourselves, O Americans, the authors of those laws on which your happiness depends.'

You have now in the field armies sufficient to repel the whole force of your enemies and their base and mercenary auxiliaries. The hearts of your soldiers beat high with the spirit of freedom; they are animated with the justice of their cause, and while they grasp their swords can look up to Heaven for assistance. Your adversaries are composed of wretches who laugh at the rights of humanity, who turn religion into derision, and would, for higher wages, direct their swords against their leaders or their country. Go on, then, in your generous enterprise, with gratitude to Heaven for past success, and confidence of it in the future. For my own part, I ask no greater blessing than to share with you the common danger and common glory. If I have a wish dearer to my soul than that my ashes may be mingled with those of a Warren and a Montgomery, it is that these American states may never cease to be free and independent.

·

## WILLIAM PITT, 1st EARL OF CHATHAM
18 November 1777

### 'You cannot conquer America'

*William Pitt, Earl of Chatham, was living in a dark, lonely hell which engulfed his spirits. For two years the shadow of death lay across him — but in 1777 he revived to find his innermost fears realized. War had broken out between Britain and America, and France was discussing with American representatives how help could be given to them.*

*The loss of America, Chatham believed, would bring ruin to England and leave her at the mercy of France. Yet, as he declared in this, one of his last great speeches, America could never be conquered.*

My lords, this ruinous and ignominious situation, where we cannot act with success, nor suffer with honour, calls upon us to remonstrate in the strongest and loudest language of truth to rescue the ear of Majesty from the delusions which surround it. The desperate state of our arms abroad is in part known: no man thinks more highly of them than I do: I love and honour the English troops: I know their virtues and their valour: I know they can achieve anything except impossibilities: and I know that the conquest of English America is an impossibility. You cannot, I venture to say it, you CANNOT conquer America. Your armies last war effected everything that could be effected; and what was it? It cost a numerous army, under the command of a most able general [*Lord Amherst*], now a noble lord in this House, a long and laborious campaign, to expel five thousand Frenchmen from French America. My lords, you cannot conquer America. What is your present situation there? We do not know the worst; but we know that in three campaigns we have done nothing, and suffered much. Besides the sufferings, perhaps total loss of the Northern force; the best appointed army that ever took the field, commanded by Sir William Howe, has retired from the American lines; he was obliged to relinquish his attempt, and with great delay and danger, to adopt a new and distant plan of operations. We shall soon know, and in any event have reason to lament, what may have happened since. As to conquest, therefore, my lords, I repeat it is impossible. You may swell every expense, and every effort still more extravagantly; pile and accumulate every assistance you can buy or borrow; traffic and barter with every little pitiful German prince that sells and sends his subjects to the shambles of a foreign country; your efforts are for ever vain and impotent – doubly so from this mercenary aid on which you rely; for it irritates, to an incurable resentment, the minds of your enemies – to overrun them with the sordid sons of rapine and of plunder; devoting them and their possessions to the rapacity of hireling cruelty! If I were an American, as I am an Englishman, while a foreign troop was landed in my country, I never would lay down my arms; never! never! never!

Your own army is infected with the contagion of these illiberal allies. The spirit of plunder and of rapine is gone forth among them. I know it – and notwithstanding what the noble Earl [*Earl Percy*] who moved the Address has given as his opinion of our American army, I know from authentic information, and the most experienced officers, that our discipline is deeply wounded. Whilst this is notoriously our sinking situation, America grows and flourishes; whilst our strength and discipline are lowered, theirs are rising and improving.

But, my lords, who is the man that, in addition to these disgraces and mischiefs of our army, has dared to authorize and associate to our arms the tomahawk and scalping-knife of the savage? To call into civilized alliance the wild and inhuman savage of the woods; to delegate to the merciless Indian the defence of disputed rights; and to wage the horrors of his barbarous war against our brethren? My lords, these enormities cry aloud for redress and punishment: and unless thoroughly done away, they will be an indelible stain on the national character. It is not the least of our national misfortunes that the strength and character of our army are thus impaired: infected with the mercenary spirit of robbery and rapine – familiarized to horrid scenes of savage cruelty, it can no longer boast the noble and generous principles which dignify a soldier; no longer sympathize with the dignity of the royal banner, nor feel 'the pride, pomp, and circumstance of glorious war, that make ambition virtue!' What makes ambition virtue? The sense of honour. But is the sense of honour consistent with a spirit of plunder, or the practice of murder? Can it flow from mercenary motives, or can it prompt to cruel deeds? Besides these murderers and plunderers, let me ask our ministers – what other allies have they acquired? What other powers have they associated to their cause? Have they entered into alliance with the King of the Gypsies? Nothing, my lords, is too low or too ludicrous to be consistent with their counsels.

The independent views of America have been stated and asserted as the foundation of this address. My lords, no man wishes more for the due dependence of America on this country than I do: to preserve it, and not confirm that state of independence into which your measures hitherto have driven them, is the object which we ought to unite in attaining. The Americans, contending for their rights against arbitrary exactions, I love and admire; it is the struggle of free and virtuous patriots: but, contending for independency and total disconnection from England, as an Englishman I cannot wish them success, for, in a due constitutional dependency, including the ancient supremacy of this country in regulating their commerce and navigation, consists the mutual happiness and prosperity both of England and America. She derived assistance and protection from us, and we reaped from her the most important advantages; she was, indeed, the fountain of our wealth, the nerve of our strength, the nursery and basis of our naval power.

It is our duty, therefore, my lords, if we wish to save our country, most seriously to endeavour the recovery of these most beneficial subjects: and in this perilous crisis perhaps the present moment may be the only one in which we can hope for success; for, in their negotiations with France, they have, or think they have, reason to complain: though it be notorious that they have received from that power important supplies and assistance of various kinds, yet it is certain they expected it in a more decisive and immediate degree. America is in ill humour with France on some points that have not entirely answered her expectations: let us wisely take advantage of every possible moment of reconciliation. Besides, the natural disposition of America herself still leans towards England – to the old habits of connection and mutual interest that united both countries. This was the established sentiment of all the continent; and still, my lords, in the great and principal part, the sound part of America, this wise and affectionate disposition prevails; and there is a very considerable part of America yet sound – the middle and the southern provinces. Some parts may be factious and blind to their true interests; but if we express a wise and benevolent disposition to communicate with them those immutable rights of nature, and those constitutional liberties, to which they are equally entitled with ourselves, by a conduct so just and humane, we shall confirm the favourable, and conciliate the adverse. I say, my lords, the rights and liberties to which they are equally entitled with ourselves, but no more. I would participate to them every enjoyment and freedom which the colonizing subjects of a free state can possess, or wish to possess; and I do not see why they should not enjoy every fundamental right in their property, and every original substantial liberty which Devonshire or Surrey, or the county I live in, or any other county in England can claim; reserving always, as the sacred right of the mother-country, the due constitutional dependency of the colonies. The inherent supremacy of the state, in regulating and protecting the navigation and commerce of all her subjects, is necessary for the mutual benefit and preservation of every part, to constitute and preserve the prosperous arrangement of the whole empire.

The sound parts of America, of which I have spoken, must be sensible of these great truths and of their real interests. America is not in that state of desperate and contemptible rebellion which this country has been deluded to believe. It is not a wild and lawless banditti, who, having nothing to lose, might hope to snatch something from public convulsions; many of their leaders and great men have a great stake in this great contest: the gentleman who conducts their armies, I am told, has an estate of four or five thousand pounds a year: and when I consider these things, I cannot but lament the inconsiderate violence of our penal acts – our declarations of treason and rebellion, with all the fatal effects of attainder and confiscation.

As to the disposition of foreign powers, which is asserted to be pacific and friendly, let us judge, my lords, rather by their actions and the nature of things than by interested assertions. The uniform assistance supplied to America by France suggests a different conclusion. The most important interests of France, in aggrandizing and enriching herself with what she most wants, supplies of every naval store from America, must inspire her with different sentiments. The extraordinary prepara-tions of the House of Bourbon by land and by sea, from Dunkirk to the Streights, equally ready and willing to overwhelm these defenceless islands, should rouse us to a sense of their real disposition and our own danger. Not five thousand troops in England! – hardly three thousand in Ireland! What can we oppose to the combined force of our enemies? Scarcely twenty ships of the line fully or sufficiently manned that any admiral's reputation would permit him to take the command of! The river of Lisbon in the possession of our enemies! The seas swept by American privateers! Our Channel torn to pieces by them! In this complicated crisis of danger – weakness at home and calamity abroad, terrified and insulted by the neighbouring powers, unable to act in America, or acting only to be destroyed – where is the man with the forehead to promise or hope for success in such a situation? or from perseverance in the measures that have driven us to it? Who has the forehead to do so? Where is that man? I should be glad to see his face.

You cannot conciliate America by your present measures; you cannot subdue her by your present, or by any measures. What, then, can you do? You cannot conquer, you cannot gain, but you can address, you can lull the fears and anxieties of the moment into an ignorance of the danger that should produce them. But, my lords, the time demands the language of truth: we must not now apply the flattering unction of servile compliance, or blind complaisance. In a just and necessary war, to maintain the rights or honour of my country, I would strip the shirt from my back to support it. But in such a war as this, unjust in its principle, impracticable in its means, and ruinous in its consequences, I would not contribute a single effort, nor a single shilling. I do not call for vengeance on the heads of those who have been guilty; I only recommend them to make their retreat: let them walk off; and let them make haste, or they may be assured that speedy and condign punishment will overtake them.

My lords, I have submitted to you, with the freedom and truth which I think my duty, my sentiments on your present awful situation. I have laid before you the ruin of your power, the disgrace of your reputation, the pollution of your discipline, the contamination of your morals, the complication of calamities, foreign and domestic, that overwhelm your sinking country. Your dearest interests, your own liberties, the constitution itself, totters to the foundation. All this disgraceful danger, this multitude of misery, is the monstrous offspring of this unnatural war. We have been deceived and deluded too long: let us now stop short: this is the crisis – maybe the only crisis, of time and situation, to give us a possibility of escape from the fatal effects of our delusions. But if, in an obstinate and infatuated perseverance in folly, we meanly echo back the peremptory words this day presented to us, nothing can save this devoted country from complete and final ruin. We madly rush into multiplied miseries and 'confusion worse confounded'.

Is it possible, can it be believed, that ministers are yet blind to this impending destruction? I did hope, that instead of this false and empty vanity, this overweening pride, engendering high conceits, and presumptuous imaginations – that ministers would have humbled themselves in their errors, would have confessed and retracted them, and by an active, though a late repentance, have endeavoured to redeem them. But, my lords, since they had neither sagacity to foresee, nor justice nor humanity to shun, these oppressive calamities; since not even severe experience can make them feel, nor the imminent ruin of their country awaken them from their stupefaction, the guardian care of Parliament must interpose. I shall therefore, my lords, propose to you an amendment to the address to His Majesty, to be inserted immediately after the two first paragraphs of congratulation on the birth of a princess: to recommend an immediate cessation of hostilities, and the commencement of a treaty to restore peace and liberty to America, strength and happiness to England, security and permanent prosperity to both countries. This, my lords, is yet in our power; and let not the wisdom and justice of your lordships neglect the happy, and, perhaps, the only opportunity. By the establishment of irrevocable law, founded on mutual rights, and ascertained by treaty, these glorious enjoyments may be firmly perpetuated. And let me repeat to your lordships, that the strong bias of America, at least of the wiser and sounder parts of it, naturally inclines to this happy and constitutional reconnection with you. Notwithstanding the temporary intrigues with France, we may still be assured of their ancient and confirmed partiality to us. America and France cannot be congenial: there is something decisive and confirmed in the honest American that will not assimilate to the futility and levity of Frenchmen.

My lords, to encourage and confirm that innate inclination to this country, founded on every principle of affection, as well as consideration of interest – to restore that favourable disposition into a permanent and powerful reunion with this country – to revive the mutual strength of the empire; again, to awe the House of Bourbon, instead of meanly truckling, as our present calamities compel us, to every insult of French caprice and Spanish punctilio – to re-establish our commerce – to reassert our rights and our honour – to confirm our interests, and renew our glories for ever (a consummation most devoutly to be endeavoured! and which, I trust, may yet arise from reconciliation with America) – I have the honour of submitting to you the following amendment, which I move to be inserted after the two first paragraphs of the address:

'And that this House does most humbly advise and supplicate His Majesty to be pleased to cause the most speedy and effectual measures to be taken for restoring peace in America; and that no time may be lost in proposing an immediate cessation of hostilities there, in order to the opening a treaty for the final settlement of the tranquillity of these invaluable provinces, by a removal of the unhappy causes of this ruinous civil war; and by a just and adequate security against the return of the like calamities in times to come. And this House desire to offer the most dutiful assurances to His Majesty, that they will, in due time, cheerfully cooperate with the magnanimity and tender goodness of His Majesty for the preservation of his people, by such explicit and most solemn declarations, and provisions of fundamental and irrevocable laws, as may be judged necessary for the ascertaining and fixing for ever the respective rights of Great Britain and her colonies.'

•

## WILLIAM PITT, 1ST EARL OF CHATHAM
### 7 April 1778

*'If we must fall, let us fall like men!'*

*By the spring of 1778 Chatham was a dying man, but when the Duke of Richmond proposed to press for American independence, he decided to make one last effort to thwart a policy that he believed would ruin England. As he passed to his seat the assembled lords rose and made way for him.*

*So shrunk was he with illness and suffering that from his bushy wig little could be seen of his countenance but the great aquiline nose and the flashing eyes. As he rose to speak, leaning on his crutches and supported on each side, he took one hand from his crutch and raised it to heaven. Gaunt, tragic, Lear-like in his madness, says J.H. Plumb, his feeble voice stumbled from phrase to phrase, the scene made more poignant by the flashes of rhetoric his hearers knew so well.*

My lords, I rejoice that the grave has not closed upon me; that I am still alive to lift up my voice against the dismemberment of this ancient and most noble monarchy! Pressed down as I am by the hand of infirmity, I am little able to assist my country in this most perilous conjuncture; but, my lords, while I have sense and memory, I will never consent to deprive the royal offspring of the House of Brunswick, the heirs of the Princess Sophia, of their fairest inheritance. Where is the man that will dare to advise such a measure? My lords, his Majesty succeeded to an empire as great in extent as its reputation was unsullied. Shall we tarnish the lustre of this nation by an ignominious surrender of its rights and fairest possessions? Shall this great kingdom, that has survived, whole and entire, the Danish depredations, the Scottish inroads, and the Norman Conquest; that has stood the threatened invasion of the Spanish Armada, now fall prostrate before the House of Bourbon? Surely, my lords, this nation is no longer what it was! Shall a people, that seventeen years ago was the terror of the world, now stoop so low as to tell its ancient inveterate enemy, take all we have, only give us peace? It is impossible!

I wage war with no man, or set of men. I wish for none of their employments; nor would I cooperate with men who still persist in unretracted error: or who, instead of acting on a firm decisive line of conduct, halt between two opinions, where there is no middle path. In God's name, if it is absolutely necessary to declare either for peace or war, and the former cannot be preserved with honour, why is not the latter commenced without hesitation? I am not, I confess, well informed of the resources of this kingdom; but I trust it has still sufficient to maintain its just rights, though I know them not. My lords, any state is better than despair. Let us at least make one effort; and if we must fall, let us fall like men!

*When Chatham tried to rise again, he fell back in his seat and was carried insensible to his house. He died on 11 May and was buried in Westminster Abbey.*

•

## BENJAMIN FRANKLIN
### 17 September 1787

### '*I agree to this Constitution with all its faults*'

*The Constitutional Convention, held in closed sessions at Independence Hall, Philadelphia, was a unique occasion in American history, the crowning act of the American revolution. Under George Washington as president, fifty-five delegates succeeded in devising a permanent framework for the government of the American nation.*

*At eighty-one, twice the age of half the delegates, Benjamin Franklin (1706–90) attended the debates regularly. He was too old and frail to make any great mark. His chief contribution was to keep the delegates in a good humour with his sayings, jokes and stories.*

*After more than three months, the Constitution was unanimously agreed on 15 September. Two days later the convention met to receive and to sign the official parchment version. The great occasion was opened by Franklin with his last public speech, which was read for him by James Wilson, a lawyer with the Pennsylvania delegation. There was no hard sell from Franklin. This was the best Constitution that could be devised, he said, and this was the spirit in which he himself intended to accept it.*

I confess that I do not entirely approve of this Constitution at present;

but, sir, I am not sure I shall never approve of it, for, having lived long, I have experienced many instances of being obliged, by better information or fuller consideration, to change opinions even on important subjects, which I once thought right, but found to be otherwise. It is therefore that, the older I grow, the more apt I am to doubt my own judgement of others. Most men, indeed, as well as most sects in religion, think themselves in possession of all truth, and that wherever others differ from them, it is so far error. Steele, a Protestant, in a dedication, tells the pope that the only difference between our two churches in their opinions of the certainty of their doctrine is, the Romish Church is infallible, and the Church of England is never in the wrong. But, though many private persons think almost as highly of their own infallibility as of that of their sect, few express it so naturally as a certain French lady, who, in a little dispute with her sister, said: 'But I meet with nobody but myself that is always in the right.'

In these sentiments, sir, I agree to this Constitution with all its faults – if they are such – because I think a general government necessary for us, and there is no form of government but what may be a blessing to the people if well administered; and I believe, further, that this is likely to be well administered for a course of years, and can only end in despotism, as other forms have done before it, when the people shall become so corrupted as to need despotic government, being incapable of any other. I doubt, too, whether any other convention we can obtain may be able to make a better Constitution; for, when you assemble a number of men, to have the advantage of their joint wisdom, you inevitably assemble with those men all their prejudices, their passions, their errors of opinion, their local interests, and their selfish views. From such an assembly can a perfect production be expected?

It therefore astonishes me, sir, to find this system approaching so near to perfection as it does; and I think it will astonish our enemies, who are waiting with confidence to hear that our counsels are confounded like those of the builders of Babel, and that our states are on the point of separation, only to meet hereafter for the purpose of cutting one another's throats. Thus I consent, sir, to this Constitution, because I expect no better, and because I am not sure that it is not the best. The opinions I have had of its errors I sacrifice to the public good. I have never whispered a syllable of them abroad. Within these walls they were born, and here they shall die. If every one of us, in returning to our constituents, were to report the objections he has had to it, and endeavor to gain partisans in support of them, we might prevent its being generally received, and thereby lose all the salutary effects and great advantages resulting naturally in our favor among foreign nations, as well as among ourselves, from our real or apparent unanimity. Much of the strength and efficiency of any government, in procuring and securing happiness to the people, depends on opinion, on the general opinion of the goodness of that government, as well as of the wisdom and integrity of its governors. I hope, therefore, for our own sakes, as a part of the people, and for the sake of our posterity, that we shall act heartily and unanimously in recommending this Constitution wherever our influence may extend, and turn our future thoughts and endeavors to the means of having it well administered.

On the whole, sir, I can not help expressing a wish that every member of the convention who may still have objections to it, would, with me, on this occasion, doubt a little of his own infallibility, and, to make manifest our unanimity, put his name to this instrument.

●

# ALEXANDER HAMILTON
## June 1788

### 'The thing is a dream'

*The Constitution had to be ratified by at least nine states if it was to come into operation. Most moved quickly, and by April 1788 six had accepted. Maryland ratified on 26 April and South Carolina in May. Meanwhile there were furious battles in New Hampshire, Virginia and New York, where the anti-federalists were in a majority of 46 to 19.*

*That majority was overturned solely by the oratory of Alexander Hamilton (1757–1804), who had been George Washington's aide-de-camp in 1777 at the age of twenty and afterwards one of the most eminent lawyers in New York. Hamilton was one of the first advocates of a stronger central government for the thirteen states; after the Philadelphia convention he conceived the idea of the Federalist Papers and wrote fifty-one of the eighty-five himself.*

*So he was well prepared for the combat in Poughkeepsie courthouse when New York's ratifying convention, packed with his foes, opened on 17 June (with New Hampshire and Virginia still to decide). Single-handed, he kept the federalist minority together, made three major speeches, and converted many of the anti-federalists. He secured final victory by three votes after news reached New York that Virginia had ratified.*

Gentlemen indulge too many unreasonable apprehensions of danger to the state governments; they seem to suppose that the moment you put men into a national council they become corrupt and tyrannical, and lose all their affection for their fellow citizens. But can we imagine that the senators will ever be so insensible of their own advantage as to sacrifice the genuine interest of their constituents? The state governments are essentially necessary to the form and spirit of the general system. As long, therefore, as Congress has a full conviction of this necessity, they must, even upon principles purely national, have as firm an attachment to the one as to the other. This conviction can never leave them, unless they become madmen. While the Constitution continues to be read and its principle known, the states must, by every rational man, be considered as essential, component parts of the Union; and therefore the idea of sacrificing the former to the latter is wholly inadmissible . . .

There are certain social principles in human nature from which we may draw the most solid conclusions with respect to the conduct of individuals and of communities. We love our families more than our neighbors; we love our neighbors more than our countrymen in general. The human affections, like the solar heat, lose their intensity as they depart from the center, and become languid in proportion to the expansion of the circle on which they act. On these principles, the attachment of the individual will be first and forever secured by the state governments; they will be a mutual protection and support. Another source of influence, which has already been pointed out, is the various official connections in the states. Gentlemen endeavour to evade the force of this by saying that these offices will be insignificant. This is by no means true. The state officers will ever be important, because they are necessary and useful. Their powers are such as are extremely interesting to the people; such as affect their property, their liberty, and life.

What is more important than the administration of justice and the execution of the civil and criminal laws? Can the state governments become insignificant while they have the power of raising money independently and without control? If they are really useful, if they are calculated to promote the essential interests of the people, they must have their confidence and support. The states can never lose their powers till the whole people of America are robbed of their liberties. These must go together; they must support each other, or meet one common fate. On the gentleman's principle, we may safely trust the state governments, though we have no means of resisting them; but we cannot confide in the national government, though we have an effectual constitutional guard against every encroachment. This is the essence of their argument, and it is false and fallacious beyond conception.

With regard to the jurisdiction of the two governments, I shall certainly admit that the Constitution ought to be so formed as not to prevent the states from providing for their own existence; and I maintain that it is so formed, and that their power of providing for themselves is sufficiently established. This is conceded by one gentleman, and in the next breath the concession is retracted. He says Congress has but one exclusive right in taxation – that of duties on imports; certainly, then, their other powers are only concurrent. But to take off the force of this obvious conclusion he immediately says that the laws of the United States are supreme; and that where there is one supreme there cannot be a concurrent authority; and further, that where the laws of the Union are supreme, those of the states must be subordinate; because there cannot be two supremes. This is curious sophistry. That two supreme powers cannot act together is false. They are inconsistent only when they are aimed at each other or at one indivisible object. The laws of the United States are supreme as to all their proper, constitutional objects; the laws of the states are supreme in the same way. These supreme laws may act on different objects without clashing; or they may operate on different parts of the same common object with perfect harmony.

From the delinquency of those states which have suffered little by the war, we naturally conclude that they have made no efforts; and a knowledge of human nature will teach us that their ease and security have been a principal cause of their want of exertion. While danger is distant, its impression is weak; and while it affects only our neighbors, we have few motives to provide against it. Sir, if we have national objects to pursue, we must have national revenues. If you make requisitions, and they are not complied with, what is to be done? It has been observed, to coerce the states is one of the maddest projects that was ever devised. A failure of compliance will never be confined to a single state. This being the case, can we suppose it wise to hazard a civil war? Suppose Massachusetts, or any large state, should refuse, and Congress should attempt to compel them, would they not have influence to procure assistance, especially from those states which are in the same situation as themselves? What picture does this idea present to our view? A complying state at war with a noncomplying state; Congress marching the troops of one state into the bosom of another; this state collecting auxiliaries, and forming, perhaps, a majority against its federal head. Here is a nation at war with itself. Can any reasonable man be well disposed towards a government which makes war and carnage the only means of supporting itself – a government that can exist only by the sword? Every such war must involve the innocent with the guilty. This single consideration should be sufficient to dispose every peaceable citizen against such a government.

But can we believe that one state will ever suffer itself to be used as an instrument of coercion? The thing is a dream; it is impossible. Then we are brought to this dilemma – either a federal standing army is to enforce the requisitions or the federal treasury is left without supplies and the government without support. What, sir, is the cure for this great evil? Nothing but to enable the national laws to operate on individuals in the same manner as those of the states do. This is the true reasoning upon the subject, sir. The gentlemen appear to acknowledge its force; and yet, while they yield to the principle, they seem to fear its application to the government . . .

It has been said that ingenious men may say ingenious things, and that those who are interested in raising the few upon the ruins of the many may give to every cause an appearance of justice. I know not whether these insinuations allude to the characters of any who are here present or to any of the reasonings in this house. I presume that the gentlemen would not ungenerously impute such motives to those who differ from themselves. I declare I know not any set of men who are to derive peculiar advantages from this Constitution. Were any permanent honors or emoluments to be secured to the families of those who have been active in this cause, there might be some grounds for suspicion. But what reasonable man, for the precarious enjoyment of rank and power, would establish a system which would reduce his nearest friends and his posterity to slavery and ruin? If the gentlemen reckon me among the obnoxious few, if they imagine that I contemplate with ambitious eye the immediate honors of the government, yet let them consider that I have my friends, my family, my children, to whom ties of nature and of habit have attached me. If, today, I am among the favored few, my children, tomorrow, may be among the oppressed; these dear pledges of my patriotism may, at a future day, be suffering the severe distresses to which my ambition has reduced them. The changes in the human condition are uncertain and frequent: many, on whom Fortune has bestowed her favor, may trace their family to a more unprosperous station; and many, who are now in obscurity, may look back upon the affluence and exalted rank of their ancestors. But I will no longer trespass on your indulgence. I have troubled the committee with these observations, to show that it cannot be the wish of any reasonable man to establish a government unfriendly to the liberties of the people. Gentlemen ought not, then, to presume that the advocates of this Constitution are influenced by ambitious views. The suspicion, sir, is unjust; the charge is uncharitable.

*New Yorkers acknowledged the great services of Alexander Hamilton. When they hauled a model ship of state through the city, in celebration of the ratification decision, they named her the Hamilton.*

*When Washington became President, Hamilton was the first Secretary of the Treasury.*

•

# CLASHES AMONG THE GLADIATORS

## SIR ROBERT WALPOLE
### 13 February 1741

### *'I am conscious of no crime'*

*When George I, who could not speak English, grew bored with Parliament and ceased to attend, Sir Robert Walpole (1676–1745) established his supremacy by chairing on behalf of the King a small group of ministers which was the forerunner of the British Cabinet. He came to be seen as England's first prime minister and was in power for twenty-one years, to 1742.*

*By 1741, however, he had been in power too long and could count on the support of only three members of his Cabinet. A general election was imminent when the opposition introduced to Parliament a motion petitioning the King to remove Walpole from his counsels for ever. After a long and vehement discussion Walpole wound up the debate, as his biographer John Morley put it, with an animation and dignity worthy of a great minister defending a long and powerful government of the affairs of a great nation.*

It has been observed by several gentlemen, in vindication of this motion, that if it should be carried, neither my life, liberty, nor estate will be affected. But do the honourable gentlemen consider my character and reputation as of no moment? Is it no imputation to be arraigned before this House, in which I have sat forty years, and to have my name transmitted to posterity with disgrace and infamy? I will not conceal my sentiments, that to be *named* in Parliament as a subject of inquiry, is to me a matter of great concern. But I have the satisfaction, at the same time, to reflect, that the impression to be made depends upon the consistency of the charge and the motives of the prosecutors.

Had the charge been reduced to specific allegations, I should have felt myself called upon for a specific defence. Had I served a weak or wicked master, and implicitly obeyed his dictates, obedience to his commands must have been my only justification. But as it has been my good fortune to serve a master who wants no bad ministers, and would have hearkened to none, my defence must rest on my own conduct. The consciousness of innocence is also a sufficient support against my present prosecutors. A further justification is derived from a consideration of the views and abilities of the prosecutors. Had I been guilty of great enormities, they want neither zeal and inclination to bring them forward, nor ability to place them in the most prominent point of view. But as I am conscious of no crime, my own experience convinces me that none can be justly imputed . . .

Gentlemen have talked a great deal of patriotism. A venerable word, when duly practised. But I am sorry to say that of late it has been so much hackneyed about, that it is in danger of falling into disgrace. The very idea of true patriotism is lost, and the term has been prostituted to the very worst of purposes. A patriot, sir! Why, patriots spring up like mushrooms! I could raise fifty of them within the four-and-twenty hours. I have raised many of them in one night. It is but refusing to gratify an unreasonable or an insolent demand, and up starts a patriot. I have never been afraid of making patriots; but I disdain and despise all their efforts. This pretended virtue proceeds from personal malice and disappointed ambition. There is not a man among them whose particular aim I am not able to ascertain, and from what motive they have entered into the lists of opposition . . .

If my whole administration is to be scrutinized and arraigned, why are the most favourable parts to be omitted? If facts are to be accumulated on one side, why not on the other? And why may not I be permitted to speak in my own favour? Was I not called by the voice of the King and the nation to remedy the fatal effects of the South Sea project, and to support declining credit? Was I not placed at the head of the treasury when the revenues were in the greatest confusion? Is credit revived, and does it now flourish? Is it not at an incredible height? and if so, to whom must that circumstance be attributed? Has not tranquillity been preserved both at home and abroad, notwithstanding a most unreasonable and violent opposition? Has the true interest of the nation been pursued, or has trade flourished? Have gentlemen produced one instance of this exorbitant power; of the influence which I extend to all parts of the nation; of the tyranny with which I oppress those who oppose, and the liberality with which I reward those who support me? But having first invested me with a kind of mock dignity, and styled me a prime minister, they impute to me an unpardonable abuse of that chimerical authority which they only have created and conferred. If they are really persuaded that the army is annually established by me, that I have the sole disposal of posts and honours, that I employ this power in the destruction of liberty and the diminution of commerce, let me awaken them from their delusion. Let me expose to their view the real condition of the public weal. Let me show them that the Crown has made no encroachments, that all supplies have been granted by Parliament, that all questions have been debated with the same freedom as before the fatal period in which my counsels are said to have gained the ascendancy – an ascendancy from which they deduce the loss of trade, the approach of slavery, the preponderance of prerogative, and the extension of influence. But I am far from believing that they feel those apprehensions which they so earnestly labour to communicate to others; and I have too high an opinion of their sagacity not to conclude that, even in their own judgement, they are complaining of grievances that they do not suffer, and promoting rather their private interest than that of the public.

What is this unbounded sole power which is imputed to me? How has it discovered itself, or how has it been proved?

What have been the effects of the corruption, ambition, and avarice with which I am so abundantly charged?

Have I ever been suspected of being corrupted? A strange phenomenon, a corrupter himself not corrupt! Is ambition imputed to me? Why then do I still continue a commoner? I, who refused a white staff and a peerage? I had, indeed, like to have forgotten the little ornament about my shoulders [the garter], which gentlemen have so repeatedly mentioned in terms of sarcastic obloquy. But surely, though this may be regarded with envy or indignation in another place, it cannot be supposed to raise any resentment in *this* House, where many may be pleased to see those honours which their ancestors have worn, restored again to the Commons.

Have I given any symptoms of an avaricious disposition? Have I obtained any grants from the Crown since I have been placed at the head of the treasury? Has my conduct been different from that which others in the same station would have followed? Have I acted wrong in giving the place of auditor to my son, and in providing for my own family? I trust that their advancement will not be imputed to me as a crime, unless it shall be proved that I placed them in offices of trust and responsibility for which they were unfit.

But while I unequivocally deny that I am sole and prime minister, and that to my influence and direction all the measures of the government must be attributed, yet I will not shrink from the responsibility which attaches to the post I have the honour to hold; and should, during the long period in which I have sat upon this bench, any one step taken by government be proved to be either disgraceful or disadvantageous to the nation, I am ready to hold myself accountable.

To conclude, sir, though I shall always be proud of the honour of any trust or confidence from His Majesty, yet I shall always be ready to remove from his councils and presence when he thinks fit; and therefore I should think myself very little concerned in the event of the present question, if it were not for the encroachment that will thereby be made upon the prerogatives of the Crown. But I must think that an address to His Majesty to remove one of his servants, without so much as alleging any particular crime against him, is one of the greatest encroachments that was ever made upon the prerogatives of the Crown. And therefore, for the sake of my master, without any regard for my own, I hope all those that have a due regard for our constitution, and for the rights and prerogatives of the Crown, without which our constitution cannot be preserved, will be against this motion.

*The speech was a success and the motion for an address to the King defeated. But Walpole was compelled to resign a year later.*

•

## WILLIAM PITT, 1st EARL OF CHATHAM
### 9 January 1770

### 'Where law ends, there tyranny begins'

*John Wilkes was expelled from Parliament and outlawed in 1764 after his paper,* The North Briton, *was convicted of seditious libel.*

*The subsequent Wilkes controversy highlighted an important constitutional conflict, between those who believed parliamentary privileges should be safeguarded from the Crown and the mob, and those who believed that the Commons had no right to outlaw a member or flout the electorate.*

*In this speech to the House of Lords, made after an absence of three years, Chatham placed himself firmly on the side of the freedom of the people and the principles of liberty on which the Constitution had been based since Magna Carta.*

My lords, I affirm, and am ready to maintain, that the late decision of the House of Commons upon the Middlesex election is destitute of every one of those properties and conditions which I hold to be essential to the legality of such a decision. It is not founded in reason; for it carries with it a contradiction, that the representative should perform the office of the constituent body. It is not supported by a single precedent . . .

It contradicts Magna Carta and the Bill of Rights, by which it is provided, that no subject shall be deprived of his freehold, unless by the judgement of his peers, or the law of the land; and that elections of members to serve in Parliament shall be free; and so far is this decision from being submitted to by the people that they have taken the strongest measures and adopted the most positive language to express their discontent. Whether it will be questioned by the legislature, will depend upon your lordships' resolution; but that it violates the spirit of the constitution will, I think, be disputed by no man who has heard this day's debate, and who wishes well to the freedom of his country; yet, if we are to believe the noble lord, this great grievance, this manifest violation of the first principles of the constitution, will not admit of a remedy; is not even capable of redress, unless we appeal at once to Heaven. My lords, I have better hopes of the constitution, and a firmer confidence in the wisdom and constitutional authority of this House. It is to your ancestors, my lords, it is to the English barons that we are indebted for the laws and constitution we possess. Their virtues were rude and uncultivated, but they were great and sincere. Their understandings were as little polished as their manners, but they had hearts to distinguish right from wrong; they had heads to distinguish truth from falsehood; they understood the rights of humanity, and they had spirit to maintain them.

My lords, I think that history has not done justice to their conduct, when they obtained from their sovereign that great acknowledgement of national rights contained in Magna Carta; they did not confine it to themselves alone, but delivered it as a common blessing to the whole people. They did not say, These are the rights of the great barons, or these are the rights of the great prelates; no, my lords, they said, in the simple Latin of the times, *nullus liber homo*, and provided as carefully for the meanest subject as for the greatest. These are uncouth words, and sound but poorly in the ears of scholars; neither are they addressed to the criticism of scholars, but to the hearts of free men. These three words, *nullus liber homo*, have a meaning which interests us all; they deserve to be remembered – they are worth all the classics. Let us not, then, degenerate from the glorious example of our ancestors. Those iron barons (for so I may call them when compared with the silken barons of modern days) were the guardians of the people; yet their virtues, my lords, were never engaged in a question of such importance as the present. A breach has been made in the constitution – the battlements are dismantled – the citadel is open to the first invader – the walls totter – the place is no longer tenable. What then remains for us but to stand foremost in the breach, to repair it, or to perish in it? . . .

There is one ambition at least which I ever will acknowledge, which I will not renounce but with my life – it is the ambition of delivering to my posterity those rights of freedom which I have received from my ancestors. I am not now pleading the cause of an individual, but of every freeholder in England . . . Unlimited power is apt to corrupt the minds of those who possess it; and this I know, my Lords, that where law ends, there tyranny begins.

•

## EDMUND BURKE
### 3 November 1774

### 'He is not a member of Bristol, but he is a member of Parliament'

*At the general election of 1774, Edmund Burke was asked to stand by the electors of Bristol. After his election, he delivered an address at the city's Guildhall in which he gave his famous definition of a Member of Parliament's duty to his constituents, still quoted frequently more than two centuries later.*

I owe myself, in all things, to *all* the freemen of this city. My particular friends have a demand on me that I should not deceive their expectations. Never was cause or man supported with more constancy, more activity, more spirit. I have been supported with a zeal indeed and heartiness in my friends, which (if their object had been at all proportioned to their endeavours) could never be sufficiently commended. They supported me upon the most liberal principles. They wished that the members for Bristol should be chosen for the city, and for their country at large, and not for themselves.

So far they are not disappointed. If I possess nothing else, I am sure I possess the temper that is fit for your service. I know nothing of Bristol but by the favours I have received and the virtues I have seen exerted in it.

I shall ever retain, what I now feel, the most perfect and grateful attachment to my friends – and I have no enmities, no resentment. I never can consider fidelity to engagements and constancy in friendships but with the highest approbation, even when those noble qualities are employed against my own pretensions. The gentleman who is not fortunate as I have been in this contest, enjoys in this respect a consolation full of honour both to himself and to his friends. They have certainly left nothing undone for his service.

As for the trifling petulance which the rage of party stirs up in little minds, though it should show itself even in this court, it has not made the slightest impression on me. The highest flight of such clamorous birds is winged in an inferior region of the air. We hear them, and we look upon them just as you, gentlemen, when you enjoy the serene air on your lofty rocks, look down upon the gulls that skim the mud of your river when it is exhausted of its tide.

I am sorry I cannot conclude without saying a word on a topic touched upon by my worthy colleague. I wish that topic had been passed by at a time when I have so little leisure to discuss it. But since he has thought proper to throw it out, I owe you a clear explanation of my poor sentiments on that subject.

He tells you that 'the topic of instructions has occasioned much altercation and uneasiness in this city'; and he expresses himself (if I understand him rightly) in favour of the coercive authority of such instructions.

Certainly, gentlemen, it ought to be the happiness and glory of a representative to live in the strictest union, the closest correspondence, and the most unreserved communication with his constituents. Their wishes ought to have great weight with him; their opinion high respect; their business unremitted attention. It is his duty to sacrifice his repose, his pleasure, his satisfactions, to theirs; and, above all, ever, and in all cases, to prefer their interest to his own.

To deliver an opinion is the right of all men; that of constituents is a weighty and respectable opinion, which a representative ought always to rejoice to hear, and which he ought always most seriously to consider. But authoritative instructions, mandates issued which the member is bound blindly and implicitly to obey, to vote and to argue for, though contrary to the clearest conviction of his judgement and conscience: these are things utterly unknown to the laws of this land, and which arise from a fundamental mistake of the whole order and tenor of our constitution.

Parliament is not a congress of ambassadors from different and hostile interests, which interests each must maintain, as an agent and advocate, against other agents and advocates; but Parliament is a deliberative assembly of one nation with one interest – that of the whole: where, not local purposes, not local prejudices ought to guide, but the general good, resulting from the general reason of the whole. You choose a member, indeed; but when you have chosen him, he is not a member of Bristol, but he is a member of Parliament. If the local constituent should have an interest or should form an hasty opinion, evidently opposite to the real good of the rest of the community, the member for that place ought to be as far, as any other, from any endeavour to give it effect. I beg pardon for saying so much on this subject. I have been unwillingly drawn into it, but I shall ever use a respectful frankness of communication with you. Your faithful friend, your devoted servant, I shall be to the end of my life; a flatterer you do not wish for.

But his unbiased opinion, his mature judgement, his enlightened conscience, he ought not to sacrifice to you – to any man, or to any set of men living. These he does not derive from your pleasure; no, nor from the law and the constitution. They are a trust from Providence, for the abuse of which he is deeply answerable. Your representative owes you, not his industry only, but his judgement; and he betrays, instead of serving, you if he sacrifices it to your opinion.

My worthy colleague says his will ought to be subservient to yours. If that be all, the thing is innocent. If government were a matter of will upon any side, yours, without question, ought to be superior. But government and legislation are matters of reason and judgement, and not of inclination; and what sort of reason is that in which the determination precedes the discussion? in which one set of men deliberate, and another decide? and where those who form the conclusion are perhaps three hundred miles distant from those who hear the arguments?

*Burke neglected Bristol, and his constituents resented his outspoken position on the major issues of the day. Six years later, he withdrew his candidacy.*

●

### JOHN WILKES
22 February 1775

*'The wounds given to the Constitution . . . are still bleeding'*

*After being expelled from Parliament and outlawed in 1764, John Wilkes (1725–97) clashed continually with the King, George III, and the Commons, especially after he returned to Britain and was again elected to Parliament by Middlesex. He was elected and expelled four times, until the government declared his unsuccessful opponent duly elected. The people of London rose against the threat of tyranny from a corrupt Parliament.*

*Wilkes, whose clashes with the King and the Commons established fundamental liberties of the individual and led to the setting up of the Bill of Rights Society – the first to use modern methods of agitation – put his case in this speech to the Commons.*

The motion which I shall have the honour of submitting to the House affects, in my opinion, the very vitals of this Constitution, the great primary sources of the power of the people, whom we represent, and by whose authority only, delegated to us for a time, we are a part of the legislative body of this kingdom. The proceedings of the last Parliament in the business of the Middlesex elections gave a just alarm to almost every elector in the nation. The fatal precedents then attempted to be established were considered as a direct attack on the inalienable rights of the people. The most respectable bodies in this kingdom expressed their abhorrence of the measure: they proceeded so far as to petition the Crown for the dissolution of that Parliament, as having been guilty of a flagrant abuse of their trust. Above sixty thousand of our fellow subjects carried their complaints to the foot of the throne; a number surely deserving the highest regard from a minister, if his whole attention had not been engrossed by the small number of the six thousand who return the majority of members to this House. The people, sir, were in a ferment, which has not yet subsided. They made my cause their own, for they saw the powers of government exerted against the Constitution, which was wounded through my sides; and the envenomed shafts of a wicked administration pointed at our laws and liberties, no less at a hated individual. The plan was carried on for some years with a spirit of malevolence and rancour which would have disgraced the very worst, but with a perseverance which would have done honour to the best cause. I do not mean, sir, to go through the variety of persecutions and injuries which that person suffered, I hope, with a becoming fortitude. I have forgiven them. All the great powers of the state at one time appeared combined to pour their vengeance on me. Even imperial Jove pointed his thunderbolts, red with uncommon wrath, at my devoted head. I was scorched, but not consumed. The broad shield of the law protected me. A generous public, and my noble friends, the freeholders of Middlesex, the ever-steady friends of liberty and their country, poured balm into my wounds; they are healed. Scarcely a scar remains:

but I feel, I deeply feel, the wounds given to the Constitution; they are still bleeding; this House only can heal them: they only can restore the Constitution to its former state of purity, health, and vigour . . .

In the first formation of this government, in the original settlement of our Constitution, the people expressly reserved to themselves a very considerable part of the legislative power, which they consented to share jointly with a King and House of Lords. From the great population of our island, this power could not be exercised personally, and therefore the many were compelled to delegate that power to a few; who thus became their deputies and agents only, or their representatives. It follows directly, from the very idea of choice, that such choice must be free and uncontrolled, admitting of no restrictions but the law of the land, to which King and lords are equally subject, and what must arise from the nature of the trust. A peer of Parliament, for instance, cannot be elected a member of the House of Commons, because he already forms part of another branch of the same legislative body. A lunatic has a natural incapacity. Other instances might be mentioned, but those two are sufficient. The freedom of election is, then, the common right of the people, their fair and just share of power; and I hold it to be the most glorious inheritance of every subject of this realm, the noblest and, I trust, the most solid part of that beautiful fabric, the English Constitution . . .

But, sir, if you can expel whom you please, and reject those disagreeable to you, the House will be self-created and self-existing. The original idea of your representing the people will be lost. The consequences of such a principle are to the highest degree alarming. A more forcible engine of despotism cannot be put into the hands of any minister. I wish gentlemen would attend to the plain consequences of such proceedings, and consider how they may be brought home to themselves. A member hated or dreaded by the minister is accused of any crime; for instance, of having written a pretended libel. I mention this instance as the crime least likely to be committed by most of the members of this House. No proof whatever is given on oath before you, because you cannot administer an oath. The minister invades immediately the rights of juries. Before any trial, he gets the paper voted a libel, and the member he wishes expelled to be the author – which fact you are not competent to try. Expulsion means, as is pretended, incapacity. The member is adjudged incapable; he cannot be re-elected, and thus is he excluded from Parliament. A minister by such manoeuvres may garble a House of Commons till not a single enemy of his own, or friend of his country, is left here, and the representation of the people is in a great degree lost.

Corruption had not lent despotism wings to fly so high in the time of Charles I, or the minister of that day would have been contented with expelling Hampden and the four other heroes, because they had immediately been adjudged incapable, and he would thereby have incapacitated them from thwarting in Parliament the arbitrary measures of a wicked court. Upon all these considerations, in order to quiet the minds of the people, to restore our violated Constitution to its original purity, to vindicate the injured rights of this country in particular, and of all the electors of this kingdom, and that not the least trace of the violence and injustice of the last Parliament may disgrace our records, I humbly move, 'That the resolution of this House of the seventeenth of February, 1769, "That John Wilkes, Esq., having been in this session of Parliament expelled this House, *was* and *is* incapable of sitting in the present Parliament," be expunged from the journals of this House, as being subversive of the rights of the whole body of electors of this kingdom.'

•

## CHARLES JAMES FOX
### 1 December 1783

### 'The most odious species of tyranny'

*Charles James Fox (1749–1806), a lover of liberty, was the greatest parliamentary gladiator in the history of British politics. A brilliant, impetuous speaker, he was the only man who could stand up to William Pitt the Younger without being worsted. According to Edmund Burke he was the greatest speaker the world ever saw.*

*'His speeches were things of the moment, never prepared . . . mere flashes of genius, but the Commons valued them above all the classic periods and intricate exposition of his rivals,' says one biographer.*

*The Fox–North coalition government was formed in 1783 after William Pitt the Younger refused to become prime minister. Fox immediately introduced his India Reform Bill, transferring the affairs of the East India Company to seven commissioners appointed first by Parliament and later by the Crown. He described in this speech to the Commons the rapacity of the company which, although it had laid the foundations for British rule, had left many provinces impoverished and shorn of rights and sovereignty.*

Freedom, according to my conception of it, consists in the safe and sacred possession of a man's property, governed by laws defined and certain; with many personal privileges, natural, civil, and religious, which he cannot surrender without ruin to himself; and of which to be deprived by any other power is despotism. This bill, instead of subverting, is destined to give stability to these principles; instead of narrowing the basis of freedom, it tends to enlarge it; instead of suppressing, its object is to infuse and circulate the spirit of liberty.

What is the most odious species of tyranny? Precisely that which this bill is meant to annihilate. That a handful of men, free themselves, should execute the most base and abominable despotism over millions of their fellow creatures; that innocence should be the victim of oppression; that industry should toil for rapine; that the harmless labourer should sweat, not for his own benefit, but for the luxury and rapacity of tyrannic depredation; in a word, that thirty millions of men, gifted by Providence with the ordinary endowments of humanity, should groan under a system of despotism unmatched in all the histories of the world.

What is the end of all government? Certainly the happiness of the governed. Others may hold other opinions, but this is mine, and I proclaim it. What are we to think of a government whose good fortune is supposed to spring from the calamities of its subjects, whose aggrandizement grows out of the miseries of mankind? This is the kind of government exercised under the East India Company upon the natives of Hindustan; and the subversion of that infamous government is the main object of the bill in question. But in the progress of accomplishing this end, it is objected that the charter of the company should not be violated; and upon this point, sir, I shall deliver my opinion without disguise. A charter is a trust to one or more persons for some given benefit. If this trust be abused, if the benefit be not obtained, and its failure arise from palpable guilt, or (what in this case is full as bad) from palpable ignorance or mismanagement, will any man gravely say that that trust should not be resumed and delivered to other hands, more especially in the case of the East India Company, whose manner of executing this trust, whose laxity and languor have produced, and tend to produce, consequences diametrically opposite to the ends of confiding that trust, and of the institution for which it was granted? I beg of gentlemen to be aware of the lengths to which their arguments upon the intangibility of this charter may be carried. Every syllable virtually impeaches the establishment by which we sit in this House, in the enjoyment of this freedom, and of every other blessing of our government. These kinds of arguments are batteries against the main pillar of the British Constitution. Some men are consistent with their own private opinions, and discover the inheritance of family maxims, when they question the principles of the Revolution; but I have no scruple in subscribing to the articles of that creed which produced it. Sovereigns are sacred, and reverence is due to every king; yet, with all my attachments to the person of a first magistrate, had I lived in the reign of James II, I should most certainly have contributed my efforts and borne part in those illustrious struggles which vindicated an empire from hereditary servitude, and recorded this valuable doctrine, 'that trust abused is revocable'.

No man, sir, will tell me that a trust to a company of merchants stands upon the solemn and sanctified ground by which a trust is committed to a monarch; and I am at a loss to reconcile the conduct of men who approve that resumption of violated trust, which rescued and re-established our unparalleled and admirable Constitution with a thousand valuable improvements and advantages at the Revolution, and who, at this moment, rise up the champions of the East India Company's charter, although the incapacity and incompetency of that company to a due and adequate discharge of the trust deposited in them by that charter are themes of ridicule and contempt to the world; and although, in consequence of their mismanagement, connivance, and imbecility, combined with the wickedness of their servants, the very name of an Englishman is detested, even to a proverb, through all Asia, and the national character is become degraded and dishonoured. To rescue that name from odium and redeem this character from disgrace are some of the objects of the present bill; and, gentlemen should, indeed, gravely weigh their opposition to a measure which, with a thousand other points not less valuable, aims at the attainment of these objects.

Those who condemn the present bill as a violation of the chartered rights of the East India Company condemn, on the same ground, I say again, the Revolution as a violation of the chartered rights of King James II. He, with as much reason, might have claimed the property of dominion; but what was the language of the people? 'No; you have no property in dominion; dominion was vested in you, as it is in every chief magistrate, for the benefit of the community to be governed; it was a sacred trust delegated by compact; you have abused that trust; you have exercised dominion for the purposes of vexation and tyranny – not of comfort, protection, and good order; and we, therefore, resume the power which was originally ours; we recur to the first principles of all government – the will of the many, and it is our will that you shall no longer abuse your dominion.' The case is the same with the East India Company's government over a territory, as it has been said by my honourable friend [Mr Burke], of two hundred and eighty thousand square miles in extent, nearly equal to all Christian Europe, and containing thirty millions of the human race. It matters not whether dominion arise from conquest or from compact. Conquest gives no right to the conqueror to be a tyrant; and it is no violation of right to abolish the authority which is misused . . .

•

## EDMUND BURKE
### 1 December 1783

### '*He is doing indeed a great good*'

*Fox's India Reform Bill alienated the City – and the beneficial effect of the bill on his own fortunes was also noted. He did, however, win the support of Edmund Burke, who in this speech made on the same night described contemptuously the parade of young officials sent out to India – and ended with a eulogy of Fox.*

The natives scarcely know what it is to see the grey head of an Englishman. Young men (boys almost) govern there, without society, and without sympathy with the natives. They have no more social habits with the people than if they still resided in England; nor, indeed, any species of intercourse but that which is necessary to making a sudden fortune, with a view to a remote settlement. Animated with all the avarice of age, and all the impetuosity of youth, they roll in one after another; wave after wave; and there is nothing before the eyes of the natives but an endless, hopeless prospect of new flights of birds of prey and passage, with appetites continually renewing for a food that is continually wasting . . .

And now, having done my duty to the bill, let me say a word to the author. I should leave him to his own noble sentiments if the unworthy and illiberal language with which he has been treated, beyond all example of parliamentary liberty, did not make a few words necessary; not so much in justice to him as to my own feelings. I must say, then, that it will be a distinction honourable to the age that the rescue of the greatest number of the human race that ever were so grievously oppressed, from the greatest tyranny that was ever exercised, has fallen to the lot of abilities and dispositions equal to the task; that it has fallen to one who has the enlargement to comprehend, the spirit to undertake, and the eloquence to support, so great a measure of hazardous benevolence. His spirit is not owing to his ignorance of the state of men and things; he well knows what snares are spread about his path, from personal animosity, from court intrigues, and possibly from popular delusion. But he has put to hazard his ease, his security, his interest, his power, even his darling popularity, for the benefit of a people whom he has never seen. This is the road that all heroes have trod before him. He is traduced and abused for his supposed motives. He will remember that obloquy is a necessary ingredient in the composition of all true glory: he will remember that it was not only in the Roman customs, but it is in the nature and constitution of things, that calumny and abuse are essential parts of triumph. These thoughts will support a mind which only exists for honour, under the burden of temporary reproach. He is doing indeed a great good; such as rarely falls to the lot, and almost as rarely coincides with the desires, of any man. Let him use his time. Let him give the whole length of the reins to his benevolence. He is now on a great eminence, where the eyes of mankind are turned to him. He may live long, he may do much. But here is the summit. He never can exceed what he does this day . . .

I have spoken what I think, and what I feel, of the mover of this bill. An honourable friend of mine, speaking of his merits, was charged with having made a studied panegyric; I don't know what his was. Mine, I am sure, is a studied panegyric; the fruit of much meditation; the result of the observation of near twenty years. For my own part, I am happy that I have lived to see this day; I feel myself overpaid for the labours of eighteen years when, at this late period, I am able to take my share, by one humble vote, in destroying a tyranny that exists to the disgrace of this nation, and the destruction of so large a part of the human species.

•

## CHARLES JAMES FOX
### 17 December 1783

### 'What is the difference between an absolute and a limited monarchy?'

*As the controversy over Fox's East India bill intensified, the King let it be known that he would deem those who voted for Fox his enemies. A debate on ministerial responsibility and the influence of the Crown was initiated – when Fox made this coruscating attack on the 'secret influence' of George III.*

So much has been said about the captivity of the throne, while His Majesty acts only in concert with his ministers, that one would imagine the spirit and soul of the British Constitution were yet unknown in this House. It is wisely established as a fundamental maxim, that the King can do no wrong; that whatever blunders or even crimes may be chargeable on the executive power, the Crown is still faultless? But how? Not by suffering tyranny and oppression in a free government to pass with impunity; certainly not: but the minister who advises or executes an unconstitutional measure, does it at his peril; and he ought to know, that Englishmen are not only jealous of their rights, but legally possessed of powers, competent on every such emergency to redress their wrongs. What is the distinction between an absolute and a limited monarchy? but that the sovereign, in the one, is a despot, and may do what he pleases; but in the other, is himself subjected to the laws, and consequently not at liberty to advise with any one on public affairs not responsible for that advice; and the Constitution has clearly directed his negative to operate under the same wise restrictions. These prerogatives are by no means vested in the Crown to be exerted in a wanton and arbitrary manner. The good of the whole is the exclusive object to which all the branches of the legislature and their different powers invariably point. Whoever interferes with this primary and supreme direction, must, in the highest degree, be unconstitutional. Should, therefore, His Majesty be disposed to check the progress of the legislature in accomplishing any measure of importance, either by giving countenance to an invidious whisper, or the exertion of his negative, without at the same time consulting the safety of his ministers, here would be an instance of maladministration for which, on that supposition, the Constitution has provided no remedy. And God forbid that ever the Constitution of this country should be found defective in a point so material and indispensable to public welfare.

Sir, it is a public and crying grievance that we are not the first who have felt this secret influence. It seems to be a habit against which no change of men or measures can operate with success. It has overturned a more able and popular minister [*Lord Chatham*] than the present, and bribed him with a peerage, for which his best friends never cordially forgave him. The scenes, the times, the politics, and the system of the court, may shift with the party that predominates, but this dark mysterious engine is not only formed to control every ministry, but to enslave the Constitution.

To this infernal spirit of intrigue we owe that incessant fluctuation in

His Majesty's councils, by which the spirit of government is so much relaxed, and all its minutest objects so fatally deranged. During the strange and ridiculous interregnum of last year, I had not a doubt in my own mind with whom it originated; and I looked to an honourable gentleman [*Jenkinson*] opposite to me, the moment the grounds of objection to the East India bill were stated. The same illiberal and plodding cabal who then invested the throne, and darkened the royal mind with ignorance and misconception, have once more been employed to act the same part. But how will the genius of Englishmen brook the insult? Is this enlightened and free country, which has so often and successfully struggled against every species of undue influence, to revert to those Gothic ages, when princes were tyrants, ministers minions, and government intriguing? Much and gloriously did this House fight and overcome the influence of the Crown by purging itself of ministerial dependants: but what was the contractors' bill, the board of trade, or a vote of the revenue officers, compared to a power equal to one-third of the legislature, unanswerable for, and unlimited in its acting? Against these we had always to contend; but we knew their strength, we saw their disposition, they fought under no covert, they were a powerful, not a sudden enemy. To compromise the matter, therefore, sir, it would become this House to say, rather than yield to a stretch of prerogative thus unprecedented and alarming, withdraw your secret influence, and, whatever entrenchments have been made on the Crown, we are ready to repair: take back those numerous and tried dependants who so often secured you a majority in Parliament; we submit to all the mischief which even this accession of strength is likely to produce: but for God's sake strangle us not in the very moment we look for success and triumph by an infamous string of bedchamber janissaries! . . .

For my own part, I ever thought public confidence the only substantial basis of a sound administration. The people of England have made me what I am; it was at their instance I have been called to a station in their service; and, perhaps, it would not be treating them well, hastily to abandon the post to which they have generously raised me. The whole of that respectable arrangement in which I am an individual, are, in my opinion, bound in honour to do something at least for thirty millions of innocent people, whose expectations have been raised and flattered by our exertions; who have long struggled under every oppression, and grappled with their fate in vain; whose wretched and deplorable circumstances affect the British character in every corner of the world with infamy and horror; and who, at this moment, in spite of every exertion both of the legislature and court of directors, groan under the scourge, the extortion, and the massacre, of a cruel and desperate man, whom, in my conscience and from my heart, I detest and execrate.

*Fox's bill was carried by the Commons, but defeated in the Lords the same day. He was dismissed next day. William Pitt the Younger became prime minister and the long contest between two of Britain's greatest parliamentarians began.*

•

## EDMUND BURKE
### 15–19 February 1788

### 'I impeach Warren Hastings'

*After serving as Governor-General of India for eleven years, Warren Hastings returned to England in 1786 a hero. He was fêted by the East India Company, befriended by George III and recognized for his services by Pitt. Yet he was soon accused of arbitrary and tyrannical government. Burke led the attack on him, with Richard Sheridan in support. On 3 April 1787, the Commons voted to impeach Hastings and the scene was set for the greatest political trial in England's history.*

*As the seven-year trial, heard over 145 days, opened in Westminster Hall before the House of Lords, Burke, speaking for six days, supported the prosecution and delivered a thundering indictment of Hastings and his conduct of office.*

The crimes, which we charge in these articles, are not lapses, defects, errors, of common human frailty, which, as we know and feel, we can allow for. We charge this offender with no crimes, that have not arisen from passions, which it is criminal to harbour; with no offences, that have not their root in avarice, rapacity, pride, insolence, ferocity, treachery, cruelty, malignity of temper; in short, in nothing, that does not argue a total extinction of all moral principle; that does not manifest an inveterate blackness of heart, dyed in grain with malice, vitiated, corrupted, gangrened to the very core. If we do not plant his crimes in those vices, which the breast of man is made to abhor, and the spirit of all laws, human and divine, to interdict, we desire no longer to be heard upon this occasion. Let everything that can be pleaded on the ground of surprise or error, upon those grounds be pleaded with success: we give up the whole of those predicaments. We urge no crimes, that were not crimes of forethought. We charge him with nothing, that he did not commit upon deliberation; that he did not commit against advice, supplication, and remonstrance; that he did not commit against the direct command of lawful authority; that he did not commit after reproof and reprimand, the reproof and reprimand of those, who are authorized by the laws to reprove and reprimand him. The crimes of Mr Hastings are crimes not only in themselves, but aggravated by being crimes of contumacy. They were crimes not against forms, but against those eternal laws of justice, which are our rule and our birthright. His offences are not, in formal, technical language, but in reality, in substance, and effect, *high* crimes and high misdemeanours.

So far as to the crimes. As to the criminal, we have chosen him on the same principle, on which we selected the crimes. We have not chosen to bring before you a poor, puny, trembling delinquent, misled, perhaps, by those, who ought to have taught him better, but who have afterwards oppressed him by their power, as they had first corrupted him by their example. Instances there have been many, wherein the punishment of minor offences, in inferior persons, has been made the means of screening crimes of an high order, and in men of high description. Our course is different. We have not brought before you an obscure offender, who, when his insignificance and weakness are weighed against the power of the prosecution, gives even to public justice something of the appearance of oppression; no, my lords, we have brought before you the first man of India in rank, authority, and station. We have brought before you the chief of the tribe, the head of the whole body of eastern offenders; a captain-general of iniquity, under whom all the fraud, all the peculation, all the tyranny, in India, are embodied, disciplined, arrayed, and paid. This is the person, my lords, that we bring before you. We have brought before you such a person, that, if you strike at him with the firm and decided arm of justice, you will not have need of a great many more examples. You strike at the whole corps, if you strike at the head . . .

My lords, I do not mean now to go farther than just to remind your lordships of this – that Mr Hastings' government was one whole system of oppression, of robbery of individuals, of spoliation of the public, and of supersession of the whole system of the English government, in order to vest in the worst of the natives all the power that could possibly exist in any government; in order to defeat the ends which all governments ought, in common, to have in view. In the name of the Commons of England, I charge all this villainy upon Warren Hastings, in this last moment of my application to you.

I, therefore, charge Mr Hastings with having destroyed, for private purposes, the whole system of government by the six provincial councils, which he had no right to destroy.

I charge him with having delegated to others that power, which the act of Parliament had directed him to preserve unalienably in himself.

I charge him with having formed a committee to be mere instruments and tools, at the enormous expense of £62,000 per annum.

I charge him with having appointed a person their dewan, to whom these Englishmen were to be subservient tools; whose name to his own knowledge, was by the general voice of India, by the general recorded voice of the company, by recorded official transactions, by everything, that can make a man known, abhorred, and detested, stamped with infamy; and with giving him the whole power, which he had thus separated from the council general, and from the provincial councils.

I charge him with taking bribes of Gunga Govin Sing.

I charge him with not having done that bribe service, which fidelity even in iniquity requires at the hands of the worst of men.

I charge him with having robbed those people, of whom he took the bribes.

I charge him with having fraudulently alienated the fortunes of widows.

I charge him with having, without right, title, or purchase, taken the lands of orphans, and given them to wicked persons under him.

I charge him with having removed the natural guardians of a minor rajah, and with having given that trust to a stranger, Debi Sing, whose wickedness was known to himself and all the world; and by whom the rajah, his family, and dependants were cruelly oppressed.

I charge him with having committed to the management of Debi Sing three great provinces; and thereby, with having wasted the country, ruined the landed interest, cruelly harassed the peasants, burnt their houses, seized their crops, tortured and degraded their persons, and destroyed the honour of the whole female race of that country.

In the name of the Commons of England, I charge all this villainy upon Warren Hastings, in this last moment of my application to you.

My lords, what is it, that we want here to a great act of national justice? Do we want a cause, my lords? You have the cause of oppressed princes, of undone women of the first rank, of desolated provinces, and of wasted kingdoms.

Do you want a criminal, my lords? When was there so much iniquity ever laid to the charge of any one? No, my lords, you must not look to punish any other such delinquent from India. Warren Hastings has not left substance enough in India to nourish such another delinquent.

My lords, is it a prosecutor you want? You have before you the Commons of Great Britain as prosecutors; and, I believe, my lords, that the sun, in his beneficent progress round the world, does not behold a more glorious sight than that of men, separated from a remote people by the material bounds and barriers of nature, united by the bond of a social and moral community; all the Commons of England resenting, as their own, the indignities and cruelties, that are offered to all the people of India.

Do we want a tribunal? My lords, no example of antiquity, nothing in the modern world, nothing in the range of human imagination, can supply us with a tribunal like this. My lords, here we see virtually in the mind's eye that sacred majesty of the Crown, under whose authority you sit, and whose power you exercise. We see in that invisible authority, what we all feel in reality and life, the beneficent powers and protecting justice of his majesty. We have here the heir apparent to the Crown, such as the fond wishes of the people of England wish an heir apparent of the Crown to be. We have here all the branches of the royal family in a situation between majesty and subjection, between the sovereign and the subject – offering a pledge in that situation for the support of the rights of the Crown, and the liberties of the people, both which extremities they touch. My lords, we have a great hereditary peerage here; those, who have their own honour, the honour of their ancestors, and of their posterity, to guard; and who will justify, as they have always justified, that provision in the Constitution, by which justice is made an hereditary office. My lords, we have here a new nobility, who have arisen and exalted themselves by various merits, by great military services, which have extended the fame of this country from the rising to the setting sun: we have those, who by various civil merits and various civil talents have been exalted to a situation, which they well deserve, and in which they will justify the favour of their sovereign, and the good opinion of their fellow subjects; and make them rejoice to see those virtuous characters, that were the other day upon a level with them, now exalted above them in rank, but feeling with them in sympathy what they felt in common with them before. We have persons exalted from the practice of the law, from the place, in which they administered high, though subordinate, justice, to a seat here, to en-lighten with their knowledge, and to strengthen with their votes those principles, which have distinguished the courts, in which they have presided.

My lords, you have here also the lights of our religion; you have the bishops of England. My lords, you have that true image of the primitive church in its ancient form, in its ancient ordinances, purified from the superstitions and the vices, which a long succession of ages will bring upon the best institutions. You have the representatives of that religion, which says, that their God is love, that the very vital spirit of their institution is charity; a religion, which so much hates oppression, that, when the God, whom we adore, appeared in human form, he did not appear in a form of greatness and majesty, but in sympathy with the lowest of the people – and thereby made it a firm and ruling principle, that their welfare was the object of all government; since the person, who was the Master of Nature, chose to appear himself in a subordinate situation. These are the considerations, which influence them, which animate them, and will animate them, against all oppression; knowing, that He, who is called first among them, and first among us all, both of the flock that is fed, and of those who feed it, made Himself 'the servant of all'.

My lords, these are the securities, which we have in all the constituent parts of the body of this house. We know them, we reckon, we rest upon them, and commit safely the interests of India and of humanity into your hands. Therefore, it is with confidence, that, ordered by the Commons –

I impeach Warren Hastings, Esq., of high crimes and misdemeanours.

I impeach him in the name of the Commons of Great Britain in Parliament assembled, whose parliamentary trust he has betrayed.

I impeach him in the name of all the Commons of Great Britain, whose national character he has dishonoured.

I impeach him in the name of the people of India, whose laws, rights, and liberties he has subverted; whose properties he has destroyed, whose country he has laid waste and desolate.

I impeach him in the name, and by virtue of those eternal laws of justice, which he has violated.

I impeach him in the name of human nature itself, which he has cruelly outraged, injured, and oppressed in both sexes, in every age, rank, situation, and condition of life.

My lords, at this awful close, in the name of the Commons and surrounded by them, I attest the retiring, I attest the advancing generations, between which, as a link in the great chain of eternal order, we stand. We call this nation, we call the world to witness, that the Commons have shrunk from no labour; that we have been guilty of no prevarication; that we have made no compromise with crime; that we have not feared any odium whatsoever, in the long warfare which we have carried on with the crimes, with the vices, with the exorbitant wealth, with the enormous and overpowering influence of Eastern corruption.

My lords, it has pleased Providence to place us in such a state that we appear every moment to be upon the verge of some great mutations. There is one thing, and one thing only, which defies all mutation: that which existed before the world, and will survive the fabric of the world itself – I mean justice; that justice which, emanating from the Divinity, has a place in the breast of every one of us, given us for our guide with regard to ourselves and with regard to others, and which will stand, after this globe is burned to ashes, our advocate or our accuser, before the great Judge, when He comes to call upon us for the tenor of a well-spent life.

My lords, the Commons will share in every fate with your lordships; there is nothing sinister which can happen to you, in which we shall not all be involved; and, if it should so happen that we shall be subjected to some of those frightful changes which we have seen – if it should happen that your lordships, stripped of all the decorous distinctions of human society, should, by hands at once base and cruel, be led to those scaffolds and machines of murder upon which great kings and glorious queens have shed their blood, amidst the prelates, amidst the nobles, amidst the magistrates, who supported their thrones – may you in those moments feel that consolation which I am persuaded they felt in the critical moments of their dreadful agony!

My lords, if you must fall, may you so fall! but, if you stand – and stand I trust you will – together with the fortune of this ancient monarchy, together with the ancient laws and liberties of this great and illustrious kingdom, may you stand as unimpeached in honour as in power; may you stand, not as a substitute for virtue, but as an ornament of virtue, as a security for virtue; may you stand long, and long stand the terror of tyrants; may you stand the refuge of afflicted nations; may you stand a sacred temple, for the perpetual residence of an inviolable justice!

●

# RICHARD BRINSLEY SHERIDAN
## 13 June 1788

### '*Justice . . . august and pure*'

*Richard Sheridan (1751–1816), the Irish dramatist and author of* The School for Scandal *and* The Rivals, *a devoted friend of Fox, made his parliamentary reputation with several great speeches during the Hastings trial. The speech he gave as manager of the impeachment was delivered at four separate sittings in June. This is an extract from the peroration on the fourth day, in which he discusses whether Hastings is responsible for the actions of Mr Middleton, his confidential agent, even though Middleton himself claims the responsibility for them.*

The inquiry which now only remains, my lords, is, whether Mr Hastings is to be answerable for the crimes committed by his agents? It has been fully proved that Mr Middleton signed the treaty with the superior begum in October 1778. He also acknowledged signing some others of a different date, but could not recollect the authority by which he did it! These treaties were recognized by Mr Hastings, as appears by the evidence of Mr Purling, in the year 1780. In that of October 1778, the *jaghire* was secured, which was allotted for the support of the women in the khord mahal. But still the prisoner pleads that he is not accountable for the cruelties which were exercised. His is the plea which tyranny, aided by its prime minister, treachery, is always sure to set up. Mr Middleton has attempted to strengthen this ground by endeavouring to claim the whole infamy in these transactions, and to monopolize the guilt! He dared even to aver, that he had been condemned by Mr Hastings for the ignominious part he had acted. He dared to avow this, because Mr Hastings was on his trial, and he thought he never would be arraigned; but in the face of this court, and before he left the bar, he was compelled to confess that it was for the *lenience*, and not the *severity* of his proceedings, that he had been reproved by the prisoner.

It will not, I trust, be concluded that because Mr Hastings has not marked every passing shade of guilt, and because he has only given the bold outline of cruelty, he is therefore to be acquitted. It is laid down by the law of England, that law which is the perfection of reason, that a person ordering an act to be done by his agent is answerable for that act with all its consequences, '*Quod facit per alium, facit per se.*' Middleton was appointed, in 1777, the confidential agent, the *second self* of Mr Hastings. The Governor-General ordered the measure. Even if he never saw, nor heard afterward of its consequences, he was therefore answerable for every pang that was inflicted, and for all the blood that was shed. But he did hear, and that instantly, of the whole. He wrote to accuse Middleton of forbearance and of neglect! . . .

After this, my lords, can it be said that the prisoner was ignorant of the acts, or not culpable for their consequences? It is true, he did not direct the guards, the famine, and the bludgeons; he did not weigh the fetters, nor number the lashes to be inflicted on his victims; but yet he is just as guilty as if he had borne an active and personal share in each transaction. It is as if he had commanded that the heart should be torn from the bosom, and enjoined that no blood should follow. He is in the same degree accountable to the law, to his country, and to his conscience, and to his God!

The prisoner has endeavoured also to get rid of a part of his guilt, by observing that he was but one of the supreme council, and that all the rest had sanctioned those transactions with their approbation. Even if it were true that others did participate in the guilt, it cannot tend to diminish his criminalty . . .

When, my lords, the Board of Directors received the advices which Mr Hastings thought proper to transmit, though unfurnished with any other materials to form their judgement, they expressed very strongly their doubts, and properly ordered an inquiry into the circumstances of the alleged disaffection of the begums, declaring it, at the same time, to be a debt which was due to the honour and justice of the British nation. This inquiry, however, Mr Hastings thought it absolutely necessary to elude . . .

All this, however, my lords is nothing to the magnificent paragraph which concludes this communication.

'Besides,' says he, 'I hope it will not be a departure from official language to say, that the majesty of justice ought not to be approached without solicitation. She ought not to descend to inflame or provoke, but to withhold her judgement until she is called on to determine.'

But, my lords, do you, the judges of this land, and the expounders of its rightful laws – do you approve of this mockery and call it the character of justice, which takes the form of right to excite wrong? No, my lords, justice is not this halt and miserable object; it is not the ineffective bauble of an Indian pagod; it is not the portentous phantom of despair; it is not like any fabled monster, formed in the eclipse of reason, and found in some unhallowed grove of superstitious darkness and political dismay! No, my lords. In the happy reverse of all this, I turn from the disgusting caricature to the real image! Justice I have now before me august and pure! The abstract idea of all that would be perfect in the spirits and the aspirings of men! – where the mind rises; where the heart expands; where the countenance is ever placid and benign; where her favourite attitude is to stoop to the unfortunate; to hear their cry and to help them; to rescue and relieve, to succour and save; majestic, from its mercy; venerable, from its utility; uplifted, without pride; firm, without obduracy; beneficent in each preference; lovely, though in her frown!

On that justice I rely: deliberate and sure, abstracted from all party purpose and political speculation; not on words, but on facts. You, my lords, who hear me, I conjure, by those rights which it is your best privilege to preserve; by that fame which it is your best pleasure to inherit; by all those feelings which refer to the first term in the series of existence, the original compact of our nature, our controlling rank in the creation. This is the call on all to administer to truth and equity, as they would satisfy the laws and satisfy themselves, with the most exalted bliss possible or conceivable for our nature; the self-approving consciousness of virtue, when the condemnation we look for will be one of the most ample mercies accomplished for mankind since the creation of the world! My lords, I have done.

*Hastings was finally acquitted but sentenced to pay costs of £71,800. The East India Company indemnified him by a pension of £4,000 a year for life.*

•

## WILLIAM WILBERFORCE
### 12 May 1789

### 'Let us make reparation to Africa'

*An anti-slavery society was formed in Britain in 1787 by Thomas Clarkson, Granville Sharp and William Wilberforce (1759–1833), the son of a wealthy Hull merchant who was elected MP for Hull in 1784 and became a close friend of William Pitt the Younger. Wilberforce was seriously ill in 1788 and exacted from Pitt, now prime minister, a promise that Pitt would try to abolish the slave trade. Supported by Fox and Burke, Pitt kept his promise and a bill was drawn up. By 1789, Wilberforce had recovered and the man who spent his life struggling against slavery and became the conscience of England made this powerful speech to the House of Commons.*

When we consider the vastness of the continent of Africa; when we reflect how all other countries have for some centuries past been advancing in happiness and civilization; when we think how in this same period all improvement in Africa has been defeated by her intercourse with Britain; when we reflect that it is we ourselves that have degraded them to that wretched brutishness and barbarity which we now plead as the justification of our guilt; how the slave trade has enslaved their minds, blackened their character, and sunk them so low in the scale of animal beings that some think the apes are of a higher class, and fancy the orang-outang has given them the go-by. What a mortification must we feel at having so long neglected to think of our guilt, or attempt any reparation! It seems, indeed, as if we had determined to forbear from all interference until the measure of our folly and wickedness was so full and complete; until the impolicy which eventually belongs to vice was become so plain and glaring that not an individual in the country should refuse to join in the abolition; it seems as if we had waited until the persons most interested should be tired out with the folly and nefariousness of the trade, and should unite in petitioning against it.

Let us then make such amends as we can for the mischiefs we have done to the unhappy continent; let us recollect what Europe itself was no longer ago than three or four centuries. What if I should be able to show this House that in a civilized part of Europe, in the time of our Henry VII, there were people who actually sold their own children? What if I should tell them that England itself was that country? What if I should point out to them that the very place where this inhuman traffic was carried on was the city of Bristol? Ireland at that time used to drive a considerable trade in slaves with these neighbouring barbarians; but a great plague having infested the country, the Irish were struck with a panic, suspected (I am sure very properly) that the plague was a punishment sent from heaven for the sin of the slave trade, and therefore abolished it. All I ask, therefore, of the people of Bristol is, that they would become as civilized now as Irishmen were four hundred years ago. Let us put an end at once to this inhuman traffic – let us stop this effusion of human blood. The true way to virtue is by withdrawing from temptation; let us then withdraw from these wretched Africans, those temptations to fraud, violence, cruelty, and injustice, which the slave trade furnishes. Wherever the sun shines, let us go round the world with him, diffusing our beneficence; but let us not traffic, only that we may set kings against their subjects, subjects against their kings, sowing discord in every village, fear and terror in every family, setting millions of our fellow-creatures a-hunting each other for slaves, creating fairs and markets for human flesh through one whole continent of the world, and, under the name of policy, concealing from ourselves all the baseness and iniquity of such a traffic.

Why may we not hope, ere long, to see Hanse-towns established on the coast of Africa as they were on the Baltic? It is said the Africans are idle, but they are not too idle, at least, to catch one another; seven hundred to one thousand tons of rice are annually bought of them; by the same rule why should we not buy more? At Gambia one thousand of them are seen continually at work; why should not some more thousands be set to work in the same manner? It is the slave trade that causes their idleness and every other mischief. We are told by one witness: 'They sell one another as they can'; and while they can get brandy by catching one another, no wonder they are too idle for any regular work.

I have one word more to add upon a most material point but it is a point so self-evident that I shall be extremely short. It will appear from everything which I have said, that it is not regulation, it is not mere palliatives, that can cure this enormous evil. Total abolition is the only possible cure for it. The Jamaica report, indeed, admits much of the evil, but recommends it to us so to regulate the trade, that no persons should be kidnapped or made slaves contrary to the custom of Africa. But may they not be made slaves unjustly, and yet by no means contrary to the custom of Africa? I have shown they may, for all the customs of Africa are rendered savage and unjust through the influence of this trade; besides, how can we discriminate between the slaves justly and unjustly made? or, if we could, does any man believe that the British captains can, by any regulation in this country, be prevailed upon to refuse all such slaves as have not been fairly, honestly, and uprightly enslaved? But granting even that they should do this, yet how would the rejected slaves be recompensed? They are brought, as we are told, from three or four thousand miles off, and exchanged like cattle from one hand to another, until they reach the coast. We see then that it is the existence of the slave trade that is the spring of all this internal traffic, and that the remedy cannot be applied without abolition. Again, as to the middle passage, the evil is radical there also; the merchant's profit depends upon the number that can be crowded together, and upon the shortness of their allowance. Astringents, escarotis, and all the other arts of making them up for sale, are of the very essence of the trade; these arts will be concealed both from the purchaser and the legislature; they are necessary to the owner's profit, and they will be practised. Again, chains and arbitrary treatment must be used in transporting them; our seamen must be taught to play the tyrant, and that depravation of manners among them (which some very judicious persons have treated of as the very worst part of the business) cannot be hindered, while the trade itself continues. As to the slave merchants, they have already told you that if two slaves to a ton are not permitted, the trade cannot continue; so that the objections are done away by themselves on this quarter; and in the West Indies, I have shown that the abolition is the only possible stimulus whereby a regard to population, and consequently to the happiness of the Negroes, can be effectually excited in those islands.

I trust, therefore, I have shown that upon every ground the total abolition ought to take place. I have urged many things which are not my own leading motives for proposing it, since I have wished to show every description of gentlemen, and particularly the West India planters, who deserve every attention, that the abolition is politic upon their own principles also. Policy, however, sir, is not my principle, and I am not ashamed to say it. There is a principle above everything that is political; and when I reflect on the command which says: 'Thou shalt do no murder,' believing the authority to be divine, how can I dare to set up any reasonings of my own against it? And, sir, when we think of eternity, and of the future consequences of all human conduct, what is there in this life that should make any man contradict the dictates of his conscience, the principles of justice, the laws of religion, and of God? Sir, the nature and all the circumstances of this trade are now laid open to us; we can no longer plead ignorance, we cannot evade it, it is now an object placed before us, we cannot pass it; we may spurn it, we may kick it out of our way, but we cannot turn aside so as to avoid seeing it; for it is brought now so directly before our eyes that this House must decide, and must justify to all the world, and to their own consciences, the rectitude of the grounds and principles of their decision. A society has been established for the abolition of this trade, in which Dissenters, Quakers, churchmen – in which the most conscientious of all persuasions have all united, and made a common cause in this great question. Let not Parliament be the only body that is insensible to the principles of national justice. Let us make reparation to Africa, so far as we can, by establishing a trade upon true commercial principles, and we shall soon find the rectitude of our conduct rewarded by the benefits of a regular and a growing commerce.

•

## WILLIAM PITT THE YOUNGER
### 2 April 1792

### 'A barbarous traffic in slaves'

*William Pitt (1759–1806), younger son of William Pitt, 1st Earl of Chatham, was Chancellor of the Exchequer at twenty-three and Prime Minister at twenty-four, a position he held almost continuously until his death at forty-six.*

*As Pitt rose in the Commons late at night to fulfil a promise to William Wilberforce that he would try to abolish the slave trade, he was ill and exhausted and had to take medicine before he could continue. He gathered strength and delivered one of his most celebrated speeches.*

The result of all I have said is that there exists no impediment, on the ground of pledged faith, or even on that of national expediency, to the abolition of this trade. On the contrary, all the arguments drawn from those sources plead for it, and they plead much more loudly, and much more strongly in every part of the question, for an immediate than for a gradual abolition. But now, sir, I come to Africa. That is the ground on which I rest, and here it is that I say my right honourable friends do not carry their principles to their full extent. Why ought the slave trade to be abolished? Because it is incurable injustice. How much stronger, then, is the argument for immediate than gradual abolition! By allowing it to continue even for one hour, do not my right honourable friends weaken their own argument of its injustice? If on the ground of injustice it ought to be abolished at last, why ought it not now? Why is injustice to be suffered to remain for a single hour? From what I hear without doors, it is evident that there is a general conviction entertained of its being far from just; and from that very conviction of its injustice, some men have been led, I fear, to the supposition that the slave trade never could have been permitted to begin but from some strong and irresistible necessity: a necessity, however, which if it was fancied to exist at first, I have shown cannot be thought by any man whatever to exist now. This plea of necessity has caused a sort of acquiescence in the continuance of this evil. Men have been led to place it among the rank of those necessary evils which are supposed to be the lot of human creatures, and to be permitted to fall upon some countries or individuals rather than upon others by that Being whose ways are inscrutable to us, and whose dispensations, it is conceived, we ought not to look into.

The origin of evil is indeed a subject beyond the reach of human understandings; and the permission of it by the Supreme Being is a subject into which it belongs not to us to inquire. But where the evil in question is a moral evil which a man can scrutinize, and where that moral evil has its origin with ourselves, let us not imagine that we can clear our consciences by this general, not to say irreligious and impious, way of laying aside the question. If we reflect at all on this subject, we must see that every necessary evil supposes that some other and greater evil would be incurred were it removed. I therefore desire to ask, what can be that greater evil which can be stated to overbalance the one in question? I know of no evil that ever has existed, nor can imagine any evil to exist, worse than the tearing of seventy or eighty thousand persons annually from their native land, by a combination of the most civilized nations inhabiting the most enlightened part of the globe, but more especially under the sanction of the laws of that nation which calls herself the most free and the most happy of them all.

Even if these miserable beings were proved guilty of every crime before you take them off, ought we to take upon ourselves the office of executioners? And even if we condescend so far, still can we be justified in taking them, unless we have clear proof that they are criminals? But, if we go much further – if we ourselves tempt them to sell their fellow creatures to us – we may rest assured that they will take care to provide by every possible method a supply of victims increasing in proportion to our demand. Can we, then, hesitate in deciding whether the wars in Africa are their wars or ours? It was our arms in the river Cameroon, put into the hands of the trader, that furnished him with the means of pushing his trade; and I have no more doubt that they are British arms, put into the hands of Africans, which promote universal war and desolation than I can doubt their having done so in that individual instance.

I have shown how great is the enormity of this evil, even on the supposition that we take only convicts and prisoners of war. But take the subject in the other way, and how does it stand? Think of 80,000 persons carried out of their native country by we know not what means! for crimes imputed! for light or inconsiderable faults! for debt perhaps! for the crime of witchcraft! or a thousand other weak and scandalous pretexts! Reflect on these 80,000 persons thus annually taken off! There is something in the horror of it that surpasses all the bounds of imagination. Admitting that there exists in Africa something like to courts of justice; yet what an office of humiliation and meanness is it in us, to take upon ourselves to carry into execution the iniquitous sentences of such courts, as if we also were strangers to all religion and to the first principles of justice! But that country, it is said, has been in some degree civilized, and civilized by us. It is said they have gained some knowledge of the principles of justice. Yes, we give them enough of our intercourse to convey to them the means and to initiate them in the study of mutual destruction. We give them just enough of the forms of justice to enable them to add the pretext of legal trials to their other modes of perpetrating the most atrocious iniquity. We give them just enough of European improvements to enable them the more effectually to turn Africa into a ravaged wilderness. Some evidences say that the Africans are addicted to the practice of gambling; that they even sell their wives and children, and ultimately themselves.

Are these, then, the legitimate sources of slavery? Shall we pretend that we can thus acquire an honest right to exact the labour of these people? Can we pretend that we have a right to carry away to distant regions men of whom we know nothing by authentic inquiry, and of whom there is every reasonable presumption to think that those who sell them to us have no right to do so? But the evil does not stop here. Do you think nothing of the ruin and the miseries in which so many other individuals, still remaining in Africa, are involved in consequence of carrying off so many myriads of people? Do you think nothing of their families left behind? of the connections broken? of the friendships, attachments, and relationships that are burst asunder? Do you think nothing of the miseries in consequence that are felt from generation to generation? of the privation of that happiness which might be communicated to them by the introduction of civilization, and of mental and moral improvement? – a happiness which you withhold from them so long as you permit the slave trade to continue.

Thus, sir, has the perversion of British commerce carried misery instead of happiness to one whole quarter of the globe. False to the very principles of trade, misguided in our policy, and unmindful of our duty, what astonishing mischief have we brought upon that continent! If, knowing the miseries we have caused, we refuse to put a stop to them, how greatly aggravated will be the guilt of this country! Shall we then delay rendering this justice to Africa? I am sure the immediate abolition of the slave trade is the first, the principal, the most indispensable act of policy, of duty, and of justice that the legislature of this country has to take, if it is indeed their wish to secure those important objects to which I have alluded, and which we are bound to pursue by the most solemn obligations. There is, however, one argument set up as a universal answer to everything that can be urged on our side. The slave-trade system, it is supposed, has taken such deep root in Africa that it is absurd to think of its being eradicated; and the abolition of that share of trade carried on by Great Britain is likely to be of very little service. You are not sure, it is said, that other nations will give up the trade if you should renounce it. I answer, if this trade is as criminal as it is asserted to be, God forbid that we should hesitate in relinquishing so iniquitous a traffic; even though it should be retained by other countries! I tremble at the thought of gentlemen indulging themselves in the argument which I am combating. 'We are friends,' say they, 'to humanity. We are second to none of you in our zeal for the good of Africa – but the French will not abolish – the Dutch will not abolish. We wait, therefore, on prudential principles, till they join us or set us an example.'

How, sir, is this enormous evil ever to be eradicated, if every nation is thus prudentially to wait till the concurrence of all the world shall have been obtained? Let me remark, too, that there is no nation in Europe that has, on the one hand, plunged so deeply into this guilt as Great Britain; or that is so likely, on the other, to be looked up to as an example. But does not this argument apply a thousand times more strongly in a contrary way? How much more justly may other nations point to us, and say, 'Why should we abolish the slave trade when Great Britain has not abolished it? Britain, free as she is, just and honourable as she is, and deeply involved as she is in this commerce above all nations, not only has not abolished, but has refused to abolish.' This, sir, is the argument with which we furnish the other nations of Europe if we again refuse to put an end to the slave trade. Instead, therefore, of imagining that by choosing to presume on their continuing it, we shall have exempted ourselves from guilt, and have transferred the whole criminality to them; let us rather reflect that on the very principle urged against us we shall henceforth have to answer for their crimes as well as our own.

It has also been urged, that there is something in the disposition and nature of the Africans themselves which renders all prospect of civilization on that continent extremely unpromising. 'It has been known,' says Mr Frazer, in his evidence, 'that a boy has been put to death who was refused to be purchased as a slave.' This single story was deemed by that gentleman a sufficient proof of the barbarity of the Africans, and of the inutility of abolishing the slave trade. My honourable friend, however, has told you that this boy had previously run away from his master three times; that the master had to pay his value, according to the custom of his country, every time he was brought back; and that, partly from anger at the boy for running away so frequently, and partly to prevent a repetition of the same expense, he determined to put him to death. This, sir, is the signal instance that has been dwelt upon of African barbarity. This African, we admit, was unenlightened and altogether barbarous: but let us now ask what would a civilized and enlightened West Indian, or a body of West Indians, have done in any case of a parallel nature? I will quote you, sir, a law passed in the West Indies in 1722; by which law this same crime of running away is, by the legislature of the island, punished with death, in the very first instance. I hope, therefore, we shall hear no more of the moral impossibility of civilizing the Africans, nor have our understandings again insulted by being called upon to sanction the trade until other nations shall have set the example of abolishing it . . .

Having detained the House so long, all that I will further add shall relate to that important subject, the civilization of Africa. Grieved am I to think that there should be a single person in this country who can look on the present uncivilized state of that continent as a ground for continuing the slave trade – as a ground not only for refusing to attempt the improvement of Africa, but even for intercepting every ray of light which might otherwise break in upon her. Here, as in every other branch of this extensive question, the argument of our adversaries pleads against them; for surely, sir, the present deplorable state of Africa, especially when we reflect that her chief calamities are to be ascribed to us, calls for our generous aid rather than justifies any despair on our part of her recovery, and still less any further repetition of our injuries. I will not much longer fatigue the attention of the House; but this point has impressed itself so deeply on my mind that I must trouble the committee with a few additional observations. Are we justified, I ask, on any one ground of theory, or by any one instance to be found in the history of the world from its very beginning to this day, in forming the supposition which I am now combating? Are we justified in supposing that the particular practice which we encourage in Africa, of men selling each other for slaves, is any symptom of a barbarism that is incurable? Are we justified in supposing that even the practice of offering up human sacrifices proves a total incapacity for civilization?

I believe it will be found that both the trade in slaves and the still more savage custom of offering up human sacrifices obtained in former periods throughout many of those nations which now, by the blessings of Providence, and by a long progression of improvements, are advanced the farthest in civilization. I believe that, if we reflect an instant, we shall find that this observation comes directly home to ourselves; and that, on the same ground on which we are now disposed to proscribe Africa forever from all possibility of improvement, we might, in like manner, have been proscribed and forever shut out from all the blessings which we now enjoy. There was a time, sir, when even human sacrifices are said to have been offered in this island. But I would peculiarly observe on this day, for it is a case precisely in point, that the very practice of the slave trade once prevailed among us. Slaves, as we may read in Henry's *History of Great Britain*, were formerly an established article of our exports. 'Great numbers,' he says, 'were exported like cattle, from the British coast, and were to be seen exposed for sale in the Roman market.' It does not distinctly appear by what means they were procured; but there is unquestionably no small resemblance, in this particular point, between the case of our ancestors and that of the present wretched natives of Africa; for the historian tells you that 'adultery, witchcraft, and debt were probably some of the chief sources of supplying the Roman market with British slaves; that prisoners taken in war were added to the number; and that there might be among them some unfortunate gamesters who, after having lost all their goods, at length staked themselves, their wives, and their children.'

Every one of these sources of slavery has been stated to be at this hour a source of slavery in Africa. And these circumstances, sir, with a solitary instance or two of human sacrifices, furnish the alleged proofs that Africa labours under a natural incapacity for civilization; that it is enthusiasm and fanaticism to think that she can ever enjoy the knowledge and the morals of Europe; that Providence never intended her to rise above a state of barbarism; that Providence has irrevocably doomed her to be only a nursery for slaves for us free and civilized Europeans. Allow of this principle, as applied to Africa, and I should be glad to know why it might not also have been applied to ancient and uncivilized Britain. Why might not some Roman senator, reasoning on the principles of some honourable gentlemen, and pointing to British barbarians, have predicted with equal boldness, 'There is a people that will never rise to civilization; there is a people destined never to be free; a people without the understanding necessary for the attainment of useful arts; depressed by the hand of nature below the level of the human species; and created to form a supply of slaves for the rest of the world'? Might not this have been said in all respects as fairly and as truly of Britain herself, at that period of her history, as it can now be said by us of the inhabitants of Africa? We, sir, have long since emerged from barbarism; we have almost forgotten that we were once barbarians; we are now raised to a situation which exhibits a striking contrast to every circumstance by which a Roman might have characterized us, and by which we now characterize Africa.

There is, indeed, one thing wanting to complete the contrast, and to clear us altogether from the imputation of acting even to this hour as barbarians; for we continue to this hour a barbarous traffic in slaves; we continue it even yet, in spite of all our great and undeniable pretensions to civilization. We were once as obscure among the nations of the earth, as savage in our manners, as debased in our morals, as degraded in our understandings, as these unhappy Africans are at present. But in the lapse of a long series of years, by a progression slow, and for a time almost imperceptible, we have become rich in a variety of acquirements, favoured above measure in the gifts of Providence, unrivalled in commerce, pre-eminent in arts, foremost in the pursuits of philosophy and science, and established in all the blessings of civil society: we are in the possession of peace, of happiness, and of liberty; we are under the guidance of a mild and beneficent religion; and we are protected by impartial laws, and the purest administration of justice; we are living under a system of government which our own happy experience leads us to pronounce the best and wisest which has ever yet been framed – a system which has become the admiration of the world.

From all these blessings we must forever have been shut out, had there been any truth in those principles which some gentlemen have not hesitated to lay down as applicable to the case of Africa. Had those principles been true, we ourselves had languished to this hour in that miserable state of ignorance, brutality, and degradation in which history proves our ancestors to have been immersed. Had other nations adopted these principles in their conduct towards us; had other nations applied to Great Britain the reasoning which some of the senators of this very island now apply to Africa, ages might have passed without our emerging from barbarism; and we, who are enjoying the blessings of a British civilization, of British laws, and British liberty, might, at this hour, have been little superior, either in morals, in knowledge, or refinement, to the rude inhabitants of the coast of Guinea.

If, then, we feel that this perpetual confinement in the fetters of brutal ignorance would have been the greatest calamity which could have befallen us; if we view with gratitude and exultation the contrast between the peculiar blessings we enjoy and the wretchedness of the ancient inhabitants of Britain; if we shudder to think of the misery which would still have overwhelmed us had Great Britain continued to be the mart for slaves to the more civilized nations of the world, God forbid that we should any longer subject Africa to the same dreadful scourge, and preclude the light of knowledge, which has reached every other quarter of the globe, from having access to her coasts! I trust we shall no longer continue this commerce, to the destruction of every improvement on that wide continent; and shall not consider ourselves as conferring too great a boon in restoring its inhabitants to the rank of human beings. I trust we shall not think ourselves too liberal if, by abolishing the slave trade, we give them the same common chance of civilization with other parts of the world, and that we shall now allow to Africa the opportunity – the hope – the prospect of attaining to the same blessings which we ourselves, through the favourable dispensations of Divine Providence, have been permitted, at a much more early period, to enjoy.

If we listen to the voice of reason and duty, and pursue this night the line of conduct which they prescribe, some of us may live to see a reverse of that picture from which we now turn our eyes with shame and regret. We may live to behold the natives of Africa engaged in the calm occupations of industry, in the pursuits of a just and legitimate commerce. We may behold the beams of science and philosophy breaking in upon their land, which, at some happy period in still later times, may blaze with full lustre; and, joining their influence to that of pure religion, may illuminate and invigorate the most distant extremities of that immense continent. Then may we hope that even Africa, though last of all the quarters of the globe, shall enjoy at length, in the evening of her days, those blessings which have descended so plentifully upon us in a much earlier period of the world. Then also will Europe, participating in her improvement and prosperity, receive an ample recompense for the tardy kindness (if kindness it can be called) of no longer hindering that continent from extricating herself out of the darkness which, in other more fortunate regions, has been so much more speedily dispelled –

> Nos primus equis oriens afflavit anhelis;
> Illic sera rubens accendit lumina Vesper.*

Then, sir, may be applied to Africa those words, originally used indeed with a different view –

> His demum exactis –
> Devenere locos laetos, et amoena virecta
> Fortunatorum nemorum, sedesque beatas:
> Largior hic campos Aether, et lumine vestit
> Purpureo.†

It is in this view, sir – it is as an atonement for our long and cruel injustice towards Africa – that the measure proposed by my honourable friend most forcibly recommends itself to my mind. The great and happy change to be expected in the state of her inhabitants is, of all the various and important benefits of the abolition, in my estimation, incomparably the most extensive and important. I shall vote, sir, against the adjournment; and I shall also oppose to the utmost every proposition which in any way may tend either to prevent or even to postpone for an hour the total abolition of the slave trade; a measure which, on all the various grounds which I have stated, we are bound, by the most pressing and indispensable duty, to adopt.

*The slave trade was not abolished – but Pitt laid the foundations for its eventual abolition after his death by his great rival, Fox, in 1806.*

•

---

* 'And when dayspring touches us with his panting horses' breath, there crimson Hesperus kindles his lamp at evenfall' (Virgil, *Georgics*, I, 251 ff., translated by J.W. Mackail).
† 'Now at length, this fully done, they came to the happy place, the green pleasances and blissful seats of the Fortunate Woodlands. Here an ampler air clothes the meadows in . . . lustrous sheen' (Virgil, *Aeneid*, VI, 637 ff., translated by J.W. Mackail).

# CHARLES JAMES FOX
25 November 1795

## 'The spirit of freedom'

*After several indignities to George III, the Treason and Sedition Bills were introduced for better securing the King's person and government – and suppressing seditious meetings.*

*Fox spoke to postpone discussion of the bills and made a classic case for freedom of speech.*

Our government is valuable, because it is free. What, I beg gentlemen to ask themselves, are the fundamental parts of a free government? I know there is a difference of opinion upon this subject. My own opinion is, that freedom does not depend upon the executive government, nor upon the administration of justice, nor upon any one particular or distinct part, nor even upon forms so much as it does on the general freedom of speech and of writing. With regard to freedom of speech, the bill before the House is a direct attack upon that freedom. No man dreads the use of a universal proposition more than I do myself. I must nevertheless say, that speech ought to be completely free, without any restraint whatever, in any government pretending to be free. By being completely free, I do not mean that a person should not be liable to punishment for abusing that freedom, but I mean freedom in the first instance. The press is so at present, and I rejoice it is so; what I mean is, that any man may write and print what he pleases, although he is liable to be punished, if he abuses that freedom; this I call perfect freedom in the first instance. If this is necessary with regard to the press, it is still more so with regard to speech. An *imprimatur* has been talked of, and it will be dreadful enough; but a *dicatur* will be still more horrible. No man has been daring enough to say, that the press should not be free: but the bill before them does not, indeed, punish a man for speaking, it prevents him from speaking. For my own part, I never heard of any danger arising to a free state from the freedom of the press, or freedom of speech; so far from it, I am perfectly clear that a free state cannot exist without both. The honourable and learned gentleman has said, will we not preserve the remainder by giving up this liberty? I admit that, by passing of the bill, the people will have lost a great deal.

A great deal! Aye, all that is worth preserving. For you will have lost the spirit, the fire, the freedom, the boldness, the energy of the British character, and with them its best virtue. I say, it is not the written law of the constitution of England, it is not the law that is to be found in books, that has constituted the true principle of freedom in any country, at any time. No! it is the energy, the boldness of a man's mind, which prompts him to speak, not in private, but in large and popular assemblies, that constitutes, that creates, in a state, the spirit of freedom. This is the principle which gives life to liberty; without, the human character is a stranger to freedom. If you suffer the liberty of speech to be wrested from you, you will then have lost the freedom, the energy, the boldness of the British character. It has been said, that the right honourable gentleman rose to his present eminence by the influence of popular favour, and that he is now kicking away the ladder by which he mounted to power. Whether such was the mode by which the right honourable gentleman attained his present situation I am a little inclined to question; but I can have no doubt that if this bill shall pass, England herself will have thrown away that ladder, by which she has risen to wealth (but that is the last consideration), to honour, to happiness, and to fame. Along with energy of thinking and liberty of speech, she will forfeit the comforts of her situation, and the dignity of her character, those blessings which they have secured to her at home, and the rank by which she has been distinguished among the nations. These were the sources of her splendour, and the foundation of her greatness —

> . . . Sic fortis Etruria crevit,
> Scilicet et rerum facta est pulcherrima Roma.*

We need only appeal to the example of that great city whose prosperity the poet has thus recorded. In Rome, when the liberty of speech was gone, along with it vanished all that had constituted her the mistress of the world. I doubt not but in the days of Augustus there were persons who perceived no symptoms of decay, who exulted even in their fancied prosperity, when they contemplated the increasing opulence and splendid edifices of that grand metropolis, and who even deemed that they possessed their ancient liberty, because they still retained those titles of

---

* 'Thus Etruria grew strong, and Rome became the most glorious thing on earth' (Virgil, *Georgics*, II, 533–4).

offices which had existed under the republic. What fine panegyrics were then pronounced on the prosperity of the empire! – *Tum tutus bos prata perambulat*\* This was flattery to Augustus: to that great destroyer of the liberties of mankind, as much an enemy to freedom, as any of the detestable tyrants who succeeded him. So with us, we are to be flattered with an account of the form of our government, by King, Lords, and Commons – *Eadem magistratuum vocabula*†. There were some then, as there are now, who said that the energy of Rome was not gone; while they felt their vanity gratified in viewing their city; which had been converted from brick into marble. They did not reflect that they had lost that spirit of manly independence which animated the Romans of better times, and that the beauty and splendour of their city served only to conceal the symptoms of rottenness and decay. So if this bill passes you may for a time retain your institution of juries and the forms of your free Constitution, but the substance is gone, the foundation is undermined; – your fall is certain and your destruction inevitable. As a tree that is injured at the root and the bark taken off, the branches may live for a while, some sort of blossom may still remain; but it will soon wither, decay, and perish: so take away the freedom of speech or of writing, and the foundation of all your freedom is gone. You will then fall, and be degraded and despised by all the world for your weakness and your folly, in not taking care of that which conducted you to all your fame, your greatness, your opulence, and prosperity. But before this happens, let the people once more be tried. I am a friend to taking the sense of the people, and therefore a friend to this motion. I wish for every delay that is possible in this important and alarming business. I wish for this adjournment – *Spatium requiemque furori*‡. Let us put a stop to the madness of this bill; for if you pass it, you will take away the foundation of the liberty of the people of England, and then farewell to any happiness in this country!

•

---

\* Horace, *Odes*, IV, 17: 'For safe the herds range field and fen' (Sir Theodore Martin).

†*Domi res tranquilla, eadem magistratuum vocabula* (Tacitus, *Annals*, 1, 3). 'At home all was quiet; the titles of the magistrates were unchanged.'

‡ *Tempus inane peto, requiem spatiumque furori* (Virgil, *Aeneid*, IV, 433).
       'My prayer is for a transient grace
       To give this madness breathing space' (Conington).

# THE RIGHTS OF MAN

# MIRABEAU
## 3 February 1789

### '*Woe to the privileged orders!*'

*When the French Revolution began, the power of oratory was highly prized. At several critical moments, as Simon Schama says in* Citizens, *his history of the revolution, the ability to sway audiences made the difference between life and death, triumph and disaster. Public diction was public power.*

*The most powerful orator of the first two years of the revolution was Honoré Gabriel Riquetti, Comte de Mirabeau (1749–91), a 'lecherous noble' who cast himself as champion of the people, a role he seized in three speeches at the Estates of Provence in 1789, in which he attacked the power of the nobles and argued for increased representation for the Third Estate. It was this scathing peroration from his third speech that made his fame and propelled him towards a decisive role in Paris. 'In him a new social order raises its head, angry and threatening,' says Louis Barthou, a former French prime minister. 'The whole spirit of the Revolution already appears in his language and his attitude.'*

In all countries, in all ages, have aristocrats implacably pursued the friends of the people; and when, by I know not what combination of fortune, such a friend has uprisen from the very bosom of the aristocracy, it has been at him pre-eminently that they have struck, eager to inspire wider terror by the elevation of their victim. So perished the last of the Gracchi by the hands of the patricians. But, mortally smitten, he flung dust towards heaven, calling the avenging gods to witness: and from that dust sprang Marius – Marius, less illustrious for having exterminated the Cimbri than for having beaten down the despotism of the nobility in Rome.

But you, Commons, listen to one who, unseduced by your applauses, yet cherishes them in his heart. Man is strong only by union; happy only by peace. Be firm, not obstinate; courageous, not turbulent; free, not undisciplined; prompt, not precipitate. Stop not, except at difficulties of moment; and be then wholly inflexible. But disdain the contentions of self-love, and never thrust into the balance the individual against the country. Above all, hasten, as much as in you lies, the epoch of those States-General from which you are charged with flinching – the more acrimoniously charged, the more your accusers dread the results; of those States-General through which so many pretensions will be scattered, so many rights re-established, so many evils reformed, of those States-General, in short, through which the monarch himself desires that France should regenerate herself.

For myself, who, in my public career, have had no other fear but that of wrongdoing – who, girt with my conscience and armed with my principles, would brave the universe – whether it shall be my fortune to serve you with my voice and my exertions in the national assembly, or whether I shall be enabled to aid you there with my prayers only, be sure that the vain clamours, the wrathful menaces, the injurious protestations – all the convulsions, in a word, of expiring prejudices – shall not intimidate me! What! shall he now pause in his civic course who, first among all the men of France, emphatically proclaimed his opinions on national affairs, at a time when circumstances were much less urgent than now and the task one of much greater peril?

Never! No measure of outrages shall bear down my patience. I have been, I am, I shall be, even to the tomb, the man of the public liberty, the man of the Constitution. If to be such be to become the man of the people rather than of the nobles, then woe to the privileged orders! For privileges shall have an end, but the people is eternal!

•

MIRABEAU
26 September 1789

*'Hideous bankruptcy is here . . . And yet you deliberate!'*

*One of the major causes of the French Revolution was the huge public debt, partly caused by France's role in the American War of Independence, which threatened the nation with bankruptcy. Jacques Necker, the director-general of finance, had won a loan of 80 million francs from the Assembly in August but when the situation remained desperate returned with a proposal to levy an exceptional patriotic tax of one quarter of annual income. His proposal provoked uproar but Mirabeau spoke in Necker's support and was asked to draft a proposal. Meanwhile the Assembly vacillated and the debate went on until late in the evening.*

*Then Mirabeau – angry, indignant, disgusted by the timidity and pettiness of the debate and now master of his oratorical power – rose to speak for the third time. Necker's solution was obviously not ideal. 'But heaven preserve me in such a*

*critical situation from opposing my views to his!' Then the tone of his speech*
*changed. He spoke intimately, as though man to man, as though announcing the*
*revelation of a secret, the explanation of a mystery. At the end, he won a standing*
*ovation, a unanimous vote, and clinched his control of the Assembly.*

Two centuries of depredations and brigandage have made the chasm in
which the kingdom is ready to engulf itself. We must close this fearful
abyss. Well, here is a list of French proprietors! Choose among the
richest, thus sacrificing the least number of citizens! But choose! For
must not a small number perish to save the mass of the people? Well,
these two thousand notables possess enough to make up the deficit. This
will restore order in the finances and bring peace and prosperity to the
kingdom!

Strike, immolate without pity these wretched victims, cast them into
the abyss until it is closed. You recoil in horror, inconsistent and
pusillanimous men! Do you not see that in decreeing bankruptcy, or
what is still more odious, in rendering it inevitable, without decreeing it,
you do a deed a thousand times more criminal, and – folly inconceivable
– gratuitously criminal? For at least this horrible sacrifice would cause
the disappearance of the deficit. But do you imagine that in refusing to
pay, you will cease to owe? Do you believe that the thousands, the
millions of men who will lose in an instant, by the terrible explosion or
its repercussion, all that made the consolation of their lives, and constituted, perhaps, the sole means of their support, would leave you
peaceably to enjoy your crime? Stoical contemplators of the incalculable
evils which this catastrophe would disgorge upon France! Impassive
egoists who think that these convulsions of despair and misery shall pass
like so many others, and the more rapidly as they are the more violent!
Are you sure that so many men without bread will leave you tranquilly
to the enjoyment of those dainties, the number and delicacy of which
you are unwilling to diminish. No! you will perish, and in the universal
conflagration you do not hesitate to kindle, the loss of your honour will
not save a single one of your detestable enjoyments!

Look where we are going! . . . I hear you speak of patriotism, and the
*élan* of patriotism, of invocations to patriotism. Ah! do not prostitute the
words 'country' and 'patriotism'! Is it so very magnanimous – the effort
to give a portion of one's revenue to save all of one's possessions? This,
gentlemen, is only simple arithmetic; and he who hesitates cannot disarm
indignation except by the contempt he inspires through his stupidity.
Yes, gentlemen, this is the plainest prudence, the commonest wisdom! It

is your gross material interests I invoke! I shall not say to you as formerly: will you be the first to exhibit to the nations the spectacle of a people assembled to make default in their public obligations? I shall not say again: what titles have you to liberty? What means remain to you to preserve it, if in your first act you surpass the turpitude of the most corrupt governments; if the first care of your vigilant cooperation is not for the guarantee of your constitution? I tell you, you will all be dragged into a universal ruin, and you yourselves have the greatest interests in making the sacrifices the government asks of you. Vote, then, for this extraordinary subsidy; and it may be sufficient! Vote for it, for if you have any doubts on the means adopted (vague and unenlightened doubts), you have none as to its necessity or our inability to provide an immediate substitute. Vote, then, because public necessity admits no delay and we shall be held accountable for any delay that occurs. Beware of asking for time! Misfortune never grants it!

Gentlemen, apropos of a ridiculous disturbance at the Palais Royal, of a laughable insurrection, which never had any importance save in the weak imaginations or perverted designs of a few faith-breakers, you have heard these mad words: 'Catiline is at the gates of Rome! And yet you deliberate!'

And certainly there has been about us no Catiline, no peril, no faction, no Rome. But today bankruptcy – hideous bankruptcy is here – it threatens to consume you, your properties, your honour! And yet you deliberate!

•

## RICHARD PRICE
### 4 November 1789

### 'Tremble all ye oppressors of the world!'

*The fall of the Bastille was hailed by Charles James Fox as the greatest event in human history. For most of the British, however, the French Revolution was a remote event: it was the dissenters, the reformers, the poets – among them Wordsworth, who wrote 'Bliss was it in that dawn to be alive' – who rejoiced.*

*As the centenary of Britain's 1688 Glorious Revolution approached, 1788 was celebrated as a festival of liberty. The dissenting parson Dr Richard Price (1723–91), whose pamphlet on civil liberty had inspired the Americans in declaring independence, preached to the London Revolution Society that the people must frame a government for themselves. A year later, the November 1789 meeting of the society became historic when Price preached his Unitarian sermon on 'the love of our country' and proposed an address, unanimously adopted, that offered congratulations to the French National Assembly.*

*It was this sermon, soon published as a pamphlet, which provoked Edmund Burke into action against the Revolution. His* Reflections on the Revolution in France *was published in November 1790 and written to answer Price.*

We are met to thank God for that event in this country to which the name of the Revolution has been given; and which, for more than a century, it has been usual for the friends of freedom, and more especially Protestant Dissenters, under the title of the Revolution Society, to celebrate with expressions of joy and exultation. My highly valued and excellent friend who addressed you on this occasion last year has given you an interesting account of the principal circumstances that attended this event, and of the reasons we have for rejoicing in it. By a bloodless victory, the fetters which despotism had been long preparing for us were broken; the rights of the people were asserted, a tyrant expelled, and a sovereign of our own choice appointed in his room. Security was given to our property, and our consciences were emancipated. The bounds of free inquiry were enlarged; the volume in which are the words of eternal life was laid more open to our examination; and that era of light and liberty was introduced among us by which we have been made an example to other kingdoms and became the instructors of the world. Had it not been for this deliverance, the probability is that, instead of being thus distinguished, we should now have been a base people, groaning under the infamy and misery of popery and slavery. Let us, therefore, offer thanksgivings to God, the author of all our blessings . . .

We have particular reason, as Protestant Dissenters, to rejoice on this occasion. It was at this time we were rescued from persecution, and obtained the liberty of worshipping God in the manner we think most acceptable to Him. It was then our meetinghouses were opened, our worship was taken under the protection of the law, and the principles of toleration gained a triumph. We have, therefore, on this occasion, peculiar reasons for thanksgiving. But let us remember that we ought not to satisfy ourselves with thanksgivings. Our gratitude, if genuine, will be accompanied with endeavours to give stability to the deliverance our country has obtained, and to extend and improve the happiness with which the Revolution has blessed us. Let us, in particular, take care not to forget the principles of the Revolution. This Society has, very properly, in its Reports, held out these principles, as an instruction to the public. I will only take notice of the three following:

First: the right to liberty of conscience in religious matters.

Secondly: the right to resist power when abused. And,

Thirdly: the right to choose our own governors; to cashier them for misconduct; and to frame a government for ourselves.

On these three principles, and more especially the last, was the Revolution founded. Were it not true that liberty of conscience is a sacred right; that power abused justifies resistance; and that civil authority is a delegation from the people – were not, I say, all this true, the Revolution would have been not an *assertion*, but an invasion of rights; not a revolution, but a rebellion. Cherish in your breasts this conviction, and act under its influence; detecting the odious doctrines which, had they been acted upon in this country, would have left us at this time wretched slaves – doctrines which imply that God made mankind to be oppressed and plundered; and which are no less a blasphemy against Him than an insult on common sense . . .

You may reasonably expect that I should now close this address to you. But I cannot yet dismiss you. I must not conclude without recalling, particularly, to your recollection a consideration to which I have more than once alluded, and which, probably, your thoughts have been all along anticipating; a consideration with which my mind is impressed more than I can express. I mean, the consideration of the favourableness of the present times to all exertions in the cause of public liberty.

What an eventful period is this! I am thankful that I have lived to it; and I could almost say, *Lord, now lettest thou thy servant depart in peace, for mine eyes have seen thy salvation.* I have lived to see a diffusion of knowledge which has undermined superstition and error – I have lived to see the rights of men better understood than ever; and nations panting for liberty which seemed to have lost the idea of it. I have lived to see thirty millions of people, indignant and resolute, spurning at slavery, and demanding liberty with an irresistible voice; their king led in triumph, and an arbitrary monarch surrendering himself to his subjects. After sharing in the benefits of one revolution, I have been spared to be a witness to two other revolutions, both glorious. And now, methinks, I see the ardour for liberty catching and spreading; a general amendment beginning in human affairs; the dominion of priests giving way to the dominion of reason and conscience.

Be encouraged, all ye friends of freedom and writers in its defence! The times are auspicious. Your labours have not been in vain. Behold kingdoms, admonished by you, starting from sleep, breaking their fetters, and claiming justice from their oppressors! Behold, the light you have struck out, after setting America free, reflected to France, and there kindled into a blaze that lays despotism in ashes and warms and illuminates Europe!

Tremble all ye oppressors of the world! Take warning all ye supporters of slavish governments and slavish hierarchies! Call no more (absurdly and wickedly) reformation innovation. You cannot now hold the world in darkness. Struggle no longer against increasing light and liberality. Restore to mankind their rights; and consent to the correction of abuses, before they and you are destroyed together.

•

## PIERRE VERGNIAUD
### 3 July 1792

### 'Your blood shall redden the earth'

*Until the Revolution, Pierre Vergniaud (1753–93) was a lawyer in Bordeaux. In 1791 he entered the National Assembly, where his eloquence soon made him leader of the Girondins and President of the Assembly. He challenges Mirabeau (who was executed in 1793) as the greatest orator of the revolution.*

*In July 1792, Vergniaud rose in the Assembly to warn of the imminent danger of invasion by Prussian forces and to declare that national security demanded the dethronement of the King.*

*The assembly was packed to capacity. Every deputy was in the room, many booted and spurred, many spitting on the floor. A dead silence fell on the hall as Vergniaud started to deliver one of the greatest speeches of his life – a speech which shook the throne to its foundations.*

The King has refused his sanction to your resolution upon the religious troubles. I do not know whether the sombre spirit of the Médicis and the Cardinal de Lorraine still wanders beneath the arches of the palace of the Tuileries; if the sanguinary hypocrisy of the Jesuits La Chaise and Le Tellier lives again in the soul of some monster burning to see a revival of Saint Bartholomew and the Dragonades; I do not know whether the King's heart is disturbed by the fantastic ideas suggested to him and his conscience disordered by the religious terrors with which he is environed.

But it is not possible to believe, without wronging him and accusing him of being the most dangerous enemy of the Revolution, that he wishes to encourage, by impunity, the criminal attempts of pontifical ambition, and to give to the proud agents of the tiara the disastrous power with which they have equally oppressed peoples and kings. It is not possible to believe, without wronging him and accusing him of being the enemy of the people, that he approves or even looks with indifference on the underhanded schemes employed to divide the citizens, to cast the leaven of hatred into the bosoms of sensitive souls, and to stifle in the name of the Divinity the sweetest sentiments of which He has composed the felicity of mankind. It is impossible to believe, without wronging him and accusing him of being the enemy of the law, that he withholds his consent to the adoption of repressive measures against fanaticism, in order to drive citizens to excesses that despair inspires and the laws condemn; that he prefers to expose unsworn priests, even when they do not disturb the peace, to arbitrary vengeance rather than to subject them to a law that, affecting only agitators, would cover the innocent with an inviolable aegis. Finally, it is not possible to believe, without wronging him and accusing him of being the enemy of the Empire, that he wishes to perpetuate sedition and to eternalize the disorders and all the revolutionary movements that are urging the Empire toward civil war, and which, through civil war, would plunge it into dissolution . . .

It is in the name of the King that the French princes have tried to enlist all the courts of Europe against the nation; it is to avenge the dignity of the King that the treaty of Pillnetz was concluded and the monstrous alliance between the courts of Vienna and Berlin formed; it is to defend the King that we have seen the old companies of lifeguards, under the colours of rebellion, hastening to Germany; it is in order to come to the King's aid that the emigrants are soliciting and obtaining places in the Austrian army and are prepared themselves to rend their country; it is to join those valiant knights of the royal prerogative that other worthies full of honour and delicacy abandon their post in the face of the enemy, violate their oaths, steal the military chests, strive to corrupt their soldiers, and thus plunge their glory in dastardliness, perjury, subordination, theft, and assassination; it is against the nation, or the National Assembly alone, and in order to maintain the splendour of the throne, that the King of Bohemia and Hungary makes war upon us, and the King of Prussia marches upon our frontiers; it is in the name of the King that liberty is attacked, and if they succeeded in its overthrow it would be in his name that they indemnify the allied powers for their expenses; because we understand the generosity of kings; we know with what disinterestedness they dispatch their armies to desolate a foreign land, and up to what point they would exhaust their treasuries to maintain a war that could not be profitable to them. Finally, of all the evils they are striving to heap upon our heads, and of all those we have to fear, the name alone of the King is the pretext or the cause . . .

Will you wait until weary of the hardships of the Revolution or corrupted by the habit of grovelling around a castle and the insidious preachings of moderantism [*the principles of the moderate party in politics*] – until weak men become accustomed to speak of liberty without enthusiasm and slavery without horror? How does it happen that the constituted authorities block one another in their course; that armed forces forget that they exist to obey; that soldiers or generals undertake to influence the legislative body, and distempered citizens to direct, by the machinery of violence, the action of the chief of the executive authority? Do they wish to establish a military government? That is perhaps the most imminent, the most terrible of our dangers. Murmurs are arising against the court: who shall dare to say they are unjust? It is suspected of treacherous plans; what facts can be cited to dispel these suspicions?

They speak of popular movements, of martial law; they try to familiarize the imagination with the blood of the people; the palace of the King of the French is suddenly changed to a redoubt; yet where are his enemies? Against whom are these cannons and these bayonets pointed? The defenders of the Constitution have been repulsed by the ministry; the reins of the empire have been hanging loose at the moment when it needed as much vigour as patriotism to hold them. Everywhere discord is fomenting, fanaticism triumphing. Instead of taking a firm and patriotic attitude to save it from the storm, the government lets itself be driven before the tempest; its instability inspires foreign powers with scorn; the boldness of those who vomit armies and swords against us chills the good will of the peoples who wish in secret for the triumph of liberty . . .

This means is worthy of the august mission that you fill, of the generous people whom you represent; it might even gain some celebrity for the name of that people and make you worthy to live in the memory of men: it will be to imitate the brave Spartans who sacrificed themselves at Thermopylae; those venerable men who, leaving the Roman Senate, went to await, at the thresholds of their homes, the death that marched in the van of the savage conqueror. No, you will not need to offer up prayers that avengers may spring from your ashes. Ah! The day your blood shall redden the earth, tyranny, its pride, its protectors, its palaces, its satellites, will vanish away forever before the national omnipotence. And if the sorrow of not having made your country happy embitters your last moments you will at least take with you the consolation that your death will hasten the ruin of the people's oppressors and that your devotion will have saved liberty . . .

*The King was executed in January 1793.*

•

## GEORGES JACQUES DANTON
### 2 September 1792

### 'To dare, to dare again, ever to dare!'

*Georges Jacques Danton (1759–94) was one of the few revolutionaries who almost never wrote his speeches, which is why he is remembered only by fragments such as this stirring and famous address. Danton had set himself up as an orator and agitator at the left-wing Cordeliers Club. By 1791 he had obtained a post under the Commune of Paris where he built his reputation as a tribune of the people, the 'Mirabeau of the mob'. He became Minister of Justice in August when the Commune forced the Assembly to suspend the King until he could be brought to trial.*

*Meanwhile the Prussians were advancing into France – the news that Verdun had fallen arrived in Paris on the day Danton made this speech. It was against this background that Danton called France to arms and made the speech of his life. As he spoke the September massacres were starting in the city outside.*

*'See Danton enter,' says Thomas Carlyle in his history of the French Revolution, 'the black brows clouded, the colossus figure tramping heavy; grim energy looking from all the features of the rugged man . . . So speaks the stentor-voice!'*

*'If ever there was an attempt to influence by rhetoric a popular emotion which could not be checked, and to direct energy from a destructive to a fruitful object, it is to be found in this famous speech,' Hilaire Belloc wrote in his life of Danton. The closing words are engraved on his statue.*

It seems a satisfaction for the ministers of a free people to announce to them that their country will be saved. All are stirred, all are enthused, all burn to enter the combat.

You know that Verdun is not yet in the power of our enemies, and that its garrison swears to immolate the first who breathes a proposition of surrender.

One portion of our people will guard our frontiers, another will dig and arm the entrenchments, the third with pikes will defend the interior of our cities. Paris will second these great efforts. The commissioners of the Commune will solemnly proclaim to the citizens the invitation to arm and march to the defence of the country. At such a moment you can proclaim that the capital deserves the esteem of all France. At such a moment this National Assembly becomes a veritable committee of war. We ask that you concur with us in directing this sublime movement of the people, by naming commissioners to second and assist all these great measures. We ask that any one refusing to give personal service or to furnish arms shall meet the punishment of death. We ask that proper instructions be given to the citizens to direct their movements. We ask that carriers be sent to all the departments to notify them of the decrees that you proclaim here. The tocsin we shall sound is not the alarm signal of danger, it orders the charge on the enemies of France. (*Applause*) To conquer we have need to dare, to dare again, ever to dare! And the safety of France is insured.

•

## MAXIMILIEN ROBESPIERRE
### 3 December 1792

### *'Louis must perish because our country must live!'*

*Maximilien François Marie Isidore de Robespierre (1758–94), a lawyer from Arras, was the first modern dictator, a political Calvinist known as the Incorruptible, to whom men were nothing and principles everything. His political career began in 1789, when he was elected to the Estates-General, where he distinguished himself as a champion of the Rights of Man and became a leader of the left in the Constituent Assembly and the Jacobin Club.*

*Robespierre had once been the eloquent defender of the abolition of capital punishment and trial by jury. His transition from political reformer to revolutionary is demonstrated in this speech demanding the King's execution without trial. It is a speech which shows Robespierre settling his conscience and examining the actions required of a terrorist, the oratory of a man who senses his destiny and sees himself as peculiarly fitted for his task.*

What is the conduct prescribed by sound policy to cement the republic? It is to engrave deeply into all hearts a contempt for royalty, and to strike terror into the partisans of the King. To place his crime before the world as a problem, his cause as the object of the most imposing discussion that ever existed, to place an immeasurable space between the memory of what he was and the title of a citizen, is the very way to make him most dangerous to liberty. Louis XVI was king, and the republic is established. The question is solved by this single fact. Louis is dethroned by his crimes, he conspired against the republic; either he is condemned or the republic is not acquitted. To propose the trial of Louis XVI is to question the Revolution. If he may be tried, he may be acquitted; if he may be acquitted, he may be innocent. But, if he be innocent, what becomes of the Revolution? If he be innocent, what are we but his calumniators? The coalition is just; his imprisonment is a crime; all the patriots are guilty; and the great cause which for so many centuries has been debated between crime and virtue, between liberty and tyranny, is finally decided in favour of crime and despotism!

Citizens, beware! you are misled by false notions. The majestic movements of a great people, the sublime impulses of virtue present themselves as the eruption of a volcano, and as the overthrow of political society. When a nation is forced to recur to the right of insurrection, it returns to its original state. How can the tyrant appeal to the social compact? He has destroyed it! What laws replace it? Those of nature: the people's safety. The right to punish the tyrant or to dethrone him is the same thing. Insurrection is the trial of the tyrant – his sentence is his fall from power; his punishment is exacted by the liberty of the people. The people dart their thunderbolts, that is, their sentence; they do not condemn kings, they suppress them – thrust them back again into nothingness. In what republic was the right of punishing a tyrant ever deemed a question? Was Tarquin tried? What would have been said in Rome if any one had undertaken his defence? Yet we demand advocates for Louis! They hope to gain the cause; otherwise we are only acting an absurd farce in the face of Europe. And we dare to talk of a republic! Ah! we are so pitiful for oppressors because we are pitiless towards the oppressed!

Two months since, and who would have imagined there could be a question here of the inviolability of kings? Yet today a member of the National Convention, Citizen Pétion, brings the question before you as though it were one for serious deliberation! O crime! O shame! The tribune of the French people has echoed the panegyric of Louis XVI. Louis combats us from the depths of his prison, and you ask if he be guilty, and if he may be treated as an enemy. Will you allow the Constitution to be invoked in his favour? If so, the Constitution condemns you; it forbids you to overturn it. Go, then, to the feet of the tyrant and implore his pardon and clemency.

But there is another difficulty – to what punishment shall we condemn him? The punishment of death is too cruel, says one. No, says another, life is more cruel still, and we must condemn him to live. Advocates, is it from pity or from cruelty you wish to annul the punishment of crimes? For myself I abhor the penalty of death; I neither love nor hate Louis; I hate nothing but his crimes. I demanded the abolition of capital punishment in the Constituent Assembly, and it is not my fault if the first principles of reason have appeared moral and judicial heresies. But you who never thought this mercy should be exercised in favour of those whose offences are pardonable, by what fatality are you reminded of your humanity to plead the cause of the greatest of criminals? You ask an exception from the punishment of death for him who alone could render it legitimate! A dethroned king in the very heart of a republic not yet cemented! A king whose very name draws foreign wars on the nation! Neither prison nor exile can make his an innocent existence. It is with regret I pronounce the fatal truth! Louis must perish rather than a hundred thousand virtuous citizens! Louis must perish because our country must live!

•

THOMAS ERSKINE
18 December 1792

'The rights of man'

*After meeting Benjamin Franklin in London in 1774, Thomas Paine (1737–1809) emigrated to America, where he became a radical journalist and fought against Britain in the revolutionary war. After a mission to France, he returned to England and published* The Rights of Man, *a reply to Edmund Burke's*

Reflections on the Revolution in France. *It supported the French Revolution and appealed for the overthrow of the British monarchy.*

*He was indicted for treason but had escaped to Paris when a 'special' jury of the Court of the King's Bench was called to try him.*

*Erskine, who sympathized with the French Revolution and was now the most celebrated lawyer in England, defended Paine. His courage cost him the attorney-generalship.*

I say, in the name of Thomas Paine, and in his words as author of *The Rights of Man* as written in the very volume that is charged with seeking the destruction of property:

> The end of all political associations is the preservation of the rights of man, which rights are liberty, property, and security; that the nation is the source of all sovereignty derived from it; the right of property being secured and inviolable, no one ought to be deprived of it, except in cases of evident public necessity, legally ascertained, and on condition of a previous just indemnity.

These are undoubtedly the rights of man – the rights for which all governments are established – and the only rights Mr Paine contends for; but which he thinks (no matter whether right or wrong) are better to be secured by a republican Constitution than by the forms of the English government. He instructs me to admit that, when government is once constituted, no individuals, without rebellion, can withdraw their obedience from it – that all attempts to excite them to it are highly criminal, for the most obvious reasons of policy and justice – that nothing short of the will of a whole people can change or affect the rule by which a nation is to be governed – and that no private opinion, however honestly inimical to the forms or substance of the law, can justify resistance to its authority, while it remains in force. The author of *The Rights of Man* not only admits the truth of all this doctrine, but he consents to be convicted, and I also consent for him, unless his work shall be found studiously and painfully to inculcate these great principles of government which it is charged to have been written to destroy.

Let me not, therefore, be suspected to be contending that it is lawful to write a book pointing out defects in the English government, and exciting individuals to destroy its sanctions and to refuse obedience. But, on the other hand, I do contend that it is lawful to address the English nation on these momentous subjects; for had it not been for this inalienable right (thanks be to God and our fathers for establishing it!), how should we have had this Constitution which we so loudly boast of? If, in the march of the human mind, no man could have gone before the establishments of the time he lived in, how could our establishment, by reiterated changes, have become what it is? If no man could have awakened the public mind to errors and abuses in our government, how could it have passed on from stage to stage, through reformation and revolution, so as to have arrived from barbarism to such a pitch of happiness and perfection that the Attorney-General considers it as profanation to touch it further or to look for any future amendment?

In this manner power has reasoned in every age – government, in its own estimation, has been at all times a system of perfection; but a free press has examined and detected its errors, and the people have, from time to time, reformed them. This freedom has alone made our government what it is; this freedom alone can preserve it; and therefore, under the banners of that freedom, today I stand up to defend Thomas Paine. But how, alas! shall this task be accomplished? How may I expect from you what human nature has not made man for the performance of? How am I to address your reasons, or ask them to pause, amidst the torrent of prejudice which has hurried away the public mind on the subject you are to judge? . . .

Was any Englishman ever so brought as a criminal before an English court of justice? If I were to ask you, gentlemen of the jury, what is the choicest fruit that grows upon the tree of English liberty, you would answer: security under the law. If I were to ask the whole people of England the return they looked for at the hands of government, for the burdens under which they bend to support it, I should still be answered: security under the law; or, in other words, an impartial administration of justice. So sacred, therefore, has the freedom of trial been ever held in England – so anxiously does Justice guard against every possible bias in her path – that if the public mind has been locally agitated upon any subject in judgement, the forum has either been changed or the trial postponed. The circulation of any paper that brings, or can be supposed to bring, prejudice, or even well-founded knowledge, within the reach of a British tribunal, on the spur of an occasion, is not only highly criminal, but defeats itself, by leading to put off the trial which its object was to pervert . . .

Milton wisely says that a disposition in a nation to this species of controversy is no proof of sedition or degeneracy, but quite the reverse (I omitted to cite the passage with the others). In speaking of this subject, he rises into that inexpressibly sublime style of writing wholly peculiar to himself. He was, indeed, no plagiary from anything human; he looked up for light and expression, as he himself wonderfully describes it, by devout prayer to that great Being who is the source of all utterance and knowledge, and who sendeth out His seraphim with the hallowed fire of His altar to touch and purify the lips of whom He pleases. 'When the cheerfulness of the people,' says this mighty poet, 'is so sprightly up, as that it hath not only wherewith to guard well its own freedom and safety, but to spare, and to bestow upon the solidest and sublimest points of controversy and new invention, it betokens us not degenerated nor drooping to a fatal decay, but casting off the old and wrinkled skin of corruption, to outlive these pangs and wax young again, entering the glorious ways of truth and prosperous virtue, destined to become great and honourable in these latter ages. Methinks I see in my mind a noble and puissant nation rousing herself, like a strong man after sleep, and shaking her invincible locks; methinks I see her as an eagle mewing her mighty youth, and kindling her undazzled eyes at the full midday beam; purging and unsealing her long-abused sight at the fountain itself of heavenly radiance; while the whole noise of timorous and flocking birds, with those also that love the twilight, flutter about, amazed at what she means, and in their envious gabble would prognosticate a year of sects and schisms.'

Gentlemen, what Milton only saw in his mighty imagination, I see in fact; what he expected, but which never came to pass, I see now fulfilling; methinks I see this noble and puissant nation, not degenerated and drooping to a fatal decay, but casting off the wrinkled skin of corruption to put on again the vigour of her youth. And it is because others as well as myself see this that we have all this uproar. France and its Constitution are the mere pretences. It is because Britons begin to recollect the inheritance of their own Constitution left them by their ancestors; it is because they are awakened to the corruptions which have fallen upon its most valuable parts, that forsooth the nation is in danger of being destroyed by a single pamphlet . . .

Gentlemen, I have but a few more words to trouble you with: I take my leave of you with declaring that all this freedom which I have been endeavouring to assert is no more than the ancient freedom which belongs to our own inbred Constitution; I have not asked you to acquit Thomas Paine upon any new lights, or upon any principle but that of the law, which you are sworn to administer – my great object has been to inculcate that wisdom and policy which are the parents of the government of Great Britain, forbid this jealous eye over her subjects; and that, on the contrary, they cry aloud in the language of the poet, adverted to by Lord Chatham on the memorable subject of America, unfortunately without effect.

> Be to their faults a little blind,
> Be to their virtues very kind;
> Let all their thoughts be unconfin'd,
> Nor clap your padlock on the mind.

Engage the people by their affections, convince their reason – and they will be loyal from the only principle that can make loyalty sincere, vigorous, or rational – a conviction that it is their truest interest, and that their government is for their good. Constraint is the natural parent of resistance, and a pregnant proof that reason is not on the side of those who use it. You must all remember Lucian's pleasant story: Jupiter and a countryman were walking together, conversing with great freedom and familiarity upon the subject of heaven and earth. The countryman listened with attention and acquiescence, while Jupiter strove only to convince him – but happening to hint a doubt, Jupiter turned hastily around and threatened him with his thunder. 'Ah! ah!' says the countryman, 'now, Jupiter, I know that you are wrong; you are always wrong when you appeal to your thunder.'

This is the case with me – I can reason with the people of England, but I cannot fight against the thunder of authority.

Gentlemen, this is my defence of free opinions. With regard to myself, I am, and always have been, obedient and affectionate to the law – to that rule of action, as long as I exist, I shall ever do as I have done today, maintain the dignity of my high profession, and perform, as I understand them, all its important duties.

*Erskine's eloquence was futile. As the Attorney-General rose to reply, the foreman of the jury announced that it had reached its verdict without any need for argument. The verdict was guilty.*

•

## GEORGES JACQUES DANTON
### 10 March 1793

### 'The people have nothing but blood'

*When Danton returned from a secret mission to Belgium in March 1793, the Austrians had reoccupied Aix-la-Chapelle and an English, Dutch and Hanoverian army was being assembled in Holland. The Convention in Paris ordered the mustering of 300,000 men. On 10 March, a rumour spread that Dumouriez,*

*France's most brilliant general, had surrendered in Holland. There were riots in*
*the streets as Danton addressed a frightened Convention.*

When the edifice is on fire, I do not join the rascals who would steal the
furniture; I extinguish the flames. I tell you, therefore, you should be
convinced by the dispatches of Dumouriez that you have not a moment
to spare in saving the republic.

Dumouriez conceived a plan which did honour to his genius. I would
render him greater justice and praise than I did recently. But three
months ago he announced to the executive power, your general committee of defence, that if we were not audacious enough to invade Holland
in the middle of winter, to declare instantly against England the war
which actually we had long been making, that we would double the
difficulties of our campaign, in giving our enemies the time to deploy
their forces. Since we failed to recognize this stroke of his genius, we
must now repair our faults.

Dumouriez is not discouraged; he is in the middle of Holland, where
he will find munitions of war; to overthrow all our enemies, he wants
but Frenchmen, and France is filled with citizens. Would we be free? If
we no longer desire it, let us perish, for we have all sworn it. If we wish
it, let all march to defend our independence. Your enemies are making
their last efforts. Pitt, recognizing he has all to lose, dares spare nothing.
Take Holland, and Carthage is destroyed, and England can no longer
exist but for liberty! Let Holland be conquered to liberty, and even the
commercial aristocracy itself, which at the moment dominates the English people, would rise against the government which had dragged it
into despotic war against a free people. They would overthrow this
ministry of stupidity, who thought the methods of the *ancien régime* could
smother the genius of liberty breathing in France. This ministry once
overthrown in the interests of commerce, the party of liberty would
show itself; for it is not dead! And if you know your duties, if your
commissioners leave at once, if you extend the hand to the strangers
aspiring to destroy all forms of tyranny, France is saved and the world is
free.

Expedite, then, your commissioners; sustain them with your energy;
let them leave this very night, this very evening.

Let them say to the opulent classes, the aristocracy of Europe must
succumb to our efforts, and pay our debt, or you will have to pay it!
The people have nothing but blood – they lavish it! Go, then, ingrates,
and lavish your wealth! (*Wild applause.*) See, citizens, the fair destinies

that await you. What! you have a whole nation as a lever, its reason as your fulcrum, and you have not yet upturned the world! To do this we need firmness and character; and of a truth we lack it. I put to one side all passions. They are all strangers to me save a passion for the public good.

In the most difficult situations, when the enemy was at the gates of Paris, I said to those governing: 'Your discussions are shameful; I can see but the enemy. (*Fresh applause.*) You tire me by squabbling, in place of occupying yourselves with the safety of the republic! I repudiate you all as traitors to our country! I place you all in the same line!' I said to them: 'What care I for my reputation? Let France be free, though my name were accursed!' What care I that I am called 'a blood-drinker'? Well, let us drink the blood of the enemies of humanity, if needful; but let us struggle, let us achieve freedom. Some fear the departure of the commissioners may weaken one or the other section of this convention. Vain fears! Carry your energy everywhere. The pleasantest declaration will be to announce to the people that the terrible debt weighing upon them will be wrested from their enemies or that the rich will shortly have to pay it. The national situation is cruel. The representatives of value are no longer in equilibrium in the circulation. The day of the working man is lengthened beyond necessity. A great corrective measure is necessary! Conquerors of Holland, reanimate in England the republican party; let us advance France, and we shall go glorified to posterity. Achieve these grand destinies: no more debates, no more quarrels, and the fatherland is saved.

•

## PIERRE VERGNIAUD
### 13 March 1793

*'The Revolution, like Saturn, devouring successively all her children'*

*Three days after Danton had summoned France to arms, Vergniaud delivered one of the greatest speeches of the Revolution – a condensed history of conditions in France on the verge of the Terror. According to Simon Schama, it was a speech, even by Vergniaud's standards, that was remarkable for its rhetorical power and political courage.*

*As the Jacobins decided on the annihilation of the Girondins, Vergniaud was selected as the Girondins' spokesman. He had been silent for six weeks when he mounted the tribune, promised to speak the truth – and spoke for his life.*

Unceasingly overwhelmed with calumnies, I have abstained from using the tribune because I thought that my presence there might excite passions, and I could not carry there the hope of being useful to my country. But today, when we are all reunited by a sentiment of danger common to us all; today, when the entire National Convention finds itself on the border of an abyss, where the slightest impetus could precipitate it forever, together with liberty; today, when the emissaries of Catiline do not merely present themselves at the gates of Rome but have the insolent audacity to come to this hall to display the signs of the counterrevolution, I cannot keep a silence which would become a veritable treason . . .

It is no longer possible to speak of respect for the laws, for humanity, for justice, for the rights of man . . . without being qualified at least as an intriguer, and more often yet, as an aristocrat and a counter-revolutionary; on the contrary, to provoke to murder, to incite to pillage, is a sure means of obtaining from the men who have seized the helm of public opinion, the palms of patriotism and the glorious title of patriots . . .

Thus from crimes to amnesty, from amnesty to crimes, a great number of citizens have reached the point of confusing seditious insurrections with the great insurrection of liberty, and of regarding the provocation of brigands as the explosion of energetic souls, and brigandage itself as a measure of public safety. It was a great step forward for the enemies of the Republic to have thus perverted reason and annihilated the ideas of morality. There remained to the people defenders who could still enlighten them; men who, from the first days of the Revolution, have consecrated themselves to its success, not through speculation, nor to find under the banner of liberty the means of soiling themselves with new crimes; not to acquire great houses and carriages while hypocritically proclaiming against wealth, but to have the glory of cooperating in the happiness of their country, sacrificing to this single ambition of their souls, profession, fortune, work, even family – in a word, all that was most dear to them. The aristocracy has tried to destroy them with calumny. It has pursued them with perfidious denunciations, by imposture, by frantic cries, sometimes in infamous libels, sometimes in even more infamous speeches from this tribune, in the popular assemblies, in the public places, every day, at every hour, every moment. We have seen develop this strange system of liberty according to which they say to you: 'You are free; but think as we do on such and such a question of political economy or we will denounce you to the vengeance of the people. You are free; but bow your head before the idol to which we burn incense or we will denounce you to the vengeance of the people. You are free; but join us in persecuting the men whose honesty and intelligence we doubt or we will designate you by ridiculous names and we will denounce you to the vengeance of the people.'

Then, Citizens, it has been permitted to fear that the Revolution, like Saturn, devouring successively all her children, will produce at last a despotism with the calamities that accompany it . . .

The fires of passion have been lighted with fury within this Assembly, and the aristocracy, putting no more limits to its hopes, has conceived the infernal project of destroying the Convention through itself . . . It has said: 'Let us inflame hatred still more; let us contrive that the National Convention itself should be the burning crater from which comes those sulphurous expressions of conspiracies or treason or counter-revolution. Let us profit by the imprudence of too ardent patriotism so that the anger of the people seems directed against one part of the Convention by the other. Our rage will do the rest; and if in the movement we will have excited some members of the Convention perish, we will at once present to France their colleagues as their assassins and executioners; the public indignation which we will have raised will soon produce a second catastrophe that will engulf the whole of the national representation.' . . .

This Tribunal, if it were organized on principles of justice, could be useful. The Convention had welcomed the idea of its formation; it was resolved to make it serve the success of the counter-revolution. They flattered themselves that it would be easy to persuade the Convention that the Ministers were guilty of the defeat of Aix-la-Chapelle, and thus to obtain at least their dismissal; that it would not be impossible to lead it to choose new ones from their own numbers; that they would find there members sufficiently corrupt, through ambition, to wish to accumulate in their hands the executives and the legislative functions, and that, through intrigue and terror, they would succeed in getting them elected. Once men invested with the inviolability inherent in the character of representatives of the people had in their hands all the wealth of the Republic, had at their disposition all the places, all the favours, the benefits to bribe, to frighten; all the means of intrigue, of corruption, of popularity, and even of sedition, they would crush with all the power of their ascendancy the National Convention, which would become in their hands a mere instrument to legalize their crimes and their tyranny; and if some citizens wished to raise a lamenting voice against this new tyranny, the Revolutionary Tribunal was there to try him as a conspirator, to make his head fall, and to impose silence.

I will say, however, that more than one Brutus watches over its [the Republic's] safety, and if, among its members, it should find decemvirs, they would live no more than a day . . .

You, unfortunate people, will you longer be the dupes of hypocrites who would rather obtain your applause than to merit it, who curry favour by flattering your passions rather than render you a single service . . . A tyrant of antiquity had an iron bed on which he had his victims stretched, mutilating those who were too tall for the bed and painfully dislocating those shorter, in order to make them the right length.

It [liberty] is often presented to you under the emblem of two tigers that are tearing each other to pieces. See it rather under the most consoling emblem of two brothers who embrace each other. That which they wish to have you adopt, daughter of hate and of jealousy, goes always armed with daggers. True equality, that of nature, instead of dividing them, unites them by the bonds of universal fraternity. It is that alone which can make your happiness and that of the world. The monsters stifle it and offer licence for your misguided worship. Licence, like all false gods, has its druids who would nourish it with human victims. May these cruel priests undergo the fate of their predecessors. May infamy forever seal the dishonoured stone which will cover their ashes.

When the people for the first time prostrated themselves before the sun to call it the father of nature, do you believe it was veiled by destroying clouds which bring the tempest? No, without doubt, brilliant in glory, it was advancing then in the immensity of space, spreading upon the universe fecundity and light.

Very well, let us dissipate by our firmness these clouds which envelop our political horizon; let us crush anarchy, no less the enemy of liberty than despotism; let us found liberty upon the laws and a wise Constitution. Soon you will see the thrones collapse, the sceptre break, and the people, stretching their arms towards you, proclaim by cries of joy, universal fraternity.

•

# PIERRE VERGNIAUD
## 10 April 1793

### *'Our moderation has saved the country'*

*On 10 April, as conditions in France worsened, with food scarce, prices high, and civil war in the Vendée, Robespierre – naming Vergniaud – charged the Girondin leaders with complicity with General Dumouriez, who had made a thwarted attempt to overthrow the Convention and restore the monarchy. According to Robespierre, the Girondins were conspiring to restore the monarchy with foreign arms, a result that would please 'bourgeois aristocrats'.*

*Vergniaud had no warning of Robespierre's attack but started to take notes when he ascended the tribune. Robespierre's speech was loudly cheered. As Vergniaud took the tribune, the galleries howled their derision, Marat shouted insults, and the mob was in control. Vergniaud silenced the mob and returned to Robespierre the insult of calling him 'Monsieur', when 'Citizen' was the only title for a patriot.*

Robespierre accuses us of having suddenly become 'Moderates' – monks of the order of St Bernard. Moderates – we? I was not such, on the tenth of August, Robespierre, when thou didst hide in thy cellar. Moderates! No, I am not such a Moderate that I would extinguish the national energy. I know that liberty is ever as active as a blazing flame – that it is irreconcilable with the inertia that is fit only for slaves! Had we tried but to feed that sacred fire which burns in my heart as ardently as in that of the men who talk incessantly about 'the impetuosity' of their character, such great dissensions would never have arisen in this Assembly. I know that in revolutionary times it was as great a folly to pretend the ability to calm on the spur of the moment the effervescence of the people as it would be to command the waves of the ocean when they are beaten by the wind. Thus it behoves the lawmaker to prevent as much as he can the storm's disaster by wise counsel. But if under the pretext of revolution it become necessary, in order to be a patriot, to become the declared protector of murder and of robbery – then I am a 'Moderate'!

Since the abolition of the monarchy, I have heard much talk of revolution. I said to myself: there are but two more revolutions possible: that of property or the Agrarian Law, and that which would carry us back to despotism. I have made a firm resolution to resist both the one and the other and all the indirect means that might lead us to them. If that can be construed as being a 'Moderate', then we are all such; for we all have voted for the death penalty against any citizen who would propose either one of them.

I have also heard much said about insurrection – of attempts to cause risings of the people – and I admit I have groaned under it. Either the insurrection has a determined object or it has not; in the latter case, it is a convulsion for the body politic, which, since it cannot do it good, must necessarily do it a great deal of harm. The wish to force insurrection can find lodgement nowhere but in the heart of a bad citizen. If the insurrection has a determined object, what can it be? To transfer the exercise of sovereignty to the Republic. The exercise of sovereignty is confided to the national representatives. Therefore, those who talk of insurrection are trying to destroy national representation; therefore, they are trying to deliver the exercise of sovereignty to a small number of men, or to transfer it upon the head of a single citizen; therefore, they are endeavouring to found an aristocratic government or to re-establish royalty. In either case, they are conspiring against the Republic and liberty, and if it become necessary either to approve them in order to be a patriot or be a 'Moderate' in battling against them, then I am a Moderate!

When the statue of liberty is on the throne, insurrection can be called into being only by the friends of royalty. By continually shouting to the people that they must rise; by continuing to speak to them, not the language of the laws, but that of the passions, arms have been furnished to the aristocracy. Taking the living and the language of sansculottism, it has cried out to the Finistère department: 'You are unhappy; the assignats are at a discount; you ought to rise *en masse.*' In this way the exaggerations have injured the Republic. We are 'Moderates'! But for whose profit have we shown this great moderation? For the profit of the *émigrés*? We have adopted against them all the measures of rigour that were imposed by justice and national interest. For the profit of inside conspirators? We have never ceased to call upon their heads the sword of the law. But I have demurred against the law that threatened to proscribe the innocent as well as the guilty. There was endless talk of terrible measures, of revolutionary measures. I also was in favour of them – these terrible measures, but only against the enemies of the country. I did not want them to compromise the safety of good citizens, for the reason that some unprincipled wretches were interested in their undoing. I wanted punishments but not proscriptions. Some men have appeared as if their patriotism consisted in tormenting others – in causing tears to flow! I would have wished that there should be none but happy people! The Convention is the centre around which all citizens should rally! It may be that their gaze fixed upon it is not always free from fear and anxiety. I would have wished that it should be the centre of all their affections and of all their hopes. Efforts were made to accomplish the revolution by terror. I should have preferred to bring it about by love. In short, I have not thought that, like the priests and the fierce ministers of the Inquisition, who spoke of their God of Mercy only when they were surrounded by autos-da-fé and stakes, we should speak of liberty surrounded by daggers and executioners!

You say we are 'Moderates'! Ah! let thanks be offered us for this moderation of which we are accused as if it were a crime! If, when in this tribune they came to wave the brands of discord and to outrage with the most insolent audacity the majority of the representatives of the people; if, when they shouted with as much fury as folly: 'No more truce! No more peace between us!' we had given way to the promptings of a just indignation; if we had accepted the counter-revolutionary challenge which was tendered to us – I declare to my accusers (and no matter what suspicions they create against us, no matter what the calumnies with which they try to tarnish us, our names still remain more esteemed than theirs) that we would have seen, coming in haste from all the provinces to combat the men of the second of September, men equally formidable to anarchy and to tyrants! And our accusers and we ourselves would be already consumed by the fire of civil war. Our moderation has saved the country from this terrible scourge, and by our silence we have deserved well of the Republic!

*Two months later the Girondins were expelled. Vergniaud's eloquence was still feared and he was not allowed to speak in his defence at his trial. He was executed with twenty-three colleagues.*

•

## CAMILLE DESMOULINS
### 1793

### *'It is a crime to be a king'*

*As a young man of twenty-nine, Camille Desmoulins (1760–94) played a dramatic part in the destruction of the Bastille when on 12 July 1789 he jumped on to a table and addressed the crowd in the Palais-Royal, urging them to take arms: 'It is I who call my brothers to freedom. I would rather die than submit to servitude.' A stutter inhibited his oratory but as editor and founder of the weekly* Revolutions de France *he was the greatest journalist of the Revolution. Desmoulins was elected by Paris to the National Convention, where he delivered this speech calling for the execution of the King.*

It is by the law of nations that this trial ought to be regulated. The slavery of nations during ten thousand years has not been able to rescind their indefensible rights. It was these rights that were a standing protest against the reigning of the Charleses, the Henrys, the Frederics, the Edwards, as they were against the despotism of Julius Caesar. It is a crime to be a king. It was even a crime to be a constitutional king, for the nation had never accepted the constitution. There is only one condition on which it could be legitimate to reign; it is when the whole people formally strips itself of its rights and cedes them to a single man, not only as Denmark did in 1660, but as happens when the entire people has passed or ratified this warrant of its sovereignty. And yet it could not bind the next generation, because death extinguishes all rights. It is the prerogative of those who exist, and who are in possession of this earth, to make the laws for it in their turn. Otherwise, let the dead leave their graves and come to uphold their laws against the living who have repealed them. All other kinds of royalty are imposed upon the people at the risk of their insurrection, just as robbers reign in the forests at the risk of the provost's punishment befalling them. And now after we have risen and recovered our rights, to plead these feudal laws, or even the Constitution, in opposition to republican Frenchmen, is to plead the black code to Negro conquerors of white men. Our constituents have not sent us here to follow those feudal laws and that pretended constitution, but to abolish it, or rather, to declare that it never existed, and to reinvest the nation with that sovereignty which another had usurped. Either we are truly republicans, giants who rise to the heights of these republican ideas, or we are not giants, but mere pygmies. By the law of nations Louis XVI as king, even a constitutional king, was a tyrant in a state of revolt against the nation, and a criminal worthy of death. And Frenchmen have no more need to try him than had Hercules to try the boar of Erymanthus, or the Romans to try Tarquin, or Caesar, who also thought himself a constitutional dictator.

But it is not only a king, it is a criminal accused of crimes that in his person we have to punish.

You must not expect me to indulge in undue exaggeration, and to call him a Nero, as I heard those do who have spoken the most favourably for him. I know that Louis XVI had the inclinations of a tiger, and if we established courts such as Montesquieu calls the courts of manners and behaviour, like that of the Areopagus at Athens, which condemned a child to death for putting out his bird's eyes; if we had an Areopagus, it would have a hundred times condemned this man as dishonouring the human race by the caprices of his wanton cruelties. But as it is not the deeds of his private life, but the crimes of his reign that we are judging, it must be confessed that this long list of accusations against Louis which our committee and our orators have presented to us, while rendering him a thousand times worthy of death, will nevertheless not suggest to posterity the horrors of the reign of Nero, but the crimes of constituents, the crimes of Louis the King, rather than the crimes of Louis Capet.

That which makes the former king justly odious to the people is the four years of perjuries and oaths, incessantly repeated into the nation's ear before the face of heaven, while all the time he was conspiring against the nation. Treason was always with every nation the most abominable of crimes. It has always inspired that horror which is inspired by poison and vipers, because it is impossible to guard against it. So the laws of the Twelve Tables devoted to the Furies the mandatary who betrayed the trust of his constituent, and permitted the latter to kill the former wherever he should find him. So, too, fidelity in fulfilling one's engagements is the only virtue on which those pride themselves who have lost all others. It is the only virtue found among thieves. It is the last bond which holds society – even that of the robbers themselves – together. This comparison, it is, which best paints royalty, by showing how much less villainous is even a robbers' cave than the Louvre, since the maxim of all kings is that of Caesar: 'It is permissible to break one's faith in order to reign.' So in his religious idiom, spoke Antoine de Lèvre to Charles V: 'If you are not willing to be a rascal, if you have a soul to save, renounce the empire.' So said Machiavelli in terms very applicable to our situation. For this reason it was, that many years ago in a petition to the National Assembly I quoted this passage: 'If sovereignty must be renounced in order to make a people free, he who is clothed with this sovereignty has some excuse in betraying the nation, because it is difficult and against nature to be willing to fall from so high a position.' All this proves that the crimes of Louis XVI are the crimes of the constituents who supported him in his position of king rather than his crimes, that is to say, of those who gave him the right by letters patent to be the 'enemy of the nation' and a traitor. But all these considerations, calculated as they may be to soften the horror of his crimes in the eyes of posterity, are useless before the law, in mitigating their punishment. What! Shall the judges forbear to punish a brigand because in his cave he has been brought up to believe that all the possessions of those who pass his cave belong to him? Because his education has so depraved his natural disposition that he could not be anything but a robber? Shall it be alleged as a reason for letting the treason of a king go unpunished, that he could not be anything but a traitor, and as a reason for not giving the nations the example of cutting down this tree, that it can only bear poisons? . . .

'But who shall judge this conspirator?' It is astonishing and inconceivable what trouble this question has given to the best heads of the Convention. Removed as we are from Nature and the primitive laws of all society, most of us have not thought that we could judge a conspirator without a jury of accusation, a jury of judgement, and judges who would apply the law, and all have imagined necessary a court more or less extraordinary. So we leave the ancient ruts only to fall into new ones, instead of following the plain road of common sense. Who shall judge Louis XVI? The whole people, if it can, as the people of Rome judged Manlius and Horatius, nor dreamt of the need of a jury of accusation, to be followed by a jury of judgement, and that in turn by a court which would apply the law to judge a culprit taken in the act. But as we cannot hear the pleas of twenty-five millions of men we must recur to the maxim of Montesquieu: 'Let a free people do all that it can by itself and the rest by representatives and commissioners!' And what is the National Convention but the commission selected by the French people to try the last king and to form the Constitution of the new republic?

Some claim that such a course would be to unite all the powers — legislative functions and judicial functions. Those who have most wearied our ears by reciting the dangers of this cumulation of powers must either deride our simplicity in believing that they respect those limits, or else they do not well understand themselves. For have not constitutional and legislative assemblies assumed a hundred times the functions of judges, whether in annulling the procedure of the Chatelet, and many other tribunals, or in issuing decrees against so many prisoners on suspicion whether there was an accusation or not? To acquit Mirabeau and 'P. Equality', or to send Lessart to Orléans, was not that to assume the functions of judges? I conclude from this that those 'Balancers', as Mirabeau called them, who continually talk of 'equilibrium', and the balance of power, do not themselves believe in what they say. Can it be contested, for example, that the nation which exercises the power of sovereignty does not 'cumulate' all the powers? Can it be claimed that the nation cannot delegate, at its will, this or that portion of its powers to whom it pleases? Can any one deny that the nation has cumulatively clothed us here with its powers, both to try Louis XVI and to construct the Constitution? One may well speak of the balance of power and the necessity of maintaining it when the people, as in England, exercises its sovereignty only at the time of elections. But when the nation, the sovereign, is in permanent activity, as formerly at Athens and Rome, and as now in France, when the right of sanctioning the laws is recognized as belonging to it, and when it can assemble every day in its municipalities and sections, and expel the faithless mandataries, the great necessity cannot be seen of maintaining the equilibrium of powers, since it is the people who, with its arm of iron, itself holds the scales ready to drive out the ambitious and the traitorous who wish to make it incline to the side opposite the general interest.

It is evident that the people sent us here to judge the King and to give them a constitution. Is the first of these two functions so difficult to fulfil? And have we anything else to do than what Brutus did when the people caused him to judge his two sons himself, and tested him by this, just as the Convention is tested now? He made them come to his tribunal, as you must bring Louis XVI before you. It produced for him the proofs of their conspiracy as you must present to Louis XVI that multitude of overwhelming proofs of his plots. They could make no answer to the testimony of a slave, as Louis XVI will not be able to answer anything to the correspondence of Laporte, and to that mass of written proofs that he paid his bodyguard at Coblentz and betrayed the nation. And it only remains for you to prove, as Brutus proved to the Roman people, that you are worthy to begin the Republic and its Constitution, and to appease the shades of a hundred thousand citizens whom he caused to perish in pronouncing the same sentence: 'Go, lictor, bind him to the stake.'

*Desmoulins was arrested with Danton in March 1794 and died on the guillotine.*

•

MAXIMILIEN ROBESPIERRE
5 February 1794

*'Terror is nothing else than justice'*

*By 1793, when he became a member of the Committee of Public Safety, Robespierre was one of the rulers of France, and chief strategist and philosopher of the second half of the Revolution. His uncompromising principles were set out in his famous speech to the Convention on the principles of morality that ought to guide the Revolution.*

After having marched for a long time at hazard, and, as it were, carried away by the movement of contrary factions, the representatives of the people have at last formed a government. A sudden change in the nation's fortune announced to Europe the regeneration that had been operated in the national representation; but up to this moment we must admit that we have been rather guided in these stormy circumstances by the love of good, and by a sense of the country's wants, than by any exact theory or precise rules of conduct.

It is time to distinguish clearly the aim of the Revolution and the term to which we would arrive. It is time for us to render account to ourselves, both of the obstacles which still keep us from that aim and of the means which we ought to take to attain it.

What is the aim to which we tend?

The peaceful enjoyment of liberty and equality; the reign of that eternal justice of which the laws have been engraved, not upon marble, but upon the hearts of all mankind – even in the hearts of the slaves who forget them or of the tyrants who have denied them! We desire a state of things wherein all base and cruel passions shall be enchained, all generous and beneficent passions awakened by the laws; wherein ambition should be the desire of glory, and glory the desire of serving the country; wherein distinctions should arise but from equality itself; wherein the citizen should submit to the magistrate, the magistrate to the people, and the people to justice; wherein the country assures the welfare of every individual; wherein every individual enjoys with pride the prosperity and the glory of his country; wherein all minds are enlarged by the continual communication of republican sentiments and by the desire of meriting the esteem of a great people; wherein arts should be the decorations of that liberty which they ennoble, and commerce the source of public wealth and not the monstrous opulence of some few houses. We desire to substitute morality for egotism, probity for honour, principles for usages, duties for functions, the empire of reason for the tyranny of fashions, the scorn of vice for the scorn of misfortune, pride for insolence, greatness of soul for vanity, the love of glory for the love of money, good citizens for good society, merit for intrigue, genius for cleverness, truth for splendour, the charm of happiness for the ennui of voluptuousness, the grandeur of man for the pettiness of the great, a magnanimous people, powerful, happy, for a people amiable, frivolous, and miserable; that is to say, all the virtues and all the miracles of a republic for all the vices and all the follies of a monarchy.

What is the nature of the government that can realize these prodigies? The democratic or republican government.

Democracy is that state in which the people, guided by laws that are its own work, executes for itself all that it can well do, and, by its delegates, all that it cannot do itself. But to found and consolidate democracy, we must first end the war of liberty against tyranny, and traverse the storm of the Revolution. Such is the aim of the revolutionary system you have organized; you ought, therefore, to regulate your conduct by the circumstances in which the Republic finds itself; and the plan of your administration ought to be the result of the spirit of revolutionary government, combined with the general principles of democracy.

The great purity of the French Revolution, the sublimity even of its object, is precisely that which makes our force and our weakness. Our force, because it gives us the ascendancy of truth over imposture, and the rights of public interest over private interest. Our weakness, because it rallies against us all the vicious; all those who in their hearts meditate the robbery of the people; all those who, having robbed them, seek impunity; all those who have rejected liberty as a personal calamity; and those who have embraced the Revolution as a trade and the Republic as a prey. Hence the defection of so many ambitious men, who have abandoned us on our route because they did not commence the journey to arrive at the same object as we did. We must crush both the interior and exterior enemies of the Republic, or perish with her. And in this situation, the first maxim of your policy should be to conduct the people by reason and the enemies of the people by terror. If the spring of popular government during peace is virtue, the spring of popular government in rebellion is at once both virtue and terror; virtue, without which terror is fatal! terror, without which virtue is powerless! Terror is nothing else than justice, prompt, secure, and inflexible! It is, therefore, an emanation of virtue; it is less a particular principle than a consequence of the general principles of democracy, applied to the most urgent wants of the country.

It has been said that terror is the instrument of a despotic government. Does yours, then, resemble despotism? Yes, as the sword which glitters in the hand of a hero of liberty resembles that with which the satellites of tyranny are armed! The government of a revolution is the despotism of liberty against tyranny. Is force, then, only made to protect crime? Is it not also made to strike those haughty heads which the lightning has doomed? Nature has imposed upon every being the law of self-preservation. Crime massacres innocence to reign, and innocence struggles with all its force in the hands of crime. Let tyranny but reign one day, and on the morrow there would not remain a single patriot. Until when will the fury of tyranny continue to be called justice, and the justice of the people barbarity and rebellion? How tender they are to oppressors – how inexorable to the oppressed! Nevertheless, it is necessary that one or the other should succumb. Indulgence for the Royalist! exclaimed certain people. Pardon for wretches! No! Pardon for innocence, pardon for the weak, pardon for the unhappy, pardon for humanity!

•

## MAXIMILIEN ROBESPIERRE
### 8 June 1794

### 'The Supreme Being'

*For Robespierre, terror and virtue were part of the same exercise in self-improvement – 'virtue, without which terror is harmful and terror, without which virtue is impotent'. So the most important arm of the Convention for Robespierre was the Committee of Public Instruction. Working with the French painter Jacques David, a fellow-revolutionary who directed the great national fêtes founded on classic customs (and inspired by Jean Jacques Rousseau), Robespierre created his most ambitious political production – the Festival of the Supreme Being.*

*David had conceived of the event as a vast revolutionary oratorio, with a choir of 2,400 voices singing the 'Marseillaise' and the new 'Hymn of the Supreme Being', the anthem of Robespierre's Republican religion. Robespierre appeared, dressed in a blue coat, a tricolour sash and plumed hat, as the last strains of the new hymn faded in the Tuileries, where thousands of Parisians were gathered for the ceremonies.*

The day forever fortunate has arrived, which the French people have consecrated to the Supreme Being. Never has the world which He created offered to Him a spectacle so worthy of His notice. He has seen reigning on the earth tyranny, crime, and imposture. He sees at this moment a whole nation, grappling with all the oppressions of the human race, suspend the course of its heroic labours to elevate its thoughts and vows toward the great Being who has given it the mission it has undertaken and the strength to accomplish it.

Is it not He whose immortal hand, engraving on the heart of man the code of justice and equality, has written there the death sentence of tyrants? Is it not He who, from the beginning of time, decreed for all the ages and for all peoples liberty, good faith, and justice?

He did not create kings to devour the human race. He did not create priests to harness us, like vile animals, to the chariots of kings and to give to the world examples of baseness, pride, perfidy, avarice, debauchery, and falsehood. He created the universe to proclaim His power. He created men to help each other, to love each other mutually, and to attain to happiness by the way of virtue.

It is He who implanted in the breast of the triumphant oppressor remorse and terror, and in the heart of the oppressed and innocent calmness and fortitude. It is He who impels the just man to hate the evil one, and the evil man to respect the just one. It is He who adorns with modesty the brow of beauty, to make it yet more beautiful. It is He who makes the mother's heart beat with tenderness and joy. It is He who bathes with delicious tears the eyes of the son pressed to the bosom of his mother. It is He who silences the most imperious and tender passions before the sublime love of the fatherland. It is He who has covered nature with charms, riches, and majesty. All that is good is His work, or is Himself. Evil belongs to the depraved man who oppresses his fellow man or suffers him to be oppressed.

The Author of Nature has bound all mortals by a boundless chain of love and happiness. Perish the tyrants who have dared to break it!

Republican Frenchmen, it is yours to purify the earth which they have soiled, and to recall to it the justice that they have banished! Liberty and virtue together came from the breast of Divinity. Neither can abide with mankind without the other.

O generous People, would you triumph over all your enemies? Practise justice, and render the Divinity the only worship worthy of Him. O People, let us deliver ourselves today, under His auspices, to the just transports of a pure festivity. Tomorrow we shall return to the combat with vice and tyrants. We shall give to the world the example of republican virtues. And that will be to honour Him still.

The monster which the genius of kings had vomited over France has gone back into nothingness. May all the crimes and all the misfortunes of the world disappear with it! Armed in turn with the daggers of fanaticism and the poisons of atheism, kings have always conspired to assassinate humanity. If they are able no longer to disfigure Divinity by superstition, to associate it with their crimes, they try to banish it from the earth, so that they may reign there alone with crime.

O People, fear no more their sacrilegious plots! They can no more snatch the world from the breast of its Author than remorse from their own hearts. Unfortunate ones, uplift your eyes toward heaven! Heroes of the fatherland, your generous devotion is not a brilliant madness. If the satellites of tyranny can assassinate you, it is not in their power entirely to destroy you. Man, whoever thou mayest be, thou canst still conceive high thoughts for thyself. Thou canst bind thy fleeting life to God, and to immortality. Let nature seize again all her splendour, and wisdom all her empire! The Supreme Being has not been annihilated.

It is wisdom above all that our guilty enemies would drive from the republic. To wisdom alone it is given to strengthen the prosperity of empires. It is for her to guarantee to us the rewards of our courage. Let us associate wisdom, then, with all our enterprises. Let us be grave and discreet in all our deliberations, as men who are providing for the interests of the world. Let us be ardent and obstinate in our anger against conspiring tyrants, imperturbable in dangers, patient in labours, terrible in striking back, modest and vigilant in successes. Let us be generous towards the good, compassionate with the unfortunate, inexorable with the evil, just towards every one. Let us not count on an unmixed prosperity, and on triumphs without attacks, nor on all that depends on fortune or the perversity of others. Sole, but infallible guarantors of our independence, let us crush the impious league of kings by the grandeur of our character, even more than by the strength of our arms.

Frenchmen, you war against kings; you are therefore worthy to honour Divinity. Being of Beings, Author of Nature, the brutalized slave, the vile instrument of despotism, the perfidious and cruel aristocrat, outrages Thee by his very invocation of Thy name. But the defenders of liberty can give themselves up to Thee, and rest with confidence upon Thy paternal bosom. Being of Beings, we need not offer to Thee unjust prayers. Thou knowest Thy creatures, proceeding from Thy hands. Their needs do not escape Thy notice, more than their secret thoughts. Hatred of bad faith and tyranny burns in our hearts, with love of justice and the fatherland. Our blood flows for the cause of humanity. Behold our prayer. Behold our sacrifices. Behold the worship we offer Thee.

•

## MAXIMILIEN ROBESPIERRE
26 July 1794

### 'Death is the beginning of immortality'

*By July 1794, the moderates in the Convention grew more outspoken in condemning a Terror that was no longer justified by war. Robespierre's influence was waning fast. Millions of jobless and landless were asking why the Committee of Public Safety was doing nothing to alleviate their condition – but Robespierre was preoccupied with stamping out vice. Plans were laid for his downfall. He signed his death sentence when he carried a law by which deputies could be tried by order of the CPS, with no proof of guilt required.*

*Robespierre decided to deliver a speech denouncing his enemies – by now he had few friends – which he composed in solitary walks through the woods at Ville d'Array and in contemplation of Rousseau's tomb.*

*On 8 Thermidor he mounted the tribune and gave, lasting two hours, the last speech of his life. Only the frequent blinking of his eyes and the nervous drumming of his fingers on the pulpit betrayed his inner agitation as he spoke in a slow, even voice from his manuscript.*

Is it I who have thrown patriots into prison and have carried the Terror into every walk of life? Is it I who – while shielding treason and neglecting the crimes of aristocracy – have waged war upon peaceful citizens, magnified into crime private opinion and trifling offence, pretending to see guilt on every hand, until the Revolution has become abhorred by the people itself?

When the victims of their tyranny would complain, they would excuse themselves by saying: Robespierre wills it; we are not to blame. They said to the nobles: it is he who has proscribed you. To the patriots: he wants to save the nobles. To the priests: he alone persecutes you; without him you would be left in peace and could triumph. To the fanatics: he wants to destroy religion. To patriots whom they persecuted: he has ordered it, or does not want to have it stopped. All manner of complaints were sent to me regarding wrongs I lacked the power to right, and people were told: your fate depends on him alone. They said: look at these pitiful condemned! Who is responsible for their fate? Robespierre! – They particularly set out to prove that the Revolutionary Tribunal was a bloody assize created and controlled by me alone, for the purpose of executing both the just and the unjust – for it was considered useful to raise up enemies against me among men both good and evil. Hardly an individual has been arrested, hardly a citizen vexed, but he was told: behold the author of your woes! But for him you would be free and happy. In all the prisons and in all the Departments this plan of attack was followed. It was I who had done everything, required everything, commanded everything, for it should not be forgotten that I bear the title of Dictator.

I will confine myself to saying that the nature and extent of this calumny – the inability to do good and prevent wrong from being done – have forced me, for the last six weeks, to abandon completely my functions as member of the Committee of Public Safety. Six weeks have passed since my dictatorship is at an end. Is the country happier now? I hope so!

They call me a tyrant. If I were one, they would crawl at my feet. I would gorge them with gold and permit them to commit crime unhindered, and they would heap gratitude upon me.

If the reins of the Republic are relaxed even for a moment, military despotism will take possession of them, and we will perish for not having known how to make use of the appointed hour in the destiny of mankind when liberty could have been firmly founded. Without the Revolutionary Government the Republic cannot be made to endure, but when that government falls into perfidious hands, then it becomes itself the instrument of counter-revolution.

I have not the gift of feigning respect for scoundrels, and even less (in accordance with a royal maxim) of making use of them. I was made to combat crime, not to govern it.

The weapons of liberty should be wielded only by hands that are clean. I have sometimes feared – I confess it – to become sullied myself by the unclean presence of perverted individuals who have insinuated themselves among the sincere friends of mankind.

The Departments of the Republic where these crimes have been perpetrated, will they forget them because we have forgotten them? Will the complaints to which we close our ears not find a more forceful echo in the hearts of the oppressed? Guilt unpunished, will it not pursue its way from crime to crime? And if the guilty escape the justice of men, will they escape Eternal Justice, which they have outraged by their horrible excesses?

No, Chaumette! No, Fouché! Death is not an eternal sleep! Citizens, erase from the tomb this inscription put there by sacrilegious hands, which casts a pall over the face of nature. Engrave rather this upon it: Death is the beginning of immortality.

*This was the speech that should be read to understand the man, said Hilaire Belloc – a theory stated with power and precision, a noble ideal based on the scaffold; a dogma and a detailed persecution side by side.*

*When he entered the Convention next day, Robespierre was greeted with shouts of 'Down with the tyrant!' He was arrested and imprisoned but escaped. He took refuge in the Hôtel de Ville, where he attempted suicide. He was guillotined with twenty-one of his followers on 28 July – 10 Thermidor.*

•

## WILLIAM PITT THE YOUNGER
### 10 November 1797

### *'Danger with indelible shame and disgrace'*

*After his campaign in Italy, Napoleon Bonaparte had seized power in Paris, and France had rejected peace overtures from Pitt. It was to be war, and Napoleon was greeted by the French revolutionaries as the conqueror of England. As England faced the greatest danger it had yet known, Pitt explained the failure of the negotiations and made his historic appeal for national unity.*

He who scruples to declare that in the present moment the government of France are acting as much in contradiction to the known wishes of the French nation, as to the just pretensions and anxious wishes of the people of Great Britain – he who scruples to declare them the authors of this calamity, deprives us of the consolatory hope which we are inclined

to cherish, of some future change of circumstances more favourable to
our wishes.

It is a melancholy spectacle, indeed, to see in any country, and on the
ruin of any pretence of liberty however nominal, shallow, or delusive, a
system of tyranny erected, the most galling, the most horrible, the most
undisguised in all its parts and attributes that has stained the page of
history, or disgraced the annals of the world; but it would be much
more unfortunate, if when we see that the same cause carries desolation
through France, which extends disquiet and fermentation through
Europe, it would be worse, indeed, if we attributed to the nation of
France that which is to be attributed only to the unwarranted and
usurped authority which involves them in misery, and would, if unre-
sisted, involve Europe with them in one common ruin and
destruction . . .

It is a matter of charge against us that we even harbour in our minds
at this moment a wish to conclude peace upon the terms which we think
admissible with the present rulers of France. I am not one of those who
can or will join in that sentiment. I have no difficulty in repeating what I
stated before, that in their present spirit, after what they have said, and
still more after what they have done, I can entertain little hope of so
desirable an event. I have no hesitation in avowing, for it would be
idleness and hypocrisy to conceal it, that for the sake of mankind in
general, and to gratify those sentiments which can never be eradicated
from the human heart, I should see with pleasure and satisfaction the
termination of a government whose conduct and whose origin is such as
we have seen that of the government of France. But that is not the
object, that ought not to be the principle, of the war, whatever wish I
may entertain in my own heart; and whatever opinion I may think it fair
or manly to avow, I have no difficulty in stating that, violent and odious
as is the character of that government, I verily believe, in the present
state of Europe, that if we are not wanting to ourselves, if, by the
blessing of Providence, our perseverance and our resources should
enable us to make peace with France upon terms in which we taint not
our character, in which we do not abandon the sources of our wealth,
the means of our strength, the defence of what we already possess; if we
maintain our equal pretensions, and assert that rank which we are
entitled to hold among nations – the moment peace can be obtained on
such terms, be the form of government in France what it may, peace is
desirable, peace is then anxiously to be sought. But unless it is attained
on such terms, there is no extremity of war, there is no extremity of

honourable contest, that is not preferable to the name and pretence of peace, which must be in reality a disgraceful capitulation, a base, an abject surrender of everything that constitutes the pride, the safety, and happiness of England . . .

If we look to the whole complexion of this transaction, the duplicity, the arrogance and the violence which has appeared in the course of the negotiation, if we take from thence our opinion of its general result, we shall be justified in our conclusion, not that the people of France, not that the whole government of France, but that that part of the government which had too much influence and has now the whole ascendancy, never was sincere; was determined to accept of no terms of peace but such as would make it neither durable nor safe, such as could only be accepted by this country by a surrender of all its interests, and by a sacrifice of every pretension to the character of a great, a powerful, or an independent nation.

This, sir, is inference no longer, you have their own open avowal. You have it stated in the subsequent declaration of France itself, that it is not against your commerce, it is not against your wealth, it is not against your possessions in the East or colonies in the West, it is not against even the source of your maritime greatness, it is not against any of the appendages of your empire, but against the very essence of your liberty, against the foundation of your independence, against the citadel of your happiness, against your constitution itself, that their hostilities are directed. They have themselves announced and proclaimed the proposition, that what they mean to bring with their invading army is the genius of *their* liberty − I desire no other word to express the subversion of the British constitution, and the substitution of the most malignant and fatal contrast − and the annihilation of British liberty, and the obliteration of everything that has rendered you a great, a flourishing, and a happy people.

This is what is at issue; for this are we to declare ourselves in a manner that deprecates the rage which our enemy will not dissemble and which will be little moved by our entreaty. Under such circumstances, are we ashamed or afraid to declare, in a firm and manly tone, our resolution to defend ourselves, or to speak the language of truth with the energy that belongs to Englishmen united in such a cause? Sir, I do not scruple for one to say, if I knew nothing by which I could state to myself a probability of the contest terminating in our favour, I would maintain, that the contest with its worst chances is preferable to an acquiescence in such demands.

If I could look at this as a dry question of prudence, if I could calculate it upon the mere grounds of interest, I would say, if we love that degree of national power which is necessary for the independence of the country and its safety; if we regard domestic tranquillity, if we look at individual enjoyment, from the highest to the meanest among us, there is not a man, whose stake is so great in the country, that he ought to hesitate a moment in sacrificing any portion of it to oppose the violence of the enemy; nor is there, I trust, a man in this happy and free nation, whose stake is so small, that would not be ready to sacrifice his life in the same cause. If we look at it with a view to safety, this would be our conduct; but if we look at it upon the principle of true honour, of the character which we have to support, of the example which we have to set to the other nations of Europe, if we view rightly the lot in which Providence has placed us, and the contrast between ourselves and all the other countries in Europe, gratitude to that Providence should inspire us to make every effort in such a cause. There may be danger; but on the one side there is danger accompanied with honour, on the other side there is danger with indelible shame and disgrace. Upon such an alternative Englishmen will not hesitate.

I wish to disguise no part of my sentiments upon the grounds on which I put the issue of the contest. I ask whether, up to the principles I have stated, we are prepared to act. Having done so, my opinion is not altered; my hopes, however, are animated from the reflection that the means of our safety are in our own hands. For there never was a period when we had more to encourage us; in spite of heavy burdens, the radical strength of the nation never showed itself more conspicuous; its revenue never exhibited greater proofs of the wealth of the country. The same objects, which constitute the blessings we have to fight for, furnish us with the means of continuing them. But it is not upon that point I rest it. There is one great resource, which I trust will never abandon us. It has shone forth in the English character, by which we have preserved our existence and fame as a nation, which I trust we shall be determined never to abandon under any extremity, but shall join hand and heart in the solemn pledge that is proposed to us, and declare to His Majesty, that we know great exertions are wanting, that we are prepared to make them, and at all events determined to stand or fall by the laws, liberties, and religion of our country.

•

# WILLIAM PITT THE YOUNGER
3 February 1800

## '*An implacable spirit of destruction*'

*Only a few weeks after he made himself First Consul, Napoleon offered peace to England on Christmas Day 1799 but was rebuffed and the war continued. Pitt derided the overweening ambition of France in this speech to a packed House of Commons, responding to a plea by Thomas Erskine for peace.*

The all-searching eye of the French Revolution looks to every part of Europe, and every quarter of the world, in which can be found an object either of acquisition or plunder. Nothing is too great for the temerity of its ambition, nothing too small or insignificant for the grasp of its rapacity. From hence Bonaparte and his army proceeded to Egypt. The attack was made, pretences were held out to the natives of that country in the name of the French King, whom they had murdered; they pretended to have the approbation of the grand seignior, whose territories they were violating; their project was carried on under the profession of a zeal for Mahometanism; it was carried on by proclaiming that France had been reconciled to the Mussulman faith, had abjured that of Christianity, or, as he in his impious language termed it, of '*the sect of the Messiah*'.

The only plea which they have since held out to colour this atrocious invasion of a neutral and friendly territory, is, that it was the road to attack the English power in India. It is most unquestionably true, that this was one and a principal cause of this unparalleled outrage; but another, and an equally substantial cause (as appears by their own statements), was the division and partition of the territories of what they thought a falling power. It is impossible to dismiss this subject without observing that this attack against Egypt was accompanied by an attack upon the British possessions in India, made on true revolutionary principles. In Europe, the propagation of the principles of France had uniformly prepared the way for the progress of its arms. To India, the lovers of peace had sent the messengers of Jacobinism, for the purpose of inculcating war in those distant regions, on Jacobin principles, and of forming Jacobin clubs, which they actually succeeded in establishing, and which in most respects resembled the European model, but which were distinguished by this peculiarity, that they were required to swear in one breath, hatred to tyranny, the love of liberty, and the destruction of all kings and sovereigns – except the good and faithful ally of the French republic, Citizen Tippoo.

What then was the nature of this system? Was it anything but what I have stated it to be; an insatiable love of aggrandizement, an implacable spirit of destruction directed against all the civil and religious institutions of every country? This is the first moving and acting spirit of the French Revolution; this is the spirit which animated it at its birth, and this is the spirit which will not desert it till the moment of its dissolution, 'which grew with its growth, which strengthened with its strength', but which has not abated under its misfortunes, nor declined in its decay; it has been invariably the same in every period, operating more or less, according as accident or circumstances might assist; but it has been inherent in the revolution in all its stages, it has equally belonged to Brissot, to Robespierre, to Tallien, to Reubel, to Barras, and to every one of the leaders of the directory, but to none more than to Bonaparte, in whom now all their powers are united. What are its characters? Can it be accident that produced them? No, it is only from the alliance of the most horrid principles with the most horrid means, that such miseries could have been brought upon Europe. It is this paradox, which we must always keep in mind when we are discussing any question relative to the effects of the French Revolution. Groaning under every degree of misery, the victim of its own crimes, and as I once before expressed it in this house, asking pardon of God and of man for the miseries which it has brought upon itself and others, France still retains (while it has neither left means of comfort, nor almost of subsistence to its own inhabitants) new and unexampled means of annoyance and destruction against all the other powers of Europe.

Its first fundamental principle was to bribe the poor against the rich, by proposing to transfer into new hands, on the delusive notion of equality, and in breach of every principle of justice, the whole property of the country; the practical application of this principle was to devote the whole of that property to indiscriminate plunder, and to make it the foundation of a revolutionary system of finance, productive in proportion to the misery and desolation which it created. It has been accompanied by an unwearied spirit of proselytism, diffusing itself over all the nations of the earth; a spirit which can apply itself to all circumstances and all situations, which can furnish a list of grievances, and hold out a promise of redress equally to all nations, which inspired the teachers of

French liberty with the hope of alike recommending themselves to those who live under the feudal code of the German empire; to the various states of Italy, under all their different institutions; to the old republicans of Holland, and to the new republicans of America; to the Catholic of Ireland, whom it was to deliver from Protestant usurpation; to the Protestant of Switzerland, whom it was to deliver from popish superstition; and to the Mussulman of Egypt, whom it was to deliver from Christian persecution; to the remote Indian, blindly bigoted to his ancient institutions; and to the natives of Great Britain, enjoying the perfection of practical freedom, and justly attached to their constitution, from the joint result of habit, of reason, and of experience. The last and distinguishing feature is a perfidy, which nothing can bind, which no tie of treaty, no sense of the principles generally received among nations, no obligation, human or divine, can restrain. Thus qualified, thus armed for destruction, the genius of the French Revolution marched forth, the terror and dismay of the world. Every nation has in its turn been the witness, many have been the victims of its principles, and it is left for us to decide, whether we will compromise with such a danger, while we have yet resources to supply the sinews of war, while the heart and spirit of the country is yet unbroken, and while we have the means of calling forth and supporting a powerful cooperation in Europe.

•

## CHARLES JAMES FOX
3 February 1800

### 'Must the bowels of Great Britain be torn out?'

*Fox had determined to put politics behind him and had not been in the Commons for three years. His friends persuaded him that the overture from Napoleon was an exception to every rule and a popular issue. As Pitt was speaking, members were surprised to see Fox walk to his seat, where Sheridan and Erskine sat on either side.*

*Fox was unusually nervous and told friends his speech might be the last he ever made to Parliament. But he never spoke better in his life, as he ridiculed his great adversary and made the case for peace.*

*The speech, made without notes, ended at 3.30 in the morning with this stirring peroration.*

Sir, what is the question this night? We are called upon to support ministers in refusing a frank, candid, and respectful offer of negotiation, and to countenance them in continuing the war. Now, I would put the question in another way. Suppose ministers have been inclined to adopt the line of conduct which they pursued in 1796 and 1797, and that tonight, instead of a question on a war address, it had been an address to His Majesty to thank him for accepting the overture and for opening a negotiation to treat for peace: I ask the gentlemen opposite – I appeal to the whole 558 representatives of the people – to lay their hands upon their hearts, and to say whether they would not have cordially voted for such an address? Would they, or would they not? Yes, sir, if the address had breathed a spirit of peace your benches would have resounded with rejoicings, and with praises of a measure that was likely to bring back the blessings of tranquillity. On the present occasion, then, I ask for the vote of none but of those who, in the secret confession of their conscience, admit, at this instant while they hear me, that they would have cheerfully and heartily voted with the minister for an address directly the reverse of this. If every such gentleman were to vote with me, I should be this night in the greatest majority that ever I had the honour to vote with in this House.

Sir, we have heard tonight a great many most acrimonious invectives against Bonaparte, against the whole course of his conduct, and against the unprincipled manner in which he seized upon the reins of government. I will not make his defence – I think all this sort of invective, which is used only to inflame the passions of this House and of the country, exceeding ill timed and very impolitic – but I say I will not make his defence. I am not sufficiently in possession of materials upon which to form an opinion on the character and conduct of this extraordinary man. Upon his arrival in France he found the government in a very unsettled state, and the whole affairs of the Republic deranged, crippled, and involved. He thought it necessary to reform the government; and he did reform it, just in the way in which a military man may be expected to carry on a reform – he seized on the whole authority to himself.

It will not be expected from me that I should either approve or apologize for such an act. I am certainly not for reforming governments by such expedients; but how this House can be so violently indignant at the idea of military despotism is, I own, a little singular, when I see the composure with which they can observe it nearer home; nay, when I see them regard it as a frame of government most peculiarly suited to the exercise of free opinion on a subject the most important of any that can engage the attention of a people. Was it not the system that was so happily and so advantageously established of late all over Ireland; and which, even now, the government may, at its pleasure, proclaim over the whole of that kingdom? Are not the persons and property of the people left in many districts at this moment to the entire will of military commanders? And is not this held out as peculiarly proper and advantageous at a time when the people of Ireland are free, and with unbiased judgement, to discuss the most interesting question of a legislative union? Notwithstanding the existence of martial law, so far do we think Ireland from being enslaved that we think it precisely the period and the circumstances under which she may best declare her free opinion! Now really, sir, I cannot think that gentlemen who talk in this way about Ireland can, with a good grace, rail at military despotism in France.

But, it seems, 'Bonaparte has broken his oaths. He has violated his oath of fidelity to the Constitution of the year 3.' Sir, I am not one of those who think that any such oaths ought ever to be exacted. They are seldom or ever of any effect; and I am not for sporting with a thing so sacred as an oath. I think it would be good to lay aside all such oaths. Whoever heard that, in revolutions, the oath of fidelity to the former government was ever regarded; or even when violated that it was imputed to the persons as a crime? In times of revolution, men who take up arms are called rebels – if they fail, they are adjudged to be traitors. But who ever heard before of their being perjured?

On the restoration of Charles II, those who had taken up arms for the Commonwealth were stigmatized as rebels and traitors, but not as men foresworn. Was the Earl of Devonshire charged with being perjured on account of the allegiance he had sworn to the house of Stuart and the part he took in those struggles which preceded and brought about the Revolution? The violation of oaths of allegiance was never imputed to the people of England, and will never be imputed to any people. But who brings up the question of oaths? He who strives to make twenty-four millions of persons violate the oaths they have taken to their present Constitution, and who desires to re-establish the house of Bourbon by such violation of their vows. I put it so, sir; because, if the question of oaths be of the least consequence, it is equal on both sides. He who desires the whole people of France to perjure themselves, and who hopes for success in his project only upon their doing so, surely cannot make it a charge against Bonaparte that he has done the same . . .

'It is not the interest of Bonaparte,' it seems, 'sincerely to enter into a negotiation, or, if he should even make peace, sincerely to keep it.' But how are we to decide upon his sincerity? By refusing to treat with him? Surely, if we mean to discover his sincerity, we ought to hear the propositions which he desires to make. 'But peace would be unfriendly to his system of military despotism.' Sir, I hear a great deal about the short-lived nature of military despotism. I wish the history of the world would bear gentlemen out in this description of military despotism. Was not the government erected by Augustus Caesar a military despotism? and yet it endured for six hundred or seven hundred years. Military despotism, unfortunately, is too likely in its nature to be permanent, and it is not true that it depends on the life of the first usurper. Though half the Roman emperors were murdered, yet the military despotism went on; and so it would be, I fear, in France. If Bonaparte should disappear from the scene, to make room, perhaps, for a Berthier, or any other general, what difference would that make in the quality of French despotism or in our relation to the country? We may as safely treat with a Bonaparte or with any of his successors, be they who they may, as we could with a Louis XVI, a Louis XVII, or a Louis XVIII. There is no difference but in the name. Where the power essentially resides, thither we ought to go for peace.

But, sir, if we are to reason on the fact, I should think that it is the interest of Bonaparte to make peace. A lover of military glory, as that general must necessarily be, may he not think that his measure of glory is full – that it may be tarnished by a reverse of fortune, and can hardly be increased by any new laurels? He must feel that, in the situation to which he is now raised, he can no longer depend on his own fortune, his own genius, and his own talents for a continuance of his success; he must be under the necessity of employing other generals, whose misconduct or incapacity might endanger his power, or whose triumphs even might affect the interest which he holds in the opinion of the French. Peace, then, would secure to him what he has achieved, and fix the inconstancy of fortune. But this will not be his only motive.

He must see that France also requires a respite – a breathing interval to recruit her wasted strength. To procure her this respite would be, perhaps, the attainment of more solid glory, as well as the means of acquiring more solid power, than anything which he can hope to gain from arms and from the proudest triumphs. May he not then be zealous to gain this fame, the only species of fame, perhaps, that is worth acquiring? Nay, granting that his soul may still burn with the thirst of military exploits, is it not likely that he is earnestly disposed to yield to the feelings of the French people, and to consolidate his power by consulting their interests? I have a right to argue in this way, when of his insincerity are reasoned upon on the other side. Sir, these aspersions are, in truth, always idle, and even mischievous. I have been too long accustomed to hear imputations and calumnies thrown out upon great and honourable characters to be much influenced by them . . .

Sir, I wish the atrocities of which we hear so much, and which I abhor as much as any man, were indeed unexampled. I fear that they do not belong exclusively to the French. When the right honourable gentleman speaks of the extraordinary successes of the last campaign, he does not mention the horrors by which some of those successes were accompanied. Naples, for instance, has been, among others, what is called 'delivered'; and yet, if I am rightly informed, it has been stained and polluted by murders so ferocious, and by cruelties of every kind so abhorrent, that the heart shudders at the recital. It has been said, not only that the miserable victims of the rage and brutality of the fanatics were savagely murdered, but that, in many instances, their flesh was eaten and devoured by the cannibals who are the advocates and the instruments of social order! Nay, England is not totally exempt from reproach, if the rumours which are circulated be true. I will mention a fact to give ministers the opportunity, if it be false, of wiping away the stain that it must otherwise fix on the British name. It is said that a party of the republican inhabitants of Naples took shelter in the fortress of the Castel de Uova. They were besieged by a detachment from the royal army, to whom they refused to surrender; but demanded that a British officer should be brought forward, and to him they capitulated. They made terms with him under the sanction of the British name. It was agreed that their persons and property should be safe, and that they should be conveyed to Toulon. They were accordingly put on board a vessel; but before they sailed their property was confiscated, numbers of them taken out, thrown into dungeons, and some of them, I understand, notwithstanding the British guarantee, actually executed.

Where then, sir, is this war, which on every side is pregnant with such horrors, to be carried? Where is it to stop? Not till you establish the house of Bourbon! And this you cherish the hope of doing, because you have had a successful campaign. Why, sir, before this you have had a successful campaign. The situation of the allies, with all they have gained, is surely not to be compared now to what it was when you had taken Valenciennes, Quesnoy, Condé, etc., which induced some gentlemen in this House to prepare themselves for a march to Paris. With all that you have gained, you surely will not say that the prospect is brighter now than it was then. What have you gained but the recovery of a part of what you before lost? One campaign is successful to you – another to them; and in this way, animated by the vindictive passions of revenge, hatred, and rancour, which are infinitely more flagitious even than those of ambition and the thirst of power, you may go on forever; as, with such black incentives, I see no end to human misery. And all this without an intelligible motive, all this because you may gain a better peace a year or two hence! So that we are called upon to go on merely as a speculation. We must keep Bonaparte for some time longer at war as a state of probation. Gracious God, sir, is war a state of probation? Is peace a rash system? Is it dangerous for nations to live in amity with each other? Is your vigilance, your policy, your common powers of observation, to be extinguished by putting an end to the horrors of war? Cannot this state of probation be as well undergone without adding to the catalogue of human sufferings? 'But we must pause!' What! must the bowels of Great Britain be torn out – her best blood be spilt – her treasure wasted – that you may make an experiment? Put yourselves – oh! that you would put yourselves – in the field of battle, and learn to judge of the sort of horrors that you excite. In former wars a man might at least have some feeling, some interest, that served to balance in his mind the impressions which a scene of carnage and of death must inflict. If a man had been present at the Battle of Blenheim, for instance, and had inquired the motive of the battle, there was not a soldier engaged who could not have satisfied his curiosity, and even perhaps allayed his feelings – they were fighting to repress the uncontrolled ambition of the *grand monarque*.

But if a man were present now at a field of slaughter, and were to inquire for what they were fighting – 'Fighting!' would be the answer; 'they are not fighting, they are pausing.' 'Why is that man expiring? Why is that other writhing with agony? What means this implacable fury?' The answer must be, 'You are quite wrong, sir; you deceive yourself – they are not fighting – do not disturb them – they are merely pausing! – this man is not expiring with agony – that man is not dead – he is only pausing! Lord help you, sir! they are not angry with one another; they have now no cause of quarrel – but their country thinks that there should be a pause. All that you see, sir, is nothing like fighting – there is no harm, nor cruelty, nor bloodshed in it whatever – it is nothing more than *a political pause*! – it is merely to try an experiment – to see whether Bonaparte will not behave himself better than heretofore; and in the meantime we have agreed to a pause, in pure friendship!' And is this the way, sir, that you are to show yourselves the advocates of order? You take up a system calculated to uncivilize the world, to destroy order, to trample on religion, to stifle in the heart, not merely the generosity of noble sentiment, but the affections of social nature; and in the prosecution of this system you spread terror and devastation all around you.

Sir, I have done. I have told you my opinion. I think you ought to have given a civil, clear, and explicit answer to the overture which was fairly and handsomely made you. If you were desirous that the negotiation should have included all your allies, as the means of bringing about a general peace, you should have told Bonaparte so; but I believe you were afraid of his agreeing to the proposal. You took that method before. 'Ay, but,' you say, 'the people were anxious for peace in 1797.' I say they are friends to peace now; and I am confident that you will one day own it. Believe me, they are friends to peace; although, by the laws which you have made restraining the expression of the sense of the people, public opinion cannot now be heard as loudly and unequivocally as heretofore. But I will not go into the internal state of this country. It is too afflicting to the heart to see the strides which have been made by means of, and under the miserable pretext of, this war against liberty of every kind, both of speech and of writing; and to observe in another kingdom the rapid approaches to that military despotism which we affect to make an argument against peace. I know, sir, that public opinion, if it could be collected, would be for peace as much now as in 1797, and I know that it is only by public opinion – not by a sense of their duty – not by the inclination of their minds – that ministers will be brought, if ever, to give us peace.

I conclude, sir, with repeating what I said before; I ask for no gentleman's vote who would have reprobated the compliance of ministers with the proposition of the French government; I ask for no gentleman's support tonight who would have voted against ministers, if they had come down and proposed to enter into a negotiation with the French; but I have a right to ask – I know that, in honour, in consistency, in conscience, I have a right to expect the vote of every gentleman who would have voted with ministers in an address to his Majesty dia-metrically opposite to the motion of this night.

•

## WILLIAM PITT THE YOUNGER
### 9 November 1805

### *'Europe is not to be saved by any single man'*

*A fortnight after Nelson's victory at the Battle of Trafalgar, the Lord Mayor's annual banquet was held in London. Pitt's health was drunk as the saviour of Europe. The ailing Prime Minister, who died ten weeks later, responded with a short speech that the British statesman Lord Curzon ranked with Abraham Lincoln's Gettysburg address and second inaugural as one of the three greatest speeches in the English language. 'Pitt's speech occupied only a few seconds in delivery, Lincoln's less than three minutes,' he said in the 1913 Rede Lecture at Cambridge, 'yet where are the world-famed pages, the crowded hours of rhetoric, compared with these?'*

I return you many thanks for the honour you have done me; but Europe is not to be saved by any single man. England has saved herself by her exertions, and will, as I trust, save Europe by her example.

•

# TOWARDS CIVIL WAR

# GEORGE WASHINGTON
23 December 1783

### 'I retire from the great theatre of action'

*Once the rearguard of the British troops had evacuated New York, George Washington was determined to leave for home. He had a last meeting with his officers at Fraunces' Tavern. At a ball given in his honour at Annapolis on 22 December, Washington danced every set so that all the ladies could dance with him. He addressed Congress the next day and submitted his resignation in a dignified and eloquent short speech.*

The great events on which my resignation depended having at length taken place; I have now the honor of offering my sincere congratulations to Congress and of presenting myself before them to surrender into their hands the trust committed to me, and to claim the indulgence of retiring from the service of my country.

Happy in the confirmation of our independence and sovereignty, and pleased with the opportunity afforded the United States of becoming a respectable nation, I resign with satisfaction the appointment I accepted with diffidence. A diffidence in my abilities to accomplish so arduous a task, which however was superseded by a confidence in the rectitude of our cause, the support of the supreme Power of the Union, and the patronage of Heaven.

The successful termination of the war has verified the most sanguine expectations, and my gratitude for the interposition of Providence, and the assistance I have received from my countrymen, increases with every review of the momentous contest.

While I repeat my obligations to the army in general, I should do injustice to my own feelings not to acknowledge in this place the peculiar services and distinguished merits of the gentlemen who have been attached to my person during the war. It was impossible the choice of confidential officers to compose my family should have been more fortunate. Permit me sir, to recommend in particular those, who have continued in service to the present moment, as worthy of the favorable notice and patronage of Congress.

I consider it an indispensable duty to close this last solemn act of my official life, by commending the interests of our dearest country to the protection of Almighty God, and those who have the superintendence of them, to his holy keeping.

Having now finished the work assigned me, I retire from the great theatre of action; and bidding an affectionate farewell to this august body under whose orders I have so long acted, I here offer my commission, and take my leave of all the employments of public life.

•

## GEORGE WASHINGTON
### 17 September 1796

### *'Observe good faith and justice towards all nations'*

*As he approached the end of his second term as president in 1796, George Washington (1732–99), after forty-five years of public service, was mentally and physically exhausted and tired of the personal attacks on him. His thoughts turned to retirement and he conceived the idea of bequeathing to Americans a legacy of the ideas that inspired him. Several hands helped to draft the farewell address – including Alexander Hamilton and James Madison – but he went over it carefully himself.*

*The address, Washington's last political will and testament, warns against the growth of party factionalism and becoming embroiled in foreign quarrels. Nations must in the end depend on themselves alone – the lesson of all revolutions.*

Friends and fellow-citizens: the period for a new election of a citizen to administer the executive government of the United States being not far distant, and the time actually arrived when your thoughts must be employed in designating the person who is to be clothed with that important trust, it appears to me proper, especially as it may conduce to a more distinct expression of the public voice, that I should now apprise you of the resolution I have formed, to decline being considered among the number of those out of whom a choice is to be made.

I beg you, at the same time, to do me the justice to be assured that this resolution has not been taken without a strict regard to all the considerations appertaining to the relation which binds a dutiful citizen to his country; and that in withdrawing the tender of service which silence, in my situation, might imply, I am influenced by no diminution of zeal for your future interest, no deficiency of grateful respect for your past kindness, but am supported by a full conviction that the step is compatible with both.

The acceptance of, and continuance hitherto, in the office to which your suffrages have twice called me, have been a uniform sacrifice of inclination to the opinion of duty, and to a deference for what appeared to be your desire. I constantly hoped that it would have been much earlier in my power, consistently with motives which I was not at liberty to disregard, to return to that retirement from which I had been reluctantly drawn. The strength of my inclination to do this, previous to the last election, had even led to the preparation of an address, to declare it to you; but mature reflection on the then perplexed and critical posture of our affairs with foreign nations, and the unanimous advice of persons entitled to my confidence, impelled me to abandon the idea.

I rejoice that the state of your concerns, external as well as internal, no longer renders the pursuit of inclination incompatible with the sentiment of duty or propriety, and am persuaded, whatever partiality may be retained for my services, that in the present circumstances of our country, you will not disapprove of my determination to retire . . .

Here, perhaps, I ought to stop. But a solicitude for your welfare, which cannot end but with my life, and the apprehension of danger, natural to that solicitude, urge me, on an occasion like the present, to offer to your solemn contemplation, and to recommend to your frequent review, some sentiments, which are the result of much reflection, of no inconsiderable observation, and which appear to me all-important to the permanency of your felicity as a people. These will be offered to you with the more freedom, as you can only see in them the disinterested warnings of a parting friend, who can possibly have no personal motive to bias his counsel. Nor can I forget, as an encouragement to it, your indulgent reception of my sentiments on a former and not dissimilar occasion.

Interwoven as is the love of liberty with every ligament of your hearts, no recommendation of mine is necessary to fortify or confirm the attachment.

The unity of government which constitutes you one people is also now dear to you. It is justly so, for it is a main pillar in the edifice of your real independence, the support of your tranquility at home, your peace abroad, of your safety, of your prosperity, of that very liberty which you so highly prize. But as it is easy to foresee, that from different causes and from different quarters, much pains will be taken, many artifices employed, to weaken in your minds the conviction of this truth;

as this is the point in your political fortress against which the batteries of internal and external enemies will be most constantly and actively (though often covertly and insidiously) directed, it is of infinite moment that you should properly estimate the immense value of your national union, to your collective and individual happiness; that you should cherish a cordial, habitual, and immovable attachment to it; accustoming yourselves to think and speak of it as of the palladium of your political safety and prosperity, watching for its preservation with jealous anxiety; discountenancing whatever may suggest even a suspicion that it can in any event be abandoned; and indignantly frowning upon the first dawning of every attempt to alienate any portion of our country from the rest, or to enfeeble the sacred ties which now link together the various parts.

For this you have every inducement of sympathy and interest. Citizens, by birth or choice, of a common country, that country has a right to concentrate your affections. The name of American, which belongs to you in your national capacity, must always exalt the just pride of patriotism more than any appellation derived from local discriminations. With slight shades of difference, you have the same religion, manners, habits and political principles. You have, in a common cause, fought and triumphed together; the independence and liberty you possess are the work of joint councils and joint efforts, of common dangers, sufferings, and successes.

But these considerations, however powerfully they address themselves to your sensibility, are greatly outweighed by those which apply more immediately to your interest. Here every portion of our country finds the most commanding motives for carefully guarding and preserving the union of the whole . . .

Let me now warn you, in the most solemn manner, against the baneful effects of the spirit of party, generally.

This spirit, unfortunately, is inseparable from our nature, having its root in the strongest passions of the human mind. It exists under different shapes, in all governments, more or less stifled, controlled, or repressed. But in those of the popular form, it is seen in its greatest rankness, and is truly their worst enemy.

The alternate domination of one faction over another, sharpened by the spirit of revenge, natural to party dissensions, which, in different ages and countries, has perpetrated the most horrid enormities, is itself a frightful despotism. But this leads, at length, to a more formal and permanent despotism. The disorders and miseries, which result, gradually incline the minds of men to seek security and repose in the absolute power of an individual; and sooner or later, the chief of some prevailing faction, more able or more fortunate than his competitors, turns this disposition to the purposes of his own elevation on the ruins of public liberty . . .

There is an opinion, that parties, in free countries, are useful checks upon the administration of the government, and serve to keep alive the spirit of liberty. This, within certain limits, is probably true; and, in governments of a monarchical cast, patriotism may look with indulgence, if not with favor, upon the spirit of party. But in those of popular character, in governments purely elective, it is a spirit not to be encouraged. From their natural tendency, it is certain there will always be enough of that spirit for every salutary purpose. And there being constant danger of excess, the effort ought to be, by force of public opinion, to mitigate and assuage it. A fire not to be quenched, it demands a uniform vigilance to prevent its bursting into a flame, lest, instead of warming, it should consume . . .

Observe good faith and justice towards all nations; cultivate peace and harmony with all; religion and morality enjoin this conduct; and can it be that good policy does not equally enjoin it? It will be worthy of a free, enlightened, and, at no distant period, a great nation, to give to mankind the magnanimous and too novel example of a people always guided by an exalted justice and benevolence. Who can doubt that, in the course of time and things, the fruits of such a plan would richly repay any temporary advantages that might be lost by a steady adherence to it? Can it be, that Providence has not connected the permanent felicity of a nation with its virtue? The experiment, at least, is recommended by every sentiment which ennobles human nature. Alas! is it rendered impossible by its vices?

In the execution of such a plan, nothing is more essential than that permanent, inveterate antipathies against particular nations, and passionate attachments for others, should be excluded; and that in place of them, just and amicable feelings towards all should be cultivated. The nation, which indulges towards another an habitual hatred, or an habitual fondness, is in some degree a slave. It is a slave to its animosity or to its affection, either of which is sufficient to lead it astray from its duty and its interest. Antipathy in one nation against another, disposes each more readily to offer insult and injury, to lay hold of slight causes of umbrage, and to be haughty and intractable, when accidental or trifling occasions of dispute occur.

Hence frequent collisions, obstinate, envenomed, and bloody contests.

The nation, prompted by ill-will and resentment, sometimes impels to war the government, contrary to the best calculations of policy. The government sometimes participates in the national propensity, and adopts through passion what reason would reject; at other times, it makes the animosity of the nation subservient to projects of hostility instigated by pride, ambition and other sinister and pernicious motives. The peace often, and sometimes, perhaps, the liberty of nations, has been the victim.

So, likewise, a passionate attachment of one nation for another produces a variety of evils. Sympathy for the favorite nation facilitating the illusion of an imaginary common interest in cases where no real common interest exists, and infusing into one the enmities of the other, betrays the former into a participation in the quarrels and wars of the latter, without adequate inducement or justification. It leads also to concessions to the favorite nation of privileges denied to others, which is apt doubly to injure the nation making the concessions; by unnecessarily parting with what ought to have been retained; and by exciting jealousy, ill-will, and a disposition to retaliate, in the parties from whom equal privileges are withheld; and it gives to ambitious, corrupted, or deluded citizens (who devote themselves to the favorite nation) facility to betray, or sacrifice the interests of their own country, without odium, sometimes even with popularity; gilding, with the appearances of a virtuous sense of obligation, a commendable deference for public opinion, or laudable zeal for public good, the base or foolish compliances of ambition, corruption, or infatuation . . .

Against the insidious wiles of foreign influence (I conjure you to believe me, fellow-citizens), the jealousy of a free people ought to be constantly awake; since history and experience prove, that foreign influence is one of the most baneful foes of republican government. But that jealousy, to be useful must be impartial; else it becomes the instrument of the very influence to be avoided, instead of a defence against it. Excessive partiality for one foreign nation, and excessive dislike of another, cause those whom they actuate, to see danger only on one side; and serve to veil and even second the arts of influence on the other. Real patriots, who may resist the intrigues of the favorite, are liable to become suspected and odious; while its tools and dupes usurp the applause and confidence of the people, to surrender their interests.

The great rule of conduct for us, in regard to foreign nations is, in extending our commercial relations, to have with them as little political connection as possible. So far as we have already formed engagements, let them be fulfilled with perfect good faith. Here let us stop.

Europe has a set of primary interests, which to us have none, or a very remote relation. Hence she must be engaged in frequent controversies, the causes of which are essentially foreign to our concerns. Hence, therefore, it must be unwise in us to implicate ourselves, by artificial ties, in the ordinary vicissitudes of her politics, or the ordinary combinations and collisions of her friendships and enmities.

Our detached and distant situation invites and enables us to pursue a different course. If we remain one people, under an efficient government, the period is not far off when we may defy material injury from external annoyance; when we may take such an attitude as will cause the neutrality we may at any time resolve upon, to be scrupulously respected; when belligerent nations, under the impossibility of making acquisitions upon us, will not lightly hazard the giving us provocation; when we may choose peace or war, as our interest, guided by justice, shall counsel.

Why forgo the advantages of so peculiar a situation? Why quit our own, to stand upon foreign ground? Why, by interweaving our destiny with that of any part of Europe, entangle our peace and prosperity in the toils of European ambition, rivalship, interest, humor, or caprice?

'Tis our true policy to steer clear of permanent alliances with any portion of the foreign world; so far, I mean, as we are now at liberty to do it; for let me not be understood as capable of patronizing infidelity to existing engagements. I hold the maximum no less applicable to public than to private affairs, that honesty is always the best policy. I repeat it, therefore, let those engagements be observed in their genuine sense. But, in my opinion, it is unnecessary, and would be unwise, to extend them.

Taking care always to keep ourselves, by suitable establishments, in a respectable defensive posture, we may safely trust to temporary alliances for extraordinary emergencies.

Harmony, and a liberal intercourse with all nations, are recommended by policy, humanity, and interest. But even our commercial policy should hold an equal and impartial hand; neither seeking not granting exclusive favors or preferences; consulting the natural course of things; diffusing and diversifying, by gentle means, the streams of commerce, but forcing nothing; establishing, with powers so disposed, in order to give trade a stable course, to define the rights of our merchants, and to enable the government to support them, conventional rules of intercourse, the best that present circumstances and mutual opinion will permit, but temporary, and liable to be, from time to time, abandoned or varied, as experience and circumstances shall dictate; constantly keeping in view, that it is folly in one nation to look for disinterested favors from another; that it must pay, with a portion of its independence, for whatever it may accept under that character; that, by such acceptance, it may place itself in the condition of having given equivalents for nominal favors, and yet of being reproached with ingratitude for not giving more. There can be no greater error than to expect to calculate upon real favors from nation to nation. It is an illusion, which experience must cure, which a just pride ought to discard . . .

Though, in reviewing the incidents of my administration, I am unconscious of intentional error, I am, nevertheless, too sensible of my defects, not to think it probable that I may have committed many errors. Whatever they may be, I fervently beseech the Almighty to avert or mitigate the evils to which they may tend. I shall also carry with me the hope that my country will never cease to view them with indulgence, and that after forty-five years of my life dedicated to its service, with an upright zeal, the faults of incompetent abilities will be consigned to oblivion, as myself must soon be to the mansions of rest.

Relying on its kindness in this, as in other things, and actuated by that fervent love towards it, which is so natural to a man who views in it the native soil of himself and his progenitors for several generations, I anticipate, with pleasing expectations, that retreat in which I promise myself to realize, without alloy, the sweet enjoyment of partaking, in the midst of my fellow-citizens, the benign influence of good laws under a free government – the ever favorite object of my heart, and the happy reward, as I trust, of our mutual cares, labors, and dangers.

*Washington's Farewell Address is read in Senate and the House of Representatives at noon on each 22 February as a tribute to him and a reminder of his beliefs.*

•

# GOUVERNEUR MORRIS
1800

## '*I am an American*'

*As a member of the Pennsylvania delegation led by Benjamin Franklin, Gouverneur Morris (1752–1816) was one of the most forceful participants at the Constitutional Convention at Philadelphia in 1787, which drafted the Constitution of the United States. He spoke against slavery and life tenure for the President and led the committee of style which cast the agreed points into plain but eloquent language.*

*When he made this speech, he had just become a senator. We join him when he starts to define the true source and principle of national greatness.*

I feel but too well that in venturing to discuss the subject of national greatness I must fall short of the ideas in your minds and disappoint your expectations. Instead of irradiating with the light of genius, I must take the more humble course of investigation and begin by inquiring what is national greatness.

Does it consist in numbers, wealth, or extent of territory? Certainly not. Swollen with the pride inspired by such circumstances, the Persians addressed their master as the Great King, but Darius felt in repeated discomfiture the superiority of a great nation led by Alexander. We see in our day a prince who may boast that the sun never sets on his domain, yet his authority superseded in his ports and insulted in his capital, it would seem as if his territory were extended around the globe only to display before all the world his ignominious condition. Such is the state of that proud monarchy which once menaced the liberties of Europe. But who trembles now at the name of Spain? There is none so abject. Nay, should there exist a government in which fear is the incurable disease, no paroxysm would be excited by the menace of Spain. To the wise a word is sufficient, and therefore it will be needless before this audience to prove that a nation small like Greece may rise to the heights of national greatness while littleness shall mark every public act of a numerous people. And equally needless must it be to express what you cannot but feel: that in proportion to the high esteem, respect, and admiration with which we view the splendor of Greece in the day of her glory is our profound contempt for those who presiding over a powerful people shall tamely submit to the multiplied repetition of indignities from all who through interest or for sport may plunder and insult them. These are feelings so natural that to disguise them would be vain, to suppress them impossible. I could indeed, were I to indulge a licentious imagination, suppose a number of men who without national spirit or sentiment shall presume to call themselves a nation – I can suppose a herd of piddling huckstering individuals base and insensible . . .

Let us pause. Perhaps there never was a society of men so completely void of virtue. But between them and the brave band at Thermopylae gradations are infinite.

Perhaps it may be asked if genius and excellence in the arts constitute national greatness. To this question the answer must be given with caution and not without some modification. The ages of Pericles, of Augustus, and of Louis XIV were indeed ages of splendor. They were unquestionably the evidence, but I must venture to believe they were the result, not the cause of national greatness. A nation truly great cannot but excel in arts as well as in arms. And as a great mind stamps with its own impression the most common arts, so national greatness will show itself alike in the councils of policy, in the works of genius, in monuments of magnificence and deeds of glory. All these are the fruits, but they are not the tree.

Here I anticipate the general and the generous question: does it not consist in liberty? That liberty is a kind and fostering nurse of greatness will be cheerfully and cordially admitted, but as we have seen national greatness where there was no freedom, so we have seen free nations where baseness rather than greatness constituted the national character. The intrepidity of the Swiss troops is generally known and acknowledged. In a contest for freedom with the duke of Burgundy the nation was great and covered itself with glory, but, alas, how changed, how fallen when distributing stipendiary aid to hostile hosts. Their valor was arrayed against itself, and brothers fell by the swords of brothers. They became at length the proverbial examples of mercenary disposition. And then neither liberty no[r] discipline nor courage rescued Helvetian fame from the charge of baseness.

Thus, then, we have seen that a people may be numerous, powerful, wealthy, free, brave, and inured to war without being great, and by reflecting on the reason why a combination of those qualities and circumstances will not alone suffice we are close to the true source and principle of national greatness.

It is in the national spirit. It is in that high, haughty, generous, and noble spirit which prizes glory more than wealth and holds honor dearer than life. It is that spirit, the inspiring soul of heroes, which raises men above the level of humanity. It is present with us when we read the story of ancient Rome. It swells our bosoms at the view of her gigantic deeds and makes us feel that we must ever be irresistible while human nature shall remain unchanged. I have called it a high, haughty, generous, and noble spirit. It is high – elevated above all low and vulgar considerations. It is haughty – despising whatever is little and mean, whether in character, council, or conduct. It is generous – granting freely to the weak and to the indigent protection and support. It is noble – dreading shame and dishonor as the greatest evil, esteeming fame and glory beyond all things human.

When this spirit prevails, the government, whatever its form, will be wise and energetic because such government alone will be borne by such men. And such a government, seeking the true interest of those over whom they preside, will find it in the establishment of a national character becoming the spirit by which the nation is inspired. Foreign powers will then know that to withhold a due respect and deference is dangerous, that wrongs may be forgiven but that insults will be avenged. As a necessary result every member of the society bears with him everywhere full protection, and when he appears his firm and manly port mark him of a superior order in the race of man. The dignity of sentiment which he has inhaled with his native air gives to his manner an ease superior to the politeness of courts and a grace unrivaled by the majesty of kings.

These are blessings which march in the train of national greatness and come on the pinions of youthful hope. I anticipate the day when to command respect in the remotest regions it will be sufficient to say, 'I am an American.' Our flag shall then wave in glory over the ocean and our commerce feel no restraint but what our own government may impose. Happy, thrice happy day. Thank God, to reach this envied state we need only to will. Yes, my countrymen, our destiny depends on our will. But if we would stand high on the record of time, that will must be inflexible.

•

## THOMAS JEFFERSON
### 4 March 1801

### *'Equal and exact justice to all men'*

*In the 1800 presidential election, Thomas Jefferson (1743–1826) and Aaron Burr each received 73 electoral votes, defeating John Adams, the second president. Jefferson, who drafted the Declaration of Independence, emerged as president only after thirty hours of debate and balloting in the House of Representatives.*

*He was the first to occupy the White House (only half finished when he was inaugurated) in the new capital city of Washington.*

*Adams made federalist nominations to official positions (including John Marshall as Chief Justice) up to midnight on 3 March and then rode out of Washington to avoid the humiliation of greeting his successor.*

*Scorning the pageantry that conflicted with his democratic principles, Jefferson rode to his inauguration on horseback in plain clothes, without attendants, tied up his horse, walked into the new Senate chamber, took the oath of office from Marshall, his cousin and enemy, and delivered his inaugural address – one of the four or five greatest an American president has ever delivered.*

During the contest of opinion through which we have passed the animation of discussions and of exertions has sometimes worn an aspect which might impose on strangers unused to think freely and to speak and to write what they think; but this being now decided by the voice of the nation, announced according to the rules of the Constitution, all will, of course, arrange themselves under the will of the law, and unite in common efforts for the common good. All, too, will bear in mind this sacred principle, that though the will of the majority is in all cases to prevail, that will to be rightful must be reasonable; that the minority possess their equal rights, which equal law must protect, and to violate would be oppression. Let us, then, fellow-citizens, unite with one heart and one mind. Let us restore to social intercourse that harmony and affection without which liberty and even life itself are but dreary things. And let us reflect that, having banished from our land that religious intolerance under which mankind so long bled and suffered, we have yet gained little if we countenance a political intolerance as despotic, as wicked, and capable of as bitter and bloody persecutions. During the throes and convulsions of the ancient world, during the agonizing spasms of infuriated man, seeking through blood and slaughter his long-lost liberty, it was not wonderful that the agitation of the billows should reach even this distant and peaceful shore; that this should be more felt and feared by some and less by others, and should divide opinions as to measures of safety. But every difference of opinion is not a difference of principle. We have called by different names brethren of the same principle. We are all Republicans, we are all Federalists. If there be any among us who would wish to dissolve this Union or to change its republican form, let them stand undisturbed as monuments of the safety with which error of opinion may be tolerated where reason is left free to combat it. I know, indeed, that some honest men fear that a republican government can not be strong, that this government is not strong enough; but would the honest patriot, in the full tide of successful experiment, abandon a government which has so far kept us free and firm on the theoretic and visionary fear that this government, the world's best hope, may by possibility want energy to preserve itself? I trust not. I believe this, on the contrary, the strongest government on earth. I believe it the only one where every man, at the call of the law, would fly to the standard of the law, and would meet invasions of the public order as his own personal concern. Sometimes it is said that man can not be trusted with the government of himself. Can he, then, be trusted with the government of others? Or have we found angels in the forms of kings to govern him? Let history answer this question.

Let us, then, with courage and confidence pursue our own Federal and Republican principles, our attachment to union and representative government. Kindly separated by nature and a wide ocean from the exterminating havoc of one quarter of the globe; too high-minded to endure the degradations of the others; possessing a chosen country, with room enough for our descendants to the thousandth and thousandth generation; entertaining a due sense of our equal right to the use of our own faculties, to the acquisitions of our own industry, to honor and confidence from our fellow-citizens, resulting not from birth, but from our actions and their sense of them; enlightened by a benign religion, professed, indeed, and practiced in various forms, yet all of them inculcating honesty, truth, temperance, gratitude, and the love of man; acknowledging and adoring an overruling Providence, which by all its dispensations proves that it delights in the happiness of man here and his greater happiness hereafter – with all these blessings, what more is necessary to make us a happy and a prosperous people? Still one thing more, fellow-citizens – a wise and frugal government, which shall restrain men from injuring one another, shall leave them otherwise free to regulate their own pursuits of industry and improvement, and shall not take from the mouth of labor the bread it has earned. This is the sum of good government, and this is necessary to close the circle of our felicities.

About to enter, fellow-citizens, on the exercise of duties which comprehend everything dear and valuable to you, it is proper you should understand what I deem the essential principles of our government, and consequently those which ought to shape its administration. I will compress them within the narrowest compass they will bear, stating the general principle, but not all its limitations. Equal and exact justice to all men, of whatever state or persuasion, religious or political; peace, commerce, and honest friendship with all nations, entangling alliances with none; the support of the state governments in all their rights, as the most competent administrations for our domestic concerns and the surest bulwarks against antirepublican tendencies; the preservation of the general government in its whole constitutional vigor, as the sheet anchor of our peace at home and safety abroad; a jealous care of the right of election by the people – a mild and safe corrective of abuses which are lopped by the sword of revolution where peaceable remedies are unprovided; absolute acquiescence in the decisions of the majority, the vital principle of republics, from which is no appeal but to force, the vital principle and immediate parent of despotism; a well disciplined militia, our best reliance in peace and for the first moments of war, till regulars may relieve them; the supremacy of the civil over the military authority; economy in the public expense, that labor may be lightly burthened; the honest payment of our debts and sacred preservation of the public faith; encouragement of agriculture, and of commerce as its handmaid; the diffusion of information and arraignment of all abuses at the bar of the public reason; freedom of religion; freedom of the press, and freedom of person under the protection of the habeas corpus, and trial by juries impartially selected.

These principles form the bright constellation which has gone before us and guided our steps through an age of revolution and reformation. The wisdom of our sages and blood of our heroes have been devoted to their attainment. They should be the creed of our political faith, the text of civic instruction, the touchstone by which to try the services of those we trust; and should we wander from them in moments of error or of alarm, let us hasten to retrace our steps and to regain the road which alone leads to peace, liberty, and safety.

I repair, then, fellow-citizens, to the post you have assigned me. With experience enough in subordinate offices to have seen the difficulties of this the greatest of all, I have learnt to expect that it will rarely fall to the lot of imperfect man to retire from this station with the reputation and the favor which bring him into it. Without pretensions to that high confidence you reposed in our first and greatest revolutionary character, whose pre-eminent services had entitled him to the first place in his country's love and destined for him the fairest page in the volume of faithful history, I ask so much confidence only as may give firmness and effect to the legal administration of your affairs. I shall often go wrong through defect of judgement. When right, I shall often be thought wrong by those whose positions will not command a view of the whole ground. I ask your indulgence for my own errors, which will never be intentional, and your support against the errors of others, who may condemn what they would not if seen in all its parts. The approbation implied by your suffrage is a great consolation to me for the past, and my future solicitude will be to retain the good opinion of those who have bestowed it in advance, to conciliate that of others by doing them all the good in my power, and to be instrumental to the happiness and freedom of all . . .

•

# RED JACKET
## 1805

### '*We also have a religion*'

*Otetani, chief of the Seneca tribe, who was born in 1758, became known as Red Jacket from the bright red coat given him by the British when he supported them during the American Revolution. As chief his title was Sagoyewatha. As the main spokesman for the Six Nations, he became a friend of George Washington.*

*Red Jacket opposed attempts to bring European values to his tribe. This eloquent address at a council of chiefs of the Six Nations was made when Christian missionaries tried to baptize his followers.*

It was the will of the Great Spirit that we should meet together this day. He orders all things and has given us a fine day for our council. He has taken His garment from before the sun and caused it to shine with brightness upon us. Our eyes are opened that we see clearly; our ears are unstopped that we have been able to hear distinctly the words you have spoken. For all these favors we thank the Great Spirit, and Him only.

Brother, this council fire was kindled by you. It was at your request that we came together at this time. We have listened with attention to what you have said. You requested us to speak our minds freely. This gives us great joy; for we now consider that we stand upright before you and can speak what we think. All have heard your voice and all speak to you now as one man. Our minds are agreed.

Brother, you say you want an answer to your talk before you leave this place. It is right you should have one, as you are a great distance from home and we do not wish to detain you. But first we will look back a little and tell you what our fathers have told us and what we have heard from the white people.

Brother, listen to what we say. There was a time when our forefathers owned this great island. Their seats extended from the rising to the setting sun. The Great Spirit had made it for the use of Indians. He had created the buffalo, the deer, and other animals for food. He had made the bear and the beaver. Their skins served us for clothing. He had scattered them over the country and taught us how to take them. He had caused the earth to produce corn for bread. All this He had done for His red children because He loved them. If we had some disputes about our hunting-ground they were generally settled without the shedding of much blood.

But an evil day came upon us. Your forefathers crossed the great water and landed on this island. Their numbers were small. They found friends and not enemies. They told us they had fled from their own country for fear of wicked men and had come here to enjoy their religion. They asked for a small seat. We took pity on them, granted their request, and they sat down among us. We gave them corn and meat; they gave us poison in return.

The white people, brother, had now found our country. Tidings were carried back and more came among us. Yet we did not fear them. We took them to be friends. They called us brothers. We believed them and gave them a larger seat. At length their numbers had greatly increased. They wanted more land; they wanted our country. Our eyes were opened and our minds became uneasy. Wars took place. Indians were hired to fight against Indians, and many of our people were destroyed. They also brought strong liquor among us. It was strong and powerful, and has slain thousands.

Brother, our seats were once large and yours were small. You have now become a great people, and we have scarcely a place left to spread our blankets. You have got our country, but are not satisfied; you want to force your religion upon us.

Brother, continue to listen. You say that you are sent to instruct us how to worship the Great Spirit agreeably to His mind; and, if we do not take hold of the religion which you white people teach we shall be unhappy hereafter. You say that you are right and we are lost. How do we know this to be true? We understand that your religion is written in a Book. If it was intended for us, as well as you, why has not the Great Spirit given to us, and not only to us, but why did He not give to our forefathers the knowledge of that Book, with the means of understanding it rightly. We only know what you tell us about it. How shall we know when to believe, being so often deceived by the white people?

Brother, you say there is but one way to worship and serve the Great Spirit. If there is but one religion, why do you white people differ so much about it? Why not all agreed, as you can all read the Book?

Brother, we do not understand these things. We are told that your religion was given to your forefathers and has been handed down from father to son. We also have a religion which was given to our forefathers and has been handed down to us, their children. We worship in that way. It teaches us to be thankful for all the favors we receive, to love each other, and to be united. We never quarrel about religion.

Brother, the Great Spirit has made us all, but He has made a great difference between His white and His red children. He has given us different complexions and different customs. To you He has given the arts. To these He has not opened our eyes. We know these things to be true. Since He has made so great a difference between us in other things, why may we not conclude that He has given us a different religion according to our understanding? The Great Spirit does right. He knows what is best for His children; we are satisfied.

Brother, we do not wish to destroy your religion or take it from you. We only want to enjoy our own.

Brother, you say you have not come to get our land or our money, but to enlighten our minds. I will now tell you that I have been at your meetings and saw you collect money from the meeting. I can not tell what this money was intended for, but suppose that it was for your minister; and, if we should conform to your way of thinking, perhaps you may want some from us.

Brother, we are told that you have been preaching to the white people in this place. These people are our neighbors. We are acquainted with them. We will wait a little while and see what effect your preaching has upon them. If we find it does them good, makes them honest, and less disposed to cheat Indians, we will then consider again of what you have said.

Brother, you have now heard our answer to your talk, and this is all we have to say at present. As we are going to part, we will come and take you by the hand, and hope the Great Spirit will protect you on your journey and return you safe to your friends.

*Red Jacket eventually sought peace with the US government and persuaded his followers to support the United States against Britain in the war of 1812.*

•

## TECUMSEH
### 1810

#### *'Once a happy race. Since made miserable'*

*Tecumseh (1768–1813) was a great general, a compelling orator and a generous and humane man, says Hugh Brogan, the historian of America. It was Tecumseh (Crouching Tiger) who realized – too late – that only by uniting in one nation might the Indians save themselves from the depradations of the white man. He delivered this speech at Vincennes, Indiana, in council with Governor Harrison.*

It is true I am a Shawanee. My forefathers were warriors. Their son is a warrior. From them I only take my existence; from my tribe I take nothing. I am the maker of my own fortune; and Oh! that I could make that of my red people, and of my country, as great as the conceptions of my mind, when I think of the Spirit that rules the universe. I would not then come to Governor Harrison, to ask him to tear the treaty and to obliterate the landmark; but I would say to him: Sir, you have liberty to return to your own country. The being within, communing with past ages, tells me that once, nor until lately, there was no white man on this continent. That it then all belonged to red men, children of the same parents, placed on it by the Great Spirit that made them, to keep it, to traverse it, to enjoy its productions, and to fill it with the same race. Once a happy race. Since made miserable by the white people, who are never contented, but always encroaching. The way, and the only way, to check and to stop this evil, is for all the red men to unite in claiming a common and equal right in the land, as it was at first, and should be yet; for it never was divided, but belongs to all for the use of each. That no part has a right to sell, even to each other, much less to strangers; those who want all, and will not do with less.

The white people have no right to take the land from the Indians, because they had it first; it is theirs. They may sell, but all must join. Any sale not made by all is not valid. The late sale is bad. It was made by a part only. Part do not know how to sell. It requires all to make a bargain for all. All red men have equal rights to the unoccupied land. The right of occupancy is as good in one place as in another. There cannot be two occupations in the same place. The first excludes all others. It is not so in hunting or traveling; for there the same ground will serve many, as they may follow each other all day; but the camp is stationary, and that is occupancy. It belongs to the first who sits down on his blanket or skins which he has thrown upon the ground; and till he leaves it no other has a right.

•

## SIMON BOLIVAR
### 15 February 1819

### 'The triple yoke of ignorance, tyranny and corruption'

*It was not only in the United States, France and Britain that men fought for freedom. In Latin America, the outstanding leader of the struggle for political independence was Simon Bolivar (1783–1830). As the 'Liberator', Bolivar personified a continent's determination to be free as he strove to establish a political order founded on justice and the rights of the individual. He sustained a fifteen-year offensive against Spanish domination. His 'Angostura' speech was delivered to the Congress of Venezuela at its inauguration in the city of Angostura.*

Legislators! I place in your hands the supreme command of Venezuela. It is now your lofty duty to devote yourselves to the well-being of the Republic; our fate and the measure of our glory is in your hands, those very hands which will sign the decrees establishing our Freedom. At this moment the Supreme Head of the Republic is no more than a simple citizen, and this he desires to remain until his dying day . . .

When America was separated from the Spanish monarchy, it found itself in a similar situation to the Roman Empire, when that enormous mass broke up in the midst of the Ancient World. The fragments that were left then formed independent nations in conformity with their situations or interests; but with the difference that each one re-established its original system. We do not even retain the vestiges of what went before: we are not Europeans, or Indians, but rather a species mid-way between the original inhabitants and the Spaniards. Americans by birth and Europeans in our rights, we find ourselves in the predicament of fighting with the Indians for the ownership of the land and contending with the opposition of invaders for the privilege of remaining in the country of our birth; thus, our case can be seen to be fraught with difficulties. What is more, our condition has always been a passive one, our political existence null; and our difficulty in attaining freedom is all the more painful because, before, we stagnated in the most wretched servitude; not only were we stripped of freedom, but even of a role of domination in our domestic affairs. Let me explain this paradox. Under the regime of absolute power, all authority goes unchallenged. The will of the despot is the supreme law arbitrarily executed by inferiors who participate in organized repression as a consequence of the authority they wield. They are in charge of civil, political, military and religious functions. But whereas the satraps of Persia were Persians, the pashas of the Great Sultan were Turks, the sultans of Tartary, Tartars; and whereas China had its own mandarins even when it had fallen under the rule of Genghis Khan, America, on the contrary, received everything from Spain and we were in fact deprived of any role of domination in our domestic affairs and internal government. This denial made it impossible for us to understand the course of public affairs; neither did we enjoy the personal esteem which the show of authority commands in the eyes of the people, and which is of such importance in great revolutions. In short, gentlemen, we were excluded and kept apart from the world's affairs in all that concerned the science of government.

Bound as we were by the triple yoke of ignorance, tyranny and corruption, we were unable to acquire learning, power or virtue. And since we were schooled by such evil tutors, the lessons we received and the examples we studied were of a most ruinous nature. We were enthralled by deception even more than by force; and corruption degraded us even more than superstition. Slavery is the daughter of darkness; an ignorant people is the blind instrument of its own destruction; ambition and intrigue take advantage of the credulity and inexperience of men who have no political, economic or civil understanding: they take to be realities what are in fact only illusions; they confuse licence with liberty, treason with patriotism, vengeance with justice. Such a people resembles an able-bodied blind man who, encouraged by his feeling of strength, strides forward with the assurance of the most clear-sighted and, stumbling into every pitfall, is no longer able to find his way. If such a degraded people should ever attain their freedom, they will not delay in losing it, for there will be no way of persuading them that happiness consists in the practice of virtue, that lawful government is more powerful than the rule of tyrants because it is more inflexible and requires that all obey its beneficent discipline, that morality and not force is the basis of the law, and that the exercise of justice is the exercise of freedom. Thus, legislators, your task is all the more difficult because the men you must form have been perverted by misleading illusions and destructive motives. Freedom, says Rousseau, is a most succulent dish, but one that is difficult to digest. Our frail fellow-citizens will have to build up their strength long before they are able to digest the life-giving nutrient of freedom. Will they, with their limbs stiffened from such long enchainment, their sight enfeebled by the darkness of their dungeons, and their spirit crushed by pernicious servitude, be able to stride firmly toward the august temple of freedom? Will they be able to gaze unblinkingly into its splendid rays, and inhale the pure air which surrounds it?

Consider your choice carefully, legislators. Do not forget that you are about to lay the foundations of a new people, and that they will rise to the greatness for which nature has equipped them if you so shape this foundation to match the eminent status that awaits them. If your choice is not governed by the guiding spirit of Venezuela, which should inspire you in choosing the right form and nature of the government you are to adopt for the happiness of the people, if, I repeat, you should fail to choose rightly, all our new beginnings will end in slavery.

•

## DANIEL WEBSTER
### 22 December 1820

### *'The first scene of our history'*

*Daniel Webster (1782–1852) made his reputation as one of America's greatest orators when he delivered the oration at Plymouth commemorating the 200th anniversary of the landing of the Pilgrims. Although the style of the speech now seems too florid, Webster was immediately compared with Demosthenes, Cicero*

*and Charles James Fox. In a letter to the eminent lawyer and member of the*
*Massachusetts House of Representatives, the former president John Adams wrote:*
*'If there should be an American who can read it without tears, I am not that*
*American. Mr Burke is no longer entitled to the praise – the most consummate*
*orator of modern times.'*

*This is an extract from the beginning of the two-hour oration, which was*
*immediately printed and published.*

*George Tickner, a young Harvard scholar and friend of Webster, wrote that*
*night: 'Three or four times I thought my temples would burst with the gush of*
*blood . . . it seemed to me as if he was like the mountain that might not be touched*
*and that burned with fire.'*

We have come to this Rock, to record here our homage for our Pilgrim
Fathers; our sympathy in their sufferings; our gratitude for their labors;
our admiration of their virtues; our veneration for their piety; and our
attachment to those principles of civil and religious liberty, which they
encountered the dangers of the ocean, the storms of heaven, the violence
of savages, disease, exile, and famine, to enjoy and to establish. And we
would leave here, also, for the generations which are rising up rapidly to
fill our places, some proof that we have endeavoured to transmit the
great inheritance unimpaired; that in our estimate of public principles
and private virtue, in our veneration of religion and piety, in our
devotion to civil and religious liberty, in our regard for whatever
advances human knowledge or improves human happiness, we are not
altogether unworthy of our origin.

There is a local feeling connected with this occasion, too strong to be
resisted; a sort of genius of the place, which inspires and awes us. We feel
that we are on the spot where the first scene of our history was laid;
where the hearths and altars of New England were first placed; where
Christianity, and civilization, and letters made their first lodgement, in a
vast extent of country, covered with a wilderness, and peopled by
roving barbarians. We are here, at the season of the year at which the
event took place. The imagination irresistibly and rapidly draws around
us the principal features and the leading characters in the original scene.
We cast our eyes abroad on the ocean, and we see where the little bark,
with the interesting group upon its deck, made its slow progress to the
shore. We look around us, and behold the hills and promontories where
the anxious eyes of our fathers first saw the places of habitation and of
rest. We feel the cold which benumbed, and listen to the winds which
pierced them. Beneath us is the Rock, on which New England received

the feet of the Pilgrims. We seem even to behold them, as they struggle with the elements, and, with toilsome efforts, gain the shore. We listen to the chiefs in council; we see the unexampled exhibition of female fortitude and resignation; we hear the whisperings of youthful impatience, and we see, what a painter of our own has also represented by his pencil, chilled and shivering childhood, houseless, but for a mother's arms, couchless, but for a mother's breast, till our own blood almost freezes . . .

The hours of this day are rapidly flying, and this occasion will soon be passed. Neither we nor our children can expect to behold its return. They are in the distant regions of futurity, they exist only in the all-creating power of God, who shall stand here a hundred years hence, to trace, through us, their descent from the Pilgrims, and to survey, as we have now surveyed, the progress of their country, during the lapse of a century. We would anticipate their concurrence with us in our sentiments of deep regard for our common ancestors. We would anticipate and partake the pleasure with which they will then recount the steps of New England's advancement. On the morning of that day, although it will not disturb us in our repose, the voice of acclamation and gratitude, commencing on the Rock of Plymouth, shall be transmitted through millions of the sons of the Pilgrims, till it lose itself in the murmurs of the Pacific seas.

We would leave for the consideration of those who shall then occupy our places, some proof that we hold the blessings transmitted from our fathers in just estimation; some proof of our attachment to the cause of good government, and of civil and religious liberty; some proof of a sincere and ardent desire to promote every thing which may enlarge the understandings and improve the hearts of men. And when, from the long distance of a hundred years, they shall look back upon us, they shall know, at least, that we possessed affections, which, running backward and warming with gratitude for what our ancestors have done for our happiness, run forward also to our posterity, and meet them with cordial salutation, ere yet they have arrived on the shore of being.

Advance, then, ye future generations! We would hail you, as you rise in your long succession, to fill the places which we now fill, and to taste the blessings of existence where we are passing, and soon shall have passed, our own human duration. We bid you welcome to this pleasant land of the fathers. We bid you welcome to the healthful skies and the verdant fields of New England. We greet your accession to the great inheritance which we have enjoyed. We welcome you to the blessings of good government and religious liberty. We welcome you to the treasures of science and the delights of learning. We welcome you to the transcendent sweets of domestic life, to the happiness of kindred, and parents, and children. We welcome you to the immeasurable blessings of rational existence, the immortal hope of Christianity, and the light of everlasting truth!

•

## DANIEL WEBSTER
### 26 January 1830

### 'Liberty and union, now and forever'

*As tension grew between North and South over the high protective tariffs that were enriching New England at the expense of the Southern states, an inquiry into limiting the sale of public land was proposed in the Senate by Senator Samuel Foote of Connecticut.*

*Robert Young Hayne, Senator for Carolina, used the debate on Foote's resolution to attack New England, to advocate an alliance between South and West, and to maintain the right of states to resist supposedly unconstitutional acts of Congress.*

*As a unionist and constitutionalist, Daniel Webster, now Senator for Massachusetts, disagreed violently with Hayne. On 26 January, Webster delivered to a crowded Senate his oratorical masterpiece (of which it is mainly the conclusion that appears below), arguing the case for a strong union.*

I must now beg to ask, sir, whence is this supposed right of the states derived? – where do they find the power to interfere with the laws of the Union? Sir, the opinion which the honorable gentleman maintains is a notion founded in a total misapprehension, in my judgement, of the origin of this government and of the foundation on which it stands. I hold it to be a popular government, erected by the people; those who administer it, responsible to the people; and itself capable of being amended and modified, just as the people may choose it should be. It is as popular, just as truly emanating from the people, as the state governments. It is created for one purpose; the state governments for another. It has its own powers; they have theirs. There is no more authority with them to arrest the operation of a law of Congress than with Congress to arrest the operation of their laws. We are here to administer a Constitution emanating immediately from the people, and trusted by them to our administration. It is not the creature of the state governments. It is of no moment to the argument that certain acts of the state legislatures are necessary to fill our seats in this body. That is not one of their original state powers, a part of the sovereignty of the state. It is a duty which the people, by the Constitution itself, have imposed on the state legislatures, and which they might have left to be performed elsewhere, if they had seen fit. So they have left the choice of President with electors; but all this does not affect the proposition that this whole government, President, Senate, and House of Representatives, is a popular government. It leaves it still all its popular character. The governor of a state (in some of the states) is chosen, not directly by the people, but by those who are chosen by the people, for the purpose of performing, among other duties, that of electing a governor. Is the government of the state, on that account, not a popular government? This government, sir, is the independent offspring of the popular will. It is not the creature of state legislatures; nay, more, if the whole truth must be told, the people brought it into existence, established it, and have hitherto supported it, for the very purpose, amongst others, of imposing certain salutary restraints on state sovereignties. The states cannot now make war; they cannot contract alliances; they cannot make, each for itself, separate regulations of commerce; they cannot lay imposts; they cannot coin money. If this Constitution, sir, be the creature of state legislatures, it must be admitted that it has obtained a strange control over the volitions of its creators . . .

The people, sir, erected this government. They gave it a Constitution, and in that Constitution they have enumerated the powers which they bestow on it. They have made it a limited government. They have defined its authority. They have restrained it to the exercise of such powers as are granted; and all others, they declare, are reserved to the states, or the people. But, sir, they have not stopped here. If they had, they would have accomplished but half their work. No definition can be so clear as to avoid possibility of doubt; no limitation so precise, as to exclude all uncertainty. Who, then, shall construe this grant of the people? Who shall interpret their will, where it may be supposed they have left it doubtful? With whom do they repose this ultimate right of deciding on the powers of the government? Sir, they have settled all this in the fullest manner. They have left it, with the government itself, in its appropriate branches. Sir, the very chief end, the main design, for which the whole Constitution was framed and adopted, was to establish a government that should not be obliged to act through state agency, or depend on state opinion and state discretion. The people had had quite enough of that kind of government, under the confederacy. Under that system, the legal action – the application of law to individuals – belonged exclusively to the states. Congress could only recommend – their acts were not of binding force, till the states had adopted and sanctioned them. Are we in that condition still? Are we yet at the mercy of state discretion, and state construction? Sir, if we are, then vain will be our attempt to maintain the constitution under which we sit.

But, sir, the people have wisely provided, in the constitution itself, a proper, suitable mode and tribunal for settling questions of constitutional law. There are in the constitution, grants of powers to Congress; and restrictions on these powers. There are, also, prohibitions on the states. Some authority must, therefore, necessarily exist, having the ultimate jurisdiction to fix and ascertain the interpretation of these grants, restrictions, and prohibitions. The Constitution has itself pointed out, ordained, and established that authority. How has it accomplished this great and essential end? By declaring, sir, that 'the Constitution and the laws of the United States, made in pursuance thereof, shall be the supreme law of the land, anything in the constitution or laws of any State to the contrary notwithstanding'.

This, sir, was the first great step. By this the supremacy of the Constitution and laws of the United States is declared. The people so will it. No state law is to be valid which comes in conflict with the constitution, or any law of the United States passed in pursuance of it. But who shall decide this question of interference? To whom lies the last appeal? This, sir, the Constitution itself decides, also, by declaring, 'that the judicial power shall extend to all cases arising under the constitution and laws of the United States'. These two provisions, sir, cover the whole ground. They are in truth, the keystone of the arch. With these, it is a constitution; without them, it is a confederacy. In pursuance of these clear and express provisions, Congress established, at its very first session, in the judicial act, a mode for carrying them into full effect, and for bringing all questions of constitutional power to the final decision of the supreme court. It then, sir, became a government. It then had the means of self-protection; and, but for this, it would, in all probability, have been now among things which are past. Having constituted the government, and declared its powers, the people have further said, that since somebody must decide on the extent of these powers, the government shall itself decide; subject, always, like other popular governments, to its responsibility to the people. And now, sir, I repeat, how is it that a state legislature acquires any power to interfere? Who, or what, gives them the right to say to the people, 'We, who are your agents and servants for one purpose, will undertake to decide that your other agents and servants, appointed by you for another purpose, have transcended the authority you gave them!' The reply would be, I think, not impertinent – 'Who made you a judge over another's servants? To their own masters they stand or fall.'

Sir, I deny this power of state legislatures altogether. It cannot stand the test of examination. Gentlemen may say, that in an extreme case, a state government might protect the people from intolerable oppression. Sir, in such a case, the people might protect themselves, without the aid of the state governments. Such a case warrants revolution. It must make, when it comes, a law for itself. A nullifying act of a state legislature cannot alter the case, nor make resistance any more lawful. In maintaining these sentiments, sir, I am but asserting the rights of the people. I state what they have declared, and insist on their right to declare it. They have chosen to repose this power in the general government, and I think it my duty to support it, like other constitutional powers.

For myself, sir, I do not admit the jurisdiction of South Carolina, or any other state, to prescribe my constitutional duty; or to settle, between me and the people, the validity of laws of Congress, for which I have voted. I decline her umpirage. I have not sworn to support the Constitution according to her construction of its clauses. I have not stipulated, by my oath of office, or otherwise, to come under any responsibility, except to the people, and those whom they have appointed to pass upon the question, whether laws, supported by my votes, conform to the Constitution of the country. And, sir, if we look to the general nature of the case, could anything have been more preposterous, than to make a government for the whole Union, and yet leave its powers subject, not to one interpretation, but to thirteen, or twenty-four, interpretations? Instead of one tribunal, established by all, responsible to all, with power to decide for all – shall constitutional questions be left to four-and-twenty popular bodies, each at liberty to decide for itself, and none bound to respect the decisions of others; and each at liberty, too, to give a new construction on every new election of its own members? Would anything, with such a principle in it, or rather with such a destitution of all principle, be fit to be called a government? No, sir. It should not be denominated a Constitution. It should be called, rather, a collection of topics, for everlasting controversy; heads of

debate for a disputatious people. It would not be a government. It
would not be adequate to any practical good, nor fit for any country to
live under. To avoid all possibility of being misunderstood, allow me to
repeat again, in the fullest manner, that I claim no powers for the
government by forced or unfair construction. I admit that it is a
government of strictly limited powers; of enumerated, specified, and
particularized powers; and that whatsoever is not granted, is withheld.
But notwithstanding all this, and however the grant of powers may be
expressed, its limit and extent may yet, in some cases, admit of doubt;
and the general government would be good for nothing, it would be
incapable of long existing, if some mode had not been provided, in
which those doubts, as they should arise, might be peaceably, but
authoritatively, solved.

And now, Mr President, let me run the honorable gentleman's doctrine
a little into its practical application. Let us look at his probable *modus
operandi*. If a thing can be done, an ingenious man can tell how it is to be
done. Now, I wish to be informed, how this state interference is to be
put in practice without violence, bloodshed, and rebellion. We will take
the existing case of the tariff law. South Carolina is said to have made up
her opinion upon it. If we do not repeal it (as we probably shall not) she
will then apply to the case the remedy of her doctrine. She will, we must
suppose, pass a law of her legislature, declaring the several acts of
Congress, usually called the tariff laws, null and void, so far as they
respect South Carolina, or the citizens thereof. So far, all is a paper
transaction, and easy enough. But the collector at Charleston is collecting
the duties imposed by these tariff laws – he therefore must be stopped.
The collector will seize the goods if the tariff duties are not paid. The
state authorities will undertake their rescue; the marshal, with his posse,
will come to the collector's aid, and here the contest begins. The militia
of the state will be called out to sustain the nullifying act. They will
march, sir, under a very gallant leader: for I believe the honorable
member himself commands the militia of that part of the state. He will
raise the nullifying act on his standard, and spread it out as his banner! It
will have a preamble, bearing, That the tariff laws are palpable, deliberate,
and dangerous violations of the constitution! He will proceed, with this
banner flying, to the custom-house in Charleston:

All the while,
Sonorous metal, blowing martial sounds.

Arrived at the custom-house, he will tell the collector that he must collect no more duties under any of the tariff laws. This he will be somewhat puzzled to say, by the way, with a grave countenance, considering what hand South Carolina, herself, had in that of 1816. But, sir, the collector would, probably, not desist at his bidding. He would show him the law of Congress, the treasury instruction, and his own oath of office. He would say, he should perform his duty, come what might. Here would ensue a pause: for they say that a certain stillness precedes the tempest. The trumpeter would hold his breath awhile, and before all this military array should fall on the custom-house, collector, clerks, and all, it is very probable some of those composing it, would request of their gallant commander-in-chief, to be informed a little upon the point of law; for they have, doubtless, a just respect for his opinions as a lawyer, as well as for his bravery as a soldier. They know he has read Blackstone and the constitution, as well as Turenne and Vauban. They would ask him, therefore, something concerning their rights in this matter. They would inquire whether it was not somewhat dangerous to resist a law of the United States. What would be the nature of their offence, they would wish to learn, if they, by military force and array, resisted the execution in Carolina of a law of the United States, and it should turn out, after all, that the law was constitutional? He would answer, of course, treason. No lawyer could give any other answer. John Fries, he would tell them, had learned that some years ago. How, then, they would ask, do you propose to defend us? We are not afraid of bullets, but treason has a way of taking people off, that we do not much relish. How do you propose to defend us? 'Look at my floating banner,' he would reply; 'see there the nullifying law!' Is it your opinion, gallant commander, they would then say, that if we should be indicted for treason, that same floating banner of yours would make a good plea in bar? 'South Carolina is a sovereign state,' he would reply. That is true – but would the judge admit our plea? 'These tariff laws,' he would repeat, 'are unconstitutional, palpably, deliberately, dangerously.' That all may be so; but if the tribunal should not happen to be of that opinion, shall we swing for it? We are ready to die for our country, but it is rather an awkward business, this dying without touching the ground! After all, that is a sort of hemp tax, worse than any part of the tariff.

Mr President, the honorable gentleman would be in a dilemma, like that of another great general. He would have a knot before him which he could not untie. He must cut it with his sword. He must say to his followers, defend yourselves with your bayonets; and this is war – civil war.

Direct collision, therefore, between force and force, is the unavoidable result of that remedy for the revision of unconstitutional laws which the gentleman contends for. It must happen in the very first case to which it is applied. Is not this the plain result? To resist, by force, the execution of a law, generally, is treason. Can the courts of the United States take notice of the indulgence of a state to commit treason? The common saying, that a state cannot commit treason herself, is nothing to the purpose. Can she authorize others to do it? If John Fries had produced an act of Pennsylvania, annulling the law of Congress, would it have helped his case? Talk about it as we will, these doctrines go the length of revolution. They are incompatible with any peaceable administration of the government. They lead directly to disunion and civil commotion; and, therefore, it is, that at their commencement, when they are first found to be maintained by respectable men, and in a tangible form, I enter my public protest against them all.

The honorable gentleman argues, that if this government be the sole judge of the extent of its own powers, whether that right of judging be in Congress, or the Supreme Court, it equally subverts state sovereignty. This gentleman sees, or thinks he sees, although he cannot perceive how the right of judging, in this matter, if left to the exercise of state legislatures, has any tendency to subvert the government of the Union. The gentleman's opinion may be, that the right ought not to have been lodged with the general government; he may like better such a constitution, as we should have under the right of state interference; but I ask him to meet me on the plain matter of fact; I ask him to meet me on the constitution itself; I ask him if the power is not found there – clear and visibly found there?

But, sir, what is this danger, and what the grounds of it? Let it be remembered, that the constitution of the United States is not unalterable. It is to continue in its present form no longer than the people who established it shall choose to continue it. If they shall become convinced that they have made an injudicious or inexpedient partition and distribution of power, between the state governments and the general government, they can alter that distribution at will.

If anything be found in the national constitution, either by original provision, or subsequent interpretation, which ought not to be in it, the people know how to get rid of it. If any construction be established, unacceptable to them, so as to become, practically, a part of the constitution, they will amend it, at their own sovereign pleasure: but while the people choose to maintain it, as it is; while they are satisfied with it, and refuse to change it, who has given, or who can give, to the state legislatures a right to alter it, either by interference, construction, or otherwise? Gentlemen do not seem to recollect that the people have any power to do anything for themselves; they imagine there is no safety for them, any longer than they are under the close guardianship of the state legislatures. Sir, the people have not trusted their safety, in regard to the general Constitution, to these hands. They have required other security, and taken other bonds. They have chosen to trust themselves, first, to the plain words of the instrument, and to such construction as the government itself, in doubtful cases, should put on its own powers, under their oaths of office, and subject to their responsibility to them: just as the people of a state trust their own state governments with a similar power. Secondly, they have reposed their trust in the efficacy of frequent elections, and in their own power to remove their own servants and agents, whenever they see cause. Thirdly, they have reposed trust in the judicial power, which, in order that it might be trustworthy, they have made as respectable, as disinterested, and as independent as was practicable. Fourthly, they have seen fit to rely, in case of necessity, or high expediency, on their known and admitted power, to alter or amend the constitution, peaceably and quietly, whenever experience shall point out defects or imperfections. And, finally, the people of the United States have, at no time, in no way, directly or indirectly, authorized any state legislature to construe or interpret their high instrument of government; much less to interfere, by their own power, to arrest its course and operation.

If, sir, the people in these respects, had done otherwise than they have done, their Constitution could neither have been preserved, nor would it have been worth preserving. And, if its plain provisions shall now be disregarded, and these new doctrines interpolated in it, it will become as feeble and helpless a being, as its enemies, whether early or more recent, could possibly desire. It will exist in every state, but as a poor dependent on state permission. It must borrow leave to be; and will be, no longer than state pleasure, or state discretion, sees fit to grant the indulgence, and to prolong its poor existence.

But, sir, although there are fears, there are hopes also. The people have preserved this, their own chosen constitution, for forty years, and have seen their happiness, prosperity, and renown, grow with its growth, and strengthen with its strength. They are now, generally, strongly attached to it. Overthrown by direct assault, it cannot be; evaded, undermined, nullified, it will not be, if we, and those who shall succeed us here, as agents and representatives of the people, shall conscientiously and vigilantly discharge the two great branches of our public trust – faithfully to preserve, and wisely to administer it.

Mr President, I have thus stated the reasons of my dissent to the doctrines which have been advanced and maintained. I am conscious of having detained you and the Senate much too long. I was drawn into the debate with no previous deliberation such as is suited to the discussion of so grave and important a subject. But it is a subject of which my heart is full, and I have not been willing to suppress the utterance of its spontaneous sentiments. I cannot, even now, persuade myself to relinquish it, without expressing, once more, my deep conviction, that, since it respects nothing less than the union of the states, it is of most vital and essential importance to the public happiness. I profess, sir, in my career, hitherto, to have kept steadily in view the prosperity and honor of the whole country, and the preservation of our federal Union. It is to that Union we owe our safety at home, and our consideration and dignity abroad. It is to that Union that we are chiefly indebted for whatever makes us most proud of our country. That Union we reached only by the discipline of our virtues in the severe school of adversity. It had its origin in the necessities of disordered finance, prostrate commerce, and ruined credit. Under its benign influences, these great interests immediately awoke, as from the dead, and sprang forth with newness of life. Every year of its duration has teemed with fresh proofs of its utility and its blessings; and, although our territory has stretched out wider and wider, and our population spread farther and farther, they have not outrun its protection or its benefits. It has been to us all a copious fountain of national, social, and personal happiness. I have not allowed myself, sir, to look beyond the Union, to see what might lie hidden in the dark recess behind. I have not coolly weighed the chances of preserving liberty when the bonds that unite us together shall be broken asunder. I have not accustomed myself to hang over the precipice of disunion, to see whether, with my short sight, I can fathom the depth of the abyss below; nor could I regard him as a safe counsellor in the affairs of this government, whose thoughts should be mainly bent on considering, not how the Union shall be best preserved, but how tolerable might be the condition of the people when it shall be broken up and destroyed. While the Union lasts, we have high, exciting, gratifying prospects spread out before us, for us and our children. Beyond that I seek not to penetrate the veil. God grant that, in my day, at least, that curtain may not rise. God grant, that on my vision never may be opened what lies behind. When my eyes shall be turned to behold, for the last time, the sun in heaven, may I not see him shining on the broken and dishonored fragments of a once glorious Union; on states dissevered, discordant, belligerent; on a land rent with civil feuds, or drenched, it may be, in fraternal blood! Let their last feeble and lingering glance, rather behold the gorgeous ensign of the republic, now known and honored throughout the earth, still full high advanced, its arms and trophies streaming in their original lustre, not a stripe erased or polluted, nor a single star obscured – bearing for its motto, no such miserable interrogatory, as What is all this worth? Nor those other words of delusion and folly, liberty first, and union afterwards – but everywhere, spread all over in characters of living light, blazing on all its ample folds, as they float over the sea and over the land, and in every wind under the whole heavens, that other sentiment, dear to every true American heart – liberty and union, now and forever, one and inseparable.

*William Safire, the American commentator on oratory, describes Webster's speech as one of the most forceful rebuttals in the history of American debate. The reply to Hayne marked Webster's zenith as an orator – generations of schoolboys were taught the art of public speaking by practising his peroration.*

•

## SETH LUTHER
### c. 1832

### 'We have borne these evils by far too long'

*Seth Luther, a carpenter, was the first American in the crusade against child labour. He learned about the conditions of American workers in the early nineteenth century from a tour of fourteen states and from reading books and newspapers. Although the ten-hour day had been won in New York by 1832, labourers elsewhere worked from dawn to dusk. Strikes in Boston and Providence were defeated – but the movement for shorter hours gathered strength and the first convention of the New England Association of Farmers, Mechanics and Other Working Men met in 1831 and pledged members to a ten-hour day with no loss of wages.*

*Luther settled to live among the cotton mills of New England with a hatred of class distinction. He delivered this address in Boston, Charlestown, Cambridgeport, Waltham and Dorchester.*

Our ears are constantly filled with the cry of national wealth, national glory, American system, and American industry . . .

This cry is kept up by men who are endeavoring by all the means in their power to cut down the wages of our own people, and who send agents to Europe to induce foreigners to come here to underwork American citizens, to support American industry and the American system.

The whole concern (as now conducted) is as great a humbug as ever deceived any people. We see the system of manufacturing lauded to the skies; senators, representatives, owners, and agents of cotton mills using all means to keep out of sight the evils growing up under it. Cotton mills, where cruelties are practiced, excessive labor required, education neglected, and vice, as a matter of course, on the increase, are denominated 'the principalities of the destitute, the palaces of the poor.' . . . A member of the United States Senate seems to be extremely pleased with cotton mills; he says in the Senate, 'Who has not been delighted with the clockwork movements of a large cotton manufactory; he had visited them often, and always with increased delight.' He says the women work in large airy apartments well warmed; they are neatly dressed, with ruddy complexions and happy countenances, they mend the broken threads and replace the exhausted balls or broaches, and at stated periods they go to and return from their meals with a light and cheerful step. (While on a visit to that pink of perfection, Waltham, I remarked that the females moved with a very light step, and well they might, for the bell rung for them to return to the mill from their homes in nineteen minutes after it had rung for them to go to breakfast; some of these females boarded the largest part of half a mile from the mill.) And the grand climax is that at the end of the week, after working like slaves for thirteen or fourteen hours every day, 'they enter the temples of God on the Sabbath, and thank Him for all His benefits' – and the American system above all requires a peculiar outpouring of gratitude. We remark that whatever girls or others may do west of the Allegheny Mountains, we do not believe there can be a single person found east of those mountains who ever thanked God for permission to work in a cotton mill.

Without being obliged to attribute wrong or mercenary motives to the honorable senator (whose talents certainly must command respect from all, let their views in other respects be what they may), we remark that we think he was most grossly deceived by the circumstances of his visit. We will give our reasons in a few words spoken (in part) on a former occasion on this subject. It is well known to all that when honorables travel, timely notice is given of their arrival and departure in places of note. Here we have a case; the honorable senator from Kentucky is about to visit a cotton mill; due notice is given; the men, girls, and boys are ordered to array themselves in their best apparel. Flowers of every hue are brought to decorate the mill and enwreath the brows of the fair sex. If nature will not furnish the materials from the lap of summer, art supplies the deficiency. Evergreens mingle with the roses, the jasmine, and the hyacinth to honor the illustrious visitor, the champion, the very Goliath of the American system. He enters! Smiles are on every brow. No cowhide, or rod, or 'well-seasoned strap' is suffered to be seen by the honorable Senator or permitted to disturb the enviable happiness of the inmates of this almost celestial habitation. The honorable gentleman views with keen eye the 'clockwork'. He sees the rosy faces of the houris inhabiting this palace of beauty; he is in ecstasy – he is almost dumb-founded – he enjoys the enchanting scene with the most intense delight. For an hour or more (not fourteen hours) he seems to be in the regions described in Oriental song, his feelings are overpowered, and he retires, almost unconscious of the cheers which follow his steps; or if he hears the ringing shout, 'tis but to convince him that he is in a land of reality and not of fiction. His mind being filled with sensations, which, from their novelty, are without a name, he exclaims, 'tis a paradise; and we reply, if a cotton mill is a 'paradise', it is 'Paradise Lost' . . .

It has been said that the speaker is opposed to the American system. It turns upon one single point – if these abuses are the American system, he is opposed. But let him see *an* American system where education and intelligence are generally diffused, and the enjoyment of life and liberty secured to all; he then is ready to support such a system. But so long as our government secures exclusive privileges to a very small part of the community, and leaves the majority the 'lawful prey' to avarice, so long does he contend against any 'system' so exceedingly unjust and unequal in its operations. He knows that we must have manufactures. It is impossible to do without them; but he has yet to learn that it is necessary, or just, that manufactures must be sustained by injustice, cruelty, ignorance, vice, and misery; which is now the fact to a startling degree. If what we have stated be true, and we challenge denial, what must be done? Must we fold our arms and say, it always was so and always will be? If we did so, would it not almost rouse from their graves the heroes of our Revolution? Would not the cold marble representing our beloved Washington start into life and reproach us for our cowardice? Let the word be – onward! onward! We know the difficulties are great, and the obstacles many; but, as yet, we 'know our rights, and knowing, dare maintain'. We wish to injure no man, and we are determined not to be injured as we have been; we wish nothing but those equal rights which were designed for us all. And although wealth, and prejudice, and slander, and abuse are all brought to bear on us, we have one consolation – 'We are the majority.'

One difficulty is a want of information among our own class, and the higher orders reproach us for our ignorance; but, thank God, we have enough of intelligence among us yet to show the world that all is not lost.

Another difficulty among us is – the press has been almost wholly, and is now in a great degree, closed upon us. We venture to assert that the press is bribed by gold in many instances; and we believe that if law had done what gold has accomplished, our country would, before this time, have been deluged with blood. But workingmen's papers are multiplying, and we shall soon, by the diffusion of intelligence, be enabled to form a front which will show all monopolists, and all tyrants, that we are not only determined to have the name of freemen, but that we will live freemen and die freemen.

Fellow citizens of New England, farmers, mechanics, and laborers, we have borne these evils by far too long; we have been deceived by all parties; we must take our business into our own hands. Let us awake. Our cause is the cause of truth – of justice and humanity. It must prevail. Let us be determined no longer to be deceived by the cry of those who produce nothing and who enjoy all, and who insultingly term us – the farmers, the mechanics, and laborers – the lower orders, and exultingly claim our homage for themselves, as the higher orders – while the Declaration of Independence asserts that 'All men are created equal.'

•

# JOHN C. CALHOUN
15–16 February 1833

### 'The controversy is . . . between power and liberty'

*Until 1828, the career of John C. Calhoun (1782–1850), who came from a slaveholding family of South Carolina, seemed destined to end in the White House. As vice-president to John Quincy Adams and Andrew Jackson, he was only one step away.*

*It was then he realized that he was becoming out of touch with his slaveholding constituency in South Carolina. In 1829 he declared that a state could nullify unconstitutional laws. When South Carolina passed a nullification ordinance in 1832, he resigned as vice-president, entered the Senate and became a champion of state rights and the interests of slaveholders.*

*President Jackson responded with his famous proclamation against nullification, restating the principles of the constitution, and introduced the Revenue Enforcement Bill [the Force Bill], giving him emergency use of the army to enforce revenue laws.*

*Speaking in the Senate over two days, Calhoun argued in this speech against Jackson the case for states against the government.*

This bill proceeds on the ground that the entire sovereignty of this country belongs to the American people, as forming one great community, and regards the states as mere fractions or counties and not as integral parts of the Union; having no more right to resist the encroachments of the government than a county has to resist the authority of a state; and treating such resistance as the lawless acts of so many individuals without possessing sovereignty or political rights. It has been said that the bill declares war against South Carolina. No. It decrees a massacre of her citizens! War has something ennobling about it, and, with all its horrors, brings into action the highest qualities, intellectual and moral. It was, perhaps, in the order of Providence that it should be permitted for that very purpose. But this bill declares no war, except, indeed, it be that which savages wage – a war, not against the community, but the citizens of whom that community is composed. But I regard it as worse than savage warfare – as an attempt to take away life under the color of law, without the trial by jury, or any other safeguard which the Constitution has thrown around the life of the citizen. It authorizes the President, or even his deputies, when they may suppose the law to be violated, without the intervention of a court or jury, to kill without mercy or discrimination!

It has been said by the Senator from Tennessee [*Grundy*] to be a measure of peace! Yes, such peace as the wolf gives to the lamb – the kite to the dove! Such peace as Russia gives to Poland, or death to its victim! A peace by extinguishing the political existence of the state, by awing her into an abandonment of the exercise of every power which constitutes her a sovereign community. It is to South Carolina a question of self-preservation; and I proclaim it, that, should this bill pass, and an attempt be made to enforce it, it will be resisted, at every hazard – even that of death itself. Death is not the greatest calamity: there are others still more terrible to the free and brave, and among them may be placed the loss of liberty and honor. There are thousands of her brave sons who, if need be, are prepared cheerfully to lay down their lives in defense of the state and the great principles of constitutional liberty for which she is contending. God forbid that this should become necessary! It never can be, unless this government is resolved to bring the question to extremity . . .

Is this a Federal Union? a Union of states, as distinct from that of individuals? Is the sovereignty in the several states, or in the American people in the aggregate? The very language which we are compelled to use when speaking of our political institutions affords proof conclusive as to its real character. The terms Union, Federal, united, all imply a combination of sovereignties, a confederation of states. They are never applied to an association of individuals. Whoever heard of the United States of New York, of Massachusetts, or of Virginia? Whoever heard the term Federal or Union applied to the aggregation of individuals into one community? Nor is the other point less clear – that the sovereignty is in the several states, and that our system is a Union of twenty-four sovereign powers, under a constitutional compact, and not of a divided sovereignty between the states severally and the United States. In spite of all that has been said, I maintain that sovereignty is in its nature indivisible. It is the supreme power in a state, and we might just as well speak of half a square, or of half a triangle, as of half a sovereignty. It is a gross error to confound the exercise of sovereign powers with sovereignty itself, or the delegation of such powers with the surrender of them. A sovereign may delegate his powers to be exercised by as many agents as he may think proper, under such conditions and with such limitations as he may impose; but to surrender any portion of his sovereignty to another is to annihilate the whole. The Senator from

Delaware calls this metaphysical reasoning, which, he says, he cannot comprehend. If by metaphysics he means that scholastic refinement which makes distinctions without difference, no one can hold it in more utter contempt than I do; but if, on the contrary, he means the power of analysis and combination – that power which reduces the most complex idea into its elements, which traces causes to their first principle, and, by the power of generalization and combination, unites the whole in one harmonious system – then, so far from deserving contempt, it is the highest attribute of the human mind. It is the power which raises man above the brute – which distinguishes his faculties from mere sagacity, which he holds in common with inferior animals. It is this power which has raised the astronomer from being a mere gazer at the stars to the high intellectual eminence of a Newton or a Laplace, and astronomy itself from a mere observation of isolated facts into that noble science which displays to our admiration the system of the universe. And shall this high power of the mind, which has effected such wonders when directed to the laws which control the material world, be forever prohibited, under a senseless cry of metaphysics, from being applied to the high purpose of political science and legislation? I hold them to be subject to laws as fixed as matter itself, and to be as fit a subject for the application of the highest intellectual power. Denunciation may, indeed, fall upon the philosophical inquirer into these first principles, as it did upon Galileo and Bacon when they first unfolded the great discoveries which have immortalized their names; but the time will come when truth will prevail in spite of prejudice and denunciation, and when politics and legislation will be considered as much a science as astronomy and chemistry . . .

It is said that the bill ought to pass because the law must be enforced. The law must be enforced! The imperial edict must be executed! It is under such sophistry, couched in general terms, without looking to the limitations which must ever exist in the practical exercise of power, that the most cruel and despotic acts ever have been covered. It was such sophistry as this that cast Daniel into the lions' den, and the three Innocents into the fiery furnace. Under the same sophistry the bloody edicts of Nero and Caligula were executed. The law must be enforced. Yes, the act imposing the 'tea tax must be executed'. This was the very argument which impelled Lord North and his administration to that mad career which forever separated us from the British crown. Under a similar sophistry, 'that religion must be protected', how many massacres have been perpetrated? and how many martyrs have been tied to the stake? What! acting on this vague abstraction, are you prepared to enforce a law without considering whether it be just or unjust, constitu-constitutional or unconstitutional? Will you collect money when it is acknowledged that it is not wanted? He who earns the money, who digs it from the earth with the sweat of his brow, has a just title to it against the universe. No one has a right to touch it without his consent, except his government, and this only to the extent of its legitimate wants; to take more is robbery, and you propose by this bill to enforce robbery by murder. Yes: to this result you must come by this miserable sophistry, this vague abstraction of enforcing the law, without a regard to the fact whether the law be just or unjust, constitutional or unconstitutional.

In the same spirit we are told that the Union must be preserved, without regard to the means. And how is it proposed to preserve the Union? By force? Does any man in his senses believe that this beautiful structure – this harmonious aggregate of states, produced by the joint consent of all – can be preserved by force? Its very introduction will be certain destruction to this Federal Union. No, no. You cannot keep the states united in their constitutional and Federal bonds by force. Force may, indeed, hold the parts together, but such union would be the bond between master and slave – a union of exaction on one side and of unqualified obedience on the other. That obedience which, we are told by the Senator from Pennsylvania [*Wilkins*], is the Union! Yes, exaction on the side of the master; for this very bill is intended to collect what can be no longer called taxes – the voluntary contribution of a free people – but tribute – tribute to be collected under the mouths of the cannon! Your customhouse is already transferred into a garrison, and that garrison with its batteries turned, not against the enemy of your country, but on subjects (I will not say citizens), on whom you propose to levy contributions. Has reason fled from our borders? Have we ceased to reflect? It is madness to suppose that the Union can be preserved by force. I tell you plainly that the bill, should it pass, cannot be enforced. It will prove only a blot upon your statute book, a reproach to the year, and a disgrace to the American Senate. I repeat, it will not be executed; it will rouse the dormant spirit of the people and open their eyes to the approach of despotism. The country has sunk into avarice and political corruption, from which nothing can arouse it but some measure on the part of the government, of folly and madness, such as that now under consideration.

Disguise it as you may, the controversy is one between power and liberty; and I tell the gentlemen who are opposed to me that, as strong as may be the love of power on their side, the love of liberty is still stronger on ours. History furnishes many instances of similar struggles, where the love of liberty has prevailed against power under every disadvantage, and among them few more striking than that of our own Revolution; where, as strong as was the parent country, and feeble as were the colonies, yet, under the impulse of liberty and the blessing of God, they gloriously triumphed in the contest.

We have now sufficient experience to ascertain that the tendency to conflict in its [the bill's] action is between the Southern and other sections. The latter, having a decided majority, must habitually be possessed of the powers of the government, both in this and in the other House; and, being governed by that instinctive love of power so natural to the human breast, they must become the advocates of the power of government and in the same degree opposed to the limitations; while the other and weaker section is as necessarily thrown on the side of the limitations. One section is the natural guardian of the delegated powers, and the other of the reserved; and the struggle on the side of the former will be to enlarge the powers, while that on the opposite side will be to restrain them within their constitutional limits. The contest will, in fact, be a contest between power and liberty, and such I consider the present – a contest in which the weaker section, with its peculiar labor, productions, and institutions, has at stake all that can be dear to freemen.

Should we be able to maintain in their full vigor our reserved rights, liberty and prosperity will be our portion; but if we yield, and permit the stronger interest to concentrate within itself all the powers of the government, then will our fate be more wretched than that of the aborigines whom we have expelled. In this great struggle between the delegated and reserved powers, so far from repining that my lot, and that of those whom I represent, is cast on the side of the latter, I rejoice that such is the fact; for, though we participate in but few of the advantages of the government, we are compensated, and more than compensated, in not being so much exposed to its corruptions. Nor do I repine that the duty, so difficult to be discharged, of defending the reserved powers against apparently such fearful odds has been assigned to us. To discharge it successfully requires the highest qualities, moral and intellectual; and should we perform it with a zeal and ability proportioned to its magnitude, instead of mere planters, our section will become distinguished for its patriots and statesmen. But, on the other hand, if we prove unworthy of the trust – if we yield to the steady encroachments of power – the severest calamity and most debasing corruption will overspread the land. Every Southern man, true to the interests of his section, and faithful to the duties which Providence has allotted him, will be forever excluded from the honors and emoluments of this government, which will be reserved for those only who have qualified themselves, by political prostitution, for admission into the Magdalen Asylum.

•

## WENDELL PHILLIPS
### 8 December 1837

### 'The priceless value of the freedom of the press'

*Wendell Phillips (1811–84) was first drawn to the abolitionist cause in 1835 when he witnessed a Boston mob set upon the abolitionist journalist William Lloyd Garrison and drag him through the streets at the end of a rope.*

*Two years later he went to a meeting at Faneuil Hall in Boston called to protest against the murder of Elijah Lovejoy by a Negro-hating mob in Alton, Illinois. Lovejoy, a white abolitionist who published an anti-slavery newspaper, was killed when a warehouse where he stored his press for safety was set on fire. Unannounced and uninvited, James T. Austin, Attorney-General of Massachusetts, rose to ridicule the meeting. Hundreds cheered when he compared Lovejoy's murderers to the members of the Boston Tea Party.*

*Phillips, who became one of the most brilliant speakers of his age, could no longer contain his anger. Amid boos and catcalls, the Boston aristocrat rose to speak – and to sway the audience against Austin to support the protest.*

Elijah Lovejoy was not only defending the freedom of the press, but he was under his own roof, in arms with the sanction of the civil authority. The men who assailed him went against and over the laws. The *mob*, as the gentleman (a previous speaker) terms it – mob, forsooth! certainly we sons of the tea-spillers are a marvelously patient generation! – the 'orderly mob' which assembled in the Old South to destroy the tea, were met to resist, not the laws, but illegal enactions. Shame on the American who calls the tea tax and stamp act *laws*! Our fathers resisted, not the King's prerogative, but the King's usurpation. To find any other account, you must read our revolutionary history upside down. Our state archives are loaded with arguments of John Adams to prove the taxes laid by the British Parliament unconstitutional – beyond its power.

It was not until this was made out that the men of New England rushed to arms. The arguments of the Council Chamber and the House of Representatives preceded and sanctioned the contest. To draw the conduct of our ancestors into a precedent for mobs, for a right to resist laws we ourselves have enacted, is an insult to their memory. The difference between the excitements of those days and our own, which the gentleman in kindness to the latter has overlooked, is simply this: the men of that day went for the right, as secured by the laws. They were the people rising to sustain the laws and Constitution of the province. The rioters of our days go for their own wills, right or wrong. Sir, when I heard the gentleman lay down principles which place the murderers of Alton side by side with Otis and Hancock, with Quincy and Adams, I thought those pictured lips [*pointing to the portraits in the hall*] would have broken into voice to rebuke the recreant American – the slanderer of the dead. The gentleman said that he should sink into insignificance if he dared to gainsay the principles of these resolutions. Sir, for the sentiments he had uttered, on soil consecrated by the prayers of Puritans and the blood of patriots, the earth should have yawned and swallowed him up.

Some persons seem to imagine that anarchy existed at Alton from the commencement of these disputes. Not at all. 'No one of us,' says an eye-witness and a comrade of Lovejoy, 'has taken up arms during these disturbances but at the command of the mayor.' Anarchy did not settle down on that devoted city till Lovejoy breathed his last. Till then the law, represented in his person, sustained itself against its foes. When he fell, civil authority was trampled under foot. He had 'planted himself on his constitutional rights, appealed to the laws, claimed the protection of the civil authority, taken refuge under the broad shield of the Constitution. When through that he was pierced and fell, he fell but one sufferer in a common catastrophe.' He took refuge under the banner of liberty – amid its folds; and when he fell, its glorious stars and stripes, the emblem of free institutions, around which cluster so many heart-stirring memories, were blotted out in the martyr's blood.

It has been stated, perhaps inadvertently, that Lovejoy or his comrades fired first. This is denied by those who have the best means of knowing. Guns were first fired by the mob. After being twice fired on, those within the building consulted together and deliberately returned the fire. But suppose they did fire first. They had a right so to do; not only the right which every citizen has to defend himself, but the further right which every civil officer has to resist violence. Even if Lovejoy fired the first gun, it would not lessen his claim to our sympathy, or destroy his title to be considered a martyr in defense of a free press. The question now is, Did he act within the Constitution and the laws? The men who fell in State Street, on the 5th of March, 1770, did more than Lovejoy is charged with. They were the *first* assailants upon some slight quarrel, they pelted the troops with every missile within reach. Did this bate one jot of the eulogy with which Hancock and Warren hallowed their memory, hailing them as the first martyrs in the cause of American liberty? If, sir, I had adopted what are called peace principles, I might lament the circumstances of this case. But all you who believe as I do, in the right and duty of magistrates to execute the laws, join with me and brand as base hypocrisy the conduct of those who assemble year after year on the 4th of July to fight over the battles of the Revolution, and yet 'damn with faint praise' or load with obloquy, the memory of this man who shed his blood in defense of life, liberty, property, and the freedom of the press!

Throughout that terrible night I find nothing to regret but this, that, within the limits of our country, civil authority should have been so prostrated as to oblige a citizen to arm in his own defense, and to arm in vain. The gentleman says Lovejoy was presumptuous and imprudent – he 'died as the fool dieth'. And a reverend clergyman of the city tells us that no citizen has a right to publish opinions disagreeable to the community! If any mob follows such publication, on him rests its guilt. He must wait, forsooth, till the people come up to it and agree with him! This libel on liberty goes on to say that the want of right to speak as we think is an evil inseparable from republican institutions! If this be so, what are they worth? Welcome the despotism of the Sultan, where one knows what he may publish and what he may not, rather than the tyranny of this many-headed monster, the mob, where we know not what we may do or say, till some fellow citizen has tried it, and paid for the lesson with his life. This clerical absurdity chooses as a check for the abuses of the press, not the law, but the dread of a mob. By so doing, it deprives not only the individual and the minority of their rights, but the majority also, since the expression of their opinion may sometime provoke disturbances from the minority. A few men may make a mob as well as many. The majority, then, have no right, as Christian men, to utter their sentiments, if by any possibility it may lead to a mob! Shades of Hugh Peters and John Cotton, save us from such pulpits!

Imagine yourself present when the first news of Bunker Hill battle reached a New England town. The tale would have run thus: 'The patriots are routed, – the redcoats victorious, – Warren lies dead upon the field.' With what scorn would that Tory have been received, who should have charged Warren with imprudence! who should have said that, bred a physician, he was 'out of place' in that battle, and 'died as the fool dieth'. How would the intimation have been received, that Warren and his associates should have merited a better time? But if success be, indeed, the only criterion of prudence, *Respice finem* – wait till the end!

Presumptuous to assert the freedom of the press on American ground! Is the assertion of such freedom before the age? So much before the age as to leave one no right to make it because it displeases the community? Who invents this libel on his country? It is this very thing which entitles Lovejoy to greater praise. The disputed right which provoked the Revolution – taxation without representation – is far beneath that for which he died. One word, gentlemen. As much as thought is better than money, so much is the cause in which Lovejoy died nobler than a mere question of taxes. James Otis thundered in this hall when the King did but touch his pocket. Imagine, if you can, his indignant eloquence had England offered to put a gag upon his lips. The question that stirred the Revolution touched our civil interests. This concerns us not only as citizens, but as immortal beings. Wrapped up in its fate, saved or lost with it, are not only the voice of the statesman, but the instructions of the pulpit and the progress of our faith.

Mr Chairman, from the bottom of my heart I thank that brave little band at Alton for resisting. We must remember that Lovejoy had fled from city to city – suffered the destruction of three presses patiently. At length he took counsel with friends, men of character, of tried integrity, of wide views, of Christian principle. They thought the crisis had come; it was full time to assert the laws. They saw around them, not a community like our own, of fixed habits, of character moulded and settled, but one 'in the gristle, not yet hardened into the bone of manhood'. The people there, children of our older states, seem to have forgotten the blood-tried principles of their fathers the moment they lost sight of our New England hills. Something was to be done to show them the priceless value of the freedom of the press, to bring back and set right their wandering and confused ideas. He and his advisers looked out on a community, staggering like a drunken man, indifferent to their rights and confused in their feelings. Deaf to argument, haply they might be stunned into sobriety. They saw that of which we cannot judge, the *necessity* of resistance. Insulted law called for it. Public opinion, fast hastening on the downward course, must be arrested.

Does not the event show they judged rightly? Absorbed in a thousand trifles, how has the nation all at once come to a stand? Men begin, as in 1776 and 1640, to discuss principles, to weigh characters, to find out where they are. Haply, we may awake before we are borne over the precipice.

•

## HENRY CLAY
### 5 February 1850

### 'The dove of peace'

*Henry Clay (1777–1852) became known as the Great Pacificator when he steered through Congress the Missouri Compromise in 1820, dividing new states between slave and free. Once again, in 1850, Clay, now the Senator for Kentucky, became the Great Compromiser during the storm over the admission of California as a free state. Clay, who believed in gradual emancipation, worked his magic for the last time, evolving a programme which admitted California (and pleased the North) but also introduced a stricter Fugitive Slave Law (which pleased the South) and which delayed the Civil War for a decade.*

*This extract is from the second of the many speeches he made during the furious debate in the Senate which lasted for months.*

It has been objected against this measure that it is a compromise. It has been said that it is a compromise of principle, or of a principle. Mr President, what is a compromise? It is a work of mutual concession – an agreement in which there are reciprocal stipulations – a work in which, for the sake of peace and concord, one party abates his extreme demands in consideration of an abatement of extreme demands by the other party: it is a measure of mutual concession – a measure of mutual sacrifice. Undoubtedly, Mr President, in all such measures of compromise, one party would be very glad to get what he wants, and reject what he does not desire but which the other party wants. But when he comes to reflect that, from the nature of the government and its operations, and from those with whom he is dealing, it is necessary upon his part, in order to secure what he wants, to grant something to the other side, he should be reconciled to the concession which he has made in consequence of the concession which he is to receive, if there is no great principle involved, such as a violation of the Constitution of the United States. I admit that such a compromise as that ought never to be sanctioned or adopted. But I now call upon any senator in his place to point out from the beginning to the end, from California to New Mexico, a solitary provision in this bill which is violative of the Constitution of the United States.

The responsibility of this great measure passes from the hands of the committee, and from my hands. They know, and I know, that it is an awful and tremendous responsibility. I hope that you will meet it with a just conception and a true appreciation of its magnitude, and the magnitude of the consequences that may ensue from your decision one way or the other. The alternatives, I fear, which the measure presents, are concord and increased discord; a servile civil war, originating in its causes on the lower Rio Grande, and terminating possibly in its consequences on the upper Rio Grande in the Santa Fé country, or the restoration of harmony and fraternal kindness. I believe from the bottom of my soul that the measure is the reunion of this Union. I believe it is the dove of peace, which, taking its aerial flight from the dome of the capitol, carries the glad tidings of assured peace and restored harmony to all the remotest extremities of this distracted land. I believe that it will be attended with all these beneficent effects. And now let us discard all resentment, all passions, all petty jealousies, all personal desires, all love of place, all hankerings after the gilded crumbs which fall from the table of power. Let us forget popular fears, from whatever quarter they may spring. Let us go to the limpid fountain of unadulterated patriotism, and, performing a solemn lustration, return divested of all selfish, sinister, and sordid impurities, and think alone of our God, our country, our consciences, and our glorious Union – that Union without which we shall be torn into hostile fragments, and sooner or later become the victims of military despotism or foreign domination.

Mr President, what is an individual man? An atom, almost invisible without a magnifying glass – a mere speck upon the surface of the immense universe; not a second in time, compared to immeasurable, never-beginning, and never-ending eternity; a drop of water in the great deep, which evaporates and is borne off by the winds; a grain of sand, which is soon gathered to the dust from which it sprung. Shall a being so small, so petty, so fleeting, so evanescent, oppose itself to the onward march of a great nation which is to subsist for ages and ages to come; oppose itself to that long line of posterity which, issuing from our loins, will endure during the existence of the world? Forbid it, God. Let us look to our country and our cause, elevate ourselves to the dignity of pure and disinterested patriots, and save our country from all impending dangers. What if, in the march of this nation to greatness and power, we should be buried beneath the wheels that propel it onward! What are we – what is any man – worth who is not ready and willing to sacrifice himself for the benefit of his country when it is necessary?

I call upon all the South. Sir, we have had hard words, bitter words, bitter thoughts, unpleasant feelings toward each other in the progress of this great measure. Let us forget them. Let us sacrifice these feelings. Let us go to the altar of our country and swear, as the oath was taken of old, that we will stand by her; that we will support her; that we will uphold her Constitution; that we will preserve her union; and that we will pass this great, comprehensive, and healing system of measures, which will hush all the jarring elements and bring peace and tranquility to our homes.

Let me, Mr President, in conclusion, say that the most disastrous consequences would occur, in my opinion, were we to go home, doing nothing to satisfy and tranquilize the country upon these great questions. What will be the judgement of mankind, what the judgement of that portion of mankind who are looking upon the progress of this scheme of self-government as being that which holds the highest hopes and expectations of ameliorating the condition of mankind – what will their judgement be? Will not all the monarchs of the Old World pronounce our glorious republic a disgraceful failure? Will you go home and leave all in disorder and confusion – all unsettled – all open? The contentions and agitations of the past will be increased and augmented by the agitations resulting from our neglect to decide them. Sir, we shall stand condemned by all human judgement below, and of that above it is not for me to speak. We shall stand condemned in our own consciences, by our own constituents, and by our own country. The measure may be defeated. I have been aware that its passage for many days was not absolutely certain. From the first to the last, I hoped and believed it would pass, because from the first to the last I believed it was founded on the principles of just and righteous concession, of mutual conciliation. I believe that it deals unjustly by no part of the Republic; that it saves their honor, and, as far as it is dependent upon Congress, saves the interests of all quarters of the country. But, sir, I have known that the decision of its fate depended upon four or five votes in the Senate of the United States, whose ultimate judgement we could not count upon the one side or the other with absolute certainty.

Its fate is now committed to the Senate, and to those five or six votes to which I have referred. It may be defeated. It is possible that, for the chastisement of our sins and transgressions, the rod of Providence may be still applied to us, may be still suspended over us. But, if defeated, it will be a triumph of ultraism and impracticability – a triumph of a most extraordinary conjunction of extremes; a victory won by abolitionism; a victory achieved by free-soilism; a victory of discord and agitation over peace and tranquility; and I pray to Almighty God that it may not, in consequence of the inauspicious result, lead to the most unhappy and disastrous consequences to our beloved country.

•

## JOHN C. CALHOUN
### 4 March 1850

### 'This cry of union'

*John C. Calhoun was a dying man when he made his last journey from South Carolina to Washington to speak in the great Senate debate initiated by Henry Clay. The news that he was going to speak brought crowds to the Senate.*

*There was silence, broken only by whispers, as he made his way to his seat assisted by friends. He rose with difficulty, thanked the Senate for allowing him to be heard and then, too weak to speak himself, passed his speech to the Virginian Senator James M. Mason, who spoke it for him.*

I have, senators, believed from the first that the agitation of the subject of slavery would, if not prevented by some timely and effective measure, end in disunion. Entertaining this opinion, I have, on all proper occasions, endeavored to call the attention of both the two great parties which divide the country, to adopt some such measure to prevent so great a disaster, but without success. The agitation has been permitted to proceed, with almost no attempt to resist it, until it has reached a period when it can no longer be disguised or denied that the Union is in danger. You have thus forced upon you the greatest and the gravest question that ever can come under your consideration: How can the Union be preserved?

To this question there can be but one answer: that the immediate cause is, the almost universal discontent which pervades all the states composing the southern section of the Union. This widely extended discontent is not of recent origin. It commenced with the agitation of the slavery question, and has been increasing ever since.

One of the causes is, undoubtedly, to be traced to the long-continued agitation of the slave question on the part of the North, and the many aggressions which they have made on the rights of the South, during that time.

There is another, lying back of it, but with which this is intimately connected, that may be regarded as the great and primary cause. It is to be found in the fact that the equilibrium between the two sections in the government, as it stood when the Constitution was ratified, and the government put in action, has been destroyed. At that time there was nearly a perfect equilibrium between the two, which afforded ample means to each to protect itself against the aggression of the other; but as it now stands, one section has exclusive power of controlling the government, which leaves the other without any adequate means of protecting itself against its encroachment and oppression.

The cry of Union! Union! the glorious Union! can no more prevent disunion, than the cry of Health! health! glorious health! on the part of the physician can save a patient lying dangerously ill. So long as the Union, instead of being regarded as a protector, is regarded in the opposite character by not much less than a majority of the states, it will be in vain to attempt to concentrate them by pronouncing eulogies on it.

Besides, this cry of Union comes commonly from those whom we cannot believe to be sincere. It usually comes from our assailants; but we cannot believe them to be sincere, for if they loved the Union, they would necessarily be devoted to the Constitution. It made the Union, and to destroy the Constitution would be to destroy the Union. But the only reliable and certain evidence of devotion to the Constitution is, to abstain, on the one hand, from violating it, and to repel, on the other, all attempts to violate it. It is only by faithfully performing those high duties that the Constitution can be preserved, and with it the Union.

Nor can we regard the profession of devotion to the Union, on the part of those who are not our assailants, as sincere, when they pronounce eulogies upon the Union evidently with the intent of charging us with disunion, without uttering one word of denunciation against our assailants. If friends of the Union, their course should be to unite with us in repelling these assaults, and denouncing the authors as enemies of the Union. Why they avoid this and pursue the course they obviously do, it is for them to explain.

Nor can the Union be saved by invoking the name of the illustrious

Southerner, whose mortal remains repose on the western bank of the Potomac. He was one of us – a slave-holder and a planter. We have studied his history, and find nothing in it to justify submission to wrong. On the contrary, his great fame rests on the solid foundation that, while he was careful to avoid doing wrong to others, he was prompt and decided in repelling wrong. I trust that, in this respect, we profited by his example.

Nor can we find anything in his history to deter us from seceding from the Union, should it fail to fulfil the objects for which it was instituted, by being permanently and hopelessly converted into the means of oppression instead of protection. On the contrary, we find much in his example to encourage us, should we be forced to the extremity of deciding between submission and disunion.

I have now, senators, done my duty, in expressing my opinions fully, freely, and candidly on this solemn occasion. In doing so, I have been governed by the motives which have governed me in all the stages of the agitation of the slavery question since its commencement, and exerted myself to arrest it, with the intention of saving the Union, if it could be done, and, if it cannot, to save the section where it has pleased Providence to cast my lot, and which, I sincerely believe, has justice and the Constitution on its side. Having faithfully done my duty to the best of my ability, both to the Union and my section, throughout the whole of this agitation, I shall have the consolation, let what will come, that I am free from all responsibility.

•

## DANIEL WEBSTER
### 7 March 1850

### '*Liberty and union*'

*It was now the turn of Daniel Webster to make the only speech in American history that is remembered by its date – the 'Seventh of March' speech. Clay had sent Webster an outline of his proposals in January. Webster now made the most important (but not the best) speech of his life, with almost no preparation, since he was a broken man, sustained by drugs. It was afterwards the subject of bitter controversy and lost him many previous admirers, mainly because he did not condemn slavery (and had not since he was first mentioned as a candidate for the presidency) and spoke in favour of the Fugitive Slave Law.*

I wish to speak today, not as a Massachusetts man, nor as a Northern man, but as an American and a member of the Senate of the United States. It is fortunate that there is a Senate of the United States; a body not yet moved from its propriety, nor lost to a just sense of its own dignity and its own high responsibilities, and a body to which the country looks, with confidence, for wise, moderate, patriotic, and healing counsels. It is not to be denied that we live in the midst of strong agitations and are surrounded by very considerable dangers to our institutions and government. The imprisoned winds are let loose. The East, the North, and the stormy South combine to throw the whole sea into commotion, to toss its billows to the skies, and disclose its profoundest depths.

I do not affect to regard myself, Mr President, as holding, or fit to hold, the helm in this combat with the political elements; but I have a duty to perform, and I mean to perform it with fidelity, not without a sense of existing dangers, but not without hope. I have a part to act, not for my own security or safety, for I am looking out for no fragment upon which to float away from the wreck, if wreck there must be, but for the good of the whole and the preservation of all; and there is that which will keep me to my duty during this struggle, whether the sun and the stars shall appear for many days.

I speak today for the preservation of the Union. 'Hear me for my cause.' I speak today out of a solicitous and anxious heart, for the restoration to the country of that quiet and that harmony which make the blessings of this Union so rich and so dear to us all. These are the topics that I propose to myself to discuss; these are the motives, and the sole motives, that influence me in the wish to communicate my opinions to the Senate and the country; and if I can do anything, however little, for the promotion of these ends, I shall have accomplished all that I expect.

We all know, sir, that slavery has existed in the world from time immemorial. There was slavery in the earliest periods of history, among the Oriental nations. There was slavery among the Jews; the theocratic government of that people issued no injunction against it. There was slavery among the Greeks. At the introduction of Christianity, the Roman world was full of slaves, and I suppose there is to be found no injunction against that relation between man and man in the teachings of the Gospel of Jesus Christ or of any of His Apostles.

Now, sir, upon the general nature and influence of slavery there exists a wide difference of opinion between the Northern portion of this country and the Southern. It is said, on the one side, that, although not the subject of any injunction or direct prohibition in the New Testament, slavery is a wrong; that it is founded merely in the right of the strongest; and that it is an oppression, like unjust wars, like all those conflicts by which a powerful nation subjects a weaker to its will; and that, in its nature, whatever may be said of it in the modifications which have taken place, it is not according to the meek spirit of the Gospel. It is not 'kindly affectioned'; it does not 'seek another's, and not its own'; it does not 'let the oppressed go free'. These are sentiments that are cherished, and of late with greatly augmented force, among the people of the Northern states. They have taken hold of the religious sentiment of that part of the country, as they have, more or less, taken hold of the religious feelings of a considerable portion of mankind. The South, upon the other side, having been accustomed to this relation between the two races all their lives; from their birth, having been taught, in general, to treat the subjects of this bondage with care and kindness, and I believe, in general, feeling great kindness for them, have not taken the view of the subject which I have mentioned. There are thousands of religious men, with consciences as tender as any of their brethren at the North, who do not see the unlawfulness of slavery; and there are more thousands, perhaps, that, whatsoever they may think of it in its origin, and as a matter depending upon natural rights, yet take things as they are, and, finding slavery to be an established relation of the society in which they live, can see no way in which, let their opinions on the abstract question be what they may, it is in the power of this generation to relieve themselves from this relation. And candor obliges me to say that I believe they are just as conscientious, many of them, and the religious people, all of them, as they are at the North who hold different opinions . . .

But we must view things as they are. Slavery does exist in the United States. It did exist in the states before the adoption of this Constitution, and at that time. Let us therefore, consider for a moment what was the state of sentiment, North and South, in regard to slavery – in regard to slavery at the time this Constitution was adopted. A remarkable change has taken place since; but what did the wise and great men of all parts of the country think of slavery then? In what estimation did they hold it at the time when this Constitution was adopted? It will be found, sir, if we will carry ourselves by historical research back to that day, and ascertain men's opinions by authentic records still existing among us, that there was no diversity of opinion between the North and the South upon the subject of slavery. It will be found that both parts of the country held it equally an evil, a moral and political evil. It will not be found that, either at the North or at the South, there was much, though there was some, invective against slavery as inhuman and cruel. The great ground of objection to it was political; that it weakened the social fabric; that, taking the place of free labor, society became less strong and labor less productive; and therefore we find from all the eminent men of the time the clearest expression of their opinion that slavery is an evil. They ascribed its existence here, not without truth, and not without some acerbity of temper and force of language, to the injurious policy of the mother country, who, to favor the navigator, had entailed these evils upon the colonies ... You observe, sir, that the term *slave* or *slavery* is not used in the Constitution. The Constitution does not require that 'fugitive slaves' shall be delivered up. It requires that persons held to service in one state, and escaping into another, shall be delivered up. Mr Madison opposed the introduction of the term *slave* or *slavery* into the Constitution; for he said that he did not wish to see it recognized by the Constitution of the United States of America that there could be property in men ...

Mr President, I should much prefer to have heard from every member on this floor declarations of opinion that this Union could never be dissolved than the declaration of opinion by anybody that, in any case, under the pressure of any circumstances, such a dissolution was possible. I hear with distress and anguish the word 'secession', especially when it falls from the lips of those who are patriotic, and known to the country, and known all over the world for their political services. Secession! Peaceable secession! Sir, your eyes and mine are never destined to see that miracle. The dismemberment of this vast country without convulsion! The breaking up of the fountains of the great deep without ruffling the surface! Who is so foolish – I beg everybody's pardon – as to expect to see any such thing? Sir, he who sees these states, now revolving in harmony around a common center, and expects to see them quit their places and fly off without convulsion, may look the next hour to see the heavenly bodies rush from their spheres, and jostle against each other in the realms of space, without causing the wreck of the universe. There can be no such thing as a peaceable secession. Peaceable secession is an utter impossibility. Is the great Constitution under which we live, covering this whole country, is it to be thawed and melted away by secession, as the snows on the mountain melt under the influence of a vernal sun, disappear almost unobserved, and run off? No, sir! No, sir!

I will not state what might produce the disruption of the Union; but, sir, I see as plainly as I can see the sun in heaven what that disruption itself must produce; I see that it must produce war . . .

And, now, Mr President, instead of speaking of the possibility or utility of secession, instead of dwelling in those caverns of darkness, instead of groping with those ideas so full of all that is horrid and horrible, let us come out into the light of the day; let us enjoy the fresh air of Liberty and Union; let us cherish those hopes which belong to us; let us devote ourselves to those great objects that are fit for our consideration and our action; let us raise our conceptions to the magnitude and the importance of the duties that devolve upon us; let our comprehension be as broad as the country for which we act, our aspirations as high as its certain destiny; let us not be pygmies in a case that calls for men. Never did there devolve on any generation of men higher trusts than now devolve upon us, for the preservation of this Constitution and the harmony and peace of all who are destined to live under it. Let us make our generation one of the strongest and brightest links in that golden chain which is destined, I fondly believe, to grapple the people of all the states to this Constitution for ages to come. We have a great, popular, constitutional government, guarded by law and by judicature, and defended by the affections of the whole people. No monarchical throne presses these states together, no iron chain of military power encircles them; they live and stand under a government popular in its form, representative in its character, founded upon principles of equality, and so constructed, we hope, as to last forever. In all its history it has been beneficent; it has trodden down no man's liberty; it has crushed no state. Its daily respiration is liberty and patriotism; its yet-youthful veins are full of enterprise, courage, and honorable love of glory and renown. Large before, the country has now, by recent events, become vastly larger. This Republic now extends, with a vast breadth, across the whole continent. The two great seas of the world wash the one and the other shore. We realize, on a mighty scale, the beautiful description of the ornamental border of the buckler of Achilles:

> Now, the broad shield complete, the artist crowned
> With his last hand, and poured the ocean round;
> In living silver seemed the waves to roll,
> And beat the buckler's verge, and bound the whole.

●

# FREDERICK DOUGLASS
## 4 July 1852

### 'I hear the mournful wail of millions'

*Frederick Douglass (c. 1815–95) the son of an unknown white man, suffered as a slave before escaping in his early twenties. By hard study, constant speaking, writing his autobiography and spending two years in England as a precaution against capture by his former owners, he became the leading black abolitionist speaker in the era before the Civil War.*

*Douglass delivered this speech at Rochester, New York, to commemorate the Declaration of Independence – a speech, which, if it had been delivered in many American cities, would have resulted in a mobbing.*

Fellow citizens, above your national, tumultuous joy, I hear the mournful wail of millions! whose chains, heavy and grievous yesterday, are, today, rendered more intolerable by the jubilee shouts that reach them. If I do forget, if I do not faithfully remember those bleeding children of sorrow this day, 'may my right hand forget her cunning, and may my tongue cleave to the roof of my mouth'! To forget them, to pass lightly over their wrongs, and to chime in with the popular theme would be treason most scandalous and shocking, and would make me a reproach before God and the world.

My subject, then, fellow citizens, is American slavery. I shall see this day and its popular characteristics from the slave's point of view. Standing there identified with the American bondman, making his wrongs mine. I do not hesitate to declare with all my soul that the character and conduct of this nation never looked blacker to me than on this Fourth of July! Whether we turn to the declarations of the past or to the professions of the present, the conduct of the nation seems equally hideous and revolting. America is false to the past, false to the present, and solemnly binds herself to be false to the future. Standing with God and the crushed and bleeding slave on this occasion, I will, in the name of humanity which is outraged, in the name of liberty which is fettered, in the name of the Constitution and the Bible which are disregarded and trampled upon, dare to call in question and to denounce, with all the emphasis I can command, everything that serves to perpetuate slavery – the great sin and shame of America! 'I will not equivocate; I will not excuse'; I will use the severest language I can command; and yet not one word shall escape me that any man, whose judgement is not blinded by prejudice, or who is not at heart a slaveholder, shall not confess to be right and just.

But I fancy I hear someone of my audience say, 'It is just in this circumstance that you and your brother abolitionists fail to make a favorable impression on the public mind. Would you argue more and denounce less, would you persuade more and rebuke less, your cause would be much more likely to succeed.' But, I submit, where all is plain there is nothing to be argued. What point in the anti-slavery creed would you have me argue? On what branch of the subject do the people of this country need light? Must I undertake to prove that the slave is a man? That point is conceded already. Nobody doubts it. The slaveholders themselves acknowledge it in the enactment of laws for their government. They acknowledge it when they punish disobedience on the part of the slave. There are seventy-two crimes in the state of Virginia which, if committed by a black man (no matter how ignorant he be), subject him to the punishment of death; while only two of the same crimes will subject a white man to the like punishment. What is this but the acknowledgement that the slave is a moral, intellectual, and responsible being? The manhood of the slave is conceded. It is admitted in the fact that Southern statute books are covered with enactments forbidding, under severe fines and penalties, the teaching of the slave to read or to write. When you can point to any such laws in reference to the beasts of the field, then I may consent to argue the manhood of the slave. When the dogs in your streets, when the fowls of the air, when the cattle on your hills, when the fish of the sea and the reptiles that crawl shall be unable to distinguish the slave from a brute, then will I argue with you that the slave is a man!

For the present, it is enough to affirm the equal manhood of the Negro race. Is it not astonishing that, while we are plowing, planting, and reaping, using all kinds of mechanical tools, erecting houses, constructing bridges, building ships, working in metals of brass, iron, copper, silver, and gold; that, while we are reading, writing, and ciphering, acting as clerks, merchants, and secretaries, having among us lawyers, doctors, ministers, poets, authors, editors, orators, and teachers; that, while we are engaged in all manner of enterprises common to other men, digging gold in California, capturing the whale in the Pacific, feeding sheep and cattle on the hillside, living, moving, acting, thinking, planning, living in families as husbands, wives, and children, and, above

all, confessing and worshiping the Christian's God, and looking hope-
fully for life and immortality beyond the grave, we are called upon to
prove that we are men!

Would you have me argue that man is entitled to liberty? that he is
the rightful owner of his own body? You have already declared it. Must
I argue the wrongfulness of slavery? Is that a question for republicans?
Is it to be settled by the rules of logic and argumentation, as a matter
beset with great difficulty, involving a doubtful application of the
principle of justice, hard to be understood? How should I look today, in
the presence of Americans, dividing and subdividing a discourse, to
show that men have a natural right to freedom? speaking of it relatively
and positively, negatively and affirmatively? To do so would be to make
myself ridiculous and to offer an insult to your understanding. There is
not a man beneath the canopy of heaven that does not know that slavery
is wrong for him.

What, am I to argue that it is wrong to make men brutes, to rob them
of their liberty, to work them without wages, to keep them ignorant of
their relations to their fellow men, to beat them with sticks, to flay their
flesh with the lash, to load their limbs with irons, to hunt them with
dogs, to sell them at auction, to sunder their families, to knock out their
teeth, to burn their flesh, to starve them into obedience and submission
to their masters? Must I argue that a system thus marked with blood,
and stained with pollution, is wrong? No! I will not. I have better
employment for my time and strength than such arguments would
imply.

What, then, remains to be argued? Is it that slavery is not divine; that
God did not establish it; that our doctors of divinity are mistaken?
There is blasphemy in the thought. That which is inhuman cannot be
divine! Who can reason on such a proposition? They that can may; I
cannot. The time for such argument is past.

At a time like this, scorching iron, not convincing argument, is
needed. O! had I the ability, and could I reach the nation's ear, I would
today pour out a fiery stream of biting ridicule, blasting reproach,
withering sarcasm, and stern rebuke. For it is not light that is needed,
but fire; it is not the gentle shower, but thunder. We need the storm, the
whirlwind, and the earthquake. The feeling of the nation must be
quickened; the conscience of the nation must be roused; the propriety
of the nation must be startled; the hypocrisy of the nation must be
exposed; and its crimes against God and man must be proclaimed and
denounced.

What, to the American slave, is your Fourth of July? I answer: a day that reveals to him, more than all other days in the year, the gross injustice and cruelty to which he is the constant victim. To him, your celebration is a sham; your boasted liberty, an unholy license; your national greatness, swelling vanity; your sounds of rejoicing are empty and heartless; your denunciation of tyrants, brass-fronted impudence; your shouts of liberty and equality, hollow mockery; your prayers and hymns, your sermons and thanksgivings, with all your religious parade and solemnity, are, to him, mere bombast, fraud, deception, impiety, and hypocrisy – a thin veil to cover up crimes which would disgrace a nation of savages. There is not a nation of savages. There is not a nation on the earth guilty of practices more shocking and bloody than are the people of the United States at this very hour.

Go where you may, search where you will, roam through all the monarchies and despotisms of the Old World, travel through South America, search out every abuse, and when you have found the last, lay your facts by the side of the everyday practices of this nation, and you will say with me that, for revolting barbarity and shameless hypocrisy, America reigns without a rival.

•

# THE AGE OF IMPROVEMENT

# HENRY BROUGHAM
## 1812

### 'I stand up . . . against the friends and followers of Mr Pitt'

*After leaving Scotland, where his liberal views denied him promotion, the Scottish lawyer Henry Brougham (1778–1868) had been an MP for two years when he first displayed his talent for invective in this speech against the policy of William Pitt the Younger at the Liverpool Election in 1812.*

*He was such a vehement speaker that one English judge described him as the 'Harangue'. He used repetition and exaggeration as powerful oratorical weapons. In this speech six sentences start with his derisive use of the word 'immortal'.*

Gentlemen, when I told you a little while ago that there were new and powerful reasons today for ardently desiring that our cause might succeed, I did not sport with you – yourselves shall now judge of them. I ask you – is the trade with America of any importance to this great and thickly peopled town? (*Cries of 'Yes! yes!'*) Is a continuance of the rupture with America likely to destroy that trade? (*Loud cries of 'It is! it is!'*) Is there any man who would deeply feel it, if he heard that the rupture was at length converted into open war? Is there a man present who would not be somewhat alarmed if he supposed that we should have another year without the American trade? Is there any one of nerves so hardy, as calmly to hear that our government have given up all negotiation – abandoned all hopes of speedy peace with America? Then I tell that man to brace up his nerves – I bid you all be prepared to hear what touches you all equally. We are by this day's intelligence at war with America in good earnest – our government have at length issued letters of marque and reprisal against the United States! (*Universal cries of 'God help us! God help us!'*) Aye, God help us! God of his infinite compassion take pity on us! God help and protect this poor town – and this whole trading country!

Now, I ask you whether you will be represented in Parliament by the men who have brought this grievous calamity on your heads, or by those who have constantly opposed the mad career which was plunging us into it? Whether will you trust the revival of your trade – the restoration of your livelihood – to them who have destroyed it, or to me whose counsels, if followed in time, would have averted this unnatural war, and

left Liverpool flourishing in opulence and peace? Make your choice –
for it lies with yourselves which of us shall be commissioned to bring back
commerce and plenty – they whose stubborn infatuation has chased those
blessings away – or we, who are only known to you as the strenuous
enemies of their miserable policy, the fast friends of your best interests.

Gentlemen, I stand up in this contest against the friends and followers
of Mr Pitt, or, as they partially designate him, the immortal statesman
now no more. Immortal in the miseries of his devoted country! Immortal
in the wounds of her bleeding liberties! Immortal in the cruel wars
which sprang from his cold miscalculating ambition! Immortal in the
intolerable taxes, and countless loads of debt which these wars have
flung upon us – which the youngest man amongst us will not live to see
the end of! Immortal in the triumphs of our enemies, and the ruin of our
allies, the costly purchase of so much blood and treasure! Immortal in
the afflictions of England, and the humiliation of her friends, through
the whole results of his twenty years' reign, from the first rays of favour
with which a delighted Court gilded his early apostacy, to the deadly
glare which is at this instant cast upon his name by the burning
metropolis of our last ally! (*The news of the burning of Moscow had arrived by
that day's post.*) But may no such immortality ever fall to my lot – let me
rather live innocent and inglorious; and when at last I cease to serve
you, and to feel for your wrongs, may I have an humble monument in
some nameless stone, to tell that beneath it there rests from his labours
in your service, 'an enemy of the immortal statesman – a friend of peace
and of the people'.

Friends! you must now judge for yourselves, and act accordingly.
Against us and against you stand those who call themselves the successors
of that man. They are the heirs of his policy; and if not of his
immortality too, it is only because their talents for the work of destruction are less transcendent than his. They are his surviving colleagues.
His fury survives in them if not his fire; and they partake of all his
infatuated principles, if they have lost the genius that first made those
principles triumphant. If you choose them for your delegates, you know
to what policy you lend your sanction – what men you exalt to power.
Should you prefer me, your choice falls upon one who, if obscure and
unambitious, will at least give his own age no reason to fear him, or
posterity to curse him – one whose proudest ambition it is to be deemed
the friend of Liberty and of Peace.

•

# GEORGE CANNING
## 1823

## 'The interest of England'

*Some critics of oratory consider George Canning (1770–1827) the only English speaker of the first half of the nineteenth century to stand comparison with John Bright.*

*A disciple of Pitt, he was serving his second stint as Foreign Secretary under Lord Liverpool when he made this speech after receiving the freedom of the naval town of Plymouth, and put his faith in the English navy as the symbol of world peace.*

Gentlemen, the end which I confess I have always had in view, and which appears to be the legitimate object of pursuit to a British states-man, I can describe in one word. The language of modern philosophy is wisely and diffusely benevolent; it professes the perfection of our species, and the amelioration of the lot of all mankind. Gentlemen, I hope that my heart beats as high for the general interest of humanity – I hope that I have as friendly a disposition towards other nations of the earth, as any one who vaunts his philanthropy most highly; but I am contented to confess, that in the conduct of political affairs, the grand object of my contemplation is the interest of England.

Not, gentlemen, that the interest of England is an interest which stands isolated and alone. The situation which she holds forbids an exclusive selfishness; her prosperity must contribute to the prosperity of other nations, and her stability to the safety of the world. But, intimately connected as we are with the system of Europe, it does not follow that we are therefore called upon to mix ourselves on every occasion, with a restless and meddling activity, in the concerns of the nations which surround us. It is upon a just balance of conflicting duties, and of rival, but sometimes incompatible, advantages, that a government must judge when to put forth its strength, and when to husband it for occasions yet to come.

Our ultimate object must be the peace of the world. That object may sometimes be best attained by prompt exertions – sometimes by absti-nence from interposition in contests which we cannot prevent. It is upon these principles that, as has been most truly observed by my worthy friend, it did not appear to the government of this country to be necessary that Great Britain should mingle in the recent contest between France and Spain.

Your worthy Recorder has accurately classed the persons who would have driven us into that contest. There were undoubtedly among them those who desired to plunge this country into the difficulties of war, partly from the hope that those difficulties would overwhelm the administration; but it would be most unjust not to admit that there were others who were actuated by nobler principles and more generous feelings who would have rushed forward at once from the sense of indignation at aggression, and who deemed that no act of injustice could be perpetrated from one end of the universe to the other, but that the sword of Great Britain should leap from its scabbard to avenge it. But as it is the province of law to control the excess even of laudable passions and propensities in individuals, so it is the duty of government to restrain within due bounds the ebullition of national sentiment, and to regulate the course and direction of impulses which it cannot blame.

Is there any one among the latter class of persons described by my honourable friend (for to the former I have nothing to say), who continues to doubt whether the government did wisely in declining to obey the precipitate enthusiasm which prevailed at the commencement of the contest in Spain? Is there anybody who does not now think, that it was the office of government to examine more closely all the various bearings of so complicated a question, to consider whether they were called upon to assist a united nation, or to plunge themselves into the internal feuds by which that nation was divided – to aid in repelling a foreign invader, or, to take part in a civil war? Is there any man that does not now see what would have been the extent of burdens that would have been cast upon this country? Is there any one who does not acknowledge that, under such circumstances, the enterprise would have been one to be characterized only by a term borrowed from that part of the Spanish literature with which we are most familiar, – quixotic; an enterprise, romantic in its origin, and thankless in the end?

But while we thus control even our feelings by our duty, let it not be said that we cultivate peace, either because we fear, or because we are unprepared for, war; on the contrary, if eight months ago the government did not hesitate to proclaim that the country was prepared for war, if war should be unfortunately necessary, every month of peace that has since passed, has but made us so much the more capable of exertion. The resources created by peace are means of war. In cherishing those resources, we but accumulate those means. Our present repose is no more a proof of inability to act, than the state of inertness and inactivity in which I have seen those mighty masses that float in the waters above your town, is a proof they are devoid of strength, and incapable of being fitted out for action. You well know, gentlemen, how soon one of those stupendous masses, now reposing on their shadows in perfect stillness, – how soon, upon any call of patriotism, or of necessity, it would assume the likeness of an animated thing, instinct with life and motion – how soon it would ruffle, as it were, its swelling plumage – how quickly it would put forth all its beauty and its bravery, collect its scattered elements of strength, and awaken its dormant thunder. Such as is one of these magnificent machines when springing from inaction into a display of its might – such is England herself, while apparently passive and motionless she silently concentrates the power to be put forth on an adequate occasion. But God forbid that that occasion should arise.

After a war sustained for nearly a quarter of a century – sometimes single-handed, and with all Europe arrayed at times against her or at her side, England needs a period of tranquillity, and may enjoy it without fear of misconstruction. Long may we be enabled, gentlemen, to improve the blessings of our present situation, to cultivate the arts of peace, to give to commerce, now reviving, greater extension and new spheres of employment, and to confirm the prosperity now generally diffused throughout this island. Of the blessings of peace, gentlemen, I trust that this borough, with which I have now the honour and happiness of being associated, will receive an ample share. I trust the time is not far distant, when that noble structure of which, as I learn from your Recorder, the box with which you have honoured me, through his hands, formed a part, that gigantic barrier against the fury of the waves that roll into your harbour, will protect a commercial marine not less considerable in its kind, than the warlike marine of which your port has been long so distinguished an asylum, when the town of Plymouth will participate in the commercial prosperity as largely as it has hitherto done in the naval glories of England.

•

ROBERT PEEL
5 March 1829

'A moral necessity'

*As Home Secretary from 1828, Robert Peel – who as Secretary for Ireland had been nicknamed 'Orange Peel' because he so powerfully opposed Catholic emancipation – made a major change in his principles and piloted the Catholic Emancipation Bill through the Commons. After Daniel O'Connell was elected for County Clare but, as a Catholic, barred from taking his seat, Peel was persuaded there would be civil war unless emancipation was granted.*

*On 4 March, Peel had told George IV he would resign if the King insisted on blocking the bill. Early next morning, the King relented. A few hours later Peel stood up to ask the House to consider the laws imposing disabilities on Roman Catholics. It was a dramatic moment in Peel's personal career. Rumours of the dissension between the King and his ministers had been flying round London and the House was packed to suffocation as Peel rose to vindicate his decision. He spoke for four hours and made the greatest speech he had yet delivered.*

I rise as a minister of the King, and sustained by the just authority which belongs to that character, to vindicate the advice given to His Majesty by a united Cabinet – to insert in his gracious speech the recommendation which has just been read respecting the propriety of taking into consideration the condition of Ireland, and the removal of the civil disabilities affecting our Roman Catholic fellow-subjects. I rise, sir, in the spirit of peace, to propose the adjustment of the Roman Catholic question – that question which has so long and so painfully occupied the attention of Parliament, and which has distracted the councils of the King for the last thirty years. I rise, sir, to discuss this great question in the spirit inculcated in one of those simple and beautiful prayers with which the proceedings of this House were on this day auspicated. In that solemn appeal to the almighty source of all wisdom and goodness, we are enjoined to lay aside all private interests, prejudices, and partial affections, that the result of our councils may tend to the maintenance of true religion and justice; the safety, honour, and happiness of the King; the public wealth, peace, and tranquillity of the realm; and the uniting and knitting together of the hearts of all persons and estates within the same in true christian charity . . .

I have been called upon to state the reasons which have swayed me in the adoption of the course I now advocate, and which is in opposition to that which I have so long pursued. And for the satisfaction of those who have made this appeal to me, and for the satisfaction of the people of this country, I will endeavour to make out the case I have been challenged to establish.

I am well aware, sir, that I speak in the presence of a House of Commons, the majority of which is prepared to vote in favour of an adjustment of this question, upon higher grounds than those on which I desire to rest my arguments. To them it is needless to appeal. But I trust that, in what I shall think it necessary to say, less with the personal object of self-vindication than with a view to satisfy the great body of the people of this empire; those who require no reasoning to convince them will bear with me while I go through the details of an argument which has pressed on my mind with the force of demonstration. Sir, I have for years attempted to maintain the exclusion of Roman Catholics from Parliament and the high offices of the state. I do not think it was an unnatural or an unreasonable struggle. I resign it, in consequence of the conviction that it can be no longer advantageously maintained; from believing that there are not adequate materials or sufficient instruments for its effectual and permanent continuance. I yield, therefore, to a moral necessity which I cannot control, unwilling to push resistance to a point which might endanger the establishments that I wish to defend . . .

Does that moral necessity exist? Is there more danger in continued resistance than in concession accompanied with measures of restriction and precaution?

My object is to prove, by argument, the affirmative answer to these questions.

In that argument, I shall abstain from all discussions upon the natural or social rights of man. I shall enter into no disquisitions upon the theories of government. My argument will turn upon a practical view of the present condition of affairs, and upon the consideration, not of what may be said, but what is to be done under circumstances of immediate and pressing difficulty.

Sir, the outline of my argument is this: we are placed in a position in which we cannot remain. We cannot continue stationary. There is an evil in divided cabinets and distracted councils which can be no longer tolerated. This is my first position. I do not say, in the first instance, what we are to do in consequence. I merely declare that our present position is untenable. Supposing this established, and supposing it conceded, that a united government must be formed; in the next place I say, that that government must choose one of two courses. They must advance, or they must recede. They must grant further political privileges to the Roman Catholics, or they must retract those already given. They must remove the barriers that obstruct the continued flow of relaxation and indulgence, or they must roll back to its source the mighty current which has been let in upon us, year after year, by the gradual withdrawal of restraint . . .

Sir, I detailed, on a former occasion, that a dreadful commotion had distracted the public mind in Ireland – that a feverish agitation and unnatural excitement prevailed, to a degree scarcely credible, throughout the entire country. I attempted to show that social intercourse was poisoned there in its very springs – that family was divided against family, and man against his neighbour – that, in a word, the bonds of social life were almost dissevered – that the fountains of public justice were corrupted – that the spirit of discord walked openly abroad – and that an array of physical force was marshalled in defiance of all law and to the imminent danger of the public peace. I ask, sir, could this state of things be suffered to exist, and what course were we to pursue? Perhaps I shall be told, as I was on a former occasion, in forcible, though familiar language, that 'This is the old story! that all this has been so for the last twenty years, and that therefore there is no reason for a change.' Why, sir, this is the very reason for the change. It is because the evil is not casual and temporary, but permanent and inveterate – it is because the detail of misery and of outrage is nothing but 'the old story', that I am contented to run the hazards of a change. We cannot determine upon remaining idle spectators of the discord and disturbance of Ireland. The universal voice of the country declares that something must be done; I am but echoing the sentiments of all reasonable men, when I repeat that something must be done.

Sir, objections, solid objections, if considered abstractedly, may be brought forward against the details of every measure of an extensive and complicated nature, like the present. Depend upon it, we shall never settle the Catholic question, if every man is determined to settle it in his own way, and according to his own peculiar views and wishes. We never shall settle it, unless we are prepared to make mutual concessions and sacrifices. I admit the possibility of danger from the grant of relief; but I ask the Protestants whether there be not a prospect, that, by uniting the Protestant mind on this subject, we shall be able to find new and sufficient securities, against any difficulties that may possibly arise out of the settlement of this question. I ask the Roman Catholics to contemplate the extent of privilege that is conferred, and the sacrifices which we make, by consenting to repeal the laws which have given an exclusive character to the legislature and government of this country. Let them meet us in the same spirit, and manifest an anxious wish to allay every reasonable apprehension. God grant that the sanguine expectations of those who for so many years have advised this settlement may be fulfilled! God grant that the removal of the disabilities, that have so long affected our Roman Catholic fellow-subjects, may be attended by the desired effect; and assuage the civil contentions of Ireland! – that, by the admission of the Roman Catholics to a full and equal participation in civil rights, and by the establishment of a free and cordial intercourse between all classes of his Majesty's subjects, mutual jealousies may be removed; and that we may be taught, instead of looking at each other as adversaries and opponents, to respect and value each other, and to discover the existence of qualities, on both sides, that were not attributed to either!

Perhaps I am not so sanguine as others in my expectations of the future; but I have not the slightest hesitation in saying, that I fully believe that the adjustment of this question, in the manner proposed, will give better and stronger securities to the Protestant interest and the Protestant establishment, than any that the present state of things admits of; and will avert evils and dangers impending and immediate. What motive, I ask, can I have for the expression of these opinions, but the honest conviction of their truth? I have watched the progress of events. I have seen, day by day, disunion and hatred increasing, and the prospects of peace obscured by the gloomy advance of discontent, and suspicion and distrust creeping on 'step by step' – to quote the words of Mr Grattan – 'like the mist at the heels of the countryman'. I well know that I might have taken a more popular and a more selfish course. I might have held language much more acceptable to the friends with whom I have long acted, and to the constituents whom I have lately lost. *His ego gratiora dictu alia esse scio; sed me vera pro gratis loqui, et si meum ingenium non moneret, necessitas cogit. Vellem equidem vobis placere: sed multo malo vos salvos esse; qualicunque erga me animo futuri estis.** In the

* 'I am aware that there are other things more pleasant to say than these; but even if my natural disposition did not incline me thereto, necessity compels me to say what is true rather than what is pleasant. I should indeed like to please you; but I had much rather you should be safe, whatever may be your future feelings towards me' (Livy, Bk III, ch. 75).

course I have taken, I have been mainly influenced by the anxious desire to provide for the maintenance of Protestant interests; and for the security of Protestant establishments. This is my defence – this is my consolation – this shall be my revenge.

Sir, I will hope for the best. God grant that the moral storm may be appeased – that the turbid waters of strife may be settled and composed – and that, having found their just level, they may be mingled, with equal flow, in one clear and common stream. But, if these expectations are to be disappointed – if, unhappily, civil strife and contention shall survive the restoration of political privileges: – if there is something inherent in the spirit of the Roman Catholic religion which disdains equality, and will be satisfied with nothing but ascendancy – still, I am content to run the hazard of the change. The contest, if inevitable, will be fought for other objects, and with other arms. The struggle will be – not for the abolition of civil distinctions – but for the predominance of an intolerant religion.

Sir, I contemplate the progress of that struggle with pain; but I look forward to its issue with perfect composure and confidence. We shall have dissolved the great moral alliance that has hitherto given strength to the cause of the Roman Catholics. We shall range on our side the illustrious authorities which have heretofore been enlisted upon theirs; – the rallying cry of 'Civil Liberty' will then be all our own. We shall enter the field with the full assurance of victory – armed with the consciousness of having done justice, and of being in the right – backed by the unanimous feeling of England – by the firm union of orthodoxy and dissent – by the applauding voice of Scotland; and, if other aid be requisite, cheered by the sympathies of every free state in either hemisphere, and by the wishes and the prayers of every freeman, in whatever clime, or under whatever form of government his lot may have been cast. I move you, sir, 'That the House resolve itself into a committee of the whole House, to consider of the laws imposing civil disabilities on His Majesty's Roman Catholic subjects.'

*The speech was a national triumph. The Act of 1829 was a sentence of death on the Anglican settlement made at the 1688 revolution. Yet Peel, once the idolized champion of the Protestant party, became an outcast and the scapegoat for the Wellington government, which lost power the following year.*

●

# THOMAS MACAULAY
2 March 1831

### 'Renew the youth of the state'

*The Whigs returned to power in 1830 pledged to reform Parliament. Under the first Reform Bill of 1830, power was transferred to the industrial towns and the counties with big populations. It meant that many boroughs would lose their MPs and one in four of the existing constituencies would disappear.*

*Thomas Babington Macaulay (1800–1859), author of the classic* History of England, *was also a distinguished orator who entered Parliament as a Whig in 1830 and soon made his reputation with his speeches defending reform. He made this speech during a debate on a motion introduced by Lord Russell to amend the representation of the people in England and Wales.*

The question of parliamentary reform is still behind. But signs, of which it is impossible to misconceive the import, do most clearly indicate that unless that question also be speedily settled, property and order, and all the institutions of this great monarchy, will be exposed to fearful peril. Is it possible that gentlemen long versed in high political affairs cannot read these signs? Is it possible that they can really believe that the representative system of England, such as it now is, will last to the year 1860? If not, for what would they have us wait? Would they have us wait merely that we may show to all the world how little we have profited by our own recent experience? Would they have us wait that we may once again hit the exact point where we can neither refuse with authority nor concede with grace? Would they have us wait that the numbers of the discontented party may become larger, its demands higher, its feelings more acrimonious, its organization more complete? Would they have us wait till the whole tragi-comedy of 1827 has been acted over again? till they have been brought into office by a cry of 'No reform', to be reformers, as they were once before brought into office by a cry of 'No popery', to be emancipators? Have they obliterated from their minds – gladly, perhaps, would some among them obliterate from their minds – the transactions of that year? And have they forgotten all the transactions of the succeeding year? Have they forgotten how the spirit of liberty in Ireland, debarred from its natural outlet, found a vent by forbidden passages? Have they forgotten how we were forced to indulge the Catholics in all the licence of rebels, merely because we chose to withhold from them the liberties of subjects? Do they wait for associations more formidable than that of the Corn Exchange, for contributions larger than the Rent, for agitators more violent than those who, three years ago, divided with the King and the Parliament the sovereignty of Ireland? Do they wait for that last and most dreadful paroxysm of popular rage, for that last and most cruel test of military fidelity? Let them wait, if their past experience shall induce them to think that any high honour or any exquisite pleasure is to be obtained by a policy like this. Let them wait, if this strange and fearful infatuation be indeed upon them, that they should not see with their eyes, or hear with their ears, or understand with their heart. But let us know our interest and our duty better.

Turn where we may, within, around, the voice of great events is proclaiming to us, reform, that you may preserve. Now, therefore, while everything at home and abroad forebodes ruin to those who persist in a hopeless struggle against the spirit of the age; now, while the crash of the proudest throne of the Continent is still resounding in our ears; now, while the roof of a British palace affords an ignominious shelter to the exiled heir of forty kings; now, while we see on every side ancient institutions subverted and great societies dissolved; now, while the heart of England is still sound; now, while old feelings and old associations retain a power and a charm which may too soon pass away; now, in this your accepted time; now, in this your day of salvation, take counsel, not of prejudice, not of party spirit, not of the ignominious pride of a fatal consistency, but of history, of reason, of the ages which are past, of the signs of this most portentous time. Pronounce in a manner worthy of the expectation with which this great debate has been anticipated, and of the long remembrance which it will leave behind. Renew the youth of the state. Save property, divided against itself. Save the multitude, endangered by its own ungovernable passions. Save the aristocracy, endangered by its own unpopular power. Save the greatest, and fairest, and most highly civilized community that ever existed from calamities which may in a few days sweep away all the rich heritage of so many ages of wisdom and glory. The danger is terrible. The time is short. If this bill should be rejected, I pray to God that none of those who concur in rejecting it may ever remember their votes with unavailing remorse amidst the wreck of laws, the confusion of ranks, the spoliation of property, and the dissolution of social order.

•

ROBERT PEEL
3 March 1831

*'The dangers which menace states'*

*As leader of the opposition, Peel, who had succeeded to the baronetcy in 1830, opposed reform. He had sat, half angry, half contemptuous, as the staggering scope of the proposed reform was revealed by Russell. On the night after Macaulay, after a weak speech by Lord Palmerston, he rose to speak.*

We should do well to consider, before we consent to the condemnation of own institutions, what are the dangers which menace states with ruin or decay. Compare our fate with other countries of Europe during the period of the last century and a half. Not one has been exempt from the miseries of foreign invasion, scarcely one has preserved its independence inviolate. In how many have there been changes of the dynasty, or the severest conflicts between the several orders of the state? In this country we have had to encounter severe trials, and have encountered them with uniform success. Amid foreign wars, the shock of disputed successions, rebellion at home, extreme distress, the bitter contention of parties, the institutions of this country have stood uninjured. The ambition of military conquerors – of men endeared, by success, to disciplined armies, never have endangered, and never could endanger the supremacy of the law, or master the control of public opinion. These were the powerful instruments that shattered with impunity the staff of Marlborough, and crumbled into dust the power of Wellington. Other states have fallen from the too great influence of a military spirit, and the absorption of power by standing armies. What is the character of the armies which our commanders led to victory? The most formidable engines that skill and valour could direct against a foreign enemy; but in peace, the pliant, submissive instruments of civil power. 'Give us,' says the member for Waterford, 'give us for the repression of outrage and insurrection the regular army, for the people respect it for its courage, and love it for its courteous forbearance, and patience, and ready subjection to the law.' And what, sir, are the practical advantages which we are now promised, as the consequence of the change we are invited to make, as the compensation for the risk we must incur? Positively not one. Up to this hour, no one has pretended that we shall gain anything by the change, excepting, indeed, that we shall conciliate the public favour. Why, no doubt, you cannot propose to share your power with half a million of men without gaining some popularity – without purchasing by such a bribe some portion of good-will. But these are vulgar arts of government; others will outbid you, not now, but at no remote period – they will offer votes and power to a million of men, will quote your precedent for the concession, and will carry your principles to their legitimate and natural consequences . . .

Let us never be tempted to resign the well-tempered freedom which we enjoy, in the ridiculous pursuit of the wild liberty which France has established. What avails that liberty which has neither justice nor wisdom for its companions – which neither brings peace nor prosperity in its train? It was the duty of the King's government to abstain from agitating this question at such a period as the present – to abstain from the excitement throughout this land of that conflict – (God grant it may be only a moral conflict!) – which must arise between the possessors of existing privileges, and those to whom they are to be transferred. It was the duty of the government to calm, not to stimulate, the fever of popular excitement. They have adopted a different course – they have sent through the land the firebrand of agitation, and no one can now recall it. Let us hope that there are limits to their powers of mischief. They have, like the giant enemy of the Philistines, lighted three hundred brands, and scattered through the country discord and dismay; but God forbid that they should, like him, have the power to concentrate in death all the energies that belong to life, and to signalize their own destruction by bowing to the earth the pillars of that sacred edifice, which contains within its walls, according even to their own admission, 'the noblest society of freemen in the world'.

*The subsequent Reform Act was passed in 1832.*

•

# HENRY BROUGHAM
7 October 1831

### 'Reject not this bill!'

*After being elected for the county of York in 1830, the Whigs persuaded Henry Brougham to accept a peerage and he became Lord Chancellor. Although speaking from the House of Lords, he made a significant contribution to the success of the Reform Bill. Many contemporaries considered his speech on the second reading of the bill – of which this was the peroration – as his masterpiece.*

My Lords, I do not disguise the intense solicitude which I feel for the event of this debate, because I know full well that the peace of the country is involved in the issue. I cannot look without dismay at the rejection of the measure. But grievous as may be the consequences of a temporary defeat – temporary it can only be; for its ultimate, and even speedy, success is certain. Nothing can now stop it. Do not suffer yourselves to be persuaded that even if the present ministers were driven from the helm, anyone could steer you through the troubles which surround you without reform. But our successors would take up the task in circumstances far less auspicious. Under them, you would be fain to grant a bill compared with which the one we now proffer you is moderate indeed. Hear the parable of the sibyl; for it conveys a wise and wholesome moral. She now appears at your gate, and offers you mildly the volumes – the precious volumes – of wisdom and peace. The price she asks is reasonable: to restore the franchise which, without any bargain, you ought voluntarily to give; you refuse her terms – her moderate terms – she darkens the porch no longer. But soon, for you cannot do without her wares, you call her back – again she comes, but with diminished treasures; the leaves of the book are in part torn away by lawless hands – in part defaced with characters of blood. But the prophetic maid has risen in her demands – it is Parliaments by the year – it is vote by the ballot – it is suffrage by the million! From this you turn away indignant, and for the second time she departs. Beware of her third coming; for the treasure you must have; and what price she may next demand, who shall tell? It may even be the mace which rests upon that woolsack. What may follow your course of obstinacy, if persisted in, I cannot take upon me to predict, nor do I wish to conjecture. But this I know full well, that, as sure as man is mortal, and to err is human, justice deferred enhances the price at which you must purchase safety and peace – nor can you expect to gather in another crop than they did who went before you, if you persevere in their utterly abominable husbandry of sowing injustice and reaping rebellion.

But among the awful considerations that now bow down my mind, there is one which stands pre-eminently above the rest. You are the highest judicature in the realm; you sit here as judges, and decide all causes, civil and criminal, without appeal. It is a judge's first duty never to pronounce sentence, in the most trifling case, without hearing. Will you make this the exception? Are you really prepared to determine, but not to hear, the mighty cause upon which a nation's hopes and fears hang? You are. Then beware of your decision! Rouse not, I beseech you, a peace-loving, but a resolute, people; alienate not from your body the affections of a whole empire. As your friend, as the friend of my order, as the friend of my country, as the faithful servant of my sovereign, I counsel you to assist with your uttermost efforts in preserving the peace, and upholding and perpetuating the Constitution. Therefore, I pray and I exhort you not to reject this measure. By all you hold most dear – by all the ties that bind every one of us to our common order and our common country, I solemnly adjure you – I warn you – I implore you – yea, on my bended knees, I supplicate you – reject not this bill!

●

## THOMAS MACAULAY
### 17 April 1833

### '*A matter of shame and remorse*'

*When the reformed British Parliament met for the first time in January 1833, it proceeded to pass bills emancipating slaves in the British Colonies, regulating child labour and granting money for elementary education. Also resubmitted was a bill from Sir Robert Grant for the removal of Jewish disabilities 'with the like exceptions as are provided to His Majesty's subjects professing the Roman Catholic faith'.*

*Speaking in the debate, Macaulay made the classic statement of the case against bigotry.*

My honourable friend should either persecute to some purpose or not persecute at all. He dislikes the word persecution, I know. He will not admit that the Jews are persecuted. And yet I am confident that he would rather be sent to the King's Bench Prison for three months or be fined a hundred pounds than be subject to the disabilities under which the Jews lie. How can he then say that to impose such disabilities is not persecution, and that to fine and imprison is persecution? All his reasoning consists in drawing arbitrary lines. What he does not wish to inflict he calls persecution. What he does wish to inflict he will not call persecution. What he takes from the Jews he calls political power. What he is too good-natured to take from the Jews he will not call political power. The Jew must not sit in Parliament; but he may be the proprietor of all the ten-pound houses in a borough. He may have more fifty-pound tenants than any peer in the kingdom. He may give the voters treats to please their palates, and hire bands of gypsies to break their heads, as if he were a Christian and a marquess. All the rest of this system is of a piece.

The Jew may be a juryman, but not a judge. He may decide issues of fact, but not issues of law. He may give a hundred thousand pounds' damages; but he may not in the most trivial case grant a new trial. He may rule the money market; he may influence the exchanges; he may be summoned to congresses of emperors and kings. Great potentates, instead of negotiating a loan with him by tying him in a chair and pulling out his grinders, may treat with him as with a great potentate, and may postpone the declaring of war or the signing of a treaty till they have conferred with him. All this is as it should be; but he must not be a Privy Councillor. He must not be called Right Honourable, for that is political power. And who is it that we are trying to cheat in this way? Even Omniscience. Yes, sir; we have been gravely told that the Jews are under the divine displeasure, and that if we give them political power God will visit us in judgement.

Do we then think that God cannot distinguish between substance and form? Does not He know that, while we withhold from the Jews the semblance and name of political power, we suffer them to possess the substance? The plain truth is that my honourable friend is drawn in one direction by his opinions and in a directly opposite direction by his excellent heart. He halts between two opinions. He tries to make a compromise between principles which admit of no compromise. He goes a certain way in intolerance. Then he stops, without being able to give a reason for stopping. But I know the reason. It is his humanity. Those who formerly dragged the Jew at a horse's tail, and singed his beard with blazing furze bushes, were much worse men than my honourable friend; but they were more consistent than he . . .

The honourable Member for Oldham tells us that the Jews are naturally a mean race, a sordid race, a money-getting race; that they are averse to all honourable callings; that they neither sow nor reap; that they have neither flocks nor herds; that usury is the only pursuit for which they are fit; that they are destitute of all elevated and amiable sentiments. Such, sir, has in every age been the reasoning of bigots. They never fail to plead in justification of persecution the vices which persecution has engendered. England has been to the Jews less than half a country; and we revile them because they do not feel for England more than a half patriotism. We treat them as slaves, and wonder that they do not regard us as brethren. We drive them to mean occupations, and then reproach them for not embracing honourable professions. We long forbade them to possess land; and we complain that they chiefly occupy themselves in trade. We shut them out from all the paths of ambition; and then we despise them for taking refuge in avarice.

During many ages we have, in all our dealings with them, abused our immense superiority of force; and then we are disgusted because they have recourse to that cunning which is the natural and universal defence of the weak against the violence of the strong. But were they always a mere money-changing, money-getting, money-hoarding race? Nobody knows better than my honourable friend the member for the University of Oxford that there is nothing in their national character which unfits them for the highest duties of citizens. He knows that, in the infancy of civilization, when our island was as savage as New Guinea, when letters and arts were still unknown to Athens, when scarcely a thatched hut stood on what was afterwards the site of Rome, this contemned people had their fenced cities and cedar palaces, their splendid Temple, their fleets of merchant ships, their schools of sacred learning, their great statesmen and soldiers, their natural philosophers, their historians, and their poets.

What nation ever contended more manfully against overwhelming odds for its independence and religion? What nation ever, in its last agonies, gave such signal proofs of what may be accomplished by a brave despair? And if, in the course of many centuries, the oppressed descendants of warriors and sages have degenerated from the qualities of their fathers, if, while excluded from the blessings of law, and bowed down under the yoke of slavery, they have contracted some of the vices of outlaws and of slaves, shall we consider this as a matter of reproach to them? Shall we not rather consider it as matter of shame and remorse to ourselves? Let us do justice to them. Let us open to them the door of the House of Commons. Let us open to them every career in which ability and energy can be displayed. Till we have done this, let us not presume to say that there is no genius among the countrymen of Isaiah, no heroism among the descendants of the Maccabees.

Sir, in supporting the motion of my honourable friend, I am, I firmly believe, supporting the honour and the interests of the Christian religion. I should think that I insulted that religion if I said that it cannot stand unaided by intolerant laws. Without such laws it was established, and without such laws it may be maintained. It triumphed over the superstitions of the most refined and of the most savage nations, over the graceful mythology of Greece and the bloody idolatry of the Northern forests. It prevailed over the power and policy of the Roman Empire. It tamed the barbarians by whom that empire was overthrown. But all these victories were gained not by the help of intolerance, but in spite of the opposition of intolerance. The whole history of Christianity proves that she has little indeed to fear from persecution as a foe, but much to fear from persecution as an ally. May she long continue to bless our country with her benignant influence, strong in her sublime philosophy, strong in her spotless morality, strong in those internal and external evidences to which the most powerful and comprehensive of human intellects have yielded assent, the last solace of those who have outlived every earthly hope, the last restraint of those who are raised above every earthly fear! But let not us, mistaking her character and her interests, fight the battle of truth with the weapons of error, and endeavour to support by oppression that religion which first taught the human race the great lesson of universal charity.

*The resolution was passed but thrown out by the House of Lords, inspired by William IV and the bench of bishops. The fight for the Jews was eventually won in 1858.*

•

## RICHARD COBDEN
### 13 March 1845

### 'You are the gentry of England'

*The Anti-Corn-Law League was founded in Manchester in 1838 and the radical Richard Cobden (1804–65) became its most important leader. Addressing mass meetings throughout the country, he and his great ally, John Bright, espoused the doctrines of free trade. The climax of the agitation to repeal the Corn Laws came in 1845, when the Irish potato crop failed and there was a bad harvest in England.*

*Cobden's greatest oratorical triumph was this speech in the House of Commons.*

There are politicians in the House – men who look with an ambition – probably a justifiable one – to the honours of office. There may be men who – with thirty years of continuous service, having been pressed into a groove from which they can neither escape nor retreat – may be holding office, high office, maintained there probably at the expense of their present convictions which do not harmonize very well with their early opinions. I make allowances for them; but the great body of the honourable gentlemen opposite came up to this House, not as politicians, but as the farmers' friends, and protectors of the agricultural interests. Well, what do you propose to do? You have heard the Prime Minister declare that, if he could restore all the protection which you have had, that protection would not benefit agriculturists. Is that your belief? If so, why not proclaim it? And if it is not your conviction, you will have falsified your mission in this House by following the right honourable baronet out into the lobby, and opposing inquiry into the condition of the very men who sent you here.

With mere politicians I have no right to expect to succeed in this motion. But I have no hesitation in telling you that, if you give me a committee of this House, I will explode the delusion of agricultural protection! I will bring forward such a mass of evidence, and give you such a preponderance of talent and of authority, that when the blue book is published and sent forth to the world, as we can now send it, by our vehicles of information, your system of protection shall not live in public opinion for two years afterward. Politicians do not want that. This cry of protection has been a very convenient handle for politicians.

The cry of protection carried the counties at the last election, and politicians gained honours, emoluments, and place by it. But is that old tattered flag of protection, tarnished and torn as it is already, to be kept hoisted still in the counties for the benefit of politicians; or will you come forward honestly and fairly to inquire into this question? I can not believe that the gentry of England will be made mere drumheads to be sounded upon by a prime minister to give forth unmeaning and empty sounds, and to have no articulate voice of their own. No! You are the gentry of England who represent the counties. You are the aristocracy of England. Your fathers led our fathers; you may lead us if you will go the right way. But, although you have retained your influence with this country longer than any other aristocracy, it has not been by opposing popular opinion, or by setting yourselves against the spirit of the age.

In other days, when the battle and the hunting-fields were the tests of manly vigour, your fathers were first and foremost there. The aristocracy of England were not like the noblesse of France, the mere minions of a court; nor were they like the hidalgos of Madrid, who dwindled into pygmies. You have been Englishmen. You have not shown a want of courage and firmness when any call has been made upon you. This is a new era. It is the age of improvement; it is the age of social advancement, not the age for war or for feudal sports. You live in a mercantile age, when the whole wealth of the world is poured into your lap. You can not have the advantages of commercial rents and feudal privileges; but you may be what you always have been, if you will identify yourselves with the spirit of the age. The English people look to the gentry and aristocracy of their country as their leaders. I, who am not one of you, have no hesitation in telling you that there is a deep-rooted, an hereditary prejudice, if I may so call it, in your favour in this country. But you never got it, and you will not keep it, by obstructing the spirit of the age. If you are indifferent to enlightened means of finding employment for your own peasantry; if you are found obstructing that advance which is calculated to knit nations more together in the bonds of peace by means of commercial intercourse; if you are found fighting against the discoveries which have almost given breath and life to material nature, and setting up yourselves as obstructives of that which destiny has decreed shall go on – why, then, you will be the gentry of England no longer, and others will be found to take your place.

•

BENJAMIN DISRAELI
15 May 1846

*'The cause of the people, the cause of England'*

*When Benjamin Disraeli (1804–81) made his maiden speech, it was drowned by shouts of laughter. 'The time must come when you will hear me,' he vowed. That time came nine years later when Disraeli opposed Sir Robert Peel, now prime minister, when he decided to repeal the Corn Laws.*

*By 1846, Disraeli hated Peel and saw him as the arch-enemy. He had already denounced Peel in January, accusing him of betraying the party system of government. The final clash between the two men occurred on 15 May in a silent, crowded chamber, with the livid gaslights hissing.*

*Disraeli stood directly behind his victim, motionless except when he drew his handkerchief out of his pocket when he was about to make a hit, his voice passionless, his countenance unmoved. For three hours he made barb after malevolent barb. The devastating satire and malicious wit of the last twenty minutes won him the biggest ovation of his parliamentary career – and effectively destroyed Peel.*

Now, sir, I must say in vindication of the right honourable gentleman that I think great injustice has been done to him throughout these debates. A perhaps justifiable misconception has universally prevailed. Sir, the right honourable gentleman has been accused of foregone treachery – of long-meditated deception – of a desire unworthy of a great statesman, even if an unprincipled one – of always having intended to abandon the opinions by professing which he rose to power. Sir, I entirely acquit the right honourable gentleman of any such intention. I do it for this reason, that when I examine the career of this minister, which has now filled a great space in the parliamentary history of this country, I find that for between forty and fifty years that right honourable gentleman has traded on the ideas and intelligence of others. His life has been one great appropriation clause. He is a burglar of others' intellect. Search the index of Beatson from the days of the Conqueror to the termination of the last reign, there is no statesman who has committed political petty larceny on so great a scale. I believe, therefore, when the right honourable gentleman undertook our cause on either side of the House that he was perfectly sincere in his advocacy; but as in the course of discussion the conventionalisms which he received from us crumbled away in his grasp, feeling no creative power to sustain men with new arguments, feeling no spontaneous sentiments to force upon him conviction, the right honourable gentleman – reduced at last to defending the noblest cause, one based on the most high and solemn principles, upon 'the burdens peculiar to agriculture' – the right honourable gentleman, faithful to the law of his nature, imbibed the new doctrines, the more vigorous, bustling, popular and progressive doctrines, as he had imbibed the doctrines of every leading man in this country for thirty or forty years, with the exception of the doctrines of parliamentary reform which the Whigs very wisely led the country upon and did not allow to grow sufficiently mature to fall into the mouth of the right honourable gentleman.

Sir, the right honourable gentleman tells us that he does not feel humiliated. Sir, it is impossible for anyone to know what are the feelings of another. Feeling depends upon temperament: it depends upon the idiosyncrasy of the individual: it depends upon the organization of the animal that feels. But this I will tell the right honourable gentleman, that, though he may not feel humiliated, his country ought to feel humiliated. Is it so pleasing to the self-complacency of a great nation, is it so grateful to the pride of England, that one who from the position he has contrived to occupy must rank as her foremost citizen, is one of whom it may be said, as Dean Swift said of another minister, 'that he is a gentleman who has the perpetual misfortune to be mistaken'? And, sir, even now, in this last scene of the drama, when the party whom he unintentionally betrayed is to be unintentionally annihilated – even now, in this the last scene, the right honourable gentleman, faithful to the law of his being, is going to pass a project which I believe it is matter of notoriety is not of his own invention. It is one which may have been modified, but which I believe has been offered to another government and by that government has been wisely rejected. Why, sir, these are matters of general notoriety. After the day that the right honourable gentleman made his first exposition of his schemes, a gentleman well known to the House, and learned in all the political secrets behind the scenes, met me and said, 'Well, what do you think of your chief's plan?' Not knowing exactly what to say, but taking up a phrase which has been much used in the House, I observed, 'Well, I suppose it is a great and comprehensive plan.' 'Oh!' he replied, 'we know all about it; it was offered to us. It is not his plan; it's Popkins's plan.' And is England to be governed by Popkins's plan? Will he go to the country with it? Will he go with it to that ancient and famous England that once was governed by statesmen – by Burleighs and by Walsinghams; by Boling-brokes and by Walpoles; by a Chatham and a Canning – will he go to it with this fantastic scheming of some presumptuous pedant? I won't believe it: I have that confidence in the common sense, I will say the common spirit, of our countrymen, and I believe they will not long endure this huckstering tyranny of the Treasury Bench – those political pedlars that bought their party in the cheapest market and sold us in the dearest.

I know, sir, that there are many who believe that the time is gone by when one can appeal to those high and honest impulses that were once the mainstay and the main element of the English character. I know, sir, that we appeal to a people debauched by public gambling – stimulated and encouraged by an inefficient and shortsighted minister. I know that the public mind is polluted with economic fancies: a depraved desire that the rich may become richer without the interference of industry and toil. I know, sir, that all confidence in public men is lost. But, sir, I have faith in the primitive and enduring elements of the English character. It may be vain now, in the midnight of their intoxication, to tell them that there will be an awakening of bitterness; it may be idle now, in the springtide of their economic frenzy, to warn them that there may be an ebb of trouble. But the dark and inevitable hour will arrive. Then, when their spirit is softened by misfortune, they will recur to those principles that made England great, and which, in our belief, can alone keep England great. Then, too, perchance they may remember, not with unkindness, those who, betrayed and deserted, were neither ashamed nor afraid to struggle for the 'good old cause' – the cause with which are associated principles the most popular, sentiments the most entirely national, the cause of labour, the cause of the people – the cause of England.

•

## SIR ROBERT PEEL
### 15 May 1846

*'I cannot charge myself with having taken any course
inconsistent with Conservative principles'*

*When Disraeli sat down, the chamber rang with prolonged protectionist cheers.
Whether maddened by his tormentor's malicious wit or infuriated at this shady
adventurer discoursing on the 'primitive and enduring elements of the English
character', Peel attempted a personal riposte. He was met with brutal screaming
and hooting and shouts of derision and struggled to obtain a hearing. He was jeered
when he spoke of his personal integrity. His voice failed him and his eyes filled
with tears. He pulled himself together, spoke with dignity, and made his last great
Corn Law speech.*

I believe it is nearly three months since I first proposed, as the organ of
Her Majesty's government, the measure which, I trust, is about to
receive tonight the sanction of the House of Commons; and considering
the lapse of time, considering the frequent discussions, considering the
anxiety of the people of this country that these debates should be
brought to a close, I feel that I should be offering an insult to the House
if I were to condescend to bandy personalities upon such an occasion.
Sir, I foresaw that the course which I have taken from a sense of public
duty would expose me to serious sacrifices. I foresaw as its inevitable
result, that I must forfeit friendship which I most highly valued, that I
must interrupt political relations in which I felt a sincere pride; but the
smallest of all the penalties which I anticipated were the continued
venomous attacks of the member for Shrewsbury [*Disraeli*]. Sir, I will
only say of that honourable gentleman that if he, after reviewing the
whole of my public life, a life extending over thirty years previous to my
accession to office in 1841, if he then entertained the opinion of me
which he now professes, it is a little surprising that in the spring of
1841, after his long experience of my public career, he should have been
prepared to give me his confidence. It is still more surprising that he
should have been ready, as I think he was, to unite his fortunes with
mine in office, thus implying the strongest proof which any public man
can give of confidence in the honour and integrity of a minister of the
Crown . . .

I foresaw the consequences that have resulted from the measures which I thought it my duty to propose. We were charged with the heavy responsibility of taking security against a great calamity in Ireland. We did not act lightly. We did not form our opinion upon merely local information, the information of local authorities likely to be influenced by an undue alarm. Before I and those who agreed with me came to that conclusion, we had adopted every means, by local inquiry and by sending perfectly disinterested persons of authority to Ireland, to form a just and correct opinion. Whether we were mistaken or not, I believe we were not mistaken, but, even if we were mistaken, a generous construction should be put upon the motives and conduct of those who are charged with the responsibility of protecting millions of the subjects of the Queen from the consequences of scarcity and famine.

Sir, whatever may be the result of these discussions, I feel severely the loss of the confidence of those from whom I heretofore received a most generous support. So far from expecting them, as some have said, to adopt my opinions, I perfectly recognize the sincerity with which they adhere to their own. I recognize their perfect right, on account of the admitted failure of my speculation, to withdraw from me their confidence. I honour their motives, but I claim, and always will claim, while entrusted with such powers and subject to such responsibility as the minister of this great country is entrusted with, and is subject to; I always will assert the right to give that advice which I conscientiously believe to be conducive to the general well-being. I was not considering, according to the language of the honourable member for Shrewsbury, what was the best bargain to make for a party. I was considering first what were the best measures to avert a great calamity and, as a secondary consideration, to relieve that interest, which I was bound to protect, from the odium of refusing to acquiesce in measures which I thought to be necessary for the purpose of averting that calamity. Sir, I cannot charge myself or my colleagues with having been unfaithful to the trust committed to us. I do not believe that the great institutions of this country have suffered during our administration of power . . .

Sir, if I look to the prerogative of the Crown, if I look to the position of the Church, if I look to the influence of the aristocracy, I cannot charge myself with having taken any course inconsistent with Conservative principles, calculated to endanger the privileges of any branch of the legislature, or any institutions of the country. My earnest wish has been, during my tenure of power, to impress the people of this country with a belief that the legislature was animated by a sincere desire to frame its legislation upon the principles of equity and justice. I have a strong belief that the greatest object, which we or any other Government can contemplate, should be to elevate the condition of that class of the people with whom we are brought into no direct relationship by the exercise of the elective franchise. I wish to convince them that our object has been to apportion taxation, that we shall relieve industry and labour from any undue burden, and transfer it, so far as is consistent with the public good, to those who are better enabled to bear it. I look to the present peace of this country; I look to the absence of all disturbance, to the non-existence of any commitment for a seditious offence; I look to the calm that prevails in the public mind; I look to the absence of all disaffection; I look to the increased and growing public confidence on account of the course you have taken in relieving trade from restrictions and industry from unjust burdens: and where there was dissatisfaction, I see contentment; where there was turbulence, I see there is peace; where there was disloyalty, I see there is loyalty: I see a disposition to confide in you, and not to agitate questions that are at the foundations of your institutions. Deprive me of power tomorrow, you can never deprive me of the consciousness that I have exercised the powers committed to me from no corrupt or interested motives, from no desire to gratify ambition, or attain any personal object; that I have laboured to maintain peace abroad consistently with the national honour and defending every public right, to increase the confidence of the great body of the people in the justice of your decisions, and by the means of equal law to dispense with all coercive powers, to maintain loyalty to the Throne and attachment to the Constitution, from a conviction of the benefit that will accrue to the great body of the people.

*The Corn Law Bill was passed by a majority of 98 on 25 June, with 232 Conservative backbenchers voting against Peel and only 112 on his side.*

•

BENJAMIN DISRAELI
2 July 1849

*'I suffer, and I see no hope'*

*When Parliament met in 1849, Disraeli led the opposition. His views had changed: he now believed that protectionism was a lost cause and that the party needed to accept free trade. He was determined to educate the party to accept reality.*

Some three years ago, as it appears to me, we thought fit to change the principle upon which the economic system of this country has been previously based. Hitherto this country has been, as it were, divided into a hierarchy of industrial classes, each one of which was open to all, but in each of which every Englishman was taught to believe that he occupied a position better than the analogous position of individuals in any other country in the world. For example, the British merchant was looked upon as the most creditable, the wealthiest, and the most trustworthy merchant in the world; the English farmer ranked as the most skilful agriculturalist, while the English manufacturer was acknowledged as the most skilful and successful, without a rival in ingenuity and enterprise. So with the British sailor – the name was a proverb; and chivalry was confessed to have found a last resort in the breast of a British officer. It was the same in our learned professions. Our physicians and lawyers held higher positions than those in other countries. I have heard it stated that the superiority of these classes was obtained at the cost of the hierarchy – at the cost of the labouring population of the country. But . . . I know of no great community existing since, I will say, the fall of the Roman Empire where the working population have been upon the whole placed in so advantageous a position as the working classes of England . . . In this manner, in England society was based upon the aristocratic principle in its complete and most magnificent development. You set to work to change the basis upon which this society was established, you disdain to attempt the accomplishment of the best; and what you want to achieve is the cheapest. But I have shown you that its infallible consequence is to cause the impoverishment and embarrassment of the people . . . But the wealth of England does not merely consist in the number of acres we have tilled and cultivated, nor in our havens filled with shipping, nor in our unrivalled factories, nor in the intrepid history of our mines. Not these merely form the principal wealth of our country; we have a more precious treasure, and that is the character of our people. That is what you have injured. In destroying what you call class legislation, you have destroyed that noble and indefatigable ambition which has been the best source of all our greatness, of all our prosperity, and all our power.

I know of nothing more remarkable in the present day than the general discontent which prevails, accompanied as it is on all sides by an avowed inability to suggest any remedy. The feature of the present day is depression and perplexity. That English spirit which was called out and supported by your old system seems to have departed from us. It was a system which taught men to aspire, and not to grovel. It was a system that gave strength to the subject, and stability to the state; that made the people of this country undergo adversity and confront it with a higher courage than any other people; and that animated them, in the enjoyment of a prosperous fortune, with a higher degree of enterprise. I put it to any gentleman – I care not to what party he belongs, what his political opinions, or what his pursuits in life – if there be not now only one universal murmur – a murmur of suffering without hope . . .

As far as I can judge, men in every place – in the golden saloon, and in the busy mart of industry; in the port, in the Exchange, by the loom, or by the plough, every man says, 'I suffer, and I see no hope.'

*Disraeli was defeated by 140 votes.*

•

# HENRY PALMERSTON
1850

## '*The strong arm of England*'

*Lord Palmerston (1784–1865) was Foreign Secretary under three British prime ministers – Gray, Melbourne and Russell – Home Secretary under Lord Aberdeen and Prime Minister from 1855–8 and 1859–65. There were nine administrations between 1846 and 1867 but it was the age of Palmerston. His ambition was to be minister of a nation rather than a political party. At the height of his power, he believed that a Pax Britannica had replaced the old Pax Romana.*

*He delivered this famous 'Civis Romanus sum' speech when he was forced to defend himself in Parliament against severe criticism of his action in sending British ships to blockade the Greek coast in 1850, without consulting France and Russia who were joint guarantors with Britain of the independence of Greece.*

The government of a great country like this is undoubtedly an object of fair and legitimate ambition to men of all shades of opinion. It is a noble thing to be allowed to guide the policy, and to influence the destinies of such a country, and if ever it was an object of honourable ambition, more than ever must it be so at the moment at which I am speaking. For while we have seen, as stated by the right honourable baronet, the member for Ripon [*Sir James Graham*], the political earthquake rocking Europe from side to side – while we have seen thrones shaken, shattered, levelled; institutions overthrown and destroyed – while, in almost every country of Europe, the conflict of civil war has deluged the land with blood, from the Atlantic to the Black Sea, from the Baltic to the Mediterranean; this country has presented a spectacle honourable to the people of England, and worthy of the admiration of mankind.

We have shown that liberty is compatible with order; that individual liberty is reconcilable with obedience to the law. We have shown the example of a nation, in which every class of society accepts with cheerfulness the lot which Providence has assigned to it; while at the same time every individual of each class is constantly striving to raise himself in the social scale – not by injustice and wrong, not by violence and illegality, but by persevering good conduct, and by the steady and energetic exertion of the moral and intellectual faculties with which his Creator has endowed him. To govern such a people as this is indeed an object worthy of the ambition of the noblest man who lives in the land; and, therefore, I find no fault with those who may think any opportunity a fair one for endeavouring to place themselves in so distinguished and honourable a position. But I contend that we have not in our foreign policy done anything to forfeit the confidence of the country. We may not, perhaps, in this matter or in that, have acted precisely up to the opinions of one person or of another – and hard indeed it is, as we all know by our individual and private experience, to find any number of men agreeing entirely in any matter, on which they may not be equally possessed of the details of the facts, and circumstances, and reasons, and conditions, which led them to action. But, making allowance for those differences of opinion which may fairly and honourably rise amongst those who concur in general views, I maintain that the principles which can be traced through all our foreign transactions, as the guiding rule and directing spirit of our proceedings, are such as deserve approbation. I therefore fearlessly challenge the verdict which this House, as representing a political, a commercial, a constitutional country, is to give on the question now brought before it; whether the principles on which the foreign policy of Her Majesty's government has been conducted, and the sense of duty which has led us to think ourselves bound to afford protection to our fellow-subjects abroad, are proper and fitting guides for those who are charged with the government of England; and whether, as the Roman, in days of old, held himself free from indignity; so also a British subject, in whatever land he may be, shall feel confident that the watchful eye and the strong arm of England will protect him against injustice and wrong.

•

## BENJAMIN DISRAELI
### 16 December 1852

### *'England does not love coalitions'*

*After introducing his first Budget, Disraeli endured six nights of taunts, ridicule and insult from the opposition. So the excitement was intense when he rose to wind up the debate, looking as if he had drunk too much, at 10.20 on the night of 16 December. Violent thunder crashed outside the newly built Palace of Westminster as he ridiculed colleagues – but his jibes and taunts about personalities went too far for the taste of the House.*

The right honourable gentleman charges me with proposing recklessly to increase the direct taxation of the country? Why, he seems to forget that he is the minister who with the property and income tax you have now producing its full amount, with a window-tax that brought nearly £2,000,000, came down to the House of Commons one day and proposed to a startled assembly to double nearly that property and income tax. Recklessness! Why, sir, if recklessness be carelessness of consequences; if it be the conduct of a man who has not well weighed the enterprise in which he is embarked, what are we to esteem this behaviour of the right honourable gentleman? We hear much of the duplication of the house-tax – an immense amount; but if the right honourable gentleman had carried the duplication of the property and income tax, I think he might fairly have been charged with recklessly increasing the direct taxation of the country. The most curious thing, however, is that the minister who came forward to make a proposition which nothing but the most grave conjuncture of circumstances might have justified, at the first menace of opposition withdrew his proposition. Talk of recklessness! Why, what in the history of finance is equal to the recklessness of the right honourable gentleman? And what was the ground on which he withdrew this enormous proposition – a proposition which only the safety of the state would have justified him in making? When he was beaten, baffled, humiliated, he came down to the House of Commons and said that he had sufficient revenue without resorting to that proposition! The future historian will not be believed when he states that a minister came down with a proposition nearly to double the income tax, and when that proposition was rejected, the next day announced that the ways and means were ample without it. But then the right honourable gentleman tells me – in not very polished, and scarcely in parliamentary language – that I do not know my business. He may have learned his business. The House of Commons is the best judge of that; I care not to be his critic. Yet if he have learned his business, he has still to learn that petulance is not sarcasm, and that insolence is not invective . . .

Some advice has been offered to me which I ought perhaps to notice. I have been told to withdraw my Budget. I was told that Mr Pitt withdrew his Budget, and I know that more recently other persons have done so too. Sir, I do not aspire to the fame of Mr Pitt, but I will not submit to the degradation of others. No, sir; I have seen the consequences of a government not being able to pass their measures – consequences not honourable to the government, not advantageous to the country, and not in my opinion, conducive to the reputation of this House, which is most dear to me.

I remember a Budget which was withdrawn, and re-withdrawn, and withdrawn again in the year 1848. What was the consequence of that government thus existing upon sufferance? What was the consequence to the finances of the country? Why, that injurious, unjust and ignoble transaction respecting the commutation of the window-tax and house-duty, which now I am obliged to attempt to remedy. The grievance is deeper than mere questions of party consideration. When parties are balanced – when a government cannot pass its measures – the highest principles of public life, the most important of the dogmas of politics, degenerate into party questions. Look at this question of direct taxation – the most important question of the day. It is a question which must sooner or later force itself upon everybody's attention; and I see before me many who I know sympathize, so far as that important principle is concerned, with the policy of the government. Well direct taxation, although applied with wisdom, temperance and prudence, has become a party question. Talk of administrative reform! Talk of issuing commissions to inquire into our dockyards! Why, if I were, which is not impossible, by intense labour to bring forward a scheme which might save a million annually to the country, administrative reform would become a party question to-morrow. Yes! I know what I have to face. I have to face a coalition. The combination may be successful. But coalitions, although successful, have always found this, that their triumph has been short. This too I know, that England does not love coalitions. I appeal from the coalition to that public opinion which governs this country – to that public opinion whose mild and irresistible influence can control even the decrees of parliaments, and without whose support the most august and ancient institutions are but 'the baseless fabric of a vision'.

•

## WILLIAM GLADSTONE
### 16 December 1852

### 'A Budget . . . which may peril our safety'

*As he sat awaiting his turn to reply to Disraeli, William Gladstone (1809–98), his immediate predecessor as Chancellor, admired the 'superlative acting' and 'brilliant oratory' of his opponent's speech, even though it had driven the opposition into a condition of apoplectic rage.*

*As Gladstone rose, his usually calm features were livid and distorted with passion. His voice shook and it was some time before he could find words or make himself heard as the Conservatives screamed at him. Assuming, according to* The Times *report, a high tone of moral feeling, he lectured Disraeli on the impropriety of his behaviour.*

*Robert Blake, in his biography of Disraeli, says: 'The artist who wished to immortalize an instant of time that would illuminate the political history of the mid-Victorian era would have done well to choose the moment when Gladstone rose to answer Disraeli . . . Gladstone on his feet, handsome, tall, still possessing the youthful good looks, the open countenance, which had charmed his contemporaries at Eton and Christ Church; Disraeli seated on the Treasury bench, aquiline, faintly sinister, listening with seeming indifference to the eloquent rebuke of the orator. It was a scene that was not easily forgotten.'*

*The duel between Disraeli and Gladstone coloured the parliamentary life of a whole generation.*

I begin by telling the right honourable gentleman the Chancellor of the Exchequer that I postpone for some minutes the inquiry whether he knows business or not, that there are some things which he, too, has yet to learn . . .

And I tell the right honourable gentleman more – that the licence of language he has used – the phrases he has applied to the characters of public men – [*Loud cries of 'Hear, hear!'*] – that the phrases he has applied to the characters of public men, whose career – [*The remainder of the sentence was drowned in renewed cries from both sides of the House*].

I confess that I could not hear those phrases used and remain totally unmoved. I do not address myself to those gentlemen belonging to the great party opposite, from whom I have never received anything but courtesy and forbearance – [*Interruption*] – but I will tell them this, that they must bear to have their Chancellor of the Exchequer, who is so free in his comments upon the conduct of others, brought to the bar of the opinion of this Committee, and tried by those laws of decency and propriety – [*Cheers and confusion, which drowned the remainder of the sentence*]. Sir, we are accustomed here to attach to the words of the minister of the Crown a great authority – and that disposition to attach authority, as it is required by the public interest, so it has been usually justified by the conduct and character of those ministers; but I must tell the right honourable gentleman that he is not entitled to charge with insolence men who – [*Renewed cheers again drowned the remaining words of the sentence*]. I must tell the right honourable gentleman that whatever he has learned – and he has learned much – he has not yet learned the limits of discretions of moderation, and of forbearance, that ought to restrain the conduct and language of every member of this House, the disregard of which is an offence in the meanest amongst us, but it is of tenfold weight when committed by the leader of the House of Commons . . .

I vote against the Budget of the Chancellor of the Exchequer, not only because I disapprove upon general grounds of the principles of that Budget but emphatically and peculiarly because in my conscience – though it may be an erroneous belief – it is my firm conviction that the Budget is one, I will not say the most liberal, nor the most radical, but I will say the most subversive in its tendencies and ultimate effects which I have ever known submitted to this House. It is the most regardless of those general rules of prudence which it is absolutely necessary we should preserve, and which it is perfectly impossible that this House, as a popular assembly, should observe unless the government sets us the example, and uses its influence to keep us in the right course. Sir, the House of Commons is a noble assembly, worthy of its historical and traditional associations; but it is too much to expect that we should teach the executive its duty in elementary matters of administration and finance. If I vote against the government, I vote in support of those Conservative principles which I thank God are common in a great degree to all parties in the British House of Commons, but of which I thought it was the peculiar pride and glory of the Conservative party to be the champions and the leaders. Are you not the party of 1842? Are you not the party who, in times of difficulty, chose to cover a deficit, and to provide a large surplus? And are you the same party to be united now in a time of prosperity, to convert a large surplus into a deficiency? I appeal to you by what you then were. I appeal to you to act now as you did then. Us you have cast off. I do not blame you for that. I am, indeed, always disposed to view with regret the rupture of party ties – my disposition is rather to retain them. I confess that I look, if not with suspicion, at least with disapprobation, on any one who is disposed to treat party connections as matters of small importance. My opinion is that party ties closely appertain to those principles of confidence which we entertain for the House of Commons. But us you have cast off for inconsistency. Have we ever complained of that? Have we ever made it matter of charge against you? No, certainly not; you owe us no grudge on that account. But you must remember that you also have a character to maintain – that you also are on your trial – that you also are bound to look with suspicion on those principles of financial policy which depart from those rules that not only all statesmen, but the common sense of the country, agree to be essential to the prosperity of this nation. You are now asked to vote for a Budget which consecrates, as it were, the principle of a deficiency, and which endangers the public credit of the country, and which may peril our safety – if, indeed, the circumstances of the present day are circumstances of uneasiness; and if the government have thought it right to call upon you for increased exertions in providing for the defences of the country, I say, then, that I vote against this Budget, feeling that in giving that vote I do the work, so far as depends upon me, which you ought to join with me in doing. I do not express that sentiment in an offensive manner, but I say it because I feel deeply attached to the institutions of the country. I look back with regret upon the days when I sat nearer to many of my honourable friends opposite than I now am, and I feel it my duty to use that freedom of speech which I am sure, as Englishmen, you will tolerate, when I tell you that if you give your assent and your high authority to this most unsound and destructive principle on which the financial scheme of the Government is based – you may refuse my appeal now – you may accompany the right honourable gentleman the Chancellor of the Exchequer into the lobby; but my belief is that the day will come when you will look back upon this vote – as its consequences sooner or later unfold themselves – you will look back upon this vote with bitter, but with late and ineffectual regret.

*Gladstone's speech destroyed the Budget and set out principles of taxation which he followed in a series of Budgets as Chancellor from 1858 to 1866. The first Derby–Disraeli administration fell.*

•

## JOHN BRIGHT
### 31 March 1854

### '*I am told indeed that the war is popular*'

*Lord Salisbury described John Bright (1811–89) as the greatest master of English oratory of his generation – fit to rank with Pitt and Fox. By the 1850s, as MP for Durham and Manchester, Bright's reputation as an outstanding radical leader had already been secured by his agitation against the Corn Laws and his criticism of British foreign policy.*

*With Cobden, he strongly opposed the Crimean War (and both lost their seats for it in 1857). War was declared on 29 March. Two days later Bright, speaking for an hour and a half, made the first of his great Crimean war speeches.*

I am told indeed that the war is popular, and that it is foolish and eccentric to oppose it. I doubt if the war is very popular in this House. But as to what is, or has been, popular, I may ask, what was more popular than the American war? There were persons lately living in Manchester who had seen the recruiting party going through the principal streets of that city, accompanied by the parochial clergy in full canonicals, exhorting the people to enlist to put down the rebels in the American colonies. Where is now the popularity of that disastrous and disgraceful war, and who is the man to defend it? But if honourable members will turn to the correspondence between George III and Lord North, on the subject of that war, they will find that the King's chief argument for continuing the war was, that it would be dishonourable in him to make peace so long as the war was popular with the people. Again, what war could be more popular than the French war? Has not the noble Lord [Lord John Russell] said, not long ago, in this House, that peace was rendered difficult if not impossible by the conduct of the English press in 1803? For myself, I do not trouble myself whether my conduct in Parliament is popular or not. I care only that it shall be wise and just as regards the permanent interests of my country, and I despise from the bottom of my heart the man who speaks a word in favour of this war, or of any war which he believes might have been avoided, merely because the press and a portion of the people urge the government to enter into it.

I recollect a passage of a distinguished French writer and statesman which bears strongly upon our present position: he says, 'The country which can comprehend and act upon the lessons which God has given it in the past events of its history, is secure in the most imminent crises of its fate.' The past events of our history have taught me that the intervention of this country in European wars is not only unnecessary, but calamitous; that we have rarely come out of such intervention having succeeded in the objects we fought for; that a debt of £800,000,000 sterling has been incurred by the policy which the noble Lord approves, apparently for no other reason than that it dates from the time of William III; and that, not debt alone has been incurred, but that we have left Europe at least as much in chains as before a single effort was made by us to rescue her from tyranny. I believe, if this country, seventy years ago, had adopted the principle of non-intervention in every case where her interests were not directly and obviously assailed, that she would have been saved from much of the pauperism and brutal crimes by which our government and people have alike been disgraced. This country might have been a garden, every dwelling might have been of marble, and every person who treads its soil might have been sufficiently educated. We should indeed have had less of military glory. We might have had neither Trafalgar nor Waterloo; but we should have set the high example of a Christian nation, free in its institutions, courteous and just in its conduct towards all foreign states, and resting its policy on the unchangeable foundation of Christian morality.

•

## JOHN BRIGHT
### 23 February 1855

### '*The Angel of Death has been abroad throughout the land*'

*John Bright's greatest speech was made on the day Lord Palmerston, the Prime Minister, announced that four members of his government, including Gladstone, had resigned, believing that they had been censured by the House for their part in the conduct of the war. Meanwhile a British mission was in Vienna negotiating with the Russians.*

*The speech made its reputation by a single sentence, one of the most famous phrases ever uttered by an English orator, which came to Bright as he lay in bed that morning. 'I would give all that I ever had to have made that speech,' Disraeli told Bright afterwards.*

*The House was packed and every seat in the gallery taken when Bright, aware that the country and the Chamber was against him, rose to speak for a small, powerless minority.*

I shall not say one word here about the state of the army in the Crimea, or one word about its numbers or its condition. Every member of this House, every inhabitant of this country, has been sufficiently harrowed with details regarding it. To my solemn belief, thousands – nay, scores of thousands of persons – have retired to rest, night after night, whose slumbers have been disturbed or whose dreams have been based upon the sufferings and agonies of our soldiers in the Crimea. I should like to ask the noble Lord at the head of the government – although I am not sure if he will feel that he can or ought to answer the question – whether the noble Lord the member for London has power, after discussions have commenced, and as soon as there shall be established good grounds for believing that the negotiations for peace will prove successful, to enter into any armistice? ['*No! no!*']

I know not, sir, who it is that says 'No, no,' but I should like to see any man get up and say that the destruction of 200,000 human lives lost on all sides during the course of this unhappy conflict is not a sufficient sacrifice. You are not pretending to conquer territory – you are not pretending to hold fortified or unfortified towns; you have offered terms of peace which, as I understand them, I do not say are not moderate; and breathes there a man in this House or in this country whose appetite for blood is so insatiable that, even when terms of peace have been offered and accepted, he pines for that assault in which of Russian, Turk, French and English, as sure as one man dies, 20,000 corpses will strew the streets of Sebastopol? I say I should like to ask the noble Lord – and I am sure that he will feel, and that this House will feel, that I am speaking in no unfriendly manner towards the government of which he is at the head – I should like to know, and I venture to hope that it is so, if the noble lord the member for London has power, at the earliest stage of these proceedings at Vienna, at which it can properly be done – and I should think that it might properly be done at a very early stage – to adopt a course by which all further waste of human life may be put an end to, and further animosity between three great nations be, as far as possible, prevented?

I appeal to the noble lord at the head of the government and to this House; I am not now complaining of the war – I am not now complaining of the terms of peace, nor, indeed, of anything that has been done – but I wish to suggest to this House what, I believe, thousands and tens of thousands of the most educated and of the most Christian portion of the people of this country are feeling upon this subject, although, indeed, in the midst of a certain clamour in the country, they do not give public expression to their feelings. Your country is not in an advantageous state at this moment; from one end of the kingdom to the other there is a general collapse of industry. Those members of this House not intimately acquainted with the trade and commerce of the country do not fully comprehend our position as to the diminution of employment and the lessening of wages. An increase in the cost of living is finding its way to the homes and hearts of a vast number of the labouring population.

At the same time there is growing up – and, notwithstanding what some honourable members of this House may think of me, no man regrets it more than I do – a bitter and angry feeling against that class which has for a long period conducted the public affairs of this country. I like political changes when such changes are made as the result, not of passion, but of deliberation and reason. Changes so made are safe, but changes made under the influence of violent exaggeration, or of the violent passions of public meetings, are not changes usually approved by this House or advantageous to the country. I cannot but notice, in speaking to gentlemen who sit on either side of this House, or in speaking to any one I meet between this House and any of those localities we frequent when this House is up – I cannot, I say, but notice that an uneasy feeling exists as to the news which may arrive by the very next mail from the East.

I do not suppose that your troops are to be beaten in actual conflict with the foe, or that they will be driven into the sea; but I am certain that many homes in England in which there now exists a fond hope that the distant one may return – many such homes may be rendered desolate when the next mail shall arrive. The Angel of Death has been abroad throughout the land; you may almost hear the beating of his wings. There is no one, as when the first-born were slain of old, to sprinkle with blood the lintel and the two sideposts of our doors, that he may spare and pass on; he takes his victims from the castle of the noble, the mansion of the wealthy, and the cottage of the poor and the lowly, and it is on behalf of all these classes that I make this solemn appeal.

I tell the noble lord, that if he be ready honestly and frankly to endeavour, by the negotiations about to be opened at Vienna, to put an end to this war, no word of mine, no vote of mine, will be given to shake his power for one single moment, or to change his position in this House. I am sure that the noble lord is not inaccessible to appeals made to him from honest motives and with no unfriendly feeling. The noble lord has been for more than forty years a member of this House. Before I was born, he sat upon the Treasury bench, and he has spent his life in the service of his country. He is no longer young, and his life has extended almost to the term allotted to man. I would ask, I would entreat the noble lord to take a course which, when he looks back upon his whole political career – whatever he may therein find to be pleased with, whatever to regret – cannot but be a source of gratification to him. By adopting that course he would have the satisfaction of reflecting that, having obtained the object of his laudable ambition – having become the foremost subject of the Crown, the director of, it may be, the destinies of his country, and the presiding genius in her councils – he had achieved a still higher and nobler ambition: that he had returned the sword to the scabbard – that at his word torrents of blood had ceased to flow – that he had restored tranquillity to Europe, and saved this country from the indescribable calamities of war.

*When Bright finished, there was an intense silence. Not since Pitt had a speech caused so deep an impression.*

*The Crimean war was the first time in Victorian England that the new force of middle-class politics, expressed through the press and public meetings, at which Bright excelled, changed the foreign policy of the government.*

•

### JOHN BRIGHT
### 4 December 1861

### *'If all other tongues are silent, mine shall speak'*

*John Bright was at the forefront of the struggle to swing Britain behind President Lincoln and against the slaveholders of the south when civil war was threatened in the United States. Christmas 1861 was the moment of greatest danger in the relations of Britain and America after Charles Wilkes, captain of an American warship, stopped the* Trent, *a British merchant steamer, and seized Mason and Slidell, envoys of the Slaveholders' Confederation, on their way to seek British and French support. Wilkes put them in jail and many in Britain wanted a declaration of war.*

*Bright made this speech repudiating the warmongers and hymning the free Union at a public banquet in his home town of Rochdale, when he was invited to speak about the American Civil War. His statement of the case for the North against the slaveholders did much to form a Northern party in England.*

Two centuries ago, multitudes of the people of this country found a refuge on the North American continent, escaping from the tyranny of the Stuarts and from the bigotry of Laud. Many noble spirits from our country made great experiments in favour of human freedom on that continent. Bancroft, the great historian of his own country, has said, in his own graphic and emphatic language, 'The history of the colonization of America is the history of the crimes of Europe.' From that time down to our own period, America has admitted the wanderers from every clime. Since 1815, a time which many here remember, and which is within my lifetime, more than three millions of persons have emigrated from the United Kingdom to the United States. During the fifteen years from 1845 or 1846 to 1859 or 1860 – a period so recent that we all remember the most trivial circumstances that have happened in that time – during those fifteen years more than two million three hundred and twenty thousand persons left the shores of the United Kingdom as emigrants for the States of North America.

At this very moment, then, there are millions in the United States who personally, or whose immediate parents, have at one time been citizens of this country. They found a home in the Far West; they subdued the wilderness; they met with plenty there, which was not afforded them in their native country; and they have become a great people. There may be persons in England who are jealous of those states. There may be men who dislike democracy, and who hate a republic; there may be even those whose sympathies warm towards the slave oligarchy of the South. But of this I am certain, that only misrepresentation the most gross or calumny the most wicked can sever the tie which unites the great mass of the people of this country with their friends and brethren beyond the Atlantic.

Now, whether the Union will be restored or not, or the South achieve an unhonoured independence or not, I know not, and I predict not. But this I think I know – that in a few years, a very few years, the twenty millions of freemen in the North will be thirty millions, or even fifty millions – a population equal to or exceeding that of this kingdom. When that time comes, I pray that it may not be said amongst them, that, in the darkest hour of their country's trials, England, the land of their fathers, looked on with icy coldness and saw unmoved the perils and calamities of their children. As for me, I have but this to say: I am but one in this audience, and but one in the citizenship of this country; but if all other tongues are silent, mine shall speak for that policy which gives hope to the bondsmen of the South, and which tends to generous thoughts, and generous words, and generous deeds, between the two great nations who speak the English language, and from their origin are alike entitled to the English name.

•

JOHN BRIGHT
18 December 1862

'*A mighty fabric of human bondage*'

*A year after his speech on the 'Trent affair', Bright returned again to the American Civil War in a speech at Birmingham.*

Is there a man here that doubts for a moment that the object of the war on the part of the South – they began the war – that the object of the war on the part of the South is to maintain in bondage four millions of human beings? That is only a small part of it. The further object is to perpetuate for ever the bondage of all the posterity of those four millions of slaves . . .

The object is, that a handful of white men on that continent shall lord it over many millions of blacks, made black by the very Hand that made us white. The object is, that they should have the power to breed Negroes, to work Negroes, to lash Negroes, to chain Negroes, to buy and sell Negroes, to deny them the commonest ties of family, or to break their hearts by rending them at their pleasure, to close their mental eye to but a glimpse even of that knowledge which separates us from the brute – for in their laws it is criminal and penal to teach the Negro to read – to seal from their hearts the Book of our religion, and to make chattels and things of men and women and children.

Now I want to ask whether this is to be the foundation, as it is proposed, of a new slave empire, and whether it is intended that on this audacious and infernal basis England's new ally is to be built up.

Now I should have no kind of objection to recognize a country because it was a country that held slaves – to recognize the United States, or to be in amity with it. The question of slavery there, and in Cuba and in Brazil, is, as far as respects the present generation, an accident, and it would be unreasonable that we should object to trade with and have political relations with a country, merely because it happened to have within its borders the institution of slavery, hateful as that institution is. But in this case it is a new state intending to set itself up on the sole basis of slavery. Slavery is blasphemously declared to be its chief corner-stone.

I have heard that there are, in this country, ministers of state who are in favour of the South; that there are members of the aristocracy who are terrified at the shadow of the Great Republic; that there are rich men on our commercial exchanges, depraved, it may be, by their riches, and thriving unwholesomely within the atmosphere of a privileged class; that there are conductors of the public press who would barter the rights of millions of their fellow-creatures that they might bask in the smiles of the great.

But I know that there are ministers of state who do not wish that this insurrection should break up the American nation; that there are members of our aristocracy who are not afraid of the shadow of the Republic; that there are rich men, many, who are not depraved by their riches; and that there are public writers of eminence and honour who will not barter human rights for the patronage of the great. But most of all, and before all, I believe – I am sure it is true in Lancashire, where the working men have seen themselves coming down from prosperity to ruin, from independence to a subsistence on charity – I say that I believe that the unenfranchised but not hopeless millions of this country will never sympathize with a revolt which is intended to destroy the liberty of a continent, and to build on its ruins a mighty fabric of human bondage . . .

Slavery has been, as we all know, the huge, foul blot upon the fame of the American Republic; it is a hideous outrage against human right and against divine law; but the pride, the passion of man, will not permit its peaceable extinction. The slave owners of our colonies, if they had been strong enough, would have revolted too. I believe there was no mode short of a miracle more stupendous than any recorded in Holy Writ that could in our time, or in a century, or in any time, have brought about the abolition of slavery in America, but the suicide which the South has committed and the war which it has begun . . .

I blame men who are eager to admit into the family of nations a state which offers itself to us, based upon a principle, I will undertake to say, more odious and more blasphemous than was ever heretofore dreamed of in Christian or Pagan, in civilized or in savage times. The leaders of this revolt propose this monstrous thing – that over a territory forty times as large as England, the blight and curse of slavery shall be for ever perpetuated.

I cannot believe, for my part, that such a fate will befall that fair land, stricken though it now is with the ravages of war. I cannot believe that civilization, in its journey with the sun, will sink into endless night in order to gratify the ambition of the leaders of this revolt, who seek to

> Wade through slaughter to a throne,
> And shut the gates of mercy on mankind.

I have another and a far brighter vision before my gaze. It may be but a vision, but I will cherish it. I see one vast confederation stretching from the frozen North in unbroken line to the glowing South, and from the wild billows of the Atlantic westward to the calmer waters of the Pacific main – and I see one people, and one language, and one law, and one faith, and, over all that wide continent, the home of freedom, and a refuge for the oppressed of every race and of every clime.

●

# WILLIAM GLADSTONE
27 April 1866

### *'You cannot fight against the future'*

*Gladstone introduced the Representation of the People Bill on 12 March. His Reform Bill lowered the property qualification for voting, added some 400,000 votes to the electorate, and provoked a major political storm.*

*Disraeli said that the bill was conceived in the spirit of the American rather than the British Constitution – and taunted Gladstone with a speech he had made thirty-five years earlier at the Oxford Union in which he had said that the suffrage was 'a moral right'.*

*Speaking for two and a half hours, until 3.30 a.m., Gladstone delivered this stinging rebuke.*

Let us for a moment consider the enormous and silent changes which have been going forward among the labouring population. May I use the words to honourable and right honourable gentlemen once used by way of exhortation by Sir Robert Peel to his opponents, 'elevate your vision'? Let us try and raise our views above the fears, the suspicions, the jealousies, the reproaches, and the recriminations of this place and this occasion. Let us look onward to the time of our children and of our children's children. Let us know what preparation it behoves us should be made for that coming time. Is there or is there not, I ask, a steady movement of the labouring classes, and is or is not that movement a movement onwards and upwards? . . .

Has my right honourable friend, in whom mistrust rises to its utmost height, ever really considered the astonishing phenomena connected with some portion of the conduct of the labouring classes, especially in the Lancashire distress? Has he considered what an amount of self-denial was exhibited by these men in respect to the American war? They knew that the source of their distress lay in the war, yet they never uttered or entertained the wish that any effort should be made to put an end to it, as they held it to be a war for justice and for freedom. Could any man have believed that a conviction so still, so calm, so firm, so energetic, could have planted itself in the minds of a population without becoming a known patent fact throughout the whole country? But we knew nothing of it. And yet when the day of trial came we saw that noble sympathy on their part with the people of the North; that determination that, be their sufferings what they might, no word should proceed from them that would hurt a cause which they so firmly believed to be just. On one side there was a magnificent moral spectacle; on the other side was there not also a great lesson to us all, to teach us that in those little tutored, but yet reflective minds, by a process of quiet instillation, opinions and sentiments gradually form themselves of which we for a long time remain unaware, but which, when at last they make their appearance, are found to be deep-rooted, mature and ineradicable? . . .

Sir, the hour has arrived when this protracted debate must come to an end [*Cheers*] . . .

But a very few words more, and I have done. May I speak briefly to honourable gentlemen opposite, as some of them have addressed advice to gentlemen on this side of the House. I would ask them, 'Will you not consider, before you embark in this new crusade, whether the results of those other crusades in which you have heretofore engaged have been so satisfactory to you as to encourage you to repeat the operation?' Great battles you have fought, and fought them manfully. The battle of maintaining civil disabilities on account of religious belief, the battle of resisting the first Reform Act, the obstinate and long-continued battle of protection, all these great battles have been fought by the great party that I see opposite; and, as to some portion of those conflicts, I admit my own share of the responsibility. But I ask, again, have their results – have their results towards yourselves – been such as that you should be disposed to renew struggles such as these? Certainly those who compose the Liberal party here, at least in that capacity have no reason or title to find fault. The effect of your course has been to give them for five out of every six, or for six out of every seven years since the epoch of the Reform Act the conduct and management of public affairs. The effect has been to lower, to reduce, and contract your just influence in the country, and to abridge your legitimate share in the administration of the government. It is good for the public interest that you should be strong; but if you are to be strong, you can only be so by showing, in addition to the kindness and the personal generosity which I am sure you feel towards the people, a public, a political trust and confidence in them. What I now say can hardly be said with an evil motive, I am conscious of no such sentiment towards any man or party. But, sir, we are assailed; this bill is in a state of crisis and of peril, and the government along with it. We stand or fall with it, as has been declared by my noble friend Lord Russell. We stand with it now; we may fall with it a short time hence. If we do so fall, we, or others in our places, shall rise with it hereafter. I shall not attempt to measure with precision the forces that are to be arrayed against us in the coming issue. Perhaps the great division of tonight is not the last that must take place in the struggle. At some point of the contest you may possibly succeed. You may drive us from our seats. You may bury the bill that we have introduced, but we will write upon its gravestone for an epitaph this line, with certain confidence in its fulfilment –

Exoriare aliquis nostris ex ossibus ultor.*

You cannot fight against the future. Time is on our side. The great social forces which move onwards in their might and majesty, and which the tumult of our debates does not for a moment impede or disturb – those great social forces are against you; they are marshalled on our side; and the banner which we now carry in this fight, though perhaps at some moment it may droop over our sinking heads, yet it soon again will float in the eye of heaven, and it will be borne by the firm hands of the united people of the three kingdoms, perhaps not to an easy, but to a certain and to a not distant victory.

*Gladstone lost his bill in June and announced the resignation of his government. Lord Derby formed a Conservative government. Disraeli succeeded Gladstone as Chancellor and leader of the Commons and introduced the successful 1867 Reform Bill.*

•

# BENJAMIN DISRAELI
## 3 April 1872

### 'Sanitas sanitatum, omnia sanitas'

*Disraeli seldom made speeches to mass audiences, but in 1872 he made two that clinched his command of the Conservative party.*

*The first was at the Free Trade Hall in Manchester, the favourite platform of Cobden and Bright, where he sustained himself through a three-and-a-quarter-hour speech by consuming two bottles of 'white brandy'.*

* Arise you avenger from my bones (Virgil, *Aeneid*, Bk IV).

*He presented the Conservatives as the patriotic party, denounced radical forces determined to destroy the Church and House of Lords, even the monarchy, declared that the first consideration of a minister should be the health of the people, and ended with a rallying cry to England as a powerful country with an imperial destiny.*

The Conservative party are accused of having no programme of policy. If by a programme is meant a plan to despoil churches and plunder landlords, I admit we have no programme. If by a programme is meant a policy which assails or menaces every institution and every interest, every class and every calling in the country, I admit we have no programme. But if to have a policy with distinct ends, and these such as most deeply interest the great body of the nation, be a becoming programme for a political party, then I contend we have an adequate programme and one which, here or elsewhere, I shall always be prepared to assert and to vindicate.

Gentlemen, the programme of the Conservative party is to maintain the Constitution of the country. I have not come down to Manchester to deliver an essay on the English Constitution; but when the banner of republicanism is unfurled – when the fundamental principles of our institutions are controverted – I think, perhaps, it may not be inconvenient that I should make some few practical remarks upon the character of our Constitution – upon that monarchy limited by the coordinate authority of the estates of the realm, which, under the title of Queen, Lords, and Commons, has contributed so greatly to the prosperity of this country, and with the maintenance of which I believe that prosperity is bound up.

Gentlemen, since the settlement of that Constitution, now nearly two centuries ago, England has never experienced a revolution, though there is no country in which there has been so continuous and such considerable change. How is this? Because the wisdom of your forefathers placed the prize of supreme power without the sphere of human passions. Whatever the struggle of parties, whatever the strife of factions, whatever the excitement and exaltation of the public mind, there has always been something in this country round which all classes and parties could rally, representing the majesty of the law, the administration of justice, and involving, at the same time, the security for every man's rights and the fountain of honour. Now, gentlemen, it is well clearly to comprehend what is meant by a country not having a revolution for two centuries. It means, for that space, the unbroken exercise and enjoyment of the ingenuity of man. It means, for that space, the continuous application of the discoveries of science to his comfort and convenience. It means the accumulation of capital, the elevation of labour, the establishment of those admirable factories which cover your district; the unwearied improvement of the cultivation of the land, which has extracted from a somewhat churlish soil harvests more exuberant than those furnished by lands nearer to the sun. It means the continuous order which is the only parent of personal liberty and political right. And you owe all these, gentlemen, to the Throne.

There is another powerful and most beneficial influence which is also exercised by the Crown. Gentlemen, I am a party man. I believe that, without party, parliamentary government is impossible. I look upon parliamentary government as the noblest government in the world, and certainly the one most suited to England. But without the discipline of political connection, animated by the principle of private honour, I feel certain that a popular assembly would sink before the power or the corruption of a minister. Yet, gentlemen, I am not blind to the faults of party government. It has one great defect. Party has a tendency to warp the intelligence, and there is no minister, however resolved he may be in treating a great public question, who does not find some difficulty in emancipating himself from the traditionary prejudice on which he has long acted. It is, therefore, a great merit in our Constitution that before a minister introduces a measure to Parliament, he must submit it to an intelligence superior to all party, and entirely free from influences of that character . . .

Gentlemen, I am not here to maintain that there is nothing to be done to increase the well-being of the working classes of this country, generally speaking. There is not a single class in the country which is not susceptible of improvement; and that makes the life and animation of our society. But in all we do we must remember that much depends upon the working classes themselves; and what I know of the working classes in Lancashire makes me sure that they will respond to this appeal. Much also may be expected from that sympathy between classes which is a distinctive feature of the present day; and, in the last place, no inconsiderable results may be obtained by judicious and prudent legislation. But, gentlemen, in attempting to legislate upon social matters the great object is to be practical – to have before us some distinct aims and some distinct means by which they can be accomplished.

Gentlemen, I think public attention as regards these matters ought to be concentrated upon sanitary legislation. That is a wide subject, and, if properly treated, comprises almost every consideration which has a just claim upon legislative interference. Pure air, pure water, the inspection of unhealthy habitations, the adulteration of food – these and many kindred matters may be legitimately dealt with by the legislature; and I am bound to say the legislature is not idle upon them; for we have at this time two important measures before Parliament on the subject. One – by a late colleague of mine, Sir Charles Adderley – is a large and comprehensive measure, founded upon a sure basis, for it consolidates all existing public acts, and improves them.

The other measure by the government is of a partial character. What it comprises is good, so far as it goes, but it shrinks from that bold consolidation of existing acts which I think one of the great merits of Sir Charles Adderley's bill, which permits us to become acquainted with how much may be done in favour of sanitary improvement by existing provisions.

Gentlemen, I cannot impress upon you too strongly my conviction of the importance of the legislature and society uniting together in favour of these important results. A great scholar and a great wit, three hundred years ago, said that, in his opinion, there was a great mistake in the Vulgate, which, as you all know, is the Latin translation of the Holy Scriptures, and that, instead of saying 'Vanity of vanities, all is vanity' – *Vanitas vanitatum, omnia vanitas* – the wise and witty king really said: *'Sanitas sanitatum, omnia sanitas.'* Gentlemen, it is impossible to overrate the importance of the subject. After all, the first consideration of a minister should be the health of the people. A land may be covered with historic trophies, with museums of science and galleries of art, with universities and with libraries; the people may be civilized and ingenious; the country may be even famous in the annals and action of the world, but, gentlemen, if the population every ten years decreases, and the stature of the race every ten years diminishes, the history of that country will soon be the history of the past . . .

I doubt not there is in this hall more than one publican who remembers that last year an act of Parliament was introduced to denounce him as a 'sinner'. I doubt not there are in this hall a widow and an orphan who remember the profligate proposition to plunder their lonely heritage. But, gentlemen, as time advanced it was not difficult to perceive that extravagance was being substituted for energy by the government. The unnatural stimulus was subsiding. Their paroxysms ended in prostration. Some took refuge in melancholy, and their eminent chief alternated between a menace and a sigh. As I sat opposite the treasury bench the ministers reminded me of one of those marine landscapes not very unusual on the coast of South America. You behold a range of exhausted volcanoes. Not a flame flickers on a single pallid crest. But the situation is still dangerous. There are occasional earthquakes, and ever and anon the dark rumbling of the sea . . .

•

## BENJAMIN DISRAELI
### 24 June 1872

### *'The issue is not a mean one'*

*A few weeks later, at Crystal Palace in London, Disraeli refined his Manchester speech and set out the historic principles of the Conservative party – to maintain Britain's institutions, advance the empire and elevate the condition of the people.*

Gentlemen, the Tory party, unless it is a national party, is nothing. It is not a confederacy of nobles, it is not a democratic multitude; it is a party formed from all the numerous classes in the realm – classes alike and equal before the law, but whose different conditions and different aims give vigour and variety to our national life.

Gentlemen, a body of public men distinguished by their capacity took advantage of these circumstances. They seized the helm of affairs in a manner the honour of which I do not for a moment question, but they introduced a new system into our political life. Influenced in a great degree by the philosophy and the politics of the Continent, they endeavoured to substitute cosmopolitan for national principles; and they baptized the new scheme of politics with the plausible name of 'Liberalism'. Far be it from me for a moment to intimate that a country like England should not profit by the political experience of Continental nations of not inferior civilization; far be it from me for a moment to maintain that the party which then obtained power and which has since generally possessed it did not make many suggestions for our public life that were of great value, and bring forward many measures which, though changes, were nevertheless improvements. But the tone and tendency of Liberalism cannot be long concealed. It is to attack the institutions of the country under the name of Reform, and to make war on the manners and customs of the people of this country under the pretext of Progress. During the forty years that have elapsed since the commencement of this new system – although the superficial have seen upon its surface only the contentions of political parties – the real state of affairs has been this: the attempt of one party to establish in this country cosmopolitan ideas, and the efforts of another – unconscious efforts, sometimes, but always continued – to recur to and resume those national principles to which they attribute the greatness and glory of the country.

The Liberal party cannot complain that they have not had fair play. Never had a political party such advantages, never such opportunities. They are still in power; they have been for a long period in power. And yet what is the result? I speak not I am sure the language of exaggeration when I say that they are viewed by the community with distrust and, I might even say, with repugnance. And, now, what is the present prospect of the national party? I have ventured to say that in my opinion Liberalism, from its essential elements, notwithstanding all the energy and ability with which its tenets have been advocated by its friends – notwithstanding the advantage which has accrued to them, as I will confess, from all the mistakes of their opponents, is viewed by the country with distrust. Now in what light is the party of which we are members viewed by the country, and what relation does public opinion bear to our opinions and our policy? . . .

Now, I have always been of opinion that the Tory party has three great objects. The first is to maintain the institutions of the country – not from any sentiment of political superstition, but because we believe that they embody the principles upon which a community like England can alone safely rest. The principles of liberty, of order, of law, and of religion ought not to be entrusted to individual opinion or to the caprice and passion of multitudes, but should be embodied in a form of permanence and power. We associate with the monarchy the ideas which it represents – the majesty of law, the administration of justice, the fountain of mercy and of honour. We know that in the estates of the realm and the privileges they enjoy, is the best security for public liberty and good government. We believe that a national profession of faith can only be maintained by an established Church, and that no society is safe unless there is a public recognition of the providential government of the world, and of the future responsibility of man. Well, it is a curious circumstance that during all these same forty years of triumphant Liberalism, every one of these institutions has been attacked and assailed – I say, continuously attacked and assailed. And what, gentlemen, has been the result? For the last forty years the most depreciating comparisons have been instituted between the sovereignty of England and the sovereignty of a great republic. We have been called upon in every way, in Parliament, in the press, by articles in newspapers, by pamphlets, by every means which can influence opinion, to contrast the simplicity and economy of the sovereignty of the United States with the cumbrous cost of the sovereignty of England . . .

Now, if you consider the state of public opinion with regard to those estates of the realm, what do you find? Take the case of the House of Lords. The House of Lords has been assailed during this reign of Liberalism in every manner and unceasingly. Its constitution has been denounced as anomalous, its influence declared pernicious; but what has been the result of this assault and criticism of forty years? Why, the people of England, in my opinion, have discovered that the existence of a second chamber is necessary to constitutional government; and, while necessary to constitutional government, is, at the same time, of all political inventions the most difficult. Therefore, the people of this country have congratulated themselves that, by the aid of an ancient and famous history, there has been developed in this country an assembly which possesses all the virtues which a senate should possess – independence, great local influence, eloquence, all the accomplishments of political life, and a public training which no theory could supply.

The assault of Liberalism upon the House of Lords has been mainly occasioned by the prejudice of Liberalism against the land laws of this country. But in my opinion, and in the opinion of wiser men than myself, and of men in other countries beside this, the liberty of England depends much upon the landed tenure of England – upon the fact that there is a class which can alike defy despots and mobs, around which the people may always rally, and which must be patriotic from its intimate connection with the soil. Well, gentlemen, so far as these institutions of the country – the monarchy and the Lords spiritual and temporal – are concerned, I think we may fairly say, without exaggeration, that public opinion is in favour of those institutions, the maintenance of which is one of the principal tenets of the Tory party, and the existence of which has been unceasingly criticised for forty years by the Liberal party. Now, let me say a word about the other estate of the realm, which was first attacked by Liberalism.

One of the most distinguishing features of the great change effected in 1832 was that those who brought it about at once abolished all the franchises of the working classes. They were franchises as ancient as those of the baronage of England; and, while they abolished them, they proposed no substitute. The discontent upon the subject of the representa-

tion which has from that time more or less pervaded our society dates
from that period, and that discontent, all will admit, has now ceased. It
was terminated by the Act of Parliamentary Reform of 1867–8. That Act
was founded on a confidence that the great body of the people of this
country were 'Conservative'. When I say 'Conservative', I use the word
in its purest and loftiest sense. I mean that the people of England, and
especially the working classes of England, are proud of belonging to a
great country, and wish to maintain its greatness – that they are proud
of belonging to an imperial country, and are resolved to maintain, if
they can, their empire – that they believe, on the whole, that the
greatness and the empire of England are to be attributed to the ancient
institutions of the land.

Gentlemen, I venture to express my opinion, long entertained, and
which has never for a moment faltered, that this is the disposition of
the great mass of the people; and I am not misled for a moment by
wild expressions and eccentric conduct which may occur in the metropolis of this country. There are people who may be, or who at least
affect to be, working men, and who, no doubt, have a certain influence
with a certain portion of the metropolitan working classes, who talk
Jacobinism . . .

I say with confidence that the great body of the working class of
England utterly repudiate such sentiments. They have no sympathy with
them. They are English to the core. They repudiate cosmopolitan
principles. They adhere to national principles. They are for maintaining
the greatness of the kingdom and the empire, and they are proud of
being subjects of our sovereign and members of such an empire . . .

No institution of England, since the advent of Liberalism, has been so
systematically, so continuously assailed as the established Church. Gentlemen, we were first told that the Church was asleep, and it is very
possible, as everybody, civil and spiritual, was asleep forty years ago,
that that might have been the case. Now we are told that the Church is
too active, and that it will be destroyed by its internal restlessness and
energy. I see in all these efforts of the Church to represent every mood
of the spiritual mind of man, no evidence that it will fall, no proof that
any fatal disruption is at hand. I see in the Church, as I believe I see in
England, an immense effort to rise to national feelings and recur to
national principles. The Church of England, like all our institutions,
feels it must be national, and it knows that, to be national, it must be
comprehensive. Gentlemen, I have referred to what I look upon as the
first object of the Tory party – namely, to maintain the institutions of

the country, and reviewing what has occurred, and referring to the present temper of the times upon these subjects, I think that the Tory party, or, as I will venture to call it, the National party, has everything to encourage it. I think that the nation, tested by many and severe trials, has arrived at the conclusion which we have always maintained, that it is the first duty of England to maintain its institutions, because to them we principally ascribe the power and prosperity of the country.

Gentlemen, there is another and second great object of the Tory party. If the first is to maintain the institutions of the country, the second is, in my opinion, to uphold the empire of India, as a burden upon this country, viewing everything in a financial aspect, and totally passing by those moral and political considerations which make nations great, and by the influence of which alone men are distinguished from animals.

Well, what has been the result of this attempt during the reign of Liberalism for the disintegration of the empire? It has entirely failed. But how has it failed? Through the sympathy of the colonies with the mother country. They have decided that the empire shall not be destroyed, and in my opinion no minister in this country will do his duty who neglects any opportunity of reconstructing as much as possible our colonial empire, and of responding to those distant sympathies which may become the source of incalculable strength and happiness to this land. Therefore, gentlemen, with respect to the second great object of the Tory party also – the maintenance of the empire – public opinion appears to be in favour of our principles – that public opinion which, I am bound to say, thirty years ago, was not favourable to our principles, and which, during a long interval of controversy, in the interval had been doubtful.

Gentlemen, another great object of the Tory party, and one not inferior to the maintenance of the empire, or the upholding of our institutions, is the elevation of the condition of the people. Let us see in this great struggle between Toryism and Liberalism that has prevailed in this country during the last forty years what are the salient features. It must be obvious to all who consider the condition of the multitude with a desire to improve and elevate it, that no important step can be gained unless you can effect some reduction of their hours of labour and humanize their toil. The great problem is to be able to achieve such results without violating those principles of economic truth upon which the prosperity of all states depends. You recollect well that many years ago the Tory party believed that these two results might be obtained – that you might elevate the condition of the people by the reduction of their toil and the mitigation of their labour, and at the same time inflict no injury on the wealth of the nation. You know how that effort was encountered – how these views and principles were met by the triumphant statesmen of Liberalism. They told you that the inevitable consequence of your policy was to diminish capital, that this, again, would lead to the lowering of wages, to a great diminution of the employment of the people, and ultimately to the impoverishment of the kingdom.

These were not merely the opinions of ministers of state, but those of the most blatant and loud-mouthed leaders of the Liberal party. And what has been the result? Those measures were carried, but carried, as I can bear witness, with great difficulty and after much labour and a long struggle. Yet they were carried; and what do we now find? That capital was never accumulated so quickly, that wages were never higher, that the employment of the people was never greater, and the country never wealthier . . .

This is a numerous assembly; this is an assembly individually influential; but it is not on account of its numbers, it is not on account of its individual influence, that I find it to me deeply interesting. It is because I know that I am addressing a representative assembly. It is because I know that there are men here who come from all districts and all quarters of England, who represent classes and powerful societies, and who meet here not merely for the pleasure of a festival, but because they believe that our assembling together may lead to national advantage. Yes, I tell all who are here present that there is a responsibility which you have incurred today, and which you must meet like men. When you return to your homes, when you return to your counties and to your cities, you must tell to all those whom you can influence that the time is at hand, that, at least, it cannot be far distant, when England will have to decide between national and cosmopolitan principles. The issue is not a mean one. It is whether you will be content to be a comfortable England, modelled and moulded upon Continental principles and meeting in due course an inevitable fate, or whether you will be a great country – an imperial country – a country where your sons, when they rise, rise to paramount positions, and obtain not merely the esteem of their countrymen, but command the respect of the world.

Upon you depends the issue . . .

*The Manchester and Crystal Palace speeches are still cited as the major contribution of Disraeli to an enduring concept of progressive Conservatism, though Robert Blake points out that social reform occupies only three of forty-five pages in the major edition of his speeches. Social legislation was a major preoccupation of his government in 1875–6.*

•

# WILLIAM GLADSTONE

### THE MIDLOTHIAN CAMPAIGN

*Gladstone's Midlothian campaign in 1879 marked a turning point in British political history. It was the first time a British statesman had gone on the stump to woo the electorate. He made five major indoor speeches as well as many others at railway stations on his journey or to waiting crowds.*

*Every word he spoke was reported all over the country, says his biographer Philip Magnus. 'People flocked to Midlothian from all parts of Scotland, including the storm-vexed Hebrides, to hear the magic voice, to watch the eagle eye, to enjoy the superb gestures and to share in what Disraeli called a "pilgrimage of passion" and Gladstone a "festival of freedom".'*

•

## 25 November 1879, Edinburgh

### 'God speed the right'

*As Gladstone travelled to Scotland by train, crowds of workers gathered to cheer him as he passed and he spoke to them at the stations in Carlisle, Hawick and Galashiels. As he arrived at Edinburgh, bonfires blazed on the hills and fireworks cascaded in the sky. Next day he delivered the first speech of the Midlothian campaign.*

It is no longer the government with which you have to deal. You have to deal with the majority of the House of Commons. The majority of the House of Commons has completely acquitted the government. Upon every occasion when the government has appealed to it, the majority of the House of Commons has been ready to answer to the call. Hardly a man has ever hesitated to grant the confidence that was desired, however outrageous in our view the nature of the demand might be. Completely and bodily, the majority of the House of Commons has taken on itself the responsibility of the government – and not only the collective majority of the House of Commons, gentlemen. If you had got to deal with them by a vote of censure on that majority in the lump, that would be a very ineffective method of dealing. They must be dealt with individually. That majority is made up of units. It is the unit with which you have got to deal. And let me tell you that the occasion is a solemn one; for as I am the first to aver that now fully and bodily the majority of the House of Commons has, in the face of the country, by a multitude of repeated and deliberate acts, made itself wholly and absolutely responsible in the whole of these transactions that I have been commenting upon, and in many more; and as the House of Commons has done that, so upon the coming general election will it have to be determined whether that responsibility, so shifted from an Administration to a Parliament, shall again be shifted from a Parliament to a nation. As yet the nation has had no opportunity. Nay, as I pointed out early in these remarks, the government do not seem disposed to give them the opportunity. To the last moment, so far as we are informed by the best authorities, they intend to withhold it. The nation, therefore, is not yet responsible. If faith has been broken, if blood has been needlessly shed, if the name of England has been discredited and lowered from that lofty standard which it ought to exhibit to the whole world, if the country has been needlessly distressed, if finance has been thrown into confusion, if the foundations of the Indian Empire have been impaired, all these things as yet are the work of an Administration and a Parliament; but the day is coming, and is near at hand, when that event will take place which will lead the historian to declare whether or not they are the work, not of an Administration and not of a Parliament, but the work of a great and a free people. If this great and free and powerful people is disposed to associate itself with such transactions, if it is disposed to assume upon itself what some of us would call the guilt, and many of us must declare to be the heavy burden, of all those events that have been passing before our eyes, it rests with them to do it. But, gentlemen, let every one of us resolve in his inner conscience, before God and before man – let him resolve that he at least will have no share in such a proceeding; that he will do his best to exempt himself; that he will exempt himself from every participation in what he believes to be mischievous and ruinous misdeeds; that, so far as his exertions can avail, no trifling, no secondary consideration shall stand in the way of them, or abate them; that he will do what in him lies to dissuade his countrymen from arriving at a resolution so full of mischief, of peril, and of shame.

Gentlemen, this is the issue which the people of this country will have to try. Our minds are made up. You and they have got to speak. I for my part have done and will do the little that rests with me to make clear the nature of the great controversy that is to be decided; and I say from the bottom of my soul, 'God speed the right.'

•

26 November 1879, Dalkeith

## 'Remember the rights of the savage'

I am not here before you as one of those who have ever professed to believe that the state which society has reached permits us to make a vow of universal peace, and of renouncing, in all cases, the alternative of war. But I am here to say that a long experience of life leads me, not towards any abstract doctrine upon the subject, but to a deeper and deeper conviction of the enormous mischiefs of war, even under the best and most favourable circumstances, and of the mischiefs indescribable and the guilt unredeemed of causeless and unnecessary wars. Look back over the pages of history; consider the feelings, with which we now regard wars that our forefathers in their time supported with the same pernicious fanaticism, of which we have had some developments in this country within the last three years. Consider, for example, that the American War, now condemned by 999 out of every 1,000 persons in this country, was a war which for years was enthusiastically supported by the mass of the population. And then see how powerful and deadly are the fascinations of passion and of pride; and, if it be true that the errors of former times are recorded for our instruction, in order that we may avoid their repetition, then I beg and entreat you, be on your guard against these deadly fascinations; do not suffer appeals to national pride to blind you to the dictates of justice.

Remember the rights of the savage, as we call him. Remember that the happiness of his humble home, remember that the sanctity of life in the hill villages of Afghanistan among the winter snows, is as inviolable in the eye of Almighty God as can be your own. Remember that He who has united you together as human beings in the same flesh and blood, has bound you by the law of mutual love; that that mutual love is not limited by the shores of this island, is not limited by the boundaries of Christian civilization; that it passes over the whole surface of the earth, and embraces the meanest along with the greatest in its unmeasured scope. And, therefore, I think that in appealing to you ungrudgingly to open your own feelings, and bear your own part in a political crisis like this, we are making no inappropriate demand, but are beseeching you to fulfil a duty which belongs to you, which, so far from involving any departure from your character as women, is associated with the fulfilment of that character, and the performance of its duties; the neglect of which would in future times be to you a source of pain and just mortification, and the fulfilment of which will serve to gild your own future years with sweet remembrances, and to warrant you in hoping that, each in your own place and sphere, you have raised your voice for justice, and have striven to mitigate the sorrows and misfortunes of mankind.

•

## 27 November 1879, West Calder

### *'Liberty for ourselves, Empire over the rest of mankind'*

*Triumphal arches had been erected along the route as Gladstone travelled to West Calder, and its streets were lit by hundreds of fairy lanterns at night.*

I am sorry to find that that which I call the pharisaical assertion of our own superiority has found its way alike into the practice and seemingly into the theories of the government. I am not going to assert anything which is not known, but the Prime Minister has said that there is one day in the year – namely, the 9th of November, Lord Mayor's Day – on which the language of sense and truth is to be heard amidst the surrounding din of idle rumours generated and fledged in the brains of irresponsible scribes. I do not agree, gentlemen, in that panegyric upon the 9th of November . . .

On that day the Prime Minister, speaking out – I do not question for a moment his own sincere opinion – made what I think one of the most unhappy and ominous allusions ever made by a minister of this country. He quoted certain words, easily rendered as 'Empire and Liberty' – words (he said) of a Roman statesman, words descriptive of the state of Rome – and he quoted them as words which were capable of legitimate application to the position and circumstances of England. I join issue with the Prime Minister upon that subject, and I affirm that nothing can be more fundamentally unsound, more practically ruinous, than the establishment of Roman analogies for the guidance of British policy.

What, gentlemen, was Rome? Rome was indeed an imperial state, you may tell me – I know not, I cannot read the counsels of Providence – a state having a mission to subdue the world; but a state whose very basis it was to deny the equal rights, to proscribe the independent existence, of other nations. That, gentlemen, was the Roman idea. It has been partially and not ill described in three lines of a translation from Virgil by our great poet Dryden, which run as follows:

> O Rome! 'tis thine alone with awful sway
> To rule mankind, and make the world obey,
> Disposing peace and war thine own majestic way.

We are told to fall back upon this example. No doubt the word 'Empire' was qualified with the word 'Liberty'. But what did the two words 'Liberty' and 'Empire' mean in a Roman mouth? They meant simply this – 'Liberty for ourselves, Empire over the rest of mankind.'

I do not think, gentlemen, that this ministry, or any other ministry, is going to place us in the position of Rome. What I object to is the revival of the idea – I care not how feebly, I care not even how, from a philosophic or historic point of view, how ridiculous the attempt at this revival may be. I say it indicates an intention – I say it indicates a frame of mind, and that frame of mind, unfortunately, I find, has been consistent with the policy of which I have given you some illustrations – the policy of denying to others the rights that we claim ourselves. No doubt, gentlemen, Rome may have had its work to do, and Rome did its work. But modern times have brought a different state of things. Modern times have established a sisterhood of nations, equal, independent; each of them built up under that legitimate defence which public law affords to every nation, living within its own borders, and seeking to perform its own affairs; but if one thing more than another has been detestable to Europe, it has been the appearance upon the stage from time to time of men who, even in the times of the Christian civilization, have been thought to aim at universal dominion. It was this aggressive disposition on the part of Louis XIV, King of France, that led your forefathers, gentlemen, freely to spend their blood and treasure in a cause not immediately their own, and to struggle against the method of policy which, having Paris for its centre, seemed to aim at an universal monarchy.

•

5 December 1879, Glasgow

*'The blessed ends of prosperity and justice, liberty and peace'*

*In the morning, Gladstone addressed the students of Glasgow University as Lord Rector. Then in the afternoon he spoke to 6,000 in St Andrew's Hall. Thousands had to be turned away.*

Well, gentlemen, what then is the general upshot of this review, in which I have been engaged since I came to Scotland; which I have had, I feel it more than any can, no power adequately to conduct, but yet which I hope I have not gone through without bringing out into the light, and bringing home to the mind and the heart, some truths at least which it is material for this nation to know? What is the general upshot? Let us look at it together. I will use the fewest words. We have finance in confusion; we have legislation in intolerable arrear; we have honour compromised by the breach of public law; we have public distress aggravated by the destruction of confidence; we have Russia aggrandized and yet estranged; we have Turkey befriended as we say, but mutilated, and sinking every day; we have Europe restless and disturbed – Europe, which, after the Treaty of Paris, at all events so far as the Eastern Question was concerned, had something like rest for a period approaching twenty years, has, almost ere the ink of the Treaty of Berlin is dry, been agitated from end to end with rumours and alarms, so that on the last 10th of November we were told that the Prime Minister thought that peace might be preserved, but on the previous 9th of November – namely, four months after the Treaty – it had been much more doubtful. In Africa you have before you the memory of bloodshed, of military disaster, the record of 10,000 Zulus – such is the computation of Bishop Colenso – slain for no other offence than their attempt to defend against your artillery with their naked bodies their hearths and homes, their wives and families. You have the invasion of a free people in the Transvaal; and you have, I fear, in one quarter or another – I will not enter into details, which might be injurious to the public interest – prospects of further disturbance and shedding of blood. You have Afghanistan ruined; you have India not advanced, but thrown back in government, subjected to heavy and unjust charges, subjected to what may well be termed, in comparison with the mild government of former years, a system of oppression; and with all this you have had at home, in matters which I will not now detail, the law broken, and the rights of Parliament invaded. Gentlemen, amidst the whole of this pestilent activity – for so I must call it – this distress and bloodshed which we have either produced or largely shared in producing, not in one instance down to the Treaty of Berlin, and down to the war in Afghanistan – not in one instance did we either do a deed, or speak an effectual word, on behalf of liberty. Such is the upshot, gentlemen, of the sad enumeration. To call this policy Conservative is, in my opinion, a pure mockery, and an abuse of terms. Whatever it may be in its motive, it is in its result disloyal, it is in its essence thoroughly subversive. There is no democrat, there is no agitator, there is no propounder of anti-rent doctrines, whatever mischief he may do, who can compare in mischief with possessors of authority who thus invert, and who thus degrade, the principles of free government in the British Empire. Gentlemen, I wish to end as I began. Is this the way, or is this not the way, in which a free nation, inhabiting these islands, wishes to be governed? Will the people, be it now or be it months hence, ratify the deeds that have been done, and assume upon themselves that tremendous responsibility? The whole humble aim, gentlemen, of my proceedings has been to bring home, as far as was in my power, this great question to the mind and to the conscience of the community at large. If I cannot decide the issue – and of course I have no power to decide it – I wish at least to endeavour to make it understood by those who can. And I cherish the hope that

> When the hurly-burly's done,
> When the battle's lost and won,

I may be able to bear home with me, at least, this consolation, that I have spared no effort to mark the point at which the roads divide – the one path which plunges into suffering, discredit, and dishonour, the other which slowly, perhaps, but surely, leads a free and a high-minded people towards the blessed ends of prosperity and justice, of liberty and peace.

*Gladstone was returned to power four months later.*

•

# WILLIAM GLADSTONE
## 26 April 1883

### 'The most inexpressible calamity'

*Charles Bradlaugh was an atheist and a reputed republican, causes that Gladstone detested. As an atheist, Bradlaugh claimed the right to take the oath of allegiance by affirming, since the words 'So help me God' had no meaning for him. His claim was rejected and he was repeatedly expelled from the Commons, only to be re-elected.*

*In April 1883, Gladstone won round the Archbishop of Canterbury and moved a bill to enable unbelievers to affirm, as Quakers and Jews were already entitled to do. His speech on the second reading, with a section of the Liberal party in open revolt, was one of his noblest performances.*

Many members of this House will recollect, perhaps, the noble and majestic lines – for such they are – of the Latin poet –

> Omnis enim per se divom natura necesse est,
> Immortali aevo summa cum pace fruatur;
> Sejuncta a nostris rebus, semotaque longe.
> Nam privata dolore omni, privata periclis,
> Ipsa suis pollens opibus, nihil indiga nostri,
> Nec bene promeritis capitur nec tangitur ira.

'Divinity exists' – as these, I must say, magnificent words set forth – 'in remote, inaccessible recesses of which we know nothing; but with us it has no dealing, with us it has no relation.' Sir, I have purposely gone back to ancient times, because the discussion is less invidious than the discussion of modern schools of opinion. But, sir, I do not hesitate to say that the specific evil, the specific form of irreligion, with which in educated society in this country you have to contend, and with respect to which you ought to be on your guard, is not blank atheism. That is a rare form of opinion, and it is seldom met with. But what is frequently met with are those various forms of opinion which teach us that whatever there be beyond the visible scene, whatever there be beyond this short span of life, you know and can know nothing of it, and that it is a visionary and a bootless undertaking to endeavour to establish relations with it. That is the specific mischief of the age; but that mischief you do not attempt to touch. Nay, more; you glory in the state of the law that now prevails. All differences of religion you wish to tolerate. You wish to allow everybody to enter your Chamber who admits the existence of Deity. You would seek to admit Voltaire. That is a specimen of your toleration. But Voltaire was not a taciturn foe of Christianity. He was the author of that painful and awful phrase that goes to the heart of every Christian – and goes, I believe, to the heart of many a man professing religion who is not a Christian – *ecrasez l'infame*. Voltaire was a believer in God; he would not have had the slightest difficulty in taking the oath; and you are working up the country to something like a crusade on this question; endeavouring to strengthen in the minds of the people the false notion that you have got a real test, a real safeguard; that Christianity is still generally safe, with certain unavoidable exceptions, under the protecting aegis of the oath within the walls of this Chamber. And it is for that you are entering on a great religious war! I hold, then, that this contention of our opponents is disparaging to religion; it is idle; and it is also highly irrational.

After all that has been said, and after the flood of accusations and invective that has been poured out, I have thought it right at great length and very seriously to show that, at all events, whether we be beaten or not, we do not decline the battle, and that we are not going to allow it to be said that the interests of religion are put in peril, and that they are to find their defenders only on the opposite side of the House. That sincere and conscientious defenders of those interests are to be found there I do not question at this moment; but I do contend with my whole heart and soul that the interests of religion, as well as the interests of civil liberty, are concerned in the passage of this measure. My reasons, Sir, for the passing of the bill may be summed up in a few words. If I were asked to put a construction on this Oath as it stands, I probably should give it a higher meaning than most gentlemen opposite. It is my opinion, as far as I can presume to form one, that the Oath has in it a very large flavour of Christianity. There are other forms of positive attestation, recognized by other systems of religion, which may enable the oath to be taken by the removal of the words 'So help me God', and the substitution of some other words, or some symbolical act, involving the idea of Deity, and responsibility to the Deity. But I think we ought to estimate the real character of this oath according to the intention of the legislature. The oath does not consist of spoken words alone. The spoken words are accompanied by the corroborative act of kissing the Book. What is the meaning of that? According to the intention of the legislature, I certainly should say that that act is an import of the acceptance of the divine revelation. There have been other forms in other countries. I believe in Scotland the form is still maintained of holding up the right hand instead of kissing the Book. In Spain the form is, I believe, that of kissing the Cross. In Italy, I think, at one time, the form was that of laying the hand on the Gospel. All these different forms meant, according to the original intention, an acceptance of Christianity. But you do not yourselves venture to say that the law could be applied in that sense. A law of this kind is like a coin spick-and-span brand-new from the Mint carrying upon it its edges in all their sharpness and freshness; but it wears down in passing from hand to hand, and, though there is a residuum, yet the distinctive features disappear.

Whatever my opinion may be as to the original vitality of the oath, I think there is very little difference of opinion as to what it has now become. It has become, as my honourable friend says, a theistic test. It is taken as no more than a theistic test. It does, as I think, involve a reference to Christianity. But while this is my personal opinion, it is not recognized by authority, and, at any rate, does not prevail in practice; for some gentlemen in the other House of Parliament, if not in this also, have written works against the Christian religion, and yet have taken the oath. But, undoubtedly, it is not good for any of us to force this test so flavoured, or even if not so flavoured, upon men who cannot take it with a full and a cordial acceptance. It is bad – it is demoralizing to do so. It is all very well to say – 'Oh, yes; but it is their responsibility.' That is not, in my view, a satisfactory answer.

A seat in this House is to the ordinary Englishman in early life, or, perhaps, in middle and mature life, when he has reached a position of distinction in his career, the highest prize of his ambition. But if you place between him and that prize not only the necessity of conforming to certain civil conditions, but the adoption of certain religious words, and if these words are not justly measured to the condition of his conscience and of his convictions, you give him an inducement – nay, I do not go too far when I say you offer him a bribe to tamper with those convictions – to do violence to his conscience in order that he may not be stigmatized by being shut out from what is held to be the noblest privilege of the English citizen – that of representing his fellow-citizens in Parliament. And, therefore, I say that, besides our duty to vindicate the principle of civil and religious liberty, which totally detaches religious controversy from the enjoyment of civil rights, it is most important that the House should consider the moral effect of this test. It is a purely theistic test. Viewed as a theistic test, it embraces no acknowledgement of Providence, of divine government, of responsibility, or of retribution. It involves nothing but a bare and abstract admission – a form void of all practical meaning and concern. This is not a wholesome, but an unwholesome lesson. Yet more. I own that although I am now, perhaps, going to injure myself by bringing the name of Mr Bradlaugh into this controversy, I am strongly of opinion that the present controversy should come to a close. I have no fear of atheism in this House. Truth is the expression of the divine mind; and however little our feeble vision may be able to discern the means by which God will provide for its preservation, we may leave the matter in his hands, and we may be quite sure that a firm and courageous application of every principle of justice and of equity is the best method we can adopt for the preservation and influence of truth.

I must painfully record my opinion that grave injury has been done to religion in many minds – not in instructed minds, but in those which are ill-instructed or partially instructed, which have a large claim on our consideration – in consequence of steps which have, unhappily, been taken. Great mischief has been done in many minds through the resistance offered to the man elected by the constituency of Northampton, which a portion of the community believe to be unjust. When they see the profession of religion and the interests of religion ostensibly associated with what they are deeply convinced is injustice, they are led to questions about religion itself, which they see to be associated with injustice. Unbelief attracts a sympathy which it would not otherwise enjoy; and the upshot is to impair those convictions and that religious faith, the loss of which I believe to be the most inexpressible calamity which can fall either upon a man or upon a nation.

*The bill was lost by three votes. In 1888 Bradlaugh piloted an Affirmation Bill through the Commons.*

•

# THE AGE OF LINCOLN

### 'On the Red Man's trail'

*An Indian burial ground at Suquamish in the state of Washington contains the grave of Seattle, the great Indian chief. The inscription on the granite shaft reads: 'Seattle, chief of the Suquamish and Allied Tribes, died June 7, 1866, the firm friend of the Whites, and for him the City of Seattle was named by its founders.'*

*As a boy Seattle witnessed the arrival in Puget Sound of the British explorer Vancouver in the* Discovery. *The friendliness of the explorers convinced him that peace, not war, was the right path to follow. He converted to Christianity and inaugurated morning and evening prayers among his people. At first whites shared his people's fish and venison, but relations with the Indians deteriorated with the arrival of more and more settlers. Several tribes tried to drive whites out in 1854–5.*

*So in January 1855 Isaac I. Stevens, Washington's first governor and Superintendent of Indian affairs, called Seattle's bands together and told them of a treaty which would place them on reservations. Seattle was the first to sign. Seattle, more than six feet tall, broad-shouldered, deep-chested, replied to Stevens in a resounding voice which could be heard by all his people along the beach. (This is a translation by Dr Henry A. Smith, who had mastered the Salish language, which is accepted as accurate.)*

Yonder sky that has wept tears of compassion upon our fathers for centuries untold, and which to us looks eternal, may change. Today it is fair, tomorrow it may be overcast with clouds.

My words are like the stars that never set. What Seattle says the Great Chief at Washington can rely upon with as much certainty as our paleface brothers can rely upon the return of the seasons.

The son of the White Chief says his father sends us greetings of friendship and good will. This is kind of him, for we know he has little need of our friendship in return because his people are many. They are like the grass that covers the vast prairies, while my people are few; they resemble the scattering trees of a storm-swept plain.

The Great – and I presume – good White Chief sends us word that he wants to buy our lands but is willing to allow us to reserve enough to live on comfortably. This indeed appears generous, for the Red Man no longer has rights that he need respect, and the offer may be wise, also, for we are no longer in need of a great country.

There was a time when our people covered the whole land as the waves of a wind-ruffled sea covers its shell-paved floor, but that time has long since passed away with the greatness of tribes now almost forgotten. I will not dwell on nor mourn over our untimely decay, nor reproach my paleface brothers with hastening it, for we, too, may have been somewhat to blame.

Youth is impulsive. When our young men grow angry at some real or imaginary wrong, and disfigure their faces with black paint, their hearts also are disfigured and turn black, and then they are often cruel and relentless and know no bounds, and our old men are unable to restrain them.

Thus it has ever been. Thus it was when the white man first began to push our forefathers westward. But let us hope that the hostilities between the Red Man and his paleface brother may never return. We would have everything to lose and nothing to gain.

It is true that revenge by young braves is considered gain, even at the cost of their own lives, but old men who stay at home in times of war, and mothers who have sons to lose, know better.

Our good father at Washington – for I presume he is now our father as well as yours, since King George has moved his boundaries farther north – our great and good father, I say, sends us word that if we do as he desires he will protect us.

His brave warriors will be to us a bristling wall of strength, and his great ships of war will fill our harbors so that our ancient enemies far to the northward – the Sinsiams, Hydas and Tsimpsians – will no longer frighten our women and old men. Then will he be our father and we his children.

But can that ever be? Your God is not our God! Your God loves your people and hates mine! He folds His strong arms lovingly around the white man and leads him as a father leads his infant son – but He has forsaken His red children, if they are really His. Our God, the Great Spirit, seems, also, to have forsaken us. Your God makes your people wax strong every day – soon they will fill all the land.

My people are ebbing away like a fast-receding tide that will never flow again. The white man's God cannot love His red children or He would protect them. We seem to be orphans who can look nowhere for help.

How, then, can we become brothers? How can your God become our

God and renew our prosperity and awaken in us dreams of returning greatness?

Your God seems to us to be partial. He came to the white man. We never saw Him, never heard His voice. He gave the white man laws, but had no word for His red children whose teeming millions once filled this vast continent as the stars fill the firmament.

No. We are two distinct races, and must ever remain so, with separate origins and separate destinies. There is little in common between us.

To us the ashes of our ancestors are sacred and their final resting place is hallowed ground, while you wander far from the graves of your ancestors and, seemingly, without regret.

Your religion was written on tablets of stone by the iron finger of an angry God, lest you might forget it. The Red Man could never comprehend nor remember it.

Our religion is the traditions of our ancestors – the dreams of our old men, given to them in the solemn hours of night by the Great Spirit, and the visions of our Sachems, and is written in the hearts of our people.

Your dead cease to love you and the land of their nativity as soon as they pass the portals of the tomb – they wander far away beyond the stars, are soon forgotten and never return.

Our dead never forget this beautiful world that gave them being. They still love its winding rivers, its great mountains and its sequestered vales, and they ever yearn in tenderest affection over the lonely-hearted living, and often return to visit, guide and comfort them.

Day and night cannot dwell together. The Red Man has ever fled the approach of the white man, as the changing mist on the mountain side flees before the blazing sun.

However, your proposition seems a just one, and I think that my people will accept it and will retire to the reservation you offer them. Then we will dwell apart in peace, for the words of the Great White Chief seem to be the voice of Nature speaking to my people out of the thick darkness, that is fast gathering around them like a dense fog floating inward from a midnight sea.

It matters little where we pass the remnant of our days. They are not many. The Indian's night promises to be dark. No bright star hovers above his horizon. Sad-voiced winds moan in the distance. Some grim Fate of our race is on the Red Man's trail, and wherever he goes he will still hear the sure approaching footsteps of his fell destroyer and prepare to stolidly meet his doom, as does the wounded doe that hears the approaching footsteps of the hunter.

A few more moons, a few more winters – and not one of all the mighty hosts that once filled this broad land and that now roam in fragmentary bands through these vast solitudes or lived in happy homes, protected by the Great Spirit, will remain to weep over the graves of a people once as powerful and as hopeful as your own!

But why should I repine? Why should I murmur at the fate of my people? Tribes are made up of individuals and are no better than they. Men come and go like the waves of the sea. A tear, a tamanamus, a dirge and they are gone from our longing eyes forever. It is the order of Nature. Even the white man, whose God walked and talked with him as friend to friend, is not exempt from the common destiny. We may be brothers, after all. We will see.

We will ponder your proposition, and when we decide we will tell you. But should we accept it, I here and now make this the first condition – that we will not be denied the privilege, without molestation, of visiting at will the graves of our ancestors, friends and children.

Every part of this country is sacred to my people. Every hillside, every valley, every plain and grove has been hallowed by some fond memory or some sad experience of my tribe. Even the rocks, which seem to lie dumb as they swelter in the sun along the silent sea shore in solemn grandeur, thrill with memories of past events connected with the lives of my people.

The very dust under your feet responds more lovingly to our footsteps than to yours, because it is the ashes of our ancestors, and our bare feet are conscious of the sympathetic touch, for the soil is rich with the life of our kindred.

The noble braves, fond mothers, glad, happy-hearted maidens, and even the little children, who lived and rejoiced here for a brief season, and whose very names are now forgotten, still love these sombre solitudes and their deep fastnesses which, at eventide, grow shadowy with the presence of dusky spirits.

And when the last Red Man shall have perished from the earth and his memory among the white men shall have become a myth, these shores will swarm with the invisible dead of my tribe; and when your children's children shall think themselves alone in the fields, the store, the shop, upon the highway, or in the silence of the pathless woods, they will not be alone. In all the earth there is no place dedicated to solitude.

At night, when the streets of your cities and villages will be silent and you think them deserted, they will throng with the returning hosts that once filled and still love this beautiful land.

The white man will never be alone. Let him be just and deal kindly with my people, for the dead are not powerless.

Dead – did I say? There is no death. Only a change of worlds!

•

## WILLIAM LLOYD GARRISON
1854

### '*Man above all institutions!*'

*By 1854, it was twenty-three years since the brilliant journalist William Lloyd Garrison (1805–79) had founded* The Liberator, *the abolitionist journal whose sale was never more than 3,000 but which by its eloquence and courage kept the slavery issue alive until the Thirteenth Amendment prohibiting slavery was passed in 1865. As this speech demonstrates, he refused the slightest compromise with slavery; indeed, he advocated Northern secession in 1843 because the compact between North and South was 'a covenant with death and an agreement with hell'.*

I am a believer in that portion of the Declaration of American Independence in which it is set forth, as among self-evident truths, 'that all men are created equal; that they are endowed by their Creator with certain inalienable rights; that among these are life, liberty, and the pursuit of happiness'. Hence, I am an abolitionist. Hence, I cannot but regard oppression in every form – and most of all, that which turns a man into a thing – with indignation and abhorrence. Not to cherish these feelings would be recreancy to principle. They who desire me to be dumb on the subject of slavery, unless I will open my mouth in its defense, ask me to give the lie to my professions, to degrade my manhood, and to stain my soul. I will not be a liar, a poltroon, or a hypocrite, to accommodate any party, to gratify any sect, to escape any odium or peril, to save any interest, to preserve any institution, or to promote any object. Convince me that one man may rightfully make another man his slave, and I will no longer subscribe to the Declaration of Independence. Convince me that liberty is not the inalienable birthright of every human being, of whatever complexion or clime, and I will give that instrument to the consuming fire. I do not know how to espouse freedom and slavery together. I do not know how to worship God and Mammon at the same time. If other men choose to go upon all fours, I choose to stand erect, as God designed every man to stand. If, practically falsifying its heaven-attested principles, this nation denounces me for refusing to imitate its example, then, adhering all the more tenaciously to those principles, I will not cease to rebuke it for its guilty inconsistency. Numerically, the contest may be an unequal one, for the time being; but the author of liberty and the source of justice, the adorable God, is more than multitudinous, and he will defend the right. My crime is that I will not go with the multitude to do evil. My singularity is that when I say that freedom is of God and slavery is of the devil, I mean just what I say. My fanaticism is that I insist on the American people abolishing slavery or ceasing to prate of the rights of man . . .

The abolitionism which I advocate is as absolute as the law of God, and as unyielding as his throne. It admits of no compromise. Every slave is a stolen man; every slaveholder is a man stealer. By no precedent, no example, no law, no compact, no purchase, no bequest, no inheritance, no combination of circumstances, is slaveholding right or justifiable. While a slave remains in his fetters, the land must have no rest. Whatever sanctions his doom must be pronounced accursed. The law that makes him a chattel is to be trampled underfoot; the compact that is formed at his expense, and cemented with his blood, is null and void; the church that consents to his enslavement is horribly atheistical; the religion that receives to its communion the enslaver is the embodiment of all criminality. Such, at least, is the verdict of my own soul, on the supposition that I am to be the slave; that my wife is to be sold from me for the vilest purposes; that my children are to be torn from my arms, and disposed of to the highest bidder, like sheep in the market. And who am I but a man? What right have I to be free, that another man cannot prove himself to possess by nature? Who or what are my wife and children, that they should not be herded with four-footed beasts, as well as others thus sacredly related? . . .

If the slaves are not men; if they do not possess human instincts, passions, faculties, and powers; if they are below accountability, and devoid of reason; if for them there is no hope of immortality, no God, no heaven, no hell; if, in short, they are what the slave code declares them to be, rightly 'deemed, sold, taken, reputed and adjudged in law to be chattels personal in the hands of their owners and possessors, and their executors, administrators and assigns, to all intents, constructions, and purposes whatsoever'; then, undeniably, I am mad, and can no longer discriminate between a man and a beast. But, in that case, away with the horrible incongruity of giving them oral instruction, of teaching them the catechism, of recognizing them as suitably qualified to be members of Christian churches, of extending to them the ordinance of baptism, and admitting them to the communion table, and enumerating many of them as belonging to the household of faith! Let them be no more included in our religious sympathies or denominational statistics than are the dogs in our streets, the swine in our pens, or the utensils in our dwellings. It is right to own, to buy, to sell, to inherit, to breed, and to control them, in the most absolute sense. All constitutions and laws which forbid their possession ought to be so far modified or repealed as to concede the right.

But, if they are men; if they are to run the same career of immortality with ourselves; if the same law of God is over them as over all others; if they have souls to be saved or lost; if Jesus included them among those for whom he laid down his life; if Christ is within many of them 'the hope of glory'; then, when I claim for them all that we claim for ourselves, because we are created in the image of God, I am guilty of no extravagance, but am bound, by every principle of honor, by all the claims of human nature, by obedience to Almighty God, to 'remember them that are in bonds as bound with them', and to demand their immediate and unconditional emancipation . . .

These are solemn times. It is not a struggle for national salvation; for the nation, as such, seems doomed beyond recovery. The reason why the South rules, and the North falls prostrate in servile terror, is simply this: with the South, the preservation of slavery is paramount to all other considerations – above party success, denominational unity, pecuniary interest, legal integrity, and constitutional obligation. With the North, the preservation of the Union is placed above all other things – above honor, justice, freedom, integrity of soul, the Decalogue and the Golden Rule – the infinite God himself. All these she is ready to discard for the Union. Her devotion to it is the latest and the most terrible form of idolatry. She has given to the slave power a carte blanche, to be filled as it may dictate – and if, at any time, she grows restive under the yoke, and shrinks back aghast at the new atrocity contemplated, it is only necessary for that power to crack the whip of disunion over her head, as it has done again and again, and she will cower and obey like a plantation slave – for has she not sworn that she will sacrifice everything in heaven and on earth, rather than the Union?

What then is to be done? Friends of the slave, the question is not

whether by our efforts we can abolish slavery, speedily or remotely –
for duty is ours, the result is with God; but whether we will go with
the multitude to do evil, sell our birthright for a mess of pottage,
cease to cry aloud and spare not, and remain in Babylon when the
command of God is 'Come out of her, my people, that ye be not
partakers of her sins, and that ye receive not of her plagues.' Let us
stand in our lot, 'and having done all, to stand'. At least, a remnant
shall be saved. Living or dying, defeated or victorious, be it ours to
exclaim, 'No compromise with slavery! Liberty for each, for all, forever! Man above all institutions! The supremacy of God over the
whole earth!'

●

## ABRAHAM LINCOLN
### 16 October 1854

### 'The monstrous injustice of slavery'

*At forty-five, Abraham Lincoln (1809–65) had not been active in politics for
several years. Yet when the 1820 Missouri Compromise was repealed by Stephen
Douglas, Senator for Lincoln's state of Illinois, and the Kansas–Nebraska Act
of 1854 was passed, opening Federal territories that were not yet states to slavery,
he was aroused as he had never been before. He re-entered politics to work for the
repeal of the legislation.*

*He had been brooding deeply on the slavery issue, studying the debates in the
House of Representatives, poring over books in the state library and jotting down
notes for use in speeches when he set out to run for the state legislature.*

*When Douglas returned to Illinois to inspire his followers, Lincoln was
ready for him. At the state fair in Springfield on 3 October, Douglas arraigned
his opponents. As he finished, Lincoln announced that he would reply next day.*

*Without coat or collar, in ill-fitting trousers, Lincoln began his written speech
haltingly but his hesitancy soon disappeared. He was soon wet with sweat and his
matted hair became tousled as he flung back his head. Time and time again the
hall rang with applause. He spoke for four hours with a new and unexpected
power. The speech was not reported until Lincoln repeated it twelve days later at
Peoria (which is the text used below).*

I think, and shall try to show, that it is wrong; wrong in its direct effect,
letting slavery into Kansas and Nebraska – and wrong in its prospective

principle, allowing it to spread to every other part of the wide world, where men can be found inclined to take it.

This declared indifference, but as I must think, covert *real* zeal for the spread of slavery, I cannot but hate. I hate it because of the monstrous injustice of slavery itself. I hate it because it deprives our republican example of its just influence in the world – enables the enemies of free institutions, with plausibility, to taunt us as hypocrites – causes the real friends of freedom to doubt our sincerity, and especially because it forces so many really good men amongst ourselves into an open war with the very fundamental principles of civil liberty – criticizing the Declaration of Independence, and insisting that there is no right principle of action but self-interest . . .

The doctrine of self-government is right – absolutely and eternally right – but it has no just application as here attempted. Or perhaps I should rather say that whether it has such just application depends upon whether a Negro is not or is a man. If he is not a man, why in that case he who is a man may, as a matter of self-government, do just as he pleases with him. But if the Negro *is* a man, is it not to that extent a total destruction of self-government to say that he too shall not govern himself? When the white man governs himself that is self-government; but when he governs himself, and also governs *another* man, that is *more* than self-government – that is despotism. If the Negro is a *man*, why then my ancient faith teaches me that 'all men are created equal'; and that there can be no moral right in connection with one man's making a slave of another.

Judge Douglas frequently, with bitter irony and sarcasm, paraphrases our argument by saying 'The white people of Nebraska are good enough to govern themselves, but they are not good enough to govern a few miserable Negroes!'

Well I doubt not that the people of Nebraska are, and will continue to be, as good as the average of people elsewhere. I do not say the contrary. What I do say is, that no man is good enough to govern another man, without that other's consent. I say this is the leading principle – the sheet anchor of American republicanism. Our Declaration of Independence says:

'We hold these truths to be self evident: that all men are created equal; that they are endowed by their Creator with certain inalienable rights; that among these are life, liberty, and the pursuit of happiness. That to secure these rights, governments are instituted among men, deriving their just powers from the consent of the governed.'

I have quoted so much at this time merely to show that according to our ancient faith the just powers of governments are derived from the consent of the governed. Now the relation of masters and slaves is, *pro tanto*, a total violation of this principle. The master not only governs the slave without his consent; but he governs him by a set of rules altogether different from those which he prescribes for himself. Allow *all* the governed an equal voice in the government, and that, and that only, is self-government . . .

Some men, mostly Whigs, who condemn the repeal of the Missouri Compromise, nevertheless hesitate to go for its restoration, lest they be thrown in company with the abolitionist. Will they allow me as an old Whig to tell them good humoredly that I think this is very silly? Stand with anybody that stands right. Stand with him while he is right and part with him when he goes wrong. Stand with the abolitionist in restoring the Missouri Compromise; and stand against him when he attempts to repeal the fugitive slave law. In the latter case you stand with the southern disunionist. What of that? you are still right. In both cases you are right. In both cases you oppose the dangerous extremes. In both you stand on middle ground and hold the ship level and steady. In both you are national and nothing less than national. This is good old Whig ground. To desert such ground, because of any company, is to be less than a Whig – less than a man – less than an American . . .

Little by little, but steadily as man's march to the grave, we have been giving up the old for the new faith. Near eighty years ago we began by declaring that all men are created equal; but now from that beginning we have run down to the other declaration, that for some men to enslave others is a 'sacred right of self-government'. These principles cannot stand together. They are as opposite as God and Mammon; and whoever holds to the one must despise the other . . .

Fellow countrymen – Americans South, as well as North, shall we make no effort to arrest this? Already the Liberal party throughout the world express the apprehension 'that the one retrograde institution in America is undermining the principles of progress, and fatally violating the noblest political system the world ever saw'. This is not the taunt of enemies, but the warning of friends. Is it quite safe to disregard it – to despise it? Is there no danger to liberty itself in discarding the earliest practice and first precept of our ancient faith? In our greedy chase to make profit of the Negro, let us beware, lest we 'cancel and tear to pieces' even the white man's charter of freedom.

Our republican robe is soiled, and trailed in the dust. Let us repurify it. Let us turn and wash it white, in the spirit if not the blood of the Revolution. Let us turn slavery from its claims of 'moral right', back upon its existing legal rights, and its arguments of 'necessity'. Let us return it to the position our fathers gave it; and there let it rest in peace. Let us readopt the Declaration of Independence, and with it the practices and policy which harmonize with it. Let North and South – let all Americans – let all lovers of liberty everywhere – join in the great and good work. If we do this, we shall not only have saved the Union; but we shall have so saved it as .to make, and to keep it, forever worthy of the saving. We shall have so saved it that the succeeding millions of free happy people, the world over, shall rise up and call us blessed, to the latest generations . . .

*With this speech, Lincoln began the rise which was to lead him to the presidency. Within two years he was leader of the Republican Party in Illinois.*

•

## ABRAHAM LINCOLN
## 16 June 1858

### *'A house divided against itself cannot stand'*

*During the early summer of 1858, ninety-five Republican county conventions nominated Lincoln as their choice as Republican senator to fight Stephen Douglas – and his nomination was assured when the state convention met at Springfield on 16 June and he was unanimously adopted.*

*Lincoln had prepared his acceptance speech carefully, writing it on scraps of paper deposited in his hat. When he showed it to a few friends the day before, all but his legal partner Willian Hernden were astonished and horrified. Lincoln's mind was made up. 'Friends,' he said, 'this thing has been retarded long enough. The time has come when these sentiments should be uttered; and if it is decreed that I should go down because of this speech, then let me go down linked to the truth – let me die in the advocacy of what is just and right.'*

*Most of the speech was a detailed study of the history of legal judgements on slavery. The famous opening and some of the peroration follow.*

If we could first know where we are, and whither we are tending, we could better judge what to do, and how to do it. We are now far into the fifth year since a policy was initiated with the avowed object and confident promise of putting an end to slavery agitation. Under the operation of that policy, that agitation has not only not ceased, but has constantly augmented. In my opinion, it will not cease until a crisis shall have been reached and passed. 'A house divided against itself cannot stand.' I believe this government cannot endure permanently half slave and half free. I do not expect the Union to be dissolved – I do not expect the house to fall – but I do expect it will cease to be divided. It will become all one thing or all the other. Either the opponents of slavery will arrest the further spread of it, and place it where the public mind shall rest in the belief that it is in the course of ultimate extinction; or its advocates will push it forward till it shall become alike lawful in all the states, old as well as new – North as well as South.

Have we no tendency to the latter condition?

Let anyone who doubts carefully contemplate that now almost complete legal combination – piece of machinery, so as to speak – compounded of the Nebraska doctrine and the Dred Scott decision. Let him consider not only what work the machinery is adapted to do, and how well adapted, but also let him study the history of its construction, and trace, if he can, or rather fail, if he can, to trace the evidence of design and concert of action among its chief architects, from the beginning.

The new year of 1854 found slavery excluded from more than half the states by state Constitutions, and from most of the national territory by Congressional prohibition. Four days later commenced the struggle which ended in repealing that Congressional prohibition. This opened all the national territory to slavery, and was the first point gained.

But, so far, Congress only had acted, and an endorsement by the people, real or apparent, was indispensable to save the point already gained and give chance for more.

This necessity had not been overlooked, but had been provided for, as well as might be, in the notable argument of 'Squatter Sovereignty', otherwise called 'sacred right of self-government', which latter phrase, though expressive of the only rightful basis of any government, was so perverted in this attempted use of it as to amount to just this: that if any one man choose to enslave another, no third man shall be allowed to object. That argument was incorporated into the Nebraska Bill itself, in the language which follows:

It being the true intent and meaning of this act not to legislate slavery into any territory or state, nor to exclude it therefrom, but to leave the people thereof perfectly free to form and regulate their domestic institutions in their own way, subject only to the Constitution of the United States.

Then opened the roar of loose declamation in favor of 'Squatter Sovereignty', and 'sacred right of self-government'. 'But,' said opposition members, 'let us amend the bill so as to expressly declare that the people of the territory may exclude slavery.' 'Not we,' said the friends of the measure; and down they voted the amendment.

While the Nebraska Bill was passing through Congress, a law case involving the question of a Negro's freedom, by reason of his owner having voluntarily taken him first into a free state and then into a territory covered by the Congressional prohibition, and held him as a slave for a long time in each, was passing through the United States Circuit Court for the District of Missouri; and both Nebraska Bill and lawsuit were brought to a decision in the same month of May, 1854. The Negro's name was 'Dred Scott', which name now designates the decision finally made in the case . . .

The several points of the Dred Scott decision, in connection with Senator Douglas's 'care-not' policy, constitute the piece of machinery, in its present state of advancement. This was the third point gained. The working points of that machinery are:

First, that no Negro slave, imported as such from Africa, and no descendant of such slave, can ever be a citizen of any state, in the sense of that term as used in the Constitution of the United States. This point is made in order to deprive the Negro, in every possible event, of the benefit of that provision of the United States Constitution which declares that: 'The citizens of each state shall be entitled to all privileges and immunities of citizens in the several states.'

Second, that 'subject to the Constitution of the United States', neither Congress nor a territorial legislature can exclude slavery from any United States territory. This point is made in order that individual men may fill up the territories with slaves, without danger of losing them as property, and thus to enhance the chances of permanency to the institution through all the future.

Third, that whether the holding a Negro in actual slavery in a free state makes him free, as against the holder, the United States courts will not decide, but will leave to be decided by the courts of any slave state the Negro may be forced into by the master. This point is made, not to be pressed immediately; but, if acquiesced in for a while, and apparently

endorsed by the people at an election, then to sustain the logical
conclusion that what Dred Scott's master might lawfully do with Dred
Scott, in the free state of Illinois, every other master may lawfully do
with any other one, or one thousand slaves, in Illinois or in any other
free state.

Auxiliary to all this, and working hand in hand with it, the Nebraska
doctrine, or what is left of it, is to educate and mold public opinion, at
least Northern public opinion, not to care whether slavery is voted
down or voted up. This shows exactly where we now are; and partially,
also, whither we are tending . . .

By the Nebraska Bill, the people of a state, as well as a territory, were
to be left 'perfectly free', 'subject only to the Constitution'. Why
mention a state? They were legislating for territories, and not for or
about states. Certainly the people of a state are and ought to be subject
to the Constitution of the United States; but why is mention of this
lugged into this merely territorial law? Why are the people of a territory
and the people of a state therein lumped together, and their relation to
the Constitution therein treated as being precisely the same? While the
opinion of the court, by Chief Justice Taney, in the Dred Scott case, and
the separate opinions of all the concurring judges, expressly declare that
the Constitution of the United States neither permits Congress nor a
territorial legislature to exclude slavery from any United States territory,
they all omit to declare whether or not the same Constitution permits a
state, or the people of a state, to exclude it. Possibly this is a mere
omission; but who can be quite sure, if McLean or Curtis [Supreme
Court Justices] had sought to get into the opinion a declaration of
unlimited power in the people of a state to exclude slavery from their
limits, just as Chase and Mace [Supreme Court justices] sought to get
such declaration, in behalf of the people of a territory, into the Nebraska
Bill — I ask, who can be quite sure that it would not have been voted
down in the one case as it had been in the other? The nearest approach
to the point of declaring the power of a state over slavery is made by
Judge Nelson. He approaches it more than once, using the precise idea,
and almost the language, too, of the Nebraska Act. On one occasion, his
exact language is, 'except in cases where the power is restrained by the
Constitution of the United States, the law of the state is supreme over
the subject of slavery within its jurisdiction'. In what cases the power of
the states is so restrained by the United States Constitution is left an
open question, precisely as the same question, as to the restraint on the
power of the territories, was left open in the Nebraska Act. Put this and

that together, and we have another nice little niche, which we may ere long see filled with another Supreme Court decision, declaring that the Constitution of the United States does not permit a state to exclude slavery from its limits. And this may especially be expected if the doctrine of 'care not whether slavery be voted down or voted up' shall gain upon the public mind sufficiently to give promise that such a decision can be maintained when made.

Such a decision is all that slavery now lacks of being alike lawful in all the states. Welcome or unwelcome, such decision is probably coming, and will soon be upon us, unless the power of the present political dynasty shall be met and overthrown. We shall lie down pleasantly dreaming that the people of Missouri are on the verge of making their state free, and we shall awake to the reality instead that the Supreme Court has made Illinois a slave state. To meet and overthrow the power of that dynasty is the work now before all those who would prevent that consummation. This is what we have to do. How can we best do it?

There are those who denounce us openly to their own friends, and yet whisper us softly, that Senator Douglas is the aptest instrument there is with which to effect that object. They wish us to infer all from the fact that he now has a little quarrel with the present head of the dynasty; and that he has regularly voted with us on a single point, upon which he and we have never differed. They remind us that he is a great man, and that the largest of us are very small ones. Let this be granted. But 'a living dog is better than a dead lion'. Judge Douglas, if not a dead lion, for this work, is at least a caged and toothless one. How can he oppose the advances of slavery? He does not care anything about it. His avowed mission is impressing the 'public heart' to care nothing about it. A leading Douglas Democratic newspaper thinks Douglas's superior talent will be needed to resist the revival of the African slave trade. Does Douglas believe an effort to revive that trade is approaching? He has not said so. Does he really think so? But if it is, how can he resist it? For years he has labored to prove it a sacred right of white men to take Negro slaves into the new territories. Can he possibly show that it is less a sacred right to buy them where they can be bought cheapest? And unquestionably they can be bought cheaper in Africa than in Virginia. He has done all in his power to reduce the whole question of slavery to one of a mere right of property; and, as such, how can he oppose the foreign slave trade – how can he refuse that trade in that 'property' shall be 'perfectly free' – unless he does it as a protection to the home production? And as the home producers will probably not ask the protection, he will be wholly without a ground of opposition.

Senator Douglas holds, we know, that a man may rightfully be wiser today than he was yesterday – that he may rightfully change when he finds himself wrong. But can we, for that reason, run ahead and infer that he will make any particular change, of which he, himself, has given no intimation? Can we safely base our action upon any such vague inference? Now, as ever, I wish not to misrepresent Judge Douglas's position, question his motives, or do aught that can be personally offensive to him. Whenever, if ever, he and we can come together on principle so that our cause may have assistance from his great ability, I hope to have interposed no adventitious obstacle. But clearly, he is not now with us – he does not pretend to be – he does not promise ever to be.

Our cause, then, must be entrusted to, and conducted by, its own undoubted friends – those whose hands are free, whose hearts are in the work – who do care for the result. Two years ago the Republicans of the nation mustered over thirteen hundred thousand strong. We did this under the single impulse of resistance to a common danger, with every external circumstance against us. Of strange, discordant, and even hostile elements, we gathered from the four winds, and formed and fought the battle through, under the constant hot fire of a disciplined, proud, and pampered enemy. Did we brave all them to falter now? – now, when that same enemy is wavering, dissevered, and belligerent? The result is not doubtful. We shall not fail – if we stand firm, we shall not fail. Wise counsels may accelerate, or mistakes delay it, but, sooner or later, the victory is sure to come.

•

## ABRAHAM LINCOLN
### 30 October 1858

### 'I have labored for and not against the Union'

*Lincoln made more than sixty speeches during the campaign, including seven in head-to-head debates with Douglas. At Springfield, on 30 October, he reviewed his senatorial campaign in his final address.*

My friends, today closes the discussions of this canvass. The planting and the culture are over; and there remains but the preparation, and the harvest.

I stand here surrounded by friends – some political, all personal, friends, I trust. May I be indulged, in this closing scene, to say a few words of myself. I have borne a laborious and, in some respects to myself, a painful part in the contest. Through all, I have neither assailed nor wrestled with any part of the Constitution. The legal right of the Southern people to reclaim their fugitives I have constantly admitted. The legal right of Congress to interfere with their institution in the states, I have constantly denied. In resisting the spread of slavery to new territory, and with that, what appears to me to be a tendency to subvert the first principle of free government itself, my whole effort has consisted. To the best of my judgement I have labored for and not against the Union. As I have not felt, so I have not expressed any harsh sentiment toward our Southern brethren. I have constantly declared, as I really believed, the only difference between them and us is the difference of circumstances.

I have meant to assail the motives of no party or individual; and if I have, in any instance (of which I am not conscious), departed from my purpose, I regret it.

I have said that in some respects the contest has been painful to me. Myself, and those with whom I act, have been constantly accused of a purpose to destroy the Union; and bespattered with every imaginable odious epithet; and some who were friends, as it were but yesterday, have made themselves most active in this. I have cultivated patience, and made no attempt at a retort.

Ambition has been ascribed to me. God knows how sincerely I prayed from the first that this field of ambition might not be opened. I claim no insensibility to political honors; but today could the Missouri restriction be restored, and the whole slavery question replaced on the old ground of 'toleration' by necessity where it exists, with unyielding hostility to the spread of it, on principle, I would, in consideration, gladly agree that Judge Douglas should never be out, and I never in, an office, so long as we both or either live.

*Douglas beat Lincoln by 54 votes to 46, but the debates attracted national attention, turned Lincoln into a national figure and put the presidency within his reach. Lincoln said of his defeat: 'Like the boy that stumped his toe – it hurt too bad to laugh and he was too big to cry.'*

*He had his vindication two years later when he won the Republican nomination for the presidency and triumphed over his Democrat rival.*

•

## JOHN BROWN
2 November 1859

### 'The blood of millions'

*When murder stalked the plains of Kansas in 1856, the chief troublemaker was the abolitionist fanatic John Brown (1800–1859). With five of his sons, Brown murdered five unarmed men in cold blood to avenge an attack on slaves in Lawrence – and then had to fight for his life against a mob seeking yet another instalment of revenge as a reign of terror led to the burning of crops, the stealing of horses and men cut down by ambush.*

*Three years later, with some eighteen followers, Brown seized the Federal arsenal at Harpers Ferry, Virginia, killing several citizens, including a free Negro, with the aim of instigating a slave revolt. They held off Virginia militiamen and a detachment of US marines under Colonel Robert E. Lee until all but two were dead or wounded.*

*At his trial Brown was found guilty of treason, inspiring a slave rebellion, and first-degree murder. Two days later he spoke from the dock.*

I have, may it please the court, a few words to say. In the first place, I deny everything but what I have all along admitted – the design on my part to free the slaves. I intended certainly to have made a clean thing of that matter, as I did last winter when I went into Missouri and there took slaves without the snapping of a gun on either side, moved them through the country, and finally left them in Canada. I designed to have done the same thing again on a larger scale. That was all I intended. I never did intend murder, or treason, or the destruction of property, or to excite or incite slaves to rebellion, or to make insurrection.

I have another objection; and that is, it is unjust that I should suffer such a penalty. Had I interfered in the manner which I admit, and which I admit has been fairly proved (for I admire the truthfulness and candor of the greater portion of the witnesses who have testified in this case) – had I so interfered in behalf of the rich, the powerful, the intelligent, the so-called great, or in behalf of any of their friends – either father, mother, brother, sister, wife, or children, or any of that class – and suffered, and sacrificed what I have in this interference, it would have been all right; and every man in this court would have deemed it an act worthy of reward rather than punishment.

This court acknowledges, as I suppose, the validity of the law of God. I see a book kissed here which I suppose to be the Bible, or at least the New Testament. That teaches me that all things whatsoever I would that men should do to me I should do even so to them. It teaches me, further, to 'remember them that are in bonds as bound with them'. I endeavored to act up to that instruction. I say I am yet too young to understand that God is any respecter of persons. I believe that to have interfered as I have done – as I have always freely admitted I have done – in behalf of His despised poor was not wrong, but right. Now, if it is deemed necessary that I should forfeit my life for the furtherance of the ends of justice, and mingle my blood further with the blood of my children and with the blood of millions in this slave country whose rights are disregarded by wicked, cruel, and unjust enactments – I submit; so let it be done!

Let me say one word further.

I feel entirely satisfied with the treatment I have received on my trial. Considering all the circumstances, it has been more generous than I expected. But I feel no consciousness of guilt. I have stated from the first what was my intention and what was not. I never had any design against the life of any person, nor any disposition to commit treason, or excite slaves to rebel, or make any general insurrection. I never encouraged any man to do so, but always discouraged any idea of that kind.

Let me say also a word in regard to the statements made by some of those connected with me. I hear it has been stated by some of them that I have induced them to join me. But the contrary is true. I do not say this to injure them, but as regretting their weakness. There is not one of them but joined me of his own accord, and the greater part of them at their own expense. A number of them I never saw, and never had a word of conversation with, till the day they came to me; and that was for the purpose I have stated.

Now I have done.

*John Brown's raid began the chain of events that led to rebellion and war. Wendell Phillips thought that emancipation began at Harpers Ferry. After his execution Brown was immortalized in song, to the tune of the 'Battle Hymn of the Republic', sung by Union soldiers in the war: 'John Brown's body lies a-moldering in the grave, but his soul goes marching on.'*

•

ABRAHAM LINCOLN
27 February 1860

*'Let us have faith that right makes might'*

*Lincoln was already tipped as the Republican presidential candidate and starting to attract powerful support in the East when he was invited to lecture in New York. His sponsor was the Young Men's Central Republican Union, whose leaders wanted to thwart William Seward's bid for the presidency.*

*Though there was a snowstorm that night there was an audience of 1,500, the cream of New York's intellectual and cultural life, with Horace Greeley, editor of the* New York Tribune, *on the platform. Lincoln was escorted to the platform by another editor, William Callard Bryant of the* New York Evening Post.

*Any fear on the part of Lincoln, uncomfortably conscious of his new broadcloth suit, that his Western mannerisms and rural accent would amuse sophisticated Easterners was quickly dispelled by the warmth of his reception. As he addressed to fellow Republicans this stirring peroration on how they should treat the Southerners, the audience rose to its feet; shouting, waving hats and handkerchiefs, in a sustained ovation.*

*The speech was published in full next day in four New York papers, and the* Chicago Tribune *published it as a pamphlet.*

A few words now to Republicans. It is exceedingly desirable that all parts of this great Confederacy shall be at peace, and in harmony, one with another. Let us Republicans do our part to have it so. Even though much provoked, let us do nothing through passion and ill temper. Even though the Southern people will not so much as listen to us, let us calmly consider their demands, and yield to them, if, in our deliberate view of our duty, we possibly can. Judging by all they say and do, and by the subject and nature of their controversy with us, let us determine, if we can, what will satisfy them.

Will they be satisfied if the territories be unconditionally surrendered to them? We know they will not. In all their present complaints against us, the territories are scarcely mentioned. Invasions and insurrections are the rage now. Will it satisfy them, if, in the future, we have nothing to do with invasions and insurrections? We know it will not. We so know, because we know we never had anything to do with invasions and insurrections; and yet this total abstaining does not exempt us from the charge and the denunciation.

The question recurs, what will satisfy them? Simply this: We must not only let them alone, but we must, somehow, convince them that we do let them alone. This, we know by experience, is no easy task. We have been so trying to convince them from the very beginning of our organization, but with no success. In all our platforms and speeches we have constantly protested our purpose to let them alone; but this has had no tendency to convince them. Alike unavailing to convince them, is the fact that they have never detected a man of us in any attempt to disturb them.

These natural, and apparently adequate means all failing, what will convince them? This, and this only: cease to call slavery *wrong*, and join them in calling it *right*. And this must be done thoroughly – done in *acts* as well as in *words*. Silence will not be tolerated – we must place ourselves avowedly with them. Senator Douglas's new sedition law must be enacted and enforced, suppressing all declarations that slavery is wrong, whether made in politics, in presses, in pulpits, or in private. We must arrest and return their fugitive slaves with greedy pleasure. We must pull down our free state Constitutions. The whole atmosphere must be disinfected from all taint of opposition to slavery, before they will cease to believe that all their troubles proceed from us.

I am quite aware they do not state their case precisely in this way. Most of them would probably say to us: 'Let us alone, *do* nothing to us, and *say* what you please about slavery.' But we do let them alone – have never disturbed them – so that, after all, it is what we say, which dissatisfies them. They will continue to accuse us of doing, until we cease saying.

I am also aware they have not, as yet, in terms, demanded the overthrow of our free-state Constitutions. Yet those constitutions declare the wrong of slavery, with more solemn emphasis, than do all other sayings against it; and when all these other sayings shall have been silenced, the overthrow of these constitutions will be demanded, and nothing be left to resist the demand. It is nothing to the contrary, that they do not demand the whole of this just now. Demanding what they do, and for the reason they do, they can voluntarily stop nowhere short of this consummation. Holding, as they do, that slavery is morally right, and socially elevating, they cannot cease to demand a full recognition of it, as a legal right, and a social blessing.

Nor can we justifiably withhold this, on any ground save our conviction that slavery is wrong. If slavery is right, all words, acts, laws, and constitutions against it, are themselves wrong, and should be silenced and swept away. If it is right, we cannot justly object to its nationality –

its universality; if it is wrong, they cannot justly insist upon its extension – its enlargement. All they ask, we could readily grant, if we thought slavery right; all we ask, they could as readily grant, if they thought it wrong. Their thinking it right, and our thinking it wrong, is the precise facts upon which depends the whole controversy. Thinking it right, as they do, they are not to blame for desiring its full recognition, as being right; but, thinking it wrong, as we do, can we yield to them? Can we cast our votes with their view, and against our own? In view of our moral, social, and political responsibilities, can we do this?

Wrong as we think slavery is, we can yet afford to let it alone where it is, because that much is due to the necessity arising from its actual presence in the nation; but can we, while our votes will prevent it, allow it to spread into the national territories, and to overrun us here in these free states? If our sense of duty forbids this, then let us stand by our duty, fearlessly and effectively. Let us be diverted by none of those sophistical contrivances wherewith we are so industriously plied and belabored – contrivances such as groping for some middle ground between the right and the wrong, vain as the search for a man who should be neither a living man nor a dead man – such as a policy of 'don't care' on a question about which all true men do care – such as Union appeals beseeching true Union men to yield to Disunionists, reversing the divine rule, and calling, not the sinners, but the righteous to repentance – such as invocations to Washington, imploring men to unsay what Washington said, and undo what Washington did.

Neither let us be slandered from our duty by false accusations against us, nor frightened from it by menaces of destruction to the government nor of dungeons to ourselves. Let us have faith that right makes might, and in that faith, let us, to the end, dare to do our duty as we understand it.

•

## JEFFERSON DAVIS
### 21 January 1861

### 'A final adieu'

*Once Abraham Lincoln was elected president, Southern states prepared to leave the Union. On 21 January 1861, senators from Florida, Alabama and then Mississippi announced to the Senate that they were leaving (South Carolina senators sent their resignation by letter).*

*The Senator for Mississippi was Jefferson Davis (1808–89), a war hero and*

*former Secretary of War who had succeeded John C. Calhoun as leader of the*
*extreme right State Rights party and a supporter of slavery. Davis, who became*
*president of the Confederacy – the Confederated States of America – made his fare-*
*well to the Union in simple, dignified style, speaking more in sorrow than in anger.*

I rise, Mr President, for the purpose of announcing to the Senate that I
have satisfactory evidence that the state of Mississippi, by a solemn
ordinance of her people in convention assembled, has declared her
separation from the United States. Under these circumstances, of course,
my functions are terminated here. It has seemed to me proper, however,
that I should appear in the Senate to announce that fact to my associates,
and I will say but very little more. The occasion does not invite me to
go into argument, and my physical condition would not permit me to do
so if it were otherwise; and yet it seems to become me to say something
on the part of the state I here represent, on an occasion so solemn as this.

It is known to senators who have served with me here that I have for
many years advocated, as an essential attribute of state sovereignty, the
right of a state to secede from the Union. Therefore, if I had not
believed there was justifiable cause; if I had thought that Mississippi was
acting without sufficient provocation, or without an existing necessity, I
should still, under my theory of the government, because of my allegiance
to the state of which I am a citizen, have been bound by her action. I,
however, may be permitted to say that I do think that she has justifiable
cause, and I approve of her act. I conferred with her people before that
act was taken, counseled them then that, if the state of things which they
apprehended should exist when the convention met, they should take
the action which they have now adopted.

I hope none who hear me will confound this expression of mine with
the advocacy of the right of a state to remain in the Union, and to
disregard its constitutional obligations by the nullification of the law.
Such is not my theory. Nullification and secession, so often confounded,
are indeed antagonistic principles. Nullification is a remedy which it is
sought to apply within the Union, and against the agent of the states. It
is only to be justified when the agent has violated his constitutional
obligation, and a state, assuming to judge for itself, denies the right of
the agent thus to act, and appeals to the other states of the Union for a
decision; but when the states themselves, and when the people of the
states, have so acted as to convince us that they will not regard our
constitutional rights, then, and then for the first time, arises the doctrine
of secession in its practical application.

A great man who now reposes with his fathers, and who has been often arraigned for a want of fealty to the Union, advocated the doctrine of nullification, because it preserved the Union. It was because of his deep-seated attachment to the Union, his determination to find some remedy for existing ills short of a severance of the ties which bound South Carolina to the other states, that Mr Calhoun advocated the doctrine of nullification, which he proclaimed to be peaceful, to be within the limits of state power, not to disturb the Union, but only to be a means of bringing the agent before the tribunal of the states for their judgement.

Secession belongs to a different class of remedies. It is to be justified upon the basis that the states are sovereign. There was a time when none denied it. I hope the time may come again, when a better comprehension of the theory of our government, and the inalienable rights of the people of the states, will prevent any one from denying that each state is a sovereign, and thus may reclaim the grants which it has made to any agent whomsoever.

I therefore say I concur in the action of the people of Mississippi, believing it to be necessary and proper, and should have been bound by their action if my belief had been otherwise; and this brings me to the important point which I wish on this last occasion to present to the Senate. It is by this confounding of nullification and secession that the name of the great man whose ashes now mingle with his mother earth has been invoked to justify coercion against a seceded state. The phrase 'to execute the laws' was an expression which General Jackson applied to the case of a state refusing to obey the laws while yet a member of the Union. That is not the case which is now presented. The laws are to be executed over the United States, and upon the people of the United States. They have no relation to any foreign country. It is a perversion of terms, at least it is a great misapprehension of the case, which cites that expression for application to a state which has withdrawn from the Union. You may make war on a foreign state. If it be the purpose of gentlemen, they may make war against a state which has withdrawn from the Union; but there are no laws of the United States to be executed within the limits of a seceded state. A state finding herself in the condition in which Mississippi has judged she is, in which her safety requires that she should provide for the maintenance of her rights out of the Union, surrenders all the benefits (and they are known to be many), deprives herself of the advantages (they are known to be great), severs all the ties of affection (and they are close and enduring), which have bound her to the Union; and thus divesting herself of every benefit, taking upon herself every burden, she claims to be exempt from any power to execute the laws of the United States within her limits.

I well remember an occasion when Massachusetts was arraigned before the bar of the Senate, and when then the doctrine of coercion was rife and to be applied against her because of the rescue of a fugitive slave in Boston. My opinion then was the same that it is now. Not in a spirit of egotism, but to show that I am not influenced in my opinion because the case is my own, I refer to that time and that occasion as containing the opinion which I then entertained, and on which my present conduct is based. I then said, if Massachusetts, following her through a stated line of conduct, chooses to take the last step which separates her from the Union, it is her right to go, and I will neither vote one dollar nor one man to coerce her back, but will say to her, Godspeed, in memory of the kind associations which once existed between her and the other states.

It has been a conviction of pressing necessity, it has been a belief that we are to be deprived in the Union of the rights which our fathers bequeathed to us, which has brought Mississippi into her present decision. She has heard proclaimed the theory that all men are created free and equal, and this made the basis of an attack upon her social institutions; and the sacred Declaration of Independence has been invoked to maintain the position of the equality of the races. That Declaration of Independence is to be construed by the circumstances and purposes for which it was made. The communities were declaring their independence; the people of those communities were asserting that no man was born – to use the language of Mr Jefferson – booted and spurred to ride over the rest of mankind; that men were created equal – meaning the men of the political community; that there was no divine right to rule; that no man inherited the right to govern; that there were no classes by which power and place descended to families, but that all stations were equally within the grasp of each member of the body politic. These were the great principles they announced; these were the purposes for which they made their declaration; these were the end to which their enunciation was directed. They have no reference to the slave; else, how happened it that among the items of arraignment made against George III was that he endeavored to do just what the North had been endeavoring of late to do – to stir up insurrection among our slaves? Had the Declaration announced that the Negroes were free and equal, how was the prince to be arraigned for stirring up insurrection among them? And how was this to be enumerated among the high crimes which caused the colonies to sever their connection with the mother country? When our Constitution was formed, the same idea was rendered more palpable, for there we find provision made for that very class of persons as property; they were not put upon the footing of equality with white men – not even upon that of paupers and convicts; but, so far as representation was concerned, were discriminated against as a lower caste, only to be represented in the numerical proportion of three-fifths.

Then, senators, we recur to the compact which binds us together; we recur to the principles upon which our government was founded; and when you deny them, and when you deny to us the right to withdraw from a government which, thus perverted, threatens to be destructive of our rights, we but tread in the path of our fathers when we proclaim our independence, and take the hazard. This is done not in hostility to others, not to injure any section of the country, not even for our own pecuniary benefit; but from the high and solemn motive of defending and protecting the rights we inherited, and which it is our sacred duty to transmit unshorn to our children.

I find in myself, perhaps, a type of the general feeling of my constituents toward yours. I am sure I feel no hostility to you, senators from the North. I am sure there is not one of you, whatever sharp discussion there may have been between us, to whom I cannot now say, in the presence of my God, I wish you well; and such, I am sure, is the feeling of the people whom I represent toward those whom you represent. I therefore feel that I but express their desire when I say I hope, and they hope, for peaceful relations with you, though we must part. They may be mutually beneficial to us in the future, as they have been in the past, if you so will it. The reverse may bring disaster on every portion of the country; and if you will have it thus, we will invoke the God of our fathers, who delivered them from the power of the lion, to protect us from the ravages of the bear; and thus, putting our trust in God, and in our own firm hearts and strong arms, we will vindicate the right as best we may.

In the course of my service here, associated at different times with a great variety of senators, I see now around me some with whom I have served long; there have been points of collision; but whatever of offense there has been to me, I leave here; I carry with me no hostile remembrance. Whatever offense I have given which has not been redressed, or for which satisfaction has not been demanded, I have, senators, in this hour of our parting, to offer you my apology for any pain which, in heat of discussion, I have inflicted. I go hence unencumbered of the remembrance of any injury received, and having discharged the duty of making the only reparation in my power for any injury offered.

Mr President and senators, having made the announcement which the occasion seemed to me to require, it only remains for me to bid you a final adieu.

•

### ABRAHAM LINCOLN
### 11 February 1861

### *'My feeling of sadness at this parting'*

*After his election as president, Lincoln remained in Springfield, where he was besieged by office-seekers, for nearly four months. He made a pilgrimage to his father's grave and the house of his stepmother.*

*At last, at eight o'clock on a cold and drizzly morning, he and his family made their way to Great Western Station and the special train with a single passenger car that would take them on the twelve-day journey to Washington.*

*Lincoln stood at the rail, head down, an expression of tragic sadness on his face. Slowly his chin lifted and he looked at the faces of the neighbours who had come to wish him success. A hush fell on the crowd as Lincoln made his farewell to the town he was never to see again.*

No one, not in my situation, can appreciate my feeling of sadness at this parting. To this place, and the kindness of these people, I owe everything. Here I have lived a quarter of a century, and have passed from a young to an old man. Here my children have been born, and one is buried. I now leave, not knowing when or whether ever I may return, with a task before me greater than that which rested upon Washington. Without the assistance of that Divine Being who ever attended him, I cannot succeed. With that assistance, I cannot fail. Trusting in Him who can go with me, and remain with you, and be everywhere for good, let us confidently hope that all will yet be well. To His care commending you, as I hope in your prayers you will commend me, I bid you an affectionate farewell.

•

## ABRAHAM LINCOLN
### 4 March 1861

### 'We are not enemies, but friends'

*When Lincoln began work on his inaugural at Springfield, he asked for one of Henry Clay's 1850 speeches, a copy of the Constitution, Andrew Jackson's proclamation on nullification and Daniel Webster's reply to Hayne, which he considered the greatest example of American oratory. The address was set in type at Springfield and studied by advisers on the journey to Washington. He accepted but adapted a conciliatory last paragraph suggested by William Seward.*

*There had been rumours of an attempt to kill Lincoln during the journey to the capital, and only two weeks earlier Jefferson Davis had been elected president of the Confederation. So Washington had been turned into an armed camp for the inauguration. At noon President Buchanan collected his successor from Willard's Hotel to escort him to the Capitol in an open carriage. Files of soldiers lined the streets, cavalry guarded every intersection, and riflemen on rooftops watched windows across the street. Two batteries of artillery were posted near the Capitol.*

*In a black suit, black boots and a white shirt, carrying a gold-headed cane and his tall hat, Lincoln rose to deliver his address. As he saw nowhere to put his hat and cane, his defeated rival Stephen Douglas reached out to hold them for him.*

*Unrolling his manuscript and adjusting his spectacles, Lincoln faced the crowd of 20,000 and then warned them in a clear voice that carried to the edge of the crowd that he was prepared to fight a war to maintain the Union but that secession was unnecessary.*

This country, with its institutions, belongs to the people who inhabit it. Whenever they shall grow weary of the existing government, they can exercise their *constitutional* right of amending it, or their *revolutionary* right to dismember or overthrow it. I cannot be ignorant of the fact that many worthy and patriotic citizens are desirous of having the national Constitution amended. While I make no recommendation of amendments, I fully recognize the rightful authority of the people over the whole subject to be exercised in either of the modes prescribed in the instrument itself; and I should under existing circumstances favor rather than oppose a fair opportunity being afforded the people to act upon it . . .

The chief magistrate derives all his authority from the people, and they have conferred none upon him to fix terms for the separation of the states. The people themselves can do this also if they choose; but the executive, as such, has nothing to do with it. His duty is to administer the present government, as it came to his hands, and to transmit it, unimpaired by him, to his successor.

Why should there not be a patient confidence in the ultimate justice of the people? Is there any better or equal hope in the world? In our present differences, is either party without faith of being in the right? If the Almighty Ruler of nations, with His eternal truth and justice, be on your side of the North, or on yours of the South, that truth, and that justice, will surely prevail, by the judgement of this great tribunal, the American people.

By the frame of the government under which we live, this same people have wisely given their public servants but little power for mischief; and have, with equal wisdom, provided for the return of that little to their own hands at very short intervals.

While the people retain their virtue and vigilance, no administration, by any extreme of wickedness or folly, can very seriously injure the government in the short space of four years.

My countrymen, one and all, think calmly and well upon this whole subject. Nothing valuable can be lost by taking time. If there be an object to hurry any of you, in hot haste, to a step which you would never take deliberately, that object will be frustrated by taking time; but no good object can be frustrated by it. Such of you as are now dissatisfied still have the old Constitution unimpaired, and, on the sensitive point, the laws of your own framing under it; while the new administration will have no immediate power, if it would, to change either. If it were admitted that you who are dissatisfied hold the right side in the dispute, there still is no single good reason for precipitate action. Intelligence, patriotism, Christianity, and a firm reliance on Him who has never yet forsaken this favored land are still competent to adjust, in the best way, all our present difficulty.

In your hands, my dissatisfied fellow countrymen, and not in mine, is the momentous issue of civil war. The government will not assail you. You can have no conflict, without being yourselves the aggressors. You have no oath registered in heaven to destroy the government, while *I* shall have the most solemn one to 'preserve, protect, and defend' it.

I am loath to close. We are not enemies, but friends. We must not be enemies. Though passion may have strained, it must not break, our bonds of affection. The mystic chords of memory, stretching from every battlefield, and patriot grave, to every living heart and hearthstone, all over this broad land, will yet swell the chorus of the Union, when again touched, as surely they will be, by the better angels of our nature.

•

## EDWARD EVERETT
### 19 November 1863

### 'A new bond of union'

*When the cemetery for the soldiers who fell in the Battle of Gettysburg was dedicated, the main speaker was Edward Everett (1794–1865), the most celebrated American orator of his age. Everett had been four times Governor of Massachusetts, Ambassador to Great Britain, President of Harvard, Secretary of State, and a senator. He gave his oration on George Washington 128 times and raised nearly 60,000 dollars for the purchase of Mount Vernon as a national monument.*

*Everett was the 'star' of the day of dedication. As the official procession made its way to the cemetery and a crowd of 15,000, President Lincoln looked ungainly on a horse too small for him. Souvenir hunters searched the battlefield for bullets. Coffins lay scattered across the battlefield.*

*Everett spoke confidently in his rich mellow voice until, after two hours, he reached his peroration.*

Now, friends, fellow citizens of Gettysburg and Pennsylvania, and you from remoter states, let me again, as we part, invoke your benediction on these honored graves. You feel, though the occasion is mournful, that it is good to be here. You feel that it was greatly auspicious for the cause of the country that the men of the East, and the men of the West, the men of nineteen sister states, stood side by side on the perilous ridges of the battle. You now feel it a new bond of union that they shall lie side by side on the perilous ridges of the battle. You now feel it a new bond of union that they shall lie side by side till a clarion, louder than that which marshaled them to the combat, shall awake their slumbers. God bless the Union; it is dearer to us for the blood of brave men which has been shed in its defense. The spots on which they stood and fell; these pleasant heights; the thriving village whose streets so lately rang with the strange din of war; the fields beyond the ridge, where the noble Reynolds held the advancing foe at bay, and, while he his own life, assured by his forethought and self-sacrifice the triumph of the two succeeding days; the little streams which wind through the hills, on whose banks in aftertimes the wandering plowman will turn up, with the rude weapons of savage warfare, the fearful missiles of modern artillery; Seminary Ridge, the Peach Orchard, Cemetery, Culp, and Wolf Hill, Round Top, Little Round Top, humble names, henceforward dear and famous – no lapse of time, no distance of space, shall cause you to be forgotten. 'The whole earth,' said Pericles, as he stood over the remains of his fellow citizens, who had fallen in the first year of the Peloponnesian War – 'the whole earth is the sepulcher of illustrious men.' All time, he might have added, is the millennium of their glory. Surely I would do no injustice to the other noble achievements of the war, which have reflected such honor on both arms of the service, and have entitled the armies and the navy of the United States, their officers and men, to the warmest thanks and the richest rewards which a grateful people can pay. But they, I am sure, will join us in saying, as we bid farewell to the dust of these martyr-heroes, that wheresoever throughout the civilized world the accounts of this great warfare are read, and down to the latest period of recorded time, in the glorious annals of our common country there will be no brighter page than that which relates to the battles of Gettysburg.

•

## ABRAHAM LINCOLN
### 19 November 1863

### '*Government of the people, by the people, for the people*'

*When Edward Everett finished the main oration, a hymn was sung and then Lincoln made some dedicatory 'remarks'. The crowd had scattered and by the time the stragglers got near the platform the speech was over. Everett's florid speech is forgotten. Lincoln spoke 270 words in about three minutes, interrupted by applause five times, and made the greatest and noblest speech of modern times, a speech that stands comparison with the Sermon on the Mount or the funeral oration of Pericles.*

*It is the speech most often quoted, most frequently recorded (recently by Margaret Thatcher and General Norman Schwarzkopf), and which remains the subject of scholarly inquiry (most recently in* Lincoln at Gettysburg *by Garry Wills).*

*So what is its secret? That was the question President John Kennedy asked his speechwriter Theodore Sorensen when he was preparing his inaugural in 1960. Sorensen's answer was that Lincoln used short words. According to Wills, Lincoln was influenced by the rhetoric of the Greek revival, the imagery of the rural cemetery movement and the influence of transcendentalism, as well as his own political experience.*

*The Gettysburg address was certainly not written on the back of an envelope. It was drafted and redrafted – right up to the morning of 19 November – to win the ideological as well as the military civil war. Lincoln added the words 'under God' as he spoke.*

*Lincoln summed up for his audience their deepest beliefs. 'In their name, summoned by Lincoln's sober language,' says Hugh Brogan, 'they could continue to fight in stern Puritan hopefulness.'*

*For Wills, the Gettysburg address rendered obsolete the florid style of Everett and forged a new lean language to redeem the first modern war.*

Fellow-countrymen – Four score and seven years ago our fathers brought forth on this continent a new nation, conceived in Liberty, and dedicated to the proposition that all men are created equal.

Now we are engaged in a great civil war, testing whether that nation, or any nation so conceived and so dedicated, can long endure. We are met on a great battlefield of that war. We have come to dedicate a portion of that field, as a final resting-place for those who here gave their lives that that nation might live. It is altogether fit and proper that we should do this.

But, in a larger sense, we cannot dedicate – we cannot consecrate – we cannot hallow this ground. The brave men, living and dead, who struggled here, have consecrated it, far above our poor power to add or detract. The world will little note, nor long remember, what we say here, but it can never forget what they did here. It is for us, the living, rather, to be dedicated here to the unfinished work which they who fought here have thus far so nobly advanced. It is rather for us to be here dedicated to the great task remaining before us – that from these honoured dead we take increased devotion to that cause for which they gave the last full measure of devotion – that we here highly re-solve that these dead shall not have died in vain – that this nation, under God, shall have a new birth of freedom – and that government of ʾhe people, by the people, for the people, shall not perish from the

# ABRAHAM LINCOLN
## 4 March 1865

### *'With malice toward none'*

*Lincoln swept to an overwhelming victory in the 1864 presidential election with an electoral vote of 212 out of 233. On the day of his inauguration, the Civil War was almost over – it ended thirty-seven days later. So his second inaugural address looked beyond the war and appealed for reconciliation and reconstruction. It ranks with the Gettysburg address as one of the greatest speeches of modern times.*

*With characteristic modesty, Lincoln wrote afterwards that he thought the address would 'wear as well as – perhaps better than – anything I have produced, but I believe that it is not immediately popular. Men are not flattered by being shown there is a difference between the Almighty and them.'*

At this second appearing to take the oath of the presidential office there is less occasion for an extended address than there was at the first. Then a statement somewhat in detail of a course to be pursued seemed fitting and proper. Now, at the expiration of four years, during which public declarations have been constantly called forth on every point and phase of the great contest which still absorbs the attention and engrosses the energies of the nation, little that is new could be presented. The progress of our arms, upon which all else chiefly depends, is as well known to the public as to myself, and it is, I trust, reasonably satisfactory and encouraging to all. With high hope for the future, no prediction in regard to it is ventured.

On the occasion corresponding to this four years ago all thoughts were anxiously directed to an impending civil war. All dreaded it, all sought to avert it. While the inaugural address was being delivered from this place, devoted altogether to saving the Union without war, urgent agents were in the city seeking to destroy it without war – seeking to dissolve the Union and divide effects by negotiation. Both parties deprecated war, but one of them would make war rather than let the nation survive, and the other would accept war rather than let it perish, and the war came.

One-eighth of the whole population were colored slaves, not distributed generally over the Union, but localized in the southern part of it. These slaves constituted a peculiar and powerful interest. All knew that this interest was somehow the cause of the war. To strengthen, perpetu-ate, and extend this interest was the object for which the insurgents would rend the Union even by war, while the Government claimed no right to do more than to restrict the territorial enlargement of it. Neither party expected for the war the magnitude or the duration which it has already attained. Neither anticipated that the cause of the conflict might cease with or even before the conflict itself should cease. Each looked for an easier triumph, and a result less fundamental and astounding. Both read the same Bible and pray to the same God, and each invokes His aid against the other. It may seem strange that any men should dare to ask a just God's assistance in wringing their bread from the sweat of other men's faces, but let us judge not, that we be not judged. The prayers of both could not be answered. That of neither has been answered fully.

The Almighty has His own purposes. 'Woe unto the world because of offenses; for it must needs be that offenses come, but woe to that man by whom the offense cometh.' If we shall suppose that American slavery is one of those offenses which, in the providence of God, must needs come, but which, having continued through His appointed time, He now wills to remove, and that He gives to both North and South this terrible war as the woe due to those by whom the offense came, shall we discern therein any departure from those divine attributes which the believers in a living God always ascribe to Him? Fondly do we hope, fervently do we pray, that this mighty scourge of war may speedily pass away. Yet, if God wills that it continue until all the wealth piled by the bondsman's two hundred and fifty years of unrequited toil shall be sunk, and until every drop of blood drawn with the lash shall be paid by another drawn with the sword, as was said three thousand years ago, so still it must be said 'the judgements of the Lord are true and righteous altogether'.

With malice toward none, with charity for all, with firmness in the right as God gives us to see the right, let us strive on to finish the work we are in, to bind up the nation's wounds, to care for him who shall have borne the battle and for his widow and his orphan, to do all which may achieve and cherish a just and lasting peace among ourselves and with all nations.

*was assassinated a month later.*

•

## CHIEF JOSEPH
### 1877

### 'I will fight no more'

*For Indians, the nineteenth century was an era of defeat as the whites asserted their dominance over the continent. The few victories they won provoked still greater punishment, as after Little Big Horn, when Crazy Horse and Sitting Bull wiped out an American regiment.*

*As leader of the Nez Percé tribe, Chief Joseph fought a long but unsuccessful campaign against his oppressors but surrendered after being given generous promises. All were broken. An eye-witness of his defeat said: 'In his long career, Chief Joseph cannot accuse the government of the United States of one single act of justice.' This was his noble speech of surrender.*

Tell General Howard I know his heart. What he told me before, I have it in my heart. I am tired of fighting. Our chiefs are killed; Looking-Glass is dead, Ta-Hool-Hool-Shute is dead. The old men are all dead. It is the young men who say yes or no. He who led on the young men is dead. It is cold, and we have no blankets; the little children are freezing to death. My people, some of them, have run away to the hills, and have no blankets, no food. No one knows where they are – perhaps freezing to death. I want to have time to look for my children, and see how many of them I can find. Maybe I shall find them among the dead. Hear me, my chiefs! I am tired; my heart is sick and sad. From where the sun now stands I will fight no more forever.

•

## HENRY W. GRADY
### 22 December 1886

### 'Fields that ran red with human blood in April were green with the harvest in June'

*Henry Woodfin Grady (1850–89) was editor and part owner of the Atlanta Constitution when – twenty years after the Civil War – he was the first Southerner invited to address the prestigious New England Club of New York*

*City. Among his audience was William Sherman, the general who marched through Georgia.*

I accept the term 'The New South' as in no sense disparaging to the old. Dear to me, sir, is the home of my childhood and the traditions of my people. I would not, if I could, dim the glory they won in peace and war, or by word or deed take aught from the splendor and grace of their civilization – never equaled and, perhaps, never to be equaled in its chivalric strength and grace. There is a New South, not through protest against the old, but because of new conditions, new adjustments, and, if you please, new ideas and aspirations. It is to this that I address myself, and to the consideration of which I hasten lest it become the Old South before I get to it. Age does not endow all things with strength and virtue, nor are all new things to be despised. The shoemaker who put over his door 'John Smith's shop. Founded in 1760' was more than matched by his young rival across the street who hung out this sign: 'Bill Jones. Established 1886. No old stock kept in this shop.'

Dr Talmadge has drawn for you, with a master's hand, the picture of your returning armies. He has told you how, in the pomp and circumstance of war, they came back to you, marching with proud and victorious tread, reading their glory in a nation's eyes! Will you bear with me while I tell you of another army that sought its home at the close of the late war – an army that marched home in defeat and not in victory – in pathos and not in splendor, but in glory that equaled yours, and to hearts as loving as ever welcomed heroes home? Let me picture to you the footsore Confederate soldier, as, buttoning up in his faded gray jacket the parole which was to bear testimony to his children of his fidelity and faith, he turned his face southward from Appomattox in April 1865. Think of him as ragged, half starved, heavy-hearted, enfeebled by want and wounds; having fought to exhaustion, he surrenders his gun, wrings the hands of his comrades in silence, and, lifting his tear-stained and pallid face for the last time to the graves that dot the old Virginia hills, pulls his gray cap over his brow and begins the slow and painful journey. What does he find – let me ask you, who went to your homes eager to find, in the welcome you had justly earned, full payment for four years' sacrifice – what does he find when, having followed the battle-stained cross against overwhelming odds, dreading death not half so much as surrender, he reaches the home he left so prosperous and beautiful? He finds his house in ruins, his farm devastated, his slaves free, his stock killed, his barns empty, his trade destroyed, his money worthless; his social system, feudal in its magnificence, swept away; his people without law or legal status, his comrades slain, and the burdens of others heavy on his shoulders. Crushed by defeat, his very traditions are gone; without money, credit, employment, material, or training; and besides all this, confronted with the gravest problem that ever met human intelligence – the establishing of a status for the vast body of his liberated slaves.

What does he do – this hero in gray with a heart of gold? Does he sit down in sullenness and despair? Not for a day. Surely God, who had stripped him of his prosperity, inspired him in his adversity. As ruin was never before so overwhelming, never was restoration swifter. The soldier stepped from the trenches into the furrow; horses that had charged Federal guns marched before the plow, and fields that ran red with human blood in April were green with the harvest in June; women reared in luxury cut up their dresses and made breeches for their husbands, and, with a patience and heroism that fit women always as a garment, gave their hands to work. There was little bitterness in all this. Cheerfulness and frankness prevailed. 'Bill Arp' [a current humorist] struck the keynote when he said: 'Well, I killed as many of them as they did of me, and now I am going to work.' Or the soldier returning home after defeat and roasting some corn on the roadside, who made the remark to his comrades: 'You may leave the South if you want to, but I am going to Sandersville, kiss my wife, and raise a crop, and if the Yankees fool with me any more I will whip 'em again.' I want to say to General Sherman – who is considered an able man in our parts, though some people think he is a kind of careless man about fire – that from the ashes he left us in 1864 we have raised a brave and beautiful city; that somehow or other we have caught the sunshine in the bricks and mortar of our homes, and have builded therein not one ignoble prejudice or memory . . .

But what of the Negro? Have we solved the problem he presents or progressed in honor and equity toward the solution? Let the record speak to the point. No section shows a more prosperous laboring population than the Negroes of the South; none in fuller sympathy with the employing and landowning class. He shares our school fund, has the fullest protection of our laws and the friendship of our people. Self-interest, as well as honor, demands that he should have this. Our future, our very existence, depend upon our working out this problem in full and exact justice. We understand that when Lincoln signed the Emancipation Proclamation your victory was assured; for he then committed you to the cause of human liberty, against which the arms of man cannot prevail; while those of our statesmen who trusted to make slavery the cornerstone of the Confederacy doomed us to defeat as far as they could, committing us to a cause that reason could not defend or the sword maintain in the light of advancing civilization. Had Mr Toombs [first Secretary of State of the Confederacy] said, which he did not say, that he would call the roll of his slaves at the foot of Bunker Hill, he would have been foolish, for he might have known that whenever slavery became entangled in war it must perish, and that the chattel in human flesh ended for ever in New England when your fathers – not to be blamed for parting with what didn't pay – sold their slaves to our fathers – not to be praised for knowing a paying thing when they saw it.

· The relations of the Southern people with the Negro are close and cordial. We remember with what fidelity for four years he guarded our defenseless women and children, whose husbands and fathers were fighting against his freedom. To his eternal credit be it said that whenever he struck a blow for his own liberty he fought in open battle, and when at last he raised his black and humble hands that the shackles might be struck off, those hands were innocent of wrong against his helpless charges, and worthy to be taken in loving grasp by every man who honors loyalty and devotion. Ruffians have maltreated him, rascals have misled him, philanthropists established a bank for him, but the South, with the North, protests against injustice to this simple and sincere people. To liberty and enfranchisement is as far as law can carry the Negro. The rest must be left to conscience and common sense. It should be left to those among whom his lot is cast, with whom he is indissolubly connected and whose prosperity depends upon their possessing his intelligent sympathy and confidence. Faith has been kept with him in spite of calumnious assertions to the contrary by those who assume to speak for us or by frank opponents. Faith will be kept with him in the future, if the South holds her reason and integrity . . .

This is said in no spirit of time-serving or apology. The South has nothing for which to apologize. She believes that the late struggle between the states was war and not rebellion, revolution and not conspiracy, and that her convictions were as honest as yours. I should be unjust to the dauntless spirit of the South and to my own convictions if I did not make this plain in this presence. The South has nothing to take back. In my native town of Athens is a monument that crowns its central hill – a plain white shaft. Deep cut into its shining side is a name dear to me above the names of men, that of a brave and simple man who died in brave and simple faith. Not for all the glories of New England – from Plymouth Rock all the way – would I exchange the heritage he left me in his soldier's death. To the foot of that shaft I shall send my children's children to reverence him who ennobled their name with his heroic blood. But, sir, speaking from the shadow of that memory, which I honor as I do nothing else on earth, I say that the cause in which he suffered and for which he gave his life was adjudged by higher and fuller wisdom than his or mine, and I am glad that the omniscient God held the balance of battle in His Almighty hand, and that human slavery was swept for ever from American soil – the American Union saved from the wreck of war . . .

•

## BOOKER T. WASHINGTON
### 18 September 1893

### *'A new heaven and a new earth'*

*Booker Taliaferro Washington (1856–1915) was born a Virginia slave of a white father in a mud-floor shack – but freed by Abraham Lincoln's Emancipation Proclamation when he was six. Although he had to work in a salt furnace, he studied at night, enrolled in an elementary school and went on to Hampton Institute and the Wayland Seminary in Washington DC. He became president of the Negro school at Tuskegee, Alabama, and devoted the rest of his life to its success, attracting the support of Carnegie and Rockefeller.*

*As Tuskegee grew into a school with a faculty of 200, Washington became the Afro-American leader of his generation. He persuaded blacks to exploit white supremacy by accepting it – but many, including William Du Bois, the leading black intellectual, thought his views betrayed black rights and condemned blacks to permanent inferiority.*

*Washington became so famous that he was in demand as a speaker throughout the nation, especially on race relations. It was this address in Atlanta at the States and International Exposition that made him the recognized leader of the blacks.*

A ship lost at sea for many days suddenly sighted a friendly vessel. From the mast of the unfortunate vessel was seen a signal: 'Water, water; we die of thirst!' The answer from the friendly vessel at once came back: 'Cast down your bucket where you are.' A second time the signal, 'Water, water; send us water!' ran up from the distressed vessel, and was answered: 'Cast down your bucket where you are.' The captain of the distressed vessel, at last heeding the injunction, cast down his bucket, and it came up full of fresh, sparkling water from the mouth of the Amazon River. To those of my race who depend upon bettering their condition in a foreign land, or who underestimate the importance of cultivating friendly relations with the Southern white man, who is his next-door neighbor, I would say: 'Cast down your bucket where you are' – cast it down in making friends in every manly way of the people of all races by whom we are surrounded.

Cast it down in agriculture, mechanics, in commerce, in domestic service, and in the professions. And in this connection it is well to bear in mind that whatever other sins the South may be called to bear, when it comes to business, pure and simple, it is in the South that the Negro is given a man's chance in the commercial world, and in nothing is this exposition more eloquent than in emphasizing this chance.

Our greatest danger is that in the great leap from slavery to freedom we may overlook the fact that the masses of us are to live by the productions of our hands, and fail to keep in mind that we shall prosper in proportion as we learn to dignify and glorify common labor, and put brains and skill into the common occupations of life; shall prosper in proportion as we learn to draw the line between the superficial and the substantial, the ornamental gewgaws of life and the useful. No race can prosper till it learns that there is as much dignity in tilling a field as in writing a poem. It is at the bottom of life we must begin, and not at the top. Nor should we permit our grievances to overshadow our opportunities . . .

As we have proved our loyalty to you in the past, in nursing your children, watching by the sickbed of your mothers and fathers, and often following them with tear-dimmed eyes to their graves, so in the future, in our humble way, we shall stand by you with a devotion that no foreigner can approach, ready to lay down our lives, if need be, in defence of yours, interlacing our industrial, commercial, civil, and religious life with yours in a way that shall make the interests of both races one. In all things that are purely social we can be as separate as the fingers, yet one as the hand in all things essential to mutual progress.

There is no defense or security for any of us except in the highest intelligence and development of all. If anywhere there are efforts tending to curtail the fullest growth of the Negro, let these efforts be turned into stimulating, encouraging, and making him the most useful and intelligent citizen. Effort or means so invested will pay a thousand per cent interest. These efforts will be twice blessed – blessing him that gives and him that takes . . .

Gentlemen of the exposition, as we present to you our humble effort at an exhibition of our progress, you must not expect overmuch. Starting thirty years ago with ownership here and there in a few quilts and pumpkins and chickens (gathered from miscellaneous sources), remember the path that has led from these to the invention and production of agricultural implements, buggies, steam engines, newspapers, books, statuary, carving, paintings, the management of drugstores and banks, has not been trodden without contact with thorns and thistles. While we take pride in what we exhibit as a result of our independent efforts, we do not for a moment forget that our part in this exhibition would fall far short of your expectations but for the constant help that has come to our educational life, not only from the Southern states, but especially from Northern philanthropists, who have made their gifts a constant stream of blessing and encouragement.

The wisest among my race understand that the agitation of questions of social equality is the extremest folly, and that progress in the enjoyment of all the privileges that will come to us must be the result of severe and constant struggle rather than of artificial forcing. No race that has anything to contribute to the markets of the world is long in any degree ostracized. It is important and right that all privileges of the law be ours, but it is vastly more important that we be prepared for the exercise of those privileges. The opportunity to earn a dollar in a factory just now is worth infinitely more than the opportunity to spend a dollar in an opera house.

In conclusion, may I repeat that nothing in thirty years has given us more hope and encouragement, and drawn us so near to you of the white race, as this opportunity offered by the exposition; and here bending, as it were, over the altar that represents the results of the struggles of your race and mine, both starting practically empty-handed three decades ago, I pledge that, in your effort to work out the great and intricate problem which God has laid at the door of the South, you shall have at all times the patient, sympathetic help of my race; only let this be constantly in mind that, while from representations in these buildings of the products of field, of forest, of mine, of factory, letters, and art, much good will come, yet far above and beyond material benefits will be the higher good that, let us pray God, will come in a blotting out of sectional differences and racial animosities and suspicions, in a determination to administer absolute justice, in a willing obedience among all classes to the mandates of law. This, coupled with our material prosperity, will bring into our beloved South a new heaven and a new earth.

•

## BOOKER T. WASHINGTON
### 1896

### '*The sacrifice was not in vain*'

*A significant recognition of the power and influence of Booker T. Washington was the award to him by Harvard of an honorary degree. This is part of the speech he delivered to Harvard alumni.*

If through me, a humble representative, seven millions of my people in the South might be permitted to send a message to Harvard – Harvard that offered up on death's altar, young Shaw, and Russell, and Lowell and scores of others, that we might have a free and united country – that message would be, 'Tell them that the sacrifice was not in vain. Tell them that by the way of the shop, the field, the skilled hand, habits of thrift and economy, by way of industrial school and college, we are coming. We are crawling up, working up, yea, bursting up. Often through oppression, unjust discrimination, and prejudice, but through them we are coming up, and with proper habits, intelligence, and property, there is no power on earth that can permanently stay our progress.'

If my life in the past has meant anything in the lifting up of my people and the bringing about of better relations between your race and mine, I assure you from this day it will mean doubly more. In the economy of God, there is but one standard by which an individual can succeed – there is but one for a race. This country demands that every race measure itself by the American standard. By it a race must rise or fall, succeed or fail, and in the last analysis mere sentiment counts for little. During the next half century and more, my race must continue passing through the severe American crucible. We are to be tested in our patience, our forbearance, our perseverance, our power to endure wrong, to withstand temptations, to economize, to acquire and use skill; our ability to compete, to succeed in commerce, to disregard the superficial for the real, the appearance for the substance, to be great and yet small, learned and yet simple, high and yet the servant of all. This, this is the passport to all that is best in the life of our Republic, and the Negro must possess it, or be debarred.

While we are thus being tested, I beg of you to remember that wherever our life touches yours, we help or hinder. Wherever your life touches ours, you make us stronger or weaker. No member of your race in any part of our country can harm the meanest member of mine, without the proudest and bluest blood in Massachusetts being degraded. When Mississippi commits crime, New England commits crime, and in so much lowers the standard of your civilization. There is no escape – man drags man down, or man lifts man up.

In working out our destiny, while the main burden and center of activity must be with us, we shall need in a large measure in the years that are to come as we have in the past, the help, the encouragement, the guidance that the strong can give the weak. Thus helped, we of both races in the South soon shall throw off the shackles of racial and sectional prejudices and rise as Harvard University has risen and as we all should rise, above the clouds of ignorance, narrowness, and selfishness, into that atmosphere, that pure sunshine, where it will be our highest ambition to serve man, our brother, regardless of race or previous condition.

•

## WILLIAM JENNINGS BRYAN
### 8 July 1896

### 'You shall not crucify mankind upon a cross of gold'

*All his life William Jennings Bryan (1860–1925), a Protestant fundamentalist and teetotaller, was the champion of rural America. He was born in Salem, Illinois, studied law in Chicago and practised in Nebraska, where he was elected to Congress as a Democrat in 1891. He sympathized with the Populist movement and thought rural poverty could be cured by the free coinage of silver, which would give the poor cheap money.*

*Out of office in 1895, he devoted himself to securing a silver delegation to the 1896 Democratic Convention, where a demand for the free coinage of both gold and silver was included in the platform and aroused fierce controversy. There was pandemonium in the hall. Only when Bryan rose to speak did the 20,000 delegates start to listen. It was then that he made the famous 'Cross of Gold' speech, with its declaration of holy war against the rich and mighty – a speech that recommitted the Democratic party to its original principles of working for the weak and the poor.*

I would be presumptuous, indeed, to present myself against the distinguished gentlemen to whom you have listened if this were a mere measuring of abilities; but this is not a contest between persons. The humblest citizen in all the land, when clad in the armor of a righteous cause, is stronger than all the hosts of error. I come to speak to you in defense of a cause as holy as the cause of liberty – the cause of humanity . . .

When you (*turning to the gold delegates*) come before us and tell us that we are about to disturb your business interests, we reply that you have disturbed our business interests by your course.

We say to you that you have made the definition of a business man too limited in its application. The man who is employed for wages is as much a business man as his employer; the attorney in a country town is as much a business man as the corporation counsel in a great metropolis; the merchant at the crossroads store is as much a business man as the merchant of New York; the farmer who goes forth in the morning and toils all day, who begins in spring and toils all summer, and who by the application of brain and muscle to the natural resources of the country creates wealth is as much a business man as the man who goes upon the board of trade and bets upon the price of grain; the miners who go down a thousand feet into the earth, or climb two thousand feet upon the cliffs, and bring forth from their hiding places the precious metals to be poured into the channels of trade are as much business men as the few financial magnates who, in a back room, corner the money of the world. We come to speak of this broader class of business men.

Ah, my friends, we say not one word against those who live upon the Atlantic Coast, but the hardy pioneers who have braved all the dangers of the wilderness, who have made the desert to blossom as the rose – the pioneers away out there (*pointing to the West*) who rear their children near to nature's heart, where they can mingle their voices with the voices of the birds – out there where they have erected schoolhouses for the education of their young, churches where they praise their Creator, and cemeteries where rest the ashes of their dead – these people, we say, are as deserving of the consideration of our party as any people in this country. It is for these that we speak. We do not come as aggressors. Our war is not a war of conquest; we are fighting in the defense of our homes, our families, and posterity. We have petitioned, and our petitions have been scorned; we have entreated, and our entreaties have been disregarded; we have begged, and they have mocked when our calamity came. We beg no longer; we entreat no more; we petition no more. We defy them! . . .

And now, my friends, let me come to the paramount issue. If they ask us why it is that we say more on the money question than we say upon the tariff question, I reply that, if protection has slain its thousands, the gold standard has slain its tens of thousands. If they ask us why we do not embody in our platform all the things that we believe in, we reply that when we have restored the money of the Constitution all other necessary reforms will be possible; but that until this is done there is no other reform that can be accomplished.

Why is it that within three months such a change has come over the country? Three months ago when it was confidently asserted that those who believe in the gold standard would frame our platform and nominate our candidates, even the advocates of the gold standard did not think that we could elect a president. And they had good reason for their doubt, because there is scarcely a state here today asking for the gold standard which is not in the absolute control of the Republican party. But note the change. Mr McKinley was nominated at St Louis upon a platform which declared for the maintenance of the gold standard until it can be changed into bimetallism by international agreement. Mr McKinley was the most popular man among the Republicans, and three months ago everybody in the Republican party prophesied his election. How is it today? Why, the man who was once pleased to think that he looked like Napoleon – that man shudders today when he remembers that he was nominated on the anniversary of the Battle of Waterloo. Not only that, but as he listens he can hear with ever-increasing distinctness the sound of the waves as they beat upon the lonely shores of St Helena.

Why this change? Ah, my friends, is not the reason for the change evident to anyone who will look at the matter? No private character, however pure, no personal popularity, however great, can protect from the avenging wrath of an indignant people a man who will declare that he is in favor of fastening the gold standard upon this country, or who is willing to surrender the right of self-government and place the legislative control of our affairs in the hands of foreign potentates and powers.

We go forth confident that we shall win. Why? Because upon the paramount issue of this campaign there is not a spot of ground upon which the enemy will dare to challenge battle. If they tell us that the gold standard is a good thing, we shall point to their platform and tell them that their platform pledges the party to get rid of the gold standard and substitute bimetallism. If the gold standard is a good thing, why try to get rid of it? I call your attention to the fact that some of the very people who are in this convention today and who tell us that we ought to declare in favor of international bimetallism – thereby declaring that the gold standard is wrong and that the principle of bimetallism is better – these very people four months ago were open and avowed advocates of the gold standard, and were then telling us that we could not legislate two metals together, even with the aid of all the world. If the gold standard is a good thing, we ought to declare in favor of its retention and not in favor of abandoning it; and if the gold standard is a bad thing, why should we wait until other nations are willing to help us to let go? Here is the line of battle, and we care not upon which issue they force the fight; we are prepared to meet them on either issue or on both. If they tell us that the gold standard is the standard of civilization, we reply to them that this, the most enlightened of all the nations of the earth has never declared for a gold standard and that both the great parties this year are declaring against it. If the gold standard is the standard of civilization, why, my friends, should we not have it? If they come to meet us on that issue we can present the history of our nation. More than that; we can tell them that they will search the pages of history in vain to find a single instance where the common people of any land have ever declared themselves in favor of the gold standard. They can find where the holders of fixed investments have declared for a gold standard, but not where the masses have.

Mr [John Griffin] Carlisle [Kentucky statesman] said in 1878 that this was a struggle between 'the idle holders of idle capital' and 'the struggling masses, who produce the wealth and pay the taxes of the country'; and, my friends, the question we are to decide is: upon which side will the Democratic party fight; upon the side of 'the idle holders of idle capital' or upon the side of 'the struggling masses'? That is the question which the party must answer first, and then it must be answered by each individual hereafter. The sympathies of the Democratic party, as shown by the platform, are on the side of the struggling masses who have ever been the foundation of the Democratic party. There are two ideas of government. There are those who believe that, if you will only legislate to make the well-to-do prosperous, their prosperity will leak through on those below. The

Democratic idea, however, has been that if you legislate to make the masses prosperous, their prosperity will find its way up through every class which rests upon them.

You come to us and tell us that the great cities are in favor of the gold standard; we reply that the great cities rest upon our broad and fertile prairies. Burn down your cities and leave our farms, and your cities will spring up again as if by magic; but destroy our farms and the grass will grow in the streets of every city in the country.

My friends, we declare that this nation is able to legislate for its own people on every question, without waiting for the aid or consent of any other nation on earth; and upon that issue we expect to carry every state in the Union. I shall not slander the inhabitants of the fair state of Massachusetts nor the inhabitants of the state of New York by saying that, when they are confronted with the proposition, they will declare that this nation is not able to attend to its own business. It is the issue of 1776 over again. Our ancestors, when but three millions in number, had the courage to declare their political independence of every other nation; shall we, their descendants, when we have grown to seventy millions, declare that we are less independent than our forefathers? No, my friends, that will never be the verdict of our people. Therefore, we care not upon what lines the battle is fought. If they say bimetallism is good, but that we cannot have it until other nations help us, we reply that, instead of having a gold standard because England has, we will restore bimetallism, and then let England have bimetallism because the United States has it. If they dare to come out in the open field and defend the gold standard as a good thing, we will fight them to the uttermost. Having behind us the producing masses of this nation and the world, supported by the commercial interests, the laboring interests, and the toilers everywhere, we will answer their demand for a gold standard by saying to them: you shall not press down upon the brow of labor this crown of thorns, you shall not crucify mankind upon a cross of gold.

*At the thundering close of his speech, Bryan got a unanimous ovation. Next day he was nominated as presidential candidate. He used the 'Cross of Gold' theme in 600 campaign speeches, heard by an estimated 5 million people, but was beaten by William McKinley.*

•

# THE CRY OF IRELAND

# HENRY GRATTAN
## 19 April 1780

### 'The breath of liberty'

*Ireland's fight for freedom began in the reign of Henry VII, when the Poynings Act compelled Ireland to submit bills to the English King and Privy Council before they could be acted on by the Irish Parliament. The sixth Act of George I subsequently declared Ireland a subordinate kingdom. It was the oratory of Henry Grattan (1740–1820), who became the acknowledged leader of what the poet Byron called the 'eloquent war', which finally won Ireland the power to make its own laws independent of the English Parliament.*

*Grattan was called to the Irish bar in 1772. After being disinherited by his father, the MP for Dublin, for his support of Henry Flood, the Irish nationalist, he entered the Irish Parliament in 1775 and carried the amendment to the address calling for Irish free trade in 1779.*

*A year later, still only thirty-four, he spoke to his motion that the King and the Lords and Commons of Ireland should be the only powers competent to make laws for Ireland.*

England now smarts under the lesson of the American War; the doctrine of imperial legislature she feels to be pernicious; the revenues and monopolies annexed to it she has found to be untenable; she lost the power to enforce it; her enemies are a host, pouring upon her from all quarters of the earth; her armies are dispersed; the sea is not hers; she has no minister, no ally, no admiral, none in whom she long confides, and no general whom she has not disgraced; the balance of her fate is in the hands of Ireland; you are not only her last connection, you are the only nation in Europe that is not her enemy. Besides, there does, of late, a certain damp and spurious supineness overcast her arms and councils, miraculous as that vigour which has lately inspirited yours – for with you everything is the reverse; never was there a Parliament in Ireland so possessed of the confidence of the people; you are the greatest political assembly now sitting in the world; you are at the head of an immense army; nor do we only possess an unconquerable force, but a certain unquenchable public fire, which has touched all ranks of men like a visitation.

Turn to the growth and spring of your country, and behold and admire it; where do you find a nation who, upon whatever concerns the rights of mankind, expresses herself with more truth or force, perspicuity or justice? not the set phrase of scholastic men, not the tame unreality of court addresses, not the vulgar raving of a rabble, but the genuine speech of liberty, and the unsophisticated oratory of a free nation.

See her military ardour, expressed, not only in forty thousand men, conducted by instinct as they were raised by inspiration, but manifested in the zeal and promptitude of every young member of the growing community. Let corruption tremble; let the enemy, foreign or domestic, tremble; but let the friends of liberty rejoice at these means of safety and this hour of redemption. Yes; there does exist an enlightened sense of rights, a young appetite for freedom, a solid strength, and a rapid fire, which not only put a declaration of right within your power, but put it out of your power to decline one. Eighteen counties are at your bar; they stand there with the compact of Henry, with the charter of John, and with all the passions of the people. 'Our lives are at your service, but our liberties – we received them from God; we will not resign them to man.' . . . The people of that country [Great Britain] are now waiting to hear the Parliament of Ireland speak on the subject of their liberty; it begins to be made a question in England whether the principal persons wish to be free; it was the delicacy of former Parliaments to be silent on the subject of commercial restrictions, lest they should show a knowledge of the fact, and not a sense of the violation; you have spoken out, you have shown a knowledge of the fact, and not a sense of the violation.

On the contrary, you have returned thanks for a partial repeal made on a principle of power; you have returned thanks as for a favour, and your exultation has brought your charters, as well as your spirit, into question, and tends to shake to her foundation your title to liberty; thus you do not leave your rights where you found them. You have done too much not to do more; you have gone too far not to go on; you have brought yourselves into that situation in which you must silently abdicate the rights of your country, or publicly restore them. It is very true you may feed your manufacturers, and landed gentlemen may get their rents, and you may export woollen, and may load a vessel with baize, serges, and kerseys, and you may bring back again directly from the plantations sugar, indigo, specklewood, beetle root, and panelas. But liberty, the foundation of trade, the charters of the land, the independency of Parliament, the securing, crowning, and the consummation of everything are yet to come. Without them the work is imperfect, the foundation is wanting, the capital is wanting, trade is not free, Ireland is a colony without the benefit of a charter, and you are a provincial synod without the privileges of a Parliament . . .

There is no policy left for Great Britain but to cherish the remains of her Empire, and do justice to a country who is determined to do justice to herself, certain that she gives nothing equal to what she received from us when we gave her Ireland.

With regard to this country, England must resort to the free principles of government, and must forgo that legislative power which she has exercised to do mischief to herself; she must go back to freedom, which, as it is the foundation of her Constitution, so it is the main pillar of her empire; it is not merely the connection of the Crown, it is a constitutional annexation, an alliance of liberty, which is the true meaning and mystery of the sisterhood, and will make both countries one arm and one soul, replenishing from time to time, in their immortal connection, the vital spirit of law and liberty from the lamp of each other's light. Thus combined by the ties of common interest, equal trade, and equal liberty, the constitution of both countries may become immortal, a new and milder empire may arise from the errors of the old, and the British nation assume once more her natural station – the head of mankind.

That there are precedents against us I allow – acts of power I would call them, not precedent; and I answer the English pleading such precedents, as they answered their kings when they urged precedents against the liberty of England: such things are the weakness of the times; the tyranny of one side, the feebleness of the other, the law of neither; we will not be bound by them; or rather, in the words of the Declaration of Right: 'No doing judgement, proceeding, or anywise to the contrary, shall be brought into precedent or example.' Do not then tolerate a power – the power of the British Parliament over this land, which has no foundation in utility or necessity, or empire, or the laws of England, or the laws of Ireland, or the laws of nature, or the laws of God – do not suffer it to have a duration in your mind.

Do not tolerate that power which blasted you for a century, that power which shattered your loom, banished your manufacturers, dishonoured your peerage, and stopped the growth of your people; do not, I say, be bribed by an export of woollen, or an import of sugar, and permit that power which has thus withered the land to remain in your country and have existence in your pusillanimity.

Do not suffer the arrogance of England to imagine a surviving hope in the fears of Ireland; do not send the people to their own resolves for liberty, passing by the tribunals of justice and the high court of

Parliament; neither imagine that, by any formation of apology, you can palliate such a commission to your hearts, still less to your children, who will sting you with their curses in your grave for having interposed between them and their Maker, robbing them of an immense occasion, and losing an opportunity which you did not create and can never restore.

Hereafter, when these things shall be history, your age of thraldom and poverty, your sudden resurrection, commercial redress, and miraculous armament, shall the historian stop at liberty, and observe – that here the principal men among us fell into mimic trances of gratitude – they were awed by a weak ministry, and bribed by an empty treasury – and when liberty was within their grasp, and the temple opened her folding doors, and the arms of the people clanged, and the zeal of the nation urged and encouraged them on, that they fell down, and were prostituted at the threshold?

I might, as a constituent, come to your bar, and demand my liberty. I do call upon you, by the laws of the land and their violation, by the instruction of eighteen counties, by the arms, inspiration, and providence of the present moment, tell us the rule by which we shall go – assert the law of Ireland – declare the liberty of the land.

I will not be answered by a public lie in the shape of an amendment; neither, speaking for the subject's freedom, am I to hear of faction. I wish for nothing but to breathe, in this our island, in common with my fellow subjects, the air of liberty. I have no ambition, unless it be the ambition to break your chain and contemplate your glory. I never will be satisfied so long as the meanest cottager in Ireland has a link of the British chain clanking to his rags; he may be naked, he shall not be in iron; and I do see the time is at hand, the spirit is gone forth, the declaration is planted; and though great men shall apostatize, yet the cause will live; and though the public speaker should die, yet the immortal fire shall outlast the organ which conveyed it, and the breath of liberty, like the word of the holy man, will not die with the prophet, but survive him.

I shall move you, 'That the King's most excellent Majesty, and the Lords and Commons of Ireland, are the only power competent to make laws to bind Ireland.'

*The motion was lost.*

•

# HENRY GRATTAN
## 16 April 1782

### 'A free people'

*Two years later, again on a motion from Henry Grattan, the Irish Parliament was summoned to debate Irish rights – but on the advice of Charles James Fox the King had already yielded.*

*There was great excitement in Dublin on the day of the debate. The streets were lined with volunteer regiments. Grattan's address was carried without a dissenting voice in either House.*

I am now to address a free people: ages have passed away, and this is the first moment in which you could be distinguished by that appellation.

I have spoken on the subject of your liberty so often, that I have nothing to add, and have only to admire by what heaven-directed steps you have proceeded until the whole faculty of the nation is braced up to the act of her own deliverance.

I found Ireland on her knees, I watched over her with a paternal solicitude; I have traced her progress from injuries to arms, and from arms to liberty. Spirit of Swift! spirit of Molyneux! your genius has prevailed. Ireland is now a nation. In that new character I hail her, and bowing to her august presence, I say, *Esto perpetua!*

She is no longer a wretched colony, returning thanks to her governor for his rapine, and to her king for his oppression; nor is she now a squabbling, fretful sectary, perplexing her little wits, and firing her furious statutes with bigotry, sophistry, disabilities, and death, to transmit to posterity insignificance and war . . .

You, with difficulties innumerable, with dangers not a few, have done what your ancestors wished, but could not accomplish; and what your posterity may preserve, but will never equal: you have moulded the jarring elements of your country into a nation. You had not the advantages which were common to other great countries; no monuments, no trophies, none of those outward and visible signs of greatness, such as inspire mankind and connect the ambition of the age which is coming on with the example of that going off, and form the descent and concatenation of glory: no; you have not had any great act recorded among all your misfortunes, nor have you one public tomb to assemble the crowd, and spread to the living the language of integrity and freedom.

Your historians did not supply the want of monuments; on the contrary, these narrators of your misfortunes, who should have felt for your wrongs, and have punished your oppressors with oppressions, natural scourges, the moral indignation of history, compromised with public villainy and trembled; they excited your violence, they suppressed your provocation, and wrote in the chain which entrammelled their country. I am come to break that chain, and I congratulate my country, who, without any of the advantages I speak of, going forth, as it were, with nothing but a stone and a sling, and what oppression could not take away, the favour of Heaven, accomplished her own redemption, and left you nothing to add and everything to admire.

*An act giving Ireland its freedom was passed by both British Houses of Parliament a month later.*

•

## JOHN PHILPOT CURRAN
### 29 January 1794

### 'Universal emancipation'

*Archibald Hamilton Rowan was prosecuted for signing an appeal to the Volunteers, who were favouring revolutionary France, after Dublin Castle had issued a proclamation for repressing seditious associations. John Philpot Curran's defence of Rowan was later described by Alfred Brougham, the English statesman, as the greatest speech in ancient or modern times.*

*The famous passage on universal emancipation was praised as a fine specimen of climacteric energy by a nineteenth-century American commentator. 'As sentence follows after sentence, each heightens and deepens the effect, till the passage closes with the magnificent climax at the end, like the swell and crash of an orchestra.' As Curran ended this part of his speech, there was a sudden burst of applause from the hall.*

Gentlemen, the representation of our people is the vital principle of their political existence; without it they are dead, or they live only to servitude; without it there are two estates acting upon and against the third, instead of acting in co-operation with it; without it, if the people are oppressed by their judges, where is the tribunal to which the judges can be amenable? without it, if they are trampled upon and plundered by a minister, where is the tribunal to which the offender shall be amenable; without it, where is the ear to hear, or the heart to feel, or the hand to redress their sufferings? Shall they be found, let me ask you, in the accursed bands of imps and minions that bask in their disgrace, and fatten upon their spoils, and flourish upon their ruin? But let me not put this to you as a merely speculative question. It is a plain question of fact: rely upon it, physical man is everywhere the same; it is only the various operations of moral causes that gives variety to the social or individual character and condition. How otherwise happens it that modern slavery looks quietly at the despot, on the very spot where Leonidas expired? The answer is Sparta has not changed her climate, but she has lost that government which her liberty could not survive.

I call you, therefore, to a plain question of fact. This paper recommends a reform in Parliament, I put that question to your consciences; do you think it needs that reform? I put it boldly and fairly to you, do you think the people of Ireland are represented as they ought to be? Do you hesitate for an answer? If you do, let me remind you, that until last year, three millions of your countrymen have by the express letter of the law, been excluded from the reality of actual, and even from the phantom of virtual representation. Shall we then be told that this is the affirmation of a wicked and seditious incendiary? If you do not feel the mockery of such a charge, look at your country; in what state do you find it? Is it in a state of tranquillity and general satisfaction? These are traces by which good are ever to be distinguished from bad governments, without any very minute inquiry or speculative refinement. Do you feel that a veneration for the law, a pious and humble attachment to the Constitution, form the political morality of the people? Do you find that comfort and competency among your people which are always to be found where a government is mild and moderate, where taxes are imposed by a body who have an interest in treating the poorer orders with compassion, and preventing the weight of taxation from pressing sore upon them? . . .

This paper, gentlemen, insists upon the necessity of emancipating the Catholics of Ireland, and that is charged as part of the libel. If they had waited another year, if they had kept this prosecution impending for another year, how much would remain for a jury to decide upon I should be at a loss to discover. It seems as if the progress of public information was eating away the ground of the prosecution, this part of the libel has unluckily received the sanction of the legislature. In that interval our Catholic brethren have obtained that admission, which, it seems, it was a libel to propose; in what way to account for this, I am really at a loss. Have any alarms been occasioned by the emancipation of our Catholic brethren? Has the bigoted malignity of any individual been crushed? or has the stability of the government, or that of the country been weakened; or is one million of subjects stronger than four millions? Do you think that the benefit they received should be poisoned by the sting of vengeance? If you think so, you must say to them – 'You have demanded emancipation, and you have got it; but we abhor your persons, we are outraged at your success, and we will stigmatize by criminal prosecution the adviser of that relief which you have obtained from the voice of your country.' I ask you, do you think, as honest men, anxious for the public tranquillity, conscious that there are wounds not yet completely cicatrized, that you ought to speak this language at this time, to men who are too much disposed to think that in this very emancipation they have been saved from their own Parliament by the humanity of their sovereign?

Or do you wish to prepare them for the revocation of these improvident concessions? Do you think it wise or humane at this moment to insult them, by sticking up in a pillory the man who dared to stand forth as their advocate? I put it to your oaths; do you think that a blessing of that kind, that a victory obtained by justice over bigotry and oppression, should have a stigma cast upon it by an ignominious sentence upon men bold and honest enough to propose that measure? to propose the redeeming of religion from the abuses of the church, the reclaiming of three millions of men from bondage, and giving liberty to all who had a right to demand it; giving I say, in the so much censured words of this paper, giving 'universal emancipation!' I speak in the spirit of the British law, which makes liberty commensurate with and inseparable from British soil; which proclaims even to the stranger and sojourner, the moment he sets his foot upon British earth, that the ground on which he treads is holy, and consecrated by the genius of universal emancipation. No matter in what language his doom may have been pronounced; no matter what complexion incompatible with freedom, an Indian or an African sun may have burnt upon him; no matter in what disastrous battle his liberty may have been cloven down; no matter with what solemnities he may have been devoted upon the altar of slavery; the first moment he touches the sacred soil of Britain, the altar and the god sink together in the dust; his soul walks abroad in her own majesty; his body swells beyond the measure of his chains, that burst from around him; and he stands redeemed, regenerated, and disenthralled, by the irresistible genius of universal emancipation.

•

### WOLFE TONE
10 November 1798

### 'Whatever be the sentence of the court, I am prepared for it'

*Although he was a Protestant, Wolfe Tone (1763–98) organized a Catholic convention in Dublin in 1792 which persuaded the Irish parliament to pass the Catholic Relief Act, giving Catholics the vote on the same terms as Protestants a year later. He was forced into exile in 1794 during the French revolutionary wars and sought the help of France to overthrow the British in Ireland.*

*A French invasion expedition with forty-three ships, 15,000 men and Tone as adjutant was sent to Ireland in 1796 but was split up by storms and returned home. Two years later, the Irish rebellion gave Tone another opportunity but a small French force of 3,000 men was intercepted by the British off Donegal. Tone hoped to pass as a French officer but was betrayed by a former fellow-student. He made this proud, defiant speech to his court-martial.*

I mean not to give you the trouble of bringing judicial proof to convict me legally of having acted in hostility to the government of his Britannic Majesty in Ireland. I admit the fact. From my earliest youth I have regarded the connection between Great Britain and Ireland as the curse of the Irish nation, and felt convinced that, whilst it lasted, this country could never be free nor happy. My mind has been confirmed in this opinion by the experience of every succeeding year, and the conclusions which I have drawn from every fact before my eyes. In consequence, I was determined to employ all the powers which my individual efforts could move, in order to separate the two countries. That Ireland was not able of herself to throw off the yoke, I knew; I therefore sought for aid wherever it was to be found. In honourable poverty I rejected offers which, to a man in my circumstances, might be considered highly advantageous. I remained faithful to what I thought the cause of my country, and sought in the French Republic an ally to rescue three millions of my countrymen.

I believe there is nothing in what remains for me to say which can give any offence; I mean to express my feelings and gratitude towards the Catholic body, in whose cause I was engaged. I have laboured to create a people in Ireland by raising three millions of my countrymen to the rank of citizens. I have laboured to abolish the infernal spirit of religious persecution, by uniting the Catholics and Dissenters. To the former I owe more than ever can be repaid. The services I was so fortunate as to render them they rewarded munificently; but they did more: when the public cry was raised against me – when the friends of my youth swarmed off and left me alone – the Catholics did not desert me; they had the virtue even to sacrifice their own interests to a rigid principle of honour; they refused, though strongly urged, to disgrace a man who, whatever his conduct towards the government might have been, had faithfully and conscientiously discharged his duty towards them; and in so doing, though it was in my own case, I will say they showed an instance of public virtue of which I know not whether there exists another example.

I shall, then, confine myself to some points relative to my connection with the French army. Attached to no party in the French Republic – without interest, without money, without intrigue – the openness and integrity of my views raised me to a high and confidential rank in its armies. I obtained the confidence of the Executive Directory, the approbation of my generals, and I will venture to add, the esteem and affection of my brave comrades. When I review these circumstances, I feel a secret and internal consolation which no reverse of fortune, no sentence in the power of this court to inflict, can deprive me of, or weaken in any degree. Under the flag of the French Republic I originally engaged with a view to save and liberate my own country. For that purpose I have encountered the chances of war amongst strangers; for that purpose I repeatedly braved the terrors of the ocean covered, as I knew it to be, with the triumphant fleets of that power which it was my glory and my duty to oppose. I have sacrificed all my views in life; I have courted poverty; I have left a beloved wife unprotected, and children whom I adored, fatherless. After such a sacrifice, in a cause which I have always considered – conscientiously considered – as the cause of justice and freedom, it is no great effort at this day, to add the sacrifice of my life. But I hear it said that this unfortunate country has been a prey to all sorts of horrors. I sincerely lament it. I beg, however, it may be remembered that I have been absent four years from Ireland. To me these sufferings can never be attributed. I designed by fair and open war to procure the separation of the two countries. For open war I was prepared, but instead of that a system of private assassination has taken place. I repeat, whilst I deplore it, that it is not chargeable on me. Atrocities, it seems, have been committed on both sides. I do not less deplore them. I detest them from my heart; and to those who know my character and sentiments I may safely appeal for the truth of this assertion; with them I need no justification. In a case like this success is everything. Success, in the eyes of the vulgar, fixes its merits. Washington succeeded, and Kosciusko* failed. After a combat nobly sustained – a combat which would have excited the respect and sympathy of a generous enemy – my fate has been to become a prisoner to the eternal disgrace of those who gave the orders. I was brought here in irons like a felon. I mention this for the sake of others; for me, I am indifferent to it. I am aware of the fate which awaits me, and scorn equally the tone of complaint and that of supplication. As to the connection between this country and Great Britain, I repeat it – all that has been imputed to me (words, writings, and actions), I here deliberately avow. I have spoken and acted with reflection and on principle, and am ready to meet the consequences. Whatever be the sentence of the court I am prepared for it. Its members will surely discharge their duty – I shall take care not to be wanting in mine.

*Wolfe Tone was condemned to the scaffold but committed suicide before his execution could take place.*

•

## HENRY GRATTAN
### 26 May 1800

### 'Thou art not conquered'

*One of Henry Grattan's most electric speeches – made against the Union – was delivered when he was prostrated with disease and so feeble that he could not walk without help.*

The Constitution may for a time be so lost; the character of the country

* The polish soldier and patriot Tadeusz Kosciusko (1746–1817) led an uprising against the Russians but was taken prisoner in 1794.

cannot be so lost. The ministers of the Crown will, or may, perhaps, at length find that it is not so easy to put down for ever an ancient and respectable nation, by abilities, however great, and by power and by corruption, however irresistible. Liberty may repair her golden beams, and with redoubled heat animate the country: the cry of loyalty will not long continue against the principles of liberty; loyalty is a noble, a judicious and a capacious principle, but in these countries loyalty, distinct from liberty, is corruption, not loyalty.

The cry of the connection will not, in the end, avail against the principles of liberty. Connection is a wise and a profound policy; but connection without an Irish Parliament is connection without its own principle, without analogy of condition, without the pride of honour that should attend it; is innovation, is peril, is subjugation – not connection.

The cry of disaffection will not, in the end, avail against the principles of liberty.

Identification is a solid and imperial maxim, necessary for the preservation of freedom, necessary for that of empire; but, without union of hearts – with a separate government – and without a separate Parliament, identification is extinction, is dishonour, is conquest – not identification.

Yet I do not give up the country. I see her in a swoon, but she is not dead. Though in her tomb she lies helpless and motionless, still there is on her lips a spirit of life, and on her cheek a glow of beauty –

> Thou art not conquered; beauty's ensign yet
> Is crimson in thy lips and in thy cheeks,
> And death's pale flag is not advanced there.

While a plank of the vessel sticks together, I will not leave her. Let the courtier present his flimsy sail, and carry the light bark of his faith, with every new breath of wind. I will remain anchored here, with fidelity to the fortune of my country, faithful to her freedom, faithful to her fall.

•

# ROBERT EMMET
## 19 September 1803

### 'I am going to my cold and silent grave'

*As soon as he had left Trinity College, Dublin, Robert Emmet (1778–1803) travelled on the Continent, seeking help for the Irish cause and interviewing Napoleon and Talleyrand in 1802. He returned to Ireland in 1803 to spend his £3,000 fortune on muskets and pikes and plotted to seize Dublin Castle. The uprising failed. Emmet escaped but was captured when he returned from his hiding place in the Wicklow mountains to say farewell to his sweetheart, Sarah Curran.*

*His trial at Green Street courthouse lasted from early morning until ten o'clock at night. The jury did not leave their box and found him guilty. When asked whether he had anything to say before sentence of death was pronounced upon him, he delivered this defiant speech.*

I am asked what have I to say why sentence of death should not be pronounced on me, according to law. I have nothing to say that can alter your predetermination, nor that it will become me to say, with any view to the mitigation of that sentence which you are to pronounce, and I must abide by. But I have that to say which interests me more than life, and which you have laboured to destroy. I have much to say why my reputation should be rescued from the load of false accusation and calumny which has been cast upon it. I do not imagine that, seated where you are, your mind can be so free from prejudice as to receive the least impression from what I am going to utter. I have no hopes that I can anchor my character in the breast of a court constituted and trammelled as this is.

I only wish – and that is the utmost that I expect – that your lordships may suffer it to float down your memories untainted by the foul breath of prejudice, until it finds some more hospitable harbour to shelter it from the storms by which it is buffeted. Were I only to suffer death, after being adjudged guilty by your tribunal, I should bow in silence, and meet the fate that awaits me without a murmur; but the sentence of the law which delivers my body to the executioner will, through the ministry of the law, labour in its own vindication to consign my character to obloquy; for there must be guilt somewhere; whether in the sentence of the court, or in the catastrophe, time must determine. A man in my situation has not only to encounter the difficulties of fortune, and the force of power over minds which it has corrupted or subjugated, but the difficulties of established prejudice. The man dies, but his memory lives. That mine may not perish, that it may live in the respect of my countrymen, I seize upon this opportunity to vindicate myself from some of the charges alleged against me. When my spirit shall be wafted to a more friendly port – when my shade shall have joined the bands of those martyred heroes who have shed their blood on the scaffold and in the field, in the defence of their country and of virtue, this is my hope: I wish that my memory and my name may animate those who survive me, while I look down with complacency on the destruction of that perfidious government which upholds its domination by blasphemy of the Most High; which displays its power over man as over the beasts of the forest; which sets man upon his brother, and lifts his hand, in the name of God, against the throat of his fellow who believes or doubts a little more or a little less than the government standard – a government which is steeled to barbarity by the cries of the orphans and the tears of the widows it has made.

I appeal to the immaculate God – I swear by the throne of Heaven, before which I must shortly appear – by the blood of the murdered patriots who have gone before me – that my conduct has been, through all this peril, and through all my purposes, governed only by the conviction which I have uttered, and by no other view than that of the emancipation of my country from the super-inhuman oppression under which she has so long and too patiently travailed; and I confidently hope that, wild and chimerical as it may appear, there is still union and strength in Ireland to accomplish this noblest of enterprises. Of this I speak with the confidence of intimate knowledge, and with the consolation that appertains to that confidence. Think not, my lords, I say this for the petty gratification of giving you a transitory uneasiness. A man who never yet raised his voice to assert a lie will not hazard his character with posterity by asserting a falsehood on a subject so important to his country, and on an occasion like this. Yes, my lords, a man who does not wish to have his epitaph written until his country is liberated will not leave a weapon in the power of envy, or a pretence to impeach the probity which he means to preserve, even in the grave to which tyranny consigns him . . .

I have always understood it to be the duty of a judge, when a prisoner has been convicted, to pronounce the sentence of the law. I have also understood that judges sometimes think it their duty to hear with patience and to speak with humanity; to exhort the victim of the laws, and to offer, with tender benignity, their opinions of the motives by which he was actuated in the crime of which he was adjudged guilty. That a judge has thought it his duty as to have done, I have no doubt; but where is the boasted freedom of your institutions – where is the vaunted impartiality, clemency, and mildness of your courts of justice, if an unfortunate prisoner, whom your policy, and not justice, is about to deliver into the hands of the executioner, is not suffered to explain his motives sincerely and truly, and to vindicate the principles by which he was actuated? My lords, it may be a part of the system of angry justice to bow a man's mind by humiliation to the proposed ignominy of the scaffold; but worse to me than the purposed shame or the scaffold's terrors would be the shame of such foul and unfounded imputations as have been laid against me in this court. You, my lord, are a judge; I am the supposed culprit. I am a man; you are a man also. By a revolution of power we might change places, though we never could change characters. If I stand at the bar of this court and dare not vindicate my character, what a farce is your justice! If I stand at this bar and dare not vindicate my character, how dare you calumniate it? Does the sentence of death, which your unhallowed policy inflicts on my body, condemn my tongue to silence and my reputation to reproach? Your executioner may abridge the period of my existence; but while I exist, I shall not forbear to vindicate my character and motives from your aspersions; and, as a man, to whom fame is dearer than life, I will make the last use of that life in doing justice to that reputation which is to live after me, and which is the only legacy I can leave to those I honour and love, and for whom I am proud to perish. As men, my lords, we must appear on the great day at one common tribunal; and it will then remain for the Searcher of All Hearts to show a collective universe who was engaged in the most virtuous actions, or swayed by the purest motive – my country's oppressors, or –

Why did your lordships insult me? Or rather, why insult justice, in demanding of me why sentence of death should not be pronounced against me? I know, my lords, that form prescribes that you should ask the question. The form also presents the right of answering. This, no doubt, may be dispensed with, and so might the whole ceremony of the trial, since sentence was already pronounced at the Castle before the jury was empanelled. Your lordships are but the priests of the oracle, and I insist on the whole of the forms.

I am charged with being an emissary of France. An emissary of France! and for what end? It is alleged that I wish to sell the independence of my country; and for what end? Was this the object of my ambition?

And is this the mode by which a tribunal of justice reconciles contradiction? No; I am no emissary; and my ambition was to hold a place among the deliverers of my country, not in power nor in profit, but in the glory of the achievement. Sell my country's independence to France! and for what? Was it a change of masters? No, but for ambition. O my country! was it personal ambition that could influence me? Had it been the soul of my actions, could I not by my education and fortune, by the rank and consideration of my family, have placed myself amongst the proudest of your oppressors? My country was my idol! To it I sacrificed every selfish, every endearing sentiment; and for it I now offer up myself, O God! No, my lords; I acted as an Irishman, determined on delivering my country from the yoke of a foreign and unrelenting tyranny, and the more galling yoke of a domestic faction, which is its joint partner and perpetrator in the patricide, from the ignominy existing with an exterior of splendour and a conscious depravity. It was the wish of my heart to extricate my country from this doubly riveted despotism – I wished to place her independence beyond the reach of any power on earth. I wished to exalt her to that proud station in the world. Connection with France was, indeed, intended, but only as far as mutual interest would sanction or require. Were the French to assume any authority inconsistent with the purest independence, it would be the signal for their destruction. We sought their aid – and we sought it as we had assurance we should obtain it – as auxiliaries in war, and allies in peace. Were the French to come as invaders or enemies, uninvited by the wishes of the people, I should oppose them to the utmost of my strength. Yes! my countrymen, I should advise you to meet them upon the beach with a sword in one hand and a torch in the other. I would meet them with all the destructive fury of war. I would animate my countrymen to immolate them in their boats, before they had contaminated the soil of my country. If they succeeded in landing, and if forced to retire before superior discipline, I would dispute every inch of ground, burn every blade of grass, and the last entrenchment of liberty should be my grave. What I could not do myself, if I should fall, I should leave as a last charge to my countrymen to accomplish; because I should feel conscious that life, any more than death, is unprofitable when a foreign nation holds my country in subjection. But it was not as an enemy that the succours of France were to land. I looked, indeed, for the assistance of France; but I wished to prove to France and to the world that Irishmen deserved to be assisted; that they were indignant at slavery, and ready to assert the independence and liberty of their country. I wished to procure for my country the guarantee which Washington procured for America; to procure an aid which, by its example, would be as important as its valour; disciplined, gallant, pregnant with science and experience; that of a people who would perceive the good, and polish the rough points of our character. They would come to us as strangers, and leave us as friends, after sharing in our perils and elevating our destiny. These were my objects: not to receive new taskmasters, but to expel old tyrants. It was for these ends I sought aid from France; because France, even as an enemy, could not be more implacable than the enemy already in the bosom of my country.

I have been charged with that importance in the emancipation of my country as to be considered the keystone of the combination of Irishmen; or as your lordship expressed it, 'the life and blood of the conspiracy'. You do me honour overmuch; you have given to the subaltern all the credit of a superior. There are men engaged in this conspiracy who are not only superior to me, but even to your own conceptions of yourself, my lord – men before the splendour of whose genius and virtues I should bow with respectful deference, and who would think themselves disgraced by shaking your bloodstained hand.

What, my lord, shall you tell me, on the passage to the scaffold, which that tyranny (of which you are only the intermediary executioner) has erected for my murder, that I am accountable for all the blood that has been and will be shed in this struggle of the oppressed against the oppressor – shall you tell me this, and must I be so very a slave as not to repel it? I do not fear to approach the Omnipotent Judge to answer for the conduct of my whole life; and am I to be appalled and falsified by a mere remnant of mortality here? By you, too, although, if it were possible to collect all the innocent blood that you have shed in your un-hallowed ministry in one great reservoir, your lordship might swim in it.

Let no man dare, when I am dead, to charge me with dishonour; let no man attaint my memory, by believing that I could have engaged in any cause but that of my country's liberty and independence; or that I could have become the pliant minion of power, in the oppression and misery of my country. The proclamation of the provisional government speaks for our views; no inference can be tortured from it to countenance barbarity or debasement at home, or subjection, humiliation, or treachery from abroad. I would not have submitted to a foreign oppressor, for the same reason that I would resist the foreign and domestic oppressor. In the dignity of freedom, I would have fought upon the threshold of my country, and its enemy should enter only by passing over my lifeless corpse. And am I, who lived but for my country, and who have subjected myself to the dangers of the jealous and watchful oppressor, and the bondage of the grave, only to give my countrymen their rights, and my country her independence – am I to be loaded with calumny, and not suffered to resent it? No; God forbid!

If the spirits of the illustrious dead participate in the concerns and cares of those who were dear to them in this transitory life, O, ever dear and venerated shade of my departed father! look down with scrutiny upon the conduct of your suffering son, and see if I have, even for a moment, deviated from those principles of morality and patriotism which it was your care to instil into my youthful mind, and for which I am now about to offer up my life. My lords, you are impatient for the sacrifice. The blood which you seek is not congealed by the artificial terrors which surround your victim – it circulates warmly and unruffled through the channels which God created for noble purposes, but which you are now bent to destroy for purposes so grievous that they cry to heaven. Be yet patient! I have but a few more words to say – I am going to my cold and silent grave – my lamp of life is nearly extinguished – my race is run – the grave opens to receive me, and I sink into its bosom. I have but one request to ask at my departure from this world; it is – the charity of its silence. Let no man write my epitaph; for, as no man who knows my motives dares now vindicate them, let not prejudice or ignorance asperse them. Let them and me rest in obscurity and peace, and my tomb remain uninscribed, and my memory in oblivion, until other times and other men can do justice to my character. When my country takes her place among the nations of the earth, then, and not till then, let my epitaph be written. I have done.

*Emmet was hanged and then decapitated the next day.*

•

## DANIEL O'CONNELL
### 23 February 1814

### *'The eternal right to freedom of conscience'*

*As Henry Grattan became an old and broken man, it was Daniel O'Connell (1775–1847), the 'Liberator', who became the orator of Irish nationalism. O'Connell was called to the Irish bar in 1798, became a successful and affluent barrister, opposed the 1800 Act of Union which left the Protestant ascendancy intact, defended the persecuted, and led the agitation for the rights of Catholics. Roy Foster, the historian of Ireland, describes him as the greatest leader of Catholic Ireland.*

*In this speech, O'Connell, who was often accused of being too loyal to the British Crown, offers England Ireland's help in return for concessions to Catholics.*

As long as truth or justice can be supposed to influence man; as long as man is admitted to be under the control of reason; so long must it be prudent and wise to procure discussions on the sufferings and the rights of the people of Ireland. Truth has proclaimed the treacherous iniquity which deprived us of our chartered liberty; truth destroys the flimsy pretext under which this iniquity is continued; truth exposes our merits and our sufferings; whilst reason and justice combine to demonstrate our right – the right of every human being to freedom of conscience – a right without which every honest man must feel that to him, individually, the protection of government is a mockery, and the restriction of penal law a sacrilege.

Truth, reason and justice are our advocates; and even in England let me tell you that those powerful advocates have some authority. They are, it is true, more frequently resisted there than in most other countries; but yet they have some sway among the English at all times. Passion may confound and prejudice darken the English understanding; and interested passion and hired prejudice have been successfully employed against us at former periods; but the present season appears singularly well calculated to aid the progress of our cause, and to advance the attainment of our important objects.

I do not make the assertion lightly. I speak after deliberate investigation, and from solemn conviction, my clear opinion that we shall, during the present session of Parliament, obtain a portion at least, if not the entire, of our emancipation. We cannot fail, unless we are disturbed in our course by those who graciously style themselves our friends, or are betrayed by the treacherous machinations of part of our own body.

Yes, everything, except false friendship and domestic treachery, forebodes success. The cause of man is in its great advance. Humanity has been rescued from much of its thraldom. In the states of Europe, where the iron despotism of the feudal system so long classed men into two species – the hereditary masters and the perpetual slaves; when rank supplied the place of merit, and to be humbly born operated as a perpetual exclusion – in many parts of Europe man is reassuming his natural station, and artificial distinctions have vanished before the force of truth and the necessities of governors . . .

It is a moment of glorious triumph to humanity; and even one instance of liberty, freely conceded, makes compensation for a thousand repetitions of the ordinary crimes of military monarchs. The crime is followed by its own punishment; but the great principle of the rights of man establishes itself now on the broadest basis, and France and Germany now set forth an example for England to imitate . . .

The cause of liberty has made, and is making, great progress in states heretofore despotic. In all the countries in Europe, in which any portion of freedom prevails, the liberty of conscience is complete. England alone, of all the states pretending to be free, leaves shackles upon the human mind; England alone, amongst free states, exhibits the absurd claim of regulating belief by law, and forcing opinion by statute. Is it possible to conceive that this gross, this glaring, this iniquitous absurdity can continue? Is it possible, too, to conceive that it can continue to operate, not against a small and powerless sect, but against the millions, comprising the best strength, the most affluent energy of the empire? – a strength and an energy daily increasing, and hourly appreciating their own importance. The present system, disavowed by liberalized Europe, disclaimed by sound reason, abhorred by genuine religion, must soon and for ever be abolished.

Let it not be said that the princes of the Continent were forced by necessity to give privileges to their subjects, and that England has escaped from a similar fate. I admit that the necessity of procuring the support of the people was the mainspring of royal patriotism on the Continent; but I totally deny that the ministers of England can dispense with a similar support. The burdens of the war are permanent; the distresses occasioned by the peace are pressing; the financial system tottering, and to be supported in profound peace only by a war taxation. In the meantime, the resources of corruption are mightily diminished. Ministerial influence is necessarily diminished by one-half of the effective force of indirect bribery; full two-thirds must be disbanded. Peculation and corruption must be put upon half pay, and no allowances. The ministry lose not only all those active partisans; those outrageous loyalists, who fattened on the public plunder during the seasons of immense expenditure; but those very men will themselves swell the ranks of the malcontents, and probably be the most violent in their opposition. They have no sweet consciousness to reward them in their present privations; and therefore they are likely to exhaust the bitterness of their souls on their late employers. Every cause conspires to render this the period in which the ministry should have least inclination, least interest, least power, to oppose the restoration of our rights and liberties . . .

There is further encouragement at this particular crisis. Dissension has ceased in the Catholic body. Those who paralysed our efforts, and gave our conduct the appearance and reality of weakness, and wavering, and inconsistency, have all retired. Those who were ready to place the entire of the Catholic feelings and dignity, and some of the Catholic religion too, under the feet of every man who pleased to call himself our friend, and to prove himself our friend, by praising on every occasion, and upon no occasion, the oppressors of the Catholics, and by abusing the Catholics themselves; the men who would link the Catholic cause to this patron and to that, and sacrifice it at one time to the minister, and at another to the opposition, and make it this day the tool of one party, and the next the instrument of another party; the men, in fine, who hoped to traffic upon our country and our religion – who would buy honours, and titles, and places, and pensions, at the price of the purity, and dignity, and safety of the Catholic Church in Ireland; all those men have, thank God, quitted us, I hope for ever. They have returned into silence and secession, or have frankly or covertly gone over to our enemies. I regret deeply and bitterly that they have carried with them some few who, like my Lord Fingal, entertain no other motives than those of purity and integrity, and who, like that noble lord, are merely mistaken.

But I rejoice at this separation – I rejoice that they have left the single-hearted, and the disinterested, and the indefatigable, and the independent, and the numerous, and the sincere Catholics to work out their emancipation unclogged, unshackled, and undismayed. They have bestowed on us another bounty also – they have proclaimed the causes of their secession – they have placed out of doubt the cause of the diversions. It is not intemperance, for that we abandoned; it is not the introduction of extraneous topics, for those we disclaimed; it is simply and purely, veto or no veto – restriction or no restriction – no other words; it is religion and principle that have divided us; thanks, many thanks to the tardy and remote candour of the seceders, that has at length written in large letters the cause of their secession – it is the Catholic Church of Ireland – it is whether that Church shall continue independent of a Protestant ministry or not. We are for its independence – the seceders are for its dependence.

Those are our present prospects of success. First, man is elevated from slavery almost everywhere, and human nature has become more dignified, and, I may say, more valuable. Secondly, England wants our cordial support, and knows that she has only to secede to us justice in order to obtain our affectionate assistance. Thirdly, this is the season of successful petition, and the very fashion of the times entitles our petition to succeed. Fourthly, the Catholic cause is disencumbered of hollow friends and interested speculators. Add to all these the native and inherent strength of the principle of religious freedom and the inert and accumulating weight of our wealth, our religion, and our numbers, and where is the sluggard that shall dare to doubt our approaching success?

Besides, even our enemies must concede to us that we act from principle, and from principle only. We prove our sincerity when we refuse to make our emancipation a subject of traffic and barter, and ask for relief only upon those grounds which, if once established, would give to every other sect the right to the same political immunity. All we ask is 'a clear stage and no favour'. We think the Catholic religion the most rationally consistent with the divine scheme of Christianity, and, therefore, all we ask is that everybody should be left to his unbiased reason and judgement. If Protestants are equally sincere, why do they call the law, and the bribe, and the place, and the pension, in support of their doctrines? Why do they fortify themselves behind pains, and penalties, and exclusions, and forfeitures? Ought not our opponents to feel that they degrade the sanctity of their religion when they call in the profane aid of temporal rewards and punishments, and that they proclaim the superiority of our creed when they thus admit themselves unable to contend against it upon terms of equality, and by the weapons of reason and argument, and persevere in refusing us all we ask – 'clear stage and no favour'.

I close with conjuring the Catholics to persevere in their present course.

Let us never tolerate the slightest inroad on the discipline of our ancient, our holy Church. Let us never consent that she should be made the hireling of the ministry. Our forefathers would have died, nay, they perished in hopeless slavery rather than consent to such degradation.

Let us rest upon the barrier where they expired, or go back into slavery rather than forward into irreligion and disgrace! Let us also advocate our cause on the two great principles – first, that of an eternal separation in spirituals between our Church and the State; secondly, that of the eternal right to freedom of conscience – a right which, I repeat it with pride and pleasure, would exterminate the Inquisition in Spain and bury in oblivion the bloody orange flag of dissension in Ireland!

•

## RICHARD LALOR SHEIL
### 24 October 1828

*'Men with starvation in their faces'*

*The Irish dramatist Richard Lalor Sheil (1791–1851) helped Daniel O'Connell found the Catholic Association in 1825 and was one of the foremost champions of Irish freedom and Catholic emancipation – the subject of his memorable speech to a mass meeting at Penenden Heath in Kent. After the momentous Clare election, in which O'Connell was elected but could not take his seat, the British government began to consider Catholic emancipation.*

*Protestants were alarmed and announced a mass meeting at Penenden Heath. Sheil bought the freehold of a small area of the heath so that he could speak. A big crowd of Catholic sympathizers turned up and there was uproar. Sheil's supporters included William Cobbett and Jeremy Bentham, who wrote: 'So masterly a union of logic and rhetoric as Mr Sheil's speech scarcely have I ever beheld.'*

*Sheil started with an impassioned denunciation of 'calumniators of Catholicism' and then asked what had been the result of English oppression.*

You behold in Ireland a beautiful country, with wonderful advantages, agricultural and commercial – a resting-place for trade on its way to either hemisphere; indented with havens, watered by numerous rivers; with a fortunate climate in which fertility is raised upon a rich soil, and inhabited by a bold, intrepid, and, with all their faults, a generous and enthusiastic people. Such is Ireland as God made her – what is Ireland as you have made her? This fine country, swarming with a population the most miserable in Europe, of whose wretchedness, if you are the authors, you are beginning to be the victims – the poisoned chalice is returned in its just circulation to your lips. Harvests the most abundant are reaped by men with starvation in their faces; all the great commercial facilities of the country are lost – the rivers that should circulate opulence, and turn the machinery of a thousand manufactures, flow to the ocean without wafting a boat or turning a wheel – the wave breaks in solitude in the silent magnificence of deserted and shipless harbours. In place of being a source of wealth and revenue to the empire, Ireland cannot defray its own expenses; her discontent costs millions of money; she debilitates and endangers England. The great mass of her population are alienated and dissociated from the state – the influence of the constituted and legitimate authorities is gone; a strange, anomalous, and unexampled kind of government has sprung up, and exercises a despotic sway; while the class, inferior in numbers, but accustomed to authority, and infuriated at its loss, are thrown into formidable reaction – the most ferocious passions rage from one extremity of the country to the other. Hundreds and thousands of men, arrayed with badges, gather in the south, and the smaller faction, with discipline and with arms, are marshalled in the north – the country is like one vast magazine of powder, which a spark might ignite into an explosion, and of which England would not only feel, but, perhaps, never recover from the shock. And is this state of things to be permitted to continue? It is only requisite to present the question in order that all men should answer – something must be done. What is to be done? Are you to re-enact the Penal Code? Are you to deprive Catholics of their properties, to shut up their schools, to drive them from the Bar, to strip them of the elective franchise, and reduce them to Egyptian bondage?

It is easy for some visionary in oppression, to imagine these things. In the drunkenness of sacerdotal debauch, men have been found to give vent to such sanguinary aspirations, and the teachers of the Gospel, the ministers of a mild and merciful Redeemer, have uttered in the midst of their ferocious wassails, the bloody orison, that their country should be turned into one vast field of massacre, and that upon the pile of carnage the genius of Orange ascendancy should be enthroned. But these men are maniacs in ferocity, whose appetites for blood you will scarcely undertake to satiate. You shrink from the extirpation of a whole people. Even suppose that, with an impunity as ignominious as it would be sanguinary, that horrible crime could be effected, then you must needs ask, what is to be done? In answering that question you will not dismiss from your recollection that the greatest statesmen who have for the last fifty years directed your councils and conducted the business of this mighty empire, concurred in the opinion, that, without a concession of the Catholic claims, nothing could be done for Ireland . . . But supposing that authority, that the coincidence of the wisest and of the best in favour of Ireland was to be held in no account, consider how the religious disqualifications must necessarily operate. Can that be a wise course of government which creates not an aristocracy of opulence, and rank, and talent, but an aristocracy in religion, and places seven millions of people at the feet of a few hundred thousand? Try this fashion of government by a very obvious test, and make the case your own. If a few hundred thousand Presbyterians stood towards you in the relation in which the Irish Protestants stand towards the Catholics, would you endure it? Would you brook a system under which Episcopalians should be rendered incapable of holding seats in the House of Commons, should be excluded from sheriffships, and corporate offices, and from the bench of justice, and from all the higher offices in the administration of the law; and should be tried by none but Presbyterian juries, flushed with the insolence of power and infuriated with all the ferocity of passion? How would you brook the degradation which would arise from such a system, and the scorn and contumelies which would flow from it? Would you listen with patience to men who told you that there was no grievance in all this – that your complaints were groundless, and that the very right of murmuring ought to be taken away? Are Irishmen and Roman Catholics so differently constituted from yourselves, that they are to behold nothing but blessings in a system which you would look upon as an unendurable wrong?

Protestants and Englishmen, however debased you may deem our country, believe me that we have enough of human nature left within us – we have enough of the spirit of manhood, all Irishmen as we are, to resent a usage of this kind. Its results are obvious. The nation is divided into two castes. The powerful and the privileged few are patricians in religion, and trample upon and despise the plebeian Christianity of the millions who are laid prostrate at their feet. Every Protestant thinks himself a Catholic's better; and every Protestant feels himself the member of a privileged corporation. Judges, sheriffs, crown counsel, crown attorneys, juries, are Protestants to a man. What confidence can a Catholic have in the administration of public justice? We have the authority of an eminent Irish judge, the late Mr Fletcher, who declared that, in the north, the Protestants were uniformly acquitted, and the Catholics were as undeviatingly condemned. A body of armed Orangemen fall upon and put to death a defenceless Catholic; they are put upon their trial, and when they raise their eyes and look upon the jury, as they are commanded to do, they see twelve of their brethren in massacre empanelled for their trial; and, after this, I shall be told that all the evils of Catholic disqualification lie in the disappointed longing of some dozen gentlemen after the House of Commons. No; it is the ban, the opprobrium, the brand, the note and mark of dishonour, the scandalous partiality, the flagitious bias, the sacrilegious and perjured leaning, and the monstrous and hydra-headed injustice, that constitute the grand and essential evils of the country. And you think it wonderful that we should be indignant at all this.

*After Catholic emancipation, in 1830, Sheil became an MP, vice-president of the Board of Trade in 1839, a privy councillor and Master of the Mint.*

•

## DANIEL O'CONNELL
### 1833

### 'We are eight millions, and you treat us thus'

*Daniel O'Connell made this fierce speech to the House of Commons in 1833 when it was debating the Irish Disturbances Bill.*

I do not rise to fawn or cringe to this House; I do not rise to supplicate you to be merciful towards the nation to which I belong – towards a nation which, though subject to England, yet is distinct from it. It is a distinct nation; it has been treated as such by this country, as may be proved by history, and by seven hundred years of tyranny. I call upon this House, as you value the liberty of England, not to allow the present nefarious bill to pass. In it are involved the liberties of England, the liberty of the press, and of every other institution dear to Englishmen.

Against the bill I protest in the name of the Irish people, and in the face of heaven. I treat with scorn the puny and pitiful assertions that grievances are not to be complained of, that our redress is not to be agitated; for, in such cases, remonstrances cannot be too strong, agitation cannot be too violent, to show to the world with what injustice our fair claims are met, and under what tyranny the people suffer.

There are two frightful clauses in this bill. The one which does away with trial by jury, and which I have called upon you to baptize; you call it a court-martial – a mere nickname; I stigmatize it as a revolutionary tribunal. What, in the name of heaven, is it, if it is not a revolutionary tribunal. It annihilates the trial by jury: it drives the judge off his bench – the man who, from experience, could weigh the nice and delicate points of a case – who could discriminate between the straightforward testimony and the suborned evidence – who could see, plainly and readily, the justice or injustice of the accusation. It turns out this man who is free, unshackled, unprejudiced – who has no previous opinions to control the clear exercise of his duty. You do away with that which is more sacred than the throne itself; that for which your king reigns, your Lords deliberate, your Commons assemble.

If ever I doubted before of the success of our agitation for repeal, this bill, this infamous bill, the way in which it has been received by the House, the manner in which its opponents have been treated, the personalities to which they have been subjected, the yells with which one of them has this night been greeted – all these things dissipate my doubts, and tell me of its complete and early triumph. Do you think those yells will be forgotten? Do you suppose their echo will not reach the plains of my injured and insulted country; that they will not be whispered in her green valleys, and heard from her lofty hills? Oh! they will be heard there; yes, and they will not be forgotten. The youth of Ireland will bound with indignation; they will say, 'We are eight millions, and you treat us thus, as though we were no more to your country than the Isle of Guernsey or Jersey!'

I have done my duty; I stand acquitted to my conscience and my country: I have opposed this measure throughout; and I now protest against it as harsh, oppressive, uncalled for, unjust, as establishing an infamous precedent by retaliating crime against crime – as tyrannous, cruelly and vindictively tyrannous.

•

## DANIEL O'CONNELL
### 1 October 1843

### *'Ireland shall be free'*

*When Daniel O'Connell was elected MP for County Clare in 1828 he could not take his seat because he was a Catholic. A year later, threatened by civil war, the Wellington government granted Catholic emancipation. At Westminster, O'Connell built up his own party of Irish MPs and won reforms for Ireland, including a national system of elementary education, a new Poor Law and the beginning of municipal power for Catholics. They did not meet his ambitions, however, and in 1840 he founded the Repeal Association to end the Union and revived his mass meetings. Thirty were held between March and August.*

*The two most famous were at Tara, attended by a million people according to* The Times, *and at Mullaghmast.*

*At Mullaghmast, O'Connell was dressed in his robes of office as a Dublin alderman and was presented with an antique Irish headdress by the sculptor John Hogan. 'Sir,' he said, 'I only regret that this cap is not of gold.' O'Connell afterwards was known as Ireland's uncrowned king. He then addressed a meeting of 400,000.*

At Mullaghmast (and I have chosen this for this obvious reason), we are on the precise spot where English treachery – aye, and false Irish treachery, too – consummated a massacre that has never been imitated, save in the massacre of the Mamelukes by Mahomet Ali. It was necessary to have Turks atrocious enough to commit a crime equal to that perpetrated by Englishmen. But do not think that the massacre at Mullaghmast was a question between Protestants and Catholics – it was no such thing. The murdered persons were to be sure Catholics, but a great number of the murderers were also Catholic and Irishmen, because there were then, as well as now, many Catholics who were traitors to Ireland. But we have now this advantage, that we may have many honest Protestants joining us – joining us heartily in hand and heart, for old Ireland and liberty. I thought this a fit and becoming spot to celebrate, in the open day, our unanimity in declaring our determination not to be misled by any treachery. Oh, my friends, I will keep you clear of all treachery – there shall be no bargain, no compromise with England – we shall take nothing but repeal, and a Parliament in College Green. You will never, by my advice, confide in any false hopes they hold out to you; never confide in anything coming from them, or cease from your struggle, no matter what promise may be held to you, until you hear me say I am satisfied; and I will tell you where I will say that – near the statue of King William, in College Green. No; we came here to express our determination to die to a man, if necessary, in the cause of old Ireland. We came to take advice of each other, and, above all, I believe you came here to take my advice. I can tell you I have the game in my hand – I have the triumph secure – I have the repeal certain, if you but obey my advice.

I will go slow – you must allow me to do so – but you will go sure. No man shall find himself imprisoned or persecuted who follows my advice. I have led you thus far in safety; I have swelled the multitude of repealers until they are identified with the entire population or nearly the entire population of the land, for seven eighths of the Irish people are now enrolling themselves repealers. I don't want more power; I have power enough; and all I ask of you is to allow me to use it. I will go on quietly and slowly, but I will go on firmly, and with a certainty of success. I am now arranging a plan for the formation of the Irish House of Commons . . .

Among the nations of the earth, Ireland stands number one in the physical strength of her sons and in the beauty and purity of her daughters. Ireland, land of my forefathers, how my mind expands, and my spirit walks abroad in something of majesty, when I contemplate the high qualities, inestimable virtues, and true purity and piety and religious fidelity of the inhabitants of your green fields and productive mountains. Oh, what a scene surrounds us! It is not only the countless thousands of brave and active and peaceable and religious men that are here assembled, but nature herself has written her character with the finest beauty in the verdant plains that surround us. Let any man run round the horizon with his eye, and tell me if created nature ever produced anything so green and so lovely, so undulating, so teeming with production. The richest harvests that any land can produce are those reaped in Ireland; and then here are the sweetest meadows, the greenest fields, the loftiest mountains, the purest streams, the noblest rivers, the most capacious harbours – and her water power is equal to turn the machinery of the whole world.

Oh, my friends, it is a country worth fighting for – it is a country worth dying for; but above all, it is a country worth being tranquil, determined, submissive, and docile for; disciplined as you are in obedience to those who are breaking the way, and trampling down the barriers between you and your constitutional liberty, I will see every man of you having a vote, and every man protected by the ballot from the agent or landlord. I will see labour protected, and every title to possession recognized, when you are industrious and honest. I will see prosperity again throughout your land – the busy hum of the shuttle and the tinkling of the smithy shall be heard again. We shall see the nailer employed even until the middle of the night, and the carpenter covering himself with his chips. I will see prosperity in all its gradations spreading through a happy, contented, religious land. I will hear the hymn of a happy people go forth at sunrise to God in praise of His mercies – and I will see the evening sun set down amongst the uplifted hands of a religious and free population. Every blessing that man can bestow and religion can confer upon the faithful heart shall spread throughout the land. Stand by me – join with me – I will say be obedient to me, and Ireland shall be free.

*A week later another mass meeting was banned by Peel. It was then abandoned by*

O'Connell, an action which ruined his reputation with many of his supporters, who broke away and founded the violent Young Ireland movement. He died a broken man in Genoa in 1847 on his way to Rome.

•

## PATRICK PEARSE
## 1 August 1915

### 'Ireland unfree shall never be at peace'

*Patrick Pearse (1879–1916) was a founder member of the Irish Volunteers and was inducted into the Irish Republican Brotherhood in 1913. His panegyric at the graveside of O'Donovan Rossa was the apogee of his oratorical career and part of a carefully prepared campaign in the year leading up to the Easter Rising. Rossa, one of the most bitter but also most courageous of the old Fenians, had died after a long illness in America and was to be buried at Glasnevin Cemetery in Dublin. The funeral was arranged as a propaganda exercise and there were hundreds of thousands at Glasnevin.*

*It was Pearse's greatest test and he rose to the occasion with a speech which was his masterpiece. In his idealization of Rossa, Pearse sketched himself and heralded the approaching revolution. His peroration was open defiance of the British in Dublin Castle.*

*The souvenir of the funeral said: 'Cold, lifeless print cannot convey even an idea of the depth and intensity of feeling in which his words were couched. Calm and deliberate, in soft yet thrilling accents, his oration was almost sublime. Here was no rhetoric, no mathematical oratory; it was the soul of a patriot breathing words of love and devotion, of hope and truth and courage, no threnody, but a paean of triumph such as might have come from out of the tomb by which we were . . .'*

It has seemed right, before we turn away from this place in which we have laid the mortal remains of O'Donovan Rossa, that one among us should, in the name of all, speak the praise of that valiant man, and endeavour to formulate the thought and the hope that are in us as we stand around his grave. And if there is anything that makes it fitting that I, rather than some other, I rather than one of the grey-haired men who were young with him and shared in his labour and in his suffering, should speak here, it is perhaps that I may be taken as speaking on behalf of a new generation that has been rebaptized in the Fenian faith, and that has accepted the responsibility of carrying out the Fenian programme. I propose to you then that, here by the grave of this unrepentant Fenian, we renew our baptismal vows; that, here by the grave of this unconquered and unconquerable man, we ask of God, each one for himself, such unshakeable purpose, such high and gallant courage, such unbreakable strength of soul as belonged to O'Donovan Rossa.

Deliberately here we avow ourselves, as he avowed himself in the dock, Irishmen of one allegiance only. We of the Irish Volunteers, and you others who are associated with us in today's task and duty, are bound together and must stand together henceforth in brotherly union for the achievement of the freedom of Ireland. And we know only one definition of freedom: it is Tone's definition, it is Mitchel's definition, it is Rossa's definition. Let no man blaspheme the cause that the dead generations of Ireland served by giving it any other name and definition than their name and their definition.

We stand at Rossa's grave not in sadness but rather in exaltation of spirit that it has been given to us to come thus into so close a communion with that brave and splendid Gael. Splendid and holy causes are served by men who are themselves splendid and holy. O'Donovan Rossa was splendid in the proud manhood of him, splendid in the heroic grace of him, splendid in the Gaelic strength and clarity and truth of him. And all that splendour and pride and strength was compatible with a humility and a simplicity of devotion to Ireland, to all that was olden and beautiful and Gaelic in Ireland, the holiness and simplicity of patriotism of a Michael O'Clery or of an Eoghan O'Growney. The clear true eyes of this man almost alone in his day visioned Ireland as we of today would surely have her: not free merely, but Gaelic as well; not Gaelic merely, but free as well.

In a closer spiritual communion with him now than ever before or perhaps ever again, in a spiritual communion with those of his day, living and dead, who suffered with him in English prisons, in communion of spirit too with our own dear comrades who suffer in English prisons today, and speaking on their behalf as well as our own, we pledge to Ireland our love, and we pledge to English rule in Ireland our hate. This is a place of peace, sacred to the dead, where men should speak with all charity and with all restraint; but I hold it a Christian thing, as O'Donovan Rossa held it, to hate evil, to hate untruth, to hate oppression, and, hating them, to strive to overthrow them. Our foes are strong and wise and wary but, strong and wise and wary as they are, they cannot undo the miracles of God who ripens in the hearts of young men the seeds sown by the young men of a former generation. And the seeds sown by the young men of '65 and '67 are coming to their miraculous ripening today. Rulers and Defenders of Realms had need to be wary if they would guard against such processes. Life springs from death; and from the graves of patriot men and women spring living nations. The Defenders of this Realm have worked well in secret and in the open. They think that they have pacified Ireland. They think that they have purchased half of us and intimidated the other half. They think that they have foreseen everything, think that they have provided against everything; but the fools, the fools, the fools! – they have left us our Fenian dead, and while Ireland holds these graves, Ireland unfree shall never be at peace.

•

## ROGER CASEMENT
### 1916

### 'In Ireland alone, in this twentieth century, is loyalty held to be a crime'

*On his retirement from the British consular service in 1911, Roger Casement became a fervent Irish nationalist. At the outbreak of the First World War, he sought to recruit Irish prisoners of war for the German army. He went to Berlin to secure German aid for Irish independence but the Germans preferred the British Empire to a free Ireland and considered Casement a nuisance.*

*On the eve of the Easter Rising, he travelled to Ireland in a German U-boat to warn that there would be no German aid and that a rising would not succeed. He landed near Tralee but was quickly arrested by the British. He was taken to London and tried for high treason at the Old Bailey by an English Lord Chief Justice and an English jury. He was refused permission to conduct his own case and was allowed to speak only after the jury found him guilty.*

*His defiance in the dock and the powerful oratory of his defence explains why, for the Irish, he remains a patriot martyr. The speech has been described [by William Blunt] as the finest document in patriotic literature, finer than anything in Plutarch or elsewhere in Pagan literature. Years later Jawaharlal Nehru, leader of the Indian movement for independence from the British, said it seemed to point out exactly how a subject nation should feel.*

My Lord Chief Justice, as I wish my words to reach a much wider audience than I see before me here, I intend to read all that I propose to say. What I shall read now is something I wrote more than twenty days ago. I may say, my lord, at once, that I protest against the jurisdiction of this court in my case on this charge, and the argument, that I am now going to read, is addressed not to this court, but to my own countrymen.

There is an objection, possibly not good in law, but surely good on moral grounds, against the application to me here of this old English statute, 565 years old, that seeks to deprive an Irishman today of life and honour, not for 'adhering to the King's enemies', but for adhering to his own people.

When this statute was passed, in 1351, what was the state of men's minds on the question of a far higher allegiance – that of a man to God and His kingdom? The law of that day did not permit a man to forsake his Church, or deny his God, save with his life. The 'heretic', then, had the same doom as the 'traitor'.

Today a man may forswear God and His heavenly kingdom, without fear or penalty – all earlier statutes having gone the way of Nero's edicts against the Christians, but that constitutional phantom 'the King' can still dig up from the dungeons and torture-chambers of the Dark Ages a law that takes a man's life and limb for an exercise of conscience.

If true religion rests on love, it is equally true that loyalty rests on love. The law that I am charged under has no parentage in love, and claims the allegiance of today on the ignorance and blindness of the past.

I am being tried, in truth, not by my peers of the live present, but by the fears of the dead past; not by the civilization of the twentieth century, but by the brutality of the fourteenth; not even by a statute framed in the language of the land that tries me, but emitted in the language of an enemy land – so antiquated is the law that must be sought today to slay an Irishman, whose offence is that he puts Ireland first.

Loyalty is a sentiment, not a law. It rests on love, not on restraint. The government of Ireland by England rests on restraint, and not on law; and since it demands no love, it can evoke no loyalty . . .

Judicial assassination today is reserved only for one race of the King's subjects – for Irishmen, for those who cannot forget their allegiance to the realm of Ireland. The Kings of England, as such, had no rights in Ireland up to the time of Henry VIII, save such as rested on compact and mutual obligation entered into between them and certain princes, chiefs, and lords of Ireland. This form of legal right, such as it was, gave no King of England lawful power to impeach an Irishman for high treason under this statute of King Edward III of England until an Irish Act, known as Poyning's Law, the tenth of Henry VII, was passed in 1494 at Drogheda, by the Parliament of the Pale in Ireland, and enacted as law in that part of Ireland. But, if by Poyning's Law an Irishman of the Pale could be indicted for high treason under this Act, he could be indicted in only one way, and before one tribunal – by the laws of the Realm of Ireland and in Ireland. The very law of Poyning, which, I believe, applies this statute of Edward III to Ireland, enacts also for the Irishman's defence 'all these laws by which England claims her liberty'.

And what is the fundamental charter of an Englishman's Liberty? That he shall be tried by his peers. With all respect, I assert this court is to me, an Irishman, charged with this offence, a foreign court – this jury is for me, an Irishman, not a jury of my peers to try me on this vital issue, for it is patent to every man of conscience that I have a right, an indefeasible right, if tried at all, under this statute of high treason, to be tried in Ireland, before an Irish court and by an Irish jury. This court, this jury, the public opinion of this country, England, cannot but be prejudiced in varying degrees against me, most of all in time of war. I did not land in England. I landed in Ireland. It was to Ireland I came; to Ireland I wanted to come; and the last place I desired to land was in England.

But for the Attorney-General of England there is only 'England'; there is no Ireland; there is only the law of England, no right of Ireland; the liberty of Ireland and of an Irishman is to be judged by the power of England. Yet for me, the Irish outlaw, there is a land of Ireland, a right of Ireland, and a charter for all Irishmen to appeal to, in the last resort, a charter, that even the very statutes of England itself cannot deprive us of – nay more, a charter that Englishmen themselves assert as the funda- mental bond of law that connects the two kingdoms. This charge of high treason involves a moral responsibility, as the very terms of the indictment against myself recite, inasmuch as I committed the acts I am charged with to the 'evil example of others in like case'. What was the evil example I set to others in the like case, and who were these others? The 'evil example' charged is that I asserted the right of my own country and the 'others' I appealed to, to aid my endeavour, were my own countrymen. The example was given, not to Englishmen, but to Irishmen, and the 'like case' can never arise in England, but only in Ireland. To Englishmen I set no evil example, for I made no appeal to them. I asked no Englishman to help me. I asked Irishmen to fight for their rights. The 'evil example' was only to other Irishmen, who might come after me, and in 'like case' seek to do as I did. How, then, since neither my example, nor my appeal was addressed to Englishmen, can I be rightfully tried by them?

If I did wrong in making that appeal to Irishmen to join with me in an effort to fight for Ireland, it is by Irishmen, and by them alone, I can be rightfully judged. From this court and its jurisdiction I appeal to those I am alleged to have wronged, and to those I am alleged to have injured by my 'evil example' and claim that they alone are competent to decide my guilt or innocence. If they find me guilty, the statute may affix the penalty, but the statute does not override or annul my right to seek judgement at their hands.

This is so fundamental a right, so natural a right, so obvious a right, that it is clear that the Crown were aware of it when they brought me by force and by stealth from Ireland to this country. It was not I who landed in England, but the Crown who dragged me here, away from my own country to which I had returned with a price upon my head, away from my own countrymen whose loyalty is not in doubt, and safe from the judgement of my peers whose judgement I do not shrink from. I admit no other judgement but theirs. I accept no verdict save at their hands.

I assert from this dock that I am being tried here, not because it is just, but because it is unjust. Place me before a jury of my own countrymen, be it Protestant or Catholic, Unionist or Nationalist, Sinn Féineach or Orangemen, and I shall accept the verdict, and bow to the statute and all its penalties. But I shall accept no meaner finding against me, than that of those, whose loyalty I have endangered by my example, and to whom alone I made appeal. If they adjudge me guilty, then guilty I am. It is not I who am afraid of their verdict — it is the Crown. If this is not so, why fear the test? I fear it not. I demand it as my right.

This is the condemnation of English rule, of English-made law, of English government in Ireland, that it dare not rest on the will of the Irish people, but exists in defiance of their will: that it is a rule, derived not from right, but from conquest.

Conquest, my Lord, gives no title; and, if it exists over the body, it fails over the mind. It can exert no empire over men's reason and judgement and affections; and it is from this law of conquest without title to the reason, judgement, and affection of my own countrymen that I appeal.

I can answer for my own acts and speeches. While one English party was responsible for preaching a doctrine of hatred, designed to bring about civil war in Ireland, the other, and that the party in power, took no active steps to restrain a propaganda that found its advocates in the Army, Navy, and Privy Council – in the House of Parliament, and in the State Church – a propaganda the methods of whose expression were so 'grossly illegal and utterly unconstitutional' that even the Lord Chancellor of England could find only words and no repressive action to apply to them. Since lawlessness sat in high places in England, and laughed at the law as at the custodians of the law, what wonder was it that Irishmen should refuse to accept the verbal protestations of an English Lord Chancellor as a sufficient safeguard for their lives and liberties? I know not how all my colleagues on the Volunteer Committee in Dublin reviewed the growing menace, but those with whom I was in closest cooperation redoubled, in face of these threats from without, our efforts to unite all Irishmen from within. Our appeals were made to Protestant and Unionist as much almost as to Catholic and Nationalist Irishmen.

We hoped that, by the exhibition of affection and goodwill on our part toward our political opponents in Ireland, we should yet succeed in winning them from the side of an English party whose sole interest in our country lay in its oppression in the past, and in the present in its degradation to the mean and narrow needs of their political animosities. It is true that they based their actions, so they averred, on 'ears for the empire', and on a very diffuse loyalty that took in all the peoples of the empire, save only the Irish. That blessed word *empire* that bears so paradoxical resemblance to charity! For if charity begins at home, *empire* begins in other men's homes, and both may cover a multitude of sins. I, for one, was determined that Ireland was much more to me than *empire*, and, if charity begins at home, so must loyalty. Since arms were so necessary to make our organization a reality, and to give to the minds of Irishmen, menaced with the most outrageous threats, a sense of security, it was our bounden duty to get arms before all else. I decided, with this end in view, to go to America, with surely a better right to appeal to Irishmen there for help in an hour of great national trial, than those envoys of *empire* could assert for their weekend descents on Ireland, or their appeals to Germany.

If, as the right honourable gentleman, the present Attorney-General, asserted in a speech at Manchester, Nationalists would neither fight for Home Rule nor pay for it, it was our duty to show him that we knew how to do both. Within a few weeks of my arrival in the United States, the fund that had been opened to secure arms for the Volunteers of Ireland amounted to many thousands of pounds. In every case the money subscribed, whether it came from the purse of the wealthy man, or from the still readier pocket of the poor man, was Irish gold.

We have been told, we have been asked to hope, that after this war Ireland will get Home Rule, as a reward for the lifeblood shed in a cause which, whomever else its success may benefit, can surely not benefit Ireland. And what will Home Rule be in return for what its vague promise has taken, and still hopes to take away from Ireland? It is not necessary to climb the painful stairs of Irish history – that treadmill of a nation, whose labours are as vain for her own uplifting as the convict's exertions are for his redemption, to review the long list of British promises made only to be broken – of Irish hopes, raised only to be dashed to the ground. Home Rule, when it comes, if come it does, will find an Ireland drained of all that is vital to its very existence unless it be that unquenchable hope we build on the graves of the dead. We are told that if Irishmen go by the thousand to die, not for Ireland, but for Flanders, for Belgium, for a patch of sand in the deserts of Mesopotamia, or a rocky trench on the heights of Gallipoli, they are winning self-government for Ireland. But if they dare to lay down their lives on their native soil, if they dare to dream even that freedom can be won only at home by men resolved to fight for it there, then they are traitors to their country, and their dream and their deaths are phases of a dishonourable phantasy.

But history is not so recorded in other lands. In Ireland alone, in this twentieth century, is loyalty held to be a crime. If loyalty be something less than love and more than law, then we have had enough of such loyalty for Ireland and Irishmen. If we are to be indicted as criminals, to be shot as murderers, to be imprisoned as convicts, because our offence is that we love Ireland more than we value our lives, then I do not know what virtue resides in any offer of self-government held out to brave men on such terms. Self-government is our right, a thing born in us at birth, a thing no more to be doled out to us, or withheld from us, by another people than the right to life itself – than the right to feel the sun, or smell the flowers, or to love our kind. It is only from the convict these things are withheld, for crime committed and proven – and Ireland, that has wronged no man, has injured no land, that has sought no dominion over others – Ireland is being treated today among the nations of the world as if she were a convicted criminal. If it be treason to fight against such an unnatural fate as this, then I am proud to be a rebel, and shall cling to my 'rebellion' with the last drop of my blood. If there be no right of rebellion against the state of things that no savage tribe would endure without resistance, then I am sure that it is better for men to fight and die without right than to live in such a state of right as this. Where all your rights have become only an accumulated wrong, where men must beg with bated breath for leave to subsist in their own land, to think their own thoughts, to sing their own songs, to gather the fruits of their own labours, and, even while they beg, to see things inexorably withdrawn from them – then, surely, it is a braver, a saner and truer thing to be a rebel, in act and in deed, against such circumstances as these, than to tamely accept it, as the natural lot of men.

*Casement was condemned to death and hanged. His so-called Black Diaries containing homosexual passages were circulated by British agents to discredit him and discourage any movement for a reprieve. Thanks to Casement, Sinn Féin got the credit for the Easter Rising – and the independence of Ireland triumphed when he was hanged.*

•

# WOMEN'S LIBERATION

# FRANCES WRIGHT
## 4 July 1828

### 'Let us rejoice as human beings'

*Frances Wright (1795–1852) was born a Scottish heiress but emigrated to the United States in 1818 and was the first woman to win fame as a public speaker. As an early suffragette she campaigned for the emancipation of women; as a social reformer, she lectured on science, religion and education and was often in danger of being mobbed.*

*She tried but failed to establish a colony for free blacks in Tennessee but went on to join Robert Owen's colony at New Harmony in Indiana. She also helped to form the first American Labour party, the Workingmen's Party of New York, in 1829.*

*It was at New Harmony that she delivered this Independence Day address.*

From the era which dates the national existence of the American people dates also a mighty step in the march of human knowledge. And it is consistent with that principle in our conformation which leads us to rejoice in the good which befalls our species, and to sorrow for the evil, that our hearts should expand on this day. On this day, which calls to memory the conquest achieved by knowledge over ignorance, willing cooperation over blind obedience, opinion over prejudice, new ways over old ways – when, fifty-two years ago, America declared her national independence, and associated it with her republic federation. Reasonable is it to rejoice on this day, and useful to reflect thereon; so that we rejoice for the real, and not any imaginary, good; and reflect on the positive advantages obtained, and on those which it is ours farther to acquire.

Dating, as we justly may, a new era in the history of man from the Fourth of July, 1776, it would be well – that is, it would be useful – if on each anniversary we examined the progress made by our species in just knowledge and just practice. Each Fourth of July would then stand as a tidemark in the flood of time by which to ascertain the advance of the human intellect, by which to note the rise and fall of each successive error, the discovery of each important truth, the gradual melioration in our public institutions, social arrangements, and, above all, in our moral feelings and mental views . . .

In continental Europe, of late years, the words patriotism and patriot have been used in a more enlarged sense than it is usual here to attribute to them, or than is attached to them in Great Britain. Since the political struggles of France, Italy, Spain, and Greece, the word patriotism has been employed, throughout continental Europe, to express a love of the public good; a preference for the interests of the many to those of the few; a desire for the emancipation of the human race from the thrall of despotism, religious and civil: in short, patriotism there is used rather to express the interest felt in the human race in general than that felt for any country, or inhabitants of a country, in particular. And patriot, in like manner, is employed to signify a lover of human liberty and human improvement rather than a mere lover of the country in which he lives, or the tribe to which he belongs. Used in this sense, patriotism is a virtue, and a patriot a virtuous man. With such an interpretation, a patriot is a useful member of society, capable of enlarging all minds and bettering all hearts with which he comes in contact; a useful member of the human family, capable of establishing fundamental principles and of merging his own interests, those of his associates, and those of his nation in the interests of the human race. Laurels and statues are vain things, and mischievous as they are childish; but could we imagine them of use, on *such* a patriot alone could they be with any reason bestowed . . .

If such a patriotism as we have last considered should seem likely to obtain in any country, it should be certainly in this. In this which is truly the home of all nations and in the veins of whose citizens flows the blood of every people on the globe. Patriotism, in the exclusive meaning, is surely not made for America. Mischievous everywhere, it were here both mischievous and absurd. The very origin of the people is opposed to it. The institutions, in their principle, militate against it. The day we are celebrating protests against it. It is for Americans, more especially, to nourish a nobler sentiment; one more consistent with their origin, and more conducive to their future improvement. It is for them more especially to know why they love their country; and to *feel* that they love it, not because it *is* their country, but because it is the palladium of human liberty – the favored scene of human improvement. It is for them, more especially, to examine their institutions; and to *feel* that they honor them because they are based on just principles. It is for them, more especially, to examine their institutions, because they have the means of improving them; to examine their laws, because at will they can alter them. It is for them to lay aside luxury whose wealth is in industry; idle parade whose strength is in knowledge; ambitious distinctions whose principle is equality. It is for them not to rest, satisfied with words, who can seize upon things; and to remember that equality means, not the mere equality of political rights, however valuable, but equality of instruction and equality in virtue; and that liberty means, not the mere voting at elections, but the free and fearless exercise of the mental faculties and that self-possession which springs out of well-reasoned opinions and consistent practice. It is for them to honor principles rather than men – to commemorate events rather than days; when they rejoice, to know for what they rejoice, and to rejoice only for what has brought and what brings peace and happiness to men. The event we commemorate this day has procured much of both, and shall procure in the onward course of human improvement more than we can now conceive of. For this – for the good obtained and yet in store for our race – let us rejoice! But let us rejoice as men, not as children – as human beings rather than as Americans – as reasoning beings, not as ignorants. So shall we rejoice to good purpose and in good feeling; so shall we improve the victory once on this day achieved, until all mankind hold with us the Jubilee of Independence.

•

## ELIZABETH CADY STANTON
### 19 July 1848

*'We now demand our right to vote'*

*As a girl Elizabeth Cady Stanton (1815–1902) was allowed to study classics and mathematics at a boys' school and to read the books in her father's law office, where she heard the complaints of women who sought his help. That was how she became aware of the humiliating status of women. When she married Henry Stanton, a well-known abolitionist, in 1840, the word 'obey' was omitted from the ceremony.*

*When she accompanied her husband that year to the world anti-slavery convention, she noticed that women were excluded and struck up a friendship with Lucretia Mott, a fellow Quaker abolitionist. They became allies and planned a women's rights convention – held eight years later at Seneca Falls, New York.*

*The Convention adapted the Declaration of Independence to read: 'We hold these truths to be self-evident: that all men and women are created equal.' It demanded the vote, property rights, and admission to higher education and church offices. Stanton delivered the keynote address.*

We have met here today to discuss our rights and wrongs, civil and political, and not, as some have supposed, to go into the detail of social life alone. We do not propose to petition the legislature to make our husbands just, generous, and courteous, to seat every man at the head of a cradle, and to clothe every woman in male attire. None of these points, however important they may be considered by leading men, will be touched in this convention. As to their costume, the gentlemen need feel no fear of our imitating that, for we think it in violation of every principle of taste, beauty, and dignity; notwithstanding all the contempt cast upon our loose, flowing garments, we still admire the graceful folds, and consider our costume far more artistic than theirs. Many of the nobler sex seem to agree with us in this opinion, for the bishops, priests, judges, barristers, and lord mayors of the first nation on the globe, and the Pope of Rome, with his cardinals, too, all wear the loose flowing robes, thus tacitly acknowledging that the male attire is neither dignified nor imposing. No, we shall not molest you in your philosophical experiments with stocks, pants, high-heeled boots, and Russian belts. Yours be the glory to discover, by personal experience, how long the kneepan can resist the terrible strapping down which you impose, in how short time the well-developed muscles of the throat can be reduced to mere threads by the constant pressure of the stock, how high the heel of a boot must be to make a short man tall, and how tight the Russian belt may be drawn and yet have wind enough left to sustain life.

But we are assembled to protest against a form of government existing without the consent of the governed – to declare our right to be free as man is free, to be represented in the government which we are taxed to support, to have such disgraceful laws as give man the power to chastise and imprison his wife, to take the wages which she earns, the property which she inherits, and, in case of separation, the children of her love; laws which make her the mere dependent on his bounty. It is to protest against such unjust laws as these that we are assembled today, and to have them, if possible, forever erased from our statute books, deeming them a shame and a disgrace to a Christian republic in the nineteenth century. We have met

> To uplift woman's fallen divinity
> Upon an even pedestal with man's.

And, strange as it may seem to many, we now demand our right to vote according to the declaration of the government under which we live. This right no one pretends to deny. We need not prove ourselves equal to Daniel Webster to enjoy this privilege, for the ignorant Irishman in the ditch has all the civil rights he has. We need not prove our muscular power equal to this same Irishman to enjoy this privilege, for the most tiny, weak, ill-shaped stripling of twenty-one has all the civil rights of the Irishman. We have no objection to discuss the question of equality, for we feel that the weight of argument lies wholly with us, but we wish the question of equality kept distinct from the question of rights, for the proof of the one does not determine the truth of the other. All white men in this country have the same rights, however they may differ in mind, body, or estate.

The right is ours. The question now is: how shall we get possession of what rightfully belongs to us? We should not feel so sorely grieved if no man who had not attained the full stature of a Webster, Clay, Van Buren, or Gerrit Smith could claim the right of the elective franchise. But to have drunkards, idiots, horse-racing, rum-selling rowdies, ignorant foreigners, and silly boys fully recognized, while we ourselves are thrust out from all the rights that belong to citizens, it is too grossly insulting to the dignity of woman to be longer quietly submitted to. The right is ours. Have it, we must. Use it, we will. The pens, the tongues, the fortunes, the indomitable wills of many women are already pledged to secure this right. The great truth that no just government can be formed without the consent of the governed we shall echo and re-echo in the ears of the unjust judge, until by continual coming we shall weary him . . .

There seems now to be a kind of moral stagnation in our midst. Philanthropists have done their utmost to rouse the nation to a sense of its sins. War, slavery, drunkenness, licentiousness, gluttony, have been dragged naked before the people, and all their abominations and deformities fully brought to light, yet with idiotic laugh we hug those monsters to our breasts and rush on to destruction. Our churches are multiplying on all sides, our missionary societies, Sunday schools, and prayer meetings and innumerable charitable and reform organizations are all in operation, but still the tide of vice is swelling, and threatens the destruction of everything, and the battlements of righteousness are weak against the raging elements of sin and death. Verily, the world waits the coming of some new element, some purifying power, some spirit of mercy and love. The voice of woman has been silenced in the state, the church, and the home, but man cannot fulfill his destiny alone, he cannot redeem his race unaided. There are deep and tender chords of sympathy and love in the hearts of the downfallen and oppressed that woman can touch more skillfully than man.

The world has never yet seen a truly great and virtuous nation, because in the degradation of woman the very fountains of life are poisoned at their source. It is vain to look for silver and gold from mines of copper and lead. It is the wise mother that has the wise son. So long as your women are slaves you may throw your colleges and churches to the winds. You can't have scholars and saints so long as your mothers are ground to powder between the upper and nether millstone of tyranny and lust. How seldom, now, is a father's pride gratified, his fond hopes realized, in the budding genius of his son! The wife is degraded, made the mere creature of caprice, and the foolish son is heaviness to his heart. Truly are the sins of the fathers visited upon the children to the third and fourth generation. God, in His wisdom, has so linked the whole human family together that any violence done at one end of the chain is felt throughout its length, and here, too, is the law of restoration, as in woman all have fallen, so in her elevation shall the race be recreated.

'Voices' were the visitors and advisers of Joan of Arc. Do not 'voices' come to us daily from the haunts of poverty, sorrow, degradation, and despair, already too long unheeded. Now is the time for the women of this country, if they would save our free institutions, to defend the right, to buckle on the armor that can best resist the keenest weapons of the enemy – contempt and ridicule. The same religious enthusiasm that nerved Joan of Arc to her work nerves us to ours. In every generation God calls some men and women for the utterance of truth, a heroic action, and our work today is the fulfilling of what has long since been foretold by the Prophet – Joel 2:28: 'And it shall come to pass afterward, that I will pour out my spirit upon all flesh; and your sons and your daughters shall prophesy.' We do not expect our path will be strewn with the flowers of popular applause, but over the thorns of bigotry and prejudice will be our way, and on our banners will beat the dark storm clouds of opposition from those who have entrenched themselves behind the stormy bulwarks of custom and authority, and who have fortified their position by every means, holy and unholy. But we will steadfastly abide the result. Unmoved we will bear it aloft. Undauntedly we will unfurl it to the gale, for we know that the storm cannot rend from it a shred, that the electric flash will but more clearly show to us the glorious words inscribed upon it, 'Equality of Rights' . . .

•

## SOJOURNER TRUTH
### 28 May 1851

### 'A'n't I a woman?'

*Sojourner Truth (c. 1797–1883) was a slave who fled in 1827 from the house-hold in New York state where she worked and found refuge with a religious group which helped her to find and free two of her children who had been sold into slavery.*

*She moved to New York City in 1829, found work as a domestic and became active in religious movements. After 'voices' told her to take the name of Sojourner Truth, she became a preacher against the evils of slavery, drawing big crowds in Ohio, Indiana, Missouri and Kansas.*

*She delivered this speech at the State Women's Rights Convention in Akron, Ohio.*

Wall, childern, whar dar is so much racket dar must be somethin' out o' kilter. I tink dat 'twixt de niggers of de Souf and de womin at de Norf, all talkin' 'bout rights, de white men will be in a fix pretty soon. But what's all dis her talkin' 'bout?

Dat man ober dar say dat womin needs to be helped into carriages, and lifted over ditches, and to hab de best place everywhar. Nobody eber helps me into carriages, or ober mud-puddles, or gibs me any best place. And a'n't I a woman? Look at me! Look at my arm! I have ploughed and planted, and gathered into barns, and no man could head me! And a'n't I a woman? I could work as much and eat as much as a man – when I could get it – and bear de lash as well! And a'n't I a woman? I have borne thirteen childern, and see 'em mos' all sold off to slavery, and when I cried out with my mother's grief, none but Jesus heard me! And a'n't I a woman?

Den dey talks 'bout dis ting in de head; what dis dey call it? (*Intellect*, whispered someone near.) Dat's it, honey. What's dat go to do wid womin's right o nigger's rights? If my cup won't hold but a pint, and yourn holds a quart, wouldn't ye be mean not to let me have my little half-measure full?

Den dat little man in black dar, he say women can't have as much rights as man, 'cause Christ wan't a woman. Whar did your Christ come from? Whar did your Christ come from? From God and a woman! Man had nothin' to do wid Him.

If de fust woman God ever made was strong enough to turn de world upside down all alone, dese women togedder ought to be able to turn it back, and get it right side up again! And now dey is asking to do it, de men better let 'em. (*Long continued cheering.*)

Bleeged to ye for hearin on me, and now old Sojourner han't got nothin' more to say. (*Roars of applause.*)

•

## LUCY STONE
### 1855

### *'Disappointment is the lot of women'*

*Five years before she delivered this speech, the American feminist Lucy Stone (1818–93) had called the first national Women's Rights Convention at Worcester, Massachusetts. Yet in 1855 most educational institutions and professions were closed to women. Stone's father did not approve of education for women and she did not start her studies at Oberlin College until she was twenty-five. She soon became a public speaker.*

*'Doing a Lucy Stone' became a standard catchphrase after she married Henry Brown Blackwell and kept her maiden name as a symbol of equality.*

From the first years to which my memory stretches, I have been a disappointed woman. When, with my brothers, I reached forth after the sources of knowledge, I was reproved with 'It isn't fit for you; it doesn't belong to women.' Then there was but one college in the world where women were admitted, and that was in Brazil. I would have found my way there, but by the time I was prepared to go, one was opened in the young State of Ohio – the first in the United States where women and negroes could enjoy opportunities with white men. I was disappointed when I came to seek a profession worthy an immortal being – every employment was closed to me, except those of the teacher, the seamstress, and the housekeeper. In education, in marriage, in religion, in everything, disappointment is the lot of woman. It shall be the business of my life to deepen this disappointment in every woman's heart until she bows down to it no longer. I wish that women, instead of being walking show-cases, instead of begging of their fathers and brothers the latest and gayest new bonnet, would ask of them their rights.

The question of Woman's Rights is a practical one. The notion has prevailed that it was only an ephemeral idea; that it was but women claiming the right to smoke cigars in the streets, and to frequent bar-rooms. Others have supposed it a question of comparative intellect; others still, of sphere. Too much has already been said and written about woman's sphere. Trace all the doctrines to their source and they will be found to have no basis except in the usages and prejudices of the age. This is seen in the fact that what is tolerated in woman in one country is not tolerated in another. In this country women may hold prayer-meetings, etc., but in Mohammedan countries it is written upon their mosques, 'Women and dogs, and other impure animals, are not permitted to enter.' Wendell Phillips says, 'The best and greatest thing one is capable of doing, that is his sphere.' I have confidence in the Father to believe that when He gives us the capacity to do anything He does not make a blunder. Leave women, then, to find their sphere. And do not tell us before we are born even, that our province is to cook dinners, darn stockings, and sew on buttons. We are told woman has all the rights she wants; and even women, I am ashamed to say, tell us so. They mistake the politeness of men for rights – seats while men stand in this hall to-night, and their adulations; but these are mere courtesies.

We want rights. The flour-merchant, the housebuilder, and the post-man charge us no less on account of our sex; but when we endeavor to earn money to pay all these, then, indeed we find the difference. Man, if he have energy, may hew out for himself a path where no mortal has ever trod, held back by nothing but what is in himself; the world is all before him, where to choose; and we are glad for you, brothers, men, that it is so. But the same society that drives forth the young man, keeps woman at home – a dependent – working little cats on worsted, and little dogs on punctured paper; but if she goes heartily and bravely to give herself to some worthy purpose, she is out of her sphere and she loses caste. Women working in tailor-shops are paid one-third as much as men. Some one in Philadelphia has stated that women make fine shirts for twelve and a half cents apiece; that no woman can make more than nine a week, and the sum thus earned, after deducting rent, fuel, etc., leaves her just three and a half cents a day for bread. Is it a wonder that women are driven to prostitution? Female teachers in New York are paid fifty dollars a year, and for every such situation there are five hundred applicants. I know not what you believe of God, but I believe He gave yearnings and longings to be filled, and that He did not mean all our time should be devoted to feeding and clothing the body. The present condition of woman causes a horrible perversion of the marriage relation.

It is asked of a lady, 'Has she married well?' 'Oh yes, her husband is rich.' Woman must marry for a home, and you men are the sufferers by this; for a woman who loathes you may marry you because you have the means to get money which she can not have. But when woman can enter the lists with you and make money for herself, she will marry you only for deep and earnest affection.

•

## SOJOURNER TRUTH
### 9 May 1867

#### '*I have a right to have just as much as a man*'

*Sojourner Truth settled in Battle Creek, Michigan, in the late 1850s and solicited food and clothing for the Negro volunteer regiments preparing for the Civil War – and was later recognized in Washington for her efforts by President Lincoln. She continued speaking for black rights and women's suffrage, as in this speech to the National Convention of American Equal Rights Association at the Church of Puritans in New York City.*

My friends, I am rejoiced that you are glad, but I don't know how you will feel when I get through. I come from another field – the country of the slave. They have got their liberty – so much good luck to have slavery partly destroyed; not entirely. I want it root and branch destroyed. Then we will all be free indeed. I feel that if I have to answer for the deeds done in my body just as much as a man, I have a right to have just as much as a man. There is a great stir about colored men getting their rights, but not a word about the colored women; and if colored men get their rights, and not colored women theirs, you see the colored men will be masters over the women, and it will be just as bad as it was before. So I am for keeping the thing going while things are stirring; because if we wait till it is still, it will take a great while to get it going again. White women are a great deal smarter, and know more than colored women, while colored women do not know scarcely anything. They go out washing, which is about as high as a colored woman gets, and their men go about idle, strutting up and down; and when the women come home, they ask for their money and take it all, and then scold because there is no food. I want you to consider on that, chil'n. I call you chil'n; you are somebody's chil'n, and I am old enough to be mother of all that is here. I want women to have their rights. In the courts women have no right, no voice; nobody speaks for them. I wish woman to have her voice there among the pettifoggers. If it is not a fit place for women, it is unfit for men to be there.

I am above eighty years old; it is about time for me to be going. I have been forty years a slave and forty years free, and would be here forty years more to have equal rights for all. I suppose I am kept here because something remains for me to do; I suppose I am yet to help to break the chain. I have done a great deal of work; as much as a man, but did not get so much pay. I used to work in the field and bind grain, keeping up with the cradler; but men doing no more, got twice as much pay; so with the German women. They work in the field and do as much work, but do not get the pay. We do as much, we eat as much, we want as much. I suppose I am about the only colored woman that goes about to speak for the rights of the colored women. I want to keep the thing stirring, now that the ice is cracked. What we want is a little money. You men know that you get as much again as women when you write, or for what you do. When we get our rights we shall not have to come to you for money, for then we shall have money enough in our own pockets; and may be you will ask us for money. But help us now until we get it. It is a good consolation to know that when we have got this battle fought we shall not be coming to you any more. You have been having our rights so long, that you think, like a slaveholder, that you own us. I know that it is hard for one who has held the reins for so long to give up; it cuts like a knife. It will feel all the better when it closes up again. I have been in Washington about three years, seeing about these colored people. Now colored men have the right to vote. There ought to be equal rights now more than ever, since colored people have got their freedom. I am going to talk several times while I am here; so now I will do a little singing. I have not heard any singing since I came here.

(*Accordingly, suiting the action to the word, Sojourner sang, 'We are going home.'*)

There, children, in heaven we shall rest from all our labors; first do all we have to do here. There I am determined to go, not to stop short of that beautiful place, and I do not mean to stop till I get there, and meet you there, too.

•

ELIZABETH CADY STANTON
1868

*'The male element is a destructive force'*

*Twenty years after her address at Seneca Falls, Elizabeth Cady Stanton addressed the Women's Suffrage Convention in Washington DC and described the vices emanating from the 'male element'.*

I urge a sixteenth amendment, because 'manhood suffrage', or a man's government, is civil, religious, and social disorganization. The male element is a destructive force, stern, selfish, aggrandizing, loving war, violence, conquest, acquisition, breeding in the material and moral world alike discord, disorder, disease, and death. See what a record of blood and cruelty the pages of history reveal! Through what slavery, slaughter, and sacrifice, through what inquisitions and imprisonments, pains and persecutions, black codes and gloomy creeds, the soul of humanity has struggled for the centuries, while mercy has veiled her face and all hearts have been dead alike to love and hope!

The male element has held high carnival thus far; it has fairly run riot from the beginning, overpowering the feminine element everywhere, crushing out all the diviner qualities in human nature, until we know but little of true manhood and womanhood, of the latter comparatively nothing, for it has scarce been recognized as a power until within the last century. Society is but the reflection of man himself, untempered by woman's thought; the hard iron rule we feel alike in the church, the state, and the home. No one need wonder at the disorganization, at the fragmentary condition of everything, when we remember that man, who represents but half a complete being, with but half an idea on every subject, has undertaken the absolute control of all sublunary matters.

People object to the demands of those whom they choose to call the strong-minded, because they say 'the right of suffrage will make the women masculine'. That is just the difficulty in which we are involved today. Though disfranchised, we have few women in the best sense; we have simply so many reflections, varieties, and dilutions of the masculine gender. The strong, natural characteristics of womanhood are repressed and ignored in dependence, for so long as man feeds woman she will try to please the giver and adapt herself to his condition. To keep a foothold in society, woman must be as near like man as possible, reflect his ideas, opinions, virtues, motives, prejudices, and vices. She must respect his statutes, though they strip her of every inalienable right, and conflict with that higher law written by the finger of God on her own soul.

She must look at everything from its dollar-and-cent point of view, or she is a mere romancer. She must accept things as they are and make the best of them. To mourn over the miseries of others, the poverty of the poor, their hardships in jails, prisons, asylums, the horrors of war, cruelty, and brutality in every form, all this would be mere sentimentalizing. To protest against the intrigue, bribery, and corruption of public life, to desire that her sons might follow some business that did not involve lying, cheating, and a hard, grinding selfishness, would be arrant nonsense.

In this way man has been molding woman to his ideas by direct and positive influences, while she, if not a negation, has used indirect means to control him, and in most cases developed the very characteristics both in him and herself that needed repression. And now man himself stands appalled at the results of his own excesses, and mourns in bitterness that falsehood, selfishness, and violence are the law of life. The need of this hour is not territory, gold mines, railroads, or specie payments but a new evangel of womanhood, to exalt purity, virtue, morality, true religion, to lift man up into the higher realms of thought and action.

We ask woman's enfranchisement, as the first step toward the recognition of that essential element in government that can only secure the health, strength, and prosperity of the nation. Whatever is done to lift woman to her true position will help to usher in a new day of peace and perfection for the race.

In speaking of the masculine element, I do not wish to be understood to say that all men are hard, selfish, and brutal, for many of the most beautiful spirits the world has known have been clothed with manhood; but I refer to those characteristics, though often marked in woman, that distinguish what is called the stronger sex. For example, the love of acquisition and conquest, the very pioneers of civilization, when expended on the earth, the sea, the elements, the riches and forces of nature, are powers of destruction when used to subjugate one man to another or to sacrifice nations to ambition.

Here that great conservator of woman's love, if permitted to assert itself, as it naturally would in freedom against oppression, violence, and war, would hold all these destructive forces in check, for woman knows the cost of life better than man does, and not with her consent would one drop of blood ever be shed, one life sacrificed in vain.

With violence and disturbance in the natural world, we see a constant effort to maintain an equilibrium of forces. Nature, like a loving mother, is ever trying to keep land and sea, mountain and valley, each in its place, to hush the angry winds and waves, balance the extremes of heat and cold, of rain and drought, that peace, harmony, and beauty may reign supreme. There is a striking analogy between matter and mind,. and the present disorganization of society warns us that in the dethronement of woman we have let loose the elements of violence and ruin that she only has the power to curb. If the civilization of the age calls for an extension of the suffrage, surely a government of the most virtuous educated men and women would better represent the whole and protect the interests of all than could the representation of either sex alone.

•

## SUSAN B. ANTHONY
### 1872

### '*Are women persons?*'

*Susan B. Anthony (1820–1906), the most effective American suffragist of the nineteenth century, attended the Seneca Falls Convention but did not meet Elizabeth Stanton until 1850. They became lifelong friends. Once the civil war was over, they campaigned for votes for women. Anthony edited* Revolution, *a journal demanding female suffrage and equal education and employment rights. She formed the National Women's Suffrage Association with Stanton in 1869. Three years later she led a march by women to the polls during the presidential election. She was convicted for her 'crime' but refused to pay the $100 fine. Asserting her equal rights, she defended her action in this speech.*

Friends and fellow-citizens: I stand before you tonight under indictment for the alleged crime of having voted at the last presidential election, without having a lawful right to vote. It shall be my work this evening to prove to you that in thus voting, I not only committed no crime, but, instead, simply exercised my citizen's rights, guaranteed to me and all United States citizens by the National Constitution, beyond the power of any State to deny.

The preamble of the Federal Constitution says:

'We, the people of the United States, in order to form a more perfect union, establish justice, insure domestic tranquillity, provide for the common defense, promote the general welfare, and secure the blessings of liberty to ourselves and our posterity, do ordain and establish this Constitution for the United States of America.'

It was we, the people; not we, the white male citizens; nor yet we, the male citizens; but we, the whole people, who formed the Union. And we formed it, not to give the blessings of liberty, but to secure them; not to the half of ourselves and the half of our posterity, but to the whole people – women as well as men. And it is a downright mockery to talk to women of their enjoyment of the blessings of liberty while they are denied the use of the only means of securing them provided by this democratic-republican government – the ballot.

For any State to make sex a qualification that must ever result in the disfranchisement of one entire half of the people is to pass a bill of attainder, or an *ex post facto* law, and is therefore a violation of the supreme law of the land. By it the blessings of liberty are forever withheld from women and their female posterity. To them this government has no just powers derived from the consent of the governed. To them this government is not a democracy. It is not a republic. It is an odious aristocracy; a hateful oligarchy of sex; the most hateful aristocracy ever established on the face of the globe; an oligarchy of wealth, where the rich govern the poor. An oligarchy of learning, where the educated govern the ignorant, or even an oligarchy of race, where the Saxon rules the African, might be endured; but this oligarchy of sex, which makes father, brothers, husband, sons, the oligarchs over the mother and sisters, the wife and daughters of every household – which ordains all men sovereigns, all women subjects, carries dissension, discord and rebellion into every home of the nation.

Webster, Worcester and Bouvier all define a citizen to be a person in the United States, entitled to vote and hold office.

The only question left to be settled now is: Are women persons? And I hardly believe any of our opponents will have the hardihood to say they are not. Being persons, then, women are citizens; and no State has a right to make any law, or to enforce any old law, that shall abridge their privileges or immunities. Hence, every discrimination against women in the Constitutions and laws of the several states is today null and void, precisely as is every one against Negroes.

*The nineteenth amendment to the Constitution, which gave American women the vote in 1920, was called the Anthony amendment.*

•

### ELIZABETH CADY STANTON
### 25 March 1888

#### '*The true woman*'

*Forty years on from the Seneca Falls Convention, the theme of the 1888 International Council of Women was women's universal sisterhood. Elizabeth Stanton reported on progress.*

The civil and political position of woman, when I first understood its real significance, was enough to destroy all faith in the vitality of republican principles. Half a century ago the women of America were bond slaves, under the old common law of England. Their rights of person and property were under the absolute control of fathers and husbands. They were shut out of the schools and colleges, the trades and professions, and all offices under government; paid the most meager wages in the ordinary industries of life, and denied everywhere the necessary opportunities for their best development. Worse still, women had no proper appreciation of themselves as factors in civilization. Believing self-denial a higher virtue than self-development, they ignorantly made ladders of themselves by which fathers, husbands, brothers, and sons reached their highest ambitions, creating an impassable gulf between them and those they loved that no magnetic chords of affection or gratitude could span. Nothing was more common forty years ago than to see the sons of a family educated, while the daughters remained in ignorance; husbands at ease in the higher circles, in which their wives were unprepared to move. Like the foolish virgins in the parable, women everywhere in serving others forgot to keep their own lamps trimmed and burning, and when the great feasts of life were spread to them the doors were shut . . .

Whether our feet are compressed in iron shoes, our faces hidden with veils and masks, whether yoked with cows to draw the plow through its furrows, or classed with idiots, lunatics, and criminals in the laws and constitutions of the state, the principle is the same, for the humiliations of spirit are as real as the visible badges of servitude. A difference in government, religion, laws, and social customs makes but little change in the relative status of woman to the self-constituted governing classes, so long as subordination in all nations is the rule of her being. Through suffering we have learned the open sesame to the hearts of each other. There is a language of universal significance, more subtle than that used in the busy marts of trade, that should be called the mother-tongue, by which with a sigh or a tear, a gesture, a glance of the eye, we know the experiences of each other in the varied forms of slavery. With the spirit forever in bondage, it is the same whether housed in golden cages, with every want supplied, or wandering in the dreary deserts of life friendless and forsaken. Now that our globe is girdled with railroads, steamships, and electric wires, every pulsation of your hearts is known to us . . .

Experience has fully proved, that sympathy as a civil agent is vague and powerless until caught and chained in logical propositions and coined into law. When every prayer and tear represents a ballot, the mothers of the race will no longer weep in vain over the miseries of their children. The active interest women are taking in all the great questions of the day is in strong contrast with the apathy and indifference in which we found them half a century ago, and the contrast in their condition between now and then is equally marked. Those who inaugurated the movement for woman's enfranchisement, who for long years endured the merciless storm of ridicule and persecution, mourned over by friends, ostracized in social life, scandalized by enemies, denounced by the pulpit, scarified and caricatured by the press, may well congratulate themselves on the marked change in public sentiment that this magnificent gathering of educated women from both hemispheres so triumphantly illustrates.

Now even married women enjoy, in a measure, their rights of person and property. They can make contracts, sue and be sued, testify in courts of justice, and with honor dissolve the marriage relation when it becomes intolerable. Now most of the colleges are open to girls, and they are rapidly taking their places in all the profitable industries, and in many of the offices under government. They are in the professions, too, as lawyers, doctors, editors, professors in colleges, and ministers in the pulpits. Their political status is so far advanced that they enjoy all the rights of citizens in two territories, municipal suffrage in one state, and school suffrage in half the states of the Union. Here is a good record of the work achieved in the past half-century; but we do not intend to rest our case until all our rights are secured, and, noting the steps of progress in other countries, on which their various representatives are here to report, we behold with satisfaction everywhere a general uprising of women, demanding higher education and an equal place in the industries of the world. Our gathering here today is highly significant, in its promises of future combined action. When, in the history of the world, was there ever before such an assemblage of able, educated women, celebrated in so many varied walks of life, and feeling their right and ability to discuss the vital questions of social life, religion, and government? When we think of the vantage-ground woman holds today, in spite of all the artificial obstacles she has surmounted, we are filled with wonder as to what the future mother of the race will be when free to seek her complete development.

Thus far women have been the mere echoes of men. Our laws and constitutions, our creeds and codes, and the customs of social life are all of masculine origin. The true woman is as yet a dream of the future. A just government, a humane religion, a pure social life await her coming. Then, and not till then, will the golden age of peace and prosperity be ours. This gathering is significant, too, in being held in the greatest republic on which the sun ever shone – a nation superior to every other on the globe in all that goes to make up a free and mighty people – boundless territory, magnificent scenery, mighty forests, lakes and rivers, and inexhaustible wealth in agriculture, manufactures, and mines – a country where the children of the masses in our public schools have all the appliances of a complete education – books, charts, maps, every advantage, not only in the rudimental but in many of the higher branches, alike free at their disposal. In the Old World the palace on the hill is the home of nobility; here it is the public school or university for the people, where the rich and the poor, side by side, take the prizes for good manners and scholarship. Thus the value of real character above all artificial distinctions – the great lesson of democracy – is early learned by our children.

This is the country, too, where every man has a right to self-govern-ment, to exercise his individual conscience and judgement on all matters of public interest. Here we have no entangling alliances in church and state, no tithes to be paid, no livings to be sold, no bartering for places by dignitaries among those who officiate at the altar, no religious test for those elected to take part in government.

Here, under the very shadow of the Capitol of this great nation, whose dome is crowned with the Goddess of Liberty, the women from many lands have assembled at last to claim their rightful place, as equal factors, in the great movements of the nineteenth century, so we bid our distinguished guests welcome, thrice welcome, to our triumphant democracy. I hope they will be able to stay long enough to take a bird's-eye view of our vast possessions, to see what can be done in a moral as well as material point of view in a government of the people. In the Old World they have governments and people; here we have a government of the people, by the people, for the people – that is, we soon shall have when that important half, called women, are enfranchised, and the laboring masses know how to use the power they possess. And you will see here, for the first time in the history of nations, a church without a pope, a state without a king, and a family without a divinely ordained head, for our laws are rapidly making fathers and mothers equal in the marriage relation. We call your attention, dear friends, to these patent facts, not in a spirit of boasting, but that you may look critically into the working of our republican institutions; that when you return to the Old World you may help your fathers to solve many of the tangled problems to which as yet they have found no answer. You can tell the Czar of Russia and the Tories of England that self-government and 'home rule' are safe and possible, proved so by a nation of upward of 60 millions of people . . .

•

## EMMELINE PANKHURST
### 24 March 1908

### 'The laws that men have made'

*Emmeline Pankhurst (1858–1928), leader of the British suffragettes, formed the Women's Franchise League in 1889 but it was not until 1903 that she was persuaded by her daughter Christabel (1880–1958) to found the more militant Women's Social and Political Union. After a meeting in 1906 with Herbert Asquith, Britain's Liberal Prime Minister, she despaired of winning the vote and began to resort to militant tactics. She was first arrested, in the year of this speech at the Portman Rooms in London, after suffragettes tried to 'rush' the House of Commons and was sent to prison for three months. British women won the vote in 1918 at the end of the First World War.*

Men politicians are in the habit of talking to women as if there were no laws that affect women. 'The fact is,' they say, 'the home is the place for women. Their interests are the rearing and training of children. These are the things that interest women. Politics have nothing to do with these things, and therefore politics do not concern women.' Yet the laws decide how women are to live in marriage, how their children are to be trained and educated, and what the future of their children is to be. All that is decided by Act of Parliament. Let us take a few of these laws, and see what there is to say about them from the women's point of view.

First of all, let us take the marriage laws. They are made by men for women. Let us consider whether they are equal, whether they are just, whether they are wise. What security of maintenance has the married woman? Many a married woman having given up her economic independence in order to marry, how is she compensated for that loss? What security does she get in that marriage for which she gave up economic independence? Take the case of a woman who has been earning a good income. She is told that she ought to give up her employment when she becomes a wife and a mother. What does she get in return? All that a married man is obliged by law to do for his wife is to provide for her shelter of some kind, food of some kind, and clothing of some kind. It is left to his good pleasure to decide what the shelter shall be, what the food shall be, what the clothing shall be. It is left to him to decide what money shall be spent on the home, and how it shall be spent; the wife has no voice legally in deciding any of these things. She has no legal claim upon any definite portion of his income. If he is a good man, a conscientious man, he does the right thing. If he is not, if he chooses almost to starve his wife, she has no remedy. What he thinks sufficient is what she has to be content with.

I quite agree, in all these illustrations, that the majority of men are considerably better than the law compels them to be, so the majority of women do not suffer as much as they might suffer if men were all as bad as they might be, but since there are some bad men, some unjust men, don't you agree with me that the law ought to be altered so that those men could be dealt with?

Take what happens to the woman if her husband dies and leaves her a widow, sometimes with little children. If a man is so insensible to his duties as a husband and father when he makes his will, as to leave all his property away from his wife and children, the law allows him to do it. That will is a valid one. So you see that the married woman's position is not a very secure one. It depends entirely on her getting a good ticket in the lottery. If she has a good husband, well and good: if she has a bad one, she has to suffer, and she has no remedy. That is her position as a wife, and it is far from satisfactory.

Now let us look at her position if she has been very unfortunate in marriage, so unfortunate as to get a bad husband, an immoral husband, a vicious husband, a husband unfit to be the father of little children. We turn to the Divorce Court. How is she to get rid of such a man? If a man has got married to a bad wife, and he wants to get rid of her, he has but to prove against her one act of infidelity. But if a woman who is married to a vicious husband wants to get rid of him, not one act nor a thousand acts of infidelity entitle her to a divorce; she must prove either bigamy, desertion, or gross cruelty, in addition to immorality before she can get rid of that man.

Let us consider her position as a mother. We have repeated this so often at our meetings that I think the echo of what we have said must have reached many. By English law no married woman exists as the mother of the child she brings into the world. In the eyes of the law she is not the parent of her child. The child, according to our marriage laws, has only one parent, who can decide the future of the child, who can decide where it shall live, how it shall live, how much shall be spent upon it, how it shall be educated, and what religion it shall profess. That parent is the father.

These are examples of some of the laws that men have made, laws that concern women. I ask you, if women had had the vote, should we have had such laws? If women had had the vote, as men have the vote, we should have had equal laws. We should have had equal laws for divorce, and the law would have said that as Nature has given to children two parents, so the law should recognize that they have two parents.

I have spoken to you about the position of the married woman who does not exist legally as a parent, the parent of her own child. In marriage, children have one parent. Out of marriage children have also one parent. That parent is the mother – the unfortunate mother. She alone is responsible for the future of her child; she alone is punished if her child is neglected and suffers from neglect. But let me give you one illustration. I was in Herefordshire during the by-election. While I was there, an unmarried mother was brought before the bench of magistrates charged with having neglected her illegitimate child. She was a domestic servant, and had put the child out to nurse. The magistrates – there were colonels and landowners on that bench – did not ask what wages the mother got; they did not ask who the father was or whether he contributed to the support of the child. They sent that woman to prison for three months for having neglected her child. I ask you women here tonight, if women had had some share in the making of laws, don't you think they would have found a way of making all fathers of such children equally responsible with the mothers for the welfare of those children?

•

## EMMA GOLDMAN
June 1917

### '*The political criminal of today must needs be . . .*
### *the saint of the new age*'

*Emma Goldman (1869–1940) was born in Russia and worked in a St Petersburg glove factory before emigrating in 1885 to the United States, where she became an anarchist and earned the nickname 'Red Emma' for her agitation against tyrannical employers. She founded Mother Earth, the anarchist monthly, in 1906 in partnership with Alexander Berkman.*

*When Woodrow Wilson declared war on Germany in 1917 and introduced a draft bill for conscription, Goldman and Berkman distributed 100,000 copies of a No-Conscription manifesto, founded a No-Conscription League, and organized anti-war rallies. Their offices were raided, and Goldman and Berkman were arrested and put on trial, where they conducted their own defence. Goldman made this speech to the jury.*

Gentlemen, when we asked whether you would be prejudiced against us if it were proven that we propagated ideas and opinions contrary to those held by the majority, you were instructed by the Court to say, 'If they are within the law.' But what the court did not tell you is, that no new faith – not even the most humane and peaceable – has ever been considered 'within the law' by those who were in power. The history of human growth is at the same time the history of every new idea heralding the approach of a brighter dawn, and the brighter dawn has always been considered illegal, outside of the law.

Gentlemen of the jury, most of you, I take it, are believers in the teachings of Jesus. Bear in mind that he was put to death by those who considered his views as being against the law. I also take it that you are proud of your Americanism. Remember that those who fought and bled for your liberties were in their time considered as being against the law, as dangerous disturbers and trouble-makers. They not only preached violence, but they carried out their ideas by throwing tea into the Boston harbor. They said that 'Resistance to tyranny is obedience to God.' They wrote a dangerous document called the Declaration of Independence. A document which continues to be dangerous to this day, and for the circulation of which a young man was sentenced to ninety days prison in a New York Court, only the other day. They were the Anarchists of *their* time – they were never within the law.

Your Government is allied with the French Republic. Need I call your attention to the historic fact that the great upheaval in France was brought about by extra-legal means? The Dantes, the Robespierres, the Marats, the Herberts, aye even the man who is responsible for the most stirring revolutionary music, the Marseillaise (which unfortunately has deteriorated into a war tune), even Camille Desmoulins, were never within the law. But for those great pioneers and rebels, France would have continued under the yoke of the idle Louis XVI, to whom the sport of shooting jack rabbits was more important than the destiny of the people of France . . .

Never can a new idea move within the law. It matters not whether that idea pertains to political and social changes or to any other domain of human thought and expression – to science, literature, music; in fact, everything that makes for freedom and joy and beauty must refuse to move within the law. How can it be otherwise? The law is stationary, fixed, mechanical, 'a chariot wheel' which grinds all alike without regard to time, place and condition, without ever taking into account cause and effect, without ever going into the complexity of the human soul.

Progress knows nothing of fixity. It cannot be pressed into a definite mold. It cannot bow to the dictum, 'I have ruled,' 'I am the regulating finger of God.' Progress is ever renewing, ever becoming, ever changing – never is it within the law.

If that be crime, we are criminals even like Jesus, Socrates, Galileo, Bruno, John Brown and scores of others. We are in good company, among those whom Havelock Ellis, the greatest living psychologist, describes as the political criminals recognized by the whole civilized world, except America, as men and women who out of deep love for humanity, out of a passionate reverence for liberty and an all-absorbing devotion to an ideal are ready to pay for their faith even with their blood. We cannot do otherwise if we are to be true to ourselves – we know that the political criminal is the precursor of human progress – the political criminal of today must needs be the hero, the martyr and the saint of the new age.

But, says the Prosecuting Attorney, the press and the unthinking rabble, in high and low station, 'that is a dangerous doctrine and unpatriotic at this time'. No doubt it is. But are we to be held responsible for something which is as unchangeable and unalienable as the very stars hanging in the heavens unto time and all eternity?

Gentlemen of the jury, we respect your patriotism. We would not, if we could, have you change its meaning for yourself. But may there not be different kinds of patriotism as there are different kinds of liberty? I for one cannot believe that love of one's country must needs consist in blindness to its social faults, in deafness to its social discords, in inarticulation of its social wrongs. Neither can I believe that the mere accident of birth in a certain country or the mere scrap of a citizen's paper constitutes the love of country.

I know many people – I am one of them – who were not born here, nor have they applied for citizenship, and who yet love America with deeper passion and greater intensity than many natives whose patriotism manifests itself by pulling, kicking, and insulting those who do not rise when the national anthem is played. Our patriotism is that of the man who loves a woman with open eyes. He is enchanted by her beauty, yet he sees her faults. So we, too, who know America, love her beauty, her richness, her great possibilities; we love her mountains, her canyons, her forests, her Niagara, and her deserts – above all do we love the people that have produced her wealth, her artists who have created beauty, her great apostles who dream and work for liberty – but with the same passionate emotion we hate her superficiality, her cant, her corruption, her mad, unscrupulous worship at the altar of the Golden Calf.

We say that if America has entered the war to make the world safe for democracy, she must first make democracy safe in America. How else is the world to take America seriously, when democracy at home is daily being outraged, free speech suppressed, peaceable assemblies broken up by overbearing and brutal gangsters in uniform; when free press is curtailed and every independent opinion gagged. Verily, poor as we are in democracy, how can we give of it to the world? We further say that a democracy conceived in the military servitude of the masses, in their economic enslavement, and nurtured in their tears and blood, is not democracy at all. It is despotism – the cumulative result of a chain of abuses which, according to that dangerous document, the Declaration of Independence, the people have the right to overthrow.

The District Attorney has dragged in our Manifesto, and he has emphasized the passage, 'Resist conscription.' Gentlemen of the jury, please remember that that is not the charge against us. But admitting that the Manifesto contains the expression, 'Resist conscription', may I ask you, is there only one kind of resistance? Is there only the resistance which means the gun, the bayonet, the bomb or flying machine? Is there not another kind of resistance? May not the people simply fold their hands and declare, 'We will not fight when we do not believe in the necessity of war'? May not the people who believe in the repeal of the Conscription Law, because it is unconstitutional, express their opposition in word and by pen, in meetings and in other ways? What right has the District Attorney to interpret that particular passage to suit himself? Moreover, gentlemen of the jury, I insist that the indictment against us does not refer to conscription. We are charged with a conspiracy against registration. And in no way or manner has the prosecution proven that we are guilty of conspiracy or that we have committed an overt act.

Gentlemen of the jury, you are not called upon to accept our views, to approve of them or to justify them. You are not even called upon to decide whether our views are within or against the law. You are called upon to decide whether the prosecution has proven that the defendants Emma Goldman and Alexander Berkman have conspired to urge people not to register. And whether their speeches and writings represent overt acts.

Whatever your verdict, gentlemen, it cannot possibly affect the rising tide of discontent in this country against war which, despite all boasts, is a war for conquest and military power. Neither can it affect the ever increasing opposition to conscription which is a military and industrial yoke placed upon the necks of the American people. Least of all will your verdict affect those to whom human life is sacred, and who will not become a party to the world slaughter. Your verdict can only add to the opinion of the world as to whether or not justice and liberty are a living force in this country or a mere shadow of the past.

Your verdict may, of course, affect us temporarily, in a physical sense – it can have no effect whatever upon our spirit. For even if we were convicted and found guilty and the penalty were that we be placed against a wall and shot dead, I should nevertheless cry out with the great Luther: 'Here I am and here I stand and I cannot do otherwise.'

And gentlemen, in conclusion let me tell you that my co-defendant, Mr Berkman, was right when he said the eyes of America are upon you. They are upon you not because of sympathy for us or agreement with

Anarchism. They are upon you because it must be decided sooner or later whether we are justified in telling people that we will give them democracy in Europe, when we have no democracy here? Shall free speech and free assemblage, shall criticism and opinion – which even the espionage bill did not include – be destroyed? Shall it be a shadow of the past, the great historic American past? Shall it be trampled underfoot by any detective, or policeman, anyone who decides upon it? Or shall free speech and free press and free assemblage continue to be the heritage of the American people?

Gentlemen of the jury, whatever your verdict will be, as far as we are concerned, nothing will be changed. I have held ideas all my life. I have publicly held my ideas for twenty-seven years. Nothing on earth would ever make me change my ideas except one thing; and that is, if you will prove to me that our position is wrong, untenable, or lacking in historic fact. But never would I change my ideas because I am found guilty. I may remind you of two great Americans, undoubtedly not unknown to you, gentlemen of the jury; Ralph Waldo Emerson and Henry David Thoreau. When Thoreau was placed in prison for refusing to pay taxes, he was visited by Ralph Waldo Emerson and Emerson said: 'David, what are you doing in jail?' and Thoreau replied: 'Ralph, what are you doing outside, when honest people are in jail for their ideals?' Gentlemen of the jury, I do not wish to influence you. I do not wish to appeal to your passions. I do not wish to influence you by the fact that I am a woman. I have no such desires and no such designs. I take it that you are sincere enough and honest enough and brave enough to render a verdict according to your convictions, beyond the shadow of a reasonable doubt.

Please forget that we are Anarchists. Forget that it is claimed that we propagated violence. Forget that something appeared in *Mother Earth* when I was thousands of miles away, three years ago. Forget all that, and merely consider the evidence. Have we been engaged in a conspiracy? has that conspiracy been proven? have we committed overt acts? have those overt acts been proven? We for the defense say they have not been proven. And therefore your verdict must be not guilty.

But whatever your decision, the struggle must go on. We are but the atoms in the incessant human struggle towards the light that shines in the darkness – the Ideal of economic, political and spiritual liberation of mankind!

*Goldman and Berkman were found guilty, fined $10,000 and sentenced to two* *years in prison. Goldman was deported to Russia in 1919 but returned to the United States in 1924.*

•

## DOLORES IBARRURI GOMEZ
'La Pasionaria'
23 August 1936

### *'Fascism shall not pass'*

*The Spanish writer and politician Dolores Ibarruri Gomez (1895–1989), the daughter of a Basque miner, joined the Socialist Party in 1917, worked as a journalist for the workers' press, where she used the pseudonym La Pasionaria (the passion flower), and helped to begin the Spanish Civil War with her passionate speeches against the Fascists. One hundred thousand Valencia workers cheered La Pasionaria on when she delivered this characteristically fiery denunciation of fascism to the People's Front at the Mestal stadium.*

Comrades, people of Valencia!

I have come to you in these tragic and gloomy hours, when the fate of Spain and especially the future of the working masses is being decided. I have come to you, my mouth filled with the acrid taste of gunpowder, my mind filled with the impressions of the difficulties facing our comrades who are fighting on the summits and slopes of the Guadarramas, who realize the importance of our struggle and who are prepared to die rather than fall into the clutches of fascism. I have come to you from the field of battle, from that great fight which is assuming the character of a heroic epic, for we entered battle armed only with enthusiasm, self-sacrifice and supreme devotion to the cause of the people in order to fight an enemy furnished with all the means of warfare, which he has stolen from the people . . .

If, when entering the firing line to fight the enemy who is threatening our national liberty, we have such enthusiasm in the rear, then I say to you, the working people of Valencia, what I said when I saw the weapons in the hands of the militia, when I saw the rifles in the hands of the troops loyal to the government:

Fascism shall not pass because the wall of bodies with which we have barred its way is today strengthened by weapons of defence we have captured from the enemy — a cowardly enemy, because he has not the ideals which lead us into battle. The enemy therefore has no dash and impetuosity, whereas we are borne on the wings of our ideals, of our love, not for the Spain which is dying together with the enemy, but for the Spain we want to have – a democratic Spain.

When we speak of Spain, we mean not only the name; we mean a democratic Spain, not the Spain which is clinging to her old traditions; we mean a Spain which will give the peasants land, which will socialize industry under the control of the workers, which will introduce social insurance so that the worker may not be condemned to a homeless old age; we mean a Spain which will completely and comprehensively, and in a revolutionary spirit, solve the economic problems that lie at the foundation of all revolutions. (*Loud and prolonged applause.*)

On all fronts communists, anarchists, socialists and republicans are fighting shoulder to shoulder. We have also been joined by non-party people from town and country, because they too have realized what a victory for fascism would mean to Spain.

The struggle, started within the frontiers of our country, is already assuming an international character, because the working people of the whole world know that if fascism were to triumph in Spain, every democratic country in the world would be confronted with the fascist danger. The working people have realized this, as is borne out by the messages of solidarity we are constantly receiving from all parts of the world. International fascism, too, has realized the significance of the struggle of the Spanish people against the enemies who have violated their oath of loyalty to the country and to the country's flag. These violators of their vows have broken their promises and have rebelled in vile alliance with seditionary priests and debauched sons of the aristocracy, and are committing endless crimes in all the inhabited places through which they pass. One needs the brush of Goya . . . to depict the horrors and revolting crimes committed by these elements led by arrogant fascist generals who have long ago revealed who they are and what they are capable of.

Dante's Inferno is but a pale reflection of what happens in places through which these modern vandals pass. The slaughtered children and old people, the raped and hacked bodies of women, the demolished monuments of art . . . Wherever they pass they sow death and desolation. And what is taking place in the districts captured by the fascists would have taken place all over Spain, if they had not been opposed by a people inspired by faith in its own strength . . .

We shall very soon achieve victory and return to our children . . .

*Gomez left for the Soviet Union when Franco won power in 1939. She returned to Spain in 1977 and at the age of eighty-one was re-elected to the National Assembly.*

•

## BETTY FRIEDAN
1969

### 'A woman's civil right'

*A forty-two-year-old housewife and mother of three shocked American social structures to the core in 1963 when she published* The Feminine Mystique, *the best-seller that launched the modern women's movement. Betty Friedan (1921–) contended that deeply entrenched attitudes and social barriers imprisoned women in a 'housewife trap'. She called for expanded career opportunities, equality with men and set out to destroy the myth of the happy housewife. Some women burned their bras; others cast off their aprons – or their husbands.*

*'I did not set out consciously to start a revolution when I wrote* The Feminine Mystique,*' Friedan wrote later, 'but it changed my life, as a woman and as a writer, and other women tell me it changed theirs.' She went on to become the first president of the National Organization of Women and Founder of the National Women's Political Caucus.*

*At the first national conference for repeal of abortion laws, Betty Friedan gave this powerful speech proclaiming abortion as a woman's civil right.*

Women, even though they're almost too visible as sex objects in this country, are invisible people. As the Negro was the invisible man, so women are the invisible people in America today: women who have a share in the decisions of the mainstream of government, of politics, of the church – who don't just cook the church supper, but preach the sermon; who don't just look up the ZIP codes and address the envelopes, but make the political decisions; who don't just do the housework of industry but make some of the executive decisions. Women, above all, who say what their own lives and personalities are going to be, and no longer listen to or even permit male experts to define what 'feminine' is or isn't.

The essence of the denigration of women is our definition as sex object. To confront our inequality, therefore, we must confront both society's denigration of us in these terms and our own self-denigration as people.

Am I saying that women must be liberated from sex? No. I am saying that sex will only be liberated to be a human dialogue, sex will only cease to be a sniggering, dirty joke and an obsession in this society, when women become active self-determining people, liberated to a creativity beyond motherhood, to a full human creativity.

Am I saying that women must be liberated from motherhood? No. I am saying that motherhood will only be a joyous and responsible human act when women are free to make, with full conscious choice and full human responsibility, the decisions to become mothers. Then, and only then, will they be able to embrace motherhood without conflict, when they will be able to define themselves not just as somebody's mother, not just as servants of children, not just as breeding receptacles, but as people for whom motherhood is a freely chosen part of life, freely celebrated while it lasts, but for whom creativity has many more dimensions, as it has for men.

Then, and only then, will motherhood cease to be a curse and a chain for men and for children. For despite all the lip service paid to motherhood today, all the roses sent on Mother's Day, all the commercials and the hypocritical ladies' magazines' celebration of women in their roles as housewives and mothers, the fact is that all television or night-club comics have to do is go before a microphone and say the words 'my wife', and the whole audience erupts into gales of guilty, vicious and obscene laughter.

The hostility between the sexes has never been worse. The image of women in avant-garde plays, novels and movies, and behind the family situation comedies on television is that mothers are man-devouring, cannibalistic monsters, or else Lolitas, sex objects – and objects not even of heterosexual impulse, but of sadomasochism. That impulse – the punishment of women – is much more of a factor in the abortion question than anybody ever admits.

Motherhood is a bane almost by definition, or at least partly so, as long as women are forced to be mothers – and only mothers – against their will. Like a cancer cell living its life through another cell, women today are forced to live too much through their children and husbands (they are too dependent on them, and therefore are forced to take too much varied resentment, vindictiveness, inexpressible resentment and rage out on their husbands and children).

Perhaps it is the least understood fact of American political life: the enormous buried violence of women in this country today. Like all oppressed people, women have been taking their violence out on their own bodies, in all the maladies with which they plague the MDs and the psychoanalysts. Inadvertently, and in subtle and insidious ways, they have been taking their violence out, too, on their children and on their husbands, and sometimes they're not so subtle.

The battered-child syndrome that we are hearing more and more about from our hospitals is almost always to be found in the instance of unwanted children, and women are doing the battering, as much or more than men. In the case histories of psychologically and physically maimed children, the woman is always the villain, and the reason is our definition of her: not only as passive sex object, but as mother, servant, someone else's mother, someone else's wife.

Am I saying that women have to be liberated from men? That men are the enemy? No. I am saying the *men* will only be truly liberated to love women and to be fully themselves when women are liberated to have a full say in the decisions of their lives and their society.

Until that happens, men are going to bear the guilty burden of the passive destiny they have forced upon women, the suppressed resentment, the sterility of love when it is not between two fully active, joyous people, but has in it the element of exploitation. And men will not be free to be all they can be as long as they must live up to an image of masculinity that disallows all the tenderness and sensitivity in a man, all that might be considered feminine. Men have enormous capacities in them that they have to repress and fear in order to live up to the obsolete, brutal, bear-killing, Ernest Hemingway, crew-cut Prussian, napalm-all-the-children-in-Vietnam, bang-bang-you're-dead image of masculinity. Men are not allowed to admit that they sometimes are afraid. They are not allowed to express their own sensitivity, their own need to be passive sometimes and not always active. Men are not allowed to cry. So they are only half-human, as women are only half-human, until we can go this next step forward. All the burdens and responsibilities that men are supposed to shoulder alone makes them, I think, resent women's pedestal, much as that pedestal may be a burden for women.

This is the real sexual revolution. Not the cheap headlines in the papers about at what age boys and girls go to bed with each other and whether they do it with or without the benefit of marriage. That's the least of it. The real sexual revolution is the emergence of women from passivity, from the point where they are the easiest victims for all the seductions, the waste, the worshiping of false gods in our affluent society, to full self-determination and full dignity. And it is the emergence of men from the stage where they are inadvertent brutes and masters to sensitive, complete humanity.

This revolution cannot happen without radical changes in the family as we know it today; in our concepts of marriage and love, in our architecture, our cities, our theology, our politics, our art. Not that women are special. Not that women are superior. But these expressions of human creativity are bound to be infinitely more various and enriching when women and men are allowed to relate to each other beyond the strict confines of the *Ladies' Home Journal*'s definition of the Mamma and Papa marriage.

If we are finally allowed to become full people, not only will children be born and brought up with more love and responsibility than today, but we will break out of the confines of that sterile little suburban family to relate to each other in terms of all of the possible dimensions of our personalities – male and female, as comrades, as colleagues, as friends, as lovers. And without so much hate and jealousy and buried resentment and hypocrisies, there will be a whole new sense of love that will make what we call love on Valentine's Day look very pallid.

It's crucial, therefore, that we see this question of abortion as more than a quantitative move, more than a politically expedient move. Abortion repeal is not a question of political expediency. It is part of something greater. It is historic that we are addressing ourselves this weekend to perhaps the first national confrontation of women and men. Women's voices are finally being heard aloud, saying it the way it is about the question of abortion both in its most basic sense of morality and in its new political sense as part of the unfinished revolution of sexual equality.

In this confrontation, we are making an important milestone in this marvelous revolution that began long before any of us here were born and which still has a long way to go. As the pioneers from Mary Wollstonecraft to Margaret Sanger gave us the consciousness that brought us from our several directions here, so we here, in changing the very terms of the debate on abortion to assert woman's right to choose, and to define the terms of our lives ourselves, move women further to full human dignity. Today, we moved history forward . . .

•

# A CENTURY OF WAR
# AND REVOLUTION

DAVID LLOYD GEORGE
21 September 1914

*'The great pinnacle of sacrifice'*

*Many speeches were made in the autumn of 1914 rallying the British for the war
with Germany – but none matched in sheer poetic eloquence this address by Lloyd
George, whose war speeches were described as standing like 'superannuated spells'.*

*Although there was a broad consensus about the justice of the war, the one
element required to make it acceptable to a liberal society was some kind of broad,
humane justification to explain what the war was really about.*

*'Lloyd George remained suspiciously silent during the early weeks,' says the
British historian Kenneth O. Morgan. 'But in an eloquent address to a massed
audience of his Welsh fellow-countrymen at the Queen's Hall, London, he
committed himself without reserve to a fight to the finish. He occupied, or claimed
to occupy, the highest moral ground. It was, he declared, a war on behalf of liberal
principles, a crusade on behalf of the 'little five-foot-five nations' . . .*

*'It was not surprising that a claim that the war was a holy cause, backed up not
only by the leaders of all the Christian churches but by all the Liberal pantheon of
heroes from Fox to Gladstone, met with an instant response, not least in the
smaller nations of Scotland and Wales within Britain itself.'*

This is the story of two little nations. The world owes much to little
nations . . . The greatest art in the world was the work of little nations;
the most enduring literature of the world came from little nations; the
greatest literature of England came when she was a nation of the size of
Belgium fighting a great empire. The heroic deeds that thrill humanity
through generations were the deeds of little nations fighting for their
freedom. Yes, and the salvation of mankind came through a little nation.
God has chosen little nations as the vessels by which He carries His
choicest wines to the lips of humanity, to rejoice their hearts, to exalt
their vision, to stimulate and strengthen their faith; and if we had stood
by when two little nations were being crushed and broken by the brutal
hands of barbarism, our shame would have rung down the everlasting
ages.

But Germany insists that this is an attack by a lower civilization upon
a higher one. As a matter of fact, the attack was begun by the civilization
which calls itself the higher one. I am no apologist for Russia; she has

perpetrated deeds of which I have no doubt her best sons are ashamed. What empire has not? But Germany is the last empire to point the finger of reproach at Russia. Russia has made sacrifices for freedom – great sacrifices. Do you remember the cry of Bulgaria when she was torn by the most insensate tyranny that Europe has ever seen? Who listened to that cry? The only answer of the 'higher civilization' was that the liberty of the Bulgarian peasants was not worth the life of a single Pomeranian soldier. But the 'rude barbarians' of the north sent their sons by the thousand to die for Bulgarian freedom. What about England? Go to Greece, the Netherlands, Italy, Germany, France – in all those lands I could point out places where the sons of Britain have died for the freedom of those peoples. France has made sacrifices for the freedom of other lands than her own. Can you name a single country in the world for the freedom of which modern Prussia has ever sacrificed a single life? By the test of our faith the highest standard of civilization is the readiness to sacrifice for others.

Have you read the Kaiser's speeches? They are full of the glitter and bluster of German militarism – 'mailed fist' and 'shining armour'. Poor old mailed fist! Its knuckles are getting a little bruised. Poor shining armour! The shine is being knocked out of it. There is the same swagger and boastfulness running through the whole of the speeches. The extract which was given in the *British Weekly* this week is a very remarkable product as an illustration of the spirit we have to fight. It is the Kaiser's speech to his soldiers on the way to the front:

> Remember that the German people are the chosen of God. On me, the German Emperor, the Spirit of God has descended. I am His sword, His weapon and His Vicegerent. Woe to the disobedient, and death to cowards and unbelievers.

Lunacy is always distressing, but sometimes it is dangerous; and when you get it manifested in the head of the state, and it has become the policy of a great empire, it is about time that it should be ruthlessly put away. I do not believe he meant all these speeches; it was simply the martial straddle he had acquired. But there were men around him who meant every word of them. This was their religion. Treaties? They tangle the feet of Germany in her advance. Cut them with the sword! Little nations? They hinder the advance of Germany. Trample them in the mire under the German heel. The Russian Slav? He challenges the supremacy of Germany in Europe. Hurl your legions at him and massacre him! Britain? She is a constant menace to the predominance of

Germany in the world. Wrest the trident out of her hand. Christianity? Sickly sentimentalism about sacrifice for others! Poor pap for German digestion! We will have a new diet. We will force it upon the world. It will be made in Germany – the diet of blood and iron. What remains? Treaties have gone. The honour of nations has gone. Liberty has gone. What is left? Germany. Germany is left! '*Deutschland über Alles!*'

That is what we are fighting – that claim to predominance of a material, hard civilization which, if it once rules and sways the world, liberty goes, democracy vanishes. And unless Britain and her sons come to the rescue it will be a dark day for humanity.

Have you followed the Prussian Junker and his doings? We are not fighting the German people. The German people are under the heel of this military caste, and it will be a day of rejoicing for the German peasant, artisan and trader when the military caste is broken. You know its pretensions. They give themselves the air of demigods. They walk the pavements, and civilians and their wives are swept into the gutter; they have no right to stand in the way of a great Prussian soldier. Men, women, nations – they all have to go. He thinks all he has to say is, 'We are in a hurry.' That is the answer he gave to Belgium – 'Rapidity of action is Germany's greatest asset,' which means, 'I am in a hurry; clear out of my way.' You know the type of motorist, the terror of the roads, with a sixty-horse-power car, who thinks the roads are made for him, and knocks down anybody who impedes the action of his car by a single mile an hour. The Prussian Junker is the road-hog of Europe. Small nationalities in his way are hurled to the roadside, bleeding and broken. Women and children are crushed under the wheels of his cruel car, and Britain is ordered out of his road. All I can say is this: if the old British spirit is alive in British hearts, that bully will be torn from his seat. Were he to win, it would be the greatest catastrophe that has befallen democracy since the day of the Holy Alliance and its ascendancy.

They think we cannot beat them. It will not be easy. It will be a long job; it will be a terrible war; but in the end we shall march through terror to triumph. We shall need all our qualities – every quality that Britain and its people possess – prudence in counsel, daring in action, tenacity in purpose, courage in defeat, moderation in victory; in all things faith.

It has pleased them to believe and to preach the belief that we are a decadent and degenerate people. They proclaim to the world through their professors that we are a non-heroic nation skulking behind our mahogany counters, whilst we egg on more gallant races to their destruction. This is a description given of us in Germany – 'a timorous, craven nation, trusting to its Fleet'. I think they are beginning to find their mistake out already – and there are half a million young men of Britain who have already registered a vow to their King that they will cross the seas and hurl that insult to British courage against its perpetrators on the battlefields of France and Germany. We want half a million more; and we shall get them.

I envy you young people your opportunity. They have put up the age limit for the Army, but I am sorry to say I have marched a good many years even beyond that. It is a great opportunity, an opportunity that only comes once in many centuries to the children of men. For most generations sacrifice comes in drab and weariness of spirit. It comes to you today, and it comes today to us all, in the form of the glow and thrill of a great movement for liberty, that impels millions throughout Europe to the same noble end. It is a great war for the emancipation of Europe from the thraldom of a military caste which has thrown its shadows upon two generations of men, and is now plunging the world into a welter of bloodshed and death. Some have already given their lives. There are some who have given more than their own lives; they have given the lives of those who are dear to them. I honour their courage, and may God be their comfort and their strength. But their reward is at hand; those who have fallen have died consecrated deaths. They have taken their part in the making of a new Europe – a new world. I can see signs of its coming in the glare of the battlefield.

The people will gain more by this struggle in all lands than they comprehend at the present moment. It is true they will be free of the greatest menace to their freedom. That is not all. There is something infinitely greater and more enduring which is emerging already out of this great conflict – a new patriotism, richer, nobler, and more exalted than the old. I see amongst all classes, high and low, shedding themselves of selfishness, a new recognition that the honour of the country does not depend merely on the maintenance of its glory in the stricken field, but also in protecting its homes from distress. It is bringing a new outlook for all classes. The great flood of luxury and sloth which had submerged the land is receding, and a new Britain is appearing. We can see for the first time the fundamental things that matter in life, and that have been obscured from our vision by the tropical growth of prosperity.

May I tell you in a simple parable what I think this war is doing for us? I know a valley in North Wales, between the mountains and the sea. It is a beautiful valley, snug, comfortable, sheltered by the mountains from all the bitter blasts. But it is very enervating, and I remember how the boys were in the habit of climbing the hill above the village to have a glimpse of the great mountains in the distance, and to be stimulated and freshened by the breezes which came from the hilltops, and by the great spectacle of their grandeur. We have been living in a sheltered valley for generations. We have been too comfortable and too indulgent – many, perhaps, too selfish – and the stern hand of fate has scourged us to an elevation where we can see the great everlasting things that matter for a nation – the great peaks we had forgotten, of Honour, Duty, Patriotism, and, clad in glittering white, the great pinnacle of Sacrifice pointing like a rugged finger to Heaven. We shall descend into the valleys again; but as long as the men and women of this generation last, they will carry in their hearts the image of those great mountain peaks whose foundations are not shaken, though Europe rock and sway in the convulsions of a great war.

*From the moment of his Queen's Hall speech, Lloyd George challenged Asquith, the Prime Minister. 'Unconsciously, perhaps even unwillingly, he was offering himself as the man who could run the war better,' says A.J.P. Taylor. Lloyd George became Prime Minister in 1916 and led Britain to victory.*

•

## V.I. LENIN
### 15 April 1917

### 'Long live the world socialist revolution!'

*After the Russian revolution of March 1917, Lenin travelled back to Petrograd from Switzerland, passing through Germany in a sealed train provided by the German general staff, who counted on the Bolsheviks spreading disaffection among the Russian soldiers.*

*An honour guard of Kronstadt sailors in striped jerseys and red pompon hats met Lenin at the Finland Station. A brass band played the 'Marseillaise'. Lenin was taken to the imperial waiting-room where he addressed a dense crowd and immediately snubbed any hope that the Bolsheviks would close democratic ranks with the Mensheviks. He appealed directly for civil war and international revolution.*

Dear comrades, soldiers, sailors and workers! I am happy to greet

in your persons the victorious Russian revolution, and greet you as
the vanguard of the worldwide proletarian army . . . The piratical imperialist war is the beginning of civil war throughout Europe . . .
The hour is not far distant when the peoples will turn their arms
against their own capitalist exploiters . . . The worldwide socialist
revolution has already dawned . . . Germany is seething . . . Any
day now the whole of European capitalism may crash. The Russian
revolution accomplished by you has prepared the way and opened
a new epoch. Long live the worldwide socialist revolution!

*As Lenin left the room, an officer on the platform outside saluted him and a
detachment of soldiers with bayonets stood to attention. A great roar of a cheer
went up from the revolutionary workers and sailors of Petrograd who had come to
greet him. The sailors presented arms and their commander reported to Lenin for
duty. They wanted him to speak, it was whispered. Lenin walked a few paces and
took off his bowler hat.*

I don't know yet whether you agree with the Provisional Government. But I know very well that when they give you sweet
speeches and make many promises they are deceiving you and the
whole Russian people. The people need peace. The people need
bread and land. And they give you war, hunger, no food, and the
land remains with the landowners. Sailors, comrades, you must
fight for the revolution, fight to the end.

*Lenin remained in Petrograd until 18 July, when the failure of an abortive Soviet
coup d'état forced him to escape again to Finland. He returned to Petrograd on
23 October and from his headquarters in the Smolny Institute led the rising which
captured the government offices. The Bolshevik forces went into action on 25 October.
The key points in the city were occupied. Members of the provisional government
were prisoners or fugitives. That afternoon, Lenin announced to a meeting of the
Petrograd Soviet the triumph of 'the workers' and peasants' revolution'.*

Comrades, the workers' and peasants' revolution, about the necessity of
which the Bolsheviks have always spoken, has been accomplished.

What is the significance of this workers' and peasants' revolution? Its
significance is, first of all, that we shall have a Soviet government, our
own organ of power, in which the bourgeoisie will have no share
whatsoever. The oppressed masses will themselves create a power. The
old state apparatus will be shattered to its foundations and a new
administrative apparatus set up in the form of the Soviet organizations.

From now on, a new phase in the history of Russia begins, and this, the third Russian revolution, should in the end lead to the victory of socialism.

One of our urgent tasks is to put an immediate end to the war. It is clear to everybody that in order to end this war, which is closely bound up with the present capitalist system, capital itself must be fought.

We shall be helped in this by the world working-class movement, which is already beginning to develop in Italy, Britain and Germany.

The proposal we make to international democracy for a just and immediate peace will everywhere awaken an ardent response among the international proletarian masses. All the secret treaties must be immediately published in order to strengthen the confidence of the proletariat.

Within Russia a huge section of the peasantry have said that they have played long enough with the capitalists, and will now march with the workers. A single decree putting an end to landed proprietorship will win us the confidence of the peasants. The peasants will understand that the salvation of the peasantry lies only in an alliance with the workers. We shall institute genuine workers' control over production.

We have now learned to make a concerted effort. The revolution that has just been accomplished is evidence of this. We possess the strength of mass organization, which will overcome everything and lead the proletariat to the world revolution.

We must now set about building a proletarian socialist state in Russia.

Long live the world socialist revolution! (*Stormy applause.*)

*That evening the second All-Russian Congress of Soviets proclaimed the transfer of all power throughout Russia to Soviets of Workers', Soldiers' and Peasants' Deputies. As Lenin stood at the reading-stand, he was greeted by a long-rolling ovation. When it finished, he said simply: 'We shall now proceed to construct the socialist order.' Again there was an overwhelming human roar. The congress adopted decrees on peace and on the land and approved the composition of the Council of People's Commissars – the first workers' and peasants' government.*

*Yet the Bolsheviks were massively defeated in the elections that followed. When the Constituent Assembly, the dream of Russia's revolutionaries and liberals for nearly a century, met in January 1918, it was dissolved by force.*

*The Bolsheviks seized power and went on, particularly under Lenin's successor Joseph Stalin, to construct one of the worst tyrannies of the twentieth century. 'Lenin and the party, the man and the instrument, were now indissolubly one,' says E.H. Carr. 'The foundations had been laid of the ascendancy in the party of the single leader.'*

•

## WOODROW WILSON
### 25 September 1919

#### 'Man will see the truth'

*When the Senate baulked at the League of Nations covenant, which he had negotiated with the Allied leaders in Paris, Wilson, aged sixty-three, set out on a great speaking tour through the West to rally the people to him and overcome Senator Lodge. Thirty speeches were planned in twenty days.*

*'Worn out by his labours; appalled at what might flow from the repudiation of his handiwork; filled with a prophet's vision and also, unfortunately, with the vanity of Jonah, he refused all compromise,' says Hugh Brogan. 'His eloquence was never greater. He defended the treaty with a passion worthy of a better cause ... The choice, he assured them again and again, trying to press home the lessons of his own education, lay between peace with the treaty, faults and all, or war without it.'*

*At Pueblo, Colorado, where this speech was made, he suffered complete nervous exhaustion and collapsed. The tour was cancelled and Wilson returned to the White House, where he suffered a massive stroke. The treaty was defeated in the Senate by a small margin. For the fifteen remaining months of his presidency, Wilson lay inert in the White House, doing nothing, saying nothing.*

Again and again, my fellow citizens, mothers who lost their sons in France have come to me and, taking my hand, have shed tears upon it not only, but they had added, 'God bless you, Mr President!' Why, my fellow citizens, should they pray God to bless me? I advised the Congress of the United States to create the situation that led to the death of their sons. I ordered their sons oversea. I consented to their sons being put in the most difficult parts of the battle line, where death was certain, as in the impenetrable difficulties of the forest of Argonne. Why should they weep upon my hand and call down the blessings of God upon me? Because they believe that their boys died for something that vastly transcends any of the immediate and palpable objects of the war. They believe, and they rightly believe, that their sons saved the liberty of the world. They believe that wrapped up with the liberty of the world is the continuous protection of that liberty by the concerted powers of all civilized people. They believe that this sacrifice was made in order that other sons should not be called upon for a similar gift – the gift of life, the gift of all that died – and if we did not see this thing through, if we fulfilled the dearest present wish of Germany and now dissociated ourselves from those alongside whom we fought in the war, would not something of the halo go away from the gun over the mantelpiece, or the sword? Would not the old uniform lose something of its significance? These men were crusaders. They were not going forth to prove the might of the United States. They were going forth to prove the might of justice and right, and all the world accepted them as crusaders, and their transcendent achievement has made all the world believe in America as it believes in no other nation organized in the modern world. There seems to me to stand between us and the rejection or qualification of this treaty the serried ranks of those boys in khaki, not only these boys who came home, but those dear ghosts that still deploy upon the fields of France.

My friends, on last Decoration Day I went to a beautiful hillside near Paris, where was located the cemetery of Suresnes, a cemetery given over to the burial of the American dead. Behind me on the slopes was rank upon rank of living American soldiers, and lying before me upon the levels of the plain was rank upon rank of departed American soldiers. Right by the side of the stand where I spoke there was a little group of French women who had adopted those graves, had made themselves mothers of those dear ghosts by putting flowers every day upon those graves, taking them as their own sons, their own beloved, because they had died in the same cause – France was free and the world was free because America had come! I wish some men in public life who are now opposing the settlement for which these men died could visit such a spot as that. I wish that the thought that comes out of those graves could penetrate their consciousness. I wish that they could feel the moral obligation that rests upon us not to go back on those boys, but to see the thing through, to see it through to the end and make good their redemption of the world. For nothing less depends upon this decision, nothing less than the liberation and salvation of the world . . .

You will say, 'Is the League an absolute guarantee against war?' No; I do not know any absolute guarantee against the errors of human judgement or the violence of human passion, but I ask you this: if it is not an absolute insurance against war, do you want no insurance at all? Do you want nothing? Do you want not only no probability that war will not recur, but the probability that it will recur? The arrangements of justice do not stand of themselves, my fellow citizens. The arrangements of this treaty are just, but they need the support of the combined power of the great nations of the world. And they will have that support. Now that the mists of this great question have cleared away, I believe that men will see the truth, eye to eye and face to face. There is one thing that the American people always rise to and extend their hand to, and that is the truth of justice and of liberty and of peace. We have accepted that truth and we are going to be led by it, and it is going to lead us, and through us the world, out into pastures of quietness and peace such as the world never dreamed of before.

•

## MAHATMA GANDHI
### 23 March 1922

### 'Non-violence is the first article of my faith'

*Gandhi became leader of the Indian National Congress in 1920 and the Congress adopted his programme of Satyagraha, non-violent non-cooperation, which he had earlier practised in South Africa. 'I discovered that pursuit of truth did not admit of violence being inflicted on one's opponent,' Gandhi wrote, 'but that he must be weaned from error by patience and sympathy. For what appears to be truth to one may appear to be error to the other. And patience means self-suffering. So the doctrine came to mean vindication of truth, not by the infliction of suffering on the opponent but on one's self.'*

*Supporting the Satyagraha campaign, Gandhi travelled throughout India, often speaking to meetings of more than 100,000 Indians. He was constantly shadowed by the police but it was not until 1922 that he was arrested and charged with sedition for three articles in his magazine* Young India. *The great trial at Ahmadabad, at which Gandhi pleaded guilty, followed.*

Non-violence is the first article of my faith. It is the last article of my faith. But I had to make my choice. I had either to submit to a system which I considered has done an irreparable harm to my country or incur the risk of the mad fury of my people bursting forth when they understood the truth from my lips. I know that my people have sometimes gone mad. I am deeply sorry for it; and I am therefore, here, to submit not to a light penalty but to the highest penalty. I do not ask for mercy. I do not plead any extenuating act. I am here, therefore, to invite and submit to the highest penalty that can be inflicted upon me for what in law is a deliberate crime and what appears to me to be the highest duty of a citizen. The only course open to you, Mr Judge, is, as

I am just going to say in my statement, either to resign your post or inflict on me the severest penalty if you believe that the system and law you are assisting to administer are good for the people. I do not expect that kind of conversion. But by the time I have finished with my statement you will, perhaps, have a glimpse of what is raging within my breast to run this maddest risk which a sane man can run.

*Gandhi then read his statement to the court.*

Little do town-dwellers know how the semi-starved masses of Indians are slowly sinking to lifelessness. Little do they know that their miserable comfort represents the brokerage they get for the work they do for the foreign exploiter, that the profits and the brokerage are sucked from the masses. Little do they realize that the government established by law in British India is carried on for this exploitation of the masses. No sophistry, no jugglery in figures can explain away the evidence the skeletons in many villages present to the naked eye. I have no doubt whatsoever that both England and the town-dwellers of India will have to answer, if there is a God above, for this crime against humanity which is perhaps unequalled in history. The law itself in this country has been used to serve the foreign exploiter. My experience of political cases in India leads me to the conclusion that in nine out of every ten the condemned men were totally innocent. Their crime consisted in love of their country. In ninety-nine cases out of a hundred, justice has been denied to Indians as against Europeans in the courts of India. This is not an exaggerated picture. It is the experience of almost every Indian who has had anything to do with such cases. In my opinion the administration of the law is thus prostituted consciously or unconsciously for the benefit of the exploiter.

The greatest misfortune is that Englishmen and their Indian associates in the administration of the country do not know that they are engaged in the crime I have attempted to describe. I am satisfied that many English and Indian officials honestly believe that they are administering one of the best systems devised in the world and that India is making steady though slow progress. They do not know that a subtle but effective system of terrorism and an organized display of force on the one hand and the deprivation of all powers of retaliation or self-defence on the other have emasculated the people and induced in them the habit of simulation. This awful habit has added to the ignorance and the self-deception of the administrators. Section 124-A under which I am happily charged is perhaps the prince among the political sections of the

Indian Penal Code designed to suppress the liberty of the citizen. Affection cannot be manufactured or regulated by law. If one has no affection for a person or thing one should be free to give the fullest expression to his disaffection so long as he does not contemplate, promote or incite to violence. But the section under which Mr Banker and I are charged is one under which mere promotion of disaffection is a crime. I have studied some of the cases tried under it, and I know that some of the most loved of India's patriots have been convicted under it. I consider it a privilege, therefore, to be charged under it. I have endeavoured to give in their briefest outline the reasons for my disaffection. I have no personal ill-will against any single administrator, much less can I have any disaffection towards the King's person. But I hold it to be a virtue to be disaffected towards a government which in its totality has done more harm to India than any previous system. India is less manly under the British rule than she ever was before. Holding such a belief, I consider it to be a sin to have affection for the system. And it has been a precious privilege for me to be able to write what I have in the various articles tendered in evidence against me.

In fact I believe that I have rendered a service to India and England by showing in non-cooperation the way out of the unnatural state in which both are living. In my humble opinion, non-cooperation with evil is as much a duty as is cooperation with good. But in the past, non-cooperation has been deliberately expressed in violence to the evildoer. I am endeavouring to show to my countrymen that violent non-cooperation only multiplies evil and that as evil can only be sustained by violence, withdrawal of support of evil requires complete abstention from violence. Non-violence implies voluntary submission to the penalty for non-cooperation with evil. I am here, therefore, to invite and submit cheerfully to the highest penalty that can be inflicted upon me for what in law is deliberate crime and what appears to me to be the highest duty of a citizen. The only course open to you, the Judge and the Assessors, is either to resign your posts and thus dissociate yourselves from evil if you feel that the law you are called upon to administer is an evil and that in reality I am innocent, or to inflict on me the severest penalty if you believe that the system and the law you are assisting to administer are good for the people of this country and that my activity is therefore injurious to the public weal.

*After his statement before the court, Gandhi was sentenced to six years' imprisonment and thanked the judge for his courtesy. He was imprisoned again in*

*1930, 1933 and 1942 when he went on hunger strike as part of his campaign of civil disobedience. He eventually collaborated with the English to gain independence for India, which was proclaimed twenty-five years later. A saint to many Hindus, he was assassinated in 1948.*

•

## FRANKLIN DELANO ROOSEVELT
### 4 March 1933

*'The only thing we have to fear is fear itself'*

*The Depression had hit America like an earthquake, destroying lives so totally that the people had lost their self-confidence. On Inauguration Day 1933, the banks were closed, financial transactions had ceased, and industry and business had sunk to their lowest levels. Widespread unemployment had created a feeling of utter helplessness.*

*America indeed seemed beyond help – until Franklin D. Roosevelt, crippled since 1921 when he had contracted polio and lost the use of both legs, won the 1932 presidential election by a majority of more than 12 million votes, winning forty-two states against six that voted for Hoover.*

*Now on a cold, windy March day the crippled Roosevelt (1882–1945), a man of power and vision who knew that he could save his country, took the oath and addressed the millions of Americans listening to their radios.*

*His inaugural speech was one of the turning-points of American history, says historian Hugh Brogan. In a few minutes he achieved what had eluded Hoover for four wearying years: he gave back to his countrymen their hope and energy.*

President Hoover, Mr Chief Justice, my friends:

This is a day of national consecration, and I am certain that my fellow-Americans expect that on my induction into the Presidency I will address them with a candor and a decision which the present situation of our nation impels.

This is pre-eminently the time to speak the truth, the whole truth, frankly and boldly. Nor need we shrink from honestly facing conditions in our country today. This great nation will endure as it has endured, will revive and will prosper.

So first of all let me assert my firm belief that the only thing we have to fear is fear itself – nameless, unreasoning, unjustified terror which paralyzes needed efforts to convert retreat into advance.

In every dark hour of our national life a leadership of frankness and vigor has met with that understanding and support of the people themselves which is essential to victory. I am convinced that you will again give that support to leadership in these critical days.

In such a spirit on my part and on yours we face our common difficulties. They concern, thank God, only material things. Values have shrunken to fantastic levels; taxes have risen; our ability to pay has fallen, government of all kinds is faced by serious curtailment of income; the means of exchange are frozen in the currents of trade; the withered leaves of industrial enterprise lie on every side; farmers find no markets for their produce; the savings of many years in thousands of families are gone.

More important, a host of unemployed citizens face the grim problem of existence, and an equally great number toil with little return. Only a foolish optimist can deny the dark realities of the moment.

Yet our distress comes from no failure of substance. We are stricken by no plague of locusts. Compared with the perils which our forefathers conquered because they believed and were not afraid, we have still much to be thankful for. Nature still offers her bounty and human efforts have multiplied it. Plenty is at our doorstep, but a generous use of it languishes in the very sight of the supply.

Primarily, this is because the rulers of the exchange of mankind's goods have failed through their own stubbornness and their own incompetence, have admitted that failure and abdicated. Practices of the unscrupulous money changers stand indicted in the court of public opinion, rejected by the hearts and minds of men.

True, they have tried, but their efforts have been cast in the pattern of an outworn tradition. Faced by failure of credit, they have proposed only the lending of more money.

Stripped of the lure of profit by which to induce our people to follow their false leadership, they have resorted to exhortations, pleading tearfully for restored confidence. They know only the rules of a generation of self-seekers.

They have no vision, and when there is no vision the people perish.

The money changers have fled from their high seats in the temple of our civilization. We may now restore that temple to the ancient truths.

The measure of the restoration lies in the extent to which we apply social values more noble than mere monetary profit.

Happiness lies not in the mere possession of money; it lies in the joy of achievement, in the thrill of creative effort.

The joy and moral stimulation of work no longer must be forgotten in the mad chase of evanescent profits. These dark days will be worth all they cost us if they teach us that our true destiny is not to be ministered unto but to minister to ourselves and to our fellow-men.

Recognition of the falsity of material wealth as the standard of success goes hand in hand with the abandonment of the false belief that public office and high political position are to be valued only by the standards of pride of place and personal profit; and there must be an end to a conduct in banking and in business which too often has given to a sacred trust the likeness of callous and selfish wrongdoing.

Small wonder that confidence languishes, for it thrives only on honesty, on honor, on the sacredness of obligations, on faithful protection, on unselfish performance. Without them it cannot live.

Restoration calls, however, not for changes in ethics alone. This nation asks for action, and action now.

Our greatest primary task is to put people to work. This is no unsolvable problem if we face it wisely and courageously . . .

I favor as a practical policy the putting of first things first. I shall spare no effort to restore world trade by international economic readjustment, but the emergency at home cannot wait on that accomplishment.

The basic thought that guides these specific means of national recovery is not narrowly nationalistic.

It is the insistence, as a first consideration, upon the interdependence of the various elements in, and parts of, the United States – a recognition of the old and permanently important manifestation of the American spirit of the pioneer.

It is the way to recovery. It is the immediate way. It is the strongest assurance that the recovery will endure.

In the field of world policy I would dedicate this nation to the policy of the good neighbor – the neighbor who resolutely respects himself and, because he does so, respects the rights of others – the neighbor who respects his obligations and respects the sanctity of his agreements in and with a world of neighbors.

If I read the temper of our people correctly, we now realize as we have never before, our interdependence on each other; that we cannot merely take, but we must give as well; that if we are to go forward we must move as a trained and loyal army willing to sacrifice for the good of a common discipline, because, without such discipline, no progress is made, no leadership becomes effective.

We are, I know, ready and willing to submit our lives and property to such discipline because it makes possible a leadership which aims at a larger good.

This I propose to offer, pledging that the larger purposes will bind upon us all as a sacred obligation with a unity of duty hitherto evoked only in time of armed strife.

With this pledge taken, I assume unhesitatingly the leadership of this great army of our people, dedicated to a disciplined attack upon our common problems.

Action in this image and to this end is feasible under the forms of government which we have inherited from our ancestors.

Our Constitution is so simple and practical that it is possible always to meet extraordinary needs by changes in emphasis and arrangement without loss of essential form.

That is why our constitutional system has proved itself the most superbly enduring political mechanism the modern world has produced. It has met every stress of vast expansion of territory, of foreign wars, of bitter internal strife, of world relations . . .

I am prepared under my constitutional duty to recommend the measures that a stricken nation in the midst of a stricken world may require.

These measures, or such other measures as the Congress may build out of its experience and wisdom, I shall seek, within my constitutional authority, to bring to speedy adoption.

But in the event that the Congress shall fail to take one of these two courses, and in the event that the national emergency is still critical, I shall not evade the clear course of duty that will then confront me.

I shall ask the Congress for the one remaining instrument to meet the crisis – broad executive power to wage a war against the emergency as great as the power that would be given me if we were in fact invaded by a foreign foe.

For the trust reposed in me I will return the courage and the devotion that befit the time. I can do no less.

We face the arduous days that lie before us in the warm courage of national unity; with the clear consciousness of seeking old and precious moral values; with the clean satisfaction that comes from the stern performance of duty by old and young alike.

We aim at the assurance of a rounded and permanent national life.

We do not distrust the future of essential democracy. The people of the United States have not failed. In their need they have registered a mandate that they want direct, vigorous action.

They have asked for discipline and direction under leadership. They have made me the present instrument of their wishes. In the spirit of the gift I take it.

In this dedication of a nation we humbly ask the blessing of God. May He protect each and every one of us! May He guide me in the days to come!

*By the end of the week, half a million letters had been sent to the White House, a flood that never dried up while Roosevelt was President. Words became deeds after 4 March and Roosevelt went on to win four successive elections.*

•

## ADOLF HITLER
### 26 September 1938

### *'My patience is now at an end'*

*Among all the millions of words of twentieth-century oratory, none are more chilling than the seven that Hitler uttered at the Berlin Sportspalast in September 1938: 'My patience is now at an end.'*

*The British Prime Minister, Neville Chamberlain, had visited Hitler twice in the previous ten days but had been snubbed, even after offering a plan agreed by Britain and France and accepted by the Czechs – but later repudiated by the British Cabinet – for the Sudeten districts of Czechoslovakia to be transferred to Germany without a plebiscite.*

*Chamberlain refused to give up hope and dispatched Sir Horace Wilson to Germany with a personal appeal to Hitler suggesting direct negotiations between the German and Czech governments, with the British present as a third party, in the hope of persuading him to moderate the tone of the speech he was due to make in the Sportspalast.*

*When Wilson arrived three hours before the speech was due, Hitler was in his most intransigent mood, working his resentment, hatred and opposition up to the pitch where they would provide the necessary stimulus for his speech.*

*Three hours later, Chamberlain and Beneš, the Czech President, got their answer.*

And now before us stands the last problem that must be solved and will be solved. It is the last territorial claim which I have to make in Europe, but it is the claim from which I will not recede and which, God willing, I will make good.

The history of the problem is as follows: in 1918 under the watchword 'The Right of the Peoples to Self-determination' Central Europe was torn in pieces and was newly formed by certain crazy so-called 'statesmen'. Without regard for the origin of the peoples, without regard for either their wish as nations or for economic necessities Central Europe at that time was broken up into atoms and new so-called States were arbitrarily formed. To this procedure Czechoslovakia owes its existence. This Czech state began with a single lie and the father of this lie was named Beneš. This Mr Beneš at that time appeared in Versailles and he first of all gave the assurance that there was a Czechoslovak nation. He was forced to invent this lie in order to give to the slender number of his own fellow-countrymen a somewhat greater range and thus a fuller justification. And the Anglo-Saxon statesmen, who were, as always, not very adequately versed in respect of questions of geography or nationality, did not at that time find it necessary to test these assertions of Mr Beneš. Had they done so, they could have established the fact that there is no such thing as a Czechoslovak nation but only Czechs and Slovaks and that the Slovaks did not wish to have anything to do with the Czechs but . . . (*the rest of the sentence was drowned in a tumultuous outburst of applause*).

So in the end through Mr Beneš these Czechs annexed Slovakia. Since this state did not seem fitted to live, out of hand three and a half million Germans were taken in violation of their right to self-determination and their wish for self-determination. Since even that did not suffice, over a million Magyars had to be added, then some Carpathian Russians, and at last several hundred thousand Poles.

That is this state which then later proceeded to call itself Czechoslovakia – in violation of the right of the peoples to self-determination, in violation of the clear wish and will of the nations to which this violence had been done . . .

Now the shameless part of this story begins. This state whose government is in the hands of a minority compels the other nationalities to cooperate in a policy which will oblige them one of these days to shoot at their own brothers. Mr Beneš demands of the German: 'If I wage war against Germany, then you have to shoot against the Germans. And if you refuse to do this, you are a traitor against the state and I will have you yourself shot.' And he makes the same demand of Hungary and Poland. He demands of the Slovaks that they should support aims to which the

Slovak people are completely indifferent. For the Slovak people wishes to have peace – and not adventures. Mr Beneš thus actually turns these folk either into traitors to their country or traitors to their people. Either they betray their people, are ready to fire on their fellow-country-men, or Mr Beneš says: 'You are traitors to your country and you will be shot for that by me.' Can there be anything more shameless than to compel folk of another people, in certain circumstances, to fire on their own fellow-countrymen only because a ruinous, evil, and criminal government so demands it?. I can here assert: when we had occupied Austria, my first order was: no Czech needs to serve, rather he must not serve, in the German Army. I have not driven him to a conflict with his conscience . . .

Mr Beneš now places his hopes on the world! And he and his diplomats make no secret of the fact. They state: it is our hope that Chamberlain will be overthrown, that Daladier will be removed, that on every hand revolutions are on the way. They place their hope on Soviet Russia. He still thinks then that he will be able to evade the fulfilment of his obligations.

And then I can say only one thing: now two men stand arrayed one against the other: there is Mr Beneš and here stand I. We are two men of a different make-up. In the great struggle of the peoples while Mr Beneš was sneaking about through the world, I as a decent German soldier did my duty. And now today I stand over against this man as the soldier of my people!

I have only a few statements still to make: I am grateful to Mr Chamberlain for all his efforts. I have assured him that the German people desires nothing else than peace, but I have also told him that I cannot go back behind the limits set to our patience. I have further assured him, and I repeat it here, that when this problem is solved there is for Germany no further territorial problem in Europe. And I have further assured him that at the moment when Czechoslovakia solves her problems, that means when the Czechs have come to terms with their other minorities, and that peaceably and not through oppression, then I have no further interest in the Czech state. And that is guaranteed to him! We want no Czechs!

But in the same way I desire to state before the German people that with regard to the problem of the Sudeten Germans my patience is now at an end! I have made Mr Beneš an offer which is nothing but the carrying into effect of what he himself has promised. The decision now lies in his hands: Peace or War! He will either accept this offer and now at last give to the Germans their freedom or we will go and fetch this freedom for ourselves. The world must take note that in four and a half years of war and through the long years of my political life there is one thing which no one could ever cast in my teeth: I have never been a coward!

Now I go before my people as its first soldier and behind me – that the world should know – there marches a people and a different people from that of 1918!

If at that time a wandering scholar was able to inject into our people the poison of democratic catchwords – the people of today is no longer the people that it was then. Such catchwords are for us like wasp-stings: they cannot hurt us: we are now immune.

In this hour the whole German people will unite with me! It will feel my will to be its will. Just as in my eyes it is its future and its fate which give me the commission for my action.

And we wish now to make our will as strong as it was in the time of our fight, the time when I, as a simple unknown soldier, went forth to conquer a Reich and never doubted of success and final victory.

Then there gathered close about me a band of brave men and brave women, and they went with me. And so I ask you my German people to take your stand behind me, man by man, and woman by woman.

In this hour we all wish to form a common will and that will must be stronger than every hardship and every danger.

And if this will is stronger than hardship and danger then one day it will break down hardship and danger.

We are determined!

Now let Mr Beneš make his choice!

*Alan Bullock, the distinguished Hitler biographer, describes this speech as a masterpiece of invective which even Hitler never surpassed. Rarely, he said, had the issue of war or peace been so nakedly reduced to the personal resentment and vanity of one man.*

*Chamberlain tried yet again. Three days later a settlement of the crisis was reached in Munich by the heads of government of Germany, Britain, France and Italy (Hitler, Chamberlain, Daladier and Mussolini) and the Sudetenland was annexed to Germany.*

*On 1 October German troops marched into the Sudetenland. The Second World War started on 3 September the following year.*

•

# WINSTON CHURCHILL
## 13 May 1940

### 'I have nothing to offer but blood, toil, tears and sweat'

*On becoming Prime Minister, Churchill mobilized the language and made it fight, on the first occasion only three days after he accepted office and had formed his coalition Cabinet. It was Whit Monday and Churchill made a short speech to the House of Commons. Yet on entering the chamber it was Chamberlain who got more cheers than Churchill, whose support was mostly on the Labour benches.*

*The speech was unforgettable, imposing Churchill's character and resolve on the Commons whether they liked it or not. The effect was electrifying, says Robert Rhodes James, one of his biographers. As he walked out of the chamber, he said to one of his aides: 'That got the SODS, didn't it!'*

*Churchill's war speeches were rhetorical and cheeky at the same time, Macaulay and contemporary slang mixed together, according to A.J.P. Taylor, the English historian. 'The English welcomed his romantic utterances, though themselves still speaking in more prosaic tones.'*

It must be remembered that we are in the preliminary stage of one of the greatest battles in history, that we are in action at many points in Norway and in Holland, that we have to be prepared in the Mediterranean, that the air battle is continuous and that many preparations have to be made here at home. In this crisis I hope I may be pardoned if I do not address the House at any length today. I hope that any of my friends and colleagues, or former colleagues, who are affected by the political reconstruction, will make all allowance for any lack of ceremony with which it has been necessary to act. I would say to the House, as I said to those who have joined the government: 'I have nothing to offer but blood, toil, tears and sweat.'

We have before us an ordeal of the most grievous kind. We have before us many, many long months of struggle and of suffering. You ask, what is our policy? I will say: It is to wage war, by sea, land and air, with all our might and with all the strength that God can give us: to wage war against a monstrous tyranny, never surpassed in the dark, lamentable catalogue of human crime. That is our policy. You ask, What is our aim? I can answer in one word: Victory – victory at all costs, victory in spite of all terror, victory, however long and hard the road may be; for without victory, there is no survival. Let that be realized; no survival for the British Empire; no survival for all that the British Empire has stood for, no survival for the urge and impulse of the ages, that mankind will move forward towards its goal. But I take up my task with buoyancy and hope. I feel sure that our cause will not be suffered to fail among men. At this time I feel entitled to claim the aid of all, and I say, 'Come, then, let us go forward together with our united strength.'

•

## WINSTON CHURCHILL
### 18 June 1940

### 'This was their finest hour'

*The crumbling French resistance to Hitler could not be maintained much longer. On 10 June, the government left Paris; on 16 June Marshal Pétain formed a new government. The next day France sued for peace. As Churchill predicted in this House of Commons speech, the Battle of France was over and the Battle of Britain had begun. Britain, he declared, was now resolved to fight on alone.*

*The defiant words were heard by millions when it was broadcast four hours later and it is probably the best remembered Churchill speech of the war, particularly for the magnificent peroration. Even so, as Churchill wrote later, rhetoric was no guarantee of survival.*

We do not yet know what will happen in France or whether the French resistance will be prolonged, both in France and in the French Empire overseas. The French government will be throwing away great opportunities and casting adrift their future if they do not continue the war in accordance with their Treaty obligations, from which we have not felt able to release them. The House will have read the historic declaration in which, at the desire of many Frenchmen – and of our own hearts – we have proclaimed our willingness at the darkest hour in French history to conclude a union of common citizenship in this struggle. However matters may go in France or with the French government, or other French governments, we in this island and in the British Empire will never lose our sense of comradeship with the French people. If we are now called upon to endure what they have been suffering, we shall emulate their courage, and if final victory rewards our toils they shall share the gains, aye, and freedom shall be restored to all. We abate nothing of our just demands: not one jot or tittle do we recede. Czechs, Poles, Norwegians, Dutch, Belgians have joined their causes to our own. All these shall be restored.

What General Weygand called the Battle of France is over. I expect that the Battle of Britain is about to begin. Upon this battle depends the survival of Christian civilization. Upon it depends our own British life, and the long continuity of our institutions and our empire. The whole fury and might of the enemy must very soon be turned on us. Hitler knows that he will have to break us in this island or lose the war. If we can stand up to him, all Europe may be free and the life of the world may move forward into broad, sunlit uplands. But if we fail, then the whole world, including the United States, including all that we have known and cared for, will sink into the abyss of a new Dark Age made more sinister, and perhaps more protracted, by the lights of perverted science. Let us therefore brace ourselves to our duties and so bear ourselves that, if the British Empire and its Commonwealth last for a thousand years, men will still say, 'This was their finest hour.'

●

## JOHN F. KENNEDY
### 20 January 1961

### '*A new generation of Americans*'

*For men and women born during or after the Second World War, John Kennedy's inaugural address, signalling the arrival in power of a new generation and a forty-four-year-old president, still burns in the memory, albeit that the speech has since been criticized (by the historian Hugh Brogan) as 'an essay in the higher eloquence, well enough for such an occasion though perhaps rather fustian when read in cold blood'.*

*The speech struck a stirring note as Kennedy announced that the responsibilities of government had passed to leaders 'born in this generation' and pointed out that to exclude men of under forty-four from positions of trust and command would have kept Jefferson from writing the Declaration of Independence and Washington from commanding the Continental Army.*

*Critics have since ranked Kennedy's inaugural with Jefferson (the first), Lincoln (the second), Wilson (the first) and Franklin D. Roosevelt (first and second). The speech was concise (about 1,300 words compared with some 8,000 by Harrison, the longest), the ideas were clear and forthright, the thoughts expressed simple and the delivery movingly eloquent.*

We observe today not a victory of party, but a celebration of freedom – symbolizing an end, as well as a beginning – signifying renewal, as well as change. For I have sworn before you and Almighty God the same solemn oath our forebears prescribed nearly a century and three-quarters ago.

The world is very different now. For man holds in his mortal hands the power to abolish all forms of human poverty and all forms of human life. And yet the same revolutionary beliefs for which our forebears fought are still at issue around the globe – the belief that the rights of man come not from the generosity of the state, but from the hand of God.

We dare not forget today that we are the heirs of that first revolution. Let the word go forth from this time and place, to friend and foe alike, that the torch has been passed to a new generation of Americans – born in this century, tempered by war, disciplined by a hard and bitter peace, proud of our ancient heritage – and unwilling to witness or permit the slow undoing of those human rights to which this nation has always been committed, and to which we are committed today at home and around the world.

Let every nation know, whether it wishes us well or ill, that we shall pay any price, bear any burden, meet any hardship, support any friend, oppose any foe, in order to assure the survival and the success of liberty.

This much we pledge – and more.

To those old allies whose cultural and spiritual origins we share, we pledge the loyalty of faithful friends. United, there is little we cannot do in a host of cooperative ventures. Divided, there is little we can do – for we dare not meet a powerful challenge at odds and split asunder.

To those new states whom we welcome to the ranks of the free, we pledge our word that one form of colonial control shall not have passed away merely to be replaced by a far more iron tyranny. We shall not always expect to find them supporting our view. But we shall always hope to find them strongly supporting their own freedom – and to remember that, in the past, those who foolishly sought power by riding the back of the tiger ended up inside.

To those peoples in the huts and villages across the globe struggling to break the bonds of mass misery, we pledge our best efforts to help them help themselves, for whatever period is required – not because the Communists may be doing it, not because we seek their votes, but because it is right. If a free society cannot help the many who are poor, it cannot save the few who are rich.

To our sister republics south of our border, we offer a special pledge – to convert our good words into good deeds – in a new alliance for progress – to assist free men and free governments in casting off the chains of poverty. But this peaceful revolution of hope cannot become the prey of hostile powers. Let all our neighbors know that we shall join with them to oppose aggression or subversion anywhere in the Americas. And let every other power know that this hemisphere intends to remain the master of its own house.

To that world assembly of sovereign states, the United Nations, our last best hope in an age where the instruments of war have far outpaced the instruments of peace, we renew our pledge of support – to prevent it from becoming merely a forum for invective – to strengthen its shield of the new and the weak – and to enlarge the area in which its writ may run.

Finally, to those nations who would make themselves our adversary, we offer not a pledge but a request: that both sides begin anew the quest for peace, before the dark powers of destruction unleashed by science engulf all humanity in planned or accidental self-destruction.

We dare not tempt them with weakness. For only when our arms are sufficient beyond doubt can we be certain beyond doubt that they will never be employed.

But neither can two great and powerful groups of nations take comfort from our present course – both sides overburdened by the cost of modern weapons, both rightly alarmed by the steady spread of the deadly atom, yet both racing to alter that uncertain balance of terror that stays the hand of mankind's final war.

So let us begin anew – remembering on both sides that civility is not a sign of weakness, and sincerity is always subject to proof. Let us never negotiate out of fear. But let us never fear to negotiate.

Let both sides explore what problems unite us instead of belaboring those problems which divide us.

Let both sides, for the first time, formulate serious and precise proposals for the inspection and control of arms – and bring the absolute power to destroy other nations under the absolute control of all nations.

Let both sides seek to invoke the wonders of science instead of its terrors. Together let us explore the stars, conquer the deserts, eradicate disease, tap the ocean depths, and encourage the arts and commerce.

Let both sides unite to heed in all corners of the earth the command of Isaiah – to 'undo the heavy burdens . . . and to let the oppressed go free'.

And if a beachhead of cooperation may push back the jungle of suspicion, let both sides join in creating a new endeavor, not a new balance of power, but a new world of law, where the strong are just and the weak secure and the peace preserved.

All this will not be finished in the first 100 days. Nor will it be finished in the first 1,000 days, nor in the life of this administration, nor even perhaps in our lifetime on this planet. But let us begin.

In your hands, my fellow citizens, more than in mine, will rest the final success or failure of our course. Since this country was founded, each generation of Americans has been summoned to give testimony to its national loyalty. The graves of young Americans who answered the call to service surround the globe.

Now the trumpet summons us again – not as a call to bear arms, though arms we need; not as a call to battle, though embattled we are – but a call to bear the burden of a long twilight struggle, year in and year out, 'rejoicing in hope, patient in tribulation' – a struggle against the common enemies of man: tyranny, poverty, disease, and war itself.

Can we forge against these enemies a grand and global alliance, North and South, East and West, that can assure a more fruitful life for all mankind? Will you join in that historic effort?

In the long history of the world, only a few generations have been granted the role of defending freedom in its hour of maximum danger. I do not shrink from this responsibility – I welcome it. I do not believe that any of us would exchange places with any other people or any other generation. The energy, the faith, the devotion which we bring to this endeavor will light our country and all who serve it – and the glow from that fire can truly light the world.

And so, my fellow Americans: ask not what your country can do for you – ask what you can do for your country.

My fellow citizens of the world: ask not what America will do for you, but what together we can do for the freedom of man.

Finally, whether you are citizens of America or citizens of the world, ask of us the same high standards of strength and sacrifice which we ask of you. With a good conscience our only sure reward, with history the final judge of our deeds, let us go forth to lead the land we love, asking

His blessing and His help, but knowing that here on earth God's work must truly be our own.

•

## MARTIN LUTHER KING
### 28 August 1963

### 'I have a dream'

*As the centenary of Abraham Lincoln's emancipation proclamation was celebrated in 1963, the National Association for the Advancement of Colored People, using the slogan 'Free by '63', launched a massive campaign for justice for America's blacks. The most important demonstrations were in Birmingham, Alabama (where Martin Luther King, 1929–68, led a march on the city hall, was twice thrown into gaol but won substantial measures of desegregation) and in Selma where a grand march of protest to Montgomery was addressed by King and Ralph Bunche, until then the only black American winner of the Nobel Peace Prize.*

*Then Philip Randolph, dean of the black American leaders, proposed a march on Washington for jobs and freedom. 'There was no precedent for a convocation of national scope and gargantuan size,' King wrote later. 'Complicating the situation were innumerable prophets of doom who feared that the slightest incident of violence would alienate Congress and destroy all hope of legislation.'*

*Yet 210,000 gathered at the Washington Monument in August and marched to the Lincoln Memorial, where the high point of the day was the speech by Martin Luther King, the voice of black Americans. He had written it in longhand the night before and did not finish it until 4 a.m. Now, standing before the marchers, King rose to the drama of the occasion, and delivered one of the most memorable speeches of the century. No public figure of his generation could match the skill with which he made a mastery of the spoken word the servant of his cause.*

Five score years ago, a great American, in whose symbolic shadow we stand, signed the Emancipation Proclamation. This momentous decree came as a great beacon light of hope to millions of Negro slaves who had been seared in the flames of withering injustice. It came as a joyous daybreak to end the long night of captivity.

But one hundred years later, we must face the tragic fact that the Negro is still not free. One hundred years later, the life of the Negro is still sadly crippled by the manacles of segregation and the chains of discrimination. One hundred years later, the Negro lives on a lonely island of poverty in the midst of a vast ocean of material prosperity. One hundred years later, the Negro is still languished in the corners of American society and finds himself an exile in his own land. So we have come here today to dramatize an appalling condition.

In a sense we have come to our nation's capital to cash a check. When the architects of our republic wrote the magnificent words of the Constitution and the Declaration of Independence, they were signing a promissory note to which every American was to fall heir. This note was a promise that all men would be guaranteed the unalienable rights of life, liberty, and the pursuit of happiness.

It is obvious today that America has defaulted on this promissory note insofar as her citizens of color are concerned. Instead of honoring this sacred obligation, America has given the Negro people a bad check; a check which has come back marked 'insufficient funds'. But we refuse to believe that the bank of justice is bankrupt. We refuse to believe that there are insufficient funds in the great vaults of opportunity of this nation. So we have come to cash this check – a check that will give us upon demand the riches of freedom and the security of justice. We have also come to this hallowed spot to remind America of the fierce urgency of *now*. This is no time to engage in the luxury of cooling off or to take the tranquilizing drug of gradualism.

*Now* is the time to make real the promises of Democracy.

*Now* is the time to rise from the dark and desolate valley of segregation to the sunlit path of racial justice.

*Now* is the time to open the doors of opportunity to all of God's children.

*Now* is the time to lift our nation from the quicksands of racial injustice to the solid rock of brotherhood.

It would be fatal for the nation to overlook the urgency of the moment and to underestimate the determination of the Negro. This sweltering summer of the Negro's legitimate discontent will not pass until there is an invigorating autumn of freedom and equality. Nineteen sixty-three is not an end, but a beginning. Those who hope that the Negro needed to blow off steam and will now be content will have a rude awakening if the nation returns to business as usual. There will be neither rest nor tranquility in America until the Negro is granted his citizenship rights. The whirlwinds of revolt will continue to shake the foundations of our nation until the bright day of justice emerges.

But there is something that I must say to my people who stand on the warm threshold which leads into the palace of justice. In the process of gaining our rightful place we must not be guilty of wrongful deeds. Let us not seek to satisfy our thirst for freedom by drinking from the cup of bitterness and hatred. We must forever conduct our struggle on the high plane of dignity and discipline. We must not allow our creative protest to degenerate into physical violence. Again and again we must rise to the majestic heights of meeting physical force with soul force. The marvelous new militancy which has engulfed the Negro community must not lead us to a distrust of all white people, for many of our white brothers, as evidenced by their presence here today, have come to realize that their destiny is tied up with our destiny and their freedom is inextricably bound to our freedom. We cannot walk alone.

And as we walk, we must make the pledge that we shall march ahead. We cannot turn back. There are those who are asking the devotees of civil rights, 'When will you be satisfied?' We can never be satisfied as long as the Negro is the victim of the unspeakable horrors of police brutality. We can never be satisfied as long as our bodies, heavy with the fatigue of travel, cannot gain lodging in the motels of the highways and the hotels of the cities. We cannot be satisfied as long as the Negro's basic mobility is from a smaller ghetto to a larger one. We can never be satisfied as long as a Negro in Mississippi cannot vote and a Negro in New York believes he has nothing for which to vote. No, no, we are not satisfied, and we will not be satisfied until justice rolls down like waters and righteousness like a mighty stream.

I am not unmindful that some of you have come here out of great trials and tribulations. Some of you have come fresh from narrow jail cells. Some of you have come from areas where your quest for freedom left you battered by the storms of persecution and staggered by the winds of police brutality. You have been the veterans of creative suffering. Continue to work with the faith that unearned suffering is redemptive.

Go back to Mississippi, go back to Alabama, go back to South Carolina, go back to Georgia, go back to Louisiana, go back to the slums and ghettos of our northern cities, knowing that somehow this situation can and will be changed. Let us not wallow in the valley of despair.

I say to you today, my friends, that in spite of the difficulties and frustrations of the moment I still have a dream. It is a dream deeply rooted in the American dream.

I have a dream that one day this nation will rise up and live out the true meaning of its creed: 'We hold these truths to be self-evident; that all men are created equal.'

I have a dream that one day on the red hills of Georgia the sons of former slaves and the sons of former slaveowners will be able to sit down together at the table of brotherhood.

I have a dream that one day even the state of Mississippi, a desert state sweltering with the heat of injustice and oppression, will be transformed into an oasis of freedom and justice.

I have a dream that my four little children will one day live in a nation where they will not be judged by the color of their skin but by the content of their character.

I have a dream today.

I have a dream that one day the state of Alabama, whose governor's lips are presently dripping with the words of interposition and nullification, will be transformed into a situation where little black boys and black girls will be able to join hands with little white boys and white girls and walk together as sisters and brothers.

I have a dream today.

I have a dream that one day every valley shall be exalted, every hill and mountain shall be made low, the rough places will be made plains, and the crooked places will be made straight, and the glory of the Lord shall be revealed, and all flesh shall see it together.

This is our hope. This is the faith with which I return to the South. With this faith we will be able to hew out of the mountain of despair a stone of hope. With this faith we will be able to transform the jangling discords of our nation into a beautiful symphony of brotherhood. With this faith we will be able to work together, to pray together, to struggle together, to go to jail together, to stand up for freedom together, knowing that we will be free one day.

This will be the day when all of God's children will be able to sing with new meaning

> My country, 'tis of thee,
> Sweet land of liberty,
>     Of thee I sing:
> Land where my fathers died,
> Land of the pilgrims' pride,
> From every mountainside
>     Let freedom ring.

And if America is to be a great nation this must become true. So let freedom ring from the prodigious hilltops of New Hampshire. Let freedom ring from the mighty mountains of New York. Let freedom ring from the heightening Alleghenies of Pennsylvania!

Let freedom ring from the snowcapped Rockies of Colorado!

Let freedom ring from the curvacious peaks of California!

But not only that; let freedom ring from Stone Mountain of Georgia!

Let freedom ring from Lookout Mountain of Tennessee!

Let freedom ring from every hill and molehill of Mississippi. From every mountainside, let freedom ring.

When we let freedom ring, when we let it ring from every village and every hamlet, from every state and every city, we will be able to speed up that day when all of God's children, black men and white men, Jews and Gentiles, Protestants and Catholics, will be able to join hands and sing in the words of the old Negro spiritual, 'Free at last! free at last! thank God almighty, we are free at last!'

*James Reston, one of America's most distinguished journalists, described the speech as 'an anguished echo from all the old American reformers' – from Roger Williams calling for religious liberty, Sam Adams for political liberty and Thoreau denouncing coercion to William Lloyd Garrison demanding emancipation and Eugene V. Debs crying for economic equality. King echoed them all.*

*Martin Luther King was* Time's *Man of the Year in 1963 and was awarded the Nobel Peace Prize in 1964. Civil-rights Acts, initiated by President Kennedy, were put on the statute book by President Johnson in 1964 and 1965. King was assassinated on a civil rights mission to Memphis, Tennessee, on 4 April 1968. When the* Guardian *newspaper in London analysed twentieth-century speeches, it nominated 'I have a dream' as the greatest speech of the century.*

•

## NELSON MANDELA
20 April 1964

### *'An ideal for which I am prepared to die'*

*After being sentenced to life imprisonment in 1964, Nelson Mandela (1918–) became a worldwide symbol of heroic black resistance to the apartheid regime of South Africa. He was described as the Black Pimpernel.*

*He joined the African National Congress in 1952 and became a member of a small action group whose main task was to launch Umkhonto we Sizwe (Spear of the Nation) or MK. From a safe house in Rivonia, MK planned sabotage of strategic targets — after its first terrorist attacks in 1961 bombs exploded in Johannesburg, Port Elizabeth and Durban.*

*When the ANC was banned in 1961, Mandela evaded arrest for a year but was gaoled for five years in 1962 and sent to Robben Island. His prison term was interrupted by the Rivonia trial, brought after a police raid on ANC headquarters in 1963. Mandela and his colleagues were charged under the Suppression of Communism Act.*

*The trial opened on 9 October 1963, with Mandela named as Accused Number One and facing the death penalty. The defence case opened the following April. Mandela's speech lasted four hours. He denied he was a Communist and described himself as an African patriot who admired the Magna Carta and the Bill of Rights. His concluding words inspired support throughout the world.*

Our fight is against real, and not imaginary hardships, or, to use the language of the State Prosecutor, 'so-called hardships'. We fight against two features which are the hallmarks of African life in South Africa, and which are entrenched by legislation which we seek to have repealed. These features are poverty and lack of human dignity, and we do not need Communists, or so-called 'agitators', to teach us about these things.

The whites enjoy what may well be the highest standard of living in the world, whilst Africans live in poverty and misery. Forty per cent of the Africans live in hopelessly overcrowded and, in some cases, drought-stricken reserves, where soil erosion and the overworking of the soil make it impossible for them to live properly off the land. Thirty per cent are labourers, labour tenants, and squatters on white farms and work and live under conditions similar to those of the serfs of the Middle Ages. The other thirty per cent live in towns where they have developed economic and social habits which bring them closer, in many respects, to white standards. Yet forty-six per cent of all African families in Johannesburg do not earn enough to keep them going.

The complaint of Africans, however, is not only that they are poor and whites are rich, but that the laws which are made by the whites are designed to preserve this situation. There are two ways to break out of poverty. The first is by formal education, and the second is by the worker acquiring a greater skill at his work and thus higher wages. As far as Africans are concerned, both these avenues of advancement are deliberately curtailed by legislation.

The present government has always sought to hamper Africans in their search for education. There is compulsory education for all white children at virtually no cost to their parents, be they rich or poor. Similar facilities are not provided for African children. In 1960–61, the per capita government spending on African students at state-funded schools was estimated at R12.46. In the same year, the per capita spending on white children in the Cape Province (which are the only figures available to me) was R144.57. The present Prime Minister said during the debate on the Bantu Education Bill in 1953: 'When I have control of Native education, I will reform it so that Natives will be taught from childhood to realize that equality with Europeans is not for them ... People who believe in equality are not desirable teachers for Natives. When my Department controls Native education, it will know for what class of higher education a Native is fitted, and whether he will have a chance in life to use his knowledge.'

The other main obstacle to the economic advancement of the Africans is the industrial colour bar by which all the better jobs of industry are reserved for whites only. Moreover, Africans are not allowed to form trade unions, which have recognition under the Industrial Conciliation Act. The government often answers its critics by saying that Africans in South Africa are economically better off than the inhabitants of the other countries in Africa. Our complaint is not that we are poor by comparison with people in other countries, but that we are poor by comparison with white people in our own country, and that we are prevented by legislation from altering this imbalance.

Hundreds and thousands of Africans are thrown into gaol each year under pass laws. Even worse than this is the fact that pass laws keep husband and wife apart and lead to the breakdown of family life.

Poverty and the breakdown of family life have secondary effects. Children wander about the streets of the townships because they have no schools to go to, or no money to enable them to go to school, or no parents at home to see that they go to school because both parents, if there be two, have to work to keep the family alive. This leads to a breakdown in moral standards, to an alarming rise in illegitimacy and to growing violence which erupts, not only politically but everywhere. Life in the townships is dangerous; there is not a day that goes by without somebody being stabbed or assaulted. And violence is carried out of the townships into the white living areas. People are afraid to walk alone in the streets after dark. House-breakings and robberies are increasing despite the fact that the death sentence can now be imposed for such offences. Death sentences cannot cure the festering sore. The only cure is to alter the conditions under which the Africans are forced to live, and to meet their legitimate grievances.

We want to be part of the general population, and not confined to living in our ghettos. African men want to have their wives and children to live with them where they work, and not to be forced into an unnatural existence in men's hostels. Our women want to be left with their men folk, and not to be left permanently widowed in the Reserves. We want to be allowed out after 11 p.m. and not to be confined to our rooms like little children. We want to be allowed to travel in our own country, and seek work where we want to, and not where the Labour Bureau tells us to. We want a just share in the whole of South Africa; we want security and a stake in society.

Above all, my lord, we want equal political rights, because without them our disabilities will be permanent. I know this sounds revolutionary to the whites in this country, because the majority of voters will be Africans. This makes the white man fear democracy. But this fear cannot be allowed to stand in the way of the only solution which will guarantee racial harmony and freedom for all. It is not true that the enfranchisement of all will result in racial domination. Political division, based on colour, is entirely artificial, and when it disappears, so will the domination of one colour group by another. The ANC has spent half a century fighting against racialism. When it triumphs, as it certainly must, it will not change that policy.

This then is what the ANC is fighting. Our struggle is a truly national one. It is a struggle of the African people, inspired by our own suffering and our own experience. It is a struggle for the right to live.

During my lifetime I have dedicated my life to this struggle of the African people. I have fought against white domination, and I have fought against black domination. I have cherished the ideal of a democratic and free society in which all persons live together in harmony with equal opportunities. It is an ideal which I hope to live for, and to see realized. But my lord, if needs be, it is an ideal for which I am prepared to die.

*On 11 June, Mandela and the seven other defendants were sentenced to life imprisonment. Mandela returned to Robben Island, where he was put in a stone cell measuring two metres by two metres, lit by a forty-watt bulb and set to hard labour in a quarry. He spent twenty-seven years in prison.*

•

# VACLAV HAVEL
## 1 January 1990

### 'A contaminated moral environment'

*Communism in Eastern Europe died in 1989 as one by one the Communist regimes in Poland, Czechoslovakia, Hungary, Romania and Bulgaria collapsed. The year ended with the crumbling of the Berlin Wall. It was the springtime of nations, the most exciting year in European history since 1848.*

*The motto of the year was 'Truth shall prevail' and it was a year of truth for Communism. As Timothy Garton Ash, an eyewitness to the events, puts it: 'There is a real sense in which these regimes lived by the word and perished by the word. For what, after all, happened? A few thousands, then tens of thousands, then hundreds of thousands went on to the streets. They spoke a few words, "Resign," they said. "No more shall we be slaves!" "Free elections." "Freedom!" And the walls of Jericho fell. And with the walls, the communist parties simply crumbled.'*

*That sense that truth will prevail is what made the first speech by Vaclav Havel, the playwright who was elected Czech president on 29 December 1989, so moving and uplifting in its expression of the defiant human spirit that conquered Communism during that memorable year.*

*One theme of Havel's work was that under Communism almost everybody lived a double life, saying one thing in public and another in private. It was a theme to which he returned in this speech on New Year's Day, broadcast on radio and television, with his comments on the 'contaminated moral environment' under the Communist regime.*

We live in a contaminated moral environment. We fell morally ill because we became used to saying something different from what we thought. We learned not to believe in anything, to ignore each other, to care only about ourselves. Concepts such as love, friendship, compassion, humility, or forgiveness lost their depth and dimensions, and for many of us they represented only psychological peculiarities, or they resembled gone-astray greetings from ancient times, a little ridiculous in the era of computers and spaceships. Only a few of us were able to cry out loud that the powers that be should not be all-powerful, and that special farms, which produce ecologically pure and top-quality food just for them, should send their produce to schools, children's homes, and hospitals if our agriculture was unable to offer them to all. The previous regime – armed with its arrogant and intolerant ideology – reduced man to a force of production and nature to a tool of production. In this it attacked both their very substance and their mutual relationship. It reduced gifted and autonomous people, skilfully working in their own country, to nuts and bolts of some monstrously huge, noisy, and stinking machine, whose real meaning is not clear to anyone. It cannot do more than slowly but inexorably wear down itself and all its nuts and bolts.

When I talk about contaminated moral atmosphere, I am not talking just about the gentlemen who eat organic vegetables and do not look out of the plane windows. I am talking about all of us. We had all become used to the totalitarian system and accepted it as an unchangeable fact and thus helped to perpetuate it. In other words, we are all – though naturally to differing extents – responsible for the operation of the totalitarian machinery; none of us is just its victim: we are all also its co-creators.

Why do I say this? It would be very unreasonable to understand the sad legacy of the last forty years as something alien, which some distant relative bequeathed us. On the contrary, we have to accept this legacy as a sin we committed against ourselves. If we accept it as such, we will understand that it is up to us all, and up to us only, to do something about it. We cannot blame the previous rulers for everything, not only because it would be untrue but also because it could blunt the duty that each of us faces today, namely, the obligation to act independently, freely, reasonably, and quickly. Let us not be mistaken: the best government in the world, the best parliament and the best president, cannot achieve much on their own. And it would also be wrong to expect a general remedy from them only. Freedom and democracy include participation and therefore responsibility from us all.

If we realize this, then all the horrors that the new Czechoslovak democracy inherited will cease to appear so terrible. If we realize this, hope will return to our hearts.

In the effort to rectify matters of common concern, we have something to lean on. The recent period – and in particular, the last six weeks of our peaceful revolution – has shown the enormous human, moral, and spiritual potential and civic culture that slumbered in our society under the enforced mask of apathy. Whenever someone categorically claimed that we were this or that, I always objected that society is a very mysterious creature and that it is not wise to trust only the face it presents to you. I am happy that I was not mistaken. Everywhere in the world people wonder where those meek, humiliated, sceptical, and seemingly cynical citizens of Czechoslovakia found the marvellous strength to shake from their shoulders in several weeks and in a decent and peaceful way the totalitarian yoke. And let us ask: from where did the young people who never knew another system take their desire for truth, their love of free thought, their political ideas, their civic courage and civic prudence? How did it happen that their parents – the very generation that had been considered as lost – joined them? How is it possible that so many people immediately knew what to do and none of them needed any advice or instruction? . . .

Masaryk* based his politics on morality. Let us try in a new time and in a new way to restore this concept of politics. Let us teach ourselves and others that politics should be an expression of a desire to contribute to the happiness of the community rather than of a need to cheat or rape the community. Let us teach ourselves and others that politics can be not only the art of the possible, especially if this means the art of speculation, calculation, intrigue, secret deals, and pragmatic manoeuvring, but that it can even be the art of the impossible, namely, the art of improving ourselves and the world . . .

There are free elections and an election campaign ahead of us. Let us not allow this struggle to dirty the so far clean face of our gentle revolution. Let us not allow the sympathies of the world which we have won so fast to be equally rapidly lost through our becoming entangled in the jungle of skirmishes for power. Let us not allow the desire to serve oneself to bloom once again under the fair mask of the desire to serve the common good. It is not really important now which party, club, or group will prevail in the elections. The important thing is that the winners will be the best of us, in the moral, civic, political, and professional sense, regardless of their political affiliations. The future policies and prestige of our state will depend on the personalities we select and later elect to our representative bodies . . .

In conclusion, I would like to say that I want to be a president who will speak less and work more. To be a president who will not only look out of the windows of his aeroplane but who, first and foremost, will always be present among his fellow citizens and listen to them well.

---

* Thomas Masaryk (1850–1937) was the first president of Czechoslovakia after it won independence in 1918. The name was anathema to the Communist regime.

You may ask what kind of republic I dream of. Let me reply: I dream of a republic independent, free, and democratic, of a republic economically prosperous and yet socially just, in short, of a humane republic which serves the individual and which therefore holds the hope that the individual will serve it in turn. Of a republic of well-rounded people, because without such it is impossible to solve any of our problems, human, economic, ecological, social, or political.

The most distinguished of my predecessors opened his first speech with a quotation from the great Czech educator Comenius. Allow me to round off my first speech with my own paraphrase of the same statement:

People, your government has returned to you!

•

## NELSON MANDELA
### 10 May 1994

### '*Let freedom reign*'

*Nelson Mandela was released twenty-seven years after he was imprisoned, in February 1990. Four years later, after President William de Klerk initiated a historic peace accord with the black majority of South Africans, led by Mandela, he was elected President in South Africa's first democratic elections. This was his inaugural address.*

Today all of us do, by our presence here, and by our celebrations in other parts of our country and the world, confer glory and hope to newborn liberty.

Out of the experience of an extraordinary human disaster that lasted too long must be born a society of which all humanity will be proud.

Our daily deeds as ordinary South Africans must produce an actual South African reality that will reinforce humanity's belief in justice, strengthen its confidence in the nobility of the human soul and sustain all our hopes for a glorious life for all.

All this we owe both to ourselves and to the peoples of the world who are so well represented here today.

To my compatriots, I have no hesitation in saying that each one of us is as intimately attached to the soil of this beautiful country as are the famous jacaranda trees of Pretoria and the mimosa trees of the bushveld.

Each time one of us touches the soil of this land, we feel a sense of personal renewal. The national mood changes as the seasons change.

We are moved by a sense of joy and exhilaration when the grass turns green and the flowers bloom.

That spiritual and physical oneness we all share with this common homeland explains the depth of the pain we all carried in our hearts as we saw our country tear itself apart in a terrible conflict, and as we saw it spurned, outlawed and isolated by the peoples of the world, precisely because it has become the universal base of the pernicious ideology and practice of racism and racial oppression.

We, the people of South Africa, feel fulfilled that humanity has taken us back into its bosom; that we, who were outlaws not so long ago, have today been given the rare privilege to be host to the nations of the world on our own soil. We thank all our distinguished international guests for having come to take possession with the people of our country of what is, after all, a common victory for justice, for peace, for human dignity.

We trust that you will continue to stand by us as we tackle the challenges of building peace, prosperity, non-sexism, non-racialism and democracy.

We deeply appreciate the role that the masses of our people and their political mass democratic, religious, women, youth, business, traditional and other leaders have played to bring about this conclusion. Not least among them is my second deputy president, the honourable F.W. de Klerk.

We would also like to pay tribute to our security forces, in all their ranks, for the distinguished role they have played in securing our first democratic elections and the transition to democracy, from bloodthirsty forces which still refuse to see the light.

The time for the healing of the wounds has come. The moment to bridge the chasms that divide us has come. The time to build is upon us. We have, at last, achieved our political emancipation. We pledge ourselves to liberate all our people from the continuing bondage of poverty, deprivation, suffering, gender and other discrimination.

We succeeded to take our last steps to freedom in conditions of relative peace. We commit ourselves to the construction of a complete, just and lasting peace.

We have triumphed in the effort to implant hope in the breasts of the millions of our people. We enter into a convenant that we shall build the society in which all South Africans, both black and white, will be able to walk tall, without any fear in their hearts, assured of their inalienable right to human dignity – a rainbow nation at peace with itself and the world.

As a token of its commitment to the renewal of our country, the new interim Government of National Unity will, as a matter of urgency, address the issue of amnesty for various categories of our people who are currently serving terms of imprisonment.

We dedicate this day to all the heroes and heroines in this country and the rest of the world who sacrificed in many ways and surrendered their lives so that we could be free. Their dreams have become reality. Freedom is their reward.

We are both humbled and elevated by the honour and privilege that you, the people of South Africa, have bestowed on us, as the first president of a united, democratic, non-racial and non-sexist South Africa, to lead our country out of the valley of darkness.

We understand it still that there is no easy road to freedom. We know it well that none of us acting alone can achieve success. We must therefore act together as a united people, for national reconciliation, for nation building, for the birth of a new world. Let there be justice for all. Let there be peace for all. Let there be work, bread, water and salt for all.

Let each know that for each the body, the mind and the soul have been freed to fulfil themselves.

Never, never and never again shall it be that this beautiful land will again experience the oppression of one by another and suffer the indignity of being the skunk of the world.

Let freedom reign. The sun shall never set on so glorious a human achievement. God bless Africa. Thank you.

●

# SELECT BIBLIOGRAPHY

## Anthologies

*Abraham Lincoln's Speeches and Letters*, Everyman, 1907.
*British Historical and Political Orations*, Everyman/Dutton.
Thomas Carlyle, *The Letters and Speeches of Oliver Cromwell*, Methuen, 1904.
*Cicero: Selected Political Speeches*, trans. Michael Grant, Penguin, 1969.
*The Democracy Reader*, ed. Diane Ravitch and Abigail Thernstrom, Harper Collins, 1992.
William Hazlitt, *The Eloquence of the British Senate*, 1808.
*Irish Orators and Oratory*, The Talbot Press, 1929.
*Lend Me Your Ears*, ed. William Safire, Norton, 1992.
*The Orations of Marcus Tullius Cicero*, trans. C.D. Yonge, G.E. Bell, 1877.
*Oratory, British and Irish, The Great Age*, ed. Geoffrey Locker Lampson, Humphrey, 1918.
*Selected English Speeches*, ed. Edgar R. Jones, Oxford University Press, 1913.
*Selected Speeches of John Bright*, Everyman, 1907.
*Silver Tongues*, ed. John Hayward, Michael Joseph, 1937.
*Speeches on Politics and Literature by Lord Macaulay*, Everyman.
*Speeches from Thucydides*, selected from Jowett's translation, Oxford, 1919.
*The Treasury of British Eloquence*, Nimmo, Hay and Mitchell, 1882.
*A Treasury of the World's Greatest Speeches*, ed. Houston Peterson, Grolier, 1954.
*The War Speeches and Orations of Daniel Webster*, ed. Edwin P. Whipple, Little, Brown, 1879.
*The World's Great Speeches*, ed. Lewis Copeland, Dover/Constable, 1942.

## Oratory

Robert Craig, *A History of Oratory in Parliament*, Heath, Cranton and Ouseley, 1913.
Earl Curzon of Kedleston, *Modern Parliamentary Eloquence*, Rede Lecture, Macmillan, 1913.
William Matthews, *Oratory and Orators*, Griggs.

## History

Maurice Ashley, *The Greatness of Oliver Cromwell*, Hodder & Stoughton, 1957.

Stanley Ayling, *The Elder Pitt*, Collins, 1976.

Robert Blake, *Disraeli*, Eyre & Spottiswoode/St Martin's Press, 1966/1967.

Sarah Bradford, *Disraeli*, Weidenfeld & Nicolson, 1982.

*Demosthenes: Upon the Crown*, ed. Henry Lord Brougham, Routledge.

John F. Finerty, *The People's History of Ireland*, Dodd, Mead, 1905.

John Forster, *The Statement of the Commonwealth of England*, Longman, Orme, Brown, Green and Longmans, 1840.

R.F. Foster, *Modern Ireland*, Penguin, 1989.

Antonia Fraser, *Cromwell, Our Chief of Men*, Weidenfeld & Nicolson, 1975.

Norman Gash, *Mr Secretary Peel*, Longman, 1961.

Norman Gash, *Sir Robert Peel*, Longman, 1972.

Christopher Hibbert, *The Virgin Queen*, Penguin, 1992.

H.C.G. Matthew, *Gladstone, 1809–1874*, Clarendon, 1986.

John Morley, *Walpole*, Macmillan, 1896.

J.E. Neale, *Queen Elizabeth I*, Penguin, 1990.

*The Oxford Illustrated History of Britain*, ed. Kenneth O. Morgan, Oxford University Press, 1984.

J.H. Plumb, *Sir Robert Walpole, The King's Minister*, Cresset, 1960.

S. Reed Brett, *John Pym, The Statesman of the Puritan Revolution*, John Murray, 1940.

Loren Reid, *Charles James Fox, A Man for the People*, Longman, 1969.

G.M. Trevelyan, *The Life of John Bright*, Constable, 1913.

J.H. Plumb on Lord Chatham and Sir Philip Magnus on Gladstone are strongly recommended.

## French Revolution

Louis Barthou, *Mirabeau*, Heinemann, 1913.

Ernest Belfort Bax, *Jean Paul Marat*, Grant Richards, 1920.

Hilaire Belloc, *Danton*, Nisbet, 1928.

Claude G. Bowers, *Pierre Vergniaud*, Constable, 1950.

Thomas Carlyle, *The French Revolution*, Chapman and Hall, 1898.

Alfred Cobban, *A History of Modern France*, Penguin, 1990.

Christopher Hibbert, *The French Revolution*, Penguin, 1982.

Henri de Jouvenal, *The Stormy Life of Mirabeau*, Harrap, 1929.

Ralph Korngold, *Robespierre*, Macmillan, 1937.

Simon Schama, *Citizens*, Viking, 1989.

Antonia Vallentin, *Mirabeau, Voice of the Revolution*, Hamish Hamilton, 1948.

## United States

Max Beloff, *Thomas Jefferson and American Democracy*, Hodder, 1948.

Henry Bryan Binns, *The Life of Abraham Lincoln*, Everyman/Dent, 1927.

Hugh Brogan, *The Penguin History of the United States*, Penguin.

Nicholas Murray Butler, *Building the American Nation*, Cambridge University Press/Scribner's, 1923.

James A. Harrison, *George Washington*, Putnam's, 1906.

Henry Cabot Lodge, *Daniel Webster*, Houghton Mifflin, Riverside Press, Cambridge, 1891.

John T. Morse, *Abraham Lincoln*, Osgood McIlvaine, 1893.

John T. Morse, *Thomas Jefferson*, David Douglas, Edinburgh, Houghton Mifflin, 1886.

Benjamin P. Thomas, *Abraham Lincoln*, Knopf, 1952.

W.E. Woodward, *George Washington, The Image and the Man*, Blue Ribbon, 1926.

Esmond Wright, *Washington and the American Revolution*, English Universities Press, 1957.

# THE PENGUIN BOOK OF
# MODERN SPEECHES

**EDITED BY BRIAN MACARTHUR**

The twentieth century was a century of idealism and revolution and as never before speeches were crucial in stirring the hearts and minds of millions around the world.

Whether it was Churchill rousing the British to take up arms or the dream of Martin Luther King, Fidel Castro inspiring the Cuban revolution or Salman Rushdie denouncing his fatwa, speeches have made headlines and shaped the way we see ourselves and the larger society.

Gathered here are some of the most extraordinary and memorable speeches of the modern era. Some are well known, others less so, but all, in their way, whether large or small, had a hand in shaping the world that we inhabit now.

Originally published as *The Penguin Book of Twentieth-Century Speeches*, this new edition has been updated to include the most significant speeches since the Millennium including statements on the Iraq War by George Bush, Tony Blair and Robin Cook, and speeches by Burmese heroine Aung San Suu Kyi and President Barack Obama.

'It would be hard to do better than MacArthur's selection, which is a tribute to the breadth of his knowledge' *The Times*